Congress and Its Members

Politics and Public Policy Series

Advisory Editor

Robert L. Peabody

Johns Hopkins University

Congress and Its Members

Roger H. Davidson

Congressional Research Service
University of California, Santa Barbara

Walter J. Oleszek

Congressional Research Service

Congressional Quarterly Press

a division of

CONGRESSIONAL QUARTERLY INC.
1414 22nd Street N.W., Washington, D.C. 20037

Jean L. Woy *Acquisitions Editor*

Barbara R. de Boinville *Project Editors*
John L. Moore
Susan D. Sullivan

Maceo Mayo *Production Supervisor*

Richard Pottern *Cover Design*

Jim Wells *Cover Photograph*

Photo Credits: p. 4, Frank Johnston, *Washington Post;* p. 16, Library of Congress; p. 56, *The Capital* (Annapolis); p. 96, Wide World Photos; p. 132, Alan Porter, Senate Photographic Studio; p. 166, Library of Congress; p. 179, George Tames, *New York Times;* p. 202, Steve Karafyllakis; p. 234, Marion Trikosko, *U.S. News & World Report;* p. 264, *RSP Media;* p. 290, Timothy Murphy, *U.S. News & World Report;* p. 299, Wide World Photos; p. 318, James K. W. Atherton, *Washington Post;* p. 344, Atherton, *Washington Post;* p. 372, Warren K. Leffler, *U.S. News & World Report;* p. 404, Atherton, *Washington Post;* p. 422, Atherton, *Washington Post;* p. 432, Air Photographics.

Library of Congress Cataloging in Publication Data

Davidson, Roger H.
   Congress and its members.

   Bibliography: p.
   Includes index.
   1. United States.   Congress.   2. Legislators—
United States.   I. Oleszek, Walter J.   II. Title.

JK 1061.D29   328.73   81-5446
ISBN 0-87187-202-1   AACR2

To
William A. Steiger (1938-1978)
Legislator, scholar, friend.

Foreword

Nearly 100 years ago a young Ph.D. candidate at Johns Hopkins University set forth several reasons why Congress had remained in obscurity and had generally been misunderstood:

> Like a vast picture thronged with figures of equal prominence and crowded with elaborate and obtrusive details, Congress is hard to see satisfactorily and appreciatively at a single view and from a single stand-point. Its complicated forms and diversified structure confuse the vision, and conceal the system which underlies its composition. It is too complex to be understood without an effort, without a careful and systematic process of analysis.[1]

Now approaching its 200th year, Congress is, if anything, more complex and not much better appreciated than when Woodrow Wilson attempted his analysis in *Congressional Government.* Moreover, when he wrote the book the youthful Wilson had never left Baltimore. According to his biographers, Wilson did not observe the House of Representatives or the Senate until much later, shortly before he became president.

Building upon the research and writing of scores of journalists, historians, and political scientists since World War II, Roger Davidson and Walter Oleszek have made an important contribution to the analysis of Congress. These two congressional scholars have provided a remarkably detailed and comprehensive description of two main facets of Congress: the motivations and behavior of its individual members and the ways in which the House and Senate set about making policy and passing or defeating legislation.

The authors perceive two Congresses—Congress as individual politicians, 100 senators and 435 representatives; and Congress as a collectivity with institutional purposes, chief among them initiating and passing laws. Representatives and senators, once elected, interact with one another in committees and groups and as members of the two major political parties. Individual perspectives affect but are also shaped by institutional constraints and demands. Davidson and Oleszek explore the forces that influence members of the House and Senate, including the president and executive branch, interest groups, the media, and, above all, their constituencies.

Taking advantage of their own intensive participation as staffers in several major congressional reorganizational efforts of the 1970s, the authors rely heavily on interviews, the public record, and the contributions of other scholars. The result is a book that is sensitive to the workings of Congress without losing its objectivity, that captures principal themes without bogging down in excessive detail, and that is historically grounded without losing its timeliness.

The writing of this book coincided with the beginnings of the Reagan administration. So far a new Republican administration, bolstered by control of the Senate for the first time since the 83rd Congress (1953-1955), has been able to override a Democratic-controlled House of Representatives on such major issues as cutbacks in federal programs and tax reductions. Davidson and Oleszek describe and interpret the main thrusts of these recent developments.

As the authors suggest, their primary objective has been to write a text that will help college students, especially those in courses on the legislative process, come to a better understanding of Congress. Quite likely, one or more future members of Congress will read this book and will be further motivated to take an active role in politics. The book is also aimed at citizens who want to know more about why men and women run for the House and Senate and what they do when they arrive in Washington. Not a few staff members, as well as some members of Congress, will find it a valuable reference source, especially to the considerable range of published research on the legislative branch in recent years. With the enhanced frequency of voluntary retirement and the increasing rates of turnover, party and committee leaders of Congress have lamented the absence of an "institutional memory" on the part of younger members. *Congress and Its Members* comes close to filling that gap. Davidson and Oleszek are to be commended for their "careful and systematic process of analysis" that Woodrow Wilson called for long ago.

NOTE

1. Woodrow Wilson, *Congressional Government* (1885; reprint ed., Baltimore: The Johns Hopkins Press, 1981), p. 57.

Robert L. Peabody

Preface

This book is the product of our personal fascination and professional experience with a most complex and perplexing body, the Congress of the United States. As academic political scientists, we have written technical studies about Congress and its lawmakers, lectured to college students, and tried to interpret congressional trends for wider audiences in talks and newspapers. We also have been privileged to serve during the past decade as professional staff members to several House and Senate committees and commissions—"in-house" efforts to analyze and revise congressional organization and operations. Finally, we have served as staff members of the oldest of the four legislative support agencies: the Congressional Research Service.

In writing this book, we have had in mind both general readers seeking an introduction to the modern Congress and college or university students in courses on the legislative process and national policy-making. The book has an organizing theme—the tensions between Congress as a collection of individuals and Congress as an institution—but we have tried not to allow this theme to obscure treatment of the history, structure, behavior, and policy role of Congress.

More than most, this has been a collaborative work. Robert L. Peabody reviewed the entire manuscript and made numerous useful suggestions, as did David M. Olson of the University of North Carolina at Greensboro and Burdett A. Loomis of the University of Kansas. Colleagues at the Congressional Research Service who supplied valuable information on specific subjects include Joe Cantor, Royce Crocker, Paul Dwyer, Louis Fisher, Robert Keith, Michael Kolakowski, Ronald Moe, Daniel Mulhollan, Clark Norton, Paul Rundquist, Steve Rutkus, and Allen Schick.

Our editors at Congressional Quarterly, Jean L. Woy, Barbara R. de Boinville, and John L. Moore, and their assistant, Susan D. Sullivan, deserve grateful acknowledgement for their extraordinary care and skill in improving our draft chapters and in transforming the manuscript into a book. Their prodigious efforts and professional talents were literally indispensable.

To identify all the people who contributed to our study would require endless pages. Our debt to congressional scholars, members of Congress, journalists, staff aides, and Capitol Hill friends and colleagues is immense. They have shared information, ideas, and insights that contributed immeasurably to our understanding of what makes Congress tick. Needless to say, our families exhibited the qualities needed to sustain a several-year project of this sort: encouragement, patience, and good humor. To Nancy, Douglas, and Christopher Davidson and Janet and Mark Oleszek—our loving thanks.

None of those with whom we have worked are to be held in any way accountable for our findings or opinions; most particularly, this book does not reflect the positions or views of the Congressional Research Service.

We dedicate this book to the memory of Representative William A. Steiger, R-Wis. A public servant we were privileged to consider a personal friend and colleague, Steiger taught us much about how Congress works and how individual members can at the same time fulfill institutional and electoral duties. He spent twelve uncommonly productive years in the House before his brilliant career was ended by an untimely death. His wit, insight, and commitment are as cherished as they are rare.

Roger H. Davidson
Walter J. Oleszek

Contents

Figures and Tables

Figures

Tables

I

In Search
of the
Two Congresses

"A good government implies two things: first, fidelity to the object of government, which is the happiness of the people, secondly, a knowledge of the means by which that object can be best attained."

The Federalist, No. 62 (1788)

"Legislatures are really two objects: a collectivity and an institution. As a collectivity, individual representatives act as receptors, reflecting the needs and wants of constituents. As an institution, the Legislature has to make laws, arriving at some conclusions about what ought to be done about public problems."

Charles O. Jones
"From the Suffrage of the People: An
Essay of Support and Worry for Legislatures." (1974)

These two statements—one by the authors of *The Federalist*, the other by a modern scholar—state our thesis. As the words suggest, the idea that representative assemblies contain an inherent tension between representation and lawmaking, between individual and institution, is neither new nor novel. This dualism is embedded in the Constitution, manifested in history, and validated by scholars' findings.

In elaborating the "two Congresses" notion, this book is organized into four parts, each with a brief explanatory introduction. In this part, the two Congresses theme is outlined. The second describes who the members are, how they get to the House or Senate, and what they do after they arrive. The third explores the Capitol Hill landscape—leaders, committees, staffs, and procedures—and their impact on congressional decisions. Policymaking and change within the two Congresses are the focus of the final part of the book.

1

Introduction:
The Two Congresses

TWO VIEWS OF CONGRESS

Scene 1: Capitol Hill

The 95th Congress finally adjourned early in the evening,
Sunday, October 15, 1978. The House finished at 6:46 p.m., when
departing members broke the quorum needed to conduct business;
the Senate quit half an hour later, at 7:16 p.m. During the
preceding 34 hours, all through Saturday night, lobbyists, tourists,
and others crowded the galleries to view the marathon session—
especially in the Senate, where retiring Senator James Abourezk,
D-S.D., was staging a 14-hour filibuster against President Carter's
energy bill. Once the Senate voted to limit debate on the bill, a
logjam of other business had to be disposed of—important votes,
routine approvals, and last-minute maneuvering to save or scuttle
bills.

The closing session encompassed two World Series games and
several football games—as evidenced by occasional roars emanating from the cloakrooms. Just off the House chamber, retiring
Representative Del Clawson, R-Calif., could be heard playing his
saxophone. As adjournment drew near over in the Senate, legislators were punchy. When a division (standing) vote was called on

5

tuition tax credits, Senator Birch Bayh, D-Ind., wearily asked, "At this hour does a division require the members to stand?" The presiding officer at the time, Senator Patrick Leahy, D-Vt., replied, "The chair will give them time to get to their feet." [1]

The last laugh came at everyone's expense. Just before adjournment, House Majority Whip John Brademas, D-Ind., read a statement from President Carter praising the 95th Congress as "one of the most courageous and productive." The raucous House members, ready to leave for home, laughed heartily at that.

The 95th Congress was busy, if not always memorable. Some 22,000 bills and resolutions were introduced, 800 of them passed and signed into law. The two houses took a record number of roll-call votes, 2,191. The proceedings of the Senate and House (more than 4,400 hours) required no fewer than 66,573 pages of the *Congressional Record*.

Scene 2: Long Beach, California

As the 95th Congress was dying in exhaustion, Democratic Representative Mark Hannaford was fighting for his political life 3,000 miles away in his home state. His district, the California 34th, embraced 464,000 people in the more prosperous areas of Long Beach, the middle-income suburbs of Bellflower and Lakewood, and in Orange County, part of Huntington Beach as well as the senior citizens' community of Leisure World.

Hannaford's district was Republican territory. When its 22-year GOP congressman, Craig Hosmer, retired in 1974, Hannaford—a former political science professor at Long Beach State and mayor of Lakewood—was swept into office by the Democratic tide flowing from public anger at the Watergate scandal. For two terms Hannaford hung on, winning 52 percent of the vote in 1974 and 51 percent in 1976.

Watergate made Hannaford a congressman, and the resources of incumbency helped him to stay in office four years. During his second term Hannaford sent more than 2.4 million pieces of mail to the 190,000 households in his district, using the postage-free franking privilege. Walking the streets of Lakewood, where he and his wife had raised their family, Hannaford stressed the favors he had done for the district. "You can take almost every square mile of the district and find something that we've done," he told the voters. "There are more senior citizens in my district than in any other in the country. We had a hearing here and saved the hot meals program. We got the city of Long Beach turned into an agency for the aging."

Hannaford's opponent in 1978, as in the previous two races, was Republican Dan Lungren, an attractive campaigner who happened to be the son of former President Nixon's physician. Lungren tried to pin a "big spender" image on the incumbent, and the strategy seemed to be working this time.

"Didn't you beat this same guy last time?" asked a man coming to the door of his stucco home on Lakewood's Monogram Street.

"I sure did, but he's still lusting after my job," Hannaford joked.

"What was this I read in the paper? He said you were a big spender and you admitted it?" the householder persisted.

"If I didn't spend money on newsletters, traveling home every weekend and staff, I would be cheating the people of this district," Hannaford answered. He recited laws and programs won for the district, claiming they were worth many times what he spent communicating with constituents.[2]

Hannaford's frantic campaigning failed to hold his seat for the 96th Congress. Lungren's third try proved successful. By some 13,000 votes, he defeated Hannaford, one of seven members of the Democratic "Class of '74" who were unseated. Although incumbents are not often ousted, the struggle in California's 34th District suggests what can happen in the 540 constituencies (435 representatives, 100 senators, 4 delegates, 1 resident commissioner) represented in the houses of Congress.

THE IDEA OF THE 'TWO CONGRESSES'

The final debate on the House and Senate floors and the intense struggle in the California 34th: both of these scenes point to the meaning of the United States Congress. Both, in fact, are integral aspects of Congress as a lawmaking body and a representative assembly. But how can we reconcile these disparate elements?

The answer is that there are really two Congresses, not just one. Often these two Congresses are widely separated; the tightly knit, complex world of Capitol Hill is a long way from the world of Representative Hannaford's California district—not only in thousands of miles, but in perspective and outlook as well. Moreover, the two Congresses are analytically distinct; studies indicate that public officials and citizens view the twin functions of elected assemblies—lawmaking and representing—as separate, definable tasks.

And yet, these two Congresses are closely bound together. What affects the one sooner or later affects the other. Representative Hannaford's Washington behavior was shaped largely by his diverse district and his hairline margins of victory. By the same token, the image he showed to his constituents, the way his constituents saw him, was made possible by what he accomplished on Capitol Hill.

One of these two entities, of course, is Congress as an institution. It is the Congress of textbooks, of "how-a-bill-becomes-a-law." It is Congress acting as a collegial body, performing constitutional duties and handling legislative issues. It is an intriguing subject. To tourists no less than veteran "Congress-watchers," Capitol Hill is a fascinating arena where converge many of the forces of American political life—ambitious politicians, White House and executive agencies, lobbies both powerful and weak, not to mention intricate congressional subunits and procedures that reflect the legislative struggle. The issues aired on Capitol Hill, to invoke a time-worn sentiment, affect the well-being of all of us.

Casual visitors to Capitol Hill sometimes are dismayed at their first exposure to this Congress. Often members' speeches are delivered to virtually empty House or Senate chambers; many committee hearings are routine, dull, and ill-attended. As a large body with a demanding workload, Congress works through subgroups more often than as a single body. As one representative, the late Clem Miller, D-Calif., once remarked, "Congress is a collection of committees that come together in a chamber periodically to approve one another's actions." [3] Yet these many work groups—and there are more of them now than ever before—are responsible for public business; their products often turn into binding public policy.

Yet there is a second Congress, every bit as important as the Congress of the textbooks. This is the Congress of 540 individual senators, representatives, and delegates. They are men and women of diverse ages, backgrounds, and routes to office. Their electoral fortunes depend, not upon what Congress produces as an institution, but upon the support and goodwill of voters hundreds or thousands of miles away. Journalist Richard Rovere once compared members of Congress to tribesmen whose chief concern while in Washington was what was going on around the council fires back home. This may be an exaggeration, but it contains an important truth: by no means all congressional activity takes place in Capitol Hill chambers or committee rooms.

The Historical Basis

The dual character of Congress is rooted in history. Congress's mandate to write the nation's laws is found in Article I of the Constitution, which details the powers of government as set forth by the Founders in 1787. It was no accident that the Constitution's drafters devoted the first article to the legislature nor that here were enumerated most of the government's powers. Familiar with the English Parliament's prolonged struggles with the Crown, the Constitution's authors assumed the legislature would be the chief policymaking body and the bulwark against arbitrary executives. ("In republican government, the legislative authority necessarily predominates,"observed James Madison in *The Federalist Papers*.[4]) Although in the ensuing years initiative shifted many times between the legislative and executive branches, the United States Congress remains virtually the only legislature in the world that actually tries to write the laws it passes, rather than simply ratifying laws prepared by the government in power.

"All legislative Powers herein granted shall be vested in a Congress of the United States, which shall consist of a Senate and House of Representatives," Article I, Section 1, specifies. These legislative powers are set forth in detail in the remaining nine sections of Article I. Fiscal duties—taxing and spending—are the heart of Congress's power, for they reach into almost every area of public policy. Congress also has substantial power over foreign policy (declarations of war, treaty making), government personnel (confirmations of nominees, impeachments), foreign and interstate commerce, national defense (raising and equipping armed forces), presidential selection (in cases of electoral college deadlock, presidential disability, or resignation), and constitutional amendments. Once limited in volume and simple in content, these lawmaking powers have grown to staggering proportions.

At the very same time, Congress is a representative assembly that must respond to the heavy demands of voters and constituents. Although not specifically mentioned in the Constitution, these duties flow from its provisions for electing representatives and senators.

The House of Representatives is, and was intended to be, the most representative unit of our government. Representatives are elected directly by the people for two-year terms to ensure that they do not stray too far from popular opinion. As James Madison explained, the House should have "an immediate dependence on, and an intimate sympathy with, the people." [5] For many members of the House, this means nonstop campaigning, visiting, looking after constituents, and errand running. For others the job is simpler; yet no elected official is totally "safe" from electoral defeat.

The Senate originally was intended to be one step removed from popular voting to temper the popular sentiments of the House. But the Founders were ultimately thwarted in this objective. The people's voice was assured in 1913 by ratification of the Seventeenth Amendment, which provided for direct election of senators. Even though elected for six-year terms, senators typically are servants of their constituents; most have transformed their office staffs into veritable cottage industries for generating publicity and handling constituents' inquiries. Sometimes they compete with representatives' offices, which perform the same functions for a smaller geographic area.

Thus the Constitution and subsequent historical developments affirm Congress's dual functions of *lawmaker* and *representative assembly*. The roles are tightly bound together, but nonetheless they impose separate tasks and functions.

Legislators' Tasks

This same "two Congresses" dualism—between institutional and individual duties—surfaces in legislators' role orientations and daily activities. As Speaker Sam Rayburn, D-Texas, once remarked:

> A congressman has two constituencies—he has his constituents at home, and his colleagues here in the House. To serve his constituents at home, he must also serve his colleagues here in the House.[6]

Like most of us, senators and representatives suffer from a lack of time for accomplishing what is expected of them. No problem more vexes members than that of juggling constituency and legislative tasks. Despite scheduled recesses for constituency business (called "district work" by the House and "nonlegislative periods" by the Senate), Tuesday-Thursday Capitol Hill schedules persist: the average representative makes 35 trips a year back to the district, better than one every other week.[7] Even in Washington, legislative and constituency demands must be juggled; according to one study, less than 40 percent of a representative's Washington time is allotted to duties on the floor or in committee.[8]

Members of Congress themselves, when asked to describe the functions they should perform in office, stress the twin roles of legislator and representative. Naturally, legislators differ in the weight they assign these roles, not to mention the time and resources they devote to them. Senators, whose terms are longer but whose elections are normally more competitive than representatives', used to stress legislative tasks for the first few years and then prepare for reelection by spending more time in the state renewing contacts and rebuilding fences. With the high rate of defeat at the polls, senators today tend to run for reelection all the time—like most of their House colleagues.

Legislators must often choose between the demands of these two roles. A House-sponsored survey in 1977 asked members about differences between how they *actually* spent their time and what they would like to do *ideally* as a member of Congress. By far the most frequent complaint, voiced by half of the representatives, was that constituent demands interfered with lawmaking and other Hill activity.[9]

Popular Images

The two Congresses notion conforms also with the perceptions of average persons. Recent opinion studies reveal that citizens view the Congress in Washington through different lenses than they do their individual senators and representatives.

Congress as an institution is seen primarily as a lawmaking body. It is judged mainly on the basis of citizens' overall attitudes about policies and the state of the union: Do people like the way things are going, or do they not? Are they optimistic or pessimistic about the nation's future?

By contrast, citizens view their own legislators as agents of local interest. They evaluate legislators on such criteria as service to the district, communication with constituents, and "home style"—that is, the way the officeholder deals with the home folks. In choosing senators or representatives, voters are likely to ponder such questions as: Do I trust the legislator? Does the legislator communicate with the state (or district)—answering mail and offering help to constituents? Does the legislator listen to the state (or district) and its viewpoints?

The public's divergent expectations of Congress and its members often relay conflicting signals to senators or representatives. Congress as a whole is judged by policies and results, however vaguely these are perceived by voters; individual legislators are elected, and returned to office, mainly because of personal qualifications and constituent service. To many legislators, this dictates a strategy of putting as much distance as possible between themselves and "those other politicians" back in Washington. Many candidates and incumbents run *for* Congress by running *against* Congress.[10]

PLAN OF THE BOOK

In this book the two Congresses concept is used as a tool to analyze our national legislature, which is both a policymaking body and a collectivity of independently chosen political entrepreneurs. As we have seen, this view of Congress has historical and theoretical foundations and conforms with common-sense impressions about how the institution really operates. Many of those features of Congress that most impress observers—its decentralization, its lack of hierarchy, its slow pace—are best explained by this approach. By analyzing the dual character of Congress, we can assess more precisely those sorts of policy questions that Congress is best suited to resolve and those that it accomplishes imperfectly or only with great difficulty.

We already have introduced the two Congresses theme and outlined some of the arguments for its validity. The second chapter in Part I examines the constitutional roots of Congress's dual character and traces the historical evolution of the institution.

Part II analyzes the first of these two Congresses, Congress-as-individual-politicians. The men and women elected to Congress are end products of a complex winnowing process. Aspirants are selected or eliminated, not only by the formal qualifications for office, but also by the practical hurdles they must surmount before becoming legislators. Elected officials do not mirror exactly the people they serve, nor even the voters who put them in office. Once elected, legislators represent their voters in different ways, ways that evolve as legislators age or take on new duties, or as the district's composition shifts. Legislators' public images are shaped by communications media—some sponsored by the legislators themselves, others outside their control. Sometimes legislators lose touch with the voters who elected them or alter their career goals so drastically that reelection no longer intrigues them. Thus the legislator's career terminates, voluntarily or otherwise.

Part III focuses on the second Congress, Congress-as-policymaker. This is the Congress familiar to scholars and commentators, and its workings have been meticulously recorded. Congressional policymaking is an endlessly complicated, fascinating process involving floor procedures, committees, party and factional leaders and followers, and cadres of staffs and supporting agencies. Rules and procedures in both houses are complicated, at the same time shaping and reflecting the legislative struggle.

Neither of these two Congresses functions in a vacuum. Powerful outside forces influence Congress and its members. Among these forces are such political institutions as the president, the executive establishment, the courts, and the political party coalitions. Congressional action also is shaped by public opinion, by press coverage, and by powerful lobbying groups. Even the subtle workings of social, economic, and technological change exert a powerful impact on the operations of Congress. All these forces converge upon the offices, committee rooms, and chambers of Capitol Hill.

Congress's dual nature—the unresolved dichotomy between its functions as lawmaker and representative—is dictated by the Constitution, validated by historical experience, and reinforced by the inclinations of voters and legislators alike. And yet, Congress is literally one body, not two. The same members who shape bills in committee and vote on the floor must rush to catch planes back to their districts where they are plunged into a different world made up of local problems. And the same candidates who must sell themselves at shopping center rallies must, in Washington, focus on baffling issues such as inflation rates or military weapons systems. The unique character of Congress flows directly from its dual role as a representative assembly and a lawmaking body.

In Part IV of the book we endeavor to draw together the lawmaking and representative functions of Congress. All of us are affected by laws written by representatives of given electoral districts. Whether these laws concern taxes or energy regulation or foreign assistance, they usually promote the interests of specialized constituencies, geographic or otherwise. This is consistent with the principles of a representative democracy, but in terms of "general welfare" the results are often mixed. Local interests can scatter a policy so that it fails to have the desired effects or even has adverse consequences for the citizens at large. In policy terms, *e pluribus unum* ("one out of many") may be a shining ideal or a millstone.

Sometimes people talk as if Congress is a hidebound institution inhabited by fossils. True, spittoons and inkwells still adorn the House and Senate chambers, but appearances are deceiving. Since the 1960s dramatic changes have swept virtually every nook and cranny on Capitol Hill—its membership, structures, procedures, folkways, and staffs. The causes of these changes, their results, and their long-term consequences for our government's effectiveness and vitality, are the final questions addressed in this book.

On November 3, 1774, in Bristol, England, the British statesman and philosopher Edmund Burke set forth for his constituents the dual character of a national legislature. The constituent-oriented Parliament, or Congress, he described as

> a Congress of ambassadors from different and hostile interests, which interests each must maintain, as an agent and advocate, against other agents and advocates.

The Parliament of substantive lawmaking he portrayed in different terms:

> a deliberative assembly of one nation, with one interest, that of the whole—where not local purposes, not local prejudices, ought to guide, but the general good, resulting from the general reason of the whole.[11]

From Burke we have chosen the titles for Part II, A Congress of Ambassadors, and Part III, A Deliberative Assembly of One Nation. Burke himself preferred the second concept and did not hesitate to let his voters know it; he would give local opinion a hearing, but his judgment and conscience would prevail in all cases. "Your faithful friend, your devoted servant, I shall be to the end of my life," he declared; "flatterer you do not wish for." [12]

Burke's Bristol speech is an enduring statement of the dilemma confronting members of representative assemblies. Burke was an inspired lawmaker. (He even sympathized with the cause of the American colonists.) But his candor earned him no thanks from his constituents, who turned him out of office at the first opportunity. Today, we might say Burke suffered from an inept "home style." Yet he posed the dilemma of the two Congresses so vividly that we have adopted his language to describe the conceptual distinction that forms the crux of this book. Every legislator must sooner or later come to terms with Burke's question. As citizens and voters, you will have to reach your own conclusions about the dilemma.

OUR VIEW OF CONGRESS

In describing and analyzing the two Congresses, we have tried to draw upon a wide variety of materials. Congress is the subject of a bewildering array of books, monographs, and articles. No doubt many features make Congress such a favorite object of scholarly scrutiny. It is open and accessible. Its work can be measured by statistical indicators—floor votes, for example—that permit elaborate comparative analyses. And Congress is, above all, a fascinating place—a "strategic site" from which to view the varied actors in the American political drama.

Many of these same features attract journalists and interpretive reporters to Congress. Although Congress does not draw the media attention lavished on the president and his entourage, it is extensively covered. Some of our finest commentators have written incisive, provocative analyses of Congress and the politicians who inhabit it. In short, interested observers can draw upon a large body of information about our national legislature.

Writers of an interpretive book on the U.S. Congress are thus faced with an embarrassment of riches. Indeed, studies of Congress comprise perhaps the richest body of political literature. Yet this is a mixed blessing because we have to integrate this information into something resembling a coherent whole. Moreover, much of the writing is highly detailed, specialized, or technical; we have tried to put such material into perspective, make it understandable to interested nonspecialists, and use illustrative examples whenever possible.

Another body of information about Congress, even less accessible to the average citizen, is Capitol Hill history, precedents, and lore. Some of it is recorded in public documents, but most of it is stored in the memories of legislators, their staffs, and the lobbyists and executive officials who deal with them. By and large, this information focuses on the day-to-day "real world" of Capitol Hill—its events, its personalities, and its rules and precedents.

A gap sometimes exists between those who write about Congress and those who actually live and work on Capitol Hill. Legislators and their aides are often suspicious of "those professors," who (they say) spin theories of little practical value.[13] And they are equally wary of journalists, who are to politicians as potentially dangerous as they are essential. For their part, outside commentators often dismiss Capitol Hill wisdom. Professors tend to regard the "insiders'" view as unsystematic, anecdotal, or mere gossip. Journalists suspect the insiders' view is self-serving (which it often is), designed to obscure the public's view. These conflicting views naturally spring from varying motives and divergent premises.

Is this book, then, an "insiders'" or an "outsiders'" view of Congress? Both, we hope. While it would be presumptuous to claim that we can integrate fully these two viewpoints, our backgrounds have allowed us to see Congress from both perspectives—as academic political scientists and as congressional staff members. We understand the wide gap between observing Congress as a scholar or commentator and having direct responsibilities for advising members of Congress.

It is helpful to know an institution intimately so that you can interpret it to others; yet being too close can invite distortion. We believe we know our subject well enough to appreciate its foibles and understand why it works the way it does. Yet we try to maintain a degree of professional—and scholarly—distance from it. It is far easier to describe how and why an institution functions, than to analyze its defects and suggest how it might operate more effectively. We are not entirely sanguine about the future of Congress, or indeed of representative government; and we invite students and colleagues to join us in contemplating what alternatives lie before us.

NOTES

1. U.S., Congress, Senate, *Congressional Record,* daily ed., 95th Cong., 2d sess., October 14, 1978, p. S19148.
2. Ellen Hume, "Hannaford Fights for his Political Life," *Los Angeles Times,* November 1, 1978, pt. II, p. 2.
3. Clem Miller, *Member of the House: Letters of a Congressman,* ed. John W. Baker (New York: Charles Scribner's Sons, 1962), p. 110.
4. James Madison, Alexander Hamilton, and John Jay, *The Federalist Papers,* introduction by Clinton Rossiter (New York: New American Library, 1961), no. 51, p. 322.
5. Ibid., no. 52, p. 327.
6. Sam Rayburn, *Speak, Mr. Speaker,* ed. H. G. Dulaney and Edward Hake Phillips (Bonham, Texas: Sam Rayburn Foundation, 1978), pp. 263-264.
7. Richard F. Fenno, Jr., *Home Style: House Members in Their Districts* (Boston: Little, Brown & Co., 1978), p. 35.
8. U.S., Congress, House, Commission on Administrative Review, *Administrative Reorganization and Legislative Management,* 2 vols., H. Doc. 95-232, 95th Cong., 1st sess., September 28, 1977, 2: 18-19.
9. Ibid., *Final Report,* 2 vols., H. Doc. 95-272, 95th Cong., 1st sess., December 31, 1977, 2: 875.
10. Fenno, *Home Style,* p. 168.
11. Edmund Burke, "Speech to Electors at Bristol," in *Burke's Politics,* ed. Ross J. S. Hoffman and Paul Levack (New York: Alfred A. Knopf, 1949), p. 116.
12. Ibid.
13. Fenno, *Home Style,* p. 294.

The U.S. Capitol under construction, 1868.

Evolution
of the
Modern Congress

The very first Congress met in New York City, the seat of government, in the spring of 1789. Business was delayed until a majority of members arrived to make a quorum. On April 1 the thirtieth of the 59 elected representatives reached New York; Frederick A. C. Muhlenberg of Pennsylvania promptly was chosen as Speaker of the House. Five days later the Senate achieved its quorum, although its presiding officer—Vice President John Adams—did not arrive for another two weeks.

New York City was then a bustling port town on the southern tip of Manhattan Island. Congress met in Federal Hall at the corner of Broad and Wall streets. The House occupied a large chamber on the first floor and the Senate a more intimate chamber upstairs. The new chief executive, George Washington, was still en route from his home at Mount Vernon, his trip having quickly turned into a triumphal procession with crowds and celebrations at every stop. To most of his countrymen, Washington—austere, dignified, the "epitome of propriety"—embodied a government that was otherwise little more than an idea on paper.

17

The two houses of Congress, headstrong even then, did not wait for Washington's arrival. The House began debating tariffs, a perennially fascinating legislative topic. Upstairs in the Senate, Vice President Adams, a brilliant but self-important man, needled his colleagues about the proper titles for addressing the president and himself. (Adams was dubbed "His Rotundity" by a colleague who thought the whole discussion absurd.)

On the day of the president's inauguration, April 30, Adams was still worrying about how to address the president. The issue was forced when the representatives, led by Speaker Muhlenberg, burst into the Senate chamber and seated themselves. Meanwhile, a special committee was dispatched to escort Washington to the chamber for the ceremony. The actual swearing-in was conducted on an outside balcony in front of thousands of assembled citizens. The nervous Washington haltingly read his speech. Then everyone adjourned to St. Paul's Chapel for a special prayer service. Thus the United States Congress became part of a functioning government.[1]

ANTECEDENTS OF CONGRESS

The legislative branch of the new government was untried and unknown, groping for procedures and precedents. And yet, it grew out of more than 500 years of historical development. If the architects of the Constitution of 1787 were unsure exactly how their design would work, they had strong ideas about what they intended.

The English Heritage

From the time of Edward the Confessor in the eleventh century, the central problem of political theory and practice was the relationship of the Crown to its subjects. Out of prolonged struggles, a strong, representative Parliament emerged that rivaled and eventually eclipsed the power of the Crown. The evolution of representative institutions on a national scale began in medieval Europe, when certain monarchs gained power over large territories. These territories embraced masses of people divided into social classes, groups, and communities. The monarchs called together representatives of these communities, or estates, not for creating representative government, but for the more mundane purpose of filling the royal coffers. As Charles A. Beard and John Lewis observed, "Even the most despotic medieval monarch could not tax and exploit his subjects without limits; as a matter of expediency, he had also to consider ways and means." [2]

Once brought together to provide money for the royal treasury, these groups—*parliaments,* they came to be called—evolved over a 500-

year period into the representative assemblies we know today. Four distinct stages of their development have been identified. At first the parliaments, representing estates of the realm (nobility, clergy, landed gentry, town officials), met to vote taxes for the royal treasury and engaged in very little discussion. Next, the tax-voting body became a lawmaking body, presenting grievances to the king for redress. Third, by a gradual process culminating in the seventeenth-century revolutions, parliament wrested lawmaking and tax-voting power from the king, turning itself into a sovereign body. In the nineteenth century, finally, parliamentary representation extended beyond the older privileged groups to embrace the masses, eventually every man and woman.[3]

By the time the New World colonies were founded in the 1600s, the struggle for parliamentary rights was well advanced into the third stage, at least in England. Bloody conflicts, culminating in the beheading of Charles I in 1649 and the dethroning of James II in 1688 (the so-called "Glorious Revolution"), established parliamentary influence over the Crown. Out of such struggles flowed a remarkable body of political and philosophic writings. By the eighteenth century, works by James Harrington (1611-1677), John Locke (1632-1704), and others were the common heritage of educated people—including the leaders of the American Revolution.

The Colonial Experience

This tradition of representative government migrated to the New World. As early as 1619, the thousand or so Virginia colonists elected 22 delegates, or burgesses, to a General Assembly. In 1630 the Massachusetts Bay Company established itself as the governing body for the Bay Colony, subject to annual elections. The other colonies, some of them virtually self-governing, followed suit.

Soon representative government took firm root in the colonies. The broad expanse of ocean shielding America fostered self-reliance and autonomy on the part of colonial assemblies. Claiming prerogatives similar to those of the British House of Commons, these assemblies exercised the full range of lawmaking powers—levying taxes, issuing money, and providing for colonial defense. Legislation could be vetoed by colonial governors (appointed by the Crown in the eight royal colonies); but the governors, cut off from the home government and depending on local assemblies for revenues and even their own salaries, usually preferred to reach accommodations with the locals. Royal vetoes could emanate from London, but these, too, were sparing.[4]

Other factors nourished the tree of liberty. Many of the colonists were free spirits, dissidents set on resisting all authority, especially the Crown's. Readily available land, harsh frontier life, and—by the eighteenth century—a prosperous economy fed the colonists' self-confidence. The town meeting form of government in New England and the Separatists' church assemblies helped cultivate habits of self-government. And newspapers, unfettered by royal licenses or government taxes, stimulated debate and exchange of opinions.

When England decided in the 1760s to tighten her rein upon the American colonies, therefore, she was met with stubborn opposition. Did not the colonists enjoy the same rights as Englishmen? Were not the colonial assemblies the legitimate government, deriving their authority from popular elections? As parliamentary enactments grew increasingly unpopular, the colonial legislatures took up the cause of their constituents, and the colonial governors grew more and more uncomfortable.

Especially resented by the colonists were the Stamp Act of 1765 (later repealed) and the import duties imposed in 1767. From these inflated customs receipts the home government began paying the salaries of royal governors and other officials, thus freeing them from the hold of colonial assemblies. The crisis worsened in the winter of 1773-1774 when, to protest the Tea Act, a group of colonists staged the Boston Tea Party. In retaliation, the House of Commons closed the port of Boston and passed a series of "Intolerable Acts" further strengthening royal control.

If a birthdate is to be selected for national representative assemblies in America, it would probably be September 5, 1774. On that date the First Continental Congress convened in Philadelphia. Every colony except Georgia sent delegates, who ranged from peaceable loyalists to radicals like Samuel Adams and Paul Revere. Gradually anti-British sentiment congealed, and the Congress passed a series of declarations and resolutions (each colony casting one vote) amounting to a declaration of war against the mother country.[5] After the Congress adjourned on October 22, King George III declared that the colonies were "now in a state of rebellion; blows must decide whether they are to be subject to this country or independent." [6]

If the First Continental Congress gave colonists their first taste of collective decisionmaking, the Second Continental Congress proclaimed the colonies' independence from Britain. When this body convened on May 10, 1775, many still thought war might be avoided. A petition to King George asking for "happy and permanent reconciliation" was even approved. The British responded by proclaiming a state of rebellion and launching efforts to crush it. Sentiment in the colonies swung increasingly toward independence, and by the middle of 1776 the Congress was debating Thomas Jefferson's draft resolution proposing that "these United Colonies are, and of right ought to be, free and independent states." [7] Shared legislative experience had helped bring the colonies to the threshold of independence.

More than five years of bloody conflict ensued before the colonies' independence was won. In the meantime, nearly all the colonies hastened to form new governments and draft constitutions. Unlike the English constitution, these were written documents. All of them included some sort of "bill of rights" and all paid tribute to the doctrine of separating powers among legislative, executive, and judicial branches of government. *Equal* branches of government were not created, however. Nearly all the constitutions gave the bulk of governmental powers to their legislatures. Earlier conflicts with the Crown and the royal governors had instilled in the colonists a fear of executive authority. "In actual operation," a historian wrote, "these first state constitutions produced what was tantamount to legislative omnipotence." [8]

At the national level, a parallel situation existed. Strictly speaking, from 1776 to 1787—the years of the revolutionary war and the Articles of Confederation—no national executive existed. The Continental Congress struggled on its own to direct the war effort, often with haphazard results. As the war progressed and legislative direction proved unwieldy, the Congress tended to delegate authority to its own committees and to permanent (executive) agencies. The government's frailty under the Articles, adopted in 1781, was not only a lack of delegated powers, but also the weakness of government by legislature. The Congress was paramount; a vigorous, independent executive was sorely needed.

The inability of all-powerful legislative bodies, state and national, to deal with postwar problems spurred demands for change. On the state level, newly rewritten constitutions reinstated the notion of a strong executive. At the Confederation level, it became apparent that a more "energetic" government was needed—one that could implement laws, control currency, dispose of war debts, and if necessary put down rebellion. In this spirit delegates from the states convened in Philadelphia on May 25, 1787, intending to strengthen the Articles of Confederation. Instead they drew up a new governmental charter.

CONGRESS IN THE CONSTITUTION

The structure and powers of Congress formed the very core of the Constitutional Convention's deliberations. On these questions, the 55 delegates at the Philadelphia convention were divided, and more than three months passed before they completed their work. The plan for the government, agreed upon and signed September 17, 1787, represented a compromise. Nationalist and states' rights interests, large states and small ones, northern states and southern had to be satisfied. The result was a singular blend of national and federal features based on republican principles of representation and limited government. The Constitution served the nationalists' goal of energetic central government that could function independently of the states. It also conceded the states' rights principle of limited powers shared by the various branches.

Powers of Congress

The federal government's powers are shared by three branches—legislative, executive, and judicial. Although considered one of the Constitution's most innovative features, "separation of powers" flowed naturally from English and colonial experience, which argued for dispersing governmental functions. It was advocated by philosophers such as Locke, Harrington, and Baron de Montesquieu. And the failure of the Articles of Confederation to separate these functions was widely regarded as a mistake.

The legislative branch was granted a breathtaking array of powers. Familiar with Parliament's long-term struggles with the Crown, the Founders conceived of the legislature as the chief repository of governmental powers. John Locke had observed that "the legislative is not only the supreme power, but is sacred and unalterable in the hands where the community have placed it." [9] Locke's doctrine found expression in Article I, Section 8, of the Constitution, which enumerates Congress's powers. Indeed this section embraces virtually the entire scope of governmental authority as the eighteenth-century Founders understood it. There are limits, to be sure. Most of the powers are shared with other governmental branches. But no one reading this portion of the Constitution can fail to be impressed with the Founders' vision of a vigorous legislature as a keystone of energetic government.

Raising and spending money for governmental purposes lies at the heart of Congress's prerogatives. The "power of the purse" was the lever by which parliaments historically gained bargaining advantages over kings. The Constitution's authors, well aware of this, gave Congress full power of the purse. There are two components of this power: *taxing* and *spending*.

Financing the government is carried out under a broad mandate in Article I, Section 8: "The Congress shall have power to lay and collect taxes, duties, imposts and excises, to pay the debts and provide for the common defense and general welfare of the United States." Although this wording covered all known forms of taxing, there were limitations: taxes had to be uniform throughout the country; duties were prohibited on goods traveling between states; and "capitation . . . or other direct" taxes were prohibited, unless levied according to population (Article I, Section 9). This last provision proved troublesome, especially when the Supreme Court held in 1895 *(Pollock v. Farmers' Loan and Trust Co.)* that it applied to taxes on incomes. To overcome this confusion, the Sixteenth Amendment, ratified 18 years later, explicitly conferred the power to levy income taxes.

Congressional power over government spending is no less sweeping than revenue power. According to Article I, Section 9, "No money shall be drawn from the Treasury, but in consequence of appropriations made by law." This is one of the legislature's most potent weapons in overseeing the executive branch.

Congress possesses potentially broad powers over the nation's economic and political well-being. It may coin money, incur debts, and regulate commerce. It may establish post offices, build post roads, and issue patents and copyrights. It has the duty of specifying the size of the Supreme Court and of establishing lower federal courts. It has the power to provide for a militia and call it forth to repel invasions or suppress rebellions.

Congress plays a role in foreign relations with its powers of declaring war, ratifying treaties, raising and supporting armies, providing and maintaining a navy, and making rules governing the military forces. Finally, Congress is vested with the power "to make laws which shall be necessary and proper for carrying into execution the foregoing powers" (Article I, Section 8). This provision (called the "elastic clause") probably was added simply to give Congress the means to implement the enumerated powers, but later it triggered far-reaching debates over the scope of governmental powers.

Limits on Legislative Power

Congress's enumerated powers—those "herein granted"—are not boundless. The very act of listing the powers was intended to limit government, for by implication those powers that are not listed are prohibited. This intention was made explicit by the Tenth Amendment, which reserves to the states or to the people all those powers neither explicitly delegated nor prohibited by the Constitution.

Eight specific limitations on Congress's powers are noted in Article I, Section 9. The most important bans are against *bills of attainder*, which pronounce a particular individual guilty of a crime without trial or conviction and impose a sentence upon him, and *ex post facto laws*, which make an action a crime after it has been committed or otherwise change the legal consequences of some past action. Bills of attainder and ex post facto laws are traditional tools of authoritarian regimes. Congress's enumerated powers are also limited in such matters as the slave trade, taxation, appropriations, and titles of nobility.

The original Constitution contained no Bill of Rights, or list of guarantees for citizens or states. Pressed by opponents during the ratification debate, especially in Massachusetts and Virginia, supporters of the Constitution promised early enactment of amendments to remedy this omission. The resulting 10 amendments, drawn up by the first

Congress and ratified December 15, 1791, are a basic charter of liberties that limits the reach of government. The First Amendment prohibits Congress from establishing a national religion, preventing the free exercise of religion, or abridging the freedoms of speech, press, peaceable assembly, and petition. Other amendments secure the rights of personal property and fair trial, and prohibit arbitrary arrest, questioning, or punishment.

Rights not enumerated in the Bill of Rights are not necessarily denied. In fact, subsequent amendments and legislative enactments have enlarged citizens' rights to include, among others, the rights of citizenship, of voting, and of "equal protection of the laws." Initially, the Bill of Rights was held to limit only the national government, but the Fourteenth Amendment, ratified in 1868, prohibited states from impairing "due process" or "equal protection of the laws." At first courts held that mainly economic rights were covered by these clauses. Beginning in 1925 *(Gitlow v. New York),* however, the Supreme Court began to subsume Bill of Rights guarantees under the "due process" clause. Today almost every portion of the Bill of Rights applies to the states as well as to the federal government.

Shared Powers

Most legislative powers are shared with the executive and judicial branches of government. The Constitution creates a system, not of separate institutions performing separate functions, but of separate institutions sharing functions, so that, as James Madison observed, "these departments be so far connected and blended as to give to each a constitutional control over the others." [10]

Even in lawmaking, Congress does not act alone. According to Article II, the president can convene one or both houses of Congress in special session. Although unable to introduce legislation directly, the president "shall from time to time give to the Congress information on the state of the Union, and recommend to their consideration such measures as he shall judge necessary and expedient." The president also has the power to veto congressional enactments. Within 10 days (excluding Sundays) after a bill or resolution has passed both houses of Congress, the president must sign or return it. To overrule a presidential veto, a two-thirds vote is required in each house.

Implementing laws is the duty of the president, who is enjoined by the Constitution to take care that they are faithfully executed. He is the chief officer of the executive branch. The president has the power to appoint "officers of the United States," with the Senate's advice and consent. While Congress sets up the executive departments and agencies, outlining their missions by statute, the president and his appointees set the character and pace of executive activity. Moreover, Congress has power to impeach or remove civil officers for treason, bribery, or "other high crimes and misdemeanors."

In diplomacy and national defense, traditional bastions of royal prerogative, the Constitution apportions powers between the executive and legislative branches of government. Following tradition, the president is given wide discretion in such matters: he appoints ambassadors and other envoys; he negotiates treaties; he commands the country's armed forces.

Yet here, too, functions are intermeshed. Like other principal presidential appointees, ambassadors and envoys must be approved by the Senate. Treaties do not become law of the land until they are ratified by the Senate. Although the president may dispatch troops, only Congress has the formal power to declare war. Reacting to the Vietnam war experience, Congress in 1973 passed a War Powers Resolution, reminding the president of congressional war-making powers. Through its cherished power of the purse, Congress regulates the flow of funds and equips military forces.

Judicial Review

The third of the separated branches, the judiciary, has assumed a leading role in interpreting laws and determining their constitutionality. Whether the Founders actually anticipated this function of "judicial review" is open to question. Perhaps each branch was expected to reach its own judgments on constitutional questions, especially those pertaining to its own powers. However, Chief Justice John Marshall soon preempted the other two branches with his declaration in *Marbury v. Madison* (1803) that "it is emphatically the province and duty of the judicial department to say what the law is." Until after the Civil War, Congress was the main forum for weighty constitutional debates, and only a single law was declared unconstitutional by the Court. Since the end of the nineteenth century, however, the Court's authority to interpret constitutional restraints has been conceded by both legislators and the general public.

Conflict between the Court and Congress over legislation has recurred. Since 1789, the Supreme Court has declared 106 acts of Congress unconstitutional in whole or in part.[11] Notable periods of Court activism occurred between 1864 and 1936, when 65 laws were found unconstitutional, and from 1955 to 1980, when 36 laws were found unconstitutional. Needless to say, legislators and presidents are not afraid to express views about the constitutionality of laws or the need for proposed constitutional amendments. And, when the courts have ruled, Congress sometimes reacts by trying to nullify or thwart the decision. Nonetheless, the courts play the primary role in interpreting laws and the regulations emanating from them.

Bicameralism

Not only does Congress compete for influence with other branches of government, but it is divided internally into two semi-autonomous chambers. Following the pattern initiated by Parliament and imitated by 10 of the 13 colonies, the Constitution outlines a bicameral legislature. If tradition recommended the two-house formula, the politics of the era commanded it. The larger states preferred the "nationalist" principle of popularly based representation, while the smaller states insisted on a "federal" principle ensuring representation by states.

The first branch—as the House was termed by Gouverneur Morris and James Madison, among others—rests on the nationalist idea that the legislature should answer to people rather than states. As George Mason, a revolutionary statesman, put it, the House "was to be the grand depository of the democratic principles of the government." [12] Many years later the Supreme Court ruled in *Wesberry v. Sanders* (1964) that these principles demanded that congressional districts within each state be essentially equal in population.

In contrast, the Senate embodied the federal idea: not only did each state have two Senate seats, but senators were to be chosen by the state legislatures rather than by popular election. The Senate was to provide a brake on the excesses of popular government. "The use of the Senate," explained James Madison, "is to consist in its proceeding with more coolness, with more system, and with more wisdom, than the popular branch." [13]

Historical evolution overtook the Founders' intentions. In most cases, to be sure, senators tended to voice dominant economic interests and shun the general public. Lord Bryce once remarked that the Senate seemed to care more for its "collective self-esteem" than it did for public opinion.[14] Yet state legislators frequently "instructed" their senators how to vote on key issues. In other states, legislative elections turned into statewide "canvasses" focusing on senatorial candidates. Such was the famous 1858 Illinois contest between Senator Stephen A. Douglas and Abraham Lincoln. The Democrats captured the legislature and sent Douglas back to Washington; but Lincoln's eloquent arguments against extending slavery to the territories west of the Mississippi River vaulted him into national prominence.

Direct election of senators came with the Seventeenth Amendment ratified in 1913. A byproduct of the Progressive movement, it was designed to broaden citizens' participation and blunt the power of shadowy special interests, such as party bosses and business trusts. Thus the Senate became subject to popular will.

Because states vary widely in population, the Senate is the one legislative body in the nation where "one person, one vote" emphatically does not apply. Article V assures each state of equal Senate representation and guarantees that no state will be deprived of this without its consent. Because no state is apt to give such consent, Senate representation is for all practical purposes an unamendable provision of the Constitution.

Bicameralism is perhaps the most conspicuous organizational feature of the United States Congress. Two distinct legislative processes—not just one—accompany every law that is passed. According to the Constitution, each house determines its own rules, keeps a journal of its proceedings, and serves as final judge of its members' elections and qualifications.

In addition, the Constitution assigns unique duties to the two chambers. The Senate ratifies treaties and approves presidential appointments. The House must originate all revenue measures; by tradition, it originates appropriations bills as well. In impeachments, the House prepares and tries the case while the Senate serves as the court.

The two houses jealously guard their prerogatives and resist intrusions by "the other body." Despite claims that one or the other chamber is more important—for instance, that the Senate has more prestige or the House pays more attention to legislative details—the two houses staunchly defend their equal places.

INSTITUTIONAL EVOLUTION

Written constitutions, even those as far-sighted as the 1787 one, go only a short way in explaining real-life governmental institutions. Inevitably such documents contain silences and ambiguities—issues that lie between the lines and must be resolved in the course of later events. In some respects the United States Congress has worked out as its designers expected; in other respects, however, it departs from the Founders' intentions. Moreover, institutional change or evolution occurs as Congress adapts to demands and challenges very different from those of eighteenth-century America. Institutional evolution has shaped and even transformed the two Congresses we have described—Congress-as-deliberative-body and Congress-as-representative-system.

The Size of Congress

Looking at the government of 1789 through modern lenses, one is struck by the relatively small circles of people involved. The House of Representatives, that "impetuous council," was composed of 65 members—when all of them showed up. The aristocratic Senate boasted only 26 members, two from each of the 13 original states.

In Article I, Section 2, of the Constitution, the method of apportioning House members is set forth. Herein lies the constitutional authority for the decennial census:

> The actual Enumeration shall be made within three Years after the first Meeting of the Congress of the United States, and within subsequent Term of ten Years, in such Manner as they shall by Law direct. The Number of Representatives shall not exceed one for every thirty Thousand, but each State shall have at Least one Representative.

When the first census was taken in 1790, the nation's population was less than four million—smaller than that of an average state today. The historical growth of the two houses can be seen in Table 2-1. There were 32 senators in 1800, 62 in 1850, and 90 in 1900. Since 1910, only the states of Alaska and Hawaii have been added, and the House has stabilized at 435.

In addition to its 435 full-fledged members, the House has one resident commissioner and four delegates—the House's most recent acquisitions. While they cannot vote on the House floor, these individuals sit on committees and enjoy other House privileges. Legislation granting Puerto Rico the right to elect a commissioner was approved in 1900. In March 1971 a nonvoting delegate from the District of Columbia was elected. The following year delegates were elected from the American territories of Guam, acquired from Spain following the Spanish-American War of 1898, and the Virgin Islands, purchased from Denmark in 1917. And on November 18, 1980, American Samoa elected its first nonvoting delegate to the House.

Enlarging the House is periodically suggested—especially by representatives from states losing seats after a census. However, many people agree with the late Speaker Sam Rayburn of Texas, who believed the House is already at or above its optimum size.

Size profoundly affects an organization's work. Growth compelled the House to develop strong leaders, to rely heavily on its committees, to impose strict limits on floor debate, and to devise elaborate ways of channeling the flow of floor business. It is no accident that strong leaders emerged during the House's rapid growth periods. After the initial growth spurt in the first two decades of the Republic, vigorous leadership appeared in the person of Henry Clay, whose Speakership (1811-1814, 1815-1820, and 1823-1825) demonstrated the potentialities of that office. Similarly, post-Civil War growth was accompanied by an era of strong Speakers lasting from the 1870s until 1910. Size is not the only impetus for strong leadership, but it tends to centralize procedural control.

In the smaller and more intimate Senate, vigorous leadership has been the exception rather than the rule. The relative informality of Senate procedures, not to mention the long-cherished right of unlimited debate, testify to the loose reins of leadership. Compared with the House's elaborate system of rules and its voluminous precedents, the Senate's rules are relatively brief and simple. Informal negotiations

Table 2-1 Growth in Size of House and Its Constituents, 1790-1980 Census

Year of Census	Congress	Population Base[1] (1,000s)	Number of States	Number of Representatives[2]	Apportionment Population Per Representative
	1st-2nd	—	13	65	30,000[3]
1790	3rd-7th	3,616	15	105	84,436
1800	8th-12th	4,880	16	141	34,609
1810	13th-17th	6,584	17	181	36,377
1820	18th-22nd	8,972	24	213	42,124
1830	23rd-27th	11,931	24	240	49,712
1840	28th-32nd	15,908	26	223	71,338
1850	33rd-37th	21,767	31	234	93,020
1860	38th-42nd	29,550	34	241	122,614
1870	43rd-47th	38,116	37	292	130,533
1880	48th-52nd	49,371	38	325	151,912
1890	53rd-57th	61,909	44	356	173,901
1900	58th-62nd	74,563	45	386	193,167
1910	63rd-72nd	91,604	48	435	210,583
1920[4]	—	—	—	—	—
1930	73rd-77th	122,093	48	435	280,675
1940	78th-82nd	131,006	48	435	301,164
1950	83rd-87th	149,895	48	435	334,587
1960	88th-92nd	178,559	50	435	410,481
1970	93rd-97th	204,053[5]	50	435	469,088
1980	98th-102nd	226,505	50	435	520,701

[1] Excludes the population of the District of Columbia, the population of outlying areas, the number of Indians not taxed, and (prior to 1870) two-fifths of the slave population.

[2] Actual number of representatives apportioned at the beginning of the decade.

[3] The minimum ratio of population to representatives stated in Article 1, Section 2, of the Constitution.

[4] No apportionment was made after the census of 1920.

[5] Includes 1,575,000 in population abroad.

SOURCE: U.S., Department of Commerce, Bureau of the Census, *Historical Statistics of the United States: Colonial Times to 1970,* Part 2 (Washington, D.C.: U.S. Government Printing Office, 1975), p. 1084; 1980 Census figures released by Commerce Department December 31, 1980.

among senators interested in a given measure prevail, and debate is typically regulated by unanimous consent agreements engineered by the parties' floor leaders. Although too large for its members to draw their chairs around the fireplace on a chilly winter morning—as they used to do in the early years—the Senate today retains a clubby atmosphere that the House lacks.

Electoral units, too, have grown very large. Congressional constituencies—states and districts—are among the most populous electoral units in the world. The mean congressional district now numbers half a million people, while the average state has more than four million people. This affects the bonds between citizens and their elected representatives. Whereas old-time legislators spent a great deal of time in their home districts, working at their normal trade or profession and mingling with townspeople, today's legislators keep in touch by means of frequent whirlwind visits, radio and television appearances, press releases, staff contacts, WATS lines, and computerized mass mailings.

The congressional establishment itself has changed in scale. Staffs were added gradually. In 1891 a grand total of 142 clerks, 62 for the House and 80 for the Senate, were on hand to serve members of Congress. Some senators and all representatives handled their own correspondence; keeping records and counting votes were the duties of committee clerks. Around the turn of this century, House and Senate members, their clerks, and their committees managed to fit into two ornate office buildings, one for each house. Today individual members and committees are served by more than 13,000 staff members, not to mention employees in several supporting agencies. *(See Table 8-1, p. 238.)* Housed in more than a dozen Capitol Hill buildings, they include experts in virtually every area of government policy and comprise a distinct Washington subculture.

The Legislative Workload

During the Republic's early days, the government at Washington was "at a distance and out of sight." [15] Lawmaking was a part-time occupation. As President John F. Kennedy was fond of remarking, the Clays, Calhouns, and Websters of the nineteenth century could afford to devote a whole generation or more to debating and refining the few great controversies at hand. Representative Joseph W. Martin, R-Mass., who entered the House in 1925 and went on to become Speaker (1947-1948, 1953-1954), describes the leisurely atmosphere of earlier days and the workload changes during his service:

> From one end of a session to another Congress would scarcely have three or four issues of consequence besides appropriations bills. And the issues themselves were fundamentally simpler than those that surge in upon us today in such a torrent that the individual member cannot analyze all of them adequately before he is compelled to vote. In my early years in Congress the main issues were few enough so that almost any conscientious member could with application make himself a quasi-expert at least. In the complexity and volume of today's legislation, however, most members have to trust somebody else's word or the recommendation of a committee. Nowadays bills, which thirty

years ago would have been thrashed out for hours or days, go through in ten minutes. . . .[16]

The most pressing issue considered by the Foreign Affairs Committee during one session, Martin related, was a $20,000 authorization for an international poultry show in Tulsa.

Even in the 1950s, the legislative schedule was quite manageable, as indicated in a summary of a representative's day by Speaker Sam Rayburn:

> The average member will come down to the office around eight or eight-thirty. He spends his time with visitors until around ten o'clock, then he goes to a committee meeting, and when the committee adjourns he comes to the House of Representatives, or should, and stays around the House chamber and listens.[17]

Needless to say, the days of a single morning committee meeting and time to witness the entire floor proceedings in the afternoon have gone the way of the Edsel and Hula-Hoop. Conflicting committee sessions and snatches of floor deliberation are now the order of the day.

Congress's workload—once limited in scope, small in volume, and simple in content—has grown to staggering proportions. Table 2-2 shows the soaring numbers of measures introduced and passed by Congress since 1789. The number of committee and subcommittee meetings per Congress and the number of hours Congress is in session also have increased, as Figure 2-1 illustrates. By every measure—hours in session, committee meetings, floor votes—the congressional workload has just about doubled in the past 20 years.

Legislative business has expanded in scope and complexity as well as sheer volume. Today's Congress copes with many issues that in the past were left to state or local government or were considered entirely outside the purview of governmental activity. One index of congressional committee activity ranges alphabetically from "abandoned automobiles" to "zoos," suggesting the wide variety of issues handled by modern lawmakers. Moreover, legislation tends to be lengthier and more complex than it used to be.[18] President Carter's 1977 energy package, for example, embraced more than 100 separate bills that were referred to a dozen different committees.

For most of its history, Congress was a part-time institution. Before World War I, and even after, Congress remained in session only nine months out of each 24, and the members spent the remainder of their time at home practicing law or attending to private business. In recent decades, legislative business has kept the House and Senate in almost perpetual session—punctuated by district work periods. During the average two-year Congress, the House is in session about 225 eight-hour days. The average senator or representative works an 11-hour day while Congress is in session.[19]

Table 2-2   Measures Introduced and Enacted, Selected Congresses, 1789-1981

Years	Congress	Measures Introduced			Measures Enacted		
		Total	Bills	Joint resolutions	Total	Public	Private
1789-1791	1st	144	144	—	118	108	10
1795-1797	4th	132	132	—	85	75	10
1803-1805	8th	217	217	—	111	93	18
1811-1813	12th	406	406	—	209	170	39
1819-1821	16th	480	480	—	208	117	91
1827-1829	20th	632	612	20	235	134	101
1835-1837	24th	1,107	1,055	52	459	144	315
1843-1845	28th	1,085	979	106	279	142	137
1851-1853	32nd	1,167	1,011	156	306	137	169
1859-1861	36th	1,746	1,595	151	370	157	213
1867-1869	40th	3,723	3,003	720	765	354	411
1875-1877	44th	6,230	6,001	229	580	278	302
1883-1885	48th	11,443	10,961	482	969	284	685
1891-1893	52nd	14,893	14,518	375	722	398	324
1899-1901	56th	20,893	20,409	484	1,942	443	1,499
1907-1909	60th	38,388	37,981	407	646	411	235
1915-1917	64th	30,052	29,438	614	684	458	226
1923-1925	68th	17,462	16,884	578	996	707	289
1931-1933	72nd	21,382	20,501	881	843	516	327
1939-1941	76th	16,105	15,174	931	1,662	1,005	657
1947-1948	80th	10,797	10,108	689	1,363	906	457
1955-1956	84th	17,687	16,782	905	1,921	1,028	893
1963-1964	88th	17,480	16,079	1,401	1,026	666	360
1971-1973	92nd	22,969	21,363	1,606	768	607	161
1979-1981	96th	12,583	11,722	861	736	613	123

SOURCE: U.S., Department of Commerce, Bureau of the Census, *Historical Statistics of the United States: Colonial Times to 1970,* Part 2 (Washington, D.C.: U.S. Government Printing Office, 1975), pp. 1081-1082; Bureau of the Census, *Statistical Abstract of the United States; 1980* (Washington, D.C.: U.S. Government Printing Office, 1980), p. 509; figures for the 96th Congress were provided by Bureau of the Census, Data User Services.

NOTE: Measures introduced and enacted exclude simple and concurrent resolutions.

Rules and Procedures

A mature institution is distinguished not only by the professionalism of its members, but also by the number and complexity of its rules and procedures. By that measure, today's House and Senate are mature institutions indeed. *(For a more detailed discussion of congressional rules and procedures, see Chapter 9.)*

In the early days, proceedings at the Capitol were disorderly, especially in the crowded, noisy, and badly ventilated chambers. One House historian noted that "debate has been rough and tumble, no

Figure 2-1 Legislative Workload

Committee and Subcommittee Meetings, 84th-94th Congresses

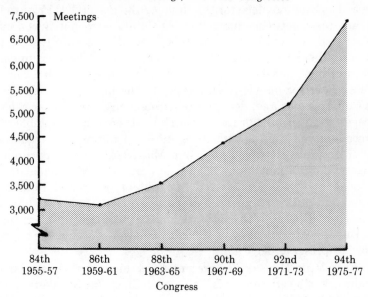

Hours in Session, 84th-96th Congresses

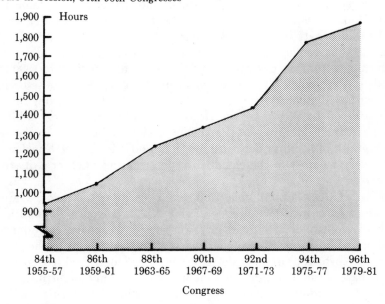

SOURCE: U.S., Congress, House, Commission on Administrative Review, *Administrative Reorganization and Reorganization Management,* 2 vols., H. Doc. 95-232, 95th Cong., 1st. sess., September 28, 1977, 2: 21.

holds barred, bruising, taunting, raucous, sometimes brutal. The floor of the House has been no place for the timid or the craven." [20] Prior to the Civil War, duels between quarreling legislators were not uncommon. One celebrated incident occurred in 1856, when Representative Preston Brooks, a southern Democrat, coldly stalked Senator Charles Sumner, a Republican from Massachusetts, and beat him senseless with a cane on the Senate floor for his views on slavery in the new territories.

As Congress matured, decorum replaced chaos, and stricter rules of order began to govern the proceedings. Today there are formidable rules and precedents as well as numerous informal norms and traditions. When, for example, Representative Jim Mattox, D-Texas, appeared on the House floor without his coat and tie on a steamy summer day in 1979, Speaker O'Neill pronounced him out of order and refused to recognize him until he reappeared in more formal garb. Meanwhile, the House sweltered because thermostats had been turned up to conserve energy. But the vast majority of O'Neill's colleagues seemed to support his effort to preserve decorum.

In the volatile House of Representatives, modern rules are largely the handiwork of a series of remarkable post-Civil War Speakers. James G. Blaine (1869-1875), Samuel J. Randall (1876-1881), John G. Carlisle (1883-1889), Charles F. Crisp (1891-1895), and especially Thomas B. Reed (1889-1891, 1895-1899) bolstered the Speaker's powers and tightened procedures, laying down new rules and precedents to tame the unruly House. Crisp strengthened the power of the Speaker to recognize members in debate by asking the member's intentions and refusing to recognize those engaging in dilatory tactics. Reed not only delivered tough rulings from the chair to limit debate, but also devised in 1890 the so-called "Reed rules." These reforms completely revised House procedure, outlawed dilatory motions, reduced to 100 the quorum in the Committee of the Whole (as the House is called when it debates bills), authorized the Committee of the Whole to close debate on any section or paragraph of a bill under consideration, and allowed the Speaker to count every member in the chamber in determining whether a quorum was present.

Most of these altered rules endured, even after the revolt against the Speakership in 1910. *(See Chapter 6.)* Today, House deliberations are tightly controlled. There are no fewer than five separate calendars or schedules of business. Most major pieces of legislation go to the Rules Committee, which drafts a "rule" governing the length and terms of the floor debate. Although individual members have many opportunities to introduce amendments under the so-called "five-minute rule" and to demand recorded votes, debate tends to be tightly controlled by the bill's floor managers, backed by the presiding officer's extensive powers. Members who want to master the rules face a formidable task, in view of the large number of rules and precedents, some of which are unpublished.

In the smaller Senate, the proceedings are less complex and hinge more on informal negotiations. It has 42 standing rules, most of them relatively simple. The Senate channels members' behavior through informal norms and folkways and through frequent use of unanimous consent agreements—agreed upon ways of proceeding. And, like the House, the Senate has an ethics committee to deal with formal charges of misconduct.

Committee System

No characteristic of Congress illustrates its institutional growth more dramatically than division of labor through the committee system. Although fashioned gradually and seemingly inexorably, the committee system rests on precedents drawn from the British House of Commons, the colonial assemblies, and the Continental Congress.[21] In 1789 the first House standing committee (Elections) was created. Until other standing committees appeared in the first two decades of the nineteenth century, most legislative business in both houses was handled by temporary committees or on the floor.

The creation and, in rare instances, abolition of committees parallels important historical events and shifting perceptions of public problems.[22] As novel political problems arose, new committees were added. The House, for example, established Commerce and Manufactures in 1795, Public Lands in 1805, Freedmen's Affairs in 1866, Roads in 1913, Science and Astronautics in 1958, and Standards of Official Conduct in 1967. Numerous committees have existed at one time or another—as many as 61 in the House and 74 in the Senate.

Today, there are 16 standing committees in the Senate and 22 in the House. *(See Table 7-1, p. 207.)* However, this is only the tip of the iceberg. Although standing committees have been trimmed—largely by the Legislative Reorganization Act of 1946 and a Senate committee realignment in 1977—subcommittees have proliferated. House committees have nearly 150 subcommittees. The House also has three select committees with seven subcommittees. In the Senate there are 105 subcommittees of standing committees. The three select committees and one special committee have a total of four subcommittees. In addition, there are four joint House-Senate committees with six subcommittees. This is more than 300 workgroups—not counting party groups, voting blocs, informal caucuses, and the like. By any measure, the House and Senate are complex organizations with many internal partitions.

The committee system is even more complex than these numbers suggest. Each chamber has rules and precedents that govern which bills should be referred to which panels. Committees in turn have guidelines for referring measures to subcommittees. Intercommittee competition over jurisdiction is commonplace in both chambers, as is the search for methods of coordinating broad-gauged measures affecting two or more committees. In the Senate cooperation normally occurs through informal consultation among committee members; in the House the Speaker has broad powers to refer legislation to two or more committees.

Altering House or Senate rules is no casual matter. (The House adopts its rules anew with each new Congress; as a continuing body, the Senate has ongoing rules although it sometimes amends them at the start of a Congress.) Most rules result from concerted effort, either by the leadership, party caucuses, or the respective rules committees. When major rules changes or committee realignments are considered, select committees may be established to make recommendations. Since World War II there have been two joint reorganization committees (1945-1946, 1965-1966), three committee realignment efforts (House, 1973-1974, 1979-1980; Senate, 1976-1977), and two study commissions (Senate, 1975-1976; House, 1976-1977). Although rules and procedural shifts do occur, time-honored ways of doing things are staunchly defended, and changes must be broached cautiously.

In short, Congress is no longer an informal institution. It bristles with norms and traditions, rules and procedures, committees and subcommittees. The modern Congress, in other words, is highly *institutionalized.* How different from the first Congress, personified by fussy John Adams worrying about what forms of address to use! The institutional complexity of today's Congress enables it to cope with a staggering workload and to contain political conflict. However, institutional complexity carries its own costs—in rigidity and the cumbersome administrative apparatus needed to keep the system afloat.

Congress and the Executive

One Saturday afternoon about four months after the First Congress convened in New York, members of the Senate were startled when their doorkeeper announced the arrival of President Washington. He had come to obtain the Senate's "advice and consent"—specified in Article II, Section 2, of the Constitution—on a treaty being negotiated with some Indian tribes in the South. The secretary of war accompanied him to answer senators' questions about the treaty. At the end of the document was a list of seven propositions to which the Senate could respond, yes or no. True to its nature, the Senate was not ready to sign on the dotted line; a debate ensued, and someone moved that the matter be referred to a committee. Washington got up "in a violent fret" and objected, "This defeats every purpose of my coming here." In the end the Senate postponed the matter, and the president withdrew with "sullen dignity." [23]

Although Washington eventually got the answers he sought, no president since then has ever gone to the Senate chamber to obtain personal advice and consent. Clearly, many details were left to be worked out between the president and Congress under the Constitution.

Like congressional rules and procedures, legislative-executive contacts display a distinct although uneven trend toward greater formal structure. Aside from the skeletal relationships specified in the Constitution itself, little in theory or precedent served to define the exact links between the president and Congress. These relationships have evolved in the subsequent course of history.

The Early Years. Symbolic of the tentative quality of executive-legislative relations in the early 1800s was the pathway that connected the White House with Capitol Hill in the new city of Washington. Unlike the broad expanse of Pennsylvania Avenue that links the two institutions today, the road was little more than a muddy footpath that ended in a swamp near the Tiber Creek—now an underground stream. Not until 1832 was there a bridge across the Tiber, and people journeying at night sometimes lost their way.[24]

The perilous road linking Capitol Hill with the White House reflected the isolation of the two governmental branches during the early decades of the new government. As one scholar observes, "Presidential involvement in the legislative process was extremely limited in the nineteenth century." [25] Close ties seemed foreclosed by the Constitution's philosophy of separation. Moreover, the relatively weak party system discouraged presidents from seeking factional allies on Capitol Hill. Individual cabinet members could gather support for various ventures and lobby for their budgets, but there was nothing approaching consistent communications between the two branches.

Pre-Modern Landmarks. Although Congress and the executive branch usually worked at arm's length during this pre-modern era, Thomas Jefferson, Andrew Jackson, and Abraham Lincoln—by common agreement the three strongest presidents of the nineteenth century—were notable exceptions. These men took an active part in the legislative process. Jefferson, the acknowledged leader of the Democratic-Republican party, worked with floor lieutenants to enact legislation drafted in the executive branch. Jefferson's success flowed from the pivotal role he played in his party and from his personal ties with lawmakers—resources he could not bequeath to his successors. Jackson's use of presidential prerogatives was quite different. Lacking a coherent legislative faction but commanding vast public adulation,

Jackson claimed a public mandate for his programs. He used patronage and the veto to bend the legislative process to his aims. Lincoln, facing civil strife, used emergency powers as a lever to force congressional action. Boldly wielding these powers during the first 11 weeks of the Civil War, he then called Congress into session and asked it to ratify what he had done. Throughout the Civil War, Lincoln proposed and lobbied for legislation and even used the veto threat to gain approval for his policies.

These three presidents used resources that were unique to themselves—Jefferson his party, Jackson his personal popularity, Lincoln his emergency powers—to gain a measure of control over Congress. These powers were personal rather than institutional; they were not passed on to succeeding occupants of the White House. In fact, quite the opposite happened: concerned about presidential "Caesarism," legislators reasserted their powers as soon as the strong presidents left the scene. The reaction following Lincoln's assassination lasted until the turn of the century, creating an unprecedented era of congressional supremacy. In his classic treatise *Congressional Government,* Woodrow Wilson declared that "the business of the President, occasionally great, is usually not much above routine. Most of the time it is mere administration, mere obedience of directions from the masters of policy, the Standing Committees." [26]

The modern presidential role in lawmaking exploits certain precedents from these early strong executives. Presidential leadership in the legislative process, however, is an invention of the present century. The administrations of Theodore Roosevelt and Woodrow Wilson broke new ground. Precedents were added by later presidents, but the "legislative presidency," as it is sometimes called, did not become a fixed part of the president's job until the post-World War II period. Only then could it be said that this role was truly institutionalized—performed because everyone, members of Congress included, expected the president to perform it as a matter of course, not because some unique combination of personality or circumstance made it possible.

The Legislative Presidency. The modern-day legislative presidency is built on a series of social and political factors: increased attention to the president, especially through the media; demands for national legislation solving economic and social problems; international crises requiring presidential responses; and legislators' dependence upon information and leadership from the executive branch. Theodore Roosevelt and Woodrow Wilson were philosophically wedded to the idea of vigorous presidential leadership. Although their successors were not always able to maintain high levels of influence, the presidency never entirely reverted to its late nineteenth-century dimensions.

The next great thrust in legislative involvement came during the Democratic administrations of Franklin Roosevelt and Harry Truman. Their legislative activism was propelled by crises—a nationwide depression, followed by global war, and then a tense "cold war" era. Since then, shifts have occurred in the form and style of executive-legislative relationships; but there has been no retreat from the activism of the Roosevelt-Truman period. Not even conservative presidents such as Dwight Eisenhower, Richard Nixon, or Ronald Reagan sought to reverse White House involvement in the legislative process. In fact, they added some precedents of their own.

Of course, contemporary presidents are not equally effective in dealing with Congress. Their personal skills vary; their success in enlisting congressional support for their programs fluctuates along with their standing in the eyes of the Washington community and of the country at large. Modern communications media ensure that presidents can grab the public's attention. Whether they are able to hold it is a presidential talent that cannot be institutionalized.

EVOLUTION OF THE LEGISLATOR'S JOB

What is it like to be a member of Congress? The job description in 1981 would be entirely different from one written in 1789. The legislator's job, like the institution of Congress, has evolved over the years. During the first Congresses, being a senator or representative was a part-time occupation. Few members considered congressional service as a career, and from most accounts the rewards were slim. Since then the demands of constituents, the career expectations of members, and the factional loyalties within Congress have changed.

Constituency Demands

Constituency demands embrace a wide range of functions, including personal appearances in the district, communication through newsletters and electronic media, explaining stands on legislative issues, assisting constituents with problems (so-called "constituency casework"), and corresponding with constituents. Of course, American legislators, especially House members, have always been expected to remain close to their voters. From the very first, representatives reported to their constituents through circularized letters.[27]

In an era of limited government, however, there was little constituent errand-running. "It was a pretty nice job that a member of Congress had in those days," recalled Representative Robert Ramspeck, D-Ga. (1929-1945), describing the Washington of 1911 when he came to take a staff job:

> At that time the government affected the people directly in only a minor way. . . . It was an entirely different job from the job we have to do today. It was primarily a legislative job, as the Constitution intended it to be.[28]

In those days, a member's mail was confined mainly to awarding rural mail routes, arranging for Spanish War pensions, sending out free seed, and only occasionally explaining legislation. At most, a single clerk was required to handle correspondence.

This unhurried pace has long since vanished. Reflecting on his 40 years on Capitol Hill, Representative Martin remarked on the dramatic upsurge of constituent awareness:

> Today the federal government is far more complex, as is every phase of national life. People have to turn to their Representative for aid. I used to think ten letters a day was a big batch; now I get several hundred a day. In earlier times, constituents didn't know their Congressman's views. With better communications, their knowledge has increased along with their expectations of what he must know.[29]

Even Martin, who left the House in 1967, would be surprised at the volume of constituency business handled by House and Senate offices. In 1980 the House Post Office logged about 150 million pieces of incoming mail—three times the 1970 figure; the Senate logged 35 million. Not only are constituents more numerous than ever before; they are better educated and served by faster communication and transportation. Public opinion surveys show that voters expect legislators to "bring home the bacon" in terms of federal services and to communicate frequently with the home folks. There is little reason to suppose these demands will fade in the future.

The Congressional Career

Careerism, or prolonged service, is a key ingredient of any human organization. It engenders loyalty, helps to define an institution's place in its social and political environment, and lends stability to the institution by ensuring the presence of experienced members. On the other hand, high careerism usually means low turnover, curbing the vitality and creativity that new members provide. This is especially critical for legislative bodies, which need representativeness as well as stability.

Levels of careerism in Congress have fluctuated throughout its history. During its early years, Congress was an institution composed of transients. The nation's capital was an unsightly place; its culture was provincial, and its summers mosquito-ridden. Members remained in Washington only a few months, spending their unpleasant sojourns in boardinghouses. "While there were a few for whom the Hill was more than a way station in the pursuit of a career," James S. Young observes, "affiliation with the congressional community tended to be brief."[30]

The early Congresses failed to command the loyalty needed to keep members in office. Congressional service was regarded as an odious duty, not as rewarding work. "My dear friend," wrote a North Carolina representative to his constituents in 1796, "there is nothing in this service, exclusive of the confidence and gratitude of my constituents, worth the sacrifice.... Having secured this, I could freely give place to any fellow citizen, that others too might obtain the consolation due to faithful service."[31] Of the 94 senators who served between 1789 and 1801, 33 resigned before completing their terms, and only six left to take other federal posts.[32] In the House, almost 6 percent of all early nineteenth-century members resigned during each Congress.

Careerism mounted after the Civil War. As late as the 1870s, more than half the House members at any given time were freshmen, and the mean length of service for members was barely two terms. By the end of the century, however, the proportion of newcomers fell to 30 percent and average House tenure reached three terms or six years.[33] About the same time senators' mean term of service topped six years or one full term.[34] Careers in both chambers continued to lengthen through the 1960s. Figure 2-2 shows changes since 1791 in the percentage of new members in the House and the mean number of terms served by House incumbents. The percentage of new senators is depicted in Figure 2-3.

Rising careerism had a number of causes. For one thing, proliferating one-party states and districts following the Civil War made possible repeated reelection of a dominant party's candidates, Democrats in the core cities and the South, Republicans in the Midwest and the rural Northeast. At the same time, the power of the legislative branch— epitomized in Woodrow Wilson's phrase, "congressional government"— made federal service attractive and rewarding. The government's subsequent growth enhanced the excitement and glamour of the national political scene, especially compared with state or local politics. Moreover, the physical environment of the nation's capital improved steadily over the years. As Representative Martin relates:

> The installation of air conditioning in the 1930s did more, I believe, than cool the Capitol: it prolonged the session. The members were no longer in such a hurry to flee Washington in July. The southerners especially had no place else to go that was half as comfortable.[35]

As members stayed longer, they needed rewards for lengthy service. When few senior members were available, presiding officers looked more to party loyalty than to seniority in naming committees or chairmen. But as careerism increased, greater respect was paid to seniority in distributing favored committee posts. In the Senate, the seniority "rule" has been largely unchallenged since 1877.[36]

Figure 2-2 Turnover and Seniority in the House, 2d-97th Congresses

Percentage of New Members, House, 1791-1981

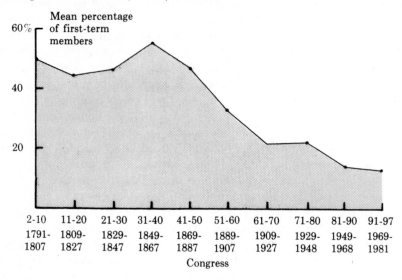

Terms Served by Incumbent Members, House, 1791-1981

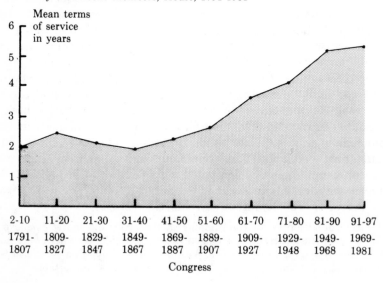

SOURCE: Nelson W. Polsby, "The Institutionalization of the U.S. House of Representatives," *American Political Science Review* (March 1968): 146-147. © 1968 by American Political Science Association. Reprinted by permission. Calculations for recent Congresses by the authors.

Figure 2-3 Percentage of New Members, Senate, 1791-1981

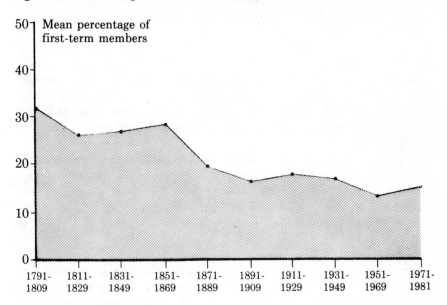

SOURCE: Randall B. Ripley, *Congress: Process and Policy,* 2d ed (New York: W.W. Norton & Co., 1978), p. 56. © 1978, 1975 by W. W. Norton & Co. Reprinted by permission. Calculations to 1981 by the authors.

In the House, seniority gained a foothold more gradually.[37] Strong post-Civil War Speakers, struggling to control the unruly chamber, sometimes ignored seniority to appoint loyal lieutenants to key committees. But in 1910, when Speaker Joseph G. Cannon (1903-1911) passed over senior members in making assignments, the House revolted, removing committee assignment power from the Speaker.[38] Since that time seniority has been virtually inviolable for selecting committee chairmen. Departures are not completely unknown, however, and in 1975 three House chairmen actually were deposed and replaced by more junior members. In choosing subcommittee chairmen, the norm of seniority is sometimes violated; lively fights then break out for these coveted posts.

The seniority principle fostered career patterns within the two houses. That is, new members found themselves at the bottom of internal career ladders that they could ascend only through continued service. Although the committee reforms of the 1970s multiplied the number of career ladders, seniority is still a prerequisite for top leadership posts.

In the early days, party leadership posts often were conferred quickly upon able legislators. Henry Clay was elected Speaker in 1811, his first year in the House. This would be unthinkable today. Thomas P. O'Neill, Jr., D-Mass., served 24 years before becoming Speaker in 1977. No one elected Speaker in this century has had fewer than 16 years of prior House service. In the Senate, the president pro tem is a largely honorific title given the majority-party senator with the longest service. Floor leadership posts have been known to go to relatively junior senators (Lyndon B. Johnson became Democratic leader after only four years in the Senate), but that is extremely rare. *(See Table 6-1 and 6-2, pp. 169, 176.)*

Apprenticeship, in short, became a norm within both chambers. In the past generation, however, many junior members grew restless with the long waiting periods required for leadership posts. As their ranks swelled, these members lobbied for broader and more equitable assignments—which opened leadership posts to more members, and earlier in their careers.

Since the late 1960s, careerism seems to have ebbed. When the 97th Congress convened in 1981, a majority in both houses had served five years or less. Three-quarters of them were elected after President Richard Nixon's resignation in 1974. This was caused mainly by voluntary retirements, not voter discontent, although reelection is rarely taken for granted. In 1980, 37 representatives were defeated—almost 10 percent of those running for reelection. Senators, whose seats are traditionally more competitive, face fiercer challenges at the polls than in the past. The 1980 elections swept from office 13 senators, including several veteran chairmen.

The voluntary retirement rate suggests that congressional life is becoming less rewarding. The lure of alternative careers, the stresses and strains of legislative service, and Congress's low public standing are some of the reasons why members of Congress are choosing to leave. Moreover, members now do not have to wait for chairmanships: with the multiplicity of subcommittees, members can try their hand at leadership and move on to other pursuits.

Factions and Parties

Parties and factions have played pivotal roles in the evolution of members' jobs. Political parties had no place in the constitutional blueprint, which was deliberately fashioned to divide and dilute factional interests. With the unveiling of Treasury Secretary Alexander Hamilton's financial program in 1790, however, a genuine partisan spirit infused Capitol Hill. The Federalists, who accepted Hamilton as their intellectual leader, espoused "energetic government" with forceful national action on public problems. The rival Republicans, who looked to Thomas Jefferson and James Madison for leadership, attracted opponents of Federalist policies and championed local autonomy, weaker national government, and programs favoring lower-class or debtor interests.

When war broke out in Europe between revolutionary France and a coalition of old regimes, the Federalists sided with the dependable (and commercially profitable) British, while the Republicans tended to admire "French principles." As early as 1794, Senator John Taylor of Virginia could write:

> The existence of two parties in Congress is apparent. The fact is disclosed almost upon every important question. Whether the subject be foreign or domestic—relative to war or peace—navigation or commerce—the magnetism of opposite views draws them wide as the poles asunder.[39]

In this country Speakers have always been political officers, and so they quickly came to reflect partisan divisions in wielding their powers. The other partisan institution in those early days was the congressional nominating caucus that selected a faction's presidential candidates. By no means all members professed clear-cut partisan or factional affiliations, however. During the so-called "Era of Good Feeling" (roughly 1815-1825), party voting was the exception rather than the rule. With the conspicuous exception of the nominating caucuses, no formal party apparatus existed. Between the quadrennial caucuses, Young explains, "the party had no officers, even of figurehead importance, for the guidance or management of legislative processes." [40] The nominating caucus collapsed after 1824, and the Jacksonians laid the foundation for something approaching a stable party system—based on grass-roots support.

Parties flourished in the years following the Civil War. Regional conflicts, along with economic upheavals produced by rapid industrialization, nurtured partisan differences. The Civil War and World War I mark the boundaries of the era of greatest partisanship on Capitol Hill and in the country at large.

From his study of the House in the McKinley period (1897-1901), David Brady concludes that "the two major parties were spatially more distinct on the urban-rural and industrial-agricultural continuum than are the two parties today." [41] This period of vigorous partisanship was characterized by the "strong Speakership" in the House of Representatives. At the grass-roots level, the parties were differentiated to a degree unheard of in the twentieth century, and party organizations were militant by American standards. By comparison, today's parties, while powerful in a procedural sense, are diffuse in representing issues or ideologies.

Since World War I, the parties have weakened but have by no means disappeared. After 1910 party caucuses or committees assumed responsibility for assigning members to committees and even sometimes formulating policy. During the 1965-1975 period, party caucuses on both sides of Capitol Hill were vehicles for reform efforts. The parties' formal apparatus is extensive. There are policy committees, campaign committees, research committees, and elaborate whip systems. About 125 staff aides are employed by party leaders and perhaps an equal number by assorted party groups.[42] In addition, party-oriented voting-bloc groups (such as the Democratic Study Group or the Republicans' Wednesday Group—both liberal House groups), "class clubs" (such as the House Democrats' New Members Caucus), and social groups complement and reinforce partisan ties.

Despite the widely proclaimed "death" of traditional political parties, partisanship and factionalism are very much alive on Capitol Hill. The first thing a visitor to the House or Senate chamber notices, in fact, is that the seats or desks are divided along partisan lines, Democrats to the left facing the dais, Republicans to the right. Seating arrangements betoken the parties' role in organizing the legislative branch. By means of party mechanisms, leaders are selected, committee assignments made, and floor debates scheduled.

If the major parties' historic role of articulating issues is waning, this role is now being performed by a baffling profusion of issue or voting-bloc groups. Among them are the Congressional Black Caucus, the Textile Caucus, the Environmental and Energy Study Conference, the High Altitude Coalition, and the Senate Steel Caucus, to name a few. Today there are nearly 70 such groups in operation.[43] A few groups are little more than paper organizations designed to attract favorable publicity for members; but a number of them are quite active. They develop common stands and tactics on issues of concern, use staff research to bolster their positions, and display voting strength by employing informal whip systems. In a sense such groups comprise a new type of party system; they function where the parties are too diverse or too divided to provide leadership or voting cues.

Factional structures provide another example of the institutionalizing process. In this instance development has been from diffuse to specific, from simple to complex, from informal to formal. Although partisanship has always accompanied legislative proceedings, it was not a central part of Washington life in the early years. In contrast, today's party institutions are visible and ubiquitous. The nation's capital reeks of partisanship—from the luxurious headquarters buildings of national associations and the lobbyists who crowd Capitol Hill offices and meeting rooms to the parties' staffs and research groups and the mushrooming issue and voting-bloc groups. Signs of institutionalized partisanship are everywhere, even if they don't always carry traditional Republican or Democratic labels.

CONCLUSION

At its birth, the United States Congress was an unstructured body. Although the general guidelines for representative assemblies were known, especially from reflecting upon the British experience, the Founders could hardly have been expected to know exactly what sort of an institution they had created. They wrote into the Constitution the powers of the legislature as they understood them and left the details to future generations. During its rich and eventful history, Congress developed into a mature organization with highly developed structures, procedures, routines, and traditions. In a word, it became institutional-ized.

This fact must be taken into account by anyone who seeks to understand Congress. Newcomers to the Capitol confront not an unde-veloped, pliable organization, but a traditional one that must be accepted on its own terms. This has a number of important conse-quences, some good and some bad.

Institutionalization enables Congress to cope with its contemporary workload. Division of labor, primarily through standing committees, permits the two houses to process a wide variety of issues at the same time. In tandem with staff resources, this specialization allows Congress to compete with the executive branch in assembling information and applying expertise to given problems. Division of labor also serves the personal and political diversity of Congress. At the same time, careerism encourages legislators to develop skills and expertise in specific issues. Procedures and traditions can contain conflict and channel the political energies that converge upon the lawmaking process.

The drawback of institutionalization is that it can turn into a kind of organizational rigidity that produces paralysis. Institutions that are too brittle can frustrate policymaking, especially in periods of rapid social or political change. Structures that are too complex can tie people in knots, producing delays and confusion. Such organizational tie-ups often produce agitation for change or reform. Even with its size and complexity, the contemporary Congress has undergone periodic waves of change or reformism. Events of the last two decades show that congressional evolution has by no means run its full course.

NOTES

1. Alvin M. Josephy, Jr., *On the Hill: A History of the American Congress* (New York: Simon & Schuster, 1980), pp. 41-48.

2. Charles A. Beard and John P. Lewis, "Representative Government in Evolution," *American Political Science Review* (April 1932): 223-240.
3. Ibid.
4. Jack P. Greene, ed., *Great Britain and the American Colonies, 1606-1763* (New York: Harper Torchbooks, 1970), p. xxxix.
5. Edmund C. Burnett, *Continental Congress* (New York: W. W. Norton & Co., 1964).
6. *Guide to Congress,* 2d ed. (Washington, D.C.: Congressional Quarterly, 1976), p. 10.
7. Burnett, *Continental Congress,* p. 171.
8. Charles C. Thach, Jr., *The Creation of the Presidency, 1775-1789: A Study in Constitutional History* (Baltimore: Johns Hopkins University Press, 1969), p. 34.
9. John Locke, *Two Tracts on Government,* ed. Philip Abrams (New York: Cambridge University Press, 1967), p. 374.
10. James Madison, Alexander Hamilton, and John Jay, *The Federalist Papers,* introduction by Clinton Rossiter (New York: New American Library, 1961), no. 48, p. 308.
11. U.S., Senate, *The Constitution of the United States of America: Analysis and Interpretation,* S. Doc. 92-80, 92d Cong., 2d sess., 1973, pp. 1597-1619. Recent figures courtesy of Johnny H. Killian, Congressional Research Service.
12. Charles Warren, *The Making of the Constitution* (Boston: Little, Brown & Co., 1928), p. 162.
13. Charles Warren, *The Supreme Court in United States History* (Boston: Little, Brown & Co., 1919), p. 195.
14. Lindsay Rogers, *The American Senate* (New York: Alfred A. Knopf, 1926), p. 21.
15. Madison, Hamilton, and Jay, *The Federalist Papers,* no. 22, p. 176.
16. Joe Martin, *My First Fifty Years in Politics,* as told to Robert J. Donovan (New York: McGraw-Hill Book Co., 1960), pp. 49-50.
17. Sam Rayburn, *Speak, Mister Speaker,* ed. H. G. Dulaney and Edward Hake Phillips (Bonham, Texas: Sam Rayburn Foundation, 1978), p. 466.
18. Allen Schick, "Complex Policymaking in the United States Senate," in *Policy Analysis on Major Issues,* U.S., Congress, Senate, Commission on the Operation of the Senate, 94th Cong., 2d sess., 1977 committee print, pp. 5-6.
19. U.S., Congress, House, Commission on Administrative Review, *Administrative Reorganization and Legislative Management,* 2 vols., H. Doc. 95-232, 95th Cong., 1st sess., September 28, 1977, 2: 17; U.S., Congress, Senate, Commission on the Operation of the Senate, *Senators: Offices, Ethics, and Pressures,* 94th Cong., 2d sess., 1977 committee print, p. xi.
20. Neil MacNeil, *Forge of Democracy: The House of Representatives* (New York: David McKay, 1963), p. 306.
21. See Jefferson's Manual, Section XI; U.S., Congress, House, *Rules of the House of Representatives,* H. Doc. 95-403, 95th Cong., 2d sess., 1979, pp. 133-137.
22. George B. Galloway, *History of the House of Representatives* (New York: Thomas Y. Crowell Co., 1961), p. 67.
23. William Maclay, *Journal of William Maclay,* ed. Edgar S. Maclay (New York: D. Appleton & Co., 1890), pp. 128-133.
24. James S. Young, *The Washington Community, 1800-1828* (New York: Columbia University Press, 1966), pp. 75-76.

25. Stephen J. Wayne, *The Legislative Presidency* (New York: Harper & Row, 1978), p. 8.
26. Woodrow Wilson, *Congressional Government* (New York: Meridian Books, 1956), p. 170.
27. Noble Cunningham, Jr., ed., *Circular Letters of Congressmen, 1789-1839*, 3 vols. (Chapel Hill: University of North Carolina Press, 1978).
28. Galloway, *History of the House*, p. 122.
29. Martin, *My First Fifty Years*, p. 101.
30. Young, *The Washington Community, 1800-1828*, p. 89.
31. Cunningham, *Circular Letters*, p. 57.
32. Roy Swanstrom, *The United States Senate, 1787-1801*, S. Doc. 64, 87th Cong., 1st sess., 1962, p. 80.
33. Nelson W. Polsby, "The Institutionalization of the House of Representatives," *American Political Science Review* (March 1968): 146-147.
34. Randall B. Ripley, *Power in the Senate* (New York: St. Martin's Press, 1969), pp. 42-43.
35. Martin, *My First Fifty Years*, p. 49.
36. Ripley, *Power in the Senate*, pp. 43-44.
37. See Samuel Kernell, "Toward Understanding 19th Century Congressional Career Patterns: Ambition, Competition, and Rotation," *American Journal of Political Science* (November 1977): 669-693.
38. Nelson W. Polsby, Miriam Gallagher, and Barry S. Rundquist, "The Growth of the Seniority System in the U.S. House of Representatives," *American Political Science Review* (September 1969): 794.
39. Swanstrom, *The United States Senate, 1787-1801*, p. 283.
40. Young, *The Washington Community, 1800-1828*, pp. 126-127.
41. David W. Brady, *Congressional Voting in a Partisan Era* (Lawrence, Kansas: The University Press of Kansas, 1973), p. 190.
42. U.S., Congress, House, Select Committee on Committees, *Final Report*, H. Rept. 96-866, 96th Cong., 2d sess., April 1, 1980, Appendix 1.
43. Daniel P. Mulhollan, Susan Webb Hammond, and Arthur G. Stevens, Jr., "Informal Groups and Agenda Setting in Congress" (Paper delivered at annual meeting of the Midwest Political Science Association. Cincinnati, Ohio, Spring 1981).

II

A Congress of Ambassadors

In the drafty studios of television station KIFI ("serving Idaho Falls, Pocatello, and Blackfoot"), Democratic Senator Frank Church was taping a weekend public affairs show. Skillfully he guided his interviewer to topics close to the hearts of eastern Idaho's potato farmers. It was an election year, and Church had exchanged his customary pinstripes for a western-style suit and the breezy informality that went with it.[1]

"I'm a big pusher of gasohol," Church declared, explaining that the mixture of gasoline and alcohol could help meet the country's energy needs. Besides, he noted, gasohol could mean a new market for Idaho farmers because "potatoes are very good alcohol producers."

Church also had called a hasty, late-night press conference in the living room of his mother-in-law's Boise home to announce that he had just learned that U.S. intelligence had detected the presence of Soviet combat troops in Cuba. This announcement, and Church's subsequent demand for removal of the troops, was aimed at countering charges that he was soft on defense and foreign policy issues.

Just the day before, Church had been in his accustomed seat as chairman of the Senate Foreign Relations Committee, managing the Carter administration's unpopular strategic arms treaty. "A problem for anyone who serves on the Foreign Relations Committee is that people get the idea he is more interested in Afghanistan than he is in the price of potatoes," Church told a reporter. In his desperate campaign for a fifth term, he therefore stressed home-grown issues.

Church's efforts both to please his constituents and attend to the Senate Foreign Relations Committee business were not successful, however. His opponent, Steven Symms, stressed local issues in his campaign and charged that Church was "out of touch" with his conservative constituents. This strategy paid off; Church narrowly lost in 1980 with 49 percent of the vote.

Everyone in the Senate and the House of Representatives faces Church's dilemma. The dilemma flows from the nature of the "two

Congresses." As legislators, senators and representatives must apply their expertise and judgment to thorny policy questions; as members of a representative assembly—"a congress of ambassadors," [2]—they must capture and hold the support of voters in their states or electoral districts. No matter how unique or valuable a member's contribution to policymaking, it is only as durable as that member's ability to gain and hold office.

The pull of local interests is seen in members' paths to office. Winning candidates usually forge close ties with their states or districts long before they arrive at Capitol Hill. Their campaign appeals must be cast in terms that local voters like. While national trends are evident, most congressional elections are decided by local personalities or local issues. In Chapter 3 we will describe the electoral game senators and representatives must play to win office.

Once in office, members of Congress quickly learn that reelection hinges upon continued constituent support. Legislators "represent" voters to win their support, but representation can take many forms. One way to represent people is to resemble them demographically; by this standard, Congress is not very representative. Another way of representing is to work and vote for policies and laws that the people favor—or that they would favor if they had the knowledge and expertise to evaluate them. Still another is to attend to constituents' problems and gain credit for resolving them. Finally, representation can mean communicating with constituents to establish an agreeable personality or style—a matter of presentation of self more than representation of issues. Such activities devour legislators' time and energies, as we will see in Chapter 4.

Another link between Congress and the people, discussed in Chapter 5, is the media coverage of Capitol Hill. Congress is a major source of national news. Individual members, for their part, realize that the right kind of publicity can boost their political career; the wrong kind can kill it. Our two Congresses tend to project divergent images, partly because they engage different levels of the press establishment. Congress's legislative output is chronicled by the national press and wire services; individual legislators are known mainly in their own bailiwicks—often through self-generated publicity. Senators, moreover, face different media markets than representatives do. Diverging channels of communication help account for the seeming paradox that citizens are critical of the institution of Congress but revere their own legislators.

Part II, A Congress of Ambassadors, reveals Congress as a collectivity of 540 members pursuing individual careers. To comprehend our national legislature, it is essential to study the men and women who compose it.

NOTES

1. Gaylord Shaw, "Senator Church Seeks to Reverse Image at Home," *Los Angeles Times,* November 5, 1979, p. 1.
2. Edmund Burke, "Speech to Electors at Bristol," in *Burke's Politics,* ed. Ross J. S. Hoffman and Paul Levack (N.Y.: Alfred A. Knopf, 1949), p. 116.

Representative Marjorie S. Holt, R-Md., mingles with
constituents at a bull roast during the 1980 campaign.

3

Making It:
The Electoral Game

Called alphabetically by name in groups of four, the senators
rise and walk to the front of the chamber. They are escorted by
colleagues from their states. The vice president of the United
States, the Senate's constitutionally designated presiding officer,
administers the oath of office. Newly elected or reelected, the
senators are now official members of "the world's greatest deliberative body," as the Senate likes to call itself. Over in the House
chamber, all 440 members have been elected or reelected and thus
must stand and be sworn in.

These new members reflect the diversity of American life.
They hail from places like Thiensville, Wisconsin; Ponca City,
Oklahoma; and Fairbanks, Alaska. Before entering Congress they
had such backgrounds as lawyer, farmer, college professor, shoe
company sales manager, airline executive, and Vietnam POW.

How did these individuals get to Congress? There is no simple
answer to that question. Yet in the broadest sense all incumbent
legislators are products of *recruitment*—a social and political
process complete with formal rules, informal norms, and countless
local twists. Social analysts agree that recruitment is a key to the
effective functioning of all institutions, including legislative bod-

ies. The first great book about politics, Plato's *Republic,* addressed the question of fitting the ablest people into leadership posts. Conservatives, following Plato, believe that societies should be ruled by the most talented people—in John Adams' phrase, the "rich and the wise and the well-born." Marxists believe recruitment reflects the class structure. Modern political scientists, regardless of ideology, seek to learn how people find their way into posts in the White House, Congress, and the courts.

Any recruitment process has both formal and informal elements. In the case of the Congress, formal elements include the constitutional framework and state and federal statutes governing nominations and elections. Equally important are informal, often unwritten, "rules of the game." For example, some people are more disposed than others to aspire to elective office; skills and attributes make some aspirants more "eligible" than others; and certain attitudes induce citizens to vote for some aspirants and against others. Taken together, these elements comprise a screening process through which some individuals pass more easily than others. The recruitment process and its "biases," both overt and hidden, affect the day-to-day operation of the House and Senate, not to mention the quality of representation and decisionmaking.

FORMAL RULES OF THE GAME

The constitutional requirements for holding congressional office are few and simple. They include *age* (25 years of age for the House of Representatives, 30 for the Senate); *citizenship* (seven years for the House, nine years for the Senate); and *residency* in the state from which the officeholder is elected. Thus, the constitutional gateways to congressional officeholding are fairly wide.

Even these minimal requirements, however, sometimes arouse controversy. During the 1960s and 1970s, when people of the post-World War II "baby boom" reached maturity and the Twenty-sixth Amendment (permitting 18-year-olds to vote) was ratified, unsuccessful efforts were made to lower the eligible age for senators and representatives.

Because of Americans' geographic mobility, residency sometimes is an issue. Voters normally prefer candidates with longstanding ties to their states or districts. In his 1978 reelection campaign, for instance, Senator John Tower, R-Texas, effectively accused his opponent, Representative Robert Krueger, of having spent most of his life "overseas or in the East" studying or teaching—a charge taken seriously in Texas. Well-known candidates sometimes succeed without such ties. New York voters elected to the Senate Robert F. Kennedy (1965-1968) and Daniel Patrick Moynihan (1977-) even though each had spent much of his life elsewhere. While House members are not bound to live in the district from which they are elected, most do so prior to their election.

Senate Apportionment

In the Senate, the "one person, one vote" rule does not apply. Article V of the Constitution assures each state, regardless of population, two Senate seats and guarantees that this equal representation cannot be taken away without the state's consent. The Founders stipulated that senators be designated by their respective state legislatures rather than by the voters themselves. Thus, the Senate was designed to add stability, wisdom, and forbearance to the actions of the popularly elected House. As we have seen, this distinction between the two houses was eroded by the Seventeenth Amendment (1913), which provided for the direct popular election of senators.

When senators were selected indirectly and states were small, the Senate tended to be a collection of spokesmen for dominant regional interests such as cotton, rails, or tobacco. Today, however, most states boast highly developed and varied economies. Many statewide electorates display ethnic, racial, and social diversity—making them microcosms of the whole nation. During the past generation, therefore, the Senate probably reflected national demographic trends more faithfully than did the House.[1] The size and diversity of statewide electorates helps make Senate races more competitive than those for the House.

House Apportionment

The 435 House seats are apportioned among the states by population. In addition, there are four nonvoting delegates (District of Columbia, Guam, Virgin Islands, and Samoa) and one resident commissioner (Puerto Rico). Once the population figures from the decennial census are gathered, apportionment is derived by a mathematical formula called the Method of Equal Proportions.[2] The idea behind this method is that proportional differences in the number of persons per representative for any pair of states should be kept to a minimum. The first 50 seats are fixed because each state is guaranteed at least one representative by the Constitution. The question then becomes: Which state deserves the 51st seat, the 52nd, and so forth? The mathematical formula yields a priority value for each seat, up to any desired number.

As the nation's population shifts, states gain or lose congressional representation. This is especially true today, when the more or less fixed size of the House means that one state's gain is another's loss. The 10-year shifts often highlight political tensions between states and regions. Earlier in this century conflicts arose between urban and rural areas and between central cities and suburbs. Today's shifts pit the older indus-

Figure 3-1 Reapportionment Gains and Losses in House Seats After 1980 Census

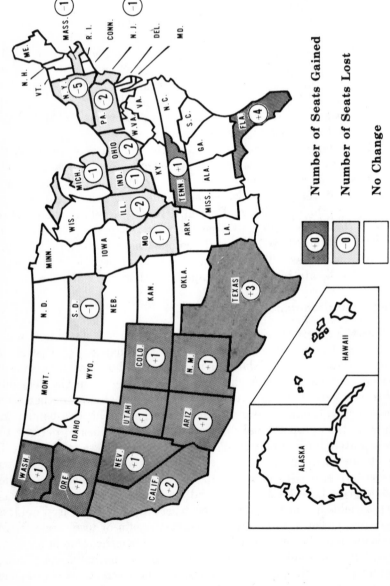

SOURCE: Adapted from *Congressional Quarterly Weekly Report,* January 10, 1981, p. 70.

trial states of the Northeast and Midwest against the growing states of the South and West—in other words, the declining "Frost Belt" versus the growing "Sun Belt." The 1980 census revealed that 10 years makes a big difference in apportionment. *(See Figure 3-1.)* Many districts slid above or below the national average of 520,000 constituents. Republican Representative Bill McCollum from Florida's 5th District had almost four times as many constituents (nearly 890,000) as Representative Robert Garcia, D-N.Y., who represents the desolated South Bronx.

Once congressional seats are apportioned among the states, district lines must be drawn. (A 1967 congressional statute prohibits *at-large* elections in states with more than a single representative.) Historically, redistricting is a fiercely political process involving intensely interested parties—state legislators, the governor, and often incumbent House members. In recent years, courts have set overall districting standards. If the political branches of state government become deadlocked on redistricting, judges sometimes step in to finish the job.

Because congressional seats are political prizes, it is not surprising that districting frequently becomes an instrument of partisan, factional, or even personal advantage. Two historical districting anomalies are malapportionment and gerrymandering.

Malapportionment. Prior to 1964, districts of grossly unequal population often existed side by side. Within a single state, districts varied by as much as 8 to 1. Rural areas were favored at the expense of growing urban areas. Rural regions tended to dominate the state legislatures, where disparities in district populations were even greater than among congressional districts. Sometimes malapportionment resulted from explicit districting acts; more often legislators simply failed to redistrict, letting population movements and demographic trends do the job for them. This was called the "silent gerrymander."

Preferring a posture of judicial self-restraint, the courts were slow to venture into the "political thicket" of districting. By the 1960s, however, the problem of unequal representation was ripe for resolution. Metropolitan areas had grown in population and political clout, but still their representation lagged in state legislatures and in Congress. Meanwhile, a new spirit of judicial activism had taken hold. In 1961 a group of Tennessee city-dwellers challenged the state's legislative districting, which had not been altered since 1901. In 1962 the Supreme Court held that federal courts had a right to review legislative districting under the Fourteenth Amendment's equal protection clause (*Baker v. Carr,* 1962). Two years later, the Court was ready to strike down state districting schemes that failed to meet standards of equality (*Reynolds v. Sims,* 1964). Chief Justice Earl Warren declared that state legislative seats, even under bicameral arrangements, must be apportioned "substantially on population."

That same year, the principle of "one person, one vote" was extended to the U.S. House of Representatives. An Atlantan who served in the Georgia Senate, James P. Wesberry, Jr., charged that the state's congressional districting violated equal protection of the laws. The Supreme Court upheld Wesberry's challenge (*Wesberry v. Sanders*, 1964). The decision was based on Article I, Section 2, of the Constitution, which directs that representatives be apportioned among the states according to their respective numbers and be chosen by the people of the several states. This language, argued Justice Hugo Black, means that "as nearly as is practicable, one man's vote in a congressional election is to be worth as much as another's."

How much equality of population is "practicable" within the states? As states struggled to comply with the *Wesberry* mandate, this question inevitably came up. Five years later the Court struck down a Missouri districting plan in which the variances among districts were no more than 3.1 percent (*Kirkpatrick v. Preisler*, 1969). In defining the phrase, "as nearly as is practicable," Justice William J. Brennan, Jr., declared that any variance in population, "no matter how small," must be justified by the state as simply unavoidable despite a good-faith effort. All of Missouri's justifications for the variances were rejected. The state had contended that variances might be permissible to give representation to distinct interest groups, follow existing political boundaries, maintain geographical compactness, or compensate for supposed anomalies in census population figures. In the only case to reach the high court following the 1971-1972 redistricting, the Court invalidated a Texas districting plan with just under 5 percent variance between the largest and smallest districts (*White v. Weiser*, 1973).

Today, House districts within states start out nearly equal in population. (Sizes vary somewhat because of apportionment, and of course inequalities build during the 10 years.) The goal of population equality, however, has been won at the expense of other goals. Parity in numbers of residents makes it harder to respect political divisions such as county lines. It also makes it hard to follow economic, social, or geographic boundaries. The congressional district, therefore, tends to be an artificial creation with little relationship to real communities of interest—economic or geographic or political. This heightens the congressional district's isolation, forcing candidates to forge their own unique groups and alliances. It also aids incumbents, who have ways of reaching voters without relying on commercial communications media.

Gerrymandering. The requirement that districts be equal in population places new emphasis on gerrymandering, the cunning art of drawing district lines to maximize partisan advantage. The gerrymander takes its name from Governor Elbridge Gerry of Massachusetts, who in 1812 created a peculiar salamander-shaped district north of Boston to benefit his Democratic party. "Packing" and "cracking" are two gerry-mandering techniques. *Packing* a district is drawing the lines to embrace as many of one party's voters as possible to make the district "safe." Needless to say, incumbents prefer safe districts that make defeat unlikely. In *cracking,* an area of partisan strength is carved among two or more districts to minimize that party's voting leverage.

Indiana's 1981 redistricting shows what shrewd party leaders can accomplish. The Republicans, controlling the governor's office and both chambers of the General Assembly, spent about $250,000 (more than the state Democratic party's entire annual budget)[3] for sophisticated computer technology to redraw the district lines. The plan, shown in Figure 3-2, contains elements of both "packing" and "cracking."

Two Democratic districts—Lee Hamilton's 9th along the Ohio River, and Adam Benjamin's industrial 1st—were packed to embrace more Democrats and improve GOP chances elsewhere. Two labor strongholds were cracked: the city of Anderson, site of the nation's largest United Auto Workers local, and nearby Muncie, site of another large UAW local. The homes of three incumbent Democratic represen-tatives are all located in a new, heavily Republican 2nd District. And one Democratic district was wiped off the map because the census cost Indiana a House seat, down from 11 to 10 members. The new districts were intended to transform the delegation's 6-to-5 Democratic edge to a 7-to-3 Republican majority.

The long-range effects of gerrymanders are not easily measured. Marginal or competitive districts (those where the winner gains less than 55 percent of the votes) are tougher for a party to capture and hold, but they have the advantage of yielding legislative seats with a modest number of voters (that is, a minimal winning coalition). Safe districts, while naturally preferred by incumbents, can waste the majority party's votes by furnishing outsized victories. One analyst argues ingeniously that before 1966, northern Republicans were some-what overrepresented in Congress because their districts tended to be marginal while Democratic districts were overwhelmingly safe.[4] This GOP "gerrymander," flowing more from geographical distribution of the two parties' voters than from intentional actions by GOP-controlled legislatures, declined around 1966 as marginal Republican seats became safer or switched to the Democrats. On the other hand, one can counter that Democrats are somewhat overrepresented in congressional elec-tions because a majority party tends to gain a bonus from winner-take-all elections, and because voter turnout rates in Democratic areas are typically lower than in GOP areas.

Another possible impact of gerrymandering is to tilt elections in incumbents' favor by creating larger numbers of safe districts. For this reason it is mentioned as a possible contributor to the rising success of

Figure 3-2 Indiana Congressional Districts After 1980 Census

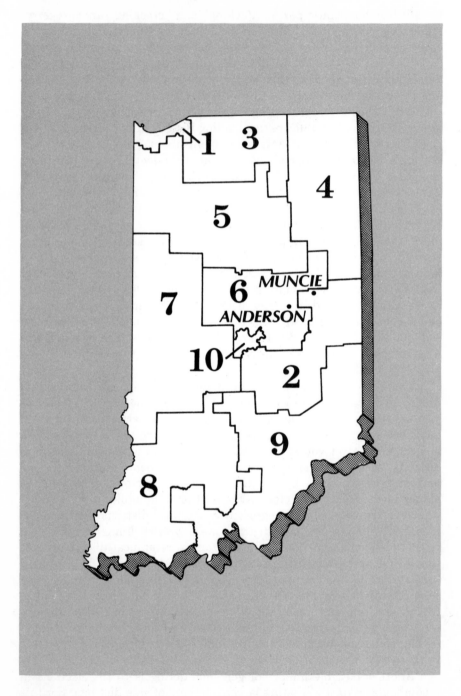

SOURCE: State of Indiana, Washington, D.C. Office.

incumbents in the late 1960s and 1970s. The evidence, however, does not point in that direction.[5] Incumbents are reelected with the same frequency in unredistricted areas as in redistricted ones. Incumbency advantages, moreover, rose not only for representatives but also for senators—whose "districts" are not gerrymandered. In short, while gerrymandering can alter the results in specific cases, its larger impact upon legislative representation is at best unclear.

Unlike malapportionment, gerrymandering is not forbidden by the Constitution or by law. Congressional reapportionment laws from the mid-nineteenth to the early twentieth century usually required that districts be equal in population and contiguous in territory. But the 1911 law specifying "continuous and compact territory" lapsed and has not been replaced despite several attempts in recent decades to enact congressional districting standards. Into this void the Supreme Court stepped with its reapportionment rulings.

Whether the Court will find certain forms of gerrymandering unconstitutional is a matter of speculation. Districts drawn deliberately to disadvantage a racial or ethnic group unquestionably would be struck down. The Court ruled against "obscene, 28-sided" boundaries in Tuskegee, Alabama, that disfranchised blacks by excluding them from the city (*Gomillion v. Lightfoot,* 1960). The Voting Rights Act of 1965, passed to stop discrimination against black voters in the South, prohibited "dilution" of minority voters—artificially cracking a bloc of minority voters between two white districts. In 1975 Congress extended the act to cover "language minorities." By 1981, however, no case involving congressional district lines had reached the Supreme Court.

THE FIELD OF CANDIDATES

Obviously, not all eligible people actually run for congressional office. It is not enough to be legally eligible; an individual must decide to make the race at a particular moment. Then the aspirant must undergo prolonged and often tedious "tests." These tests—broadly speaking, the politics of nominations, campaigns, and elections—are every bit as important as legal requirements in legislative recruitment.

Deciding to Run

Some candidates are recruited and sponsored by locally influential individuals or groups; others are self-starters who pull their own bandwagons. In former times, party groups acted as recruiters or screeners. They sought out suitable candidates and offered them support. Although less common today, party or group sponsorship survives in areas of strong political organizations or clubs.[6]

For instance, in south Philadelphia's 1st District, local Democratic chieftains in 1980 withdrew support from Representative Michael "Ozzie" Myers (convicted in the Abscam affair after his renomination) and urged voters to support former GOP Councilman Thomas Foglietta, running as an independent and backed by the Democratic organization. Foglietta won in a stunning display of candidate recruitment and party discipline. More often, parties stay in the background. The House Republican campaign committee was involved in 50 to 60 primaries in the 1976-1978-1980 election cycles. Avoiding local party fights, the committee selected promising contenders and gave them money and training to become credible candidates.

Increasingly, candidates launch their own careers, searching out supporters and financial backing. This is typical in suburbs and other areas where strong party organizations have never taken hold. In 1980 Colorado GOP Senate contender Mary Buchanan overcame party leaders (who, she said, tried to "muscle" her out of the race). Launching a petition drive after failing to capture the required 20 percent of the state convention delegates, she won a place on the primary ballot and then defeated three other candidates—all of whom were more acceptable than she was to party leaders. Eventually she lost the general election to incumbent Gary Hart. Even in party-conscious New York, self-starting candidates are common. Alphonse D'Amato, eager to challenge the state's senior senator, Jacob Javits, sought permission of Nassau County leader Joseph Margiotta. "OK, we'll let you test the waters," Margiotta agreed.[7] D'Amato beat Javits in the primary and then Representative Elizabeth Holtzman in the general election; but D'Amato's county leader gave his blessing reluctantly, yielding to D'Amato's desire to seize the moment's chance.

When party leaders lose control of their nominations, the results can be embarrassing. San Diego Democrats were shocked the morning after the 1980 primary to discover that their nominee was a member of the Ku Klux Klan. In the weeks following, California voters were treated to the spectacle of every Democratic leader in the state coming out publicly to support Representative Clair Burgener, the Republican incumbent. In November, Burgener swept the district with an unprecedented vote. The same thing happened to the GOP in Michigan's 15th District, where their 1980 challenger turned out to be a former Nazi party member. The Democratic incumbent won handily.

Of all the inducements for launching a candidacy, the likelihood of winning is probably at the top. A party with a commanding majority never lacks for candidates eager to run under the party's banner. But a party with slim chances may have to beat the bushes to find candidates, although even the most hopeless races usually can attract someone yearning for publicity.

To meet filing deadlines and line up backers, estimates of candidate strength must be made months before the final balloting. That is why wise incumbents try to show early strength and build large war chests of funds; they sense that most elections are won far in advance, by scaring off potential contenders. Similarly, any sign of weakness invites opponents. Part of the GOP's success in finding attractive candidates for the 1980 elections may have been the Carter administration's low ebb in late summer 1979 when candidacy decisions were being made.

Open seats—that is, those where incumbents have died or retired—especially attract contenders. And given the looseness of party ties, shifts in party control are quite common in races lacking an incumbent candidate. Party strategies pinpoint these districts.[8]

Primaries

Nominating procedures, set forth in state laws and conditioned by party customs, are a key element in determining the potential pool of candidates. Historically, they have been spread to ever-wider circles of participants—a development that diminishes party leaders' power and thrusts more initiative upon the candidates themselves. In most states, the *direct primary* is the formal mechanism for nominating congressional candidates. Some Republican parties in southern states use conventions, and several states combine conventions with primaries; but for virtually all members of Congress, the direct primary is the gateway to nomination.

Who should be permitted to vote in a party's primary? The states have adopted varying answers. The *closed primary,* found in 41 states, requires voters to declare party affiliation to vote on their parties' nominees. This affiliation is considered permanent until the voter follows procedures to change it. In the so-called *open primary,* conducted in seven states, voters can vote in the primary of either party (but not both) simply by requesting the party's ballot at the polling place. Two states (Alaska and Washington) use the *blanket primary,* with a single multiparty ballot that permits voters to cross party lines to vote for one candidate for each office. Party leaders naturally favor strict rules of participation, which reward party loyalty and simplify the leaders' task of influencing the outcome. Therefore, tougher rules for primary participation normally are found in states with strong party traditions.[9]

Not all primaries are competitive races. For one thing, incumbent representatives and senators are normally renominated. Local political leaders are reluctant to repudiate an incumbent, particularly one with seniority. In any event, incumbents are far better known than their challengers. Thus, in recent years no more than 3 percent of incumbent representatives have been defeated for renomination. Senate seats are somewhat more precarious, but even there less than 15 percent of incumbent senators fail to be renominated. The 1980 primaries tripped up 6 of the 398 representatives and 4 of the 29 senators seeking reelection. A fair number of representatives face no challenge at all for renomination.

When a veteran senator or representative retires, a contest for the seat usually ensues. The level of competition depends on the party's prospects in the general election. One landmark study of primaries showed a strong tie between a party's success in general elections and its number of contested primaries.[10] In one-party areas, where a party's nomination virtually assured election, a primary contest was almost certain; contests also were likely in two-party competitive areas.

The direct primary was one of the reforms adopted early in the twentieth century to overcome corrupt, boss-dominated conventions. Certainly it has permitted more participation in selecting candidates. Yet primaries normally attract a narrower segment of voters than do general elections (except in certain one-party states, where primaries dictate the final election outcomes). Less publicized than general elections, primaries tend to attract voters who are somewhat older, wealthier, better educated, more politically aware, and more ideologically committed than the electorate as a whole.[11] Primaries also have hastened the decay of political parties by encouraging would-be officeholders to appeal directly to the public and construct their own support apart from party leaders. Primaries are thus a costly way of choosing candidates: unless they begin with overwhelming advantages (such as incumbency), candidates must mount virtually the same kind of campaign in the primary that they must later repeat in the general election.

GENERAL ELECTIONS

Once nominated, the candidate's battle is only half over. Now comes the campaign—a volatile mixture of personal appearances, speechmaking, advertising, and symbolic appeals. Like all acts of communication, the campaign is designed to convey messages to potential voters. Its main function is to ensure that those who cast ballots on election day are favorably disposed toward the candidate.

Campaign Strategies

Candidates and their advisers must decide the basic tone or thrust of the campaign. This all-important decision determines the allocation of money, time, and personnel. In mapping out a successful strategy, candidates ask themselves: What sort of constituency do I have? Are my face and career familiar to voters, or am I relatively unknown? What resources—money, group support, volunteers—am I likely to attract? What issues or moods are uppermost in the minds of potential voters? The answers to such questions dictate the campaign strategy.

The type of constituency—state or congressional district—is supremely important in shaping campaign plans. Various economic and social groups, not to mention several media markets, are involved in senatorial campaigns. In contrast, most House districts are narrower entities than states and parallel no other natural geographic, community, or political dividing lines. Hence, there are often few automatic forums or media outlets for House candidates, nor are there many ready-made partisan hierarchies.[12] Would-be representatives are very much "on their own" to piece together a network of supporters.

Incumbency can be a powerful advantage. Incumbents have built-in methods of promoting support—through speeches, press coverage, newsletters, staff assistance, and constituent service. The average House member enjoys perquisites valued at more than a million dollars over a two-year term; with six-year terms, senators have resources between $4 million and $7 million. *(See box, p. 124.)*

As Table 3-1 makes clear, incumbents are good bets for reelection. Since World War II, on the average nearly 91 percent of all incumbent representatives and 73 percent of incumbent senators running for reelection have been returned to office. Casualty rates were higher than normal in 1980, when 9 senators and 31 representatives fell in general elections. And yet, the 1980 figures are not out of line when compared with other high-turnover periods—for example, the postwar generational shift (1946-1948), a midterm recession (1958), the Goldwater debacle (1964), or the Watergate fallout (1974).

Incumbency is not a sure bet, however. Given citizens' growing doubts about the honesty or efficacy of the federal government, incumbency can be turned into a liability. Challengers often try to paint incumbents as part of "the Washington crowd" and neglectful of the home folks. Sometimes incumbents are linked to unpopular local issues like busing or bilingual education. Age, failing health, or scandals are also exploited. Whether these cases add up to a trend against incumbency is uncertain. However, one target of such campaigns, Representative Morris K. Udall, D-Ariz., declared that longevity in office "is a good reason to get rid of you. Being an incumbent's not all it's cracked up to be."[13]

Majority-minority party status is difficult to assess these days because of rampant split-ticket voting. Yet partisan ratios cannot be ignored. Majority candidates in one-party areas are virtually assured of election. Their campaigns, which stress party loyalty, concentrate on voter registration drives because high voter turnout usually aids their

Table 3-1 The Advantage of Incumbency in the House and Senate, 1946-1980

	House				Senate			
Year	Seeking Re-election*	Defeated Primary	Defeated General	Percent Re-election	Seeking Re-election	Defeated Primary	Defeated General	Percent Re-elected*
1946	398	18	52	82.4	30	6	7	56.7
1948	400	15	68	79.2	25	2	8	60.0
1950	400	6	32	90.5	32	5	5	68.8
1952	389	9	26	91.0	31	2	9	64.5
1954	407	6	22	93.1	32	2	6	75.0
1956	411	6	16	94.6	29	0	4	86.2
1958	396	3	37	89.9	28	0	10	64.3
1960	405	5	25	92.6	29	0	1	96.6
1962	402	12	22	91.5	35	1	5	82.9
1964	397	8	45	86.6	33	1	4	84.8
1966	411	8	41	88.1	32	3	1	87.5
1968	409	4	9	96.8	28	4	4	71.4
1970	401	10	12	94.5	31	1	6	77.4
1972	390	12	13	93.6	27	2	5	74.1
1974	391	8	40	87.7	27	2	2	85.2
1976	384	3	13	95.8	25	0	9	64.0
1978	382	5	19	93.7	25	3	7	60.0
1980	398	6	31	90.7	29	4	9	55.2

* Counting both primary and general election defeats.

SOURCE: *Congressional Quarterly Weekly Report*, April 5, 1980, p. 908 and November 8, 1980, pp. 3302, 3320-3321.

cause. Minority-party campaigns obscure partisan differences, stress personalities, or exploit factional splits within the majority party.

Voter perceptions and attitudes are also major factors in campaign planning. Candidates who are well-known, who have high "name recognition," try to capitalize on their visibility; lesser-known candidates take out ads that repeat their names over and over again. Candidates known for openness and friendliness will highlight those qualities in ads; those who are less voluble will stress experience and competence, at the same time displaying photos or film clips reminding voters that they, too, are human. Candidates who have made tough but controversial decisions are touted as persons of courage. And so on.

As popular moods change, so do the self-images candidates seek to project. In crises, voters prefer experience, competence, and reassurance; in the wake of scandals, honesty and openness are the virtues most cherished by voters. Candidates' speeches, appearances, advertising, and appeals are designed to exploit such voter preferences. For example, many Democratic legislators who gained office in the 1960s by championing government activism in solving problems advocated balanced budgets and lower taxes when running for office 10 years later.

Often a candidate's strategy is distilled into a single theme such as "Bill Steiger is doing a good job." [14] In 1974, House incumbent William Steiger, R-Wis., used this slogan to emphasize his record. In contrast, challengers may stress their freshness and vigor, their close touch with constituent needs, or their independence from the "corrupt Washington crowd." Using a central theme or slogan helps to pull campaign efforts together and give voters a clearer impression of the candidate.

Campaign Techniques

Implementing the campaign strategy is the job of the candidate and the candidate's organization. In the past, contenders depended upon the ongoing party apparatus to wage campaign battles, and in some places this is still done. But today most party organizations have neither the permanent workers nor the financial wherewithal to mount effective campaigns. Citizen or interest-group activists and hired campaign consultants have replaced the old party pros.

If they can pay the price, today's candidates can obtain campaign services from political consulting firms. Some companies offer a wide array of services; others specialize in survey research, direct-mail appeals, advertising, coordinating volunteer efforts, or financial management and accounting. If the candidate is an incumbent, expert aides on the office payroll presumably help build support throughout the legislator's term of office. Congressional aides are supposed to refrain from actual reelection activities during the campaign itself; but in practice the distinction is hard to draw. The normal duties of a member's office staff—especially in constituent errand-running and outreach—have inescapable electoral consequences.

An important phase of the campaign is direct voter appeal through personal appearances—at shopping centers, factory gates, or even front doors. In his first Senate campaign in 1948, Lyndon Johnson swooped out of the sky in a helicopter to visit small Texas towns, grandly pitching his Stetson hat from the chopper for a bold entrance. (An aide was assigned to retrieve the hat for use at the next stop.)[15] Other candidates, preferring to stay closer to the ground, stage walking tours of their states or districts to get attention. In areas of strong party organization, voter contact is the job of ward, precinct, and block captains. Some candidates still dispense "walking-around money" to encourage local captains to get out the vote and provide small-scale financial rewards for voting.

Few neighborhoods today boast tight party organizations. Candidates and their advisers must recruit workers—usually volunteers—to make sure constituents are registered, distribute campaign leaflets, produce crowds at rallies, and win the vote on election day. Campaign workers may operate sophisticated telephone banks in central headquarters, or they may traipse door to door to drum up support for their candidate. Candidates can to some extent bypass face-to-face voter appeals by advertising and making televised appearances.

Some TV campaign efforts are quite artful. In 1980 the Republican National Committee mounted a $5 million television ad campaign to woo disgruntled voters with the message, "Vote Republican. For a Change." One TV spot featured an actor with an uncanny resemblance to House Speaker Thomas P. "Tip" O'Neill, who was portrayed as a backslapping, big-spending politician. Four years earlier Malcolm Wallop, a successful Wyoming senatorial candidate, had commercials showing a cowpoke on horseback dragging an outhouse across the open range. The audio portion of the ad reminded viewers that the Occupational Safety and Health Administration (OSHA) had decreed restroom facilities in every workplace, even out on the prairie. Another ad showed a postal letter being canceled over and over again, while the announcer talked about postal inefficiency and noted that Wallop's opponent, the incumbent, chaired the Senate's Post Office and Civil Service Committee. The ads' pointed humor underscored popular distaste of bureaucratic red tape and helped Wallop unseat the incumbent.

Media ads bring home the candidate's themes. Running in 1980 against 75-year-old Warren Magnuson, D-Wash., attorney Slade Gorton ran TV ads of himself jogging or bike riding. In turn, Magnuson, a 36-year Senate veteran, stressed his seniority and power as chairman of the Appropriations Committee. "I may walk a little slower than I used to," he said with a grin before the camera, "but the meeting can't start until

I get there, anyway." The voters chose youth over seniority, thus ending Magnuson's 37-year Senate career.

Cheaper to prepare and broadcast, radio ads remain popular, especially with House candidates. Young John LeBoutillier, trying to capture veteran Representative Lester Wolff's Long Island, New York, seat, ran a series of bold commercials depicting his Democratic opponent as a habitual junketeer. A seductive voice cooed the names of foreign cities Wolff had visited, while soft music, as in an airline lounge, was played. These ads helped LeBoutillier, a Republican, pull an upset.[16] On the other side of the country, listeners in Tucson heard two incredulous voices discussing the record of Democratic Representative Morris K. Udall. "He better explain this one," said one of the voices, which then read Udall's telephone number and urged people to call him. This ad, like some others, cropped up in several races, which indicates that ad agencies scatter their products widely.

Television is an expensive and broad-spectrum media. In contrast with TV's wide and varied appeal, radio stations reach more specialized audiences. Campaign advertisers can identify key voter groups and appeal to them.

The district's demographic features dictate which techniques will be most effective. Heavy media campaigns are most economical where a small number of newspapers or radio-TV outlets blanket the entire area, with minimum spillover into neighboring districts. For House candidates in a vast city such as New York or Los Angeles, a TV-oriented campaign would be prohibitively expensive and would waste itself on millions of viewers outside the district. Statewide senatorial campaigns, on the other hand, usually rely heavily on radio and TV spots appearing in all the state's major media markets. Some locales lack area-wide media altogether. Consider the case of New Jersey, which has the misfortune of lying between two of the nation's largest media markets, New York and Philadelphia, and therefore has few indigenous outlets, none of them statewide in scope.

Money and Other Resources

Money is "the mother's milk of politics." Just about any campaign technique can be employed with enough money. To be sure, money isn't everything in politics, but many campaigns falter for lack of it, and many others squander valuable time and energy struggling to get it. Especially useful is "early money." Available at the outset of the campaign, these funds buy advertising and radio-TV time. Candidates with tough contests in both primary and general elections face an especially vexing dilemma: Should they ration their outflow of funds and risk losing the primary, or should they wage an expensive primary campaign and risk running out of money later on?

Other important resources are volunteer support, group backing, and personal skills. Like money, nonmonetary resources are valuable because they provide candidate exposure. Support from a strong party organization or a powerful union may attract free publicity and volunteer labor. Enthusiastic volunteers or skilled operatives are essential resources. And incumbency (accompanied by taxpayers' dollars) yields visibility and opportunities for cultivating voter support that are hard for challengers to match.

Campaigns in the United States are costly. In 1980 a quarter of a billion dollars poured into House and Senate races. And the price of admission to Congress is soaring. Winning House members of the class of 1974 spent an average of $106,000. Two years later House freshmen spent an average of $141,000; in 1978 the average price of a winning campaign for freshmen members was $229,000.[17] No mystery surrounds these skyrocketing costs. Inflation, population growth, and an expanded potential electorate all account for the increase. Moreover, television ads and computerized mailings are expensive. Opening up the campaign process and relying on nonparty campaigners are other trends that have escalated costs. An old-style campaign with a caucus or convention nomination and legions of workers to canvass voters could be run more cheaply than a modern campaign with a primary nomination and voter appeals via electronic media. In short, reaching voters today is an expensive proposition.

In financial resources, some candidates are distinctly more equal than others. In 1981 the most expensive congressional campaign to date was the 1978 reelection effort of Senator Jesse Helms, R-N.C., which had a price tag of $7.5 million—or more than $12 for every vote he received. Two years later, colorful conservative Representative Robert K. Dornan spent $1.8 million to defeat Carey Peck (son of actor Gregory) in California's 27th District, a coastal ribbon of land in Los Angeles County. (Most of the money came from out-of-state mail solicitations; an estimated $1 million went to the fund-raiser, Richard Viguerie.)[18] The average Senate campaign in a competitive state costs more than $1 million; nearly a third of the House contests in 1978 required more than a quarter of a million dollars.

Although incumbents need less money than nonincumbent challengers, they receive more—a double-barreled financial advantage. Because they are better known and have government-subsidized ways of communicating with constituents, they usually can get their message across less expensively. Veteran Democratic Representative William Natcher, unopposed in 1978, reported spending just $20 (for the filing fee and postage) to gain reelection in his rural central Kentucky district. Few incumbents are so fortunate, but most of them enter their reelection races far ahead of their challengers.

At the same time, incumbents attract more money than challengers because contributors see them as better "investments." In recent House elections, incumbents have outspent challengers by 2-to-1 and 3-to-1 ratios. In 1978 almost 9 out of every 10 incumbents outspent their challengers; of those who did, only 3 percent lost their reelection bids.[19] In fact, many incumbents finish their campaigns with surpluses, which they bankroll for future races or distribute to needier candidates.

Campaign price tags depend on the type of district and the level of competition.[20] In 1978, in the 74 marginal districts (where the winner received less than 55 percent of the vote), the average combined campaign cost was $448,000—more than twice the national average of just over $200,000. Often in such elections, one or both candidates face fierce primary fights extending over many months. Many of these races are fought over open seats, where incumbency is not a factor. The average combined cost for general election candidates for the 58 open seats in 1978 was nearly double the national average.[21]

The district's demography also affects campaign costs. A 1978 study showed that suburban districts had the most expensive campaigns and urban districts the least expensive, with rural districts somewhere in between.[22] In the suburbs, partisan loyalties are notoriously weak and contests volatile. Lacking stable party organizations, candidates resort to advertising via electronic media. In cities, candidates shun media contests because of the huge cost and wasted impact upon adjoining districts. Here, too, party organizations are strongest. In rural districts, wide open spaces keep costs high: candidates must travel farther and advertise in many media markets to get their message across.

Financial inequalities in campaigning—between incumbents and nonincumbents, and between wealthy and poor donors—inevitably lead to demands for legal controls. Campaign finance laws are urged, not merely to clean up campaigns, but also to shift political influence from those who rely on financial contributions to those who depend on other resources. Several techniques have been employed to control campaign spending. The primary ones are: 1) disclosure of campaign contributions and expenditures; 2) limits on campaign contributions; 3) limits on campaign expenditures; 4) free radio and television time for candidates; and 5) public financing of campaigns.

The Federal Election Campaign Act Amendments. In the wake of several campaign financing scandals of the early 1970s, Congress decided to amend the Federal Election Campaign Act of 1971. On October 15, 1974, President Gerald Ford signed into law a broad-gauged campaign finance law, the Federal Election Campaign Act Amendments of 1974. Two years later the Supreme Court upheld certain portions of the statute and voided other portions (*Buckley v. Valeo*, 1976). To end the widespread confusion, Congress quickly passed a revised act reconciling the Court's rulings with the original congressional intent. The 1976 act was amended three years later to simplify paperwork requirements and remove some restrictions on party assistance to federal candidates and volunteer activities. Major features of the Federal Election Campaign Act as amended concern limits on individual contributions, limits on party and nonparty group contributions, and controls on campaign spending.

Individual contributions are limited to $1,000 per candidate for primaries, $1,000 more per candidate in the general elections, and a total of $5,000 in any given year. Primary, runoff, and general contests are regarded as separate elections. Individuals may contribute up to $20,000 a year to a political party and may spend an unlimited amount independently to promote parties, causes, or candidates. Expenditures over $250 must be reported, and the individual must declare that the money was not spent in collusion with the candidate. (Individuals may give up to $1,000 for a candidate and $2,000 for a party in volunteer expenses—housing, food, personal travel—without reporting it.)

National or state party committees may contribute $10,000 to each House candidate and $17,500 to each Senate candidate. However, nothing prevents the parties from mounting generalized campaigns to encourage partisan voting—as the Republicans did in 1980. In addition, there are "coordinated" expenditures. These are funds a party pays out for services requested by a candidate (for example, polling or TV ad production), who has a say in how they are spent. For Senate races, party committees may spend two cents (adjusted for inflation) for every voting-age person. In 1980 these figures ranged from $29,440 to almost $500,000. For House races, committees may spend no more than $14,720 in coordinated funds. Such funds are used in general elections but not in primaries.

Labor unions, corporations, and membership organizations may recommend to their stockholders, personnel, or members the election or defeat of a candidate. Such expenditures are unlimited, although amounts over $2,000 must be reported. The groups must declare, under penalty of perjury, that the expenditure was not made in collusion with the candidate. Unions and corporations also may spend unlimited amounts for "nonpartisan" registration or voter participation drives directed at their members, stockholders, or employees.

Under existing law, corporations and labor unions may not contribute their funds directly to candidates, but they may cover administrative or fund-raising costs of political action committees (PACs). For some years PACs have been a popular method of channeling corporate or union energies into campaign war chests. Corporate executives contribute to PACs with names such as the "Good Government Club," and most unions have a PAC, the best known of which is the AFL-CIO's

Committee on Political Education (COPE). Ostensibly such groups are voluntary; however, it does not take a confirmed cynic to suspect that subtle coercion and social pressure help keep money in the coffers.

Other types of groups are embraced by the finance law. Multi-candidate committees may give no more than $5,000 per election to a candidate. These committees must have more than 50 members and must support five or more candidates. Such committees may also give up to $15,000 per year to a political party.

There are no restrictions on how much congressional candidates or their supporters may spend, nor on how much candidates may contribute to their own cause. Senator John Heinz, R-Pa., heir to the pickle and catsup fortune, spent approximately $2.4 million of his own money to win his Senate seat in 1976. Strict accounting by candidates and political committees is mandated, however. All contributions of $50 or more must be recorded; donors of more than $100 must be identified. Accounting of funds must be made by a single committee for each candidate, and receipts and expenditures must be reported regularly.

Now that political campaigning is a regulated industry, there is an official regulator: a six-member Federal Election Commission, appointed by the president and confirmed by the Senate. The commission may issue regulations and advisory opinions, conduct investigations, and prosecute violations of the law. Buffeted by political pressures from all sides, the commission has had a stormy history.

PACS and Other Current Trends. Since the advent of modern reporting methods in the 1970s, several trends in campaign financing have emerged. Among these are the growth of PACs and PAC funds, the growth of "independent" spending, and shifts in the mix of donors.

Political action committees are thriving, partly because the 1976 law encourages them. At the end of 1974 there were 608 PACs; by the end of 1980 there were 2,551. All types of PACs grew in numbers, but corporate PACs grew most of all—from 89 in 1974 to more than 1,200 six years later. *(See Table 12-3, p. 360.)* PACs have grown in financial clout as well as numbers. Many donations go to legislators in a position to promote their policy aims—for example, members of House or Senate committees with which they deal. Common Cause estimated that 34 members of the House Agriculture Committee, which considers dairy price support levels, received $350,000 from three dairy industry PACs during the 1980 campaign.[23]

As important as donations are so-called "independent" efforts made without the candidates' cooperation or consent. According to the FEC, $2 million was spent this way for or against 144 candidates in 1976. Four years later, more than $12 million was spent to help or defeat some 400 candidates. (Some of this spending was directed at presidential races, but the bulk was to influence congressional contests.)

PACs are often formed to advance a given viewpoint or candidate. In 1980 the National Conservative Political Action Committee (NCPAC) spent $4 million to defeat six liberal senators. Four of them— George McGovern of South Dakota, John Culver of Iowa, Birch Bayh of Indiana, and Frank Church of Idaho—did in fact lose. The other two targeted senators, Alan Cranston of California and Thomas Eagleton of Missouri, won reelection. Only a few months after the elections, NCPAC targeted liberal senators such as Paul Sarbanes, D-Md., for 1982.

Most independent efforts aid a candidate. Perhaps one-fifth of such funds, however, go to *negative* campaigns to discredit a candidate (usually an incumbent). NCPAC's 1981 attack on Sarbanes is a case in point. A series of TV spots informed Maryland voters of Sarbanes's liberal record. The campaign was launched 20 months before the election, before any challenger had been named. It is not clear whether, on balance, such tactics are effective. In the case of the defeated liberal senators, all four faced uphill battles—with or without NCPAC—in states more conservative than their records showed. Some may even have rallied their forces by lashing out at "vicious out-of-state campaigns."

The campaign funding laws of the 1970s have failed to reduce inequalities between incumbents and challengers. The changes may even help incumbents and make it harder for challengers to raise the money they need to win.[24] Campaign financing laws also have failed to limit the influence of "big money" in politics. Big money is alive and well in American elections, although now it flows through more issue and candidate groups than in the past. Moreover, many of the best-funded PACs run on large numbers of mail-solicited donations rather than a few from fat cats. Finally, the "reforms" have contributed to the decline of old-style parties. Interested groups (labor unions, business and industry associations, consumer and environmental organizations, ideological movements, and a host of special-issue groups) may spend unlimited amounts in lobbying for candidates, so long as they act independently of the candidates themselves. The same is true of individuals and private associations.

Some critics advocate public funding of Senate and House campaigns. Although the 1974 act included an optional public financing scheme for presidential races—used by most major presidential contenders—Congress declined to extend public financing to its own elections. Instead, the 1974 act set spending limits for House and Senate candidates, limits well below the level normally required by challengers to unseat incumbents. Reviewing the law, the Supreme Court held that overall spending limits were unconstitutional in the absence of a public financing plan. The effect has been to leave congressional elections open to unlimited financing while imposing limits on publicly funded presidential campaigns. Public financing remains on the reformers' agenda, under the theory that placing more money in challengers' hands is the only way to ensure competition for congressional seats. Those who thrive under the existing rules, however, will resist such a change.

Money fuels campaigns but does not necessarily determine winners and losers. Some costly campaigns fail miserably, and shoestring efforts can succeed. More is known about how money is spent than about how it affects outcomes. Money is especially crucial for getting an unknown candidate's name before the electorate. The more nonincumbent challengers spend, the greater the chances that voters will recognize their names, and the better their chances against incumbents.[25]

HOW VOTERS DECIDE

Representative assemblies gain their mandate and their legitimacy from periodic elections. Moreover, elections dictate which individuals and factions will control legislative bodies. The decisions reached by voters—no matter what their level of knowledge or motivation—foretell the legislature's policies and performance. Elections do have profound results, after all, and therefore deserve close attention.

Although Congress is supposed to be the people's branch of government, citizens do not display a high degree of interest in congressional elections. In 1980, a presidential year, 45.4 percent of the voting-age population voted in House races, 13 percentage points below the 1960 figure. As Table 3-2 indicates, the long-term voting trend has been downward.

Turnout varies according to whether the election is held in a presidential or midterm year. Midterm races often lack the intense publicity and stimulus to vote provided by presidential contests. Since the 1930s, turnout in midterm congressional elections has averaged about 12 percent below that of the preceding presidential election. Midterm electorates include proportionately more people who are interested in politics and, incidentally, who are more affluent and better educated.[26] Turnout also varies according to region. Less than 20 percent of the voters turn out in certain one-party areas, especially in the South; in competitive states, turnout well above 50 percent is not uncommon.

What induces voters to cast their vote for one candidate and not another in congressional elections? Scholars don't know as much as they would like about this question because most voting studies focus on presidential races. In 1978, however, the University of Michigan's Center for Political Research launched a congressional election survey intended to be repeated every two years. Since then our understanding of voters' behavior in congressional contests has grown rapidly.

When they enter the polling booth, America's voters do not, in general, carry a lot of ideological or even issue-specific baggage. In other

Table 3-2 Turnout for Presidential and House Elections, 1932-1980

Year	Estimated Population of Voting Age	Vote Cast for Presidential Electors		Vote Cast for U.S. Representatives	
		Number	Percent	Number	Percent
1932	75,768,000	39,732,000	52.4	37,657,000	49.7
1934	77,997,000	—	—	32,256,000	41.4
1936	80,174,000	45,643,000	56.9	42,886,000	53.5
1938	82,354,000	—	—	36,236,000	44.0
1940	84,728,000	49,900,000	58.9	46,951,000	55.4
1942	86,465,000	—	—	28,074,000	32.5
1944	85,654,000	47,977,000	56.0	45,103,000	52.7
1946	92,659,000	—	—	34,398,000	37.1
1948	95,573,000	48,794,000	51.1	45,933,000	48.1
1950	98,134,000	—	—	40,342,000	41.1
1952	99,929,000	61,551,000	61.6	57,571,000	57.6
1954	102,075,000	—	—	42,580,000	41.7
1956	104,515,000	62,027,000	59.3	58,426,000	55.9
1958	106,447,000	—	—	45,818,000	43.0
1960	109,672,000	68,838,000	62.8	64,133,000	58.5
1962	112,952,000	—	—	51,267,000	45.4
1964	114,090,000	70,645,000	61.9	65,895,000	57.8
1966	116,638,000	—	—	52,908,000	45.4
1968	120,285,000	73,212,000	60.9	66,288,000	55.1
1970	124,498,000	—	—	54,173,000	43.5
1972	140,068,000	77,719,000	55.5	71,430,000	51.0
1974	145,035,000	—	—	52,495,000	36.2
1976	150,127,000	81,556,000	54.3	74,422,000	49.6
1978	155,492,000	—	—	54,693,000	35.2
1980	160,491,000	84,263,000	52.5	72,796,000	45.4

SOURCE: U.S., Commerce Department, Bureau of the Census, *Statistical Abstract of the United States*, (Washington, D.C.: U.S. Government Printing Office, 1980), p. 515.

words, they do not usually make detailed calculations about which party actually controls Congress, which party ought to control Congress, or which party favors what policies. As a general rule, voters reach their decisions on the basis of three factors: 1) party loyalties, which are declining in saliency; 2) candidate loyalties, growing in saliency and heavily weighted toward incumbents; and 3) overall judgments about the state of the nation and its economy.

Party Loyalties

Political analysts traditionally have found that party identification was the single most powerful factor in determining voters' choices. In his exhaustive study of House elections in the 1920-1964 period, Milton Cummings, Jr., weighed the effect of such things as party strength in a given constituency, "presidential tides," third parties, special local factors, and individual candidate appeals.[27] Party was far more powerful than candidate appeals in determining outcomes, although incumbency exerted an independent impact. Charles O. Jones's work yielded similar results: although House incumbents were advantaged, party affiliation was a key to election results.[28] For example, when the incumbent was not running (that is, had died, retired, or been defeated in the primary), the incumbent's party prevailed in three-quarters of the cases.

Figure 3-3 illustrates the decline in the relative importance of party identification during the last three decades. It is still true that major-ities of party identifiers cast votes for candidates of their party. However, party loyalties have weakened. Increasing proportions of citizens consider themselves independents. Of those who continue to profess partisan leanings, moreover, fewer regard themselves as strong partisans. Finally, because of weakened partisan identification, rising proportions of congressional voters defect from their party. In 1978, 22 percent of the voters (as indicated by a national sample survey) identified with one party but voted for the congressional candidate of another party. In 1956, in contrast, only 9 percent of the voters were in that category.[29] The number of congressional election "defectors" has crept upward in just about every recent election.

To the extent they persist, partisan forces presumably operate differently in presidential and midterm years. Until about 1960, presi-dential-year races displayed a high correlation between voting for president and voting for House members on a district-by-district basis. Since then, the correlation has declined as ticket-splitting has become more common. In 1976, in fact, party identifiers were slightly more loyal in presidential voting than in voting for congressional candidates. Politicians used to talk about "coattails"—the ability of popular presi-dential candidates to attract votes for other candidates of the same party. Coattail effects are still found, but they can run upward as well as downward on the ticket. In certain areas a popular presidential nominee may aid congressional candidates; just as often, presidential candidates gain from their party's local strength. In either case, spillovers from one contest to another are less frequent than they once were.

What happens in midterm elections, when presidential candidates are not on the ballot? As already noted, the midterm electorate is both smaller and different from the presidential-year electorate. Moreover, midterm elections normally result in losses for the party that captured the White House two years earlier, as Table 3-3 indicates. In midterm elections during this century, the presidential party has lost an average of 34 House seats and 4 Senate seats.

Figure 3-3 Party Identification in the United States, 1952-1980

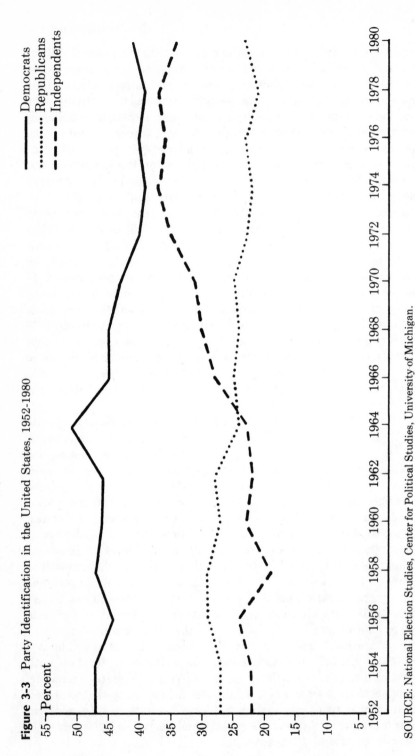

SOURCE: National Election Studies, Center for Political Studies, University of Michigan.

NOTE: Respondents were asked to identify themselves as strong Democrats, weak Democrats, Independent leaning Democrat, Independent middle of the road, Independent leaning Republican, weak Republicans, or strong Republicans. "Don't Know" responses are not shown.

For a time, the so-called "surge and decline" theory held that shrinkage of the electorate in midterm years explained the falloff in the presidential party's votes.[30] That is, a presidential surge, swollen by less motivated voters attracted by presidential campaigns, is followed two years later by a decline as these voters drop out of the electorate. But the link between presidential and congressional voting is loosening. Two other theories have been advanced to help explain midterm losses.

First, midterm elections may serve in part as referenda on the president's popularity and performance in office during the previous two years.[31] This is a plausible explanation, and the only one that accounts for such phenomena as the Democrats' 1974 post-Watergate landslide of 43 representatives and 5 senators. And yet, some years the referendum aspect of midterm elections appears negligible. In 1978, for example, Alan Abramowitz concluded that "voters' evaluations of the performance of the Carter administration apparently had little or no bearing on how they cast their ballots for Senator or Representative."[32]

A second explanation is that midterm elections reflect voter sentiment about the state of the economy. That is, the presidential party may lose heavily if the nation's economy is doing poorly.[33] Again a plausible explanation, but even this simple bit of conventional wisdom is vigorously disputed by some analysts.[34]

Candidate Appeal

After partisan loyalties, the appeal of given candidates is the strongest force in congressional voting. Not surprisingly, candidate appeal normally works in incumbents' favor. When voters abandon their party to vote for senatorial or House candidates, they usually do so to

Table 3-3 Midterm Fortunes of Presidential Parties, 1934-1978

Year	President	House	Senate
1934	Roosevelt (D)	+ 9	+10
1938	Roosevelt (D)	−71	− 6
1942	Roosevelt (D)	−50	− 8
1946	Roosevelt-Truman (D)	−54	−11
1950	Truman (D)	−29	− 5
1954	Eisenhower (R)	−18	− 1
1958	Eisenhower (R)	−47	−13
1962	Kennedy (D)	− 4	+ 4
1966	Johnson (D)	−47	− 3
1970	Nixon (R)	−12	+ 3
1974	Nixon-Ford (R)	−47	− 5
1978	Carter (D)	− 3	−12

SOURCE: Compiled by authors.

vote for incumbents. Although most pronounced in House elections, incumbency advantages are also enjoyed by senators.[35]

The incumbency factor has grown over the past generation to the point where it rivals and in many instances eclipses partisanship. In House races, one estimate fixed the incumbency advantage at about 2 percent of the vote totals during the 1954-1960 period.[36] By the late 1960s, according to a follow-up study, this advantage had grown to 5 percent.[37] In 1978, according to a nationwide election survey, incumbents captured 9 out of every 10 votes cast by party defectors. Two decades earlier, the incumbents' share of party defectors' votes was only 57 percent, or a little better than an even break. Warren Kostroski concluded that, even in Senate contests, "incumbency now serves . . . as an important alternate voting cue to party. . . ." [38]

Taken together, party and incumbency are an almost unbeatable combination.[39] In 1978 House elections covered by the Michigan survey, 95 percent of those voters identifying with the incumbent's party voted for the incumbent. Among independents, 79 percent voted for the incumbent. Even among members of the challenger's party, the split was 54 to 46 percent in the incumbent's favor. An incumbent senator's edge, although less, is nonetheless substantial. In 1978 senators running for reelection attracted 89 percent of their own party's voters and 64 percent of the independents' votes. Even among the opposition party's voters, senators captured almost a third of the ballots.

It is easy enough to say incumbents have an edge at the polls, but exactly what does that mean? It is also easy to cite congressional staff, mailing privileges and other "perks" as devices to ensure reelection. As it happens, the rise in incumbents' advantage took place in the late 1960s, about the same time new tools for communicating with voters were added—increased travel and clerk-hire allowances, for example. But all this is speculative. Nowhere can we point to a direct link between perquisites and voter approval. Perhaps incumbents prove themselves better informed and better qualified than challengers. They are, after all, a select group: they have already won election, and if they expect stiff opposition they can always retire voluntarily.

Research has uncovered several advantages of incumbency: incumbents are better known than challengers; incumbents are viewed more favorably than challengers; and incumbents (mainly in the House) often benefit from a lack of credible challengers. For various reasons, these factors favor representatives more than senators.

Incumbents, especially in the House, are better known than their opponents. This has not always been acknowledged. In a pathbreaking study published in 1962, Donald Stokes and Warren Miller disclosed how little voters usually know about the performance either of the parties or of individual legislators.[40] In fact, most voters could not recall their own representative's name. "Members of Congress and their opponents at election time," concluded the authors of another study, "remain largely unknown to most of their constituents." [41] But even if voters can't recall a candidate's name in an interview, they can identify and express opinions about the candidate when the name is presented to them—as it is in the voting booth.[42]

Gauging by name recognition rather than recall, incumbents are well-known to their electorates. In the 1978 Michigan survey, nearly all respondents were able to recognize and rate Senate and House incumbents running for reelection (96 and 93 percent, respectively). Senate challengers were recognized and rated by 86 percent of the respondents, House challengers by only 44 percent. Open-seat candidates fell somewhere between incumbents and challengers in visibility.[43] Thus, most voters are capable of recognizing and expressing views about congressional candidates, except for House challengers. These opinions have a powerful impact on voting decisions, and indeed in the eyes of some analysts are the most potent influences on congressional voting.[44]

In evaluating candidates, voters tend to favor incumbents over nonincumbents. Of the voters' comments about incumbents in the 1978 survey, four out of five were favorable. In contrast, only 57 percent of the comments about challengers were positive. Most of the comments centered around job performance or personal characteristics; relatively few dealt with issues. Voters evaluated House incumbents largely on the basis of personal characteristics and noncontroversial activities such as casework and communication with constituents. [45] Even on the issues, references to incumbents were overwhelmingly positive. Only one voter in ten claimed to know how their representative had voted on a piece of legislation during the preceding two years, but more than two-thirds of those voters claimed to have agreed with their legislator's vote.

Incumbents' popularity stems partly from their ability to shape information that constituents receive about them and their performance—through activities such as advertising, credit-claiming, and position-taking.[46] Not surprisingly, therefore, high levels of contact are reported for House and Senate incumbents; and the more contact voters have with their legislators, the more positive their evaluations are likely to be. In the 1978 survey, only 10 percent of all voters denied having exposure of any kind to their representative; only 6 percent reported no exposure to their senator. Table 3-4 illustrates the various types of contact voters report having with incumbents, challengers, and open-seat candidates. Many representatives' constituents receive mail from them or read about them in newspapers; almost a quarter have met the representative face to face. For senators, the major point of voter contact is TV appearances or newspaper and magazine coverage.

Table 3-4   Voter Contact with House and Senate Candidates, 1978

Forms of Contact	House			Senate		
	Incumbents	Challengers	Open Seats	Incumbents	Challengers	Open Seats
Any type	90%	44%	73%	94%	82%	88%
Read about in newspaper, magazine	71	32	57	73	63	78
Received mail	71	16	43	53	32	47
Saw on TV	50	24	48	80	70	78
Family or friend had contact	39	11	26	—	—	—
Heard on radio	34	15	28	45	37	49
Met personally	23	4	14	9	5	9
Saw at meeting	20	3	13	10	5	13
Talked to staff	12	2	13	6	4	9
(N)	(756)	(756)	(121)	(409)	(409)	(158)

SOURCE: 1978 National Election Study, Center for Political Studies, University of Michigan. Cited in Thomas Mann and Raymond Wolfinger, "Candidates and Parties in Congressional Elections," *American Political Science Review* (September 1980): 627.

The "visibility gap" between incumbents and challengers is wider in House than in Senate races. Whereas 9 out of every 10 voters report some form of contact with their representative, fewer than half that proportion have been exposed to challengers. Senate voters are more apt to be reached by *both* incumbent and challenger. Of those questioned in 1978, 82 percent reported contact with nonincumbent Senate candidates in their state, compared with 94 percent reporting contact with incumbent senators. In open seats, the gap is narrower. Candidates for seats with no incumbent are able to reach nearly three-quarters of their potential House voters and 90 percent of potential senatorial voters.

These figures suggest why senators are more vulnerable at the polls than their House counterparts. The 1978 survey and other studies indicate that representatives are viewed more favorably than senators— probably because they are judged primarily from noncontroversial acts like personal contact or constituent service, whereas senators cannot avoid association with divisive national issues. Second, Senate challengers are far more visible than House challengers. Senate contests are widely reported by the media, and challengers can gain almost as much exposure as incumbents. Media coverage of House races is much more fragmentary, throwing more weight to incumbents' techniques of contacting voters. Third, senators cannot manipulate voter contacts as much as representatives do. They appear to voters in a more neutral light. Senators' voter contacts occur largely through organized media that they do not control; representatives gain exposure through diverse means—personal appearances, mailings, and newsletters—that they fashion to their own advantage. "Somewhat ironically," observes Michael Robinson, "powerful senators are less able to control their images than 'invisible' House members." [47] Finally, senatorial elections are simply harder fought than House elections. There are fewer one-party states than one-party congressional districts.

"Most incumbents face obscure, politically inexperienced opponents whose resources fall far short of what is necessary to mount a formidable campaign," [48] according to Gary Jacobson. Skilled incumbents try to dampen opposition before the campaign begins. People who challenge an entrenched incumbent often face overwhelming odds. Many run the campaigns out of their own homes. Their campaign staff is made up of family members and friends. Their funds come out of their own pockets. In six of Maryland's eight congressional districts, incumbents in 1980 faced only token opposition or campaigned as if they had none at all.[49] This is the rule rather than the exception in House races, though it is increasingly rare in Senate contests.

Nonincumbents can overcome this gap with luck and attention to certain basic principles: Run for an open seat, or one where the incumbent's support is slipping. Be a credible, forceful candidate. Be prepared to spend money to erase the incumbent's visibility advantage. Blame the incumbent for "the mess in Washington." It's risky strategy. Yet every election year a handful of incumbents lose this way; and that's enough to keep most of the others on their guard.[50]

Issue Voting

According to conventional wisdom, issues and ideologies play a relatively minor role in voting, especially in congressional races. In their 1962 study of congressional voting, Stokes and Miller found that voters knew next to nothing about the performance of either the parties or individual members of Congress.[51] Recent studies tend to confirm this finding in the sense that issues themselves do not by and large decide voters' choices. Relatively few voters, according to the 1978 survey, remember how their representatives voted on any particular bill, and less than half can say whether they generally agree or disagree with how their representatives vote in Washington. Voters voice surprisingly few complaints about their representatives' voting, and legislators lose relatively few votes because of the positions they take.

These generalized findings, however, should be taken with a grain of salt. Regardless of what nationwide surveys may show, legislators and their advisers are highly sensitive to voters' anticipated reactions to issue stands. Much energy is devoted to framing positions, communicating them (sometimes in deliberately obscure words), and assessing their impact. Moreover, every professional politician can relate instances where issues tilted an election one way or another. Frequently cited are the so-called "single-interest" groups. Some citizens vote according to a single issue they regard as paramount—for example, gun control, abortion (pro or con), or certain ethnic issues. Defeats of senators such as Joseph Tydings, D-Md., in 1970 and Dick Clark, D-Iowa, in 1978 are often blamed on such voters—antigun control voters in Tydings's case and antiabortionists in Clark's. Even if small, such groups can decide close contests. That is why legislators dislike taking positions that evoke extreme responses—issues that will prompt certain voters to oppose them regardless of their stewardship on other matters.

As usual, we must distinguish between House and Senate voting. House candidates—incumbents and challengers—can more easily side-step divisive national issues and stress personal qualities and district service. Senators, on the other hand, are more closely identified with issues. A 1978 study comparing incumbents' ADA ratings with voters' self-classifications on a seven-point liberal-conservative scale found that ideology had "no discernible impact on evaluations of House candidates." [52] Contact was the prime influence on evaluations of House candidates; ideology and party identification were more important in evaluating Senate candidates.

If issues do not always directly sway voters, they exert powerful indirect effects upon election outcomes. For one thing, issues motivate that segment of voters who are opinion leaders, who can lend or withhold support far beyond their single vote. Issues are carefully monitored by organized interests, including PACs, in a position to channel funds, publicity, or volunteer workers to the candidate's cause. It is more than superstition, then, that makes legislators devote so much time and attention to cultivating these "attentive publics."

As for average voters, their choices can be influenced, if not by specific issues, by overall assessments of the state of the nation and its economy. We know, for example, that public assessments of institutions such as the presidency or Congress are based in part on considerations like these.[53] Such feelings no doubt affect congressional voting despite the candidates' best efforts to detach their appeals from national trends. Attempts to verify this relationship, by comparing aggregate vote totals with economic or social indicators, yield inconclusive results. One student's findings suggested that declining real income of citizens reduced the vote for the incumbent president's party, while rising incomes increased it.[54] Other researchers hold that economic downturns reduce the vote for the president's party but economic upturns have no corresponding effect.[55] Still others argue that "aggregate economic variables affect neither the participation rate nor the relative strengths of the two major parties" in congressional elections.[56] They concede, however, that one exception to this generalization might be the inflation that has plagued the U.S. economy in recent years. No doubt further studies will clarify these relationships. In the meantime, we can presume that aggregate factors—for example, economic indicators or levels of citizen trust in government—exert some impact upon congressional voting although the actual extent is not known.

What overall picture do we gain of voters in congressional elections? It is a rather complicated picture in which three factors—party, candidates, and issues—play varying roles. Despite weakening partisan ties, a large segment of the electorate seems to have made a "standing decision" to vote for candidates by party affiliation. Individual candidate factors are, however, of substantial and growing importance. Congressional candidates, especially incumbents, often fashion unique appeals based not on party loyalty but on "home style"—a mixture of personal style, voter contacts, and constituent service.[57] Because of their superior resources for cultivating attractive home styles, incumbents have an edge at the polls. Through media exposure, Senate challengers can often overcome this advantage; lacking such outlets for their message, House challengers can less frequently do so. Finally, issues and ideologies influence at least some voters in some elections.

ELECTION OUTCOMES

The process by which representatives and senators reach Capitol Hill is a prime aspect of the two Congresses notion we have put forth. The most pervasive attribute of electoral processes is their local character. As Thomas Mann and Raymond Wolfinger conclude, "In deciding how to cast their ballots, most voters are influenced primarily by the choice of local candidates." [58] Although national trends are the backdrop against which these local contests are fought, the candidates, the voters, and often the issues and styles, are deeply rooted in states and districts. The aggregate of all these contests is a legislative body charged with addressing national problems and issues. Recruitment processes, in short, are part of the *pluribus* from which the *unum* must emerge.

As we have seen, the electoral process is complex and multilayered. Some "rules of the game" are fixed by the Constitution and state and federal laws. Others flow from our political system—actually, from hundreds of distinct political systems in states and districts. Political groups and networks of activists in these locales exert varying levels of control over recruitment. The rigors of campaigning influence the final outcome still further. Finally, voter attitudes and motivations determine which candidates emerge victorious on election day.

Beyond these immediate results, recruitment yields a representative system for reaching decisions about society's priorities. Representation may be perfect or imperfect; resulting policies may serve citizens' needs efficiently or inefficiently; arrangements may appear fair and legitimate or may seem biased and corrupt. These are by no means trivial results, and for better or worse they flow from the vagaries of the selection process.

Party or Factional Balance

One of the most profound results of recruitment is that it yields victory or defeat for parties or factions. Despite the much-vaunted independence of candidates and voters, most races are in fact run with party labels. In 1980 no fewer than 29 different parties appeared on ballots somewhere in the United States. These included such names as: City Independent, New Union, Communist, Free Libertarian, Right to Life, Peace and Freedom, and Workers World.

In terms of governance, only two parties really count: the Democrats or the Republicans have controlled Congress since 1855. In the table on page 450 are arrayed the partisan majorities in the House and Senate since 1901. Between 1896 and 1920, it is estimated, the two parties actually had approximately equal numbers of partisans in the electorate, but lower participation rates in Democratic areas tended to favor the Republicans. The GOP's relative position improved after 1920, when women received the vote. The 1932 realignment shifted the balance to the Democrats, where it has remained until recently.

During the half-century between 1930 and 1980, the Democrats were virtually a permanent majority and the Republicans a permanent minority on Capitol Hill. In all that time, the Republicans controlled both chambers for only four years (1947-1949, 1953-1955). Democratic sweeps in 1958, 1964, and 1974 padded their majorities. Republicans eventually recovered from the first two setbacks; but by the 1970s Democratic dominance, especially in the House, was harder to overcome because incumbents were successfully exploiting their reelection assets.

For a time doomsayers predicted that the GOP might become extinct. Its outlook seemed dated and unpopular. The Watergate scandal, although by no means a Republican crime, tainted the party. Its leaders were disheartened. What was most important for congressional contests, the party's low estate scared off qualified potential candidates.

Yet the Republican party had valuable resources that eventually fueled its revival. The GOP's ideological viewpoint has always been more coherent than that of the Democrats.'[59] Potentially at least, this wins support from dedicated right-wing groups and financial backing from wealthy individuals and business firms. In the late 1970s when the Democrats failed to deal with foreign affairs and the economy, the GOP benefited from superior organization and adroit leadership from William Brock, former representative and senator from Tennessee. Brock and his staff sought out promising candidates, who were encouraged by the Democrats' disunity.

Capitalizing on the Democrats' weakness, the Republicans gained 12 seats to capture the Senate in the 1980 elections. In the House, the GOP gained 33 seats, still 26 short of a majority. Efforts to capture the House in 1982 began immediately. As we have seen, the party that controls the White House usually loses seats in the midterm election, but the GOP is aided by demographic changes. As recorded by the 1980 census, population is shifting toward the South and West, where the party is thriving, and away from northern and eastern areas, traditional Democratic bastions. Meanwhile, the Democrats, for two generations kings of the Hill, were badly divided and forced to play catch-up politics.

House majorities and minorities are exaggerated by the electoral system. This is the so-called "Matthew Effect," named for a biblical aphorism (Matthew 13:12): "For whosoever hath, to him shall be given, and he shall have more abundance; but whosoever hath not, from him shall be taken away even that he hath." A product of single-member district representation, the Matthew Effect means that the party winning the most votes captures a disproportionately large share of the legislative seats. The minority party gets fewer seats than its share of the vote would dictate.[60] In 1980 the Democrats captured 55.8 percent of the House seats with only 49.2 percent of the vote. In addition, Democrats have more safe seats than Republicans have. And Democrats are probably overrepresented because their low turnout rate means that the number of voters in Democratic districts is fewer than the number of voters in GOP districts.[61]

In the Senate the Matthew effect is not always felt. Disparities in states' size and regional party distribution often produce inconsistent results. In 1980, for instance, Democratic senatorial candidates actually outpolled GOP candidates nationally by some three million votes, but the party wound up with a 47-person minority in the chamber. The disparity stemmed from huge victories by John Glenn in Ohio (1.6 million votes), Alan Cranston in California (1.5 million), and several others. Meanwhile the GOP swept less populous states or won tight races in places like New York.

Registering Voters' Views

Are voters' views accurately reflected by the representatives they elect to Congress? This question is not easily answered. Popular control of policymakers is not the same thing as popular control of policies themselves. If this were the case, then constituents' views would be precisely mirrored by legislators' voting behavior and the laws passed by the legislature.

What sort of correlation exists between voters' attitudes and members' voting on issues? Miller and Stokes found that constituency attitudes correlated differently according to the type of policy.[62] In foreign affairs, a slight negative correlation existed between constituents' attitudes and legislators' votes; in social and economic welfare issues, the correlation was moderate; in civil rights issues, the correlation was very high. In other words, in at least one and possibly two major policy areas, the linkage was weak enough to cast some doubt on constituency control.

Political scientists explain the absence of strong linkages by noting how difficult it is to meet all the conditions needed for popular control of policies. Voters would have to identify the candidates' issue positions, and they would have to vote by referring to those positions. Differences between candidates would have to be apparent, and winners would have to vote in accord with their preelection attitudes. These conditions aren't always met. Candidates' stands aren't always clear, nor do candidates invariably differentiate themselves on issues. Voters often ignore issues in voting; and once elected, legislators frequently diverge from their preelection attitudes.

Political scientists John L. Sullivan and Robert E. O'Connor tried to test these conditions in the 1966 elections by submitting a questionnaire to all House candidates covering three issue areas—foreign affairs, civil rights, and domestic policies—and then following the successful candidates' voting records in the House.[63] Their findings suggest that elements of popular control are present. First, according to their inquiries, voters had real choices among candidates. Second, winning candidates generally voted according to their preelection stands. Third, candidates were ideologically distinct, with Democrats invariably more liberal than Republicans. To these pieces of evidence we can add another: according to the 1978 survey, most congressional voters could rank their representative on a liberal-conservative scale, and most of these claimed an affinity with their representative's ranking.[64] In other words, voters' attitudes and legislators' views are roughly parallel—even though they may diverge on numerous specific points.

If ideological or attitudinal links between voters and their representatives are rough and variable, actual contacts between constituents and individual legislators are numerous and palpable. Individual legislators do not necessarily mirror the nation as a whole in terms of demographic characteristics. Yet much of their time and effort while in office is devoted to dealing with "the folks back home." Constituency politics are ever-present in the daily lives of senators and representatives, and it is to this subject that we turn in the following chapter.

NOTES

1. Lewis A. Froman, *Congressmen and Their Constituencies* (Chicago: Rand McNally & Co., 1963).
2. *Congressional Districts in the 1970s,* 2d ed. (Washington, D.C.: Congressional Quarterly, 1974), p. 231.
3. Edward Walsh, "GOP Plays Chess with Indiana Hill Democrats," *Washington Post,* May 11, 1981, p. A4.
4. Robert S. Erikson, "Malapportionment, Gerrymandering, and Party Fortunes in Congressional Elections," *American Political Science Review* (December 1972): 1234-1235.
5. Charles S. Bullock III, "House Careerists: Changing Patterns of Longevity and Attrition," *American Political Science Review* (December 1972): 1295-1300; Albert D. Cover, "One Good Term Deserves Another: The Advantage of Incumbency in Congressional Elections," *American Journal of Political Science* (August 1977): 523-541; and John A. Ferejohn, "On the Decline of Competition in Congressional Elections," *American Political Science Review* (March 1977): 166-176.
6. Leo M. Snowiss, "Congressional Recruitment and Representation," *American Political Science Review* (September 1966): 627-639.
7. Christopher Buchanan, "House Races: New Emphasis on Open Districts," *Congressional Quarterly Weekly Report,* April 1, 1978, pp. 809-814.
8. Ibid.
9. Malcolm E. Jewell and David M. Olson, *American State Political Parties and Elections* (Homewood, Ill.: Dorsey Press, 1978), pp. 132-133.
10. V. O. Key, Jr., *Parties, Politics and Pressure Groups,* 5th ed. (New York: Thomas Y. Crowell & Co., 1964), pp. 438, 447.
11. Austin Ranney, "Parties in State Politics," in *Politics in the American States,* ed. Herbert Jacob and Kenneth Vines (Boston: Little, Brown & Co., 1976), pp. 61-99.
12. Gary Jacobson, "The Impact of Broadcast Campaigning on Electoral Outcomes," *Journal of Politics* (August 1975): 769-793; and Michael J. Robinson, "Three Faces of Congressional Media," in *The New Congress,* ed. Thomas E. Mann and Norman J. Ornstein (Washington, D.C.: American Enterprise Institute for Public Policy Research, 1981), pp. 90-91.
13. Sara Terry, "U.S. Representative Udall Finds Seniority No Longer Eases Reelection," *Christian Science Monitor,* October 21, 1980, p. 14.
14. Alan L. Clem, ed., *The Making of Congressmen: Seven Campaigns of 1974* (North Scituate, Mass.: Duxbury Press, 1976), p. 219.
15. Merle Miller, *Lyndon: An Oral Biography* (New York: G. P. Putnam's Sons, 1980), p. 120.
16. Maurice Carroll, "Generally Liberal States Prove the Folly of Generalizing," *New York Times,* November 9, 1980, p. E7.
17. Christopher Buchanan, "Candidates' Campaign Costs for Congressional Contests Have Gone Up at a Fast Pace," *Congressional Quarterly Weekly Report,* September 29, 1979, p. 2155.
18. Morton Mintz, "Outsider Money Inside a California District," *Washington Post,* February 7, 1981, p. A3.
19. Buchanan, "Candidates' Campaign Costs," p. 2152.
20. Ibid., pp. 2153-2155.
21. Gary Jacobson, *Money in Congressional Elections* (New Haven: Yale University Press, 1980), pp. 53-54, 228.

22. Buchanan, "Candidates' Campaign Costs," pp. 2154-2155.
23. Common Cause, press release, March 12, 1981.
24. Jacobson, *Money in Congressional Elections.*
25. Gary C. Jacobson, "Practical Consequences of Campaign Finance Reform: An Incumbent Protection Act?" *Public Policy* (Winter 1976): 1-32.
26. M. Margaret Conway, "Political Participation in Mid-Term Congressional Elections During the 1970s" (Paper delivered at the annual meeting of the American Political Science Association, Washington, D.C., August 31-September 3, 1979).
27. Milton C. Cummings, Jr., *Congressmen and the Electorate* (New York: Free Press, 1966).
28. Charles O. Jones, "The Role of the Campaign in Congressional Politics," in *The Electoral Process,* ed. M. Kent Jennings and L. Harmon Zeigler (Englewood Cliffs, N.J.: Prentice-Hall, 1966), pp. 21-41.
29. Thomas E. Mann and Raymond E. Wolfinger, "Candidates and Parties in Congressional Elections," *American Political Science Review* (September 1980): 617-632.
30. Angus Campbell, "Surge and Decline: A Study of Electoral Change," in *Elections and the Political Order,* ed. Campbell et al. (New York: John Wiley & Sons, 1966), pp. 40-62.
31. Edward R. Tufte, "Determinants of the Outcome of Midterm Congressional Elections," *American Political Science Review* (September 1975): 812-826; and Samuel Kernell, "Presidential Popularity and Negative Voting: An Alternative Explanation of the Midterm Congressional Decline of the President's Party," *American Political Science Review* (March 1977): 44-66.
32. Alan I. Abramowitz, "A Comparison of Voting for U.S. Senator and Representative in 1978," *American Political Science Review* (September 1980): 633-650.
33. Gerald H. Kramer, "Short-Term Fluctuations in U.S. Voting Behavior, 1896-1964," *American Political Science Review* (March 1971): 131-143; and Tufte, "Midterm Congressional Elections," pp. 812-826.
34. Francisco Arcelus and Allan H. Meltzer, "The Effect of Aggregate Economic Variables on Congressional Elections," *American Political Science Review* (December 1975): 1232-1239.
35. Barbara Hinckley, "Incumbency and the Presidential Vote in Senate Elections," *American Political Science Review* (September 1970): 836-842; Hinckley, *Congressional Elections* (Washington, D.C.: Congressional Quarterly Press, 1981), pp. 113-132; and Warren Lee Kostroski, "Party and Incumbency in Postwar Senate Elections: Trends, Patterns, and Models," *American Political Science Review* (December 1973): 1213-1234.
36. Robert S. Erikson, "The Advantage of Incumbency in Congressional Elections," *Polity* (Spring 1971): 395-405.
37. Erikson, "Malapportionment, Gerrymandering, and Party Fortunes," pp. 1234-1245.
38. Kostroski, "Party and Incumbency," p. 1233.
39. Mann and Wolfinger, "Candidates and Parties," pp. 620-621.
40. Donald E. Stokes and Warren E. Miller, "Party Government and the Saliency of Congress," *Public Opinion Quarterly* (Winter 1962): 531-546.
41. Warren E. Miller and Teresa Levitin, *Leadership and Change: Presidential Elections from 1952 to 1976* (Cambridge, Mass.: Winthrop Publishers, 1976), p. 33.
42. Alan I. Abramowitz, "Name Familiarity, Reputation and the Incumbency Effect in a Congressional Election," *Western Political Quarterly* (December

1975): 668-684; Abramowitz, "A Comparison of Voting," pp. 633-650; Thomas E. Mann, *Unsafe At Any Margin: Interpreting Congressional Elections* (Washington, D.C.: American Enterprise Institute for Public Policy Research, 1978); and Mann and Wolfinger, "Candidates and Parties."
43. Mann and Wolfinger, "Candidates and Parties," p. 623.
44. Abramowitz, "A Comparison of Voting," pp. 634-639.
45. Ibid.
46. David R. Mayhew, *Congress: The Electoral Connection* (New Haven: Yale University Press, 1974).
47. Robinson, "Three Faces of Congressional Media," p. 91.
48. Gary C. Jacobson, "Incumbents' Advantages in the 1978 U.S. Congressional Elections," *Legislative Studies Quarterly* (May 1981): 198.
49. Donald P. Baker, "It's Fall, and the Campaigning Is Easy," *Washington Post*, October 31, 1980, p. B5.
50. Mann, *Unsafe at Any Margin*.
51. Stokes and Miller, "Party Government and the Saliency of Congress."
52. Alan I. Abramowitz, "A Comparison of Voting," p. 635.
53. Glenn R. Parker, "Political Beliefs About the Structure of Government: Congress and the Presidency," *Sage Professional Papers in American Politics,* vol. 2, no. 04-018 (Beverly Hills: Sage Publications, 1974). See also V. O. Key, Jr., *The Responsible Electorate* (Cambridge, Mass.: Belknap Press, 1966).
54. Kramer, "U.S. Voting Behavior, 1896-1964," p. 131-143.
55. Howard S. Bloom and H. Douglas Price, "Voter Response to Short-Run Economic Candidates: The Asymmetric Effect of Prosperity and Recession," *American Political Science Review* (December 1975): 1240-1254.
56. Arcelus and Meltzer, "The Effects of Aggregate Economic Variables," pp. 1232-1239.
57. Richard F. Fenno, Jr., *Home Style: House Members in Their Districts* (Boston: Little, Brown & Co., 1978).
58. Mann and Wolfinger, "Candidates and Parties," p. 630.
59. Sidney Verba and Norman H. Nie, *Participation in America* (New York: Harper & Row, 1972).
60. Douglas W. Rae, *The Political Consequences of Electoral Laws,* rev. ed. (New Haven: Yale University Press, 1971).
61. Edward R. Tufte, "The Relationship Between Seats and Votes in Two-Party Systems," *American Political Science Review* (June 1973): 540-554.
62. Warren E. Miller and Donald E. Stokes, "Constituency Influence in Congress," *American Political Science Review* (March 1963): 45-57.
63. John L. Sullivan and Robert E. O'Connor, "Electoral Choice and Popular Control of Public Policy: The Case of the 1966 House Elections," *American Political Science Review* (December 1972): 1256-1268.
64. Mann and Wolfinger, "Candidates and Parties," p. 629.

Senate Majority Leader Howard H. Baker, Jr.,
at home in Tennessee.

4

Being There:
Hill Styles and Home Styles

A representative has just flown in from Washington for an evening's electioneering in the district. The representative is elated because he has just talked to the president; their lengthy phone conversation climaxed an exciting legislative struggle in which the lawmaker played a pivotal role. Yet this victory is soon cast aside as he gulps down his dinner and hurries to a campaign appearance. The back of his aide's car is piled from floor to roof with hundreds of campaign shopping bags emblazoned with the representative's name and picture. Getting in the car, the representative sighs, smiles, and says, "Back to this again." The legislator had just moved from one political world to another— from the world of high policy to "the world of the shopping bags." Political scientist Richard F. Fenno, Jr., thus introduces his study of House members in their districts. [1]

All members of Congress move back and forth between these two worlds. The familiar "textbook Congress"—lawmaking, investigating, and voting in the two chambers—is one side of the national legislature. The other Congress, the "world of the shopping bags," extends over 540 disparate constituencies, many of them far removed in geography and outlook from the nation's capital.

In this chapter we look closely at members of Congress and the two worlds in which they live and work. Who are these members? What are their jobs like on Capitol Hill and back home in their states or districts? How do these two aspects of their job fit together, and how do they clash?

HILL STYLES

Who Are the Legislators?

The Constitution names only three criteria for serving in Congress—age, citizenship, and residency. In practice, however, entrance requirements are far more restrictive. Not all Americans are equally adept at running for (much less winning) public office; for this reason, if for no other, those who serve in Congress differ in key respects from the electorate at large. It was Aristotle, after all, who first observed that elections are essentially oligarchic affairs.

By almost any measure, senators and representatives comprise an economic and social elite. They are well educated. They come from a small number of prestigious occupations. Many of them possess or amass material wealth. An estimated one-third of all senators are millionaires, and two-thirds supplement this with outside incomes of $20,000 or more. The House is more middle-class, economically speaking; but even here, at least 30 members are millionaires, and about a hundred report incomes of $20,000 or more annually beyond their congressional salaries.[2]

Occupation. Some humorist proposed that our government "of laws and not men" is really "of lawyers and not men." When the 97th Congress convened in 1981, 253 members were lawyers. As Figure 4-1 indicates, lawyers typically have outnumbered other professions in the House of Representatives; the same is true for the Senate, where Donald Matthews found that "no other occupational group even approaches the lawyers' record."[3]

In the United States, law and politics are closely linked. The legal profession stresses personal skills, such as verbalization, advocacy, and negotiation, that are useful in public office. Lawyers also can move in and out of their jobs without jeopardizing their careers. Such mobility would be unthinkable in medicine, engineering, or some other professions. (In the 97th Congress, there were seven physicians, seven engineers, and one scientist.) Many lawyers even view forays into electoral politics as a form of professional advertising.

Figure 4-1 Occupations of House Members in 11 Selected Congresses

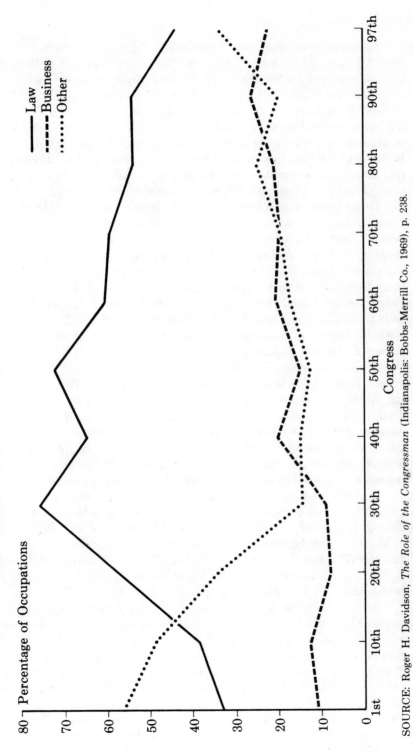

SOURCE: Roger H. Davidson, *The Role of the Congressman* (Indianapolis: Bobbs-Merrill Co., 1969), p. 238.

Business is the next most prevalent occupation, although a distant second to law. Traditionally, business people encountered difficulty in running for public office. Local proprietors (druggists or morticians, for example), while highly visible in their home towns, usually are hard pressed to leave their businesses in the hands of others. Corporate managers are neither very visible nor mobile because temporary leaves of absence can bump them off the ladder of advancement. However, business executives in service industries—publishing, broadcasting, or real estate, for example—are visible and mobile enough to be ideal candidates, and are found in growing numbers in Congress.

Other professions are represented in smaller numbers. Members of the so-called "verbalizing professions"—education, journalism, public service, and even clergy—often win seats in Congress. Almost 70 senators and representatives in the 97th Congress spent part or all of their precongressional careers in education as teachers or administrators. Despite stubborn fears about church-state separation, several clergymen are found in Congress these days. However, their numbers were curbed by Pope John Paul II's 1980 ban on public office for Roman Catholic clergy, a decision that halted the 10-year House career of Robert F. Drinan, D-Mass.

Still other occupations are represented because they are uniquely visible. Historically, military heroes have been sought after, and following World War II a surge of returning war veterans went to Congress. Two of those were John F. Kennedy and Richard M. Nixon, both of whom initially won House seats in 1946. Today, veterans still outnumber nonveterans in Congress, but the proportion is dwindling and military service no longer seems a special political asset.[4] Former hostages or prisoners of war, however, are compelling candidates.

Today's media-centered campaigns yield a type of celebrity member from various occupations. Out of the 1960s came astronaut heroes. Two of them, John Glenn, D-Ohio, and Harrison "Jack" Schmitt, R-N.M., later launched Senate careers. Other celebrities include a basketball star (Bill Bradley, D-N.J.), a Vietnam war POW (Jeremiah Denton, R-Ala.), a statewide TV personality (Jesse Helms, R-N.C.), and a professional football player (Jack Kemp, R-N.Y.).

Aside from celebrities, most members boast longstanding records of political activism before they arrive in the House or Senate. Traditionally, this meant apprenticeship in local and state elective offices, particularly state legislatures. Most senators, Matthews found, began their political careers early in life—usually soon after graduating from college—and by the time they were elected to the Senate had held three offices and spent half their adult life (about 10 years) in public office.[5] Thirty senators in 1981 had served earlier in the House. Thirty-four senators and 194 representatives served in their state legislatures.

Today's legislators often serve political apprenticeships in nonelective offices. Some were activists in the civil rights or anti-Vietnam war movements of the 1960s; others emerged from the consumer or environmental movements of the 1970s. (Such activists are far less likely than elected public servants to be lawyers—one reason for the legal profession's recent decline in Congress.) Some lawmakers serve at least part of their apprenticeship in the congressional bureaucracy itself: 57 representatives and 4 senators in the 97th Congress had worked in some capacity for a legislator, congressional committee, or other Hill agency. One steppingstone is the post of field representative for an incumbent senator or representative.

Needless to say, many key occupations are, and always have been, drastically underrepresented. Low-status occupations—including farm labor, service trades, manual and skilled labor, and domestic service—are almost unknown on Capitol Hill. In the 97th Congress only two representatives had blue-collar backgrounds: a pipe fitter and a barber. One blue-collar worker elected in recent years quit after one term because he was unhappy and self-conscious about his social status; another was convicted in the Abscam affair and ousted from the House.

Education and Religion. By every measure, Congress is a highly educated body. Virtually every member has a college degree; a majority have advanced training. Many occupations that are heavily represented require postgraduate training. Earned doctorates are not unknown, and in 1981 there were five ex-Rhodes Scholars in the Senate.

While a few prestigious private universities are overrepresented, no schools hold the dominant position that Oxford and Cambridge do in British ruling circles. One reason is the lingering norm of localism in congressional recruitment. People with close, long-term ties to the state or district are favored, and this means that local colleges and state universities have a large share of members. Of the senators sitting in 1981, 58 did their undergraduate work at in-state schools.[6]

Most members of Congress are affiliated with organized religious bodies, at least in terms of public profession of membership. Ninety-five percent of the members of the 97th Congress indicated religious affiliation, compared with about 6 out of 10 Americans. About a quarter of all House and Senate members are Roman Catholics, the largest single contingent. Twenty-three percent of the nation's population are Catholics. Most other legislators are Protestants, primarily the mainline denominations—Methodists, Episcopalians, Presbyterians, and Baptists. Jews, who comprise 3 percent of the total U.S. population, are about 6 percent of the 97th Congress. In terms of trends, Catholics and Jews have enlarged their share of Congress's membership, while mainline Protestants have declined slightly.

On most issues, religion probably has little impact on how members approach voting or other choices. However, intense social issues— among them abortion, school prayer, crime, pornography, and tuition tax credits for private schools—stir religious feelings. It is possible that members' religious ties tilt them toward the stands of extremely motivated groups on these sensitive issues.

Race and Sex. Neither the Senate nor the House accurately mirrors the nation in terms of racial, ethnic, or sexual mixture. Throughout its history, Congress has been a bastion for whites, males, and older ethnic stocks.

Black Americans, who comprise 12 percent of the nation's population, account for only 3 percent of Congress's members. In 1981, 19 blacks (including 2 nonvoting delegates) served in the House, none in the Senate. Indeed, in all our history about 50 blacks have served in Congress, three of them in the Senate and the rest in the House. Half of these served during the post-Civil War period of the nineteenth century. All were Republicans, loyal to the party of Lincoln. No blacks served in Congress from 1900 to 1928, when Oscar DePriest, a Republican, was elected from a heavily black district on Chicago's South Side. In the next 25 years only three more blacks entered Congress, but after the 1960s black representation steadily rose. A half dozen blacks have served as House committee chairmen. All but two of the twentieth-century black legislators were Democrats, reflecting blacks' current partisan allegiance.

Black legislators typically see themselves representing members of their race wherever they may live. In 1971 they formed the Congressional Black Caucus, an alliance dedicated to working for policies of interest to blacks everywhere. They point out that, although very few constituencies are represented by blacks, no fewer than 172 districts have at least a 25 percent black population.[7]

Few blacks represent white areas; most come from overwhelmingly black districts. Of the blacks serving in 1981, only Democratic Representative Ron Dellums from Berkeley, California, represented an area less than 40 percent black. The average district represented by a black has nearly a 60 percent black population. Moreover, such districts tend to be in core cities dwindling in population. This suggests that black representation may have reached a plateau unless voters' attitudes change in predominantly white areas.

Other racial minorities are similarly underrepresented. Hispanics, who compose 5 percent of the nation's population, have no senators and only 4 representatives. Three senators and three representatives are Asian Americans. Other racial minorities are represented sporadically.

Congress is overwhelmingly a male domain. Women, unable to vote until 1920, have always been underrepresented there. Starting with

Representative Jeannette Rankin, R-Mont., elected in 1916, slightly more than one hundred women have been elected or appointed to Congress. In 1981 two women served in the Senate (Nancy Landon Kassebaum, R-Kan.; Paula Hawkins, R-Fla.) and 18 in the House.

Traditionally, many women gained office on the death of husbands who were representatives or senators. Senator Margaret Chase Smith, R-Maine, and Representatives Frances Bolton, R-Ohio, and Leonor Sullivan, D-Mo., remained to have more notable careers than their husbands. As more women enter politics at all levels, the old tradition of the "widow's mandate" has weakened and women are being elected on their own merits.

Age and Tenure. Congress is sometimes portrayed as a haven of aging mossbacks waiting patiently for the seniority system to bestow them power. In one of his short stories, reporter-turned-novelist Ward Just describes the colleagues of his fictional representative, George LaRuth:

> Some of his colleagues had been there before he was born, moving now around the halls and the committee rooms as if they were extensions of the antebellum county courthouses. They smelled of tobacco and whiskey and old wool, their faces dry as parchment. LaRuth was amused to watch them on the floor; they behaved as they would at a board meeting of a family business, attentive if they felt like it, disruptive if their mood was playful. They were forgiven; it was a question of age. The House was filled with old men, and its atmosphere was one of very great age. Deference was a way of life. [8]

This is a deft portrait of the post-World War II House, when the average age of members reached a high point. Yet since then the trend has been decidedly toward youth, and deference to one's elders is no longer the norm in either chamber.

When the 97th Congress convened in January 1981, the average age in the two chambers was 49.2 years, the lowest figure in more than three decades.[9] Early in our history, members of Congress tended to be even younger. House or Senate service was a part-time job, physically demanding but not especially exalted. Politicians tended to stay a few years and then move on to other pursuits. After 1900, however, the seniority system and the political security of those from one-party areas—Democrats in the South, Republicans in the Midwest—led members to view congressional service as a long-term career. "Few die, and none retire," it was said.

In the 1970s, this aging trend reversed for several reasons. The weakening of the party system, with its apprenticeship and screening for young politicians, opened the doors to ambitious people at an earlier age. At the other end of the congressional career, today's senators and representatives tend to retire earlier than their predecessors of a generation ago. The stresses and strains of the job take their toll, and fi-

nancial rewards fall short of what members can command in the private
sector. Generous retirement provisions also encourage members to move
on at an earlier age.

In addition to being relatively mature men and women, members of
Congress tend to be Hill veterans. In 1980 the average representative
had served just under 10 years, or 4.8 House terms. The average senator
had served in that chamber an almost identical length of time—or about
8½ years, or 1.4 Senate terms. New faces and old are more equally
balanced than a decade or so ago. Then, median House tenure ap-
proached 12 years (or 6 House terms), and the median Senate tenure
was about the same (that is, almost two Senate terms). Turnover was at
a historical low point.

Nowadays between 15 and 20 percent of the members of either
chamber enter with each new election. The distribution of members in
1961 and 1981 by tenure is arrayed in Figure 4-2. When the 97th
Congress convened, 17 percent of the representatives and 18 percent of
the senators were newcomers. Nearly half of the representatives and 55
of the 100 senators had served less than six years. "The youth is fine,"
observed Senator Christopher Dodd, D-Conn., who ranked in the top
half of the House in seniority when he left in 1980 to enter the Senate,
"but what we're missing to some degree is an institutional memory." [10]
Whether this high level of turnover will continue, or whether the trend
toward longer careers will reestablish itself, cannot be determined.

Virtual Representation. Must Congress demographically mirror
the populace to be a representative institution? Probably not. Legislators from farming districts can voice farmers' concerns even though they
themselves have never plowed a field or milked a cow; whites can
champion equal opportunities for minorities. Legislators can speak for
voters of divergent social rank or life style. This is called *virtual
representation.*

By and large, Congress is a body of local political pros who find that
speaking for constituents comes naturally. Most of them keep in touch
with the home folks without even thinking about it: a majority of
representatives in one survey agreed with the statement that "I seldom
have to sound out my constituents because I think so much like them
that I know how to react to almost any proposal." [11] Nonetheless, the
symbolism of legislators matching voters' demographic characteristics
should not be minimized. When a member of an ethnic or racial
minority goes to Congress, it signals that the group has "made it"
politically. Such legislators speak for members of their racial or ethnic
group everywhere, as lawmakers of Greek heritage did in the 1974-1975
Cyprus dispute with Turkey. Electing someone to Congress, therefore, is
a badge of political legitimacy for any social group.

Figure 4-2 Seniority Distribution in Congress, 1961 and 1981

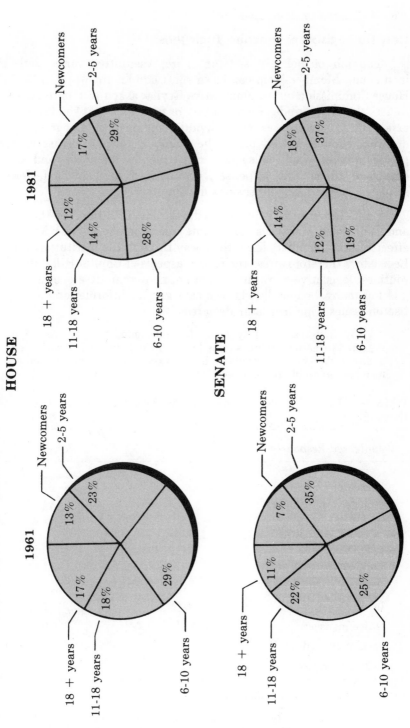

HOUSE

1961

Newcomers
2-5 years
13%
23%
17%
18%
29%
18 + years
11-18 years
6-10 years

1981

Newcomers
2-5 years
17%
29%
12%
14%
28%
18 + years
11-18 years
6-10 years

SENATE

1961

Newcomers
2-5 years
7%
35%
11%
22%
25%
18 + years
11-18 years
6-10 years

1981

Newcomers
2-5 years
18%
37%
14%
12%
19%
18 + years
11-18 years
6-10 years

How Do Legislators Describe Their Jobs?

The job of being a senator or representative varies with the incumbent. Members' jobs can be categorized in many ways. In 1977 the House Commission on Administrative Review asked 153 representatives to list "the major kinds of jobs, duties, or functions that you feel you are expected to perform as an individual member of Congress." This question elicited not so much the members' own priorities as their perceptions of what colleagues, constituents, lobbyists, and others expect of them. The responses, summarized in Table 4-1, form a snapshot of the job's dimensions and limits.[12]

Legislator. The rules, procedures, and traditions of the House and Senate lay numerous constraints upon members' behavior. To be effective, new members learn their way through the institutional maze. Legislators therefore stress the formal aspects of Capitol Hill duties and routines: legislative work, investigation, and committee specialization.

For many, being a legislator means gaining information and expertise on issues. One legislator declared:

> My first responsibility is to develop committee expertise. I'm expected to learn all there is to be known on an issue, to stay with it on a day-to-day basis. I want to be an expert, sought out by other members and able to help them. [13]

Table 4-1   House Members' Views on the Jobs Expected of Them, 1977 (N=146)

Volunteered Responses	Percentage*
Legislator	87%
Constituency servant	79
Mentor/communicator	43
Representative	26
Politico	11
Overseer	9
Institutional broker	7
Office manager	6
Jack-of-all-trades	6
(All other roles)	4

* Many members mentioned two or more jobs.

SOURCE: U.S., Congress, House, Commission on Administrative Review, *Final Report*, 2 vols., H. Doc. 95-272, 95th Cong. 1st sess., December 31, 1977, 2: 874-875.

Expertise is sought, not only because it is the way to shape public policy, but also because it sways others in the chamber.

The legislator's role dovetails with representing constituents. Most members seek committee assignments that will serve the needs of their states or districts. One former House member related how his interest in flood control and water resource development impelled him to ask for a seat on the Public Works and Transportation Committee. "The interests of my district dictated my field of specialization," he explained, "... but the decision to specialize in some legislative field is automatic for the member who wants to exercise any influence." [14]

Members soon learn that norms or folkways exist to expedite bargaining and maximize productivity. Examining the post-World War II Senate, Matthews identified six folkways governing behavior that were enforced in numerous informal ways: 1) new senators should serve an apprenticeship; 2) senators should concentrate on Senate work rather than on gaining publicity; 3) senators should specialize on issues within their committees or affecting their home states; 4) senators should be courteous to colleagues; 5) senators should extend reciprocity to colleagues—that is, they should provide willing assistance with the expectation that they will be repaid in kind one day; and 6) senators should loyally defend the Senate, "the greatest legislative and deliberative body in the world." [15]

In recent years certain Senate folkways have faded in importance.[16] New senators now participate immediately in most aspects of deliberation. Many senators, especially those with an eye on the White House, work tirelessly to attract national publicity and personal attention. Committee specialization, although still common, is less rigid than it once was because senators have numerous overlapping committee assignments and are expected to hold views on a wide range of issues. Courtesy and reciprocity are still insisted upon, but institutional loyalty—in an era of cynicism about government—often wears thin.

The House relies less on informal norms and more on formal channels of power. From interviews in the early 1970s, however, Herbert Asher uncovered seven norms: 1) friendly relationships are desirable; 2) the important work of the House is done in committee; 3) procedural rules of the House are essential; 4) members should not personally criticize a colleague on the House floor; 5) members should be prepared to trade votes; 6) members should be specialists; and 7) freshmen members should serve apprenticeships.[17]

Even this loose network of norms has been diluted.[18] Waves of new members, impatient with the notion of apprenticeship, plunge into the work of the House as soon as they learn their way around. Leadership comes earlier to members than it used to. Specialization is still attractive—more so in the House than in the Senate—but many members branch out into unrelated issues. Nor are committees the only forums for influencing legislation. Looser norms on floor participation and voting have expanded members' chances for shaping bills outside their own committees' jurisdictions. Relaxation of such norms as apprenticeship and specialization is one aspect of the current decentralization on Capitol Hill.

Constituency Servant. The role of constituency servant was mentioned by nearly 8 out of 10 respondents in the 1977 House survey. Constituent servants make sure their states or districts get their "fair share" of small business loans, school aid, public works projects, crop or business subsidies, or other federal aids. "It's a big pie down in Washington," former Representative Michael "Ozzie" Myers, D-Pa., told FBI agents posing as aides of an Arab sheik.

> Each member's sent there to bring a piece of that pie back home. And if you go down there and you don't—you come back without milkin' it after a few terms ... you don't go ... back. [19]

The words are inelegant and the context sleazy, but the nub of truth is there. Members quickly develop a sharp eye for legislative formulas and how they affect particular areas. Often they join state and local officials in lobbying for federal funds or programs.

In addition to seeking a fat portion of the federal pie, a constituency servant attempts to solve citizens' problems. This *ombudsman* role was cited by half the House members. Typically, this task is performed by legislators and their staffs as "casework"—individual cases triggered by constituent letters or visits. It is a responsibility that weighs heavily on members, even though many of them tire of it and most of them delegate it to staff aides. The philosophy of most legislators is expressed by one House member:

> Constituent work: that's something I feel very strongly about. The American people, with the growth of the bureaucracy, feel nobody cares. The only conduit a taxpayer has with the government is a congressional office. [20]

Sometimes members push constituency service to gain breathing room for legislative stands that stray from district norms. This was a strategy successfully pursued by many Democrats of the 1974 "Watergate class"—36 of whom captured seats formerly held by Republicans. Some combined a vigorous outreach program with some tailoring of positions for their districts. Colorado's Tim Wirth balanced his liberalism by coming out for a balanced budget, a stronger military, and fewer federal regulations. He also returned to his suburban Denver district at least twice every month. Another, suburban Philadelphia's Robert W. Edgar, declined to trim his liberal sails but launched an active constituent aid program. He chaired the Northeast-Midwest (Frost Belt)

Coalition and, to create jobs, lobbied for overhauling the naval aircraft carrier *U.S.S. Saratoga.* [21] Wirth and Edgar have held onto their seats. Others find constituency outreach is not enough. Liberal Democrat Andrew Maguire showed up in his New Jersey district every weekend and was known for solid constituency work. He served three terms but was ousted in 1980 by an opponent, Marge Roukema, who charged he was ideologically out of touch with the district.

Mentor/Communicator. The mentor-communicator role is linked both to legislating and constituency errand-running. Most members who stress this role view it in connection with issues that must be debated and voted on. As a 1977 respondent phrased it:

> The role of the educator is first to learn, to assess the feelings of the district on particular issues, and to educate other members as to the aims of your constituency. To take the views of Washington back to the district. It's a two-way function. [22]

Another aspect of the mentor-communicator role is the act of keeping in touch with constituents by mail, by personal appearances, and by print and electronic media.

Closely allied is the role of the issue emissary *(representative)*, articulated by a quarter of House members. Constituents expect their representatives to understand and press their views in Washington, to act as "a symbol of their connection with the federal government," in the words of one House member. This role is the essence of elective office, both in theory and in practice, and incumbents take it very seriously indeed.

Other Roles. Legislator, constituency servant, and mentor/communicator are not the only ways in which members define their roles. Some stress the duties of party leadership; others their social obligations; still others institutional brokerage—dealing with the executive branch, interest groups, and state and local governments. Some say wistfully that they must be all things to all people:

> You are expected to perform everything from the role of entertainer on occasion to being a personal advisor to your constituents. You're a jack of all trades. If you take it all seriously, it's impossible to do it. You're supposed to be a miracle-worker, to do the impossible. [23]

And a few members of Congress stress merely campaigning and gaining reelection. One former member placed this goal in perspective: "All members of Congress have a primary interest in being reelected. Some members have no other interest." [24]

How Do Legislators Spend Their Time?

Few things are more precious to senators and representatives than their time; lack of it is the most frequent complaint by legislators about

Table 4-2 A Senator's Average Day

Activity	Average Time* Hours
In Senate chamber	1:35
In committee or subcommittee	2:25
Talking with constituents, interest groups	1:40
Working with staff, reading staff papers	2:35
Mail and public information	2:10
Events outside the office (speeches, meetings)	2:10

* Due to overlap among the activities, the total time exceeds the 11-hour average day of senators. Time figures are based upon accountings for entire days in Washington.

SOURCE: U.S., Congress, Senate, Commission on the Operation of the Senate, *Toward a Modern Senate*, S. Doc. 94-278, 94th Cong., 2d sess., 1976, p. 28.

their jobs.[25] Allocating time requires exceedingly tough personal and political choices. Like the rest of us, legislators find that they lack the time to do what they want to do. They, too, must reshape their expectations, and those of others, to conform to the real world of demands and resources.

Senators' daily schedules in Washington are "long, fragmented, and unpredictable," according to a study based on time logs kept by senators' appointment secretaries.[26] A senator's average day, about 11 hours, is shown in Table 4-2. About a third of their time is spent on the Senate floor or in committee rooms. "We're like automatons," one member said. "We spend our time walking in tunnels to go to the floor to vote." [27] More than half the days the Senate is in session, it does not adjourn until 6 p.m. or later.

A House study compiled from appointment secretaries' logs revealed that representatives also have nightmarish, 11-hour days.[28] Representatives on the average start at 8:30 a.m. and finish work at 7:30 p.m. Table 4-3 indicates how much time members spend on the floor, in committee, in their offices, in other Washington locations, and outside the city. Members now spend more time in their offices and less on the floor than the 1977 survey shows. In 1978 the House launched closed-circuit TV coverage of floor sessions. Members can watch their office TV monitors to follow the action, going to the chamber when they want to speak or vote.

Scheduling is complicated by the 105 formal Senate workgroups (committees, subcommittees) and 149 House groups, not to mention joint or ad hoc panels, in the 97th Congress. These units offer more than

1,000 seats or positions in the Senate, 2,500 in the House. The average senator holds more than 10 seats and the average representative 6 seats on standing workgroups. Leadership posts abound: in the same period, all Republican senators and nearly half of all Democratic representatives chaired a committee or subcommittee. Minority-party members were by no means left out; all Democratic senators and 80 percent of the GOP representatives were ranking members of these units.

With so many assignments, members are hard pressed to control their crowded schedules. Scheduling problems are endemic. Committee quorums are difficult to achieve, and members' attentions are often

Table 4-3 A Representative's Average Day

Activity	Average Time Minutes	Average Time Hours
In the House chamber		2:53
In committee/subcommittee work		1:24
Hearings	26	
Business	9	
Markups	42	
Other	5	
In his/her office		3:19
With constituents	17	
With organized groups	9	
With others	20	
With staff aides	53	
With other representatives	5	
Answering mail	46	
Preparing legislation, speeches	12	
Reading	11	
On telephone	26	
In other Washington locations		2:02
With constituents at Capitol	9	
At events	33	
With leadership	3	
With other representatives	11	
With informal groups	8	
In party meetings	5	
Personal time	28	
Other	25	
Other		1:40
Total average representative's day		11:18

SOURCE: U.S., Congress, House, Commission on Administrative Review, *Administrative Reorganization and Legislative Management,* 2 vols., H. Doc. 95-232, 95th Cong., 1st sess., September 28, 1977, 2: 18-19.

focused elsewhere. During peak times—midweek (Tuesdays through Thursdays) and midsession (April through July)—members commonly face scheduling conflicts between two, three, or more of their committees.[29] Even within committees, scheduling is often haphazard. Quite often, working sessions are composed of the chairman, perhaps one or two colleagues, and staff aides.

Members' schedules are splintered into so many tiny bits and pieces that effective pursuit of lawmaking, oversight, and constituent service functions is hampered. According to a management study of several senators' offices, an event occurs every five minutes, on the average, to which the senator or the chief aide must personally respond.[30] Unpredictability also marks daily schedules. Often members have scant notice that their presence is expected at a meeting or hearing. Carefully developed schedules can be disrupted by changes in meeting hours, by unexpected events, or by sessions that run longer than anticipated.

Most members claim they want to spend more time on legislation. In the House survey, members were asked to compare the tasks that should be very important with those that actually take a great deal of time. The widest gaps occurred in such pursuits as studying and legislative research; overseeing executive agencies, either personally or through formal subunits; debating and voting on legislation; negotiating with other members to build support for proposals; and working in committees to develop legislation. Members were also asked about the gaps between what others expected of them and what they themselves thought they should be doing. The most commonly cited problem, mentioned by fully half the members, was that "constituent demands detract from other functions." A second complaint, cited by 36 percent of the legislators, was that "scheduling problems and time pressures detract from the work of the House." [31]

The dilemma legislators face in allocating their time is more than a mere scheduling problem. It is also a case of conflicting role expectations. The two Congresses pull members in different directions, and there is no pat formula for allocating time. As Robert Giaimo, D-Conn., House Budget Committee chairman who retired in 1980, put it:

> One problem is that you're damned if you do and damned if you don't. If you do your work here, you're accused of neglecting your district. And if you spend too much time in your district, you're accused of neglecting your work here. [32]

LOOKING HOMEWARD

Not all of a representative's or senator's duties lie in Washington, D.C. As we have stressed, legislators not only fashion policy for the nation's welfare; they also act as emissaries from their home states or districts. These dual spheres pervade legislators' consciousness and often create vexing day-to-day decisions. These choices are another reminder that members of Congress live in two distinct worlds, not just one.

What Is Representation?

Representation is one of the most pervasive and important processes of political life. Although found in virtually all political structures, representation is most typical of democratic regimes dedicated to sharing power among citizens. In small communities, decisions can be reached by face-to-face discussion, but in populous societies this sort of personalized consultation is impossible. Thus, according to traditional democratic theory, citizens control policymaking by choosing "fiduciary agents" to act on their behalf, participating in legislative deliberations in the same way that their principals, the voters, would do if they could be on hand themselves.[33] Hanna Pitkin puts it this way:

> The representative must act in such a way that, although he is independent, and his constituents are capable of action and judgment, no conflict arises between them. He must act in their interest, and this means he must not normally come into conflict with their wishes. [34]

The arrangement does not always work out precisely as democratic theory specifies. Unless it works fairly well most of the time, however, the system is defective.

Incumbent legislators give high priority to representation. As we have seen, 8 out of 10 House members interviewed in 1977 saw themselves as constituency servants. Many were mentor-communicators; others issue spokespersons. In an earlier survey of 87 members, the role most often expressed was called the tribune: the discoverer, reflector, or advocate of popular needs and wants.[35]

While legislators agree on the importance of representation, they interpret it differently. One point of departure is Edmund Burke's dictum that legislators should voice the "general reason of the whole," rather than speak merely for "local purposes" and "local prejudices." [36] Burke's viewpoint has always had its admirers, and legislators who adhere to this notion in the face of hostile public sentiment can at least hope for history's vindication. Yet electoral realities mar the Burkean ideal. Burke himself was eventually turned out of office for his candor. Modern electorates, motivated by self-interest and schooled in democratic norms, prefer their legislators to follow instructions rather than exercise independent judgments.[37]

Two dimensions are embedded in the traditional distinction between the Burkean Trustee and the Instructed Delegate. One turns on legislators' *style* of representation: whether they accept instructions

Table 4-4 Representational Roles of 87 House Members, 1960s

Representational Styles		Representational Focus	
Role	Percentage	Role	Percentage
Trustee	28%	National dominant	28%
Politico	46	Nation-district equal	23
Delegate	23	District dominant	42
Undetermined	3	Non-geographic	5
		Undetermined	3
Total	100%	Total	100%

SOURCE: Roger H. Davidson, *The Role of the Congressman* (Indianapolis: Bobbs-Merrill, Co., 1969), pp. 117, 122.

(Delegate), act upon their own initiatives (Trustee), or act upon some combination of the two (Politico). The second is the *focus* of representation: whether legislators think primarily in terms of the whole nation, their constituencies, or some combination of these. Although conceptually distinct, style and focus of representation are closely related. One study of House members in the 1960s attempted to classify members according to their basic approaches to representation; the results are shown in Table 4-4.[38]

In practice, legislators assume different representational styles according to the occasion. That is, they are Politicos. Most of them develop sophisticated ways of thinking about the choices they make, distinguishing those for which they can play the Trustee from those for which the Delegate mode is expected or appropriate. According to Thomas Cavanagh, a member ponders such factors as the nation's welfare, personal convictions, and constituency opinions. "The weight assigned to each factor varies according to the nature of the issue at hand, the availability of the information necessary for a decision, and the intensity of preference of the people concerned about the issue." [39]

In a 1977 House survey, members talked about the issues they regarded as matters of personal conscience or discretion.[40] Most of these fell into two categories: issues of overwhelming national importance, such as foreign policy and national defense, and issues that entail deep-seated convictions, such as abortion, gun control, or constitutional questions. In contrast, members said they deferred to districts on economic issues, such as public works, social needs, military spending, and farm programs. As two members explained:

On the B-1 bomber, my district has several thousand jobs involved. I'm marginally opposed, but I support it because of my district's involvement.

Take revenue sharing. It stinks, but when they need it so desperately, I'll support the constituency.[41]

Legislators tend to give unqualified support to district needs because, as they see it, no other member is likely to do so.

When members of Congress act, take a position, or cast a vote, they weigh constituencies against their own knowledge and convictions. Their solutions vary from issue to issue, but they develop distinctive patterns of priorities. One element in the calculus is the knowledge that they may be called upon to *explain* their choices to constituents—no matter how many or how few people truly care about the matter.[42] The anticipated need to explain oneself shapes a member's choices and in fact is part of the dilemma of choice.

What Are Constituencies?

No senator or representative is elected by, interacts with, or responds to, all the people in a given state or electoral district. The constituencies fixed in lawmakers' minds as they campaign or vote may be quite different from the boundaries found on maps. Fenno describes a "nest" of constituencies, ranging from the widest (geographic constituency) to the narrowest (personal constituency), which is made up of supporters, loyalists, and intimates.[43]

Geographic and Demographic Constituencies. The average House district in the 1980s exceeds half a million people, the average state four million. Because geographic constituencies are so much larger than in the early Congresses, face-to-face contacts have been replaced by what might be called a building-block approach. That is, a state or district is seen as an interlocking series of areas, neighborhoods, factions, and groupings. When a member of Congress speaks of "the state" or "the district," it is usually such a network of blocks.

Politicians are fond of talking about geographical subregions and their distinctive voting habits. Colorado, split by the Continental Divide, consists of an "eastern slope" and a "western slope." Maryland has at least three regions with distinctive traditions and voting habits: the Eastern Shore reflecting the conservative politics of the rural South; more liberal suburban areas around Washington, D.C., and urban Baltimore; and the mountainous west, marked by mining and small farming. Western Connecticut's 5th District is split between the Naugatuck Valley's old mill towns with their blue-collar voters and the comfortable bedroom communities of Fairfield County, a conservative area. Southern California's sprawling 37th District embraces smog-ridden suburbs around Riverside and Loma Linda; the irrigated farm-

116 *A Congress of Ambassadors*

land of the Coachella Valley; and the wealthy desert oases of Palm Springs and Palm Desert where Gerald Ford, Bob Hope, and Frank Sinatra reside. Most states and many House districts have similar configurations.

In fact, such distinctions are grossly simplified. Cities such as New York, Chicago, and San Francisco are melting pots that contain diverse racial, ethnic, economic, and social groups. While most cities share common problems—transportation, crime, crowding, housing, racial tensions—their demographic mixtures and political traditions vary. Nor do all suburbs follow an identical pattern. Seen from a traffic reporter's helicopter, one suburb resembles another, but the rows of houses and lawns conceal subtle differences. Migratory and zoning patterns give suburban neighborhoods some of the unique traits of inner-city neighborhoods—blue collar, white collar, white, mixed, Jewish, and so forth.

Social and economic shifts can alter the face of electoral units. In 1960 Tucson was regarded a Democratic stronghold. But in the 1980s its population is soaring. Most of the newcomers are older people retiring to the Sun Belt. "Every time there's a blizzard in Buffalo or Detroit, we get 5,000 more conservative retirees in the district," said a campaign aide to Democratic Representative Morris K. Udall.[44] Thus Udall's initial constituency has steadily eroded, and he has hung on mainly through bold campaigning and constituency service.

As a rule, demographics are linked to partisan differences in voting. Because of this, some areas are traditionally "Democratic" and others "Republican." In general, Democratic tendencies are associated with the following demographic characteristics: dense population, blue-collar workers, ethnic groupings, nonwhite residents, noncollege educated, low-income families, and rental housing. Republican areas tend to display the opposite characteristics.[45]

Although partisan differences have faded markedly in the past generation, such tendencies are still visible. In other words, one can still predict fairly accurately a legislator's party label and voting record by looking at his or her constituency. In a sense, partisan differences are constituency differences translated into issues. Members whose voting records deviate from their party's norm may simply represent areas with attributes associated with the opposition party.[46] In 1980, for example, the "deviant" Republicans included Senators Lowell Weicker of Connecticut, Jacob Javits of New York, and John Chafee of Rhode Island— all northeasterners. By the same token, the "maverick" Democrats—Ed Zorinsky of Nebraska or David Boren of Oklahoma, for example—were from midwestern, border, or southern states.[47] Many of the House "boll weevils"—conservative Democrats who backed President Reagan's budget and tax policies in defiance of their party leaders—hailed from areas where Reagan was especially popular.

Legislators are also concerned whether these demographic traits are *homogeneous* or *heterogeneous*.[48] Some constituencies are uniform and one-dimensional—mostly tobacco farmers or urban ghetto dwellers or small-town citizens. Others are diverse and embrace numerous, and not necessarily harmonious, interests. Compatibility is crucial: districts vary, not only in numbers of interests, but also in the level of conflict among them. "The less conflict a congressman perceived among his district interests," Fenno wrote, "the more likely he is to see his district as homogeneous, and the more conflict he perceives among district interests the more likely he is to see his district as heterogeneous." [49]

Seasoned political observers instinctively recognize differences between homogeneous and heterogeneous constituencies even though the concept lacks specificity and as a result has rarely been scrutinized by scholars. The following hypotheses seem plausible, however:

1. *States are more heterogeneous than House districts, in part because of their greater size.*[50] Most states embrace various regions and subregions—cities, towns, suburban areas, farms. House districts may or may not manifest this complexity. Numerous House districts are small segments of vast cities or rural areas.

2. *Because of increasing size, economic complexity, and educational levels, all constituencies, House as well as Senate, have moved historically toward greater heterogeneity.* Well into the twentieth century, it was common to say that senators represented a cotton state, or a tobacco state, or an oil state. While powerful interests still shape and sometimes dominate an area, countervailing forces are usually present. It is getting harder to find a segment of the country, even a small one, that contains just a single interest.

3. *The more heterogeneous a constituency, the more challenging the representative's task.* Conversely, homogeneous areas are more easily represented. Those voters are likely to be preoccupied with only a few issues, and legislators who maintain orthodoxy on these issues may be forgiven if their attention wanders to matters outside the voters' field of vision. Senators from wheat-producing states, of course, must work for agricultural appropriations and parity pricing; their votes on mass transit or foreign affairs may pass unnoticed. In past times, white southern voters agreed on only one issue, racial segregation, which served to give the region a kind of false unity that obscured economic and class conflicts. The region's politicians were skilled at whipping up racial feelings but free to pursue their own course on most other issues. Representing a heterogeneous constituency is far more tedious. Such members must heed a wider range of problems and stand accountable for more of their issue positions.

4. *Increasingly heterogeneous districts may lead legislators to cultivate nonissue ties with voters.* With more and more groups voicing distinctive policy interests, members of Congress are tempted to "hedge their bets"; sometimes they take multiple positions on issues and communicate them through vaguely worded letters and statements. They may also stress nonissue features of their career—style, personality, constituent service.

Another attribute of constituencies is electoral balance, especially the incumbent's safeness or vulnerability. This is not the same thing as heterogeneity, although mixed districts are probably more competitive than uniform ones. From the incumbent's vantage point, electoral competitiveness is the constituency's bottom line. Needless to say, incumbents prefer "safe" districts—ones that contain a high proportion of groups sympathetic to their partisan or ideological stance. Not only do safe districts favor reelection; they also imply that voters will be easier to please.

Truly competitive districts, especially in the House, are comparatively rare, as Table 4-5 indicates. The number of competitive districts declined in the last generation. Put differently, the proportion of elections captured by wide margins (60 percent or more of the two-party vote) has risen in the last several decades.[51] During the post-World War II years, about 6 out of every 10 elections were "safe" for the winner; after 1966 that figure increased to more than 7 out of 10. Recently, the number of competitive districts has stabilized in the House and is actually growing in the Senate, where elections tend to be more closely contested.

Politicians look at election margins differently than disinterested observers do, however. Wide margins hint at the amount of "breathing space" incumbents possess in performing their jobs. Electoral margins that seem comfortable to outsiders may terrify incumbents: downturns in electoral support are very real psychological blows and invite challengers in future contests. No wonder that incumbents worry not only about winning or losing, but also about their margins of safety.[52]

Political and Personal Constituencies. Inside the geographic and demographic constituencies are other, narrower "constituencies" that exist, often imprecisely, in candidates' or incumbents' minds as they analyze their electoral units. As Fenno describes them, they include: supporters (the reelection constituency); loyalists (the primary constituency); and intimates (the personal constituency).[53]

Supporters are people who are expected to vote favorably on election day. Of course, some of them do not. Candidates and their advisers make repeated assessments of these voters based on the area's political demography—registration figures, survey data, recent electoral trends, and so on. The more elections a candidate has encountered, the more precise ought to be the notions of where support comes from, reinforced by the most recent election results.

In waging campaigns, candidates and their managers pinpoint areas and groups with the biggest payoff—that is, sympathetic voters who can be persuaded to support and vote for the candidate. Such voters are not necessarily the candidate's most ardent supporters, but a little effort with them can pay off in a big way.

Table 4-5 House and Senate Margins of Victory, 1970-1980

Election Year	House					Senate				
	Percentage of Vote					Percentage of Vote				
	Under 55	55-59.9	60 Plus	Unopposed	(N)	Under 55	55-59.9	60 Plus	Unopposed	(N)
1970	14	15	58	14	(435)	40	23	33	3	(30)
1972	15	14	59	12	(435)	55	12	33	—	(33)
1974	24	16	46	14	(435)	41	18	35	6	(34)
1976	17	14	56	12	(435)	30	33	30	6	(33)
1978	17	14	53	16	(435)	24	33	36	6	(33)
1980	18	14	60	8	(435)	58	18	21	3	(34)

SOURCE: *Congressional Quarterly Weekly Report* and authors' calculations.

At the other end are groups rated as "hopeless" because they rarely vote for the candidate. Like most of us, legislators prefer to spend time with people whose outlook is congenial to their own. Contacts with hostile groups might seem futile, but candidates need to meet with such groups occasionally to "show the flag" and perhaps neutralize the opposition.

Because the candidate's supportive coalition may alter over time, the "last election" is carefully scanned for signs of change. In growing suburbs or volatile urban areas, population shifts often occur. Redistricting can force members to cope with unfamiliar territory. A fresh challenger or a novel issue can also threaten established patterns. Elements of uncertainty always pervade electoral politics; and politicians, like the rest of us, find uncertainty disconcerting. That is another reason why few senators or representatives are wholly confident about winning no matter how safe they may seem.

Loyalists are the politician's staunchest supporters and form the last line of electoral defense in a primary contest or other threat. They include early supporters and colleagues from pre-electoral activities. For members who rose out of antiwar, civil rights, or environmental activism, they include people first drawn together in those movements. For other members, loyalists may be concentrated in religious or ethnic groups, political or civic clubs, or "friends and neighbors" from the home territory. From home-district travels with representatives, Fenno derived the notion of "at homeness" to denote the closeness between politicians and constituents.[54] Invariably, members felt most at home with loyalists, expressing their closeness with banter and familiar talk.

Loyalists are a bedrock campaign resource, in terms of volunteer labor or financial contributions. For this reason, candidates must beware of ignoring their loyalists, who need repeated reinforcement and mobilization and are apt to be miffed if the candidate neglects to acknowledge their aid.

Intimates are close friends who supply political advice and emotional support. Nearly every candidate or incumbent knows a few of them. They may be members of the candidate's family, trusted staff members, political mentors, or individuals who shared decisive experiences early in the candidate's career.

Fenno relates the following account of an informal gathering of intimates. The session took place one Sunday afternoon in the home of a representative's chief district aide and best friend. Ostensibly watching an NFL football game on TV, the group included the representative, the district aide, a state assemblyman from the member's home county, and the district attorney of the same county. Most of them had attended the representative's initial strategy meeting four years earlier, when he had decided to run for Congress.

Between plays and at halftime, over beer and cheese, the four friends discussed every aspect of the congressman's campaign, listened to and commented on his taped radio spots, analyzed several newspaper reports, discussed local and national personalities, relived old political campaigns and hijinks, and discussed their respective political ambitions. Ostensibly they were watching the football game. Actually, the congressman was exchanging political advice, information, and perspectives with three of his oldest and closest political associates. [55]

The setting and the players differ from state to state and from district to district. But such intimates play an indispensable role: they provide unvarnished advice on political matters and serve as sounding boards for ideas and strategies. The liability of such groups is that they may give faulty advice or inaccurately assess the larger constituencies. Long-term incumbents run a special risk if their intimates lose touch with constituency shifts. Politicians confront the constant dilemma of which advisers to trust; more than most of us, they pay a public price for those who fall short.

These constituencies—supporters, loyalists, and intimates—are defined in varying ways and with varying degrees of precision by different senators and representatives. Some members are more systematic than others in assessing constituencies; some have wider circles of friends and overt supporters; some have legions of supporters but few if any intimates. The point is that "constituency" is not a simple geographical entity, but a complex and shifting perception.

Home Styles

Legislators evolve distinctive ways of projecting themselves and their records to their constituents—what Fenno calls their home style. [56] One aspect of this is the socio-psychological notion of presentation of self. [57] That is, legislators gain responses from others by expressing themselves in ways that leave distinct impressions or images. Such expressions may be verbal or nonverbal. Another facet of home style is how members explain what they have been doing while away from their home states or districts.

Legislators' home styles are communicated in various ways: personal appearances, mailings, newsletters, telephone conversations, radio or television spots, and press releases, for example. We know little about how home styles arise, but they are linked to members' personalities, backgrounds, constituency features, and resources. The concept of home style shifts the focus of constituency linkage from *representation* to *presentation*. As Fenno states, "It is the style, not the issue content, that counts most in the reelection constituency." [58]

Presentation of Self. The core ingredient of a successful home style is trust—faith that legislators are what they claim to be, and will do what they promise.[59] Winning voters' trust does not happen overnight; it takes time. Three major ingredients of trust are: 1) *qualification,* the belief that legislators are capable of handling the job, a critical threshold that nonincumbents especially must cross; 2) *identification,* the impression that legislators resemble their constituents, that they are part of the state or region; and 3) *empathy,* the sense that legislators understand constituents' problems and care about them.

Given variations among legislators and constituencies, there are countless available home styles that effectively build the trust relationship.[60] Congressman A employs a direct style rooted in face-to-face contacts with people in his primary constituency. Congressman A rarely mentions issues because most people in his district agree on them. Congressman B, a popular local athlete, uses the national defense issue to symbolize his oneness with a district supportive of military preparedness. Congressman C displays himself as an issue-oriented, highly verbal activist who is not at home with conventional politicians. And so on; the repertoire of home styles is virtually limitless.

Home styles are key ingredients in electoral success or failure. Voters are likely to remember style long after they forget issue pronouncements or votes. As one member told Fenno, "Most voters vote more on style than they do on issues." [61] Many legislators agree with and act upon this assumption.

Explaining Washington Activity. Even if the average voter is attracted less by issues than by style, incumbents are frequently challenged to explain what they have done while away from home. As we have noted, legislators make decisions in full awareness that they have to explain them to others.[62] Explaining is an integral part of decisionmaking. In home-district forums, members expect to be able to describe, interpret, and justify their actions. If constituents do not agree with the member's conclusions, they may respect the decisionmaking style.

> They don't know much about my votes. Most of what they know is what I tell them. They know more of what kind of a guy I am. It comes through in my letters: "You care about the little guy." [63]

Most incumbents have a set speech about Capitol Hill life designed to impress constituents with its complexity (and perhaps its madness), and to convey the aura of competence and influence. While few incumbents believe that a single vote can defeat them, all realize that voter disenchantment with their total record can be fatal. Thus, members stockpile reasons for virtually every position they take—often more than are needed. For thorny choices, an independent stance may be the best defense. Politicians tend to give the same account of themselves, no matter what group they are talking to. (Inconsistency, after all, is mentally costly—and can be politically costly as well.)

Legislators' accounts of Washington convey little of Congress's institutional life. Indeed, in explaining their behavior members often belittle this other Congress—portraying themselves as knight-errants battling against demonic forces and feckless colleagues.

Constituency Careers. Constituency ties evolve over the course of a senator's or representative's career. Constituency careers have at least two recognizable stages, *expansionism* and *protectionism.* In the first or expansionist stage the member constructs a reelection constituency, solidifying hard-core supporters and reaching out to attract added blocks of support.

In the second or protectionist stage the member ceases to expand the base of support, content with hoarding already-won support. Sometimes the member's primary constituency decays. Or the member loses touch with the district or shifts career goals away from reelection. Growing responsibilities in Washington can divert attention from home business. Thirteen-term veteran Charles Vanik, D-Ohio, retired in 1980 with the following comments on these tensions:

> When you become the most effective in this job, when you reach . . . the epitome of your usefulness, you do so at the price of failing to keep up local communications. . . .
>
> With me, it was a case of whether I wanted to refurbish my political base by being on the scene on an almost weekly, hourly basis back home and also of raising money, which I've lost the art of doing. [64]

Confronted with new aspirations and shifting constituency demands, not a few members decide to retire. Others struggle ineffectively and are defeated. Still others refurbish their constituency base and survive.

Allocating Members' Resources

Home style is more than a philosophy for weighing constituents' claims. It is a matter of day-to-day decisions about allocating scarce resources: How much attention should be devoted to state or district needs? How much time should be spent in the state or district? How should constituent contact be maintained? How should staff aides be deployed to deal with constituents' concerns? Decisions on such questions form an important part of legislators' home styles.

Road Tripping. One of the most vexing problems is how to balance demands for being in Washington against being in the home state or district. This is mainly a modern-day dilemma. In the nineteenth century legislators spent much of their time at home, traveling to Washington only when Congress was in session. After World War II, however, congressional sessions lengthened until they spanned virtually the entire year. Legislators began to set up permanent residence in the

Congressional Allowances, 1981

Two statements about allowances for members of Congress can be made with some certainty: they have risen significantly in recent years; and the numbers are difficult to obtain.

Listed below are the available figures for House and Senate allowances in 1981. In some cases no dollar value is given because of the difficulty in determining the range of reimbursed costs—for example, in travel or telephone reimbursements. Most of the 1981 allowances are transferable from one account to another.

	House	Senate
Salary	$ 60,662.50[1]	$ 60,662.50[1]
Washington office		
Clerk-hire	$336,384	$592,608-1,190,724[2]
Committee legislative assistants	—[4]	$183,801
Interns	$ 1,620	—
General office expenses	$ 47,300	$ 33,000 - 143,000[2]
Telephone/telegraph	15,000 long-distance minutes to district	—[3]
Stationery	—[3]	1.56 - 15.23 million pieces[2]
Office space	2-3 room suites	5-8 room suites
Furnishings	—[3]	—[3]
Equipment	Provided	Provided
District/state offices		
Rental	2500 sq. ft.	4800-8000 sq. ft.
Furnishings/equipment	$ 35,000	$ 22,550 - 31,350[2]
Mobile office	—	one
Communications		
Automated correspondence	—[3]	Provided by Senate computer center
Audio/video recordings; photography	—[3]	—[3]
Travel	Formula (min. $3,000- max. $38,000)	—[3]

[1] Salary established October 1, 1979; leaders' salaries are higher.

[2] Senators are allowed expenses based on a sliding scale linked to the state's population.

[3] Expenses are covered through the general office expenses line item. In most cases supplies and equipment are charged at rates well below retail levels.

[4] Provided for members of Appropriations, Budget, and Rules Committees.

SOURCE: Committee on House Administration; Senate Committee on Rules and Administration.

nation's capital—a practice that would have struck earlier voters as verging on arrogance. By the 1970s both houses adopted parallel schedules of sessions punctuated with brief "district work periods" (House) or "nonlegislative periods" (Senate).

At the same time the two houses authorized more paid trips to states or districts. In the early 1960s senators and representatives were allowed three government-paid trips home each year. That figure was raised rapidly in a series of moves, so that by the late 1970s senators were allowed more than 40 trips home and representatives 33. One researcher found a steady increase in the number of trips by House members during the 1970s.[65] In 1970 representatives spent close to 15 weeks during the year in their congressional districts; in 1976 members were in their districts during 22 weeks of the year.

Travel increased for all members. However, the more costly and time-consuming it is to get home, the less often will members make the trip.[66] When members' families are in Washington, they are less inclined to travel. Seniority is also a factor: in the 1970s senior members made fewer trips to their districts than junior members—perhaps reflecting junior members' greater district attentiveness.[67] Members tend to avoid their districts during periods of congressional unpopularity but spend more time there during adverse economic conditions. As election day approaches, representatives stay closer to their districts.[68]

Constituency Casework. "All God's chillun got problems," exclaimed colorful former Representative Billy Matthews, D-Fla., one day while brooding over constituent mail.[69] Helping citizens cope with the federal bureaucracy is a major job of every congressional office. While not all members are personally eager to handle casework, all of them concede the importance of such services in today's baffling world. What is more important, prompt and effective casework apparently pays off at election time.

More numerous and more sophisticated electorates, not to mention the government's bigger role in citizen's lives, have pushed legislators into the casework business in a big way. In 1977 representatives estimated their average caseload at slightly more than 10,000 cases a year.[70] Senators from small states averaged between 1,000 and 2,000 according to a 1977 study; large-state senators had from 8,000 to 70,000 cases. Senators from New York and California receive between 30,000 and 50,000 cases each year.[71]

As these figures suggest, casework loads vary from state to state and district to district. Some House offices studied by John Johannes handled no more than five or ten cases a week; others as many as 300.[72] In both chambers senior legislators apparently receive proportionately more casework requests than do junior members.[73] Perhaps senior legislators are considered more powerful and thus better equipped to resolve constituents' problems; legislators themselves certainly cultivate this image in seeking reelection. Some members stress errand-running more than others. Moreover, demographic variations among electorates can affect casework volume: some citizens are simply more apt to have contact with government agencies than others.

What are these "cases" all about? As reported by respondents in a 1977 nationwide survey, the most frequent reason for contacting a member's office (16 percent of all cases) is to express views or obtain information on legislative issues. Requests for help in finding government jobs form the next largest category, followed by cases dealing with government benefits such as Social Security, Veterans Administration, or unemployment compensation. Military cases (exemptions from service, discharges, transfers) are numerous, as are tax, legal, and immigration problems. Many are simply requests for information or government publications: copies of legislative bills and reports, executive-branch regulations, *Agricultural Yearbooks,* infant care booklets, and tourist information about the nation's capital. And there are requests for flags that have flown over the U.S. Capitol (a special flagpole on the south side of the Capitol is reserved for such flags, which are continually hoisted and lowered for that purpose).[74] Most cases come to legislators offices by letter, although phone calls or walk-ins at district or mobile offices are not uncommon. Occasionally senators or representatives themselves pick up cases from talking to constituents; many hold office hours in their districts for this purpose. When a request is received, it is usually acknowledged immediately by a letter that either fills the request or assures that an answer will be forthcoming.

If the request requires contacting a federal agency, caseworkers do this by phone, letter, or buckslip (a pre-printed referral form).[75] Usually the contact in the executive agency is a liaison officer, although some caseworkers prefer to deal directly with line officers or regional officials. Once the problem has been relayed, it is a matter of time before a decision is reached and a reply forwarded to the congressional office. The reply is then sent along to the constituent, perhaps with a covering letter signed by the member. If the agency's reply is deemed faulty, the caseworker may challenge it and ask for reconsideration, and in some cases the member may be brought in to lend weight to the appeal.

From all accounts, casework pays off in citizen support for individual legislators. In a 1977 national survey, 15 percent of all adults reported that they or members of their family had requested help from their representative.[76] Seven out of ten of them said that they were satisfied with the way their request had been handled. As Fiorina put it, "pork barreling and casework . . . are almost pure profit." [77] As we noted in Chapter 3, this is not quite the same thing as saying that casework pays off in votes; but there is every reason to assume that casework plays a part in incumbents' success at the polls. At the very least, members use constituent service for "advertising" and "credit-claiming." [78]

Fiorina argues that casework has burgeoned mainly to enhance incumbents' visibility and electoral support.[79] According to this reasoning, Congress enacts programs and creates bureaucracies with vague mandates, knowing full well that snags will arise when these services reach citizens. In turn, citizens ask elected officials to disentangle them, later showing their gratitude when reelection time rolls around.

This is a beguiling argument, but it rests on circumstantial evidence. It is possible that legislators enact laws with loopholes because they don't know how to do otherwise, not because they cunningly seek chances for future credit-claiming. Similarly, members may build up casework staffs not merely for electoral payoff, but to respond to firmly held voter expectations. Without question, voters *do* expect legislators to "bring home the bacon" and keep in touch with the home folks; most of them pay scant attention to legislative work in Washington. Many legislators, for their part, betray mixed feelings about their heavy investment in constituency service, no matter how essential they view that role to be. In short, while constituency errand-running is smart politics, it has not been proven that it sprung solely or even primarily from electoral motives.

Others criticize constituency casework as unfair or biased in practice. Citizens may not enjoy equal access to senators' or representatives' offices. Political supporters or cronies may get favored treatment at others' expense. Finally, administrative agencies may be pressured into giving special treatment to congressional requests, distorting the administration of laws.

Some critics therefore advocate an independent, nonpartisan office of constituent relations, modeled after the Scandinavian ombudsman.[80] Such a facility would have several basic attributes: 1) Although an arm of the legislature, it would work independently of both members' offices and executive agencies. 2) It would have virtually unlimited access to official papers bearing on matters under investigation. 3) It would express its conclusions about almost any aspect of the government's treatment of citizens. 4) Although lacking direct enforcing powers, it would explain its conclusions so that everyone would understand how they were reached.

Proposals for an ombudsman's office have never taken hold at the national level, although they have been adopted by some states, municipalities, and administrative agencies. No doubt the leading reason is that senators and representatives don't want to forfeit the credit-claiming and advertising benefits of casework. Moreover, there are reasons for thinking that constituent errand-running works reasonably effectively. For one thing, delegating casework to state or district offices increases its accessibility to ordinary citizens; survey data indicate such services are in fact widely sought out. Delegating casework to trained staff members also lowers the danger of political or personal favoritism. Finally, incumbent legislators have a key advantage in performing this function: they have leverage over administrative agencies because their votes create those agencies and supply them with funds. This sort of clout would not be wielded by an independent office whose power was confined to recommending and publicizing.

CONCLUSION

It is sometimes said that reelection is the overriding objective of senators and representatives.[81] This is true in a metaphorical sense: after all, election is a prerequisite to congressional service. Incumbent legislators allocate much of their time and energy, and even more of their staff and office resources, to the care and cultivation of voters. Moreover, there is no question that legislators agonize over their reelection chances and view with dismay any signs of deteriorating home-base support.

Yet senators and representatives do not live by reelection alone. Not a few turn their backs on reelection to pursue other careers or interests. For those who remain in office, reelection is not usually viewed as an end in itself, but as a lever for pursuing other goals— policymaking or Washington influence, for example. Fenno challenged one of the representatives whose constituency career he had followed, remarking that "Sometimes it must be hard to connect what you do here with what you do in Washington." "Oh no," the lawmaker replied, "I do what I do here so I can do what I want to do there." [82]

NOTES

1. Richard F. Fenno, Jr., *Home Style: House Members in Their Districts* (Boston: Little, Brown & Co., 1978), pp. xi-xii.
2. *Congressional Quarterly Weekly Report,* September 1, 1979, p. 1823.
3. Donald R. Matthews, *U.S. Senators and Their World* (Chapel Hill: University of North Carolina Press, 1960), p. 66.
4. Bill Keller, "How A Unique Lobby Force Protects Over $21 Billion in Vast Veterans' Programs," *Congressional Quarterly Weekly Report,* June 14, 1980, pp. 1627-1634.
5. Matthews, *U.S. Senators and Their World,* p. 66.
6. Andrew Hacker, "The Elected and the Anointed," *American Political Science Review* (September 1961): 541.
7. *Guide to Congress,* 2d ed. (Washington, D.C.: Congressional Quarterly, 1976), p. 528.
8. Ward Just, *The Congressman Who Loved Flaubert and Other Washington Stories* (Boston: Atlantic Monthly Press, 1973), p. 13.

9. Irwin B. Arieff, "More Catholics, Jews, Blacks, Women in the 97th Congress," *Congressional Quarterly Weekly Report,* January 24, 1981, p. 200.
10. *New York Times,* June 14, 1981, p. E5.
11. Roger H. Davidson, *The Role of the Congressman* (Indianapolis: Bobbs-Merrill Co., 1969), p. 199.
12. U.S., Congress, House, Commission on Administrative Review, *Final Report,* 2 vols., H. Doc. 95-272, 95th Cong., 1st sess., December 31, 1977, 2: 874-875.
13. Thomas E. Cavanagh, "The Two Arenas of Congress: Electoral and Institutional Incentives for Performance" (Paper delivered at the annual meeting of the American Political Science Association, New York, N.Y., August 31-September 3, 1978).
14. Frank E. Smith, *Congressman From Mississippi* (New York: Pantheon Books, 1964), pp. 129-130.
15. Matthews, *U.S. Senators.*
16. Norman J. Ornstein, Robert L. Peabody, and David W. Rohde, "The Contemporary Senate: Into the 1980s," in *Congress Reconsidered,* 2d ed., ed. Lawrence C. Dodd and Bruce I. Oppenheimer (Washington, D.C.: Congressional Quarterly Press, 1981), pp. 16-19.
17. Herbert B. Asher, "The Learning of Legislative Norms," *American Political Science Review* (June 1973): 499-513.
18. Burdett A. Loomis and Jeff Fishel, "New Members in a Changing Congress: Norms, Actions, and Satisfaction," *Congressional Studies* (Spring 1981): 81-94.
19. *New York Times,* August 14, 1980, p. B9.
20. Cavanagh, "The Two Arenas of Congress," p. 16.
21. Larry Light, "Crack 'Outreach' Programs No Longer Ensure Re-election," *Congressional Quarterly Weekly Report,* February 14, 1981, pp. 316-318.
22. Cavanagh, "The Two Arenas of Congress," p. 17.
23. Ibid., p. 18.
24. Smith, *Congressman From Mississippi,* p. 127. See also David Mayhew, *Congress: The Electoral Connection* (New Haven: Yale University Press, 1974).
25. Davidson, *The Role of the Congressman,* p. 98; and U.S., Congress, Senate, Commission on the Operation of the Senate, *Toward A Modern Senate,* S. Doc. 94-278, 94th Cong., 2d sess., 1977 committee print, p. 27.
26. Senate, *Toward A Modern Senate.*
27. Ross A. Webber, "U.S. Senators: See How They Run," *The Wharton Magazine* (Winter 1980-1981): 38.
28. House Commission on Administrative Review, *Final Report,* 1: 630-634.
29. U.S., Congress, House, Commission on Administrative Review, *Administrative Reorganization and Legislative Management,* 2 vols., H. Doc. 95-232, 95th Cong., 1st sess., September 28, 1977, 1: 27-31; and Senate, *Toward A Modern Senate,* pp. 35-38.
30. Webber, "U.S. Senators," p. 37.
31. House Commission on Administrative Review, *Final Report,* 2: 875.
32. Vernon Louviere, "For Retiring Congressmen, Enough Is Enough," *Nation's Business* (May 1980): 32.
33. William H. Riker, *The Theory of Political Coalitions* (New Haven: Yale University Press, 1962), pp. 24-38.
34. Hanna Fenichel Pitkin, *The Concept of Representation* (Berkeley: University of California Press, 1967), p. 166.
35. Davidson, *The Role of the Congressman,* p. 80.

36. Ross J. S. Hoffman and Paul Levack, eds., *Burke's Politics* (New York: Alfred A. Knopf, 1959), pp. 114-116.
37. Carl D. McMurray and Malcolm B. Parsons, "Public Attitudes Toward the Representational Role of Legislators and Judges," *Midwest Journal of Political Science* (May 1965): 167-185.
38. Davidson, *The Role of the Congressman.*
39. Thomas E. Cavanagh, "Role Orientations of House Members: The Process of Representation" (Paper delivered at the annual meeting of the American Political Science Association, Washington, D.C., August 31-September 3, 1979).
40. House Commission on Administrative Review, *Final Report.*
41. Cavanagh, "Role Orientations of House Members," p. 20.
42. John W. Kingdon, *Congressmen's Voting Decisions* (New York: Harper & Row, 1981).
43. Fenno, *Home Style,* p. 1.
44. Martin Tolchin, "Udall Re-election Imperiled by Newest Constituents," *New York Times,* October 30, 1980, p. B12.
45. See Lewis A. Froman, Jr. *Congressmen and Their Constituencies* (Chicago: Rand McNally & Co., 1963), pp. 91-93; Randall B. Ripley, *Congress: Process and Policy,* 2d ed. (New York: W. W. Norton & Co., 1978) pp. 289-291; and David M. Olson, *The Legislative Process: A Comparative Approach* (New York: Harper & Row, 1980), pp. 425-428.
46. Lewis A. Froman, Jr., "Inter-Party Constituency Differences and Congressional Voting Behavior," *American Political Science Review* (March 1963): 57-61.
47. *Congressional Quarterly Weekly Report,* January 10, 1981, p. 80.
48. Fenno, *Home Style,* pp. 4-8.
49. Ibid., p. 6.
50. Olson, *The Legislative Process,* p. 427.
51. Albert D. Cover and David R. Mayhew, "Congressional Dynamics and the Decline of Competitive Congressional Elections," in *Congress Reconsidered,* 2d ed., pp. 62-82.
52. Thomas E. Mann, *Unsafe at Any Margin: Interpreting Congressional Elections* (Washington, D.C.: American Enterprise Institute for Public Policy Research, 1978).
53. Fenno, *Home Style,* pp. 8-27.
54. Ibid., p. 21.
55. Ibid., pp. 24-25.
56. Ibid.
57. Erving Goffman, *The Presentation of Self in Everyday Life* (New York: Doubleday & Co., 1959).
58. Fenno, *Home Style,* p. 153.
59. Ibid., p. 56.
60. Ibid.
61. Ibid., p. 136.
62. Kingdon, *Congressmen's Voting Decisions.*
63. Fenno, *Home Style,* p. 153.
64. Thomas J. Brazaitas, "Vanik Deplores Lack of Courage," *Cleveland Plain Dealer,* May 11, 1980, cited in *Congressional Record,* daily ed., 96th Cong., 2d sess., May 15, 1980, p. E2437.
65. Glenn R. Parker, "Sources of Change in Congressional District Attentiveness," *American Journal of Political Science* (February 1980): 115-124.
66. Fenno, *Home Style,* p. 36.
67. Ibid., p. 209; Parker, "Sources of Change."

68. Parker, "Sources of Change."
69. Jim Wright, *You and Your Congressman* (New York: Coward-McCann, 1965), p. 35.
70. House, *Final Report,* 1: 655.
71. Janet Breslin, "Constituent Service," in *Senators: Offices, Ethics, and Pressures,* by Senate Commission on the Operation of the Senate, 94th Cong., 2d sess., 1977 committee print, p. 21.
72. John R. Johannes, "Casework as a Technique of Oversight of the Executive," *Legislative Studies Quarterly* (August 1979): 325-351.
73. House, *Final Report,* 1: 655; and Breslin, "Constituent Service," p. 21.
74. House, *Final Report,* 2: 830.
75. Johannes, "Casework as a Technique of Oversight."
76. House Commission on Administrative Review, *Final Report,* pp. 2: 830-831.
77. Morris P. Fiorina, *Congress: Keystone of the Washington Establishment* (New Haven: Yale University Press, 1977), p. 45.
78. Mayhew, *Congress: The Electoral Connection.*
79. Fiorina, *Congress: Keystone of the Washington Establishment.*
80. Walter Gellhorn, *When Americans Complain: Governmental Grievance Procedures* (Cambridge, Mass.: Harvard University Press, 1966).
81. Mayhew, *Congress: The Electoral Connection.*
82. Fenno, *Home Style,* p. 199.

5

Looking Good:
The Two Congresses
and the Public

This balmy spring afternoon, the U.S. Capitol grounds are a beehive of activity. On the Capitol steps a group of high-school-age Future Farmers of America, resplendent in blue jackets with gold emblems, pose with their representative for a photograph. Waiting impatiently out of range is another member shepherding his group of constituents—a delegation of Native Americans. Over on the lawn a Nevada TV reporter and her cameraman are interviewing the state's representative. A few yards away a lobbyist with a camera crew is talking with legislators who endorse his group's opposition to PAC campaign funding limits.

There is nothing unusual about this scene. All over Capitol Hill the complex and sometimes frantic process of communication is much in evidence. Newsmaking and newsgathering are constantly part of the lives of members of Congress—public people whose careers flourish or collapse from publicity. Unique among our government institutions, Congress works in the media's glare. "On Capitol Hill, you always have access," remarked a seasoned journalist.[1]

Communications from and about Congress pose a paradox. Although extensively reported in the media, Congress is not well understood by most Americans. Its size and complexity are partly to blame: indeed, who speaks for Congress? No news apparatus can follow the work of two chambers, more than 250 committees and subcommittees, and 540 active politicians. The average citizen can understand the president, or follow the careers of a few colorful cabinet secretaries or senators. But the whole Congress is another matter. For most citizens, it is a mystifying blur.

Nor is that the sole paradox. If Congress as an institution is widely reported but ill understood, individual members are ill reported but well understood—at least by the home folks. For senators this means, beyond their own publicity efforts, attention from statewide and metropolitan papers and broadcast outlets. For representatives, it means mainly self-generated publicity. The two Congresses, in other words, follow diverging channels of communication and, as a result, look different in the public's eyes.

In this chapter we examine the public face of the two Congresses. Congress as a news source, both in its collective work and its members' activities, is considered first. Then communication modes—those internally generated as well as those in the hands of organized media—are described. Finally we discuss the end results of the communications process. What do citizens read or hear about Congress and its members? What do people think about Congress's performance?

CONGRESS AS A NEWS SOURCE

National news media fix their attention upon the collective behavior of Congress as it probes issues, writes laws, and refines policies. News is made most often on the floor of the two chambers and in the committee and subcommittee rooms.

Floor Sessions

Congress's predecessors—the Continental and Confederation Congresses and the Constitutional Convention of 1787—met behind closed doors. When the new government met in New York in April 1789, the House broke precedent and opened its doors to the public. At first Senate sessions were closed, but in 1795 they, too, became open—responding to criticism from the press, state legislatures, and the Senate's own members.[2]

Floor deliberations are a mixture of legislative purpose and members' self-promotion. Remarks ostensibly directed at colleagues on the floor may really be aimed at publics far removed from the Hill. In earlier days, when oratory was a form of public entertainment, careers bloomed with displays of eloquence; Daniel Webster, John C. Calhoun, and Henry Clay were noted for their rhetoric. Today's eloquence is lower-keyed but still aimed at promoting people or ideas. Apart from debating measures at hand, members can highlight issues, comment on recent events, or point to constituency concerns. Certain practices and procedures enable members to gain media coverage. These include "special orders," or time set aside to discuss special issues (both chambers), one-minute speeches (House), and "extensions of remarks" (House) printed in appendixes of the *Congressional Record*. Often members' comments are reprinted and distributed in quantity to constituents or interested parties.

Only a few reporters covered the early Congresses (4 in 1813 and 12 in 1823)[3], and their accounts were highly partisan. Legislators then, as now, complained about biased reporting. In 1857 a *New York Times* reporter was held by the House Sergeant at Arms for 19 days after refusing to reveal his sources for a series of news dispatches accusing several members of corruption.[4]

Commercial firms recorded congressional debates from 1824 until 1873, when the *Congressional Record*—put out by the Government Printing Office—first appeared. Today the *Record* is nearly a verbatim transcript of the proceedings, although members may "revise and extend" their remarks and insert material (marked by black "bullets") not actually uttered. Many argue that the *Record* should print only what is actually said on the floor. Present practices, however, serve useful purposes. They allow members to recast statements they may regret, and they save precious floor time by providing an outlet for statements not delivered.

The number of journalists covering the House and Senate rose to 58 by 1868, 171 by 1900. Special press galleries were provided when the new House and Senate wings of the Capitol were finished in 1857. Following scandals alleging that lobbyists paid certain reporters to represent them, journalists adopted rules limiting admittance to press galleries. Today some 3,000 journalists are admitted. In each chamber a sizable section of the gallery, just above the dais, is set aside for reporters who, unlike other gallery visitors, can take notes on what they witness. Outside the galleries are rooms equipped for newspaper, periodical, radio-TV, and photo journalists. They guard their exclusive domains and manage the space under authority delegated by the two houses.

Until quite recently, broadcast journalists had no way of relaying floor debates directly to listeners or viewers. Although reporters can broadcast reports from studios adjacent to the chambers, the proceedings themselves were not transmitted until the late 1970s, with the ex-

ception of joint sessions for presidential addresses and other special occasions. In 1978 the Senate passed a resolution permitting radio broadcasts of the Panama Canal treaties debate. That same year the House
allowed broadcasters to transmit from the chamber's voice amplifier
system. For the first time, floor debate was transmitted directly to the
public. The House began televising its floor sessions in 1979; two years
later the Senate considered establishing a similar system.

Committee Sessions

A momentous development for Hill newsgathering was "adoption
on the part of Congress in the early years of this century of the policy of
holding, on all important bills, open committee hearings."[5] Normally
hearings are open to the public unless confidential matters are being
discussed. The all-important markup sessions—when bills are worked
over in detail—used to be closed but opened up dramatically in the
1970s. House and Senate rules now require open committee sessions
unless members vote specifically to close them.

Like floor deliberations, committee activities combine legislative
purpose with personal advertisement. Some committees are eager for
press coverage and plan their hearings to make sure they get it.
Sometimes publicity becomes, in Douglass Cater's words, "the end
product and not the sidelines of the committee's work."[6] Other committees are less receptive to attention from press or public. In one study of
76 panels in both houses, committees were found to fall into four
categories: (1) openly hostile to the media, (2) neutral (answering
questions but making few independent efforts), (3) publicity seeking,
and (4) collaborative (trading information, ideas, and sources).[7] Reasons
for the varying attitudes lie in the nature of the committee's business,
the styles of the chairman or members, and the physical layout of the
committee rooms (some, like House Rules, have scant space for reporters or visitors).

Committees seeking publicity, and that is probably the majority of
them, have many means of attracting it. Celebrity witnesses—the Henry
Kissingers, the Ralph Naders, and television and movie stars—are sure
to draw press and TV cameras, which in turn ensure members'
attendance. Investigations and reports can be geared for press consump-
tion. Field hearings can be held where the local press is apt to cover
them. Staff members can alert reporters to upcoming committee business, brief them, respond to inquiries, prepare findings in easily
digestible form, and make sure legislators are available for interviews.

Committees with an eye for publicity not only advertise committee
members but also focus public attention on pressing issues. The late
Senator Estes Kefauver, D-Tenn., gained national attention in 1951 by
chairing a sensational series of televised hearings into organized crime.

Kefauver and his staff put in months and even years of meticulous research to prepare for the hearings. Modern regulation of prescription drugs resulted from 1962 Kefauver hearings on drug testing and pricing.[8]

Television cameras appeared in certain committee hearings in the late 1940s, but in 1952 Speaker Sam Rayburn ruled that neither committee sessions nor floor deliberations could be broadcast unless the House adopted a specific rule authorizing it.[9] Not until 1970 were House committee sessions again covered electronically. Senate committees had always been open to the cameras; in a few cases, extended coverage was provided. These included the Army-McCarthy hearings of 1954, the Foreign Relations Committee's Vietnam hearings of 1966, and North Carolina Democrat Sam Ervin's 1973 Senate Watergate investigation. The House Judiciary Committee's 1974 deliberations on impeaching President Richard Nixon riveted the nation's attention and briefly revived Congress's standing in the polls.

Written products—legislation and reports—are not so readily covered by reporters. They are not usually breaking news, and they require busy reporters to sit down and study them at length. Thus, experienced committee staffs prepare summaries and press releases to simplify the reporters' job and stand ready to answer questions and provide background information.

A two-way flow of information and influence is sustained by the media. Events and issues spotlighted by the media often form the agenda for committee or floor action. Congress acts with an eye to how its action will play in the media—speeding up action because of media drumbeating or refraining from action because of supposed adverse coverage.

Televising the Congress

Although some congressional events were televised, House committee meetings (until 1970) and floor debates in both chambers took place out of camera range. Meanwhile, White House occupants from Truman on were exploiting TV's unique ability to capture attention and dramatize issues. Many commentators sensed that Congress's eclipse was somehow linked to its reliance on print media in a television age. Failure to use television, wrote David Halberstam, was a "serious institutional handicap."

> If the House was not seen performing its most important functions on television, then, as far as most people were concerned, it was not doing anything; if it was not doing anything, it might just as well not exist.[10]

By the late 1970s Congress was ready to act. Many members urged the two houses to set up a broadcasting system. (In 1944 Senator Claude

Pepper, D-Fla., who later became a representative, had introduced a joint resolution for that purpose.) Newer legislators, raised on television and dependent on it for campaigns, welcomed the cameras. In October 1977 the House authorized Speaker Thomas P. O'Neill, Jr., D-Mass., to install a closed-circuit viewing system and make audio and video signals available to the news media. Television signals were first beamed to the media on March 19, 1979. A select committee examining the issue concluded that TV coverage of floor sessions would help members and staff carry out their duties, provide a more accurate record of proceedings, and contribute to public understanding of the House.[11]

The House Broadcasting System owns six cameras mounted in the chamber and controlled remotely from a studio in the Capitol basement. Cameras focus on the Speaker's dais, two lecterns at the front of the chamber, and the majority and minority floor managers' tables. (A plan whereby the TV networks would run the system under a pooled arrangement was rejected. Leaving editorial judgments in outsiders' hands, it was reasoned, might result in shots of empty seats or members dozing in their chairs.) Coverage is gavel-to-gavel, except that cameras are turned off during roll-call votes.

The House system has several uses. Closed-circuit outlets allow members and staffs to follow floor deliberations while remaining in their offices. Radio or TV networks may broadcast the floor debate live, or they may use excerpts in news programs. Full coverage is relayed by the Cable Satellite Public Affairs Network (C-SPAN) to about 850 cable TV systems in 50 states, with some 15 million potential viewers. Finally, audio and video tapes can be archived or duplicated on request. (House rules prohibit tape purchasers from using them for political or commercial purposes.)

Televised sessions are now firmly entrenched in the House because they serve informational and political needs. Several effects have been noticed.

One-minute Speeches. These brief speeches at the beginning of the legislative day are an established informal practice and are ideal vehicles for partisan commentary. Since the TV cameras were installed, their popularity has soared. In March 1977 there were 110 one-minute speeches; four years later there were 344. At one time Democratic leaders tried to curb the speeches by moving them to the end of the day—following news deadlines. After bitter complaints and delaying tactics on the part of members, leaders promptly restored the speeches to their customary spot in the day's schedule.

Public Awareness. Although no one knows exactly how many people watch House sessions on TV, the audience is apparently small but loyal. Some legislators report comments and mail resulting from the programs; a viewers' guide has been prepared for distribution.[12] On occasion the TV audience grows quite large. In May 1979 virtually all of Alaska's TV stations transmitted House debate on the controversial Alaska lands bill. Interest was keen and viewership was high. As cable TV spreads, the impact will increase.

The House's TV experience led the Senate to consider a similar system. A resolution authorizing such a system was introduced in 1981 by Majority Leader Howard Baker, R-Tenn., as part of his leadership agenda. "Turning on the cameras to let the people see us as we really are," he told his colleagues, "can help bring a beginning of respect for public service and public servants again." He argued also that TV coverage of selected debates is an "opportunity for the Senate to actually become the great deliberative body which it was thought to be when it was created, as it has sometimes been in its past, and that we would all like it to be every day." [13] Others countered that the system would be costly and would encourage grandstanding by members.

MEMBERS' IN-HOUSE PUBLICITY

Lawmakers wage an unceasing struggle for media attention. Often party leaders gain or forfeit power because of their communication skills. In the mid-1960s House Republicans, worried about the negative publicity arising from the "Ev and Charlie show"—news conferences featuring Senate Minority Leader Everett Dirksen of Illinois and House Minority Leader Charles Halleck of Indiana—replaced Halleck with the younger and more telegenic Michigan Representative Gerald R. Ford. Republicans in the 1980s targeted the big, shambling figure of Speaker O'Neill as a symbol of the old-style, back-slapping politician. Party bodies devote much attention to their public relations. Under the leadership of Senator James A. McClure, R-Idaho, the Senate Republican Conference in 1981 launched a campaign to publicize the achievements of the GOP majority. Meanwhile, the House Democratic Caucus ran a phone-bank effort to contact the nation's editorial writers in favor of the Democratic alternative to the Reagan tax plan.

Members' offices resemble the mail distribution division of a large business. Every day stacks of printed matter are released for wide distribution. Materials include press releases, newsletters, individual and mass mailings, and programs or tapes for electronic media.

To influence legislation, members sometimes target the national media—TV networks and newspapers, such as the *New York Times* or *Washington Post*, that are read by elites. One of the most successful at promoting his work is Representative Les Aspin, D-Wis., whose views on defense built his reputation. He explains the purpose of attracting national media:

You're trying to influence the debate on the subject. You're trying to anticipate where the story is going, but you're also trying to push the story in a certain way.... You're trying to change the focus of the debate among the aficionados....[14]

Getting the attention of these media is not easy for individual legislators, especially House members. Sometimes members resort to "leaking" information to gain press exposure.

Far more often, publicity from members' offices aims not at the national media but at people back home. Enterprising legislators employ many techniques, including newsletters, mass mailings, press releases, radio and TV programs, telephone calls and interviews. Both chambers' office allowances amply support such activities. *(See box, p. 124.)* One writer estimates the total subsidy in computer time, labor, paper, and free mailing at $100 million every election year.[15]

Figure 5-1   Franked Mass Mailings by House Members, 1973-1978

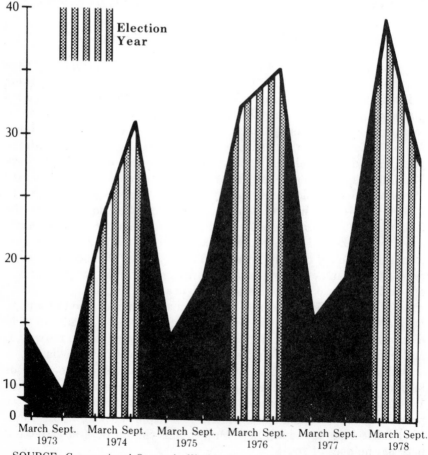

SOURCE: *Congressional Quarterly Weekly Report,* August 16, 1980, p. 2387.

'Think Direct Mail'

The cornerstone of congressional publicity is the franking privilege—the right of members to send out mail under their signatures
without cost to them. (Congress reimburses the U.S. Postal Service for
the mailings on a bulk basis.) Figures on franking usage are hard to get,
but records obtained by Common Cause indicate that House franked
mail approaches or exceeds 40 million pieces a month in election years.
(See Figure 5-1.)

The existing franking law, passed in 1973, confers wide mailing
privileges, but it forbids using the frank for mail "unrelated to the
official business, activities, and duties of members." It also bars the
frank for "mail matter which specifically solicits political support for
the sender or any other person or any political party, or a vote or
financial assistance for any candidate for any political office." In
addition, House and Senate rules forbid mass mailings 60 days before a
primary or general election. Just before the start of each 60-day period,
streams of Postal Service trucks are seen pulling away from loading
docks of the congressional office buildings.

With computerized address lists, mailings can be targeted at
groupings—physicians, nurses, schoolteachers, teamsters, or auto driv-
ers. By combining lists, groupings can be pinpointed even further—for
instance, to physicians in a certain county who are alumni of the state
university medical school. One congressional aide recounted his initi-
ation into the wonders of direct-mail technology:

> I began with a personal letter to each of the special interest groups
> we have on file. The physicians received a letter from my congressman
> enclosed with a reprint from the *Congressional Record* of his recent
> remarks on the horrors of socialized medicine. The docs ate it up. The
> nurses got a letter pointing out the congressman's recent vote to
> increase funds in the federal budget for nurse training programs, along
> with a copy of his impassioned comments on the subject.
>
> Each of these letters began, "Knowing of your intense personal
> interest in any legislation affecting physicians/nurses, I thought you
> might be interested to see...." On the average we received one
> response, invariably positive, for every two letters we sent—an abso-
> lutely phenomenal 50 percent rate of unsolicited response. Again, I was
> stunned. People cared about what we were saying. Amazing.[16]

Senate records show that senators have divided the nation's voters in a
total of 3,356 categories including "fat cats," "society and rich-guy
groups and interests," "yacht owners," and "top bureaucrats." One
senator's administrative assistant instructed his staff to "Think Direct
Mail" and to send franked mailings to two new special-interest groups a
week.[17]

The frank is as old as the nation—and so is criticism of it. A lawsuit
against the uses of franking privileges was filed by Common Cause in

1973. This suit led to the existing law. Responding to a 1976 court order, Congress agreed to release detailed information on franking practices. Based on this information, Common Cause submitted new material in July 1980. This suit asked that franked mass mailings be halted on the grounds that they violate political challengers' right to compete for office free of government-imposed handicaps. Floods of public-financed publicity, Common Cause argues, prevents opponents from effectively challenging the incumbents' records. Defenders of current franking practices respond that members must inform constituents on issues and that existing laws and rules are enough to prevent abuses.

Some members criticize franking usage. "The way Congress kicks around the frank is one of my pet peeves," says Senator Jesse Helms, R-N.C., a heavy user of privately financed mass mailings. "An appalling amount of public money is spent sending out mailings that are nothing but political puff pieces...." [18] Morris K. Udall, D-Ariz., chairman of the House Congressional Mailing Standards Commission, agrees that "the present law hasn't worked, and we have to go back and try again." However, he cautions that the task is not simple: "How do you write rules and regulations that distinguish between a thoughtful discussion of some important public issue and a self-promoting thing with the photograph of a member on every other page?"

Many offices supplement mass mailings with general-purpose news-letters blanketing home states or districts. These are upbeat accounts of the legislator's activities, complete with photos of the legislator greeting constituents or conferring with top decisionmakers. The member's committee posts are highlighted, as are efforts to boost the home area. Recipients are urged to share their views or contact local offices for help. Perhaps once a year, the newsletter may feature an opinion poll asking for views on selected issues. Whatever the results, the underlying message is that the legislator really cares what folks back home think.

Feeding the Local Press

Relations with the press receive careful attention. Most legislators have at least one staffer who serves as a press aide; some have two or three. Their job is to generate statements highlighting the member's work. Executive agencies often help by letting incumbents announce federal grants or contracts awarded in the state or district. Even if the member had nothing to do with procuring the funds, the press statement proclaims "Senator So-and-So announced today that a federal contract has been awarded to XYZ Company in Jonesville." Many offices also prepare weekly or biweekly commentaries that small-town newspapers can reprint under the lawmaker's byline.

The House and Senate have fully equipped radio and TV studios where audio or video programs or excerpts (called "actualities") can be produced for a fraction of the commercial cost.[19] The TV studios feature a series of backdrops—including the familiar Capitol dome, an office interior, or a committee room setting. Some incumbents produce regular programs that are picked up by local radio or TV outlets. More often, local outlets insert brief audio or TV clips on current issues into regular news broadcasts—to give the impression that local reporters have actually gone out and gotten the story.

Studio facilities and usage have risen, especially over the last decade. Michael Robinson's interviews with press secretaries indicate that members are using the studios more and more.[20] Representatives elected in 1968 were more than three times as likely as more senior members to use the recording studios at least once a week. As with other modes of self-advertising, junior lawmakers appear to be the most PR-conscious.

NATIONAL AND LOCAL PRESS CORPS

A vast network of print and electronic media transmits news about Congress. The "gatekeepers" of Capitol Hill news are the thousands of reporters, camera operators, editors, and producers who process the news before it ever reaches citizens in the form of newspaper articles or radio and TV items. Some news people handle only national news—stories of general interest to the nation or to specialized elites. Others concentrate on local news—news affecting a region and its people.

The Washington Press Corps

News about Congress funnels through the Washington press corps, a diverse group of about 3,000 journalists who cover national government. That is the number accredited to the congressional press galleries, perhaps a third of whom cover the House and Senate with any regularity. (Congressional press gallery accreditation is a kind of social and professional badge of honor; most Washington journalists apply, even if they spend little time on the Hill.) Some press people are as much celebrities as the people they cover; others work for such obscure journals as *Food Chemical News* or the *Wenatchee* (Wash.) *Daily World*.

Journalists tend to have middle-class origins.[21] They are also well educated; a recent study of Washington reporters found that 98 percent had attended college. The prevailing wisdom holds that reporters lean to the left politically, in contrast to conservative newspaper and radio-TV owners. Of the Washington reporters responding to a recent Brookings Institution study, 42 percent consider themselves liberal, 39 percent middle-of-the-road, and 19 percent conservative. Yet a majority of them said that journalists out of touch with the nation constituted a serious problem; four out of five thought reporters should spend more time away from the nation's capital.[22]

The "inner ring" of the press corps (Stephen Hess's term) is the main source of national news. This group includes three TV networks (NBC, CBS, ABC), two wire services (Associated Press, United Press International), three news magazines (*Time, Newsweek, U.S. News & World Report*), two journals (*Congressional Quarterly, National Journal*) and three daily newspapers (*Washington Post, New York Times,* and *Wall Street Journal*). These outlets are noteworthy not only because they cover national news in depth, but also because they help policymakers keep in touch with each other. High-level officials, and reporters themselves, gain information from these select journals.[23]

The AP and UPI bureaus are giant news services that disseminate telegraphed material to clients throughout the world. Because they serve a variety of clients, wire-service dispatches focus on current happenings—called "breaking news"—of the broadest character. However, some wire service reporters handle regional news. When a Portland editor phones that he needs a story about the Oregon congressional delegation's meeting with Forest Service officials over the Mount St. Helens disaster, some reporter will have to dig out the story. Writing for a wire service, one harassed UPI reporter complained, "is like having a thousand mothers-in-law."

In addition to the general-circulation press, the specialized press is well represented in the nation's capital. *Chronicle of Higher Education* maintains an active Washington bureau, as do *Journal of Commerce, Aviation Week,* and a host of reports and newsletters that cover national news of a specialized nature. Like the big papers, specialized journals link prime policymakers together, forming part of the so-called "subgovernments" that dominate many policy fields.

TV network crews are conspicuous around Capitol Hill, but relatively few reporters are involved. Some TV reporters specialize in Hill news, but the high cost of coverage and the tiny amount of available news time means that most reporters and crews must be ready to go wherever the news is occurring. Unlike print journalists, they cannot specialize in Congress or in given policy topics.

The Local Press

If national newsgathering is centralized, dissemination is highly dispersed. Nearly 10,000 newspapers are published in the United States, of which the 1,700 or so dailies are the most important in prestige and circulation. More than 10,000 periodicals are published. There are also nearly 9,000 radio stations and more than 1,000 TV stations throughout the country.[24] These media outlets are locally based because of the vitality of local issues and local advertising.[25]

For national news, local outlets depend heavily on the national sources we described earlier. The average paper covers national news directly only if conveyed through a local official, such as a senator or representative. According to a Ralph Nader study in the early 1970s, 72 percent of all daily newspapers have no Washington correspondent or even a "stringer" (someone who contracts to write for a "string" of newspapers).[26] For all but the largest newspapers and chains, AP or UPI copy suffices for national and international events.

Electronic outlets rely even more upon centralized news organs. Local radio and TV news staffs are usually small, employing only a handful of people. The Ralph Nader study estimated that 1 percent of all radio stations and 4 percent of TV stations had their own reporters in Washington; since then the numbers may have increased. Network TV affiliates—all but about 100 commercial stations—rely on network products. Nonaffiliated TV and radio stations draw at least four-fifths of their news from AP or UPI radio services, which are briefer versions of stories sent out to print media. The rest of the news is local, sometimes read verbatim from local newspapers.

If direct local coverage of Washington events is rare, a surprisingly large portion of the Washington press corps nonetheless deals with local aspects of national stories. One observer estimates that two-thirds of all Hill reporters (including those in radio and TV) spend most of their time on local area news.[27] The grist of their mill is the local angle of the national story—how legislative events affect the region, what "our senator" or "our representative" has to say.

Many reporters accredited to the congressional galleries concentrate on such local angles. "The bulk of the Washington press corps is made up of localizers," says a regional reporter for several southern papers.[28] This includes regional reporters for the huge wire-service bureaus. It also embraces bureaus of Newhouse, Gannett, Knight-Ridder, Cox, and other major newspaper chains that now account for two-thirds of all daily papers and three-quarters of the circulation. In addition, it embraces several hundred "stringers," who supply news to a number of unrelated papers.

Taken as a whole, however, local media outlets have inadequate resources for covering what their congressional delegations are doing in the nation's capital. Few of them have their own Washington reporters; most rely on syndicated or chain services that rarely follow individual members consistently. "If they report national news it is usually because it involves local personalities, affects local outcomes, or relates directly to local concerns." [29]

Reporters and Legislators

Reporters and sources are locked into a love-hate embrace. Each has what the other craves: sources have information on which reporters' jobs depend; reporters have the power to create publicity, the lifeblood of political careers. Whatever their private feelings, reporters sense they cannot disclose certain things if they want future interviews. Lawmakers know that cultivating the press corps pays off in good publicity. "Through close and regular contact and despite the cynical talk," wrote Donald R. Matthews, "reporters and [legislators] begin to identify with each other and to understand each other's problems." [30]

National and local journalists enter the source-reporter relationship with different perspectives and resources. Matthews observed:

> The basic tactic of the [senators] is to provide services and special favors to reporters which then may be withdrawn in the event that newsmen do not live up to their end of the bargain—i.e., render favorable coverage.... The local-story reporter, with many fewer potential sources and less prestige on the Hill, can be hurt a great deal more than the top news reporter with a wide group of potential news sources.[31]

National reporters, who may be covering an entirely different story next week, do not depend so heavily on the goodwill of a single source. They can "tell and run" with little fear of reprisal. Local reporters, on the other hand, cannot do their jobs without the aid of the local senator or representative. If the key sources dry up, the reporter's career is on the line.

WHAT THE PUBLIC SEES OR HEARS

Whatever the qualities of the press corps, whatever their relations with Capitol Hill news sources, the bottom line of the process is what the average American sees or hears about political events.

Adults are heavy media consumers. The average citizen spends more than three hours a day watching TV, two hours listening to radio, 20 minutes reading a newspaper, and 10 minutes reading magazines. Television is the broadest source of information. Since the early 1960s television has been the chief source of news; today nearly 70 percent of all citizens rely chiefly upon TV for the news. Almost half rate TV the most believable news source; half report getting *all* their news via the TV tube.[32]

About Congress

The unitary president is easier to cover than the multiheaded Congress. Examining front-page headlines and photographs from 1885 through 1974, Elmer Cornwell and Alan Balutis found "a long-term upward trend in overall presidential news, both in absolute terms and relative to news about Congress." [33] Robinson's more recent data confirm that Congress is "still very subordinate to the executive in news attention and news manipulation." [34]

Examining coverage in 1978, Hess came to a slightly different conclusion. "Washington news," he states, "is funneled through Capitol Hill. Journalists prefer Congress because it is accessible and the people who work there are likeable."[35] He found that TV stories pay more attention to the president than to Congress, but newspaper stories do not. Of the items he monitored dealing with the president and Congress, newspaper stories tilted toward Congress, 54 to 46 percent, but network TV stories broke in the president's favor by a 59-41 margin. Headlines tend to favor the president.

The national press pays more attention to the Senate than the House. The late Representative Allard K. Lowenstein, D-N.Y., once complained that if the House were ignored any more than it was already, it would become as obsolete as the House of Lords.[36] Things are not that bad, but House members do feel neglected by the national press. The Senate bias is moderate in newspapers, overwhelming on network TV. The smaller Senate, with its cluster of celebrities and presidential hopefuls, is irresistible to the TV cameras; House members, in contrast, "lack the glitter that attracts a visual medium." [37]

Majority-party legislators get more attention than minority members, according to Hess.[38] During the period of his survey, majority Democrats received a coverage "bonus" about 10 percent over their share of congressional seats. GOP representatives were doubly disadvantaged, being minority members of a less visible house. Presumably the GOP is now treated more equitably because of its rising fortunes.

As Table 5-1 shows, newspapers and TV portray the legislative process rather differently. Newspapers tend to follow measures through the legislative maze—subcommittee and committee action as well as floor action. TV's attention focuses on the climaxes of the legislative process, especially final floor actions. TV simply limits itself to the very top congressional stories. A half-hour network news program boils down

Table 5-1 Coverage of Legislative Stages by Medium

Legislative Stage in Story	*Stories (Percent)*	
	Newspapers	Television
Introduction of legislation	3	0
Subcommittees	20	7
Committees	27	24
Floor action	35	58
Conference committees	5	11

SOURCE: Stephen Hess, *The Washington Reporters* (Washington: The Brookings Institution, 1981), p. 104. © 1981 by The Brookings Institution. Reprinted by permission.

to about 22 minutes of news—perhaps 10 or 15 stories. Written out, these stories would not fill half the front page of the *New York Times*. Thus newspapers, in addition to running the top stories, have the staff resources and space to cover other activities as well.

Critics often fault electronic media for superficial news coverage. It is true that radio and TV outlets carry far less news than newspapers or journals. True, also, that the fine points of the legislative process are ill-suited to brief visual stories. What the electronic media lack in depth, however, they make up in speed and emotional impact. Often they capture the interplay of personalities or the drama of the moment as print media never can. During the filibuster against the 1964 Civil Rights Act, for instance, daily reports by then-CBS correspondent Roger Mudd were superimposed with a clock showing the second-by-second lengthening of the southern "holding action" against the bill. A page of print hardly has the unique impact of, say, 30 seconds of film showing Senator Joseph McCarthy bullying a witness or Senator Sam Ervin displaying righteous wrath at a Watergate conspirator's transgressions.

About Members

From all accounts, news media find it hard to cope with Congress's buzzing confusion—its 540 members, its hundreds of workgroups, its multitude of measures being processed at one time. This is certainly true of so-called national media that have to limit themselves to the leading stories.

National media journalists solve their problem by reporting the institution rather than its individual members. Three-fourths of the House members in Robinson's mail survey said the national media never covered them at all.[39] Most of these representatives had not appeared even once on network news during the 95th Congress.

In the Senate, reporters hover around the "big names"—celebrities, presidential contenders, or key committee leaders. An extensive study of Senate coverage from 1965 to 1974 found that Senators Robert and Edward Kennedy, Mike Mansfield, Henry Jackson, Sam Ervin, Hubert Humphrey, and Jacob Javits were among those with the widest visibility. Senators' mass-media visibility hinges on staff size, committee chairmanships, seniority, state size, inner-club status, the vote garnered in the last election, and other factors. Low-visibility senators are sometimes dismissed by reporters as "a bland, faceless lot." [40]

Most observers claim the national press is tough on Congress. Indeed, most of Robinson's respondents claimed that over the past few years the press had become tougher—because of rising cynicism, Watergate exposés, or whatever. Assessing 263 "Congress stories" on the three TV networks in early 1976, Robinson found 36 negative stories (14 percent) and not a single story that placed Congress or its members in a favorable light.[41] In February of that year, when Congress had 30 days to revamp the Federal Election Commission or see it fall, David Brinkley remarked sardonically to his TV audience that, "It is widely believed in Washington that it would take Congress thirty days to make instant coffee."

Looking askance at governmental institutions is natural for men and women of the fourth estate. Cynicism pervades the journalistic fraternity, at least at the national level. Moreover, prizes and honors come to those who expose wrongdoing. The muckraking tradition of reform-minded journalism dates to the early days of this century; scandal-mongering and sensationalism go back much farther, to the very beginnings of mass-circulation papers.[42] This tradition is kept alive by investigative reporters such as Jack Anderson whose preoccupations include wrongdoing, congressional "perks," and "junketing" trips abroad.

Capitol Hill allows free play for underlying press cynicism. Granted, the press has a rich vein of material to mine—the Abscam and "Koreagate" affairs, not to mention the personal peccadillos of Wilbur Mills, Wayne Hays, Daniel Flood, Robert Bauman, and many others. Some evidence points to a new firmness on the national press's part in handling such cases. Comparing Flood's 1978-1979 bribery scandal with a parallel case a decade earlier, Robinson concludes that the press gave greater play to the more recent scandal. "The *overall* image coming out of the nationals—papers and networks combined—is more stark, more serious, more intrusive, and more investigative in 1980 than it has ever been." [43] But if the press is tougher than ever on wayward members, it's probably because law enforcement officers are tougher, too. Matters that would have been hushed up a generation ago—not just bribery or abuse of office, but personal problems like sexual harassment, homosexuality, or alcoholism—are these days broached openly.

Local reporters are more vulnerable to reprisals from their sources than are national reporters, and they are usually less tough on Congress. Members and press aides interviewed by Robinson expressed virtually no complaints about local press coverage. As a House committee chairman put it:

> The Washington press tends to appeal to the Washington psyche—and be politically sensational or more gossipy . . . [My state's] media tends to be a little more personalized and appreciative of our problems. I always enjoy appearing before the [local] media and find that they are courteous and considerate and professional.[44]

In the Flood bribery case, Robinson found that the local press played the stories more sympathetically than did national papers like the *Washington Post* or the *New York Times*. It was not so much that they slanted their stories, but that they focused on different angles and played them differently. The local press gave wider play, for example, to Flood's home town support than did out-of-town papers.

In the long run, coverage of the average lawmaker is more revealing than coverage of scandals. In the eyes of home-district media outlets, incumbents fare very well, getting lots of positive attention. Robinson cites the case of "Congressman Press"—a mid-level House member with an average press operation and untouched by scandal. One year Congressman Press issued 144 press releases, about three a week. That year the major paper in his district ran 120 stories featuring or mentioning him; more than half the stories drew heavily on the press releases. "On average, every other week, Congressman Press was featured in a story virtually written in his own office." [45]

Even when not drawn from press releases, local stories tend to be respectful if not downright laudatory. During a reelection campaign in Wisconsin, the late Republican Representative William Steiger's press aide observed that home town stories were so lavish in their praise that no self-respecting press secretary would have dared put them out. [46] It is very rare for the local press to pillory a local representative, as the Salt Lake City press did after Representative Allan T. Howe, D-Utah, was charged with soliciting two police-decoy prostitutes in his home town. [47]

Electronic media are more benign than print media. Most local radio and TV reporters are on general assignment and do little preparation for interviews; their prime goal is to get the legislator on tape. As one legislator said, "TV people need thirty seconds of sound and video at the airport when I arrive—that's all they want." [48]

"The press has failed to show the average Congressman as he really is," a Capitol Hill reporter charged some years ago.

> . . . [T]he average Congressman lives and works today far from the beaten path of press coverage; and the abuse of the system he either fights or engages in, and the failure of the system in dozens of its intricate parts, are far removed from the attention of the public and any possible response from it. [49]

The indictment hits both national and local press. The national press gives scant attention to individual legislators, beyond a few celebrities; the local press, understaffed and underprepared, normally lets local legislators speak as they wish in person or through their own press releases. Certain qualifiers must be introduced. First, the charge applies less to senators—some of whom receive wide coverage—than to representatives, most of whom are invisible outside their own districts. Second, it does not apply to legislators enmeshed in scandals, who are treated with greater candor today than in the past.

Generalizing about something as diverse as communications media is hazardous, but certain themes are undeniable. Individual members are not reported the same way as the institution of Congress. The Senate is reported differently from the House. The national press reports things differently than the local press does. In all, the content and quality of press coverage underscore the two Congresses: Congress as collective policymaker, covered mainly by the national press, appears in a different light from the politicians who make up Congress, covered mainly by local news outlets. There are local variations, to be sure, and senators receive more searching coverage than House members. When scandals occur, all bets are off. But in general, press coverage widens the gap between the two Congresses. It also gives the two Congresses different images—negative for the institution, more positive for individual members. Not surprisingly, these images are mirrored by average citizens.

CONGRESS'S PUBLIC IMAGES

As an institution, Congress is an enigma to most citizens. Its large size, its procedural mazes, its measured pace—all blur its image for the average person. Individual legislators, in contrast, are more readily understood. And they receive higher approval.

Congressional Fever Chart

At the most general level, citizens give Congress no better than a so-so report card—perhaps C-plus. In recent surveys, about twice as many respondents say Congress is doing a "poor" or "only fair" job as give it a "pretty good" or "excellent" rating. Figure 5-2 is a fever chart of congressional popularity from 1964 to 1981. The modern zenith of popularity occurred in 1964 and 1965, when President Lyndon Johnson and Congress were fashioning "Great Society" laws during a honeymoon period following President Kennedy's assassination. Since then, the overall trend has been downward.

Public approval of Congress—and the president—rises or falls with economic conditions, wars and crises, and waves of satisfaction or cynicism.[50] Because presidential and congressional ratings usually follow parallel paths, it might be thought that people use the more visible presidency as a benchmark for assessing Congress.[51] More likely, people form overall impressions of how the government is doing and rate both institutions accordingly. Oftentimes the images of the two branches diverge. As President Nixon slid deeper into the Watergate morass, Congress's ratings climbed; approval rose 18 points over four months in 1974, which the Gallup Poll attributed mainly to the House Judiciary Committee's televised impeachment hearings.[52]

Congress is by no means the sole target of public criticism. Surveys show that after the mid-1960s public confidence in all major institutions

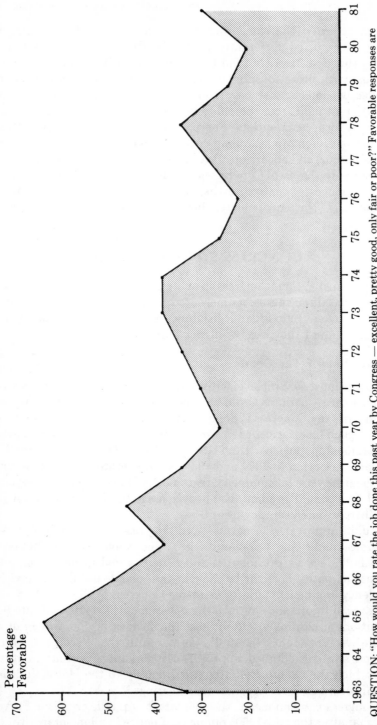

Figure 5-2 A "Fever Chart" of Congressional Popularity, 1963-1981

Percentage
Favorable

QUESTION: "How would you rate the job done this past year by Congress — excellent, pretty good, only fair or poor?" Favorable responses are "excellent" or "pretty good."

SOURCE: The Harris Survey. Figures for 1981 from NBC News-Associated Press Poll.

plummeted. Only 18 percent of the respondents in a 1980 Harris survey expressed "a great deal of confidence" in Congress, compared to 42 percent in 1966.[53] Similarly, colleges and universities commanded high confidence from only 36 percent of the people in 1980 (down from 62 percent in 1966), medicine from 34 percent (down from 73 percent). Clearly, the American people lack trust and confidence in their major institutions. Most analysts believe, however, that cynicism has not yet soured into out-and-out alienation, and that successful performance will be met with rising confidence levels.

In the wake of scandals involving members of Congress, many citizens have a jaded view of congressional ethics. Following the Abscam bribery revelations, nearly four out of five respondents in a Gallup survey agreed that some senators and representatives won election through "unethical and illegal methods in their campaigns."[54] In addition, two out of five believed that a fifth or more of Congress's members used questionable methods to get elected.

Given these negative attitudes, it is not surprising that the public finds reformism attractive. The Gallup Poll found two-to-one support for limiting the tenure of senators and representatives to 12 years.[55] This proposal has won approval overwhelmingly in surveys over the years. So have other reform proposals—ethics codes, campaign finance reforms, four-year House terms, and the like. However, views on these matters lack intensity, and few citizens are prepared to work or lobby to bring them about.

Despite their critical views, citizens expect Congress to play a strong, independent role in policymaking. Even in the 1960s, the era of the so-called "imperial presidency," people wanted Congress to take at least an equal role in foreign affairs, not to mention domestic policy.[56] More recently, a two-to-one majority said Congress should "examine in detail" President Reagan's proposed budget cuts and "go along only where it feels the program makes sense," rather than simply conceding the entire Reagan program.[57]

Let Us Now Praise Our Congresspeople

If Americans hold Congress at arms' length, they seem almost to embrace their individual senators and (especially) representatives. At the same time that surveys reveal unfavorable judgments of Congress's job, they show overall approval of the respondents' own representatives. In one 1980 survey, citizens gave their own representatives a favorable report card by a three-to-one margin (61 to 18 percent), disapproving of Congress's performance 51 to 32 percent.[58] At the same time large majorities of Americans thought members *in general* were unethical, only one in five thought their *own* congressman would accept a bribe if offered one.[59] Faint praise, to be sure; but the contrast is striking. More

Congressional Ethics

Members of Congress are bound by the Constitution, federal laws, party provisions, and House and Senate rules and conduct codes. Although many observers criticize loopholes, the panoply of regulations is quite extensive.

Constitution. Each chamber has the power to punish its members for "disorderly behavior" and, by a two-thirds vote, to expel a member. Members are immune from arrest during attendance at congressional sessions (except for treason, felony, or breach of peace); and "for any speech or debate in either house, they shall not be questioned in any other place." (Article I, Section 6) This latter provision protects lawmakers from any reprisals for expressing their views.

Criminal Laws. Federal laws make it a crime to solicit or accept a bribe; soliciting or receiving "anything of value" for performing any official act, service, or using influence in any proceeding involving the federal government; entering into or benefiting from any contracts with the government; or committing any fraud against the United States. Defendants in the so-called "Abscam" affair were convicted for violating these laws.

Ethics Codes. Adopted in 1968 and substantially tightened in 1977, the House and Senate ethics codes apply to members and key staff aides. They require extensive financial disclosure; restrict House members' outside earned income to 15 percent of salaries (senators' outside income is unlimited); prohibit unofficial office accounts that many members used to supplement official allowances; and impose stricter standards for using the congressional frank. *(See pp. 140-142.)* The House Committee on Standards of Official Conduct and the Senate Select Ethics Committee were created to implement the codes, hear charges against members, and issue advisory opinions.

Party Rules. Congressional parties can discipline members who run afoul of ethics requirements. House Democratic rules require a committee leader who is indicted to step aside temporarily; a leader who is censured or convicted is automatically replaced.

Federal Election Campaign Act Amendments of 1974. As amended in 1976 and 1979, FECA imposes extensive requirements on congressional candidates, incumbents as well as challengers. *(See Chapter 3, pp. 75-79.)*

concrete praise is found in incumbents' high rates of reelection, which persisted at the same time as low esteem of Congress as a whole.

"How come we love our Congressmen so much more than our Congress?" pondered Richard F. Fenno, Jr., a few years ago.[60] Part of the answer lies in the divergent standards by which the two Congresses—institution and individual member—are judged. In two nation-wide surveys, respondents were asked to rate their own representative's performance and express reasons for their ratings. The vast majority of the answers dealt with representatives' personalities or ability to serve the district in material ways. About three out of five answers in one survey concerned some aspects of the legislator's district service; one out of five cited the member's personal traits or reputation. Few responses pertained to policy issues. Rating Congress as a whole, most of these same people referred to policy concerns, although at a very general level.[61]

Another part of the answer lies in the media channels we have described. As we have seen, national and local coverage diverge significantly, both in focus and level of criticism. Studying the relationship between media coverage and public attitudes, Arthur H. Miller uncovered a strong relationship between a member's district press coverage and district perceptions of him or her. Local coverage of Congress as an institution, in turn, affects public attitudes toward the institution: the more national news approaches prevail in a given district, the more critical the perceptions of Congress.[62] As Robinson summarizes the situation:

> The national media, which reach everyone with their critical coverage of the institution, and the local media, which reach constituents and accommodate members, *together* serve as the single best explanation for the paradox of public opinion toward Congress.[63]

Whether or not this is true, it is certain that media play a part in public perceptions of Congress and its members. The media help also to explain apparent differences between senators and representatives. Senators, exposed to national coverage, are seen in a more neutral light than representatives, who are served by a more favorable local press. Senate contests, moreover, are covered more heavily than House races—which helps Senate challengers vault the all-important visibility gap. House challengers are rarely spotlighted by the media.

CONCLUSION

The two Congresses turn different faces toward the public. Congress as an institution is a major engine of policymaking and source of large portions of Washington news. Current news about policies is a major preoccupation of the so-called "national press"—TV networks, wire services, and leading newspapers. Their accounts of congressional policymaking are carried verbatim by local news outlets, print and electronic. Their basic mood is cool or even cynical. They tell their readers or viewers little about the personalities involved in policymaking, except for a few leaders and celebrities.

Individual lawmakers are more the province of the local press. In the case of congressional districts, outlets that pay any attention at all to legislators tend to give them respectful play. Understaffed and underbriefed, they quote the member's words or rely on office press releases. Senators draw more neutral coverage because statewide media or outlets in larger metropolitan areas tend to cover them in connection with national news. They are less able than House members to separate themselves from national policies.

The specialized press plays a key role by covering national news affecting special segments of the public. Surprisingly little is known about the specialized press, but it certainly shares in the powerful arrangements known as "subgovernments" or "iron triangles" described in Chapters 12 and 14.

Public perceptions of Congress display a predictable dichotomy. Congress is viewed in terms of generalized impressions of the state of the nation. In recent years these yielded to negative appraisals. Individual members, in contrast, are seen in rosier hues. In contrast to the institution, one's own representatives are viewed favorably and are usually reelected.

Our discussion of Congress's press relations and public image brings us to the heart of the two Congresses. If Congress and its members are viewed through different lenses, it hinges largely upon the divergent channels that communicate to the public. Everything Congress does is a product of individual politicians thrown together to chart the nation's policy. Their collective product affects all of us as citizens, and it is to that activity that we turn in Part III, A Deliberative Assembly of One Nation.

NOTES

1. Stephen Hess, *The Washington Reporters* (Washington: The Brookings Institution, 1981), p. 17.
2. Elizabeth G. McPherson, "The Southern States and the Reporting of Senate Debates: 1789-1882," *Journal of Southern History* (May 1946): 223-246. The authors are grateful for assistance on historical development given by Dennis Stephen Rutkus of the Congressional Research Service.
3. *Guide to Congress,* 2d ed. (Washington, D.C.: Congressional Quarterly, 1976), p. 600.
4. F. B. Marbut, *News from the Capitol: The Story of Washington Reporting* (Carbondale and Edwardsville, Ill: Southern Illinois University Press, 1971), pp. 97-102.

5. E. Pendleton Herring, *Group Representation Before Congress* (Baltimore: The Johns Hopkins University Press, 1929), p. 41.
6. Douglass Cater, *The Fourth Branch of Government* (Boston: Houghton Mifflin Co., 1959), p. 59.
7. Susan H. Miller, "Congressional Committee Hearings and the Media: Rules of the Game," *Journalism Quarterly* (Winter 1978): 657-663.
8. Richard Harris, *The Real Voice* (New York: Macmillan Publishing Co., 1964).
9. U.S., Congress, *Congressional Record*, 82d Cong., 2d sess., February 25, 1952, pp. 1334-1335.
10. David Halberstam, *The Powers That Be* (New York: Alfred A. Knopf, 1979), p. 248.
11. U.S., Congress, House, Select Committee on Congressional Operations, *Televising the House*, H. Doc. 95-231, 95th Cong., 1st sess., 1977.
12. U.S., Congress, House, *Viewer's Guide to the Televised Proceedings of the U.S. House of Representatives* (April 1980).
13. U.S., Congress, Senate, Committee on Rules and Administration, *Television and Radio Coverage of Proceedings in the Senate Chamber*, 97th Cong., 1st sess., 1981 committee print, pp. 4-5.
14. "How to Get the News to Come Out Your Way," *Washington Post*, June 7, 1981, p. D1.
15. David Burnham, "Congress's Computer Subsidy," *New York Times Magazine*, November 2, 1980, p. 96.
16. William Haydon, "How Congress's Computers Con the Public," *Washington Monthly* (May 1980): 45.
17. Burnham, "Congress's Computer Subsidy," p. 101.
18. Ibid., p. 98.
19. For descriptions of congressional radio-TV studios, see Ben H. Bagdikian, "Congress and the Media: Partners in Propaganda," *Columbia Journalism Review* (January-February 1974): 5-6; and Michael J. Robinson, "Three Faces of Congressional Media," in *The New Congress*, ed. Thomas E. Mann and Norman J. Ornstein (Washington, D.C.: American Enterprise Institute for Public Policy Research, 1981), pp. 62-63. Our understanding of media coverage of Congress relies heavily on the writings of Bagdikian and Robinson.
20. Robinson, "Three Faces of Congressional Media," p. 62.
21. Hess, *The Washington Reporters*, p. 165. See also Leo C. Rosten, *The Washington Correspondents* (New York: Harcourt Brace & World, 1937); and Robert O. Blanchard, "The Variety of Correspondents," in *Congress and Mass Media*, ed. Robert O. Blanchard (New York: Hastings House, 1974), pp. 168-180.
22. Ibid., p. 87.
23. Hess, *The Washington Reporters*, pp. 24-28.
24. *1981 Ayer Directory of Publications* (Bala Cynwyd, Pa.: Ayer Press, 1981), p. viii; *Broadcasting Yearbook 1980* (Washington: Broadcasting Publications, 1980), p. A2.
25. Ben H. Bagdikian, *The Information Machines* (New York: Harper & Row, 1971).
26. Bagdikian, "Congress and the Media: Partners in Propaganda," p. 5.
27. Len Allen, "Makeup of the Senate Press," in *Senate Communications with the Public*, by U.S., Congress, Senate, Commission on the Operation of the Senate, 94th Cong., 2d sess., 1977 committee print, p. 26.
28. Hess, *The Washington Reporters*, p. 61.

29. Charles Bosley, "Senate Communications with the Public," in *Senate Communications with the Public*, p. 17.
30. Donald R. Matthews, *U.S. Senators and Their World* (Chapel Hill: University of North Carolina Press, 1960), p. 213.
31. Ibid., p. 211.
32. Burns W. Roper, *Public Perceptions of Television and Other Mass Media: A Twenty-Year Review 1959-1978* (New York: The Roper Organization, 1979).
33. Elmer E. Cornwell, Jr., "Presidential News: The Expanding Public Image," *Journalism Quarterly* (Summer 1959): 282; Alan P. Balutis, "The Presidency and the Press: The Expanding Presidential Image," *Presidential Studies Quarterly* (Fall 1977): 251.
34. Robinson, "Three Faces of Congressional Media," p. 91.
35. Hess, *The Washington Reporters*, p. 98.
36. Michael Green, "Nobody Covers the House," *The Washington Monthly* (June 1970): 64.
37. Hess, *The Washington Reporters*, p. 102.
38. Ibid., pp. 103-104.
39. Robinson, "Three Faces of Congressional Media," p. 87.
40. David H. Weaver, G. Cleveland Wilhoit, Sharon Dunwoody, and Paul Hagner, "Senatorial News Coverage: Agenda-Setting for Mass and Elite Media in the United States," in *Senate Communications with the Public*, pp. 41-62.
41. Robinson, "Three Faces of Congressional Media," p. 73.
42. Roger H. Davidson, David M. Kovenock, and Michael K. O'Leary, *Congress in Crisis* (North Scituate, Mass.: Duxbury Press, 1966), pp. 45-46.
43. Robinson, "Three Faces of Congressional Media," p. 75.
44. Ibid., p. 77.
45. Ibid., pp. 80-81.
46. John F. Bibby and Roger H. Davidson, *On Capitol Hill: Studies in the Legislative Process*, 2d ed. (Hinsdale, Ill.: Dryden Press, 1972), p. 72.
47. Milton Hollstein, "Congressman Howe in the Salt Lake City Media: A Case Study of the Press as Pillory," *Journalism Quarterly* (Autumn 1977): 454-458, 465.
48. Robinson "Three Faces of Congressional Media," p. 84.
49. Green, "Nobody Covers the House," p. 66.
50. Glenn R. Parker, "Some Themes in Congressional Unpopularity," *American Journal of Political Science* (February 1977): 93-109.
51. Davidson, Kovenock, and O'Leary, *Congress in Crisis*, pp. 59-62.
52. The Gallup Poll, August 29, 1974.
53. ABC News-Harris Survey, November 24, 1980.
54. The Gallup Poll, March 20, 1980.
55. The Gallup Poll, May 17, 1981.
56. Bibby and Davidson, *On Capitol Hill*, p. 291.
57. The Harris Survey, March 30, 1981; ABC News-*Washington Post* Poll, April 1, 1981.
58. CBS News-*New York Times* Poll, August 1980.
59. CBS News-*New York Times* Poll, February 1980.
60. Richard F. Fenno, Jr., "If, As Ralph Nader Says, Congress Is 'The Broken Branch,' How Come We Love Our Congressmen So Much?" in *Congress in Change*, ed. Norman J. Ornstein (New York: Praeger Publishers, 1975), pp. 277-287.

61. Glenn R. Parker and Roger H. Davidson, "Why Do Americans Love Their Congressmen So Much More Than Their Congress?" *Legislative Studies Quarterly* (February 1979): 53-61.
62. Arthur H. Miller, "The Institutional Focus of Political Distrust" (Paper delivered at the annual meeting of the American Political Science Association, Washington, D.C., August 31-September 3, 1979).
63. Robinson, "Three Faces of Congressional Media," p. 90.

III

A Deliberative Assembly of One Nation

"**I** just wanted to tell you that the president's on the phone," Representative John Rousselot, R-Calif., announced on the House floor June 25, 1981. Speaker Thomas P. O'Neill, Jr., needed no reminder.[1] He watched a steady stream of legislators leave the floor to take calls from the president. The issue was how to consider the Republicans' budget-cut package called Gramm-Latta after its cosponsors, Phil Gramm, D-Texas, and Delbert L. Latta, R-Ohio. Republican leaders were striving for a single up-or-down vote on the budget package—sidestepping a Democratic ploy to split it into several portions. As President Reagan telephoned potential supporters, Republicans delivered a series of one-minute speeches favoring the GOP package. In the end President Reagan—and his party—won a stunning victory in the Democratic-led House. Republicans overturned the Democratic-fashioned "rule" for debate and substituted the procedure they preferred. The next day the GOP package passed.

Reagan's achievement was major and controversial: dramatic spending cuts in more than 200 national programs; consolidation of many federal activities into block grants to be administered by the states; nearly $140 billion in expected budget savings over a three-year period; and a giant stride in the direction of limiting or even reversing the growth of federal social programs.

President Reagan telescoped into five months a process that normally might require years of legislative deliberation. He adroitly orchestrated the actors that form the core of Part III: party leaders (Chapter 6), committees (Chapter 7), congressional staffs (Chapter 8), legislative procedures (Chapter 9), and Congress's relations with the White House, federal agencies, and interest groups (Chapters 10, 11, and 12, respectively).

Swift action on such momentous issues is uncommon on Capitol Hill. Probably only Franklin Roosevelt's first hundred days and Lyndon Johnson's "Great Society" are comparable in scope to President Reagan's early initiatives. Typically, Congress studies, listens, talks, and argues at great length in numerous forums: committee hearing rooms, party caucuses, and the House and Senate chambers.

This complex deliberative process is the subject of Part III as we continue to explore the two faces of Congress. As we suggested in Chapter 1, British statesman and philosopher Edmund Burke vividly described the dual character of the national legislature. The constituent-oriented Parliament, or Congress, he portrayed as "a Congress of ambassadors from different and hostile interests. . . ." The Parliament of substantive lawmaking was described in different terms:

> a deliberative assembly of one nation, with one interest, that of the whole—where not local purposes, not local prejudices, ought to guide, but the general good, resulting from the general reason of the whole.[2]

Part III focuses on Congress as a legislative and deliberative body. In Chapters 6 through 12 we take a look at the fundamental organizational and procedural components that shape congressional policymaking and presidential, bureaucratic, and interest group involvement in "the legislative struggle."[3] As we shall see, however, the deliberative assembly of one nation is never very far from local purposes and local prejudices. The individual voice is clearly heard in the institutional Congress.

NOTES

1. U.S., Congress, House, *Congressional Record,* daily ed., 97th Cong., 1st sess., June 25, 1981, p. H3365. See also *Washington Post,* June 26 and 27, 1981, p. A1.
2. Edmund Burke, "Speech to Electors at Bristol," in *Burke's Politics,* ed. Ross J. S. Hoffman and Paul Levack (New York: Alfred A. Knopf, 1949), p. 116.
3. Bertram M. Gross, *The Legislative Struggle* (New York: McGraw-Hill Book Co., 1953).

⑥

Leaders and Parties
in Congress

"A Republican Speaker in a Democratic House." An absurd
suggestion, some might say, given that the majority party always
elects the Speaker. In 1980, however, a group of House Republicans seriously considered trying to entice conservative Democrats
to join them and take control of the House during the 97th
Congress (1981-1983). "It would be hard to do," said a House GOP
member, "but I don't rule out the possibility." [1] In the end, the
scheme never materialized. A "minority candidate" could be
elected Speaker of the House or majority leader of the Senate; but
history tells us it's a remote possibility.

There is little that is bipartisan or nonpartisan about electing
the leaders of Congress. When the Democrats control the House,
the Speaker is Democratic. When the Republicans control, they
choose the Speaker. The same is true of the Senate majority
leader. In the twentieth century, it has never been any other way. [2]
Legislative organization is partisan organization. Whichever party
has the majority in the House or Senate controls not only the top
leadership posts but majorities on committees and subcommittees,
and all their chairmanships.

167

As we look in this chapter at the role of leaders and parties, we must remember that the two are bound together in the way Congress works. Each of the major political parties on Capitol Hill has a dual role, paralleling the two Congresses discussed throughout this book. In their "outside" role the parties help to recruit candidates and assist them in their campaigns. In their "inside" role the parties, especially when they are in the majority, are in charge of managing and organizing the Congress. This chapter focuses on the parties' inside function. We identify the leaders, describe their jobs, and discuss party caucuses, committees, and groups. Finally, we look at continuity and change in the congressional party system.

WHO ARE THE LEADERS?

The principal leaders of the House are the Speaker, majority leader, majority whip, minority leader, and minority whip. In 1981, with Republicans controlling the White House and the Senate, newly elected House Minority Leader Robert H. Michel of Illinois renamed his position "Republican leader." "Instead of responding to the will of a Democratic president and a Democratic Congress, in a defensive role, we're going to take the offensive," he said.[3] The key Senate positions are president pro tempore, majority leader, majority whip, minority leader, and minority whip. The Senate's minority leader in 1981, the former Democratic Majority Leader Robert C. Byrd of West Virginia, changed his title to "Democratic leader."

House

The Speaker. No other member of Congress possesses the visibility and authority of the Speaker of the House. Part of the Speaker's prestige comes from the office's formal recognition in the Constitution, which states that the House "shall chuse their Speaker." The Constitution does not require the Speaker to be a House member, but all of them have been. The Speaker is also second in line behind the vice president to succeed to the presidency. And, as the "elect of the elected," the Speaker stands near the president as a national figure.[4]

Before 1899 it was not uncommon for Speakers to have only a few years' service as representatives. Whigs Henry Clay of Kentucky and William Pennington of New Jersey were elected in their first terms. Clay still holds a record: election to the Speakership on November 4, 1811—his first day in the House. As Table 6-1 indicates, Speakers elected since 1899 have served an average of 24.1 years before their election to the Speakership. Once elected, Speakers have invariably been reelected as long as their party controlled the House.

Table 6-1 Speakers of the House, 1899-1981

Speaker	Dates of Service as Speaker	Years of Service	Years in House Before Election as Speaker
David B. Henderson, R-Iowa	1899-1903	4	16
Joseph G. Cannon, R-Ill.	1903-1911	8	28
Champ Clark, D-Mo.	1911-1919	8	16
Frederick H. Gillett, R-Mass.	1919-1925	6	26
Nicholas Longworth, R-Ohio	1925-1931	6	20
John N. Garner, D-Texas	1931-1933	2	28
Henry T. Rainey, D-Ill.	1933-1934	1	28
Joseph W. Byrns, D-Tenn.	1935-1936	1	26
William B. Bankhead, D-Ala.	1936-1940	4	19
Sam Rayburn, D-Texas	1940-1947, 1949-1953, 1955-1961	17	27
Joseph W. Martin, Jr., R-Mass.	1947-1949, 1953-1955	4	22
John W. McCormack, D-Mass.	1962-1971	9	34
Carl Albert, D-Okla.	1971-1977	6	24
Thomas P. O'Neill, Jr., D-Mass.	1977-	4+	24
	Average	5.7	24.1

SOURCE: *Members of Congress Since 1789*, 2d ed. (Washington D.C.: Congressional Quarterly, 1981), pp. 167-175.

NOTE: The House was technically without a Speaker for short periods following the deaths of Rainey and Rayburn. Congress had adjourned, and their successors were not elected until the next Congress convened.

During the Republic's first 120 years, Speakers gradually accrued power. By 1910 Speaker Joseph Cannon, R-Ill., dominated the House. He assigned members to committees; he appointed, and removed, committee chairmen; he regulated the flow of bills to the House floor as chairman of the Rules Committee; and he controlled floor debate. Taken individually, Cannon's powers were little different from those of his immediate predecessors, but taken together and exercised to their limits they bordered on the dictatorial. Moreover, Cannon's procedural grasp enabled him to stifle many of President Theodore Roosevelt's policies, such as food and drug, child labor, and antitrust laws. As Wisconsin Representative John Nelson declared to other frustrated House members, "President Roosevelt has been trying to cultivate oranges for many years in the frigid climate of the Committee on Rules, but what has he gotten but the proverbial lemons?" [5]

In 1910 the House forced Cannon to step down from the Rules Committee. The next year, when Democrats took control of the House, the new Speaker (Champ Clark of Missouri) was stripped of his authority to make committee assignments, and his power of recognition was curtailed. The Speakership then went into temporary eclipse. Power flowed to the majority leader, to the committee chairmen, and for awhile to party caucuses. "The Speaker became a figurehead, the [majority] floor leader supreme," wrote a contemporary of Cannon's.[6] Robert Luce observed:

> [The] most striking difference between the old and new methods is that, whereas leadership was then in the open, it is now under cover. Then the Speaker was the recognized centre of authority. Now nobody knows who in the last resort decides. [7]

The legacy of the historic 1910 revolt was to weaken central party leadership and its capacity to develop unified approaches to public problems. Modern Speakers, however, have regained some of the former powers of their office. "In the four years that I served as Speaker," said Republican Joseph Martin of Massachusetts, "no Republican went on an important committee without my approval." [8] Under a 1975 change, Democratic Speakers chair their party's Steering and Policy Committee, the group that assigns Democrats to committees. Another party change made that year permits the Speaker to nominate all Democratic members of the Rules Committee, including the chairman. The Speaker also acquired the authority in 1975 to refer measures to more than one committee, and to create ad hoc panels, subject to House approval.

As chief parliamentary officer and leader of the majority party, the Speaker is in a unique position to influence the course and record of the House. But his success rests less on formal rules than on personal prestige, sensitivity to member needs, ability to persuade, and skill at mediating disputes. As Speaker Sam Rayburn explained:

> The old day of pounding on the desk and giving people hell is gone. . . . A man's got to lead by persuasion and kindness and the best reason—that's the only way he can lead people.[9]

Floor Leaders. The Speaker's principal deputy—the *majority leader*—is his party's floor leader. He is elected every two years by secret ballot of the party caucus, although some Speakers essentially make the choice.[10] Unlike Republicans, House Democrats frequently elevate their next-in-line officer—from whip to majority leader to Speaker—as vacancies occur. Although succession is not guaranteed, Speaker O'Neill and his two immediate predecessors—Carl Albert, Okla., and John McCormack, Mass.—all moved from majority whip to majority leader to Speaker. No wonder strenuous contests are waged for a rung on the Democratic leadership ladder.

The floor leader is not to be confused with a *floor manager*. The floor managers, two for each bill, are frequently the chairman and ranking minority member of the committee that reported the bill. They try to steer it to a final decision.

The House majority leader usually is an experienced legislator. Jim Wright, D-Texas, for example, served 22 years on the Public Works and Transportation Committee and was slated to be its chairman in 1977 when he was elected floor leader in a four-way contest.[11] By modern custom, neither the Speaker nor the Democratic or Republican floor leaders chair committees.

House and party rules are silent concerning the majority leader's duties. His key job, defined by tradition, is to be principal floor defender and spokesman for his party. He also helps to plan the daily, weekly, and annual legislative agendas; consults with members to gauge sentiment for or against legislation; confers with the president about administration proposals, particularly when he and the president are of the same party; urges colleagues to support or defeat measures; and, in general, works diligently to advance the purposes and programs of the majority party.

The *minority leader* is the floor leader of the "loyal opposition," the titular leader of his party. (Speakers assume that role for the majority.) Minority leaders promote unity among party colleagues, monitor the progress of bills through committees and subcommittees, and forge coalitions with like-minded members of the opposition party. Bertrand Snell, R-N.Y., minority leader from 1931 to 1939, thus described the minority leader's duties:

> He is spokesman for his party and enunciates its policies. He is required to be alert and vigilant in defense of the minority's rights. It is his function and duty to criticize constructively the policies and program of the majority, and to this end employ parliamentary tactics and give close attention to all proposed legislation.[12]

The minority leader is well placed to shape his party's strategy for dealing with the majority. He can help formulate alternatives to majority-sponsored legislation, oppose outright the majority party and its leadership, or use parliamentary rules and procedures to win concessions from the majority or thwart its will. The GOP strategy of dealing with the Democrats, said Minority Leader Michel, "will be to begin first with negotiation. But with or without negotiations, we'll be continually probing the other side of the aisle. We're going to be prepared to mix it up." [13]

Like their majority counterparts, minority leaders are experienced legislators. Before Michel moved up from minority whip to Republican leader in 1981, he had spent 24 years in the House. His predecessor, John Rhodes, Ariz., was elected floor leader in 1973 after 20 years of House service.

Figure 6-1 Organization of the House of Representatives, 97th Congress (1981-1983)

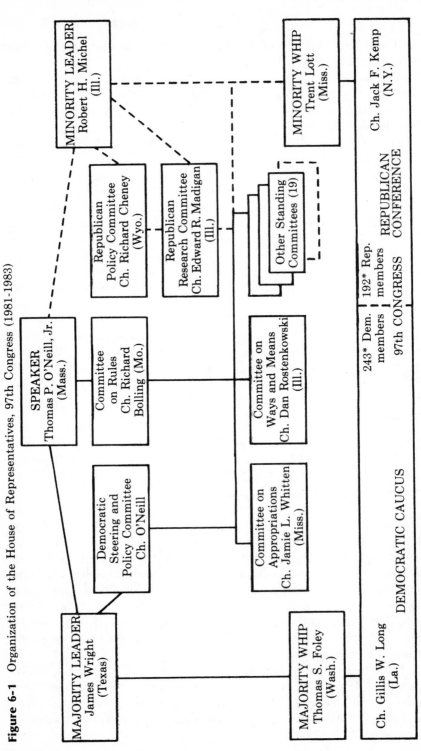

* As of January 5, 1981, when the 97th Congress convened.

The Party Whips. A whip is an assistant majority or minority leader. In the House, Republicans elect their whip; the Democratic whip is appointed by the majority leader after consultation with the Speaker, whose voice usually prevails. In 1977, Speaker O'Neill said, "I called Jim Wright and told him, 'You may think the majority leader names the whip, but the Speaker names the whip.' "[14]

As the term implies, the whip's job is to encourage party discipline and promote attendance at votes. In the modern Congress this is accomplished more by persuasion and hard work than by using punishment to "whip" members into line. And whips must be diligent in keeping track of their colleagues. Former GOP Whip Leslie Arends of Illinois (1943-1975) once resorted to a unique and successful strategem to find an absent colleague. He notified the member's local radio station, which then announced at 15-minute intervals: "If anybody spies Congressman So-and-So who should be representing us in Washington but isn't, tell him he's supposed to be in Washington tomorrow for an important vote." [15]

The whip system of each party, consisting of regional and assistant whips, aids the top leaders in gathering intelligence and counting votes. In the House, whips frequently stand by the doors to the floor, and signal their arriving colleagues to vote yea (thumbs up) or nay (thumbs down) on legislation. They also prepare weekly "whip notices" advising members of the upcoming floor agenda. *(See box on House whips, p. 174.)*

Senate

Presiding Officers. Unlike the House Speaker, the Senate majority leader is not the chief presiding officer of the chamber. In fact, the Senate has three categories of presiding officers.

First, the constitutional president of the Senate is the vice president of the United States. Except for ceremonial occasions, he seldom presides over Senate sessions, and he can vote only to break a tie. Vice presidents experienced in the ways of Congress, such as former GOP Representative George Bush or former Democratic Senator Walter Mondale, can effectively lobby senators on behalf of administration policies. Vice President Bush sits in on the weekly meetings of GOP committee chairmen and the luncheons with all Republican senators that follow those meetings. This participation is useful, he said,

> because people can come up to me and say, "Tell the president you can't do this, or you ought to do that." They let off steam on personnel problems and other things, and I get a pretty good sense of the mood that I can share with [President Reagan]. [16]

Second, the Constitution provides for a president pro tempore to preside in the vice president's absence. This officer in modern practice

House Democratic Whips . . .

Freshman Rep. Leon E. Panetta, D-Calif., was having a tough time finishing his phone call in the House cloakroom. First, Majority Leader Jim Wright, D-Texas, interrupted. Wright was followed by several other Democrats, who took turns breaking in. Then a page brought Panetta a note saying Speaker Thomas P. O'Neill, Jr., D-Mass., wanted to see him.

Panetta found no escape on the House floor. As he left the cloakroom and strode down an aisle into the crowded chamber, Jim Mooney, chief aide to Majority Whip John Brademas, D-Ind., spotted him. Mooney grabbed Norman Y. Mineta, D-Calif., and steered him toward Panetta. "Can you give us a vote on this?" asked Mineta.

Panetta said no, resisting his friend's plea to change the vote he had just cast in favor of an amendment by Joseph L. Fisher, D-Va., to cut about $7 billion from the first fiscal 1979 budget resolution (H Con Res 559).

Undaunted by the rejection, Mineta turned to court other Democrats who had voted for the amendment — and against the wishes of the Democratic leadership. Meanwhile, Wright wove his way through a crowd of younger members in the well of the chamber, urging them to switch their votes by signing little red cards stacked on a nearby table. O'Neill and Brademas stalked up an aisle, looking like hunters in search of prey. They, too, sought vote switches.

By the time the leaders stopped stalking — 10 minutes after the House scoreboard showed time had elapsed on the roll call vote — 16 Democrats had trooped down to the well to change their votes. The amendment, which had been a sure winner when time ran out, instead was defeated, 195-203.

The last-minute victory was credited to the arm-twisting of the Democratic leadership — O'Neill, Wright and Brademas. But backing up that highly visible trio were Mineta and other members of the leadership's intelligence-gathering network — the Democratic whips.

While the praise or blame for the Democratic record in the House ultimately rests with the party's leaders, many of the leadership's decisions are based on information the whips gather in their monitoring of members. It is the whips' advice that helps determine whether — and when — bills should be taken to the House floor. It is also the

is the senator of the majority party with the longest continuous service. "Because of his position as a senior member of the party, and often the chairman of a key committee, the leadership regularly consults the president pro tempore as to his views on policies and actions of the party," said Democratic leader Byrd.[17] In 1977 the Senate created the post of deputy president pro tempore for "any Member of the Senate who has held the Office of President . . . or Vice President of the United States." Senator Hubert H. Humphrey, D-Minn., vice president under Lyndon Johnson (1965-1969), was the office's first and only occupant.

. . . Counting, Coaxing, Cajoling

whips — representing the leadership — who can provide some of the muscle needed to get those bills passed.

Party whips originated in the British House of Commons, where they were named after the "whipper-in" — the rider who keeps the hounds together during a fox hunt. The first Democratic whip in the U.S. House was appointed in 1900 — three years after the Republicans named a party whip.

Unlike the British system, where political parties are well disciplined and a whip's major concern is good party attendance, whips in the U.S. House cajole as well as count noses.

In the 95th Congress, where Democrats hold a nearly 2-1 edge over Republicans and enjoy administration support on most major bills, it might seem unusual for the Democratic whips to be called on for more than an occasional nose count. But Brademas has had his troops out counting — and coaxing — votes on 63 bills or amendments since he became majority whip in 1977.

And when Brademas expanded his empire by adding seven new whips last year, he was not featherbedding, say several experienced whips. The additional people were needed to combat changes in the House that have made the whip's job of gathering votes for the leadership "a hell of a lot more difficult than it used to be," said George E. Danielson, D-Calif., who is serving his eighth year as a whip.

The major change cited by several of the whips is the independence of members elected in recent years, which makes a party loyalty appeal for votes more difficult.

"At one time you'd blow a whistle and say this is what the party wants and the members would line up and say, 'Yes sir, yes sir, yes sir,' " said Joe Moakley, D-Mass., an at-large whip in Brademas' operation and once the sole Democratic whip in the Massachusetts House.

However, younger members no longer are kept meekly disciplined by the House seniority system. "Today they get elected on Monday and they are giving a [floor] speech on Tuesday," said Moakley. . . .

SOURCE: Excerpted from Ann Cooper, "House Democratic Whips: Counting, Coaxing, Cajoling," *Congressional Quarterly Weekly Report,* May 27, 1978, pp. 1301-1306.

Third, a dozen or so majority senators, typically junior members, serve about half-hour stints each day as the presiding officer. None of the Senate's presiding officers compare to the House Speaker.

Floor Leaders. The *majority leader* is the head of the majority party in the Senate, its leader on the floor, and the leader of the Senate. Nowhere mentioned in the Constitution, the position evolved from the party post of conference (caucus) chairman during the late 1800s and early 1900s.[18] Similarly, the *minority leader* heads the minority party in

Table 6-2   Senate Floor Leaders, Democrats and Republicans, 1911-1981

Floor Leader	*Dates of Service as Floor Leader*	*Years of Service*	*Years in Senate Before Election as Floor Leader*
Democrats			
Thomas S. Martin, Va.	1911-1913, 1917-1919 †	4	16
John W. Kern, Ind.	1913-1917 †	4	2
Gilbert M. Hitchcock, Neb.	1919	1	8
Oscar W. Underwood, Ala.	1920-1923	3	5
Joseph T. Robinson, Ark.	1923-1933, 1933-1937 †	14	10
Alben W. Barkley, Ky.	1937-1947,† 1947-1949	12	10
Scott W. Lucas, Ill.	1949-1951 †	2	10
Ernest W. McFarland, Ariz.	1951-1953 †	2	10
Lyndon B. Johnson, Texas	1953-1955, 1955-1961 †	8	4
Mike Mansfield, Mont.	1961-1977 †	16	8
Robert C. Byrd, W.Va.	1977-1981,† 1981-	4	18
	Average	6.4	9.2
Republicans			
Shelby M. Cullom, Ill.	1911-1913 †	2	27
Jacob H. Gallinger, N.H.	1913-1918	5	22
Henry Cabot Lodge, Mass.	1919-1924 †	5	26
Charles Curtis, Kan.	1924-1929 †	5	15
James E. Watson, Ind.	1929-1933 †	4	13
Charles L. McNary, Ore.	1933-1945	12	16
Wallace H. White Jr., Maine	1945-1947, 1947-1949 †	4	14
Kenneth S. Wherry, Neb.	1949-1951	2	6
Robert A. Taft, Ohio	1953†	1	14
William F. Knowland, Calif.	1953-1955,† 1955-1959	6	8
Everett McKinley Dirksen, Ill.	1959-1969	10	8
Hugh Scott, Pa.	1969-1977	8	10
Howard H. Baker Jr., Tenn.	1977-1981, 1981†-	4+	10
	Average	5.2	14.5

SOURCE: Randall B. Ripley, *Power in the Senate* (New York: St. Martin's Press, 1969), p. 30; Robert L. Peabody, *Leadership in Congress:. Stability, Succession, and Change* (Boston: Little, Brown & Co., 1976), p. 328; and *Members of Congress Since 1789,* 2d ed. (Washington, D.C.: Congressional Quarterly, 1981), p. 178.

NOTE: A dagger (†) indicates dates of service as majority leader.

the Senate, and is elected biennially by secret ballot of his party colleagues. Table 6-2 identifies the modern Senate floor leaders. Historically, the majority leadership has had its ups and downs. Democrat Scott Lucas of Illinois often was frustrated in trying to enact President Harry S Truman's program. A coalition of Republicans and southern Democrats made Lucas's life difficult for two years, until Illinois voters ended his political career in 1951. Lucas's successor, Ernest McFarland of Arizona, also lost reelection after only two years as majority leader.

With these two consecutive defeats, some senators might have viewed the position of majority leader more as a liability than an asset. All this changed, however, when Republican Robert A. Taft of Ohio became majority leader in 1953. Although Taft served less then a year before his death, he enhanced the stature of the office and underscored its potential as an independent source of authority. He "proved a master of parliamentary procedures" and contributed to his party's cohesiveness, which "showed more unity on key roll-call votes in 1953 than at any time in years." [19]

Unlike Taft, who served 14 years before he became party leader, Lyndon Johnson was elected minority leader in 1953 after only four years of Senate service. In 1955 he became majority leader when the Democrats gained control of Congress during Dwight D. Eisenhower's first term. Johnson possessed a winning combination of personal attributes that helped him gain the top party office. "He doesn't have the best mind on the Democratic side," declared Richard Russell of Georgia, the de facto leader of Senate Democrats. "He isn't the best orator; he isn't the best parliamentarian. But he's the best combination of all of these qualities." [20]

Known for his powerful abilities to persuade, Johnson transformed the Democratic leadership post into one of immense authority and prestige. His extensive network of trusted aides and colleagues made him better informed about more issues than any other senator. Opposition party control of the White House gave the aggressive Johnson the luxury of choosing which policies to support and which strategies to employ to get them enacted. And his pragmatic outlook, domineering style, and arm-twisting abilities made him the premier vote-gatherer in the Senate. The majority leader's awesome display of face-to-face persuasion has been called the "Johnson Treatment."

> The treatment could last ten minutes or four hours. It came, enveloping its target, at the LBJ ranch swimming pool, in one of LBJ's offices, in the Senate cloakroom, on the floor of the Senate itself.... Its tone could be supplication, accusation, cajolery, exuberance, scorn, tears, complaint, the hint of threat.... Interjections from the target were rare. Johnson anticipated them before they could be spoken. He moved in close, his face a scant millimeter from his target, his eyebrows rising and falling. From his pockets poured clippings, memos, statistics,

mimicry, humor, and the genius of analogy made The Treatment an almost hypnotic experience and rendered the target stunned and helpless. [21]

Buttressing Johnson was an "inner club," a bipartisan group of senior senators, mainly southern Democrats such as Russell. The club, some people said, exercised real power in the Senate through its control of chairmanships and the committee assignment process.[22] There were even unwritten rules of behavior ("junior members should be seen and not heard") that encouraged new senators to defer to the "establishment."

Johnson's successor, Mike Mansfield, D-Mont., sharply curtailed the role of majority leader. He viewed himself as one among equals. "I can see a Senate with real egalitarianism, the decline of seniority as a major factor, and new senators being seen and heard and not being wallflowers," Mansfield said.[23] He permitted floor managers and individual senators to take public credit when measures were enacted. Significant organizational and procedural developments occurred in the Senate during his leadership. As one student of Congress wrote:

> The unwritten rule that freshmen Senators would play no visible role in floor debate was relaxed and eventually forgotten. He presided over an expansion in the number of subcommittees, a development which permitted relatively junior Senators to receive subcommittee chairmanships and the accompanying staff support. He rarely intruded on committee operations.[24]

When Robert C. Byrd served as majority leader from 1977 to 1981, the Senate was more democratic, more assertive, more independent, and more open to public view. Byrd had a style somewhere between that of the flamboyant Johnson and the relaxed Mansfield. "Circumstances don't permit the Lyndon Johnson style," he observed. "What I am saying is that times and things have changed. Younger Senators come into the Senate. They are more independent. The 'establishment' is a bad word. Each wants to do his 'own thing.' " [25]

Byrd recognized that he had to cater to individual members. On the other hand, the majority leader is charged with processing the Senate's workload. Caught between individual and institutional pressures, Byrd employed his formidable parliamentary skills and controls to accommodate colleagues and expedite the Senate's business.

Howard H. Baker of Tennessee succeeded Byrd as majority leader after the Republicans gained control of the Senate in 1981. As the first GOP majority leader in almost three decades, and after making an unsuccessful run for the presidency, Baker found the new position much to his liking. "I really enjoy the hell out of this job," he told an interviewer. "It is pure delight." [26]

After Baker was elected majority leader, he said he wanted to make the Senate a truly deliberative body again. "I'd like to see us restore the

Senate Majority Leader
Lyndon B. Johnson, D-Texas,
gives "The Treatment" to Senator
Theodore Francis Green, D-R.I.

Figure 6-2 Organization of the Senate, 97th Congress (1981-1983)

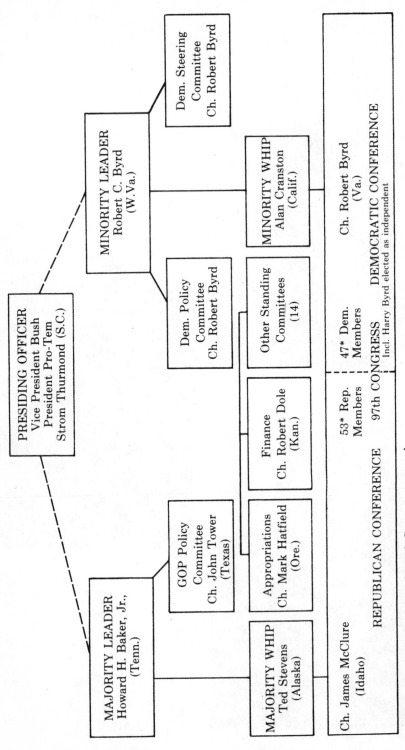

* As of January 5, 1981, when the 97th Congress convened.

nature of the Senate as a great debating institution," Baker said. "Our committees report too much legislation and we pass too many laws. We don't need more laws. We need less laws." [27] The goals of Senator Baker suggest that the floor leader's job is not institutionalized, but varies widely according to the incumbent's personal style, interests, and the circumstances in which he operates.

As we have seen, the Senate when Johnson was majority leader was a very different place than in Mansfield's, Byrd's, or Baker's day. Table 6-3 compares the Johnson (1955-1961) and post-Johnson (1961-1981) periods.

The Senate *minority leader* consults continually with the majority leader. If a member of the president's party, the minority leader has the

Table 6-3   Comparison of Majority Leaders, 1955-1981

Lyndon B. Johnson *(1955-1961)*	*Mike Mansfield* *(1961-1977)* *Robert C. Byrd* *(1977-1981)* *Howard H. Baker, Jr.* *(1981-)*
Power in the hands of seniority leaders	More even distribution of power among all senators
Large authority centralized in an aggressive majority leader	Less aggressive leadership styles
More centralized decisionmaking among fewer committees and subcommittees	Greater decentralization of decisionmaking among more committees and subcommittees
Staff resources controlled by senior members	Staff resources available to junior and minority members
Smaller workload	Larger workload of complex measures affecting new policy areas
Senate less assertive in relation to the president	Senate more assertive of its authority in relation to the president
Fewer citizen demands on senators	More constituent demands on senators
More stable membership	Less experienced membership as rapid turnovers mark senatorial career patterns
Less open institution (secret committee sessions are common)	More public institution ("sunshine in Congress")
Southern Democrats dominate the Senate	Northern and midwestern Democrats dominate the Senate; in 1981, GOP members from the West, South, and Southwest are in key positions

traditional obligation of trying to carry out the administration's program. He and his party colleagues also exercise a "watchdog" role over the majority party—offering criticisms, frustrating majority actions, and formulating alternative proposals. The minority leader's role and operating style are influenced by personality, colleagues' expectations, the party's size in the Senate, control of the White House, and the leader's view of his proper function. Comparing the leadership styles of Minority Leader Everett Dirksen, R-Ill., and his GOP predecessor, Senator William Knowland of California, a Republican senator said, "Bill Knowland saw the leadership primarily as a matter of stating a principle and standing on it. Dirksen doesn't stand on principle so much; he gets on the phone and lines up votes for our side." [28]

Party Whips. The Senate's whip system is smaller than the House's but carries out similar functions. "The best nose-counter in the Senate [Alan Cranston of California, at that time majority whip, later the minority whip] is absolutely superb when it comes to knowing how the votes will fall in place on a given issue," said Democratic leader Byrd. [29] During the 97th Congress there were 13 Democratic deputy whips in the Senate. They were appointed by Cranston after consultation with Byrd. As of mid-1981 Republicans still had not appointed any assistant whips.

HOW LEADERS EMERGE

Selection

Senators and representatives elect their top leaders before the beginning of each new Congress by secret ballot in their party caucuses. Although the whole House votes for the Speaker, it is a pro forma election. With straight party voting the as-yet-unbroken rule on this and other organizational matters, the majority party has always elected the Speaker.

Length of prior legislative service in Congress is not the only criterion that influences the election of party leaders. Other factors considered are ideological or geographical balance in the leadership, reputation for hard work and competency in procedural and organizational matters, and personal attributes such as energy, youth, or persuasive talent.

Representative Michel, for example, waged a vigorous fight in 1980 to win election as House Republican leader. His opponent, Guy Vander Jagt of Michigan, stressed oratorical ability and talent as an effective party spokesman.

> House Republicans are a forgotten minority of a forgotten body. If people pay attention they focus on [Speaker Thomas P.] Tip O'Neill. That's why we need someone who can project to the American

public. . . .Inevitably one winds up on "Face the Nation" or "Meet the Press." I think I would be a more forceful spokesman than Bob Michel.

Michel, on the other hand, emphasized parliamentary experience, service as minority whip, and bargaining skills.

> It takes more than a TV image to get things enacted into law. You can make beautiful speeches, but the bottom line is going to be enactment of the Reagan program.
>
> Let's not forget we're still down 51 votes. Guy Vander Jagt has no experience on the floor and he'd be rebuffed on the other side of the aisle because he's been such a political partisan. A day-to-day diatribe would not serve the political process. [30]

In a thorough analysis of congressional leadership, Robert Peabody found that "the most pervasive and continuing influence upon leadership selection for party office has been exerted by the personality and skill of the candidates and, especially, of the incumbent." [31] External factors, such as media and interest group activity, influence the leadership selection process indirectly. Serious GOP election losses in the 1960s contributed to House Republican leadership turnover, while Democratic image problems in the 1980s caused restiveness with their leaders.

For the most part, House and Senate leaders are in the mainstream of their party. Typically party leaders attract the support of colleagues from diverse ideological and regional backgrounds. "As a member of the leadership," said Senate Democratic leader Byrd, "it is my duty to bring north and south, liberals and conservatives together; to work out compromises. . . . I think it takes a centrist to do that." [32]

Leadership 'Perks'

By custom, rule, and law, party leaders have a number of useful prerogatives and perquisites that augment their influence. They are accorded priority in recognition on the floor, they receive higher salaries and more office space than other members, and they receive added staff. They attract national media attention that they can use to influence public and member attitudes on issues. Party practices also can enhance leadership authority. Senate Democrats permit their floor leader to chair the Policy Committee, the Steering Committee, and the Conference. Senate Republicans, on the other hand, have different members head their counterpart panels.

The Speaker by modern custom is not assigned to any committee, and the majority leader and minority leader rarely are committee members. Majority Leader Wright, however, has been a member of the Budget Committee since its creation in 1974 and his own election as floor leader three years later.

Serving as a party leader in the House is a full-time position. By contrast, every party leader in the Senate sits on several committees.

The smaller size of the Senate allows leaders to share in committee work while discharging their leadership duties. Johnson, Mansfield, and Byrd each contributed notably in space, international, and energy policy, respectively.

In 1980 Democratic leader Byrd merged his concern for coal producers in his state (West Virginia) with his privilege of recognition to modify the 1977 strip mining reclamation law. As floor leader, Byrd was recognized by the presiding officer whenever he stood up. By gaining recognition before other senators could do so, Byrd prevented others from offering amendments. This frustrated Senator Howard Metzenbaum, D-Ohio, who said, "I do feel very strongly that a member of this body should not be precluded by parliamentary procedures which favor the majority leader. . .so far as gaining recognition is concerned." [33] In the end, this tactic helped Senator Byrd in getting the Senate to amend the strip mining law.

WHAT ARE THE LEADERS' JOBS?

House and Senate leaders have basically the same job: to bring coherence and efficiency to a decentralized and individualistic legislative body. Leadership duties break down into institutional and party functions. Both kinds of functions point toward the parties' objective of influencing policymaking in conformity with their political leanings.

Institutional Jobs

Organizing the Chamber. Party leaders influence congressional organization and procedure. They help select the chief administrative officers of the House or Senate, oversee committee jurisdictional revisions, and revise congressional rules.

In 1979 the Senate modernized its rules largely through the initiative of Democratic leader Byrd, who was instrumental in rules changes that curbed the filibuster in 1975 and realigned committee jurisdictions in 1977. Notable House rules changes had occurred in 1890 when GOP Speaker Thomas B. Reed limited the minority party's ability to obstruct and conferred additional authority on the Speakership. Today's revisions sometimes have the same objectives. The majority convenes in caucus prior to the start of each Congress, drafts a rules package, and then approves it in the House on a party-line vote. Rule changes in the late 1970s strengthened the Speaker's control over floor proceedings. To expedite action on some legislation, the Speaker can now defer or cluster (back-to-back) roll call votes, or reduce the time allotted for them.

Scheduling Floor Business. Party leaders decide—after consulting with committee leaders, interested members, the president, and others—when and in what order measures should come up for debate. "In scheduling the program for the Congress one must be constantly aware of the importance of maintaining a little suspense," said House Majority Leader Wright. "I learned this from Agatha Christie. Always hold something back and keep people guessing a little bit." [34]

Once a bill is scheduled for action, the leaders' job is then to see that members vote—a more difficult task than merely herding bodies into the chamber. Party leaders may seek out certain members to speak on an issue because their endorsement can persuade other legislators to support it. Or they may delay action until the bill's sponsors are present. "The leadership must have the right members at the right place at the right time," said Byrd in 1975 when he was the Senate's majority whip.[35]

In short, leaders' scheduling prerogatives mold policy; arranging when bills reach the floor can seal their fate. In spring 1981 the Reagan administration announced plans to sell five AWACS, sophisticated radar surveillance planes, to Saudi Arabia. Concerned about undermining Israeli security, many members vigorously opposed the sale. Senate Majority Leader Baker told Reagan the proposal would have a tough time passing in Congress, and he "strongly urged the administration to give members of Congress the opportunity to have an input—to offer advice on the final shape and form of the package that might be submitted." [36] Reagan agreed to hold back the arms proposal to give Baker and others time to win support.

Party leaders are under pressure—particularly late in the session—to process essential legislation. This responsibility for the business of Congress sometimes conflicts with the scheduling preferences of election-minded members. (Again we see a tension between the "general interest of the whole," in Burke's words, and "local interests.") In 1980 Senate leaders planned little business for Mondays and Fridays to enable campaigning members to return home. Senator Barry Goldwater, R-Ariz., became frustrated with the "Tuesday to Thursday" club.

> I personally am getting a little tired of having to jam the work of this Senate into 3 days to take care of the Senators who are running for reelection, and I happen to be one of them. But my getting home is not as easy as going to New Hampshire or to Kentucky or to some other State that is literally next door. [37]

Influencing Colleagues. Party leaders also have the task of persuading members to support their legislation. In the modern Congress "twisting arms" or "breaking elbows" means pleading and cajoling to coax votes. While leaders generally seek to influence members of their own party and chamber, they also try to win cooperation from the other chamber and from the opposition party. Democratic and Republican leaders in the House and Senate regularly confer with each other to promote unity and understanding between the chambers. Senate and House GOP leaders have met every Monday afternoon since 1970 to discuss policies, strategies, and politics. Senate leaders frequently consult their counterparts in the other party on scheduling and other problems; House leaders do the same.[38]

Party leaders do not have to rely solely on their powers of persuasion, however. Their access to strategic information gives them an edge in influencing colleagues.

> Because of an improved whip system and because members will respond more candidly to leadership polls than to lobbyist or White House polls, [leaders] have perhaps the most important information in a legislative struggle—information on where the votes are and (sometimes) what it will take to win certain people over.[39]

Top leaders hold a variety of tangible and intangible rewards they can bestow or withhold. They can name legislators to special or select committees, influence assignments to standing committees, aid reelection campaigns, smooth access to the White House or executive agencies, single out legislators for high praise, and furnish numerous other services. As Speaker O'Neill commented during an interview:

> You know, you ask me what are my powers and my authority around here? The power to recognize on the floor; little odds and ends—like men get pride out of the prestige of handling the Committee of the Whole, being named Speaker for the day.... [T]here is a certain aura and respect that goes with the Speaker's office. He does have the power to be able to pick up the telephone and call people. And Members often times like to bring their local political leaders or a couple of mayors. And often times they have problems from their area and they need aid and assistance.... We're happy to try to open the door for them, having been in the town for so many years and knowing so many people. We do know where a lot of bodies are and we do know how to advise people. [40]

Adroit leaders know how to wield these "little odds and ends" to protect their party's interests. They are also sensitive to such matters as the public visibility of an issue, the extent of constituency interest in it, the size of their majority, and the likelihood of presidential intervention.[41]

Consulting the President. A traditional duty of party leaders is to meet with the president about administration goals and to convey legislative sentiment about what the executive branch is doing, or not doing. This consultative duty is performed mainly by leaders of the president's party. "My role is different when the president is in my own party," said Democratic leader Byrd when he was Senate majority leader. "With a Republican president it would be more incumbent on me to work to mold an alternative course, to speak out more, as when Lyndon Johnson was majority leader with President Eisenhower." [42]

When leaders oppose programs sponsored by their party's president, they usually step aside. Other leaders of the party who support administration views will then advocate and defend them on the floor. Alben W. Barkley, D-Ky., who was both Senate majority leader (1937-1947) and minority leader (1947-1949), went so far as to say, "[B]y and large, no matter what party is in power—no matter who is President— the majority leader of the Senate is expected to be the legislative spokesman of the administration." [43] The tug between institution and party is evident in this job.

Party Jobs

Organizing the Party. Top congressional leaders help to organize the party by selecting partisan colleagues for standing committees, revising party rules, choosing other party leaders, and appointing party committees. In 1981 Senate Democratic leader Byrd appointed several panels to develop party responses to Reagan administration programs. He also appointed a Democratic Leadership Council to "analyze what went wrong in the election and plan strategy and raise funds for the midterm elections of 1982." [44] Upset by their fall to minority status, Democrats looked forward to winning back institutional control of the Senate.

Promoting Party Unity. Another informal assignment of congressional leaders is to encourage party unity among different factional groupings and behind priority legislation. Senate GOP leader Dirksen used social gatherings to accomplish this goal.

> . . .Dirksen brought the party members together in a series of social affairs. He held cocktail parties at the Congressional Country Club outside Washington, inviting all Republican senators and sometimes their wives too. These were calculated by Dirksen to improve party harmony and to build a friendly feeling for himself with all the Republican senators. "You'd be surprised," he once said, "at the amount of goodwill they produced. You'd be surprised at how chummy they get at a party with a drink in their hands. It generates a fellowship that you can't generate in any other way." [45]

Spokesman for Party. Leaders are expected to publicize their party's policies and achievements. They give speeches in various forums, appear on radio and television talk shows, write newspaper and journal articles, or hold regular press conferences. Customarily, Speaker O'Neill meets with journalists just prior to the start of every House session; Senate Democratic leader Byrd conducts Saturday press conferences.

Leaders also are their party's spokesmen and defenders on the floor. Dirksen was an effective party champion. Known for his oratorical and debating skills, he loyally defended President Eisenhower's programs against partisan attacks. "When Senator Hubert Humphrey teasingly suggested that the Eisenhower administration was suffering from what he called the dread disease of 'budgetitis,' an unwillingness to spend money for federal programs, Dirksen retorted in kind by diagnosing Humphrey's own illness as 'spenderitis' and 'squandermania.' " [46]

Campaign Assistance. Leaders frequently assist party members who need reelection help. House Majority Leader Wright sponsors a campaign fund dispensed to numerous colleagues. Such activities provide leaders with political IOUs that can be cashed in later. "I suppose that by making some contributions to colleagues, some colleagues might sense a little closer spirit of unity with the leadership program," Wright said in 1978.[47] Senator Byrd, a noted fiddle player, often plays at gatherings in the home states of Democratic senators up for reelection.

After Republicans won the White House and Senate in 1980, Democratic congressional leaders consulted with colleagues on the party's shape and future. Speaker O'Neill assumed a prominent role in trying to revitalize his party. The House Democratic Congressional Campaign Committee formed more than a dozen task forces to help colleagues in tight races, raise funds, instruct candidates, and target vulnerable Republicans. GOP congressional leaders also began preparing for 1982 in hopes of winning control of the House and enlarging their margin in the Senate.

Congressional leaders maintain relations with national party organizations and with other groups. For example, House and Senate Democratic leaders are members of the Democratic National Committee and its executive committee. They also were actively involved in the February 1981 choice of Charles Manatt to replace John White, a Carter appointee, as head of the national committee.

THE CONGRESSIONAL PARTIES

The Democratic and Republican parties in the House and Senate are similar in some ways and different in others. The smaller Senate emphasizes individualism, reciprocity, and mutual accommodation. Partisan conflict, as a result, tends to be muted, and party leaders stress conciliation among senators regardless of party. In the larger, more impersonal House, majority party leaders sometimes ignore the wishes of the minority party, something that seldom occurs in the Senate.

Despite the different circumstances in which House and Senate leaders operate, their parties share some similar leadership components. They include, besides the leaders, party caucuses and committees, and informal party groups.

Party Caucuses

The organization of all Democrats or Republicans in the Senate is called the conference. Like their House counterparts (the Republican Conference and Democratic Caucus), Senate party conferences elect leaders, approve committee assignments, and debate party and legislative policies. On rare occasions, party caucuses strip fellow members of their committee seniority.

Democrats John Bell Williams of Mississippi and Albert Watson of South Carolina publicly endorsed Republican Barry Goldwater for president in 1964 and not Democrat Lyndon Johnson. When the Democratic Caucus met in January 1965, it assigned Williams and Watson to the last positions on their committees. In January 1967 Representative-elect Adam Clayton Powell of New York was removed from his chairmanship of the Education and Labor Committee because he had misused committee travel funds and acted contemptuously toward New York courts. The most recent case of the Democrats' disciplining a member occurred in January 1969. Representative John Rarick of Louisiana lost committee seniority because he supported George C. Wallace for president in 1968.[48]

Party caucuses are useful forums where party members and leaders can assess and sway sentiment on substantive and procedural issues. During the past decade, party caucuses have adopted procedural reforms that diluted committee chairmen's authority, strengthened the autonomy of subcommittees, and emphasized "juniority" over seniority.

Party Committees

The four congressional parties each establish committees to serve partisan needs and objectives. Of all the party committees, only the Senate majority and minority policy committees are created by law. This happened in 1947 after the House deleted a provision for policy committees from the Legislative Reorganization Act of 1946; the Senate then provided for its policy units in a legislative branch appropriations act. The policy committees provide advice on scheduling, encourage party unity, and discuss broad questions of party policy.

The Senate's policy committees do not make policy, and their influence has varied over the years. Each tends to assume greater importance when its party does not control the White House and thus needs policy guidance. For example, when Republicans lost the White House in the 1976 election, GOP Policy Committee Chairman John Tower of Texas said:

> After the election, I felt that with the Republicans out of power in the White House, I wanted to do more to arrive at Republican positions here in Congress. During the Republican Administration, of course, we were generally taking our initiatives from the White House. [49]

Party leaders do not always seek the advice of the policy committees. Majority Leader Johnson, as chairman of the Democratic Policy
Committee, seldom convened the unit. Senator Mansfield revived the
panel's role in party affairs although he deliberately kept its staff small.
Under Democratic leader Byrd, the Policy Committee's staff was
enlarged to enhance its analytical and coordinating capabilities.

The party committees in the Senate include:

Democratic

Policy (9 members)—formulates and coordinates recommendations for
party positions on specific measures and assists the party leader in scheduling measures.

Steering (22 members)—assigns Democrats to committees.

Campaign (15 members)—provides campaign aid to Democratic senatorial candidates.

Republican

Policy (23 members)—defines GOP position on specific issues, re-
searches procedural and substantive issues and drafts policy alternatives.

Committee on Committees (17 members)—assigns GOP members to
committees.

Campaign (15 members)—furnishes campaign assistance to GOP senatorial candidates.

In 1973 the House Democratic Caucus created a new Steering and
Policy Committee to give the party and its leaders "a forum for seeking
legislative coherence" and "a base for the exercise of legislative power
by an aggressive party leader." [50] The new committee would be chaired
by the Speaker and have 24 members, including its three elected
leaders, the appointed majority whip and four deputy whips, and four
other members appointed by the Speaker, as well as 12 members elected
by regional groups of House Democrats.

House Republicans have a number of party committees, too. Their
Committee on Research appoints task forces to consider alternatives to
majority legislation, stimulate committee hearings on issues, prompt
increased policy discussion among Republicans, and dramatize issues
for the November elections. Task forces on agriculture, foreign policy,
crime, and other topics have been created "where it was felt that the Republicans on standing committees could not, or would not, develop
alternatives to majority party proposals." [51] House party committees
include:

Democratic

Steering and Policy (29 members)—assigns Democrats to committees,
discusses and endorses party policy and strategy, and serves as an "executive" arm of the Democratic Caucus.

Campaign (52 members)—aids in the election of Democrats to the House.

Personnel (5 members)—oversees patronage appointments among Democratic members.

Republican

Policy (32 members)—considers policy alternatives to majority proposals and works to achieve consensus among GOP members.

Research (22 members)—conducts research for the Republicans.

Committee on Committees (Executive committee of 15 members)—assigns Republicans to the standing committees.

Campaign (21 members)—seeks to elect Republicans to the House.

Personnel (8 members)—reviews budgets of party committees and aids in supervision of Republican employees.

Informal Party Groups

Informal party groups have long been part of the congressional scene. In the pre-1970 period conservative southern Democrats formed a loosely knit alliance (the "Boll Weevils") that exercised powerful influence on legislation and congressional affairs through their disproportionate share of committee chairmanships and their coalition with conservative Republicans.

Today, a new "Boll Weevil" group of House Democrats—the Conservative Democratic Forum (CDF)—has sided with Republicans on key issues. "A new coalition has sprung up," said Speaker O'Neill. "One faction broke away from us—the conservatives and some moderates—and when they do that, Republicans gain control." [52] CDF members, who are mainly from the South, are fiscal and social conservatives who also believe in a strong military. By comparison, the earlier Boll Weevils were bound together largely by the race issue. A detailed analysis of unofficial congressional groups will be found in Chapter 12.

PARTY CONTINUITY AND CHANGE

"The Speaker runs roughshod over the minority," declared Representative Michel, then the House Republican whip. In a 1979 *Washington Star* article, Michel charged that an outsized Democratic majority led by Speaker O'Neill had "fixed" the rules of the House for the 96th Congress to steamroll the minority party. There was quick rebuttal from Representative Sidney Yates of Illinois, an O'Neill ally. Yates reminded Michel of what Republican Speaker Thomas "Czar" Reed once said to a Democratic critic. "Mr. Speaker," the critic asked, "what about the rights of the minority?" Retorted the Speaker, "The right of the minority is to draw its salary, and its function is to make a quorum." [53]

Sharp conflict of this type reflects only one pole of what might be called a "partisan continuum" in Congress. At the other pole is close cooperation (a common occurrence) between Democrats and Republicans. These dealings—and those that fall between the two poles— reflect the varied face of partisanship on Capitol Hill.

Two basic features of the congressional party system are its domination by the two major parties and its decentralization. These features reflect basic traits of the national party system and affect the way congressional parties go about their business.

The Two-Party System

The Democratic and Republican parties have dominated American politics and the Congress since the mid-nineteenth century. Scholars have posited various theories for the dualistic *national* politics of such a diverse country as the United States. Some trace the origins of the national two-party system to early conflicts between Federalists (advocates of a strong national government) and Anti-Federalists (advocates of limited national government). Continuation of dualism occurred in subsequent splits, such as North vs. South, East vs. West, agricultural vs. financial interests, and rural vs. urban areas.[54]

Constitutional, political, and legal arrangements are other bases of the two-party system. Plurality elections in single-member congressional districts encouraged creation and maintenance of two major parties. Under the winner-take-all principle, the person who wins the most votes in a state or district is elected to the Senate or House. This principle discourages the formation of third parties. In addition, many states have laws that make it difficult to create new parties.

Whatever mix of causes produced the two-party system, one thing is clear: few third-party or independent legislators have been elected to Congress during the twentieth century. The 63rd Congress (1913-1915) had the greatest minority party membership during this century: one Progressive senator and 19 representatives elected as Progressives, Progressive-Republicans, or Independents. Since 1951, only three senators and three representatives have been elected from minor parties or as independents.

Senate

Wayne L. Morse, Independent of Oregon (1945-1969)
Harry F. Byrd, Jr., Independent of Virginia (1965-   )
James L. Buckley, Conservative of New York (1971-1977)

House

H. Frazier Reams, Independent of Ohio (1951-1955)
Joe Moakley, Independent of Massachusetts (1973-   )
Thomas M. Foglietta, Independent of Pennsylvania
(1980-   )

Once elected, most independents convert to one of the major parties or vote with them in organizational matters. Control of Congress turns on the party principle. The majority party holds the major leadership posts, all committee chairmanships, and a majority on all committees. The minority party plays an important but secondary role. Third parties have no institutional status. Their participation in Democratic or Republican affairs is "by invitation only."

Party identification is probably the most important predictor of how members are likely to vote. "Party voting" fluctuates over time, as Figure 6-3 indicates, but the aggregate historical pattern highlights the reservoir of support for congressional parties.

Divided Party Control

Majority Leader Baker took charge of the Senate under at least two circumstances fairly unique to modern American politics. First, the GOP in 1980 captured control of the Senate for the first time in 26 years. As a result, Republicans assumed responsibility for passing—rather than simply opposing—legislation.

For example, a few weeks after he took office, President Reagan asked Congress to raise the public debt ceiling so that the federal government could meet its borrowing needs and pay its bills. Some Republican senators had never voted for such legislation; indeed, during the 1980 campaign they had denounced Democrats who voted for debt ceiling hikes. "We Republicans have been out on the campaign trail going after [Democrats], hammer and tong, portraying them as the party of big spending, inflation, and deficits that result," said William Armstrong, R-Colo. "Now a curious role reversal has occurred." [55] Whatever GOP senators said on the campaign trail, their support was necessary to pass the legislation—again showing the tug between individual leanings and institutional duties. In the end, the Senate passed the debt ceiling legislation 73 to 18.

Second, the two houses of Congress are controlled by different parties. As the table on page 450 makes clear, only twice before during the twentieth century has there been divided party control of Congress: the 62nd Congress (1911-1913) and the 72nd Congress (1931-1933).

How would divided party control affect bicameral and legislative-executive relations in the 97th Congress? In mid-1981 it was difficult to say, but at least three results seemed likely. First, President Reagan needed the support of some House Democrats to pass his programs. Second, conference committees were likely to assume greater importance as each chamber attempted to enact its version of disputed legislation. Finally, the minority party in each chamber would look for assistance from its "big brother" in the other body. "We're going to follow events in the House a lot more closely from now on," said a

Figure 6-3 Levels of Party Voting in Congress, 1960-1980

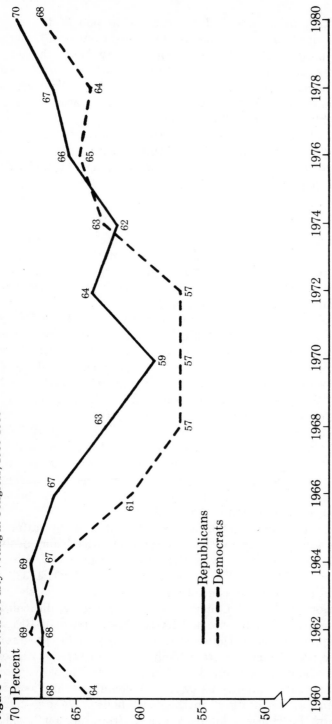

SOURCE: Party unity voting studies in *Congressional Quarterly Almanacs* for 1960, 1962, 1964, 1966, 1968, 1970, 1972, 1974, 1976, 1978, 1980. (Washington, D.C.: Congressional Quarterly).

NOTE: The graph shows the percentage of time the average Democrat or Republican in Congress voted with his party majority in partisan votes for the years listed. These "composite party unity scores" are based on votes that split the parties in the House and Senate, a majority of voting Democrats opposing a majority of voting Republicans.

Senate Democratic committee aide. "Before, we were pretty self-possessed here, but if we can't get our way as the minority, we may persuade our House contacts to put certain features into their bills and then fight for them when the measure comes to conference." [56]

Parties and Legislative Dispersion

Legislative policymaking during the twentieth century can be roughly divided into three eras: party government (early 1900s), committee government (early to mid-1900s), and subcommittee government (late 1960s forward).

Party Government. Around the turn of the century, centralized leadership was particularly evident in the House, where Speakers often were called "czars" between 1890 and 1910. Committee chairmen and rank-and-file members alike realized that success and advancement hinged on support from the Speaker. Speakers even referred to committee chairmen as their "cabinet." [57]

After the 1910 "revolt" that stripped Speaker Cannon of substantial powers, there was still a brief period (about 1911 to 1915) of party government in Congress. Democratic President Woodrow Wilson worked closely with the new Democratic majority leaders—Senator John Worth Kern of Indiana and Representative Oscar Underwood of Alabama—to enact his "New Freedom" policies. Democrats in each house used the caucus to ensure party regularity on policy matters.

On the tariff revision of 1913, for example, House Democratic leaders "resorted to the caucus, where . . . the proposed tariff bill was to be given pre-consideration and members attending bound by the caucus vote to vote with the majority of their party when the schedule should reach a vote on the floor of the House." [58] A GOP House member complained: "What is the use of offering amendments when the [Democratic] caucus majority have entered into a covenant with each other to vote down every amendment that might be offered?" [59]

The era of "King Caucus" declined after 1915, at least in part because of members' growing resentment of binding caucuses. Combined with the weakened position of elected party leaders, this ushered in the era of committee government.

Committee Government. The rise of congressional careerism, the heavier legislative workload, and the increased stress on seniority strengthened the autonomy of committees. "Dukes" or "barons" who often ruled their "fiefdoms" or "principalities" autocratically, chairmen were accommodated but not commanded by party leaders.

To build majority coalitions, party leaders became brokers and bargainers for support among members of their own party and even the opposition party. Persuasive skill replaced formal authority as the leadership's primary resource. Senior committee chairmen dominated policymaking. "On many occasions [Speaker] Rayburn virtually had to beg [Rules Chairman Howard W.] Smith to release important bills." [60] Rayburn's successors backed many of the 1970s changes as a way to dilute the chairmen's powers.

Subcommittee Government. Since the 1960s the number and power of subcommittees have grown, as we shall see in Chapter 7. Full committee chairmen exercise little influence over subcommittee activities, and party leaders find it difficult to deal with the countless power centers. The democratization of decisionmaking has made it harder for Congress to reach decisions. As a result, House and Senate leaders frequently resort to ad hoc devices to accomplish policy goals. When he was Senate majority leader, Byrd relied heavily on informal agreements to keep legislation moving. Speaker O'Neill often appoints party task forces to mobilize support behind specific bills.

"[E]very major piece of legislation that comes through here I put together an ad hoc committee," said O'Neill.[61] The Speaker appoints to these panels talented and hardworking junior Democrats, such as Philip Sharp, Ind., Butler Derrick, S.C., Richard Gephardt, Mo., and Norman Mineta, Calif. As Gephardt explained, "It helps to have a contemporary doing the lobbying. It's a normal human reaction. I'm going to feel a greater sense of kinship with people who came here when I did." [62] Task forces ensure that members loyal to the Speaker will be dispatched to round up votes on priority legislation. The success of the task forces led O'Neill in 1981 to name Representative Gephardt to a new party post: head of the task forces.

CONCLUSION

Congressional parties have elaborate organizations, and their leaders a multiplicity of roles and duties. Describing the Senate majority leader's job, Byrd said, "He facilitates, he constructs, he programs, he schedules, he takes an active part in the development of legislation, he steps in at crucial moments on the floor, offers amendments, speaks on behalf of legislation and helps to shape the outcome of the legislation." [63] Party leaders can do many things, but they cannot command their colleagues.

As a result, congressional leaders employ persuasion and other resources. These include scheduling (or not scheduling) bills for floor action, influencing committee assignments, appointing special or select committees, intervening with the White House, or arranging for campaign contributions to deserving members. The strength of today's leaders comes from control over scheduling, ability to do favors for members, personal prestige, and skill at crafting compromises and planning strategy. When the leaders lose key votes, it is seldom for lack of effort.

Compounding the party leaders' problems are new members who have sufficient analytical resources and expertise to challenge the leadership, chairmen, or the White House. In the 96th Congress Representative Dave Stockman, R-Mich., was this kind of member. (In 1981 Stockman left the House to become Reagan's director of the Office of Management and Budget.)

> When President Carter sent up his first [1979] standby gas rationing plan, Stockman, a second-term Republican, sent a point-by-point rebuttal to his House colleagues. His case, rich with numbers that countered the administration's, swayed enough members to kill the plan while congressional leaders looked on helplessly.[64]

There are plenty of opportunities in the contemporary Congress for newcomers to be seen and heard and to exert leadership in policies. This chapter focused on the formal party leaders and groups in each house. But there are members who are leaders because they can mobilize external support behind issues. Still others can be leaders if they are close to the president, as in the case of Senator Paul Laxalt, R-Nev., a longtime friend of Reagan's. "I will be a link between the White House and the Hill on a personal basis," he said.[65] And above all, there are committee leaders, both chairmen and ranking minority members.

We have seen that the "party principle" organizes Congress. But the "committee principle" significantly shapes most issues Congress will debate. These two principles are often in conflict. The first emphasizes integration, the second fragmentation. Traditionally, party leaders struggle to manage an institution that disperses policymaking authority to numerous workgroups. In our next chapter, we examine the important role of congressional committees.

NOTES

1. *Congressional Quarterly Weekly Report,* September 13, 1980, p. 2700.
2. In the Fourth Congress (1795-1797), the Federalists elected Jonathan Dayton of New Jersey Speaker even though the House was controlled by his opponents. Hubert B. Fuller, *The Speakers of the House* (Boston: Little, Brown & Co., 1909), p. 26; and Champ Clark, *My Quarter Century of American Politics,* vol. 1 (New York: Harper Bros., 1920), p. 305.
3. *New York Times,* December 10, 1980, p. B8.
4. See Chang-Wei Chiu, *The Speaker of the House of Representatives Since 1896* (New York: Columbia University Press, 1928); Mary P. Follett, *The Speaker of the House of Representatives* (New York: Longmans, Green & Co., 1896); and Paul Clancy and Shirley Elder, *Tip: A Biography of Thomas P. O'Neill, Speaker of the House* (New York: Macmillan Publishing Co., 1980).

5. U.S., Congress, *Congressional Record*, 60th Cong., 1st sess., February 5, 1908, p. 1652.
6. Lynn Haines, *Law Making in America: The Story of the 1911-1912 Session of the 62nd Congress* (Bethesda, Md.: Lynn Haines, 1912), p. 15. See James S. Fleming, "Re-establishing Leadership in the House of Representatives: The Case of Oscar W. Underwood," *Mid-America* (October 1972): 234-250.
7. Robert Luce, *Congress: An Explanation* (Cambridge, Mass.: Harvard University Press, 1926), p. 117. For studies of Speaker Cannon's leadership (1903-1911), see Kenneth W. Hechler, *Insurgency, Personalities and Politics of the Taft Era* (New York: Columbia University Press, 1940); Blair Bolles, *Tyrant from Illinois: Uncle Joe Cannon's Experiment With Personal Power* (New York: W. W. Norton & Co., 1951); and Charles O. Jones, "Joseph G. Cannon and Howard W. Smith: An Essay on the Limits of Leadership in the House of Representatives," *Journal of Politics* (September 1968): 617-646.
8. Joe Martin, *My First Fifty Years in Politics* (New York: McGraw-Hill Book Co., 1960), p. 181.
9. *U.S. News & World Report,* October 13, 1950, p. 30.
10. Randall B. Ripley, *Party Leadership in the House of Representatives* (Washington, D.C.: The Brookings Institution, 1967), p. 55. See also Ripley, *Majority Party Leadership in Congress* (Boston: Little, Brown & Co., 1969).
11. Bruce I. Oppenheimer and Robert L. Peabody, "How the Race for House Majority Leader Was Won—By One Vote," *The Washington Monthly*, November 1977, pp. 47-56.
12. Floyd M. Riddick, *Congressional Procedure* (Boston: Chapman & Grimes, 1941), pp. 345-346.
13. *Washington Post,* December 9, 1980, p. A4.
14. *New York Times,* November 18, 1977, p. A18.
15. *Nation's Business,* January 1952, pp. 52-53. See also Randall B. Ripley, "The Party Whip Organization in the United States House of Representatives," *American Political Science Review* (September 1964): 561-576; Ann Cooper, "House Democratic Whips: Counting, Coaxing, Cajoling," *Congressional Quarterly Weekly Report,* May 17, 1978, pp. 1301-1306; and Lawrence C. Dodd, "The Expanded Roles of the House Democratic Whip System: The 93rd and 94th Congresses," *Congressional Studies* (Spring 1979): 17-56.
16. *Washington Post,* March 30, 1981, p. A8.
17. U.S., Congress, Senate, *Congressional Record,* daily ed., 96th Cong., 2d sess., May 21, 1980, p. S5674.
18. Margaret Munk, "Origin and Development of the Party Floor Leadership in the United States Senate," *Capitol Studies* (Winter 1974): 23-41.
19. James T. Patterson, *Mr. Republican: A Biography of Robert A. Taft* (Boston: Houghton Mifflin Co., 1972), p. 593.
20. Robert L. Peabody, *Leadership in Congress* (Boston: Little, Brown & Co., 1976), p. 323.
21. Rowland Evans and Robert Novak, *Lyndon B. Johnson: The Exercise of Power* (New York: New American Library, 1966), p. 104.
22. See John G. Stewart, "Two Strategies of Leadership: Johnson and Mansfield," in *Congressional Behavior*, ed. Nelson W. Polsby (New York: Random House, 1971), pp. 61-92; William S. White, *Citadel: The Story of the United States Senate* (New York: Harper & Bros., 1956); Joseph S. Clark, *The Senate Establishment* (New York: Hill & Wang, 1963); and

Randall B. Ripley, *Power in the Senate* (New York: St. Martin's Press, 1969).

23. Richard E. Cohen, "Making an End to the Senate's Mansfield Era," *National Journal*, December 25, 1976, p. 1803. See also U.S., Congress, *Congressional Record*, 88th Cong., 1st sess., November 27, 1963, pp. 21754-21764.

24. John G. Stewart, "Getting the Act Together: The Senate's Leadership Role in the Policy Process," in Appendix to the Second Report With Recommendations of the Temporary Select Committee to Study the Senate Committee System, 1977, p. 11. See also Louis Baldwin, *Hon. Politician: Mike Mansfield of Montana*, (Missoula, Mont.: Mountain Press Publishing Co., 1979); and Michael Foley, *The New Senate: Liberal Influence on a Conservative Institution, 1959-1972* (New Haven: Yale University Press, 1980).

25. U.S., Congress, Senate, *Congressional Record*, daily ed., 96th Cong., 2d sess., April 18, 1980, p. S3294.

26. *Washington Post*, March 18, 1981, p. A21.

27. *New York Times*, December 3, 1980, p. A22.

28. Neil MacNeil, *Dirksen: Portrait of a Public Man* (New York: World Publishing Co., 1970), p. 172. See also Jean E. Torcom, "Leadership: The Role and Style of Everett Dirksen," in *To Be A Congressman*, ed. Sven Groennings and Jonathan P. Hawley (Washington, D.C.: Acropolis Books, 1973), pp. 185-223; and Charles O. Jones, *The Minority Party in Congress* (Boston: Little, Brown & Co., 1970).

29. *Wall Street Journal*, March 15, 1977, p. 1. See also Walter J. Oleszek, "Majority and Minority Whips of the Senate: History and Development of the Party Whip System in the United States Senate," S. Doc. 96-23, 96th Cong., 1st sess., 1979.

30. Vander Jagt and Michel quoted in the *Washington Post*, December 8, 1980, p. A2. See also Bill Keller, "New Minority Leader Michel: A Pragmatic Conservative," *Congressional Quarterly Weekly Report*, December 20, 1980, pp. 3600-3601.

31. Peabody, *Leadership in Congress*, p. 498. See also Larry S. King, "The Road to Power in Congress," *Harper's* (June 1971): 39-63.

32. U.S., Congress, Senate, *Congressional Record*, daily ed., 94th Cong., 2d sess., February 16, 1976, p. S1601.

33. Lance T. LeLoup, *The Fiscal Congress* (Westport, Conn.: Greenwood Press, 1980), p. 71.

34. U.S, Congress, House, *Congressional Record*, daily ed., 96th Cong., 2d sess., July 2, 1980, p. H6106.

35. U.S., Congress, Senate, *Congressional Record*, daily ed., 94th Cong., 1st sess., January 26, 1975, p. S1390.

36. *Washington Post*, April 27, 1981, pp. A1, A23.

37. U.S., Congress, Senate, *Congressional Record*, daily ed., 96th Cong., 2d sess., May 9, 1980, p. S5059.

38. Walter Kravitz, "Relations Between the Senate and House of Representatives: The Party Leaderships," in *Policymaking Role of Leadership in the Senate* (a compilation of papers prepared for the Commission on Operation of the Senate), 94th Cong., 2d sess., 1977, pp. 121-138.

39. Sidney Waldman, "Majority Leadership in the House of Representatives," *Political Science Quarterly* (Fall 1980): 377.

40. Michael J. Malbin, "House Democrats Are Playing with a Strong Leadership Lineup," *National Journal*, June 18, 1977, p. 942.

41. See Lewis A. Froman and Randall B. Ripley, "Conditions for Party Leadership: The Case of House Democrats," *American Political Science Review* (March 1965): 52-63.
42. *Washington Star,* June 20, 1977, p. A8.
43. Simeon S. Willis et al., *The Process of Government* (University of Kentucky: Bureau of Government Research, 1949), p. 46.
44. *New York Times,* February 18, 1981, p. A31.
45. Neil MacNeil, *Dirksen: Portrait of a Public Man,* pp. 168-169.
46. Ibid., p. 176.
47. *New York Times,* January 31, 1978, p. A13.
48. *Congressional Quarterly Weekly Report,* January 8, 1965, p. 33; Robert L. Peabody, ed., *Education of a Congressman* (New York: Bobbs-Merrill Co., 1972), pp. 251-261; and *Congressional Quarterly Weekly Report,* January 3, 1969, p. 2 and January 31, 1969, p. 203. For earlier discussions of party caucuses see Clarence J. Berdahl, "Some Notes on Party Membership in Congress," *American Political Science Review* (April 1949): 309-321, (June 1949): 492-508, (August 1949): 721-734.
49. Michael J. Malbin, "The Senate Republican Leaders—Life Without a President," *National Journal,* May 21, 1977, p. 780. See also Malcolm E. Jewell, "The Senate Republican Policy Committee and Foreign Policy," *Western Political Quarterly* (December 1959): 966-980; Hugh Bone, "An Introduction to the Senate Policy Committees," *American Political Science Review* (June 1956): 339-359; Donald Allen Robinson, "If the Senate Democrats Want Leadership: An Analysis of the History and Prospects of the Majority Policy Committee,' in *Policymaking Role of Leadership in the Senate,* pp. 40-57.
50. Norman J. Ornstein and David W. Rohde, "Political Parties and Congressional Reform" in *Parties and Elections in an Anti-Party Age,* ed. Jeff Fishel (Bloomington, Ind.: Indiana University Press, 1978), p. 286.
51. Jones, *The Minority Party in Congress,* p. 159. See also Charles O. Jones, *Party and Policy-Making: The House Republican Policy Committee* (New Brunswick, N.J.: Rutgers University Press, 1964).
52. *New York Times,* May 20, 1981, p. A20. See also *Wall Street Journal,* March 25, 1981, p. 31.
53. *Washington Star,* January 13, 1979, p. A7 and January 28, 1979, p. C2.
54. See V.O. Key, Jr., *Politics, Parties and Pressure Groups,* 5th ed (New York: Thomas Y. Crowell Co., 1964); Austin Ranney and Willmoore Kendall, *Democracy and the American Party System* (New York: Harcourt Brace Jovanovich, 1956); William Goodman, *The Two-Party System in the United States,* 3d ed. (New York: D. Van Nostrand Co., 1964); and William Nisbet Chambers and Walter Dean Burnham, eds., *The American Party System* (New York: Oxford University Press, 1975).
55. U.S., Congress, Senate, *Congressional Record,* daily ed., 97th Cong., 1st sess., February 6, 1981, p. S1127. Senator Armstrong voted against the debt ceiling extension and urged his GOP colleagues to do the same.
56. William J. Lanouette, "Don't Look for Quick Policy Shifts from the GOP Senate's Committees," *National Journal,* January 3, 1981, p. 16. See also Glen Gordon, *The Legislative Process and Divided Government: A Case Study of the 86th Congress* (University of Massachusetts, Bureau of Government Research, 1966); and David B. Truman, *The Congressional Party* (New York: John Wiley & Sons, 1959).
57. L. Horace Bushby, *Uncle Joe Cannon* (New York: Henry Holt, 1927), p. 219.

58. Elston Roady, "Party Regularity in the Sixty-third Congress" (Ph.D. diss., University of Illinois, 1951), p. 29. See also Wilder H. Haines, "The Congressional Caucus of Today," *American Political Science Review* (November 1915): 696-706.
59. U.S., Congress, *Congressional Record,* 63d Cong., 1st sess., September 13, 1913, p. 4904.
60. Richard Bolling, *House Out of Order* (New York: E. P. Dutton, 1965), p. 71. See also Bolling, *Power in the House* (New York: E. P. Dutton, 1968).
61. Clancy and Elder, *Tip,* p. 174.
62. *Washington Star,* February 27, 1979, p. A3.
63. Richard E. Cohen, "Byrd of West Virginia: A New Job, A New Image," *National Journal,* August 20, 1977, p. 1294. See also Cohen, "Congressional Leadership: Seeking a New Role," *The Washington Papers,* vol. 8, The Center for Strategic and International Studies, Georgetown University, Washington, D.C., 1980.
64. *Washington Post,* November 18, 1979, p. C5.
65. *Washington Star,* December 22, 1980, p. C1. See also Irwin B. Arieff, "Senator Paul Laxalt: Reagan's Man on the Hill," *Congressional Quarterly Weekly Report,* November 22, 1980, pp. 3396-3398; *New York Times,* November 28, 1980, p. B10; and *Washington Star,* March 29, 1981, p. A1. For a historical look at discovering congressional leaders, see Garrison Nelson, "Leadership Position-Holding in the United States House of Representatives," *Capitol Studies* (Fall 1976): 11-36.

A hearing of the House Science and Technology Committee.

7

Committees: Workshops of Congress

Over luncheon steaks in the Capitol, the chairmen and ranking minority members of the House and Senate tax committees met to discuss President Reagan's controversial three-year tax reduction plan. Journalists called the meeting "extraordinary" because so much rode on the outcome—a bipartisan tax bill or sharp legislative-executive conflict. The members and the journalists both knew that if the committee leaders agreed on what strategy to take, their colleagues would most likely go along with the decision.[1]

Congress's reliance on committees is very striking. Whether bills originate in the White House, bureaucracy, or pressure groups, they invariably are subject to committee review before being considered by the House or Senate. A committee offers a workshop, a place where a member of Congress can "get something done." The individual who feels frustrated in the spacious House or Senate chamber may very well work more effectively in the smaller committee room.

The committee-workshops enable Congress to deal coherently with a mass of complex issues. Without the committee system, a legislative body of 100 senators and 440 House members could in no way handle about 20,000 pieces of legislation biennially, a multibillion-dollar national budget, and an endless array of controversial issues. While floor actions refine final legislative products, committees are the means by which Congress sifts through an otherwise impossible jumble of bills, proposals, and issues.

In this chapter we will see how congressional committees arose, how committees are set up and their members selected, how they function, and how they adapt to pressures for change.

EVOLUTION OF THE COMMITTEE SYSTEM

Committees have tended to dominate legislative decisionmaking and routine almost from the very first Congress. Many of the early lawmakers had served in state assemblies or other forums (such as the Constitutional Convention) that functioned with and through committees.

Committees in the early Congresses, however, were mainly temporary panels created for a specific task. Once the task was completed, they went out of existence. The parent chamber closely controlled the temporary committees, assigning them clear-cut tasks, requiring them to report back favorably or unfavorably, and dissolving them when they had completed their work.

In the reverse of today's system, proposals were considered first on the House or Senate floor and then referred to specially created panels that worked out the details. The Senate, for example, would "debate a subject at length on the floor, and after the majority's desires had been crystallized, might appoint a committee to put those desires into bill form."[2] About 350 ad hoc committees were formed during the Third Congress (1793-1795) alone.[3]

By about 1816 the House and Senate developed a system of permanent or standing committees, some still in existence. Historian De Alva Alexander suggested that standing committees were better suited than ad hoc groups to cope with the larger membership and greater variety of congressional business.[4] Another scholar, George Haynes, pointed out that the "needless inconvenience of the frequent choice of select committees" taxed congressional patience.[5] Another possibility is that legislators came to value standing committees as counterweights to presidential influence in setting the legislative agenda.[6]

Permanent committees changed the way Congress made policy and distributed authority. The House and Senate now reviewed and voted upon recommendations made by specialized committees. And party leaders soon had to share authority with growing numbers of committee chairmen.

Standing committees also encouraged oversight of the executive branch. Members have called them "the eye, the ear, the hand, and very often the brain" of Congress;[7] scholars have referred to them as "little legislatures" because of their central role in making policy.[8]

As committees acquired expertise and authority, they became increasingly independent of chamber and party control. After the House revolted against Republican Speaker Joseph Cannon in 1910, power flowed to committee chairmen, who became the "dukes," "lords," and "barons" of Congress. Each chairman took on substantial powers. Along with a few strong party leaders, committee chairmen held sway over the House and Senate during most of the twentieth century. In rare instances, committee members rebelled and diminished the chairman's authority.[9] But most members heeded the advice that former Speaker John McCormack gave to freshmen: "Whenever you pass a committee chairman in the House, you bow from the waist. I do." [10]

The chairmen's authority was buttressed by a rigid seniority custom that flourished with the rise of congressional careerism.[11] The majority party member with the most years of continuous service on a committee automatically became its chairman. There were no other qualifications, such as ability or party loyalty. As a result, committee chairmen owed little or nothing to party leaders, much less presidents, for their posts. This automatic selection process did produce experienced, independent chairmen, but many members chafed under a system that concentrated authority in so few hands. The "have nots" wanted a piece of the action, too, and objected that seniority promoted the competent and incompetent alike, particularly members from "safe" areas who could ignore party policies or national sentiments.

With the rapid influx during the late 1960s and 1970s of new members who had no stake in the status quo and who allied themselves with the restless incumbents, changes were pushed through that diffused power among committee members and shattered seniority as an absolute criterion for leadership posts. Under the revised system, House and Senate committee chairmen (and ranking minority members) had to be elected by their party colleagues. In the process, three House chairmen were deposed. No longer free to wield arbitrary authority, chairmen had to abide by committee rules. And subcommittees became more important, growing in number, autonomy, and influence.[12] Congress's shift from committee government to subcommittee government, already broached in Chapter 6, is described in more detail below.

TYPES OF COMMITTEES

Congress today has a shopper's bazaar of committees. There are standing committees, subcommittees, select committees, joint committees, and conference committees. Not only are there significant differences among them, but within each general type there are variations.[13]

Standing Committees

Standing committees—16 in the Senate and 22 in the House—and their subcommittees are the central panels. For our purposes, the term "standing committee" means a permanent committee, created by public law or amendment to House or Senate rules. Standing committees continue from Congress to Congress, except in those infrequent instances where they are eliminated or new ones created. Table 7-1 compares the standing committees in the 97th Congress in terms of their size, party ratio, and number of subcommittees.

Standing committees contribute to Congress's daily and annual agenda of business. Rarely are measures considered on the House or Senate floor without first being referred to appropriate committees and approved by them.[14] Put negatively, committees are the burial ground for most legislation. Stated positively, committees select from the tens of thousands of measures introduced in each Congress those that merit floor debate. Of the thousands of bills that clear committees, fewer still are enacted into law.

Sizes and Ratios. The Legislative Reorganization Act of 1946 established the sizes of House and Senate standing committees. Both chambers have since adjusted those sizes upward, and in 1975 the House dropped from its rules any reference to committee size. Committee sizes and ratios (the number of majority and minority members on a panel) are negotiated by the majority and minority leaders.

In the Senate, noted for its reciprocity and comity among members, panels may be enlarged to accommodate senators seeking the same position. In 1973, for example, Senate Democrats created an extra seat on Foreign Relations to make room for George McGovern, D-S.D., and Hubert H. Humphrey, D-Minn., both defeated presidential candidates.

House committee enlargements are engineered, scholars suggest, by majority party leaders who want to accommodate the assignment preferences of colleagues. Under pressure from individual legislators, state party delegations, informal groups, or committee members, and bound by the traditional right of returning members to be reassigned to their committees, majority party leaders have responded by increasing the number of committee slots. Between 1947 and 1975 House committee berths increased by nearly 60 percent.[15]

Party ratios influence committee work as much as panel size does. First, biennial election results frame the bargaining between majority and minority leaders. Ratios on most committees normally reflect party strength in the full House or Senate.

Table 7-1 Standing Committees of the House and Senate, 97th Congress (1981-1983)

Committees	Size and Party Ratio		Number of Subcommittees
House			
Agriculture	43	(D 24/R 19)	8
Appropriations	55	(D 33/R 22)	13
Armed Services	44	(D 25/R 19)	7
Banking	44	(D 25/R 19)	8
Budget	30	(D 18/R 12)	9[1]
District of Columbia	9	(D 6/R 3)	3
Education and Labor	33	(D 19/R 14)	8
Energy and Commerce	42	(D 24/R 18)	6
Foreign Affairs	37	(D 21/R 16)	8
Government Operations	40	(D 23/R 17)	7
House Administration	19	(D 11/R 8)	5[2]
Interior	40	(D 23/R 17)	6
Judiciary	28	(D 16/R 12)	7
Merchant Marine	35	(D 20/R 15)	5
Post Office	26	(D 15/R 11)	7
Public Works	44	(D 25/R 19)	6
Rules	16	(D 11/R 5)	2
Science and Technology	40	(D 23/R 17)	7
Small Business	40	(D 23/R 17)	6
Standards of Official Conduct	12	(D 6/R 6)	none
Veterans' Affairs	31	(D 17/R 14)	5
Ways and Means	35	(D 23/R 12)	6
Senate			
Agriculture	17	(R 9/D 8)	8
Appropriations	29	(R 15/D 14)	13
Armed Services	17	(R 9/D 8)	6
Banking	15	(R 8/D 7)	7
Budget	22	(R 12/D 10)	none
Commerce	17	(R 9/D 8)	8
Energy and Natural Resources	20	(R 11/D 9)	6
Environment and Public Works	16	(R 9/D 7)	6
Finance	20	(R 11/D 9)	9
Foreign Relations	17	(R 9/D 8)	7
Governmental Affairs	17	(R 9/D 8)	8
Judiciary	18	(R 10/D 8)	9
Labor and Human Resources	16	(R 9/D 7)	7
Rules and Administration	12	(R 7/D 5)	none
Small Business	17	(R 9/D 8)	8
Veterans' Affairs	12	(R 7/D 5)	none

[1] 9 task forces.
[2] 5 subcommittees (and 1 policy group, 1 task force).

SOURCE: "Committees and Subcommittees of the 97th Congress," *Congressional Quarterly Special Report*, March 28, 1981.

Other practices and rules may also govern ratios. House Democratic Caucus rules state, for example, "Committee ratios should be established to create firm working majorities on each committee. In determining the ratio on the respective standing committees, the Speaker should provide for a *minimum* of three Democrats for each two Republicans." Finally, some House committees, such as Appropriations, Rules, and Ways and Means, traditionally have disproportionate ratios to ensure majority party control.

Because it has the votes, the majority party can be the final arbiter if the minority protests its allotment of committee seats. In 1981 House Republicans complained bitterly that Democrats were unfairly "packing" several major committees to thwart President Reagan's economic program. Representative Stan Parris, R-Va., objected:

> In spite of holding 44 percent of the House seats the Republicans will only receive 34 percent of the seats in the Ways and Means Committee, 40 percent of the seats on Appropriations and Budget, and a mere 31 percent of the seats on the Rules Committee, a fitting testament to the political tyranny of the majority.[16]

The ratios were set as the Democrats wanted. Several GOP members then filed suit against Democratic leaders to gain more equitable committee ratios.

Subcommittees. House rules require every standing committee with 20 or more members, except Budget, to have at least four subcommittees. (The Budget Committee has the functional equivalent of subcommittees: task forces.) This rule, adopted in 1975, was one of the reforms that weakened the committee chairmen's power. It was instituted to avoid the kind of personal dominance exerted by Ways and Means Chairman Wilbur D. Mills, D-Ark., who had abolished subcommittees.[17]

The Senate prohibits a senator from chairing more than one subcommittee on any one committee. This effectively limits the number of subcommittees to the number of majority party members on the parent committee.

Like standing committees, subcommittees vary widely in rules and procedures, staff arrangements, modes of operation, and relationships with other subcommittees and the full committee. Subcommittees sometimes even spawn offspring ("sub-subcommittees"). In 1978 a House Armed Services subcommittee created three "panels" to review specialized subjects under its purview. Subcommittees perform most of the day-to-day lawmaking and oversight work of Congress. Their growth is the result of several factors, namely:

●the complexities of problems that require policy specialization;

●the demands of interest groups calling for subcommittees handling their subject area;

•the desires of members to chair subcommittees in order to initiate lawmaking and oversight, augment personal prestige and influence, gain staff and office space, and gain a national platform; and

•the desire of majority Democrats in the early 1970s to circumscribe the power of committee chairmen.

Subcommittees are also created to enhance the reelection prospects of members—another manifestation of the "two Congresses." Senator George Aiken, R-Vt., noted that subcommittees are established to help members "in the next election back home.... I've been on subcommittees [that] never had one single meeting and yet those folks back home would think that the chairman was doing a good job there." [18]

Select or Special Committees

Select or special committees (the terms are interchangeable) are usually temporary panels that go out of business after the two-year life of the Congress in which they were created. Some select committees take on the attributes of permanent committees. The House, for example, has a Permanent Select Committee on Aging and a Permanent Select Intelligence Committee. Select committees usually do not have legislative authority; they can only study, investigate, and make recommendations.

Select panels are created for several reasons. First, they accommodate the concerns and needs of individual members. Between 1958 and 1976, sponsors of 10 of the 17 select committees authorized by the House became their chairmen. [19] Several senators who headed select or special committees during the 1970s attracted national publicity that enhanced their presidential prospects—for example, George McGovern (Select Committee on Nutrition and Human Needs), Walter Mondale (Select Committee on Equal Education Opportunity), and Frank Church (Special Committee to Study Governmental Operations with Respect to Intelligence Activities).

Second, special panels are a point of access for interest groups such as owners of small businesses, the aged, and Native Americans. Some have been stepping-stones to standing committees.

Third, select committees can supplement the standing committee system by overseeing and investigating issues that the permanent panels lack time for or prefer to ignore.

Finally, select committees can be set up to coordinate consideration of issues that overlap the jurisdictions of several standing committees. This approach is intended to reduce jurisdictional bickering. In 1981, for example, the House again authorized formation of the Select Committee on Narcotics Abuse and Control (first created in 1975). Its purpose was to coordinate the study of drug abuse.

Joint Committees

Joint committees, which include members from both chambers, have been used since the First Congress for study, investigation, oversight, and routine activities. House members of joint committees usually are appointed by the Speaker and senators by that chamber's presiding officer. The chairmanship of joint committees rotates each Congress or session between House and Senate members. In 1981 there were four joint committees:

Joint Committee	*Number of representatives*	*Number of senators*
Economic	10	10
Library	5	5
Printing	5	5
Taxation	5	5

The Joint Library Committee and the Joint Printing Committee oversee, respectively, the Library of Congress and the Government Printing Office. The Joint Taxation Committee is essentially a "holding company" for staff that works closely with the tax-writing committees of each house. The Joint Economic Committee (JEC) conducts studies and hearings on a wide range of domestic and international economic issues.

Under the chairmanship of Senator Lloyd Bentsen, D-Texas, the JEC in 1979 and 1980 explored supply-side economics approaches to business and individual tax cuts.[20] These themes became part of President Reagan's 1981 economic agenda.

Conference Committees

Before legislation can be sent to the president, it must pass both the House and Senate in identical form. Conference committees, sometimes called the "third house of Congress," reconcile differences between similar measures passed by both chambers. They are composed of members from each house. A representative highlighted their importance:

> When I came to Congress I had no comprehension of the importance of the conference committees which actually write legislation. We all know that important laws are drafted there, but I don't think one person in a million has any appreciation of their importance and the process by which they work. Part of the explanation, of course, is that there never is a printed record of what goes on in conference.[21]

We discuss the selection of conferees, rules changes affecting conferences, and conference reports in Chapter 9 on pages 285 and 286.

THE ASSIGNMENT PROCESS

Every congressional election sets off a scramble for committee seats. Legislators understand the linkage between winning desirable assignments and winning elections.[22] Newly elected representatives and senators make their preferences known quickly, and incumbents may try to move to a more prestigious panel.

Among standing committees the most powerful and so most desirable include House Ways and Means and Senate Finance, which pass on tax measures, and the House and Senate Appropriations committees, which hold the purse strings. The Budget committees, established in 1974, have also become sought-after assignments because of their guardianship of the congressional budgeting process.

Among those that seldom have waiting lists are House District of Columbia, Senate Ethics and House Standards of Official Conduct, and House Judiciary. The ethics committees in both chambers have been unpopular because legislators are reluctant to sit in judgment of their colleagues. The District of Columbia Committee is shunned by most members because it deals with local rather than national issues.

But the assignments some members avoid are the same ones that others want. For example, Senator Howell Heflin, D-Ala., a former chief justice of the Alabama Supreme Court, asked for a seat on Judiciary and accepted the chairmanship of the Ethics Committee when it became vacant.[23]

The attractiveness of committees can change over time. The House Judiciary Committee, long a coveted and choice assignment, particularly after its nationally televised impeachment inquiry of President Nixon, lost popularity after 1974. Many legislators shun the panel, wrote Judiciary Chairman Peter W. Rodino, Jr., D-N.J., because the "social issues (abortion, school prayer, school busing, gun control, the death penalty) that will be before us for decision are so volatile that to take a single 'wrong' stand or to cast one 'wrong' vote is to invite defeat at the polls." [24] Moreover, the committee authorizes little money and attracts few industry campaign donations. As Rodino explained, the panel has "no money to spread around. No grants. No loans. No loan guarantees. No subsidies." Party leaders, as a result, have to lobby members to serve on Judiciary.

In an analysis of six House committees, political scientist Richard F. Fenno, Jr., found that committee choice flows from a mix of three goals basic to all lawmakers: reelection, influence within the House, and good public policy. Of the 179 members interviewed, 81 percent "had deliberately sought and actively worked for the assignments to the committees on which they sat." [25]

Fenno found that for the most part the Appropriations and Ways and Means committees are populated by influence-oriented members;

Interior and Post Office attract reelection-oriented members; and Education and Labor and Foreign Affairs are populated by policy-oriented members. Members with similar goals find themselves on the same committees, which may make harmonious but biased committees.

Inevitably, some members receive unwelcome assignments. Black Representative Shirley Chisholm, D-N.Y., from Brooklyn, found herself in 1969 assigned to the House Agriculture Committee. "I think it would be hard to imagine an assignment that is less relevant to my background or to the needs of the predominantly black and Puerto Rican people who elected me," she said. Her protests won her a seat on the Veterans' Affairs Committee. "There are a lot more veterans in my district than there are trees," she later observed.[26] By contrast, Brooklyn Democrat Fred Richmond welcomes Agriculture Committee service and fuses local with rural issues through food stamp and other legislation.[27]

The Assignment Panels' Decision

The actual job of reviewing the requests and handing out the assignments falls to the committees on committees. Each party in each house has its own such group, under different names.

Party Assignment Committees

House Republicans. Two features characterize the GOP committee assignment group. First, the Republicans create their Committee on Committees by having each state with GOP representation elect a member to serve on the panel. Because this can be an unwieldy group, it further subdivides into an executive committee of about 15 members headed by the party's floor leader. The second feature is weighted voting. Each member casts as many votes as there are GOP members in his state delegation. The big-state members of the executive committee thus dominate assignments. Decisions of the executive committee are subject to ratification by the full Committee on Committees.

House Democrats. From 1911 to 1974 Democrats on the House Ways and Means Committee functioned as their party's committee on committees. In a significant change, the Democratic Caucus voted in December 1974 to transfer this duty to the Steering and Policy Committee. This group is headed by the Speaker and carefully balanced to reflect all significant party views. The Speaker, subject to caucus approval, appoints all Democratic members of the Rules Committee.

Senate Republicans. The GOP Conference Chairman appoints the assignment panel of about 14 members. There are also ex officio members, including the floor leader.

Senate Democrats. The Steering Committee makes assignments for Democrats. Its size (about 25 members) is set by the party conference and may fluctuate from Congress to Congress. The party's floor leader appoints members to this panel and chairs it.

The assignment panels' decisions are the first and most important acts in a three-step procedure. The second step involves approval of the assignment lists by each party's caucus. Finally, there is pro forma election by the full House or Senate.

Formal Criteria. Both formal and informal criteria guide the assignment panels in choosing committee members. Formal criteria are designed to ensure that each member is treated equitably in committee assignments.

For example, the House Democratic Caucus divides committees into three classes: exclusive, major, and nonmajor. A member assigned to an exclusive panel (Appropriations, Rules, or Ways and Means) may not serve on any other standing committee. This prevents members who receive the "plum" assignments from crowding members out of other spots.

Similarly, Senate Democratic leader Lyndon B. Johnson announced a policy ("the Johnson rule") in 1953 that all Democrats be assigned one major committee assignment before any party member received a second major assignment. Senate Republicans, under Minority Leader Everett McKinley Dirksen, adopted the practice informally in 1959 and formally in 1965.

Informal Criteria. Among the informal criteria used by parties in making assignments are the members' own wishes. "We like to give people committee assignments because they want them and because it broadens their political appeal," explained then House Minority Leader Gerald Ford, R-Mich.[28] In the weeks after an election, members tell the assignment panels which committees they would prefer. "It's a mini-political campaign," said Representative Mario Biaggi, D-N.Y., a member of his party's assignment panel; "There's nothing subtle about it. You're right in the marketplace, right at the point of sale. It all depends on your ability to negotiate with other members, and on personal friendship." [29]

In 1978, for example, Senator-elect Paul E. Tsongas, D-Mass., dropped by the office of Frank Church, D-Idaho, who was in line to become chairman of the Foreign Relations Committee. As a former Peace Corps volunteer in Africa, Tsongas hoped to land a spot on the committee, particularly on a subcommittee dealing with Africa.[30] He did not get the assignment then, but he went on Foreign Relations in 1980 when Senator Edmund S. Muskie, D-Maine, resigned to become secretary of state. A few years earlier, Senator Daniel Patrick Moynihan, D-N.Y., successfully campaigned for a seat on the Finance Committee by pointing out to the chairman, the majority leader, and most members of his party's committee on committees that a New York Democrat had not served on the Finance Committee in 100 years.[31] Other informal criteria involve the ideology, religion, locale, personality, party loyalty, professional background, race, and even sex of members. A Democrat on the House assignment panel explained why Colorado's Patricia Schroeder was placed on the Armed Services Committee as a freshman. "We thought we ought to have a woman on Armed Services because there are so many women in the service now," he said. "And Schroeder has a background in personnel. That was her field in law." [32]

Seniority. The assignment panels normally observe seniority when preparing committee membership lists. The person with the longest service is always listed first. Senate Republicans, unlike other committees on committees, apply seniority rigidly when two or more GOP senators compete for a committee vacancy.

In 1977 liberal GOP Senator Charles McC. Mathias of Maryland was blocked from the ranking minority slot on Judiciary when Senator Strom Thurmond, R-S.C., long ranking on the Armed Services Committee, moved to take the top Judiciary position. (Republicans limit their senators to one top committee position.) Thurmond outranked Mathias on Judiciary. Some speculated that Thurmond's move was a conservative tactic to prevent Mathias's elevation on Judiciary. [33] In addition, three vacant GOP slots on the panel went to conservatives Malcolm Wallop of Wyoming, Paul Laxalt of Nevada, and Orrin Hatch of Utah. Thus, Thurmond's election as ranking member of Judiciary was safely assured. In 1981 this maneuver bore results. Thurmond, not Mathias, became chairman of Judiciary when Republicans won control of the Senate for the first time in 26 years.

'Biases.' The decisions made by the assignment panels inevitably determine the ideological, geographical, or attitudinal composition of the standing committees. Committees can easily become biased toward one position or another. Farm areas are overrepresented on agriculture panels and seacoast interests on House Merchant Marine. No wonder committees are policy advocates; they propose laws that reflect the interests of their members and the outside groups that gravitate around them.

Since the 1970s there have been concerted efforts to add people with different perspectives to panels whose ideological makeup is skewed in one direction. In 1971 two House committees dominated by conservatives—Appropriations and Armed Services—had liberal legislators appointed to them despite the protests of their respective chairmen. [34]

A committee's political philosophy also influences its success on the House or Senate floor. Committees out of step ideologically with the House or Senate as a whole are likely to have legislation defeated or significantly revised through floor amendments. The House Education and Labor Committee long has been a liberal bastion. During the 1960s, for example, when the committee reported measures to the more conservative House, the legislation often was heavily amended, unlike most bills reported from the other standing committees.[35]

Approval by Party Caucuses and the Chamber

For most of the twentieth century each chamber's party caucuses either simply ratified the assignment decisions of their committees on committees or took no action on them at all. During the 1970s, however, party caucuses became major participants in the assignment process.[36]

Seniority today still encourages continuity on committees, but it has become more flexible and is under caucus control. In January 1975 House Democrats ousted three incumbent committee chairmen—W. Robert Poage of Agriculture, F. Edward Hébert of Armed Services, and Wright Patman of Banking—and replaced them with younger chairmen. A byproduct of this development has been to democratize committee decisionmaking. "The day is ended when any committee chairman can run his domain like a feudal barony, oblivious to the wishes and sensitivities of other members," said House Majority Leader Wright. "He can, however, lead with the cooperation of other members." [37]

Each chamber's rules require that all standing committees, including chairmen, be elected by the entire House or Senate. The practice, however, is for each party's leaders to offer the caucus-approved membership lists to the full chamber. These are then normally approved quickly by voice vote.

COMMITTEE LEADERSHIP

Committee leaders normally are the chairman and the ranking minority member. Committee chairmen call meetings and establish agendas, hire and fire committee staff, arrange hearings, designate conferees, act as floor managers, control committee funds and rooms, chair hearings and markups, and regulate the internal affairs and organization of the committee.

The top minority party member on a committee is also an influential figure. Among his or her powers are nominating minority conferees, hiring and firing minority staff, sitting ex officio on all subcommittees, appointing minority members to subcommittees, assisting in setting the committee's agenda, and managing legislation on the floor.

The chairman has many procedural powers. Simply refusing to schedule a bill for a hearing may be sufficient to kill it. Or a chairman may convene meetings when proponents or opponents of the legislation are unavoidably absent. The chairman's authority derives from the support of a committee majority and a variety of formal and informal resources such as substantive and parliamentary experience and control over the committee's agenda, communications, and financial resources.

How a chairman uses these powers is largely a matter of personal style. Wilbur Mills's control of Ways and Means from 1959 to 1974 was legendary. "Wilbur, why do you want to run for the president and give up your grip on the country?" once asked Representative Sam Gibbons, D-Fla.[38] Mills believed that tax legislation was too complex to be tampered with on the floor, and until 1973 the Rules Committee accommodated him with rules barring floor amendments on tax bills.

During his long tenure as chairman of the Senate Finance Committee, Russell Long, D-La., left no question who was boss. "There's no doubt he runs that committee," said Finance member Spark M. Matsunaga, D-Hawaii. "Not even Wilbur Mills was like this. Mills had factions forming against him on Ways and Means. Russell Long is close to every member on a personal basis." [39]

Traditionally, committee leaders present themselves to their constituents as members able to get things done. Because of the senior position he then held on the Appropriations Committee, said retiring Senator Milton R. Young, R-N.D., the committee "has been giving me most everything I want [for North Dakota]." [40] In 1980, however, the electoral benefits of committee leadership took on a different dimension. Several chairmen found that their high visibility made them vulnerable to defeat; voters apparently were concerned that members who stay in Washington too long neglect local needs.[41]

Chairmen of the 1980s are accountable to their party colleagues. However, they still wield considerable power. "If you work hard, you can still win most of what you want," said House Interior Chairman Morris K. Udall, D-Ariz. "But you can't do it the easy way, the way [some autocratic chairmen] did it." [42]

POLICYMAKING IN COMMITTEE

Committees foster fragmented, deliberate, collegial decisions. They ease outside groups' access to the legislative process. And they encourage bargaining and accommodation among members. To move bills through Congress's numerous decision points, from subcommittee to committee, authors of legislation must compromise differences with committee "gatekeepers." Before sending a bill to the next policymaking stage, gatekeepers may exact alterations in its substance.

Committee Jurisdictions and Lawmaking

Each standing committee's responsibilities are defined by the rules of each house, various public laws, and precedents. For example, Senate rules outline the jurisdiction of the Environment and Public Works Committee as follows:

1. Air pollution.
2. Construction and maintenance of highways.
3. Environmental aspects of Outer Continental Shelf lands.
4. Environmental effects of toxic substances, other than pesticides.
5. Environmental policy.
6. Environmental research and development.
7. Fisheries and wildlife.
8. Flood control and improvements of rivers and harbors, including environmental aspects of deepwater ports.
9. Noise pollution.
10. Nonmilitary environmental regulation and control of nuclear energy.
11. Ocean dumping.
12. Public buildings and improved grounds of the United States generally; federal buildings in the District of Columbia.
13. Public works, bridges, and dams.
14. Regional economic development.
15. Solid waste disposal and recycling.
16. Water pollution.
17. Water resources.

Such committee shall also study and review, on a comprehensive basis, matters relating to environmental protection and resource utilization and conservation, and report thereon from time to time.

Several aspects of this committee's, or any committee's, mandate bear emphasizing. First, committees do not have watertight jurisdictional compartments. Any broad subject overlaps numerous committees. The Senate has an Environment Committee, but several other panels also consider environmental legislation; the same is true in the House. These House bodies, along with a brief sketch of their environmental responsibilities, are shown below.

Agriculture	pesticides; soil conservation; some water programs
Appropriations	funding environmental programs and agencies
Banking	open space acquisition in urban areas
Government Operations	federal executive organization for the environment
Interior and Insular Affairs	water resources; power resources; land management; wildlife conservation; national parks; nuclear waste
Foreign Affairs	Law of the Sea Conference
Energy and Commerce	health effects of the environment; environmental regulations; solid waste disposal; clean air; safe drinking water

Merchant Marine and Fisheries	ocean dumping; fisheries; Law of the Sea Conference; coastal zone management; environmental impact statements
Public Works and Transportation	water pollution; sludge management
Science and Technology	environmental research and development
Small Business	effects on business of environmental regulations
Ways and Means	environmental tax expenditures.

Jurisdictional overlaps have both positive and negative results. On the plus side, they enable members to develop expertise in several policy fields, prevent any one group from dominating a topic, facilitate multiple points of access for outside interests, and promote healthy competition among committees. In 1977, airline deregulation, for example, was helped along because a Senate Judiciary subcommittee, headed by Senator Edward M. Kennedy, D-Mass., took up the issue. This prompted the panel with primary jurisdiction, the Commerce Committee, to move on deregulation even though it had been reluctant to do so.

On the other hand, "healthy competition" can quickly turn to intercommittee battles. For example, when Senator Kennedy, by then chairman of the full Judiciary Committee, announced his intention to seek passage of legislation deregulating the trucking industry, Commerce Chairman Howard Cannon, D-Nev., protested that the action was a "raid on our jurisdiction."

"What will be next?" Cannon asked. "Will Senator Kennedy want to take the bank merger act away from the Banking Committee or political action away from the Rules Committee?" [43]

House and Senate rules acknowledge jurisdictional overlap. When a bill is introduced, it is usually sent to a single committee. But a bill that addresses many problems may be jointly referred to two or more committees simultaneously or, under sequential referral, sent first to one committee and then another, and so on. In split referrals, a bill is divided into separate parts, each sent to a different committee.

The Senate has long permitted multiple referrals by unanimous consent. The House has permitted them since 1975. About 200 measures per Congress are multiply referred in the Senate. [44] The House has increasingly used multiple referrals, as shown in Table 7-2.

Multiple referrals promote public discussion of issues, access to the legislative process, and consideration of alternative approaches. They can also slow down legislative decisionmaking. House and Senate rules require all committees that received a multiply referred bill to report it out before it can be scheduled for floor debate. In general, the more committees review a measure, the longer it takes to process it. Multiple

Table 7-2 Summary of Multiple Bill Referrals in the House, 1975-1981

Congress	Measures Introduced[1]	Measures Multiply Referred	Measures Reported	Multiply Referred Measures Reported	Multiple Referrals as Percent of All Reported Bills
94th (1975-77)	19,371	1,161	1,495	38	2.5%
95th (1977-79)	18,065	1,833	1,490	80	5.4
96th (1979-81)	10,397[2]	1,241	1,224	159	13.0

[1] The number of measures that passed the House during the 94th, 95th, and 96th Congresses was 1,624, 1,615, and 1,336, respectively. Data include bills and resolutions.

[2] A resolution adopted in 1978 removed the ceiling on cosponsors for bills introduced in the House, beginning with the 96th Congress. This sharply reduced the number of identical bills introduced in each session.

SOURCE: Arthur G. Stevens, Congressional Research Service, "Indicators of Congressional Workload and Activity," May 30, 1979. Additional data were compiled from a computer search of the House Information Systems data base and Scorpio, and from the House Legislative Information and Status System (LEGIS).

referrals may also kill legislation. In 1980, for example, the House Commerce Committee reported a bill that would modernize the 1934 Communications Act that granted the American Telephone & Telegraph Company (AT&T) a monopoly over interstate telephone communications. The bill had been singly referred to Commerce under its authority for "regulation of interstate and foreign communications."

Soon after Commerce reported the telecommunications bill, the House Judiciary Committee requested and received from Speaker O'Neill a sequential referral of the bill. Judiciary Chairman Peter W. Rodino, Jr., D-N.J., argued that it had serious antitrust implications, particularly because the federal government was then engaged in a major antitrust action against AT&T. Some observers suggested, however, that referring the measure to Judiciary was a maneuver engineered by some of the bill's numerous opponents.[45] The outcome was that in 1980 the House never took up the telecommunications bill, in part because little time was left after the Judiciary Committee reviewed it and voted to report it "adversely but without prejudice." [46]

Jurisdictional statements, in short, define committees' purposes, duties, and areas of specialization, but it is often difficult to determine where one committee's turf ends and another's begins.

Patterns of Committee Decisionmaking

Most bills referred to committee are sent by the chairman to a subcommittee, which selects the bills it wants to consider and ignores the rest. Subcommittee consideration usually consists of three standard steps: public hearings, public markups, and reports.

Hearings. When committees conduct hearings on legislation, they listen to a wide variety of witnesses. These often include the sponsors of the bills, federal officials, pressure group representatives, public officials, and private citizens. During the 96th Congress, for example, the House Appropriations Committee "held 720 days of hearings, took testimony from 10,215 witnesses, published 225 volumes of hearings which comprised 202,767 printed pages."[47] Some of the important purposes served by hearings are:

- to explore the need for legislation;
- to gather information;
- to build a public record in support of legislation;
- to publicize the role of committee chairmen;
- to advertise partisan or factional viewpoints on issues;
- to advocate policy positions to executive agencies;
- to review executive implementation of public laws;
- to investigate problems and issues;
- to survey the views of outside groups and interests who support or oppose the legislation;
- to provide a forum for citizen grievances and frustrations;
- to promote public interest and support for issues.

Most hearings follow a traditional format. Witnesses read prepared statements. Each committee member then has a limited time to ask questions before the next witness is called. This procedure discourages lengthy exchanges, rebuttals, follow-up questions, or interaction among witnesses.

Occasionally committees employ a panel format in which witnesses sit together and briefly summarize their statements. In 1974 Senator Kennedy used such a format for a hearing on drug policy. The plan for the hearing follows:

> Assistant Secretary for Health Charles Edwards will present the administration's position, will respond to questions, and will then remain in the hearing room. The Pharmaceutical Manufacturers Association, on behalf of the drug industry, and in opposition to the Department of Health, Education and Welfare [now Health and Human Services] policy, will come to the witness table at the same time as the American Pharmaceutical Association on behalf of the Nation's pharmacists, and in support of the DHEW policy. After opening statements, questions will be asked alternately and each will

have a chance to comment on the other's answers. Each will then be given an opportunity to directly question the other. When this is complete, Assistant Secretary Edwards will return to the witness table to respond to questions submitted by the other witnesses, and the points raised in the course of their debate.[48]

Hearings are a necessary stage in the life of any measure. By revealing patterns of support or opposition and by airing substantive problems, hearings indicate to members whether a bill is worth taking to the full chamber. Moreover, committee members will try to use the hearings to promote or sabotage a bill.

Markups. After hearings, the bill is "marked up." This is the stage where committee members decide on the bill's actual language. Should a section be phrased "may" or "shall"? How much money or personnel should be authorized? What formula should be used to distribute funds or services? Which federal department should administer the program? What time period is appropriate for carrying out the legislation? These are only a few of the issues that committee members might have to resolve through compromise and bargaining during the markup phase. How this bargaining process works in a markup is described in the box on p. 222.

Outside pressures are often intense during markup deliberations, for under 1970s House and Senate "sunshine" rules, most markups are conducted in public. With markup rooms often filled with lobbyists watching every member's vote, compromises can be difficult to achieve. Before open markups, said a representative, you "didn't see senior vice presidents ... actually sitting there in [markup] meetings or buttonholing members as they go to the bathroom." [49] On the other hand, open markups emphasize accountability. "If you're getting zapped, at least you're getting zapped where you and everyone else can see it," commented a labor lobbyist.[50]

After conducting hearings and markups, a subcommittee sends its recommendations to the full committee, which may conduct hearings and markups on its own, ratify the subcommittee's decision, take no action, or return the matter to the subcommittee for further study.

Reports. If the full committee votes to send the bill to the House or Senate, the staff prepares a report, subject to committee approval, describing the purposes and provisions of the legislation. Often reports emphasize arguments favorable to the bill, summarizing selectively the results of staff research and hearings. Reports are noteworthy documents. Some legislators might read only the report before deciding how to vote on a bill. The bill itself may be long, highly technical, and meaningless to most readers. "A good report, therefore, does more than

Trading in Millions: Mark of a 'Markup'

...It was a typically relaxed, fraternal session. The senators, many of them in shirtsleeves, sat around a long, rectangular table, pencils in hand, worksheets before them, aides behind them. They were marking up—or drafting—the $7 billion foreign aid bill, and the manner in which they disposed of millions of dollars ... seemed almost cavalier.

Most open disputes involve only those issues that have eluded compromise elsewhere. Such was the case with a $10 million appropriation for a proposed United Nations University in Japan .... . The pledge had been made by the Carter administration, the appropriation was approved by the subcommittee, but Senator Dennis DeConcini, a conservative Democrat from Arizona, moved in full committee to withdraw it.

Senator Daniel K. Inouye, D-Hawaii ... said that as the subcommittee chairman he felt required to defend the appropriation. But his heart clearly wasn't in it. "The administration places great stress on this," Senator Inouye said. "It feels it is important. We are the ones who initiated this university."

Senator Clifford Case, Republican of New Jersey, argued: "We battled this out in subcommittee—the Japanese are putting up most of the dough—$100 million. It would be chintzy of us to pull out." Senator Edward W. Brooke, Republican of Massachusetts, maintained that the United States had made a commitment to the university. Senator Henry Bellmon, Republican of Oklahoma, replied that the commitment had been made by the administration, not the Congress. "Let *them* find the money," he said.

Senator Lowell P. Weicker, Republican of Connecticut, told his colleagues that "there are far greater needs than another university." To Mr. Inouye he said, jokingly: "If that's how you defend a line item, I hope you come into my state and campaign for my opponent." Finally, Mr. Inouye gave in: "When we were evacuating ourselves from Southeast Asia, we called upon our friends to come to our assistance," he said. "The Japanese took zero refugees and expended zero dollars. They made the most money in Vietnam. They should spend some of that money on this university." The debate took seven minutes, and then the committee voted 9-5 to delete the funds, in a move that the university's sponsors said would doom it. ...

SOURCE: Martin Tolchin, "Trading in Millions: Mark of a 'Markup,' " *The New York Times,* July 24, 1977, p. E5. © 1977 by *The New York Times.* Reprinted by permission.

explain—it also persuades," commented a former congressional staff aide.[51] Reports also guide executive agencies and federal courts in interpreting ambiguous or complex legislative language.

The Policy Environment

Each committee operates with a different external environment. Executive agencies, pressure groups, party leaders and caucuses, and the entire House or Senate all form the backdrop against which a committee operates. These environments may be consensual or conflictual. That is, major policy questions may be relatively easily settled or they may be subject to bitter controversy. Environments may also be monolithic or pluralistic; some committees have a single dominant source of outside influence, while others face numerous and competing groups or agencies. Policy environments may vary from issue to issue.

Environmental factors influence committees in at least four ways. First, they shape the content of public policies and acceptance of those policies by the full House or Senate. The House Judiciary Committee, as noted earlier, is buffeted by diverse and competing pressure groups, many passionately attached to issues such as abortion or gun control. The committee's chances for achieving agreement among its members or on the House floor depend to a large extent on its ability to accommodate such groups through artful legislative drafting.

Second, policy environments foster mutual alliances among committees, federal departments, and pressure groups. The House Merchant Marine Committee, for example, regularly advocates legislation to benefit the maritime industries and unions. This effort is backed by the Federal Maritime Commission. Such "iron triangles," discussed further in Chapters 12 and 14, may dominate policymaking in key issue areas. At the very least, "issue networks" emerge. These are rather fluid and amorphous groups of policy experts who try to influence any committee that deals with their subject area.[52]

Third, environments establish decisionmaking objectives and guidelines for committees. Clientele-oriented committees, such as the House Post Office and Civil Service Committee, try to promote the policy views of their satellite groups, such as mass-mailing firms and postal unions. The amount of public attention afforded clientele-oriented committees affects what one scholar called the "scope of the conflict." [53] Interests enjoying preferential access to decisionmakers don't encourage involvement by wider publics; interests trying to break up a group's preferential access seek to mobilize public pressures to assist them. The House Post Office and Civil Service Committee's major client groups traditionally relied on low public visibility to foster their objectives, which were to "support maximum pay increases and improvements in benefits for employee groups and oppose all rate increases for mail users." [54] This benign environment was shattered by a 1966 pre-Christmas mail breakdown in Chicago that led to postal reform proposals and a 10-day postal strike in March 1970, which helped ensure passage of a reform bill.

Finally, environmental factors influence the level of partisanship on committees. Some committees, such as the House and Senate Appropriations committees, are essentially free of party infighting; on those panels, Democrats and Republicans alike generally define their job as budget cutting. The House Education and Labor Committee, on the other hand, considers contentious social issues, such as poverty and welfare, that divide the two parties.

COMMITTEES IN CHANGE

With the Legislative Reorganization Act of 1946, Congress dramatically altered its committee structure. The 1946 Act reduced the number of standing committees and for the first time specified each panel's jurisdiction. These changes, however, resulted over the years in a proliferation of subcommittees, obsolete jurisdictions, unbalanced workloads, and far too many committee assignments for members to manage. By the 1970s many legislators questioned the effectiveness of the existing committee system.

House and Senate Reform

The pressures for change crystallized first in the House. In 1973 that chamber created a Select Committee on Committees, headed by Representative Richard Bolling, D-Mo., to propose committee revisions. Titled the Committee Reform Amendments of 1974, the plan proposed 1) eliminating several standing committees, 2) consolidating into one panel broad subject areas such as energy, transportation, and environment, 3) limiting members' committee assignments, and 4) more equitably distributing workloads among committees.

The Bolling proposal immediately aroused fierce opposition from members who stood to lose subcommittee chairmanships or who would be forced to surrender favored jurisdictions. Pressure groups, too, marshalled strong resistance. They opposed jurisdictional reshuffling because it would break convenient longtime linkages with committees responsible for their issue areas. These inside-outside alliances were strong enough to doom the committee revision plan. Instead, the House adopted a watered-down version that made only modest changes in jurisdictions contained in the 1946 Act.[55]

The Senate tried committee reform in 1977, with somewhat greater success. The Select Committee on Committees, created in 1976 and chaired by Adlai E. Stevenson, D-Ill., recast jurisdictional responsibilities along more functional lines, limited senators' assignments, and reduced from 31 to 14 all types of committees (standing, select, and joint).

On February 4, 1977, the Senate adopted about 60 percent of what the Stevenson committee asked for. Only 25 percent of the Bolling committee's plan was adopted, however.[56]

During the 96th Congress (1979-1981), the House again tried to revamp its committee system. It created another Select Committee on Committees, chaired by Jerry Patterson, D-Calif., mainly to design a separate standing committee on energy.

In December 1979 the panel recommended formation of an energy committee, to consist largely of jurisdiction taken from the Commerce Subcommittee on Energy and Power, and granted it authority for "national energy policy generally." The House overwhelmingly rejected the proposal, adopting instead one that changed the name of the Interstate and Foreign Commerce Committee to Energy and Commerce, granted it jurisdiction over "energy policy generally," and updated jurisdictional language dealing with energy. The proposal did not, however, remove energy jurisdiction from any committee that had previously exercised it.[57] Many factors contributed to the Select Committee's defeat: turf politics, inadequate leadership support, the divisiveness of the energy issue, the perception that the Patterson plan did little more than elevate a subcommittee into a full committee, the relative inexperience of the committee and its chairman, and general House antipathy toward another committee reorganization attempt. As the Select Committee dejectedly concluded:

> Rather than recommend a comprehensive reorganization in a single legislative vehicle [as did the 1973-1974 Select Committee], the present Select Committee on Committees sought to minimize opposition to reorganization by reporting a series of smaller, more manageable reorganization proposals. In short, the strategy of incremental reform seems no more likely to achieve success than have single, omnibus reorganization plans.[58]

The three efforts at committee realignment carry a key lesson: To accomplish major committee change requires skillful accommodation of members and pressure groups who stand to lose—or think they will lose—from any alteration in the status quo. The chances of success are slim without this accommodation and the hard bargaining necessary to produce a winning coalition.

Toward Subcommittee Government

Subcommittees have grown in importance in both houses, particularly in the Senate. Almost every majority party senator in recent years has chaired a subcommittee. In 1981, GOP senators averaged 2.5 chairmanships.

Senate. Formal changes in Senate rules in 1977 limited committee chairmen to one subcommittee chairmanship on any of the major committees. Moreover, no senators could serve on more than three subcommittees of any major committee. The number of Senate subcommittees was reduced from 174 in the 94th Congress to 117 in the 95th Congress to 105 in the 97th Congress.

In January 1979 the new chairman of the Judiciary Committee, Senator Kennedy, announced plans to abolish several subcommittees and end the practice of giving every Democratic freshman a subcommittee chairmanship. "It doesn't make sense to have a subcommittee for every [majority] Senator," said the committee's general counsel.[59] Opposition from incoming members caused Kennedy to abandon his plan, and new Judiciary members who wanted to chair subcommittees got them.[60] When Senator Strom Thurmond assumed the Judiciary chairmanship in 1981, he gave subcommittee chairmanships to every majority member, including freshmen.

On most committees the action now centers at the subcommittee level. "In most committees, whatever the subcommittee sends up, the full committee generally stamps and sends to the floor," observed Majority Leader Howard H. Baker, Jr.[61] In others, such as Finance, however, the full committee makes the important decisions.

House. The drift toward subcommittee government is vividly seen in the House and within the Democratic party. In the past seniority meant that chairmen were often conservatives from safe, rural districts. Liberal frustration finally turned to action during the 1970s.

The Democratic Caucus in 1971 adopted a rule that no member could be chairman of more than one legislative subcommittee. This change made it possible for younger, liberal, nonsouthern members to become subcommittee chairmen.[62]

In 1973 Democrats adopted a subcommittee "bill of rights" that created on each standing committee a mini-Democratic caucus with authority to select subcommittee chairmen and otherwise share powers that chairmen alone had previously exercised. A dramatic illustration of what these changes meant in practice occurred two years after their adoption. The chairman of the Interstate and Foreign Commerce Committee, Harley O. Staggers, D-W.Va., lost his coveted Oversight and Investigations Subcommittee chairmanship to John E. Moss, D-Calif., who won that post in the committee's caucus. Such a successful challenge would have been nearly unheard of before the 1970s; today, subcommittee leadership fights are not uncommon.

Democrats also established an equitable subcommittee assignment process. Before, junior committee members were placed on less important subcommittees, and senior members received appointment to influential ones. Party rules were adopted providing, with some exceptions, that each Democrat shall select one subcommittee before any colleague receives two.

In 1974 House Democrats continued to strengthen subcommittees. First, the caucus endorsed the principle, later incorporated in House rules, that most committees should establish at least four subcommittees. Second, the caucus directed that House rules be amended to permit each subcommittee chairman and each ranking minority sub-committee member to hire one staff aide. Finally, to ensure more accountability on party issues, the caucus subjected Appropriations subcommittee chairmen to approval by all party members.

By 1978 subcommittees had the staff, jurisdiction, and budget to be effective policymakers and overseers of administrative actions, but some members sensed that the reform movement had gone too far. Party leaders were having a harder time leading and obstructionists an easier time obstructing. A proposal was made in December 1978 to prohibit a chairman from heading a subcommittee on his committee or any other. When the change was offered in the caucus, it was rejected 85 to 21. "You can't have it both ways," said House Interior Committee Chairman Udall. "You can't put power in the subcommittee, then prevent the full committee chairman from sharing in the action." [63] By 1979 both parties had taken steps to limit the number of subcommittees per committee.

Today, subcommittee policymaking is characterized by 1) the multiplicity of interests that can present their claims to autonomous subcommittees, 2) slower decisionmaking because majority consensus is harder to achieve, given the large number of participants, 3) wider opportunities for members to exercise initiative in lawmaking and oversight, 4) workload increases as members scurry to attend meetings called by activist subcommittee leaders, and 5) heightened pressures on party leaders to schedule subcommittee-reported issues and amendments for floor consideration.

Subcommittee government, in short, mirrors the atomization of political life in the country at large. It is central to the present-day Congress. While diffused authority strengthens Congress's representative role, subcommittee government inhibits Congress's ability to formulate coordinated approaches to public problems. [64]

CONCLUSION

"The committee structure of Congress is both the chief source of strength in the congressional system, and also a source of weakness," observed former Representative Bob Eckhardt, D-Texas. [65] To be sure, committees enable Congress to address a growing array of complex, interrelated issues and process its crushing workload. Yet outmoded and proliferating committees inhibit Congress's ability to advance comprehensive responses to problems. Major consequences, in short, flow from the committee system.

First, the method of recruitment and the custom of seniority reinforce the committees' autonomy. Committees frequently are imbalanced ideologically or geographically. They are likely to advocate policies espoused by agencies and outside groups interested in their work.

Second, committees typically operate independently of one another. This longtime custom fosters an attitude of "mutual protection." Jurisdictional rivalries are endemic to the committee system.

Third, committees often develop an esprit de corps that flows across party lines. Committee members usually will defend their panels against criticisms, jurisdictional trespassing, or any attempt to bypass them.

Fourth, committees display subtle differences. Each varies in its policymaking environments, membership mixtures, decisionmaking objectives, and ability to fulfill individual member goals.

Fifth, committees dominate the House and Senate agendas. The bills they report determine what each chamber will debate and in what form.

Sixth, the 1970s reforms promoted subcommittee government and further dispersed power in Congress. This has made the job of party leaders more difficult than ever. With more centers of power, it takes party leaders longer to forge compromises and develop winning coalitions.

Finally, the committee system contributes fundamentally to policy fragmentation. A few committees—Rules and Budget, for example—can act as policy coordinators for Congress.[66] (The roles of these panels are discussed in Chapters 9 and 11.)

Because of committee fragmentation and multiple assignments, members have come to depend on staff assistance. The work of the committees, not to mention members' offices, rests more and more on these "unelected representatives."

NOTES

1. *New York Times,* June 10, 1981, p. A26 and May 19, 1981, p. D1.
2. Roy Swanstrom, *The United States Senate, 1787-1801,* Senate Doc. No. 64, 87th Cong., 1st sess., 1962, p. 224.
3. Lauros G. McConachie, *Congressional Committees* (New York: Thomas Y. Crowell Co., 1898), p. 124.
4. De Alva Stanwood Alexander, *History and Procedure of the House of Representatives* (Boston: Houghton Mifflin Co., 1916), p. 228. See George B. Galloway, *History of the House of Representatives,* 2d ed. rev., edited by Sidney Wise (New York: Thomas Y. Crowell Co., 1976).
5. George H. Haynes, *The Senate of the United States: Its History and Practice,* vol. 1 (Boston: Houghton Mifflin Co., 1938), p. 272. See Walter Kravitz, "Evolution of the Senate's Committee System," *The Annals* (January 1974): 27-38.
6. Ralph V. Harlow, *The History of Legislative Methods in the Period Before 1825* (New Haven: Yale University Press, 1917), pp. 157-158. See Nelson W. Polsby, "The Institutionalization of the U.S. House of Representatives," *American Political Science Review* (March 1968): 144-168.

7. *Cannon's Procedure in the House of Representatives,* House Doc. No. 122, 80th Cong., 1st sess., 1959, p. 83.
8. "Little Legislatures" was a term coined by Woodrow Wilson in *Congressional Government* (Boston: Houghton Mifflin Co., 1885), p. 79.
9. From 1953 to 1967, there were at least four "revolts" against House committee chairmen, including Clare Hoffman, R-Mich., of Government Operations; Wright Patman, D-Texas, of Banking; Adam Clayton Powell, D-N.Y., of Education and Labor; and Thomas Murray, D-Tenn., of Post Office and Civil Service.
10. *Wall Street Journal,* May 3, 1979, p. 1.
11. See Nelson Polsby et al., "The Growth of the Seniority System in the U.S. House of Representatives," *American Political Science Review* (September 1969): 787-807; Barbara Hinckley, *The Seniority System in Congress* (Bloomington: Indiana University Press, 1971); H. Douglas Price, "Congress and the Evolution of Legislative 'Professionalism,'" in *Congress in Change,* ed. Norman J. Ornstein (New York: Praeger Publishers, 1975), pp. 2-23; and Samuel Kernell, "Toward Understanding 19th Century Congressional Career Patterns: Ambition, Competition, and Rotation," *American Journal of Political Science* (November 1977): 669-693.
12. See Burton L. French, "Sub-Committees of Congress," *American Political Science Review* (February 1915): 68-92; Charles O. Jones, "The Role of the Congressional Subcommittee," *Midwest Journal of Political Science* (November 1962): 326-344; Thomas R. Wolanin, "Committee Seniority and the Choice of House Subcommittee Chairmen: 80th-91st Congresses," *Journal of Politics* (August 1974): 687-702; and Steven H. Haeberle, "The Institutionalization of the Subcommittee in the United States House of Representatives," *Journal of Politics* (November 1978): 1054-1065.
13. For several useful studies of committees, see George Goodwin, *The Little Legislatures* (Amherst: University of Massachusetts Press, 1970); William L. Morrow, *Congressional Committees* (New York: Charles Scribner's Sons, 1969); and Joseph Cooper, "The Study of Congressional Committees, Current Research and Future Trends," *Polity* (Fall 1971): 123-133.
14. See James W. Dyson and John W. Soule, "Congressional Committee Behavior on Roll Call Votes: The U.S. House of Representatives, 1955-1964," *Midwest Journal of Political Science* (November 1970): 626-647; and Anne L. Lewis, "Floor Success as a Measure of Committee Performance in the House," *Journal of Politics* (May 1978): 460-467.
15. Kenneth A. Shepsle, *The Giant Jigsaw Puzzle: Democratic Committee Assignments in the Modern House* (Chicago: University of Chicago Press, 1978), p. 112. See Louis Gawthrop, "Changing Membership Patterns in House Committees," *American Political Science Review* (June 1966): 366-373; Louis P. Westefield, "Majority Party Leadership and the Committee System in the House of Representatives," *American Political Science Review* (December 1974): 1593-1605; and U.S., Congress, Senate, *The Senate Committee System,* First Staff Report to the Temporary Select Committee to Study the Senate Committee System, 94th Cong., 2d sess., July 1976, Section 3: Historical Patterns of Senate Standing Committee Sizes.
16. U.S., Congress, *Congressional Record,* daily ed., 97th Cong., 1st sess., January 6, 1981, p. E30.
17. See John F. Manley, *The Politics of Finance: The House Committee on Ways and Means* (Boston: Little, Brown & Co., 1970).

18. *Washington Star,* June 28, 1976, p. A12.
19. See Stanley V. Vardys, "Select Committees of the House of Representatives," *Midwest Journal of Political Science* (August 1962): 247-265; and Bertram Waters, "The Politics of Hunger: Forming a Senate Select Committee," in *To Be A Congressman: The Promise and the Power,* ed. Sven Groennings and Jonathan Hawley (Washington, D.C.: Acropolis Books, 1973), pp. 151-168.
20. Richard E. Cohen, "Disjointed Economic Committee," *National Journal,* March 7, 1981, p. 397. For other studies of joint committees, see Harold Green and Alan Rosenthal, *Government of the Atom: The Integration of Powers* (New York: Atherton, 1963); J. Dicken Kirschten, "Is Doomsday at Hand for the Joint Atomic Energy Committee?" *National Journal,* November 20, 1976, pp. 1658-1665; *Congressional Quarterly Weekly Report,* January 8, 1977, pp. 44-45; and John F. Manley, "Congressional Staff and Public Policy-Making: The Joint Committee on Internal Revenue Taxation," *Journal of Politics* (November 1968): 1046-1067.
21. Charles L. Clapp, *The Congressman: His Job As He Sees It* (Washington, D.C.: The Brookings Institution, 1963), p. 245.
22. See, for example, Linda L. Fowler, Scott P. Douglass, and Wesley D. Clark, Jr., "The Electoral Aspects of House Committee Assignments," *Journal of Politics* (February 1980): 307-319.
23. *Congressional Quarterly Weekly Report,* November 18, 1978, p. 3328.
24. Peter Rodino, "That Old Judiciary Just Ain't What She Use to Be," *Washington Star,* March 19, 1981, p. A15. See Lynette P. Perkins, "Member Recruitment to a Mixed Goal Committee: The House Judiciary Committee," *Journal of Politics* (May 1981): 348-364.
25. Richard F. Fenno, Jr., *Congressmen in Committees* (Boston: Little, Brown & Co., 1973), p. 2.
26. Shirley Chisholm, *Unbought and Unbossed* (Boston: Houghton Mifflin Co., 1970), pp. 84, 86.
27. *New York Times,* April 3, 1977, p. 37.
28. U.S., Congress, House, *Committee Organization in the House,* House Doc. 94-187, 94th Cong., 1st sess., 1975, p. 32.
29. *New York Times,* January 25, 1981, p. E5. For discussion of the House assignment process, see Nicholas Masters, "Committee Assignments in the House of Representatives," *American Political Science Review* (June 1961): 345-357; Charles C. Bullock III, "Freshmen Committee Assignments and Re-election in the United States House of Representatives," *American Political Science Review* (September 1972): 996-1007; David Rohde and Kenneth Shepsle, "Democratic Committee Assignments in the House of Representatives: Strategic Aspects of a Social Choice Process," *American Political Science Review* (September 1973): 889-905; Irwin N. Gertzog, "The Routinization of Committee Assignments in the U.S. House of Representatives," *American Journal of Political Science* (November 1976): 693-712; Shepsle, *The Giant Jigsaw Puzzle;* and Richard E. Cohen, "The Mysterious Ways Congress Makes Committee Assignments," *National Journal,* February 3, 1979, pp. 183-188.
30. *Congressional Quarterly Weekly Report,* November 18, 1978, p. 3328.
31. *New York Times,* January 23, 1977, pp. E5 and 19.
32. *Washington Post,* March 4, 1973, p. E6.
33. *Human Events,* January 22, 1977, p. 5; *Washington Star,* February 10, 1977, p. A5; *Washington Post,* February 10, 1977, p. A5; and *New York Times,* February 11, 1977, p. A27.

34. *New York Times,* February 1, 1971, p. 18.
35. See Richard F. Fenno, Jr., "The House of Representatives and Federal Aid to Education," in *New Perspectives on the House of Representatives,* ed. Nelson W. Polsby and Robert L. Peabody (Chicago: Rand McNally & Co., 1963), pp. 195-303.
36. See David W. Rohde, "Committee Reform in the House of Representatives and the Subcommittee Bill of Rights," *The Annals* (January 1974): 39-47; Norman J. Ornstein, "The Democrats Reform Power in the House of Representatives, 1969-75," in *America in the Seventies,* ed. Allan P. Sindler (Boston: Little, Brown & Co., 1977), pp. 2-48; and Norman J. Ornstein, Robert L. Peabody, and David W. Rohde, "The Contemporary Senate: Into the 1980s," in *Congress Reconsidered,* 2d ed, edited by Lawrence C. Dodd and Bruce I. Oppenheimer (Washington, D.C.: Congressional Quarterly Press, 1981), pp. 13-30.
37. *Chicago Tribune,* August 25, 1978, p. 4.
38. *Washington Post,* September 12, 1971, p. B1. For a study of changes in Ways and Means, see Catherine E. Rudder, "Committee Reform and the Revenue Process," in *Congress Reconsidered,* 1st ed., edited by Dodd and Oppenheimer (New York: Praeger Publishers, 1977), pp. 117-139; and Irwin B. Arieff, "New Role for Rostenkowski Gets Him Into the Thick of House Power-Playing," *Congressional Quarterly Weekly Report,* May 16, 1981, p. 864.
39. Alan Ehrenhalt, "Senate Finance: The Fiefdom of Russell Long," *Congressional Quarterly Weekly Report,* September 10, 1977, p. 1905. See Richard E. Cohen, "If the Chairman's Word Isn't Law, Can This Be the Finance Committee?" *National Journal,* April 12, 1980, pp. 600-603; and Dale Tate, "Senate Finance Under Dole Retains Bipartisan Approach," *Congressional Quarterly Weekly Report,* January 31, 1981, pp. 217-219.
40. U.S., Congress, Senate, *Congressional Record,* daily ed., 96th Cong., 2d sess., March 12, 1980, p. S2432.
41. Richard E. Cohen, "A Chairmanship No Longer Guarantees A Lengthy Career in Congress," *National Journal,* October 25, 1980, pp. 1795-1799.
42. *Wall Street Journal,* May 3, 1979, p. 24.
43. *New York Times,* January 25, 1979, p. D13. Two years later, the two panels again tussled over a telecommunications bill. See U.S., Congress, Senate, *Congressional Record,* daily ed., 97th Cong., 1st sess., June 2, 1981, pp. S5643-S5652.
44. U.S., Congress, Senate, *Congressional Record,* daily ed., 96th Cong., 1st sess., February 7, 1979, pp. S1126-S1127.
45. *Wall Street Journal,* September 26, 1980, p. 12.
46. *Congressional Quarterly Weekly Report,* October 4, 1980, p. 2909. The telecommunications bill also aroused controversy during the 97th Congress. See *Washington Post,* July 7, 1981, p. A1.
47. U.S., Congress, House, *Congressional Record,* daily ed., 97th Cong., 1st sess., June 4, 1981, p. H2620.
48. U.S., Congress, Senate, *Congressional Record,* daily ed., 93rd Cong., 2d sess., January 30, 1974, pp. S765-S766.
49. *Washington Post,* May 19, 1975, p. A2.
50. Ibid. See Bob Eckhardt, "The Presumption of Committee Openness Under House Rules," *Harvard Journal on Legislation* (February 1974): 279-302; Albert Gore, "Legislative Secrecy," in *None of Your Business,* ed. Norman Dorsen and Stephen Gillers (New York: The Viking Press, 1974), pp. 137-150; and *Wall Street Journal,* July 8, 1980, p. 26.

51. Eric Redman, *The Dance of Legislation* (New York: Simon & Schuster, 1973), p. 140.
52. Hugh Heclo, "Issue Networks in the Executive Establishment," in *The New American Political System*, ed. Anthony King (Washington, D.C.: American Enterprise Institute for Public Policy Research, 1978), pp. 87-124.
53. E. E. Schattschneider, *The Semisovereign People* (New York: Holt, Rinehart & Winston, 1960).
54. Fenno, *Congressmen in Committees*, pp. 218-283. See David E. Price, "Policy Making in Congressional Committees: The Impact of 'Environmental Factors,'" *American Political Science Review* (Fall 1978): 548-574.
55. Roger H. Davidson and Walter J. Oleszek, *Congress against Itself* (Bloomington: Indiana University Press, 1977).
56. Judith H. Parris, "The Senate Reorganizes Its Committees: 1977," *Political Science Quarterly* (Summer 1979): 319-337; and Roger H. Davidson, "Two Roads of Change: House and Senate Committee Reorganization," *Congress Reconsidered*, 2d ed., pp. 107-133.
57. U.S., Congress, House, *Congressional Record*, daily ed., 96th Cong. 2d sess., March 25, 1980, p. H2139.
58. U.S., Congress, House, Select Committee on Committees, *Final Report*, H. Rept. No. 96-866, 96th Congress, 2d sess., p. 2.
59. *Roll Call*, January 25, 1979, p. 3.
60. *Washington Star*, January 24, 1979, p. A3.
61. Bernard Asbell, *The Senate Nobody Knows* (New York: Doubleday & Co., 1978), p. 338.
62. Norman J. Ornstein, "Causes and Consequences of Congressional Change: Subcommittee Reforms in the House of Representatives, 1970-1973," *Congress in Change*, pp. 102-103.
63. *Washington Post*, December 6, 1978, p. A2.
64. See Roger H. Davidson, "Subcommittee Government: New Channels for Policy Making," in *The New Congress*, ed. Thomas E. Mann and Norman J. Ornstein (Washington, D.C.: American Enterprise Institute for Public Policy Research, 1981), pp. 99-133.
65. Bob Eckhardt and Charles L. Black, Jr., *The Tides of Power* (New Haven: Yale University Press, 1976), p. 130.
66. David E. Price, "Congressional Committees in the Policy Process," in *Congress Reconsidered*, 2d ed., pp. 156-185.

Congressional Staff

"Most Friday mornings in Washington, about 40 people meet for breakfast in a private dining room in the Capitol. Together they constitute one of the most powerful groups in Washington, but the names and faces of most of them would not be familiar to the average newspaper reader." [1] And that is the way the "Chairmen's Group," the key aides to Senate committee chairmen, want it.

Besides the 540 members of Congress, there are thousands of nonvoting lawmakers on Capitol Hill. The unelected staff aides of committees and members constitute a behind-the-scenes "shadow government" that shapes the nation's policies. Legislative employees process Congress's workload, suggest policy initiatives, mobilize public opinion, advise legislators how to vote, serve constituents, and review agency implementation of laws. "We're finding that when it comes to getting something done, we are often better dealing with an aide," commented a Reagan White House staffer. "He has more influence with the member than I do. And he has access." [2]

Congress has not always relied heavily on staff. Not until 1885 and 1893, respectively, did each senator and representative receive a personal aide. Before that individual legislators either performed their duties without any assistance or hired clerks out of personal

235

funds. A similar pattern prevailed for committees. They began to hire temporary clerks during the 1850s. By 1900 standing committees in both chambers were provided funds to employ full-time aides.[3]

Inadequate committee staffing was the most urgent complaint heard by the Joint Committee on the Organization of Congress, the group that wrote the Legislative Reorganization Act of 1946:

> Such complaints came not only from Congress itself, but also were mentioned by almost every student of governmental affairs who appeared [to testify]. The shocking lack of adequate congressional fact-finding services and skilled staffs sometimes reaches such ridiculous proportions as to make Congress dependent upon "hand-outs" from Government departments and private groups or newspaper stories for its basic fund of information on which to base legislative decisions.[4]

By the 1980s Congress had come full circle. A 1980 survey found that more than 64 percent of representatives and senators thought that Congress was overstaffed.[5] "More staff creates more work, more projects to be done, more bills to be written," said Representative Morris K. Udall, D-Ariz.[6] Asserted Senator Alan K. Simpson, R-Wyo.: "The staff has the power to overwhelm individual members with a workload which leads to legislation not even tinged with the aura of common sense but which only springs from a highly technical and clinical viewpoint of the eager and 'burrowing in' staff member."[7]

In 1981 both chambers cut committee budgets 10 percent to show they were doing their part to fight inflation. For the first time committee budgets were adopted as a package rather than individually by committee. (Because the panels had not spent all that was authorized in 1980, actual funding for 1981 was about the same as the previous year.) In the Republican-controlled Senate, Majority Leader Howard H. Baker, Jr., of Tennessee engineered the cutback with the strong support of Democratic senators. Baker explained:

> As my colleagues may recall, this past September 15, [1980], I joined my distinguished counterpart from the House of Representatives, John Rhodes, and then-candidates Ronald Reagan and George Bush in pledging to reduce the operating costs of the Federal Government. We further pledged at that time to set an example for other branches of the Government by reducing the expenses and in keeping with our pledge, we established a goal of a 10-percent reduction in the Senate operating budget.[8]

The Democratic-controlled House, under considerable pressure to follow the Senate's lead and curb "stafflation," voted the reduction to stave off deeper cuts being pressed by GOP members.

In this chapter we address the growth of Congress's staff bureaucracy; the role of personal and committee staffs—who they are, what they do, and how they influence policy and elections; and the duties of the Congressional Research Service (CRS), the General Accounting Office (GAO), the Office of Technology Assessment (OTA), and the Congressional Budget Office (CBO)—four legislative support agencies that provide information and analysis to Congress.

THE LEGISLATIVE BUREAUCRACY

The cost of Congress and its staff and supporting agencies has increased dramatically. The congressional budget rose from $276.8 million in 1968 to $1.3 billion in 1981. The House and Senate employed 6,300 people in 1960, more than 14,000 two decades later. Including janitors, cooks, police, administrators, printers, and support agency personnel, about 39,000 people worked for the legislative branch in 1981. Table 8-1 highlights the rapid growth of personal and committee aides in the House and Senate since 1947.

Causes of Staff Growth

Like the executive branch, the legislative branch during the 1970s continued to grow—a trend that may have been halted or slowed by the economy-minded 97th Congress (1981-1983). Even if Congress manages to retrench, it is not likely to return to the old days of small staffs. So many aides have been recruited for Congress in recent years that the House and Senate have been forced to construct new office buildings or convert former hotels, apartments, or federal buildings into offices. Consultants have even been hired to assist legislators in office management.[9]

Numerous factors account for the staff explosion. Among them are complexity of issues, expanding workload, competition among committees and members, election of activist members, diffusion of power, constituency service, and legislative-executive conflict.

The array of complex and interdependent issues that fills Congress's agenda is staggering. Unable to specialize in everything, members need staffs for substantive and political guidance.

The modern Congress, unlike its predecessors, is a year-round institution. This means there are more committee meetings, longer floor sessions, more participants who need to be consulted before decisions can be made, and greater reliance on staff at every major phase of the legislative process. Legislators cannot handle the heavy congressional workload on their own.

Members and committees view their aides as the currency of political power on Capitol Hill because they enable them to influence a wide range of policy matters. Competition develops for the greatest influence. Senator Edward M. Kennedy, D-Mass., "assembled a large

Table 8-1 Number of Congressional Staff, Selected Years 1947-1980

Year	Personal Staff		Committee Staff	
	House	Senate	House	Senate
1947	1,440	590	167	232
1955	—	—	329	386
1957	2,441	1,115	—	—
1965	—	—	571	509
1967	4,055	1,749	—	—
1971	5,381	2,456	729	711
1972	5,827	2,683	817	844
1973	5,994	2,747	878	873
1974	6,120	3,096	1,107	948
1975	6,615	3,188	1,433	1,277
1976	6,828	3,099	1,680	1,201
1977	6,315	3,554	1,776	1,028
1978	6,295	3,268	1,844	1,151
1979	7,067	3,612	1,959	1,098
1980	8,667	4,281	1,918	1,108

SOURCE: House Select Committee on Committees, *Final Report,* House Report No. 96-866, p. 539; Harrison W. Fox, Jr., and Susan Webb Hammond, *Congressional Staffs* (New York: The Free Press, 1977), p. 171; Judy Schneider, "Congressional Staffing: 1947-1978," Congressional Research Service, August 24, 1979, p. 21; Michael J. Malbin, *Unelected Representatives* (New York: Basic Books, 1980), pp. 253-256. Schneider provided figures for 1980.

staff with one primary purpose in mind: to prepare him to take action on nearly any public issue—whether or not it is within the jurisdiction of one of his committees—on short notice." [10] Kennedy often leads floor fights against tax bills reported by the Finance Committee. He doesn't serve on the panel, but his numerous aides have helped him to become a forceful and effective spokesman on tax issues.

During the past decade younger and more activist members have been elected to Congress. These newcomers want to affect policy quickly and realize they need staff to do so. In 1975 junior senators, objecting to committee staff serving senior members first and junior members last, won the right to hire their own committee staff assistants. *(See box, p. 239.)* Senator Bob Packwood, R-Ore., explained that junior senators were asking for "an equal shot with the senior senators to committee staff so that when we are working on an antiballistic missile system or a general revenue-sharing proposal, we have the same access that the senior senators do to professional staff assistance." [11]

The shift from committee to subcommittee government, discussed in Chapters 6 and 7, has also led to an increase in staffs. In 1951 the House had 69 subcommittees; by 1981 there were about 150 subcommittees. Under House rules subcommittee chairmen and ranking minority

Measures Affecting Committee Staff

Following is a brief description of the major measures Congress has approved since 1946 that affect the hiring of congressional committee staffs:

Legislative Reorganization Act of 1946. Passage of the Legislative Reorganization Act of 1946 constituted a landmark for committee staffing: it established a permanent complement of expert staff for all standing committees, and it directed that staff be appointed on the basis of merit and not political affiliation. The latter directive is not always observed because committees prefer to hire their own Democratic or Republican "experts." Under the Act, committees were allowed to hire four professional staff aides and six clerical aides.

Legislative Reorganization Act of 1970. The 1970 Act increased from four to six the number of professional aides for most standing committees. The minority party was authorized to hire two of them and one of the six clerical aides. The 1970 Act also permitted committees to provide training for staff aides and to hire consultants.

House Committee Reform Amendments of 1974. This measure tripled the staffs of most standing committees. The number of professional aides went from 6 to 18 and clerical employees from 6 to 12, with the minority party allowed to appoint one-third of each category.

Senate Resolution 60. On June 12, 1975, the Senate adopted S Res 60, which instituted the idea of associate committee staff—aides who would help a senator with his or her committee work. The resolution authorized three committee assistants.

Senate Committee System Reorganization Amendments of 1977. This measure directed that committee staffs should be in proportion to the majority and minority members on a standing committee. It further directed that a "majority of the minority members of any committee may, by resolution, request that at least one-third of the funds of the committee for statutory, investigative, and clerical personnel ... be allocated to the minority members."

members are guaranteed one staff aide each in addition to whatever other staff assistance they obtain from the full committee or other sources.

With the growth of federal bureaucracy and the decline of party organization, members of Congress are increasingly looked upon as "ombudsmen" who can help constituents secure grants, loans, or projects for the state or district. "We're the last refuge for people with a problem," observed a representative. "That has expanded our staff from four to eighteen people." [12]

Finally, in the wake of the Vietnam war and Watergate, distrust of the executive branch ballooned. The House and Senate determined that they needed more and better staff help to evaluate executive proposals, monitor administrative performance, and initiate legislation. Imitation of the executive branch is also a factor in legislative staff growth. Senator Daniel Patrick Moynihan, D-N.Y., dubbed this the "Iron Law of Emulation." Whenever any branch of the government acquires a "new technique which enhances its power in relation to the other branches, that technique will soon be adopted by those other branches as well," he said. [13] The result: Congress created its own bureaucracy to keep up with the executive's.

Consequences of Staff Growth

Cost. The congressional staff explosion has led to a quantum jump in congressional costs, as Figure 8-1 illustrates. Included in the legislative budget are expenses for the Library of Congress, U.S. Government Printing Office, and the Architect of the Capitol.

Some members want to cut staff to save money and eliminate deadwood. (Senator William Proxmire, D-Wis., even conferred his monthly Golden Fleece Award for wasteful federal spending on Congress itself for the spiraling cost of its staff.) Others believe staff growth is necessary to preserve Congress's status as a coequal branch, serve constituent needs, and save taxpayers' dollars through increased surveillance of the administration of laws. "Congress is damned if you do and damned if you don't," said Representative David Obey, D-Wis. "If you don't increase your capability, you're ridiculed as being the sapless branch. If you do something, you're rapped for being a $1 billion Congress." [14]

Control. Many staff aides have latitude to develop, sell, and mobilize support for their ideas. On occasion, such "entrepreneurial" staff may unilaterally leak information, plant stories with the press, issue reports, harass agency officials, or invoke their member's name to do things he or she might be unaware of. (The same criticisms are leveled at White House staff.) Such actions raise questions as to whether busy legislators adequately supervise their employees. A related concern is staff domination. "I don't think a member has to become a captive of his staff," observed a representative, "but it's possible if you're not concerned about it." [15]

Figure 8-1 Costs of Running Congress, 1955-1980

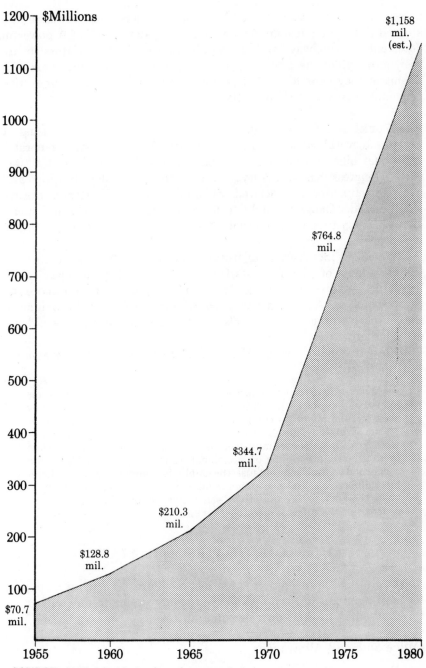

SOURCE: Annual legislative branch appropriations reports.

NOTE: Overall federal budget growth also escalated dramatically during this period.

Questions of control often are answered by the notion of derivative power. "A staff guy can have only as much influence and power as he's allowed to from his leader," commented a legislative aide.[16] A powerful deterrent to "runaway" staff is the absolute right of legislators to fire their aides. Like the president, however, legislators are prisoners of a dilemma: they cannot do their work without staff help, but they risk becoming captives of their staffs.

Workload. Paradoxically, staff both facilitate the processing of Congress's workload and contribute to it. "Additional staff generates additional bills and additional work, much of it unneeded, at a time when Congress has difficulty coping with its regular, routine, and oversight functions," declared Senator Proxmire.[17] Representative Udall added, "Congress ought to focus on the big issues. But I spend about half my time in fights that my staff or somebody else's staff gets me into." [18]

Workload increases stem from quantitative as well as qualitative trends. Many of the new staff recruits are policy activists. Even legislators predisposed to laziness can be pushed to do more by aggressive staff. All this activism contributes to the overburdening of the legislative process. It may also lead to useful work that would not get done otherwise.

Former Senator James Abourezk, D-S.D., defended congressional staff increases:

> The private constituencies that influence Congress—the arms industry, the lobby which protects corporate tax benefits, the money industry, the major oil companies—are much better off without congressional staffs. These private concerns, in concert with their guardians throughout the administration, find success much easier when there is no countervailing congressional staff to dispute their facts and conclusions....Precisely because the public is unorganized—and therefore vulnerable to the economic predators who can always find a way to press their legislative objectives—an active, if sometimes redundant, congressional staff is imperative.[19]

THE ROLE OF PERSONAL STAFF

Capitol Hill bureaucracy is not just one bureaucracy but many; yet for most members, the staff who have the largest day-to-day impact are those attached to their own personal offices.

Office Size and Allowances

Representatives and senators head sizable office enterprises that reflect their "two Congresses" responsibilities. In 1981 each House member was entitled to an annual clerk hire allowance of $336,384. With this money members may hire no more than 18 full-time and 4 part-time employees. The average House member's staff numbers about 15. (Members' allowances are detailed on page 124.)

Representatives also are entitled to an annual official expenses allowance, which in 1981 amounted to $47,300. This money is used for stationery, postage, computer services, mass mailings, and similar expenses. Additional allowances included $35,000 for office equipment and up to $38,000 for members' trips to their home districts. House members may increase their official expenses allowance by $15,000 if they lower their clerk hire allowance by a like amount.

Senators' personal staffs range in size from 13 to 71, with an average of about 31. Unlike the House, there are no limits on the number of staff a senator may employ from his or her clerk hire money, which varies according to a state's population. In 1981 the allowance ranged from $592,608 for a senator representing fewer than 2 million people to $1,190,724 for a senator from a state with 21 million. There are 16 population categories. Similarly, a senator's official expenses account varies from $33,000 to $143,000, depending upon factors such as the state's population and its distance from Washington, D.C.[20]

Organization

No two congressional offices are exactly alike. Each office is shaped by the personality, interests, constituency, and position of the individual legislator.

Members' role expectations are imprinted upon their staff organization. Those who specialize in legislation will hire experts; those who stress constituency service will closely supervise caseworkers and be prepared to intervene personally whenever needed. Political aspirants will hire seasoned press aides and will put great stock in production of press releases, targeted mailings, and radio and TV spots.

State and district needs weigh heavily in members' thinking about staff organization. Some districts require attention to government projects or programs; others have a large casework burden. A farm-state senator likely will employ at least one specialist in agricultural problems; an urban representative might hire a consumer affairs or housing expert. Moreover, traditions are important. If a legislator's predecessor had an enviable reputation for a certain type of service, the new incumbent will try to do it even better.

The member's institutional position also affects staff organization. Committee and subcommittee chairmen have committee staff at their disposal. Members without such aides rely heavily on personal staff for committee work.

Functions of Personal Staff

No matter how a congressional office is structured, it probably contains an administrative assistant (AA), legislative assistants (LAs), caseworkers, and at least one press aide.

The administrative assistant supervises the office and imparts political and legislative advice. AAs often function as the legislator's alter ego, negotiating with colleagues, constituents, and lobbyists. The office's legislative functions usually are handled by legislative assistants who work with members in committees, draft bills, write speeches, suggest policy initiatives, analyze bills, and prepare position papers. LAs also monitor committee sessions that the member cannot attend.

When Walter Mondale was a senator from Minnesota, he resolved a conflict in schedules this way:

> As the hands of the clock opposite [his] desk neared 10 a.m., he faced a decision. Should he attend a meeting of the Senate Budget Committee? Should he go to the Senate Select Committee on Intelligence hearing? Or should he attend a Labor and Public Welfare subcommittee hearing on health manpower legislation? All three were to begin at 10 a.m.
>
> "I think we may have some fireworks today," said David Aaron, his top aide on the Intelligence Committee.
>
> Senator Mondale nodded and said: "I think you're right."
>
> Then returning to his Budget Committee aide, David Carp, he asked: "How about the budget? How far are we likely to get on that today?"
>
> "I think you can skip the morning," replied Mr. Carp. "I'll keep an eye on it."
>
> Minutes later, accompanied by Mr. Aaron, Senator Mondale headed for the intelligence hearing, Mr. Carp set out for the budget meeting and another staff aide was deployed to monitor the health manpower hearing.[21]

Caseworkers help constituents deal with executive agencies and departments. They track down lost Social Security checks, expedite requests for veterans' benefits, or restore federal insurance claims. These staff aides also advise citizens, communities, and organizations on ways to qualify for federal grants, contracts, or subsidies. When projects are allocated to a state or district, it is customary for the member to announce the award and thus claim some credit for it.[22] The casework and project activities of members and staff highlight the institutional-electoral connection. No wonder most legislators work diligently to develop a reputation for providing good constituency service.

To emphasize the "personal touch," many legislators have moved Washington-based casework staff back to their home districts or states. "In 1970, there were 1,035 district-based staffers; in 1974, 1,519; and in 1979, 2,445."[23] Virtually all House and Senate members have home offices in post offices or federal buildings, and some members have as many as five or six. With the decline of party workers who helped local citizens, members' district staffs are filling this need and, simultaneously, enhancing members' reelection prospects.

Many other reasons are cited for decentralizing constituent functions. Congressional office buildings on Capitol Hill are crowded. Field offices have lower staff salaries and lower overhead, and they are also more convenient, permitting face-to-face contact with constituents and closer liaison with local and state officials, not to mention regional federal officers. This decentralizing trend, which is likely to continue, implies a heightened division between legislative functions based on Capitol Hill and constituency functions based in field offices.

Finally, many legislators hire press aides to deal with the media, particularly local and regional newspapers, radio stations, and television networks. The press aides write monthly newsletters, prepare speeches and press releases, answer inquiries from journalists, arrange for press briefings, and, in general, encourage favorable publicity for their member. For example, an event in the office of Senator Lowell Weicker, R-Conn., illustrates how favorable news can be generated from one constituent's letter.

> A woman shipped her dog by air and found that it was dead upon arrival. She then wrote Senator Weicker to complain about airline handling of animal cargo. One of the Senator's secretaries, a lover of dogs, was about to mail a routine reply when she mentioned the situation to the press secretary, Hank Price, who spotted the possibility that the "dog letter" had news value. To get information on other such cases, he phoned the Federal Aviation Agency, the Department of Agriculture, and the Civil Aeronautics Board. The last had recorded at least a dozen similar cases, while the Humane Society, which he also contacted, indicated that there had been more than one hundred cases. Upon presenting this information to the Senator, the press secretary next found himself drafting a bill for the purpose of authorizing the Secretary of Transportation to draft rules and regulations governing transport of animals by air, which Mr. Weicker introduced on the floor of the U.S. Senate. The story became front page news in Connecticut. It had human interest; "everybody" has a dog. Appreciative mail flowed heavily into the Senator's office. One constituent, whose letter is well remembered, wrote that he had never voted for a Republican in his life, but he loved animals and would vote for Lowell Weicker in future elections.[24]

Personal Staff Profile

As Table 8-2 indicates, most House and Senate personal aides are young, male, well-educated, and remain in their position about four years. The mix of personal staff attributes is a decision of each member. "It is great to have a receptionist who is from (the home state)," said a Senate AA, "but beyond her and three or four others it is not necessary to have (home state) people. In fact it is sometimes a detriment, in that they may sometimes have their own constituency." [25]

In summary, congressional offices are relatively informal and staffers are expected to display flexibility in taking on new duties. Many staff members are expert in their jobs—especially caseworkers who are knowledgeable about federal agencies and programs, those legislative assistants who are policy experts, and office managers who are familiar

Table 8-2   Age, Tenure, Sex, and Education of Personal Staff (In Percentages)

Age

	(N)	Under 30	30-39	40-59	60 or Over	Average Age
Senate						
Total population	(481)	18.5	42.4	34.4	4.7	38.6
All respondents	(244)	18.5	38.6	38.1	4.8	38.9
Not responding	(237)	18.4	49.4	27.6	4.6	37.7
House	(50)	46	22	32		
AAs	(22)	9	32	59		42
LAs	(18)	67	17	17		—
Other professional assistants	(10)	90	10	0		—

Tenure

	(N)	Less Than 4 Years	4-10 Years	11-20 Years	More Than 20 Years
House AAs	(22)	40.9	31.8	27.3	—

Sex

	(N)	Men	Women
Senate			
Total population	(470)	77.1	22.9
All respondents	(233)	80.7	19.3
Not responding	(237)	73.8	26.2
House			
(25 offices)	(62)	69.4	30.6

Education

	(N)	No College	Some College	B.A.	M.A. or M.S.	J.D. or LL.B.	Ph.D.
Senate AAs	(76)	7	5	38	14	30	5
LAs	(87)	1	1	25	13	52	8
House AAs	(265)	10	14	41	15	18	2
LAs	(189)	4.2	2.6	47	19	25	2.1

SOURCE: Harrison W. Fox, Jr., and Susan Webb Hammond, *Congressional Staffs* (New York: The Free Press, 1977), pp. 173-175, 178. © 1977 by The Free Press, a Division of Macmillan Publishing Co., Inc. Reprinted by permission.

with Hill operations. Many of them use their expertise in moving from office to office, regardless of the member's state or district.

THE ROLE OF COMMITTEE STAFF

Personal staff are fundamentally concerned with their member's reelection. Committee staff act primarily in policy and oversight capacities. To a great extent, congressional decisions are influenced by committee aides. Given the demands on members, it is hardly surprising, wrote former Senator James Buckley of New York, "that the professional staffs assigned to each committee and subcommittee should assume so important, even dominant, a role in the legislative process." [26]

Committee Staff Organization

Although each committee is different, and each has its own staff structure, common organizational patterns can be discerned.[27] Figure 8-2 shows three types of staff organization. Type I is hierarchical. The staff director is the central link between other committee aides and the chairman. The professional staff contact the chairman through the staff director, who also funnels the chairman's directives to the staff.

Type II is egalitarian. Everyone on the professional staff has direct access to the chairman. "This arrangement is more demanding for the committee or subcommittee chairman, and tends to be utilized where the professional staff is small." [28] Finally, Type III divides supervision of professional and clerical aides between the staff director and chief clerk.

Staff organization reflects tradition, preferences of committee leaders, partisan and ideological splits, and issues a committee considers. In practice, these overlapping factors help account for bipartisan or partisan, centralized or decentralized staff arrangements.

Arthur H. Vandenberg, R-Mich., chairman of the Senate Foreign Relations Committee from 1947 to 1949, believed that coherent, consistent foreign policy could best be promoted through cooperation among Congress, the president, and the two parties. As a result, the Foreign Relations staff was hired and fired by key majority and minority members and served all committee members regardless of party or seniority. The bipartisan staff tradition on Foreign Relations continued until 1979 when a "new minority" of Republicans came onto the committee, led by Senators Jesse Helms of North Carolina, S. I. Hayakawa of California, and Richard Lugar of Indiana. They wanted and received separate minority staff. "Vandenberg was fine for his time," said an aide to Senator Helms. "But times have changed." [29]

Figure 8-2   Patterns of Staff Organization

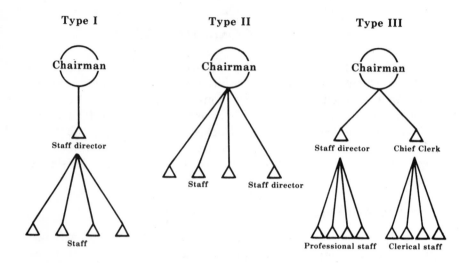

Panels may have centralized or decentralized staff patterns. During his long chairmanship of the Senate Commerce Committee (1955-1979), Warren G. Magnuson, D-Wash., apportioned the majority staff among issues and subcommittees as conditions warranted. This enabled him to exercise large influence over the activities of his subcommittees.[30] The reverse arrangement is to give subcommittees autonomous staffs, as the Senate Judiciary Committee does. James O. Eastland, D-Miss., who headed the panel from 1956 to 1979, gradually devolved authority to its subcommittees in response to the assertiveness of the Democratic members. Under Eastland, "all the full committee provided was a nonfunctional administrative shell," said a Senate aide.[31] A virtue of this system is that it permits subcommittee chairmen to appoint loyal and trusted aides. But it also results in wholesale staff shifts when the subcommittee leadership changes.[32]

Staff Authorization and Funding

In general, there are two principal types of committee staff— permanent and investigative—each authorized in a different manner. Permanent staff are established by public law or congressional rule and are funded in the annual legislative branch appropriation bill. In 1975 the House amended its rules and increased the number of permanent professional aides from 6 to 18 and clerical aides from 6 to 12.

To supplement the permanent aides, committees annually hire "investigative" staff. Although considered temporary, these aides often remain with a committee year after year. The procedure for gaining authority and funds for investigative staff is virtually identical in both houses. The committees' draft budgets, embodied in resolutions, are referred to either the Committee on House Administration or the Senate Rules and Administration Committee. Those panels then conduct hearings and markups and report the resolutions to the full chamber.

In 1981 the Senate eliminated the distinction between permanent and temporary staff and required committees to include all operating expenses in one budget request. This was done to gain better financial control over soaring staff costs.

Committees may employ consultants, take on interns, or "borrow" staff temporarily from federal agencies or legislative support agencies. As George Mahon, D-Texas, then House Appropriations Committee chairman, explained:

> We also use investigators that are recruited by our chief investigator. Some of them come from the Treasury and other departments and agencies and some are consultants who are adept in certain fields. Of course, a number of them come from the Federal Bureau of Investigation on loan. They generally come from various places in the Federal Government. That is an excellent procedure. We could not hire an army of investigators qualified in special fields and keep them on our payroll indefinitely. It would be inefficient and very costly. The criteria in selecting investigative personnel is objectivity and competence. We try to get select people. If a particular study has to do with highly technical matter, we get engineers or people from whatever profession is called for. This is the way we have done it. They work for the committee on a temporary reimbursable basis.[33]

A few committees have even established special advisory panels, composed of outside experts, to assist in policy formulation and analysis.[34]

Functions of Committee Staff

Committee staff functions differ from committee to committee. In general, however, committee staffs perform administrative (chief clerk), substantive (professional aides), political (staff director and chief counsel), and public relations (press officer) duties.

The professional staff are policy specialists who help committees develop and evaluate policies, suggest alternatives to legislation, advise members how to vote, oversee the administration of laws, and perform numerous other tasks. The main job of the staff director and chief counsel—often the chairman's handpicked aides—is to smooth the path of legislation. They maintain links with members and aides in the other body, with interest groups, and with federal agency officials; plan strategy on measures; mobilize public opinion behind bills; and forge majority coalitions in committee, on the floor, and in conference.

Organizing the office, arranging for hearing rooms, and keeping track of financial expenditures are a few of the responsibilities of the clerical staff. The press officer's duties include writing press releases that highlight committee activities, persuading journalists to cover committee hearings and meetings, and, in general, seeking favorable publicity for the committee, the chairman, and other members. On occasion, press aides may speak for the committee.

Information often flows between committee and personal aides. Personal staffers inquire about the status of bills or advise committee aides about their bosses' schedules and policy leanings. For their part, committee employees may encourage personal staffers to become involved in committee projects. Such relationships foster member involvement and backing for committee-reported measures. On occasion, rivalry and competition surface between personal and committee aides (as well as between majority and minority staffers).

Committee Staff Profile

Table 8-3 describes the age, tenure, sex, and education of committee staff. Like the personal staffers, the people who work for committees are relatively young, mobile, male, and well-educated.

Unlike staff aides of the past, who often were political operatives, staff members today are typically professionals with some expertise in their subject areas. The "best and brightest" graduates frequently gravitate to Capitol Hill to become involved in policymaking. Committee and personal staff have no job security. They can be fired with or without cause by the chairman or member who hired them.

THE POLICY ROLE OF STAFF

Congressional staffs put their imprint on practically every measure before Congress. Their influence can be direct or indirect, substantive or procedural, visible or invisible.

Shaping the Agenda

The discretionary agenda of Congress and its committees is shaped by the congressional staff. In the judgment of former Senator Norris Cotton, R-N.H.: "[M]ost of the work and most of the ideas come from the staffers. They are predominantly young men and women, fresh out of college and professional schools. They are ambitious, idealistic, and

Table 8-3 Age, Tenure, Sex, and Education of Committee Staff (In Percentages)

Age

	(N)	Under 30	30-39	40-59	60 or Over	Average Age
All committees	(313)	15.7	40.5	39.1	4.7	40.0
Senate standing	(126)	18.3	46.7	30.8	4.2	37.8
House standing	(130)	11.9	31.8	50.7	5.6	42.9

Tenure

	(N)	Less Than 4 Years	4-10 Years	11-20 Years	More Than 20 Years
All committee aides	(302)	49.7	33.1	13.9	3.3
Senate aides	(148)	56.3	29.8	11.1	2.8
House aides	(144)	44.5	35.1	16.8	3.6

Sex

	(N)	Men	Women
All committee staff	(306)	89.2	10.5
Senate standing	(126)	84.9	15.1
House standing	(129)	92.2	7.8

Education

	(N)	No College	Some College	B.A.	M.A.	J.D. or LL.B.	Ph.D.	M.D.
Committee professional staff	(313)	4.5	NA	24.8	17.2	45.0	7.6	0.7

SOURCE: Harrison W. Fox, Jr., and Susan Webb Hammond, *Congressional Staffs* (New York: The Free Press, 1977), pp. 173-175, 178. © 1977 by The Free Press, a Division of Macmillan Publishing Co., Inc. Reprinted by permission.

abounding with ideas." [35] Policy proposals emanate from many sources—the White House, administrative agencies, interest groups, state and local officials, scholars, and citizens—but staff aides are strategically positioned to advance or hinder these proposals. As one Senate committee staff director recounted: "Usually, you draw up proposals for the year's agenda, lay out the alternatives. You can put in some stuff you like and leave out some you don't. I recommend ideas that the [chairman's] interested in and also that I'm interested in." [36]

Staff aides can play the role of policy advocate or nonadvocate. Some committee staffers or "entrepreneurs" actively and aggressively promote their favorite proposals and search out legislators to sponsor and champion them. The nonadvocate, on the other hand, rarely generates issues, mainly providing information, analysis, and advice to members on request. These staff aides observe such norms as neutrality, objectivity, and anonymity. As one House staff director explained:

> In the end, the job of the staff is to help the committee do what it wants to do—to help it come to a decision and to help it implement a decision once it is reached. The staffs are nonpartisan in the sense that (1) they are not trying to play politics with the issue but are trying to help the committee come to a decision; (2) whoever comes along, they will try to give the same devoted service; and (3) they will not start from a political premise in their work but will start from a professional premise.[37]

Contrast this description of the staff's role in the legislative process with Senator Cotton's recollection:

> I recall one day sitting next to Senator Robert Griffin of Michigan in an executive session of a committee on which we both served, listening to a group of staff aides boldly disputing with members of the committee, including the chairman, and insisting their version of a bill was the result of careful study and should be accepted by the committee and reported to the Senate. Senator Griffin, grinning broadly, leaned over and whispered in my ear, "This committee spends most of its time arguing with its own staff." In that remark you have the whole [distinction between policy advocates and nonadvocates] in a nutshell.[38]

Needless to say, staff aides generally adopt the role most acceptable to the chairman and other committee members.

Conducting Investigations

Several times during the Indochina war, Senate Foreign Relations Committee Chairman J. W. Fulbright, D-Ark., dispatched aides to Vietnam and Cambodia because of inadequate information from the White House on the war's progress. Based on their on-the-scene investigations, staff reports to the committee challenged the Johnson and Nixon administrations' versions of the political and military outlook in Vietnam. In 1976 Senator John Tunney, D-Calif., armed with the information gathered in Angola by two aides, successfully sponsored an amendment halting covert CIA assistance to factions fighting there. As these two examples illustrate, Congress's investigative power undergirds its ability to make informed judgments on policy matters. And it is staff who do the essential spadework that can produce changes in policy or new laws.

Negotiating Compromises and Consensus

"I've learned that staffers are everything," said a freshman representative. Members are "stretched so thin that a lot of bargaining goes along at the staff level." [39] Staff aides negotiate with legislators, lobbyists, executive officials, and others on issues, legislative language, and political strategy. The basic negotiating objective is often to mobilize public and private resources and interests behind a congressional proposal.

Staff contributed significantly to Senate passage of the landmark Budget and Impoundment Control Act of 1974. Because many committees and senators opposed the budget reform bill reported by the Committee on Government Operations (now titled Governmental Affairs), Robert C. Byrd, D-W.Va., then majority whip, established a staff working group to hammer out a compromise.

> All standing committees were invited to designate representatives. The resulting staff effort to produce a "consensus" bill is probably without precedent in the Senate. In all, 45 staff members took part. . . . They came from ten standing committees of the Senate, four joint committees, the House Appropriations Committee, the Congressional Research Service, and the Office of Senate Legislative Counsel. . . .[40]

After 90 hours in 25 sessions during 16 days, the staff group's efforts succeeded: the consensus legislative budget bill passed, 88-0.

Giving Committee and Floor Advice

Staff aides are active in committee and floor deliberations. During hearings, the professional aides, on their own or at the specific direction of the chairman, recruit witnesses and plan when and in what order they appear. In 1977 a Senate committee staffer launched a nationwide search for a respected expert witness who would support his senator's controversial waterways bill. He succeeded. The expert's testimony won momentum for the proposal at a crucial time.[41]

Staff aides commonly accompany committees and members to the floor to give advice, draft amendments, and negotiate compromises. (The number of aides who can be present is limited, however, by House and Senate regulations.) In 1980 Senator Ted Stevens, R-Alaska, asked for a pause in Senate proceedings so that staff present on the floor could clarify a pending amendment.

> On the Melcher amendment, we do have the Commerce Committee staff here. I understand there is one matter they wish to discuss with Senator Melcher's staff, and I ask that we have a few minutes in which to do that. . . .[42]

THE ELECTORAL INFLUENCE OF STAFF

Representatives and senators wear two hats: the legislator's and the politician's. A story told by Estes Kefauver, D-Tenn., about his first day in Congress in 1939 underscores the dual roles of members. Kefauver asked Speaker William Bankhead, D-Ala., for advice on how to win reelection. Bankhead replied: "It is a simple secret. Give close and prompt attention to your mail. Your votes and speeches may make you well known and give you a reputation, but it's the way you handle your mail that determines your reelection." [43] Kefauver went on to win four more terms in the House and three in the Senate.

Although political campaigning has changed since Kefauver's day, members still recognize the importance of answering their mail promptly. In an era of "permanent campaigns," when few actions on Capitol Hill are free of political overtones, it is worth discussing several campaign functions of congressional staff.

Legal Status

No laws or congressional rules directly prohibit legislative employees from working in campaigns. Senate rules even permit two aides in a senator's office to be designated to solicit and receive campaign money. Several ethics rules and guidelines require staff aides not to neglect their "official duties," for which they are paid from public funds, by engaging in political campaigns. But this is a loose restriction. "Official duties" are defined by each member, and campaigning by aides in their free time is unlimited. To avoid criticism from opponents, however, many incumbents temporarily move their congressional staff off the public payroll and onto the campaign's.

In 1977 two lawyers sued Senator Howard W. Cannon, D-Nev., charging that his administrative assistant "worked extensively and exclusively on Senator Cannon's [1976] re-election campaign or campaign-related tasks which were not part of Senator Cannon's official legislative and representational tasks." [44] Cannon denied the charge, and a federal district court rejected the case. The two attorneys appealed. In 1981 an appeals court decided the issue posed a "political question" that the court could not answer.

The apparent effect of the decision was to permit members to keep staff aides on the congressional payroll and assign them campaign duties. That could change, however, if each house adopted regulations barring staff aides from campaign work. Several weeks after the appeals court decision, the Senate Ethics Committee "approved incorporating into the ethics code a 1977 Ethics Committee ruling that senators should take off their official payrolls staffers who are performing campaign duties to the detriment of their official Senate duties." [45]

Political-Substantive Connection

A member's political survival can depend on using information in an electoral context. A member who decides to take on an issue as a lawmaker may find that it is a two-edged sword. After more than a year of

Staff vs. Staff in Senate Race

In most contests, congressional aides doubling as campaign workers attract little attention. But that was not the case in 1978 in Colorado, where incumbent Democratic Senator Floyd K. Haskell was challenged by Republican Representative William L. Armstrong. Both campaigns used Capitol Hill staffers who had left the federal payroll. Both charged the opposition with unethical practices while claiming to be "squeaky clean" (Haskell) or "bending over backwards" to follow the law (Armstrong).

Walter Klein, Armstrong's administrative assistant, left the government payroll to manage the campaign. He said Haskell had been "derelict in drawing the distinction between political and congressional work." He accused Haskell's office of using government-paid interns to call voters. An Armstrong radio ad said Haskell "used Senate employees to raise funds for his reelection." Klein claimed that the director of Haskell's Denver office, Martin J. Wolf, was closely tied to the day-to-day workings of the campaign.

Wolf vehemently denied the charges. In two instances, he said, Senate employees had worked on campaign fund-raising after hours or had taken time off. Their names appeared in the Federal Election Commission records only because "any time anyone on the staff did anything that was political, and took more than a couple of days, they would go off the payroll and we billed their expenses to the campaign, just to make sure we were on the up and up with the FEC."

The telephoning, Wolf said, was "no different from sending out a questionnaire, it was an extension of our state operation." As for his own involvement in the campaign, Wolf said it was "virtually none at all. I really would like to [work on the campaign] but somebody's got to mind the shop."

The publicity prevented Haskell from bringing in other staff members. His legislative aide, Rob Libertore, had planned to spend the last three weeks of the campaign in Colorado, but Haskell refused to let him go. "If I showed up there," Libertore explained in an interview, "the Armstrong people would say, 'Ah, another Haskell aide.'"

SOURCE: Adapted from "Staff vs. Staff in Colorado Senate Race," *Congressional Quarterly Weekly Report,* October 28, 1978, p. 3117.

preparatory work by committee aides, Senator Kefauver launched an investigation in 1959 of overpricing by the drug industry. The next year pharmaceutical interests flooded Tennessee with money and literature urging Kefauver's defeat. "I never should have got mixed up in this drug thing," he told a committee aide. "Now I've got the drug people, the pharmacists, and the doctors all stirred up." [46]

At first things went badly for Kefauver, who refused to respond to the drug accusations. Instead, he talked about disarmament, NATO, and other matters.

Then, one day toward the close of the campaign, he was giving his more or less standard speech in a small town when the local druggist came out of his store, at the rear of the crowd, and began heckling him. At first, Kefauver ignored the man, but when he persisted, the Senator began citing facts and figures about the high cost of drugs. Suddenly, in a unique display of oratorical fervor, he flung out a long arm with forefinger pointing at the druggist, and cried, "There's one of your enemies!" The audience roared its approval, and there were shouts of "Give it to him, Estes!" [47]

During the rest of the campaign, Kefauver repeated this tactic. He would always speak near the local drugstore, using the same line and gesture with similar success. In the end he won, much to the surprise of the pollsters, the press, the drug industry and the senator himself.

Electoral Services

Congressional staff often provide the core of a member's circle of "intimates." At reelection time the administrative assistant might become the campaign manager, for example.

> The incumbent's staff, in short, allows him to attract and retain the nucleus of his personal political organization.... The incumbent fields a publicly paid team of experienced veterans to do a task they have succeeded in before, perhaps many times before, and which differs very little from their everyday jobs. [48]

Inevitably, the legitimate everyday activities of staff aides—answering mail, handling casework, maintaining computerized mailing files, or writing speeches—can yield electoral benefits.

LEGISLATIVE SUPPORT AGENCIES

Four support agencies provide Congress with information, analyses, research, and policy options. [49] The Congressional Research Service was established in 1914, the General Accounting Office in 1921, the Office of Technology Assessment in 1972, and the Congressional Budget Office in 1974. Unlike committee or personal aides, these agencies operate under strict rules of nonpartisanship and objectivity. Staffed with experts, they provide Congress with analytical talent matching that in the executive agencies, universities, or specialized groups.

Professional staff who work for the agencies operate in a congressional environment; their analyses are shaped by some of the same factors that affect committee and personal aides and that are extraneous to the quality of the research. For example, "trust" between a legislator and staffer is valued. How a report is received by a member can be colored by who prepared it. Another consideration is that Congress is an advocacy rather than an analytical body.

> Even when Congressmen and Senators seek a dispassionate, objective analysis, they are apt to be influenced by the syndrome of

"objective on our side." If members have political, ideological predispositions, or leanings on particular issues toward one particular position, they often tend to perceive as "objective" and "sound" information and analyses that substantiate and support their predispositions.[50]

Congressional Research Service

CRS is the only support agency "that is comprehensive in coverage and is equipped to provide immediate response as well as to undertake special studies and research projects," wrote the House Commission on Information and Facilities in 1975. It is the only agency that serves all members, committees, and staff aides.

CRS conducts seminars on specialized topics for members and staff, analyzes issues before Congress, undertakes legal research, maintains automated data bases, prepares digests and summaries of bills, furnishes questions for committee hearings, engages in policy analysis, and responds to thousands of requests for factual and statistical information.

Providing confidential and tailor-made information, CRS deals with every public issue, from abortion to zero population growth. Since enactment of the Legislative Reorganization Act of 1970, CRS (formerly called the Legislative Reference Service) works more closely with congressional committees and undertakes in-depth policy research, while still responding to immediate and short-term information needs. CRS's location in the Library of Congress underscores its reliance on published materials and documents rather than field investigations.

General Accounting Office

The "watchdog" of bureaucratic waste, fraud, and abuse, the GAO is Congress's main field investigator, auditor, and program evaluator. With employees located across the United States and in several foreign countries, GAO examines agency financial accounts, federal program performance, and the economy and efficiency of governmental operations.[51]

It is required by law to help committee chairmen, but most of its work for Congress is self-initiated. It seeks the views of committees, members, and staff aides to ensure that pertinent and valuable projects are undertaken. The agency accepts requests from all members, but the comptroller general assigns them priority. Most of GAO's reports (more than 1,000 each year) are available to the public.

Since the 1970s GAO has expanded its auditing and accounting role to embrace the difficult task of evaluating executive branch programs and policy decisions. Its policy recommendations and assessments cover both domestic and international issues. For example, a 1981 report concluded that "many major new weapons systems fail because of overly complex designs and a lack of attention to the abilities of the troops who must use them in the field." [52] GAO's staff has diversified from reliance on auditors, accountants, and lawyers to include social scientists, economists, scientists, engineers, systems analysts, and physicians.

Office of Technology Assessment

Heightened concern during the 1960s about Congress's capacity to address issues such as environmental degradation and supersonic transports spurred creation of OTA. Designed to inject technical and scientific thinking into legislative decisionmaking (Is saccharin harmful to people? How safe are nuclear reactors? What is the long-range potential of solar energy?), OTA's primary mandate is to conduct long-range studies of the social, biological, physical, economic, and political effects of technological issues and to provide Congress with an "early warning" of prospective issues.

Governed by a Technology Assessment Board composed of six representatives, six senators, and the OTA director, the agency assists congressional committees only, and the board must approve all assignments. In addition, the board receives the expert advice of an outside advisory group. Most of the OTA's work is accomplished through panel or contract studies. [53]

Congressional Budget Office

Created by the Budget and Impoundment Control Act of 1974, CBO is the legislative counterpart to two White House offices: the Office of Management and Budget and the Council of Economic Advisers. An integral part of the congressional budget process, the CBO assists, in order of priority, House and Senate Budget committees, House and Senate Appropriations committees, the Senate Finance Committee and House Ways and Means Committee, and finally all other congressional committees.

Among its assignments, CBO prepares five-year cost projections on proposed legislation, keeps daily score of congressional spending decisions, assesses the inflationary impact of major bills, analyzes and forecasts economic trends, evaluates the costs and benefits of fiscal options, and studies programs that affect the federal budget. The reports of CBO and other support agencies are often cited by members during congressional debates. CBO, in short, helps committees and members to evaluate and challenge the economic assumptions that underlie the president's national budget recommendations.

In March 1981, for example, CBO analysts said that President Reagan may have understated the projected budget deficit for 1982 and that the outlook was gloomy for a balanced budget by 1984 (a key Reagan objective). The president first called CBO's economic numbers "phony," but he later said they were based on assumptions different from his.[54] This dispute highlights how the neutral support agencies can become embroiled in controversy.

CONCLUSION

Thirty years ago, a noted scholar wrote that the "increasing importance of . . . staff assistants in the whole field of policy formulation is one of the most significant developments in Congress. . . ." [55] Today, the staff's role is even broader. Legislators are quick to acknowledge their dependence upon staffs. Good staff cannot make an ineffective officeholder a legislative giant, but a capable staff can make an average legislator look better and an outstanding legislator even more so. Conversely, an inept or badly managed staff can tarnish the reputation of even the most dedicated member. Given their important role, it is useful to review several major staff characteristics.

First, senators, because they are fewer in number than representatives, delegate functions to their staffs more readily. Historically, representatives prided themselves on "doing their own homework" and resented having to negotiate with Senate staff. Yet House ways have been changing. Dependence on staff—"Senatization"—is fast engulfing the House.

Second, the staff system reflects Congress's decentralized nature. Members and committees rule their own kingdoms. Staff recruitment is typically informal with many jobs found through the grapevine.

Third, although staffers tend to be adequately paid, they lack protections accorded workers in other occupations. Congressional employees can be removed at any time with or without cause.[56] For the most part, they lack seniority rights, job descriptions, salary structures, grievance procedures, and vacation, maternity, or sick leave policies. Moreover, Congress has exempted its employees from laws that regulate the work environment for people in private industry, such as the Equal Employment Opportunity Act, the Equal Pay Act, the Fair Labor Standards Act, and the Occupational Safety and Health Act.[57]

Legislators insist that this system is dictated by the political nature of their tasks and the need for trusted and loyal aides. Abuses occur, however, and there have been repeated charges of job discrimination and irregular assignments. In 1976 a Capitol Hill secretary, Elizabeth Ray, disclosed that she lacked clerical skills but had been hired to perform sexual favors for Representative Wayne Hays, D-Ohio. The resulting uproar ended Hays's congressional career and forced a wide-ranging study of House ethics and office procedures. However, it failed to yield any major alteration in the staffing system. Some House members did establish a voluntary Fair Employment Practices Committee to consider staff complaints against employers. Still, staff members are subject to the demands of a given office or committee, and still they lack overall standards of employment, salary, or grievance rights.

Fourth, staff careers are relatively short.[58] With the exception of career-oriented aides, a person with about six years of experience is an "old timer" by Hill standards. Given the high turnover of members, staff turnover is understandable. New members want to hire their own aides. Many aides view their positions as steppingstones to other jobs. Rapid staff turnover energizes Capitol Hill and infuses it with new ideas, but it also inhibits the development of staff expertise and regular review of the administration of laws.

Finally, staff growth appears to have paradoxical policy results. With "every member a king," to paraphrase Huey Long, all representatives and senators today have the means to advance individual or policy objectives in committee or on the floor. Yet Congress's ability to resolve public problems and reach consensus on legislation may be weakened because staffs permit members to be independent of committee chairmen and party leaders.

Congress has specialized offices and experts to draft proposed legislation (the House and Senate offices of legislative counsel) and to interpret the rules and precedents of each chamber (the House and Senate parliamentarians).[59] Other staff aides develop reputations for parliamentary legerdemain. In our next chapter, we focus upon Congress's rules and procedures and how they affect policymaking. Before ideas can be translated into public law, they must follow a procedural pathway noted for its twists and turns.

NOTES

1. *Washington Star,* February 2-3, 1978, p. A1.
2. *U.S. News & World Report,* March 9, 1981, p. 47.
3. Harrison W. Fox, Jr., and Susan Webb Hammond, *Congressional Staffs* (New York: The Free Press, 1977); and Kenneth Kofmehl, *Professional Staffs of Congress,* 3d ed., (West Lafayette, Ind.: Purdue University Press, 1977).
4. U.S., Congress, House, *Organization of the Congress,* House Report No. 1675, 79th Cong., 2d sess., 1946, p. 9.
5. *U.S. News & World Report,* January 14, 1980, p. 42.
6. U.S., Congress, *Congressional Record,* daily ed., 96th Cong., 2d sess., May 21, 1980, p. E2526.
7. *U.S. News & World Report,* January 14, 1980, p. 41.
8. U.S., Congress, Senate, *Congressional Record,* daily ed., 97th Cong., 1st sess., February 26, 1981, p. S15861.
9. Ross A. Webber, "U.S. Senators: See How They Run," *The Wharton Magazine* (Winter 1980-1981): 37-43.

10. Richard E. Cohen, "The Kennedy Staff: Putting the Senator Ahead," *National Journal,* December 3, 1977, p. 1882.
11. *Congressional Quarterly Weekly Report,* June 14, 1975, p. 1236. On staffing inequities for minority members, see Richard Bolling, *Power in the House* (New York: E. P. Dutton & Co., 1968), p. 264; and Patrick R. Mullen, "Congressional Reform: Minority Staffing in the House of Representatives," *Government Accounting Office Review* (Summer 1975): 32-40.
12. Thomas E. Cavanagh, "The Two Arenas of Congress: Electoral and Institutional Incentives for Performance" (Paper delivered at the annual meeting of the American Political Science Association, New York, New York, August 31-September 3, 1978), p. 31.
13. Daniel P. Moynihan, "Imperial Government," *Commentary* (June 1978): 26.
14. *New York Times,* January 16, 1977, p. 24.
15. Ibid., May 17, 1978, p. A9.
16. *Washington Post,* March 20, 1977, p. E10. See also David E. Price, "Professionals and 'Entrepreneurs': Staff Orientations and Policy Making on Three Senate Committees," *Journal of Politics* (May 1971): 316-336.
17. *Chicago Tribune,* November 11, 1979, p. 5.
18. *Wall Street Journal,* December 18, 1979, p. 1.
19. James G. Abourezk, "Many Hands Make Congress Work," *The Washington Post Book World,* August 31, 1980, p. 9.
20. Information on members' allowances is derived from the *Congressional Handbook,* Committee on House Administration, 96th Cong., 2d sess., December 1980; and from the *Senatorial Official Office Expense Account Seminar Handbook,* Senate Financial Clerk, 97th Cong., 1st sess., January 26, 1981. Paul Dwyer, Congressional Research Service, also provided information on congressional allowances.
21. *New York Times,* November 4, 1975, p. 33.
22. David Mayhew, *The Electoral Connection* (New Haven: Yale University Press, 1974); and Morris P. Fiorina, *Congress: Keystone of the Washington Establishment* (New Haven: Yale University Press, 1977).
23. Larry Light, "House Liberals Learned in 1980: Crack 'Outreach' Programs No Longer Ensure Reelection," *Congressional Quarterly Weekly Report,* February 14, 1981, p. 316.
24. Delmer D. Dunn, "Symbiosis: Congress and the Press," in *To Be A Congressman,* by Sven Groennings and Jonathan P. Hawley (Washington, D.C.: Acropolis Books, 1973), pp. 48-49.
25. Fox and Hammond, *Congressional Staffs,* p. 34.
26. James L. Buckley, *If Men Were Angels* (New York: G. P. Putnam's Sons, 1975), p. 133.
27. Samuel C. Patterson, "Congressional Committee Professional Staffing: Capabilities and Constraints," in *Legislatures in Developmental Perspective,* ed. Allan Kornberg and Lloyd D. Musolf (Durham, N.C.: Duke University Press, 1970).
28. Ibid., p. 421.
29. *Washington Post,* January 26, 1979, p. A4. See also William J. Lanouette, "A New Kind of Bipartisanship for the Foreign Relations Committee," *National Journal,* March 31, 1979, pp. 525-527.
30. David E. Price, *Who Makes the Laws?* (Cambridge, Mass.: Schenkman Publishing Co., 1972); and Price, *The Commerce Committees: A Study of the House and Senate Commerce Committees* (New York: Grossman Publishers, 1975).

262   *A Deliberative Assembly*

31. *Roll Call,* January 25, 1979, p. 25.
32. Peter H. Schuck, *A Study of the House and Senate Judiciary Committees* (New York: Grossman Publishers, 1975).
33. U.S., Congress, House, *Congressional Record,* daily ed., 95th Cong., 2d sess., August 8, 1978, p. H8069.
34. Richard Royce, "Considerations of Policy Analysis and Formulation in the Senate," in *Policymaking Role of Leadership in the Senate* (Papers prepared for the Senate, Commission on the Operation of the Senate, 94th Cong., 2d sess., 1976).
35. Norris Cotton, *In the Senate* (New York: Dodd, Mead & Co., 1978), p. 65.
36. *Washington Post,* March 20, 1977, p. E9.
37. Michael J. Malbin, *Unelected Representatives: Congressional Staff and the Future of Representative Government* (New York: Basic Books, 1980), p. 194. See also Malbin, "Delegation, Deliberation, and the New Role of Congressional Staff," in *The New Congress,* ed. Thomas E. Mann and Norman J. Ornstein (Washington, D.C.: American Enterprise Institute for Public Policy Research, 1981).
38. Cotton, *In the Senate,* p. 67.
39. *New York Times,* May 26, 1979, p. 6.
40. Allen Schick, *Congress and Money* (Washington, D.C.: The Urban Institute, 1980), p. 69.
41. T. R. Reid, *Congressional Odyssey: The Saga of a Senate Bill* (San Francisco: W. H. Freeman & Co., 1980), chap. 4.
42. U.S., Congress, Senate, *Congressional Record,* daily ed., 96th Cong., 2d sess., June 27, 1980, p. S8575.
43. Joseph B. Gorman, *Kefauver: A Political Biography* (New York: Oxford University Press, 1971).
44. Christopher Buchanan, "No Law Against It: Campaigning by Staff Aides Is Still a Common Practice," *Congressional Quarterly Weekly Report,* October 28, 1978, p. 3116.
45. *Congressional Quarterly Weekly Report,* April 11, 1981, p. 643.
46. Richard Harris, *The Real Voice* (New York: Macmillan Publishing Co., 1964), p. 116.
47. Ibid., p. 118.
48. Richard F. Fenno, Jr., *Home Style: House Members in Their Districts* (Boston: Little, Brown & Co., 1978), p. 46.
49. On the overlapping duties of support agencies, see Richard E. Cohen, "The Watchdogs for Congress Often Bark the Same Tune," *National Journal,* September 8, 1979, pp. 1484-1488. See also James Thurber, "Policy Analysis on Capitol Hill: Issues Facing the Four Analytic Support Agencies of Congress," *Policy Studies Journal* (Autumn 1977): 101-111.
50. James D. Carroll, "Policy Analysis for Congress: A Review of the Congressional Research Service," in *Congressional Support Agencies* (Papers prepared for the Senate, Commission on the Operation of the Senate, 94th Cong., 2d sess., 1976), p. 15. See also Stephen E. Frantzich, "Computerized Information Technology in the U.S. House of Representatives," *Legislative Studies Quarterly* (May 1979): 255-280; Allen Schick, "The Supply and Demand for Analysis on Capitol Hill," *Policy Analysis* (Spring 1976): 215-234; Charles O. Jones, "Why Congress Can't Do Policy Analysis (Or Words to that Effect)," *Policy Analysis* (Spring 1976): 251-264; and Norman Beckman, "Policy Analysis for the Congress," *Public Administration Review* (May/June 1977): 237-244.

51. Frederick C. Mosher, *The GAO: The Quest for Accountability in American Government* (Boulder, Colo.: Westview Press, 1979). See also Erasmus H. Kloman, *Cases in Accountability: The Work of the GAO* (Boulder, Colo.: Westview Press, 1979); and Joseph Pois, *Watchdog on the Potomac: A Study of the Comptroller General of the United States* (Washington, D.C.: University Press of America, 1979).
52. *Washington Star,* February 3, 1981, p. A4.
53. See Stephen G. Burns, "Congress and the Office of Technology Assessment," *George Washington Law Review* (August 1977): 1123-1150; *Review of the Office of Technology Assessment and Its Organic Act,* House, Science and Technology Committee, Subcommittee on Science, Research, and Technology, 95th Cong., 2d sess., 1978; John F. Burby, "Infant OTA Seeks to Alert Congress to Technological Impacts," *National Journal Reports,* September 21, 1974, pp. 1418-1429; Thomas P. Southwick, "Hill Technology Assessment Office Hit by Controversy, Future Role is Threatened," *Congressional Quarterly Weekly Report,* June 18, 1977, pp. 1202-1203; and Philip M. Butten, "Office of Technology: Bad Marks on Its First Report Cards," *Science,* July 16, 1976, pp. 213-215.
54. *Christian Science Monitor,* March 26, 1981, p. 1. See also Richard E. Cohen, "The Numbers Crunchers at the CBO Try to Steer Clear of Policy Disputes," *National Journal* June 7, 1980, pp. 938-941; *Washington Post,* June 24, 1977, p. A4; Joel Havemann, "After Two Years, CBO Gets High Marks From Congress," *National Journal,* August 13, 1977, pp. 1256-1260; Walter Williams, *The Congressional Budget Office: A Critical Link in Budget Reform* (Seattle: Institute of Governmental Research, University of Washington, 1974); and *Congressional Quarterly Weekly Report,* June 5, 1976, pp. 1430-1432.
55. Stephen K. Bailey, *Congress Makes A Law* (New York: Columbia University Press, 1950), p. 64.
56. Barbara C. Greenberg, "A Member of Congress is Liable for Damages Arising from His Sex-Based Dismissal of a Staff Member, But May Assert a Qualified Immunity Defense to Such an Action," *George Washington Law Review* (November 1977): 137-155; Florence Isbell, "Congress as Ol' Massa," *Civil Liberties Review* (January-February 1978): 46-49; and Irwin B. Arieff, "Supreme Court Supports Hill Job Bias Suits," *Congressional Quarterly Weekly Report,* June 9, 1979, pp. 1103-1104.
57. Ann Cooper, "The Last Plantation: Hill Workers Push for Job Protections Congress Denied by Labor Exemptions," *Congressional Quarterly Weekly Report,* February 11, 1978, pp. 337-346; and Allison Beck, "The Last Plantation: Will Employment Reform Come to Capitol Hill?" *Catholic University Law Review* (Winter 1979): 271-311.
58. Robert H. Salisbury and Kenneth A. Shepsle, "Congressional Staff Turnover and the Ties-That-Bind: Congressman as Enterprise," (St. Louis: Center for the Study of American Business, Washington University, 1980).
59. U.S., Congress, House, *Staff Requirements of the House Legislative Counsel,* House Doc. No. 94-327, 94th Cong., 1st sess., 1975; and Prentice Bowsher, "The Speaker's Man: Louis Deschler, House Parliamentarian," *The Washington Monthly* (April 1970): 22-27.

Congressional Rules
and Procedures

For nine days in the fall of 1977 the Senate witnessed an
unusual filibuster. Because opponents of a bill to deregulate
natural gas prices had lost a vote to choke off debate, they could
not use the conventional "talkathon" filibuster. So two Democrats,
Howard M. Metzenbaum of Ohio and James Abourezk of South
Dakota, seized upon a novel tactic: amending the bill to death.

Dubbed "the odd couple"—Metzenbaum, an urbane, reserved
symphony-goer and Abourezk, a guitar-picking, cigar-chomping
extrovert—the pair called up amendment after amendment, required that they be read in full, and requested roll call votes on
each one.[1] Their delaying tactics thoroughly frustrated the Carter
administration, the Senate, and particularly Robert C. Byrd of
West Virginia, then Democratic majority leader.

With 300 amendments still standing in the way of a final vote,
Byrd found a way to stop the filibuster. He said the cloture rule
under which the Senate was operating barred any "dilatory motion
or dilatory amendment." Making a rare appearance as presiding
officer, Vice President Walter F. Mondale helped Byrd derail the
two senators with complex parliamentary moves and controversial
rulings from the chair. The next day the Senate approved the
deregulation measure.

This episode dramatically illustrates the weight of parliamentary rules in making policy. Rules were employed by Metzenbaum

265

and Abourezk to stall the bill and by Byrd and Mondale to get it passed. Congress needs written rules to do its work. Compiling the Senate's first parliamentary manual, Thomas Jefferson stressed the importance of a known system of rules.

> It is much more material that there should be a rule to go by, than what the rule is; that there may be uniformity of proceeding in business not subject to the caprice of the Speaker or captiousness of the members. It is very material that order, decency, and regularity be preserved in a dignified public body.[2]

Jefferson surely recognized that *how* Congress operates affects *what* it does. Thus the operating rules of Congress protect majority and minority rights; divide the workload; help contain conflict; ensure fair play; and distribute power among members.

Congress's formal rules (in 1980, 381 pages for the House and 69 pages for the Senate), along with precedents and folkways, guide legislative decisions and members' behavior. Because formal rules cannot cover every contingency, precedents—accumulated decisions of House Speakers and Senate presiding officers—fill in the gaps. These precedents are codified by House and Senate parliamentarians, printed, and distributed. There are also, as in any organization, informal, unwritten codes of conduct, often called folkways. They are transmitted from incumbent members to newcomers and include such norms as courtesy to other members, specialization, and so on.[3]

For bills to become laws, they must pass successfully through numerous veto points in each house. Bills that fail to attract majority support at any critical juncture may receive a mortal wound with little chance of recovery. Congress, in short, is a procedural "obstacle course" that favors opponents of legislation and hinders proponents. This so-called "defensive advantage" promotes bargaining and compromise at each decision point. To assemble majorities, proponents deal with strategically placed members or committees who can delay or defeat their ideas. Figure 9-1 shows the major steps required to turn a bill into law.

In this chapter we explain the leading rules and procedures governing decisions: House and Senate bill introduction, committee action, floor consideration, and conference committee negotiations. Recent procedural changes will be highlighted.

INTRODUCTION OF BILLS

Only members of Congress can introduce legislation, and they receive most public law proposals from two sources: the executive branch and interest groups. But ideas for bills also originate with

Figure 9-1 How A Bill Becomes Law

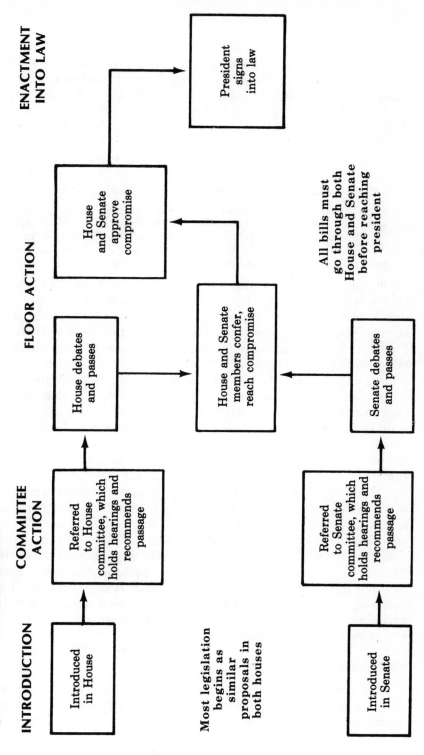

INTRODUCTION COMMITTEE ACTION FLOOR ACTION ENACTMENT INTO LAW

Introduced in House

Referred to House committee, which holds hearings and recommends passage

House debates and passes

House and Senate approve compromise

President signs into law

House and Senate members confer, reach compromise

Most legislation begins as similar proposals in both houses

Introduced in Senate

Referred to Senate committee, which holds hearings and recommends passage

Senate debates and passes

All bills must go through both House and Senate before reaching president scholars, state and local officials, congressional staffs, citizens, and members themselves. For example, sharing a taxi to Capitol Hill, Senator David Pryor, D-Ark., overheard two consultants decide to charge $25,000 instead of $12,000 because they felt the federal government would willingly pay the higher figure. Irked about "rip-offs" of this kind, Senator Pryor launched an investigation aimed at limiting the growth of a consultants' "invisible bureaucracy."[4]

A member who introduces a bill becomes its *sponsor*. This member may seek *cosponsors* to demonstrate wide support for the legislation. In 1981 Representative Elliott Levitas, D-Ga., told his colleagues that

> ...after less than 5 months of the 1st session of the 97th Congress, more than a majority of the Members of the House have now become cosponsors of H. R. 1776, the Administrative Rule-Making Control Act.... By doing so, these Members have signaled their intention to help reaffirm the authority of the Congress to write our laws.[5]

While it is easy to identify a bill's sponsor, it is difficult to pinpoint its actual initiator. Legislation is "an aggregate, not a simple production," wrote Woodrow Wilson. "It is impossible to tell how many persons, opinions, and influences have entered into its composition."[6] President John F. Kennedy, for example, usually is given credit for initiating the Peace Corps. But Theodore Sorensen, Kennedy's special counsel, recalled that the Peace Corps was "based on the Mormon and other voluntary religious service efforts, on an editorial Kennedy had read years earlier, on a speech by General Gavin, on a luncheon I had with Philadelphia businessmen, on the suggestions of his academic advisers, on legislation previously introduced and on the written response to a spontaneous late-night challenge he issued to Michigan students."[7] In short, the ideas behind many bills have tangled histories.

Much of Congress's annual agenda involves required legislation, particularly budgetary measures. Bills to authorize programs and specify how much money can be spent on them (authorization bills) and bills that actually provide the money (appropriation bills) appear on Congress's schedule at about the same time each year. Other matters recur at longer intervals, every five years perhaps. Emergency issues require Congress's immediate attention. Activist legislators also push proposals onto Congress's program, in areas such as consumer and environmental protection.[8] Bills not acted upon die automatically at the end of each two-year Congress.

Bill Drafting

"As a sculptor works in stone or clay, the legislator works in words," declared one member.[9] Words are the building blocks of policy, and legislators frequently battle over adding, deleting, or modifying terms and phrases. For example, the "safe banking" bill was renamed the

"Depository Institutions Deregulation and Monetary Control Act."
There are no unsafe banks, the banking community argued.[10]

Legislators usually rely on the House or Senate office of legislative
counsel to draft bills. Bills proposed by the executive branch or pressure
groups and sponsored by members may take one of four forms,
described in the box below.

The president plays a chief role in setting Congress's agenda.
Presidential proposals reach Capitol Hill in many forms: bills, amendments, budgetary plans, or actions subject to congressional approval or
veto. While no president gets everything he wants from Congress, White
House bills generally are treated as priority legislation. For example, in
1981 Congress devoted most of its time to President Reagan's economic

---

Types of Legislation

Bill. Most legislative proposals before Congress are in bill form, and
are designated HR (House of Representatives) or S (Senate) according to
where they originate, followed by a number assigned in the order in which
they were introduced, from the beginning of each two-year congressional
term. "Public bills" deal with general questions, and become public laws if
approved by Congress and signed by the president. "Private bills" deal
with individual matters, such as claims against the government, immigration and naturalization cases, and land titles. They become private laws if
approved and signed.

Joint Resolution. A joint resolution, designated H J Res or S J
Res, requires the approval of both houses and the president's signature,
just as a bill does, and has the force of law. There is no significant
difference between a bill and a joint resolution. The latter generally deals
with limited matters, such as a single appropriation for a specific purpose.
Joint resolutions also are used to propose constitutional amendments,
which do not require presidential signatures, but become a part of the
Constitution when three-fourths of the states have ratified them.

Concurrent Resolution. A concurrent resolution, designated H
Con Res or S Con Res, must be passed by both houses but does not
require the president's signature and does not have the force of law.
Concurrent resolutions generally are used to make or amend rules
applicable to both houses or to express their joint sentiment. A concurrent
resolution, for example, is used to fix the time for adjournment of a
Congress. It might also be used to convey the congratulations of Congress
to another country on the anniversary of its independence.

Resolution. A simple resolution, designated H Res or S Res, deals
with matters entirely within the prerogatives of one house. It requires
neither passage by the other chamber nor approval by the president, and
does not have the force of law. Most resolutions deal with the rules of one
house. They also are used to express the sentiments of a single house, as
condolences to the family of a deceased member, or to give "advice" on
foreign policy or other executive business.

program. The new president went to extraordinary lengths to lobby Congress, even visiting the Capitol to make a televised speech while recuperating from the bullet wounds he had received less than a month earlier.

Timing

"Everything in politics is timing," is a favorite byword of Speaker Thomas P. O'Neill, Jr., D-Mass. A bill's success or failure often hinges on when it is introduced or brought to the the floor. A bill that might succeed early in a session could fail as adjournment nears. Explained Representative Barber Conable, R-N.Y.:

> [A] problem exacerbating the year-end jam of legislation results from the Senate's unwillingness to impose limitations on debate. If there are several controversial bills awaiting action with a finite amount of time in which to consider them, one Senator's announced willingness to filibuster one of the measures. . .can force the dropping of a bill which a large majority of the Congress favors. Taking it up earlier would have greatly reduced its vulnerability to the filibuster.[11]

On the other hand, it is sometimes possible to rush through controversial bills during the last hectic days of a Congress.

Another timing element is public opinion. In 1977 President Carter launched a national campaign for ratification of the Panama Canal treaties. "The polls indicate that about 75 percent of the American people are opposed to 'giving up' the Canal," Senate Democratic leader Byrd said, "and you're not going to get two-thirds of the Senate to ratify the treaty until there is a substantial change in the polls." [12] He was right. In spring 1978 the Senate narrowly ratified the treaties. By then the Gallup Poll showed only 42 percent opposed.[13]

Bill Referral

Representatives may introduce bills by dropping them in the "hopper," a mahogany box near the Speaker's podium. Senators may introduce bills from the floor but usually hand them to clerks for publication in the *Congressional Record*.

After they are introduced, bills are referred to appropriate standing committees by the Senate presiding officer or the House Speaker. Committee jurisdictions and committee action are discussed in Chapter 7, so here we will pass over this stage of legislation very quickly. An important drafting consideration is the measure's scope. A comprehensive bill may attract public attention, provide bargaining room for proponents, and offer the chance "to execute a hidden ball play. The broader the scope of the measure, the more chance there is of its carrying along to enactment provisions that would otherwise stand no chance of being enacted into law." [14] On the other hand, a comprehensive bill might attract a "coalition of minorities" that can defeat it. Narrowly drafted bills, by comparison, might pass easily because they attract little public notice or controversy.

Even a bill's phraseology can affect its referral and hence its chances of passage. If a bill mentions taxes it invariably is referred to the tax panels. To sidestep these committees, Senator Pete Domenici, R-N.M., avoided the word "tax" in a 1977 bill proposing a charge on waterborne freight.

> If the waterway fee were considered a tax—which it was, basically, because it would raise revenues for the federal treasury—the rules would place it under the dominion of the Senate's tax-writing arm, the Finance Committee. But Finance was chaired by Russell B. Long, of Louisiana, whose state included two of the world's biggest barge ports and who was, accordingly, an implacable foe of waterway charges in any form. Domenici knew that Long could find several years' worth of other bills to consider before he would voluntarily schedule a hearing on S. 790 [the Domenici bill]. For this reason, [Domenici staff aides] had been careful to avoid the word *tax* in writing the bill, employing such terms as *charge* and *fee* instead.[15]

Domenici's drafting strategy worked; his bill was jointly referred to the Commerce and Environment committees.

FROM COMMITTEE TO THE FLOOR

Of the thousands of bills introduced annually, Congress takes up relatively few. Of the 14,594 measures introduced during the 96th Congress, only 2,494 were reported from committee, and only 613 became public laws.[16] Most bills considered by Congress are minor, establishing "National Baseball Week," for example. The hundred or so major and controversial bills are typically sponsored by influential members and chairmen or requested by the president. Bills with little support are simply buried in committee.

Members rely on committees to screen bills. House and Senate committees are governed by rules of procedure regarding the convening of hearings and meetings, proxy voting, and quorum requirements. House and Senate rules require, for example, that a majority of the full committee be physically present to report out any measure. If this rule is violated, a point of order can be made against the proposal on the floor.

Bills reported from committee have passed a critical stage in the lawmaking process. The next major step is reaching the House or Senate floor for debate and amendment. Our beginning point is the House, because money matters (tax and appropriation bills) originate there— the first under the Constitution and the second by custom.

SCHEDULING IN THE HOUSE

All bills reported from committee are listed in chronological order on one of several *calendars*, a system that enables the House to put measures into convenient categories. Bills that raise or spend money are assigned to the so-called Union Calendar. The House Calendar contains all other major public measures. Private bills such as immigration requests or claims against the government are assigned to the Private Calendar, and noncontroversial bills are placed on the Consent Calendar. There is no guarantee that the House will debate legislation placed on the calendars. The Speaker and majority leader largely determine if, when, and in what order bills come up.

Shortcuts for Minor Bills

House rules establish special procedures to expedite relatively minor bills. These usually consist of special days (the second and fourth Mondays in a month, for example) when such bills are to be considered.

The suspension-of-the-rules procedure allows members every Monday and Tuesday to move to suspend the rules and pass relatively noncontroversial measures. The procedure permits only 40 minutes of debate, allows no amendments, and requires two-thirds vote for passage. During the late 1970s, House members worried that weighty bills were being rushed through under suspension, particularly late in the session. As journalist Elizabeth Drew observed:

> The theory is that this is an efficient way of clearing noncontroversial proposals, but the suspension procedure is also used for other purposes: to slip bills through or to deny members an opportunity to amend them, under the pretense that if a bill is on the suspension calendar it is by definition noncontroversial.[17]

Legislators also complained that too many bills were being brought up at one time (28 during one day in 1978), confusing members as to what they were voting on. In the 95th Congress (1977-1979), 453 or 28 percent of all measures passed by the House were considered under suspension, compared with 167 or 10 percent a decade earlier.[18]

In 1979, concerned about the use of suspension, the Democratic Caucus directed the Speaker not to schedule for suspensions any bill exceeding $100 million in expenditures in any fiscal year.

Major measures reach the floor by different procedures. Tax, appropriation, and certain other measures are considered "privileged" and may be called up from the appropriate calendar for debate at almost any time. However, most major bills do not have an automatic "green light" to the floor. They get there by first obtaining a "rule" from the Rules Committee.

A Sampling of House and Senate Calendars and Whip Notices

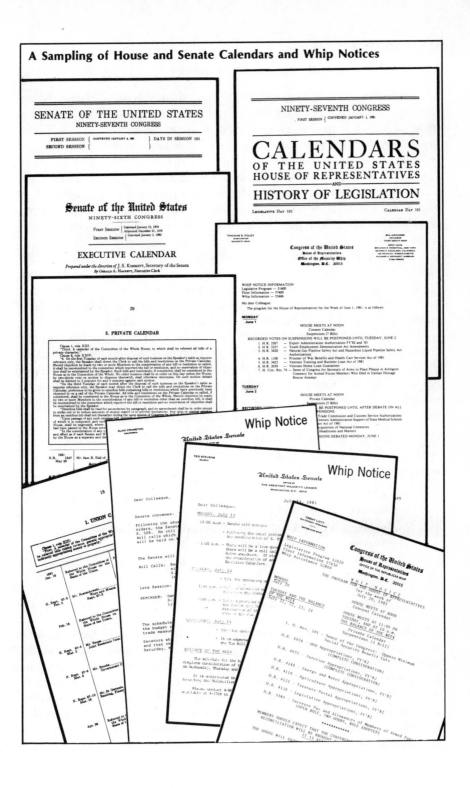

The Strategic Role of the Rules Committee

Since the First Congress, there has always been a House Rules Committee. During its early years the committee prepared or ratified a biennial set of House rules and then went out of existence. As House procedures became more complex, the committee took on added weight. In 1858 the Speaker became a member of the committee and the next year its chairman. In 1880 it became a permanent standing committee. Three years later the committee launched a procedural "revolution": it began to issue *rules* (sometimes called *special orders*)—privileged resolutions that grant priority for floor consideration to virtually all major bills.

Because House rules require bills to be taken up in the chronological order listed on the calendars, many important bills would never reach the floor before Congress adjourned. The Rules Committee can put major bills first in line. Equally important, a rule from the committee sets the conditions for debate and amendment.

A request for a rule usually is made by the chairman of the committee reporting the bill. The Rules Committee debates the request in the same way other committees consider legislation. The House parliamentarian draws up the rule with the aid of Rules staffers to reflect the committee's decision. The rule is considered on the House floor and voted on in the same manner as regular bills.

Types of Rules. There are four main kinds of rules (or special orders) granted by the Rules Committee: open, closed, modified, and waivers of points of order (parliamentary objections):

- Most bills receive an *open* rule, which means that any and all germane amendments can be proposed.

- *Closed* rules prohibit the offering of amendments, except those from the committee reporting the bill.

- *Modified* rules permit amendments to some parts of a bill but not to others.

- *Waivers* set aside specific technical violations of House rules to allow bills to reach the floor.

Since the mid-1970s, rules for handling major bills have become more complicated.[19] They may authorize only certain amendments, name the members to offer them, require that the amendments be prenoticed in the *Congressional Record,* and specify the exact order in which they are to be offered on the floor. The trend toward complex rules reflects several developments: the desire of leaders to exert greater control over floor procedures, members' restlessness with dilatory floor challenges to committee-reported bills, and wider use of multiple referrals.

Example of a Rule From the Rules Committee

Following is the text of a Rules Committee special order (rule), H Res 517, setting the terms of House debate on a 1980 tax bill, HR 5741. Principal procedures of the rule have been italicized for emphasis.

Resolved, That upon the adoption of this resolution it shall be in order to move that the House resolve itself into the *Committee of the Whole House* on the State of the Union for the consideration of the bill (HR 5741) to amend section 103 of the Internal Revenue Code of 1954 to provide that the interest on mortgage subsidy bonds will not be exempt from Federal income tax, and to exempt interest on certain savings from Federal income tax, and the first reading of the bill shall be dispensed with. After *general debate,* which shall be confined to the bill and shall continue not to exceed two hours, to be equally divided and controlled by the chairman and ranking minority member of the Committee on Ways and Means, the bill shall be considered as having been read for amendment under the *five-minute rule.* No amendments to the bill shall be in order except: (1) amendments recommended by the Committee on Ways and Means, and said amendments shall not be subject to amendment except pro forma amendments for the purpose of debate and (2) an amendment printed in the Congressional Record of December 20, 1979, by, and if offered by, Representative Glickman of Kansas, and said amendment shall not be subject to amendment except pro forma amendments for the purpose of debate. At the conclusion of the consideration of the bill for amendment, the Committee shall rise and report the bill to the House with such amendments as may have been adopted and the previous question shall be considered as ordered on the bill and amendments thereto to *final passage* without intervening motion except *one motion to recommit.*

SOURCE: U.S., Congress, House, *Congressional Record,* daily ed., 96th Cong., 2d sess., March 19, 1980, p. H1977.

In summary, rules establish the conditions under which most major bills are debated and amended. They determine the length of introductory debate, permit or prohibit amendments, and may waive points of order. They are sometimes as important to a bill's fate as being favorably reported from committee.

Arm of the Majority Leadership? Traditionally, the Rules Committee has been an agent of the majority leadership. In 1910 the House revolted against the arbitrary decisions of Speaker Joseph Cannon, R-Ill., and removed him from the committee. During subsequent decades, the committee became an independent power. It extracted substantive concessions in bills in exchange for rules. It blocked measures it opposed and advanced those it favored, often reflecting the wishes of the House's conservative coalition of Republicans and southern Democrats.

The chairman of the Rules Committee from 1955 to 1967, Howard W. "Judge" Smith, D-Va., was a master at devising delaying tactics. He might quickly adjourn meetings for lack of a quorum, allow requests for rules to languish, or refuse to schedule meetings. House consideration of the 1957 civil rights bill was temporarily delayed because Chairman Smith absented himself from the Capitol. His committee could not meet without him. Smith said he was tending to a burned barn on his Virginia farm. Retorted Speaker Rayburn: "I knew Howard Smith would do most anything to block a civil rights bill, but I never knew he would resort to arson." [20]

After 1958 liberal frustration with the coalition of conservatives who dominated the committee boiled over. The election of President Kennedy in 1960 set the stage for a titanic struggle between Speaker Rayburn and Chairman Smith over a proposal to enlarge the Rules Committee from 12 to 15 members.

> Superficially, the Representatives seemed to be quarreling about next to nothing: the membership of the committee. In reality, however, the question raised had grave import for the House and for the United States. The House's answer to it affected the tenuous balance of power between the great conservative and liberal blocs within the House. And, doing so, the House's answer seriously affected the response of Congress to the sweeping legislative proposals of the newly elected President, John Kennedy. [21]

In a dramatic vote, the House agreed to expand the Rules Committee. With the addition of two new Democrats and one Republican, the enlargement loosened the conservative coalition's grip on the panel.

With the changes of the 1970s, the Rules Committee came under even greater majority party control. In 1973 the Democratic Caucus limited the committee's sole authority to grant closed rules. And in 1975 the caucus authorized the Speaker to appoint, subject to party ratification, all Democratic members of the Rules Committee. Today the committee is tied closely to the Speaker and the Democratic Caucus. [22] As one scholar observed: "Because of its strong ties with leadership, Rules has been able to use its resources to provide a greater degree of centralized, party control in the House." [23]

In June 1981, for example, Rules' influence and strategic position was evident on the most comprehensive bill in Congress's history. The so-called "reconciliation" bill, part of Congress's budget process (see Chapter 11), contained spending cuts reported from 15 House committees in compliance with budget reductions wanted by President Reagan. Never had the House in a single bill made such massive budget cuts.

Republicans, however, charged that many of the cuts proposed by the Democratic-led committees were "phony" and threatened to offer their own budget package. The Rules Committee had the difficult task of developing a rule "that will keep the Democratic package relatively intact and head off an administration-backed [GOP] substitute." [24] Moreover, Rules had to accommodate sharp divisions within the Democratic party on whether amendments to the reconciliation bill should be permitted.

In the end, Rules crafted a procedure supported by O'Neill that would allow the House to vote separately on several amendments that cut popular programs substantially. O'Neill's "divide and conquer" strategy angered House Republicans and President Reagan. They knew that it would be hard to win individual votes on cuts in social security, student loan programs, or medicaid.

Reagan thus launched an intensive lobbying blitz for the procedure he favored: an up-or-down vote between the Democratic or Republican packages. He travelled the country seeking support for his program; he sent telegrams to about 250 congressional supporters; he dispatched aides to lobby House members; and he telephoned conservative Democrats to remind them of the grass-roots support he had in their districts.

In a stunning defeat, the Democratic rule was rejected (212 to 217) and a GOP-sponsored alternative was adopted. The president's lobbying paid off: 29 conservative Democrats sided with the Republicans. President Reagan went on to win a dramatic budget victory in part because he won the key procedural vote.

Dislodging a Bill From Committee

Committees do not necessarily reflect the point of view of the full chamber. What happens when a standing committee refuses to report a bill, or when the Rules Committee does not grant a rule? There are, in fact, procedures to circumvent committees, but they are extraordinary actions and are seldom successful.

Discharge Petition. The discharge rule permits the House to relieve a committee from jurisdiction over a stalled measure. If a committee does not report a bill within 30 days after the bill was referred to it, any member may file a discharge motion (petition) requiring the signatures of 218 members, a majority of the House. Once the signatures are obtained, the discharge motion is placed on the Discharge Calendar and can be called up by any member who signed it. If the discharge motion is passed, the bill is taken up right away. Since 1910, when the discharge rule was adopted, only two discharged measures have ever become law. Its threatened use, however, may stimulate a committee to act on a bill.

In 1980, for example, a House Judiciary subcommittee held hearings on a controversial school prayer bill after a delay of more than a year. When evangelical lobbyists persuaded about 180 House members to sign a discharge petition, the subcommittee announced the hearings "to deter other wavering House members, feeling the evangelicals' pressure, from signing the petition." [25]

If the Rules Committee refuses to report a rule within seven days after a bill has been before it, any member may enter a motion to discharge the committee. This seldom happens. The most recent instance of the Rules Committee's being discharged occurred on September 25, 1965, on a home rule proposal for the District of Columbia.

Calendar Wednesday. Adopted in 1909, the Calendar Wednesday rule provides that on Wednesdays committees may bring up from the House or Union calendars their measures that have not received a rule from the Rules Committee. The rule is cumbersome to employ, seldom used, and generally dispensed with by unanimous consent. Only two laws have ever been enacted under this procedure.

Extraction by the Rules Committee. The Rules Committee also has the power of extraction. It can introduce rules making bills in order for House debate even if they have not been reported by standing committees. Based on an 1895 precedent, this is akin to discharging committees without the 218-signature requirement. Again, this procedure is seldom used and stirs sharp controversy among members who think it usurps the rights of the other committees.

HOUSE FLOOR PROCEDURES

The House normally meets Monday through Friday, usually convening at noon. At the beginning of each day's session, bells ring throughout the Capitol and the House office buildings, summoning representatives to the floor. The signal bells also ring to notify members of votes, quorum calls, recesses, and adjournments. Typically, the opening activities include a daily prayer; approval of the *Journal* (a constitutionally required record of the previous day's proceedings); receipt of messages from the president or the Senate; announcements, if any, by the Speaker; and one-minute speeches by members on any topic.

After these preliminaries, the House generally begins considering legislation. For a major bill, a set pattern is observed: adoption of the rule, convening as a Committee of the Whole, general debate, amending, and final passage.

Adoption of the Rule

The Speaker, after consulting the majority leader and affected committee chairmen, decides when the House will debate a bill and its rule. When the scheduled day arrives, the Speaker usually recognizes one member of each party from the Rules Committee to explain the rule's contents. At the end of the debate, which frequently takes less than the allotted hour, the House votes on the rule.

Opponents of a bill will try to defeat its rule and avert House action on the bill itself. Despite the budget example described above, rules seldom are defeated because the Rules Committee is sensitive to the wishes of the House. Once the rule is adopted, the House is governed by its provisions. Most rules state that "upon the adoption of this resolution it shall be in order to move that the House resolve itself into the Committee of the Whole."

Committee of the Whole

The Committee of the Whole House on the State of the Union is a parliamentary artifice to expedite consideration of legislation. It is just the House in another form, with different rules. For example, a quorum in the committee is only 100 members, compared with 218 for the House. The Speaker appoints a majority party colleague to preside over the committee, which then begins general debate.

General Debate

A rule from the Rules Committee specifies the amount of time, usually one to two hours, for a general discussion of the bill. More controversial bills will require more time, from four to 10 hours. Control of the time is equally divided between the majority and minority floor managers—often the chairman and ranking minority member of the committee or subcommittee that reported the legislation. The majority floor manager's job is to shepherd the bill to final passage; the minority floor manager may seek to amend or kill it.

After the floor managers make their opening statements, they parcel out several minutes to colleagues on their side of the aisle who wish to speak. General debate rarely lives up to its name. Most legislators read prepared speeches, and there is little give-and-take exchange.

Sometimes debate strategy influences a bill's fate. In 1980 Representative Joseph Addabbo, D-N.Y., successfully floor managed the repeal of a law that denied millions of dollars to New York City and other areas. Asked how he did it in the face of widespread member antipathy toward New York City, Addabbo replied, "[I] made sure no New Yorkers spoke for it except upstaters." [26]

The Amending Phase (the Five-Minute Rule)

The amending process is the heart of floor decisionmaking. Amendments determine the final shape of bills and often dominate public discussion, as have Illinois Republican Henry J. Hyde's repeated amendments barring the use of federal funds for abortions.

An amendment in Committee of the Whole is considered under the five-minute rule, which gives the sponsor five minutes to defend it and an opponent five minutes to talk against it. The amendment may then be brought to a vote. Amendments, however, regularly are debated for more than 10 minutes. Legislators gain the floor by saying, "I move to strike the last word," or, "I move to strike the requisite number of words." These pro forma amendments, which make no alteration in the pending matter, simply give members five minutes of debate time.

During the amending process, members may move to strike the enabling clause—the opening phrase that makes a bill an operative law ("Be it enacted by the Senate and House of Representatives of the United States of America in Congress assembled..."). Under House rules, striking the enabling clause is equivalent to rejecting the measure. Such a motion is privileged and must be disposed of before the House takes up any further business on the bill.

Opponents may try to "load down" a bill with so many objectionable amendments that it will sink of its own weight. The reverse strategy is to propose "sweetener" amendments that attract members' support. Offering numerous amendments is an effective dilatory tactic because each amendment must be read in full, debated at least five to ten minutes, and voted upon. In 1980 a member unsuccessfully launched a 100-amendment attack on a Pacific Northwest power bill. "It was a filibuster, plain and simple," he said.[27]

The minority party's policy preferences often are expressed through amendments. "Since the liberal [Democratic] leadership more often than not refuses to schedule hearings on our bills," wrote John M. Ashbrook, R-Ohio, "we counter by offering our legislation in the form of amendments to other bills scheduled for consideration by the House." [28] The minority also guards the floor to demand explanations or votes on amendments brought up by the majority. From 1975 to 1981, the self-appointed GOP "watchdog" was Robert Bauman of Maryland. He stayed on the floor virtually nonstop and used his parliamentary skill to frustrate Speaker O'Neill and the Democrats. "Every legislative body has a Bauman," said the Speaker. "He's tough and he certainly irks the leadership when we're trying to get things done." [29]

Voting

Prior to passage of the 1970 Legislative Reorganization Act, the Committee of the Whole adopted or rejected amendments by voice or other votes with no public record of who voted, how they voted, or even whether they voted. Today, any legislator supported by 25 colleagues can obtain a recorded vote. How members decide which way to vote is discussed in Chapter 13; here we focus on the mechanics of voting.

With the installation of an electronic voting system in 1973, members insert their personalized cards (about the size of a credit card) into one of more than 40 voting stations on the floor and press the Yea, Nay, or Present button. A large electronic display board behind the press gallery provides a running tally of the total votes for or against a motion. Since the era of electronic voting, recorded votes in the House have risen sharply.

After all pending amendments have been voted upon, the Committee of the Whole "rises." The chairman hands the gavel back to the Speaker and a quorum once again becomes 218 members.

Final Passage

As specified in the rule, the full House must review the actions of its "agent," the Committee of the Whole. The Speaker announces that under the rule the *previous question* has been ordered, which means that no further debate is permitted on the bill or its amendments. The Speaker then asks if any representative wants a separate vote on any amendment. If not, all the amendments agreed to in the committee will be approved. The next important step is the recommittal motion. It provides a way for the House to return (or recommit) the bill to the committee that reported it. By custom, the request is always made by a minority party member who opposes the legislation. Recommital motions rarely succeed, but they do serve to protect the rights of the minority. Following the motion's usual defeat, the Speaker will say, "The question is on passage of the bill." Normally, final passage is by recorded vote.

Passage by the House marks the half-way point in the lawmaking process. The Senate must also approve the bill, and its procedures are substantially different from those of the House.

SCHEDULING IN THE SENATE

The smaller Senate has a relatively simple scheduling system, with one calendar for all public and private bills (the Calendar of General Orders) and another for treaties and nominations (the Executive Calendar). It has nothing comparable to the scheduling duties of the House Rules Committee, and the majority and minority leadership actively cooperate in scheduling.

Legislation typically reaches the Senate floor in two ways: by unanimous consent or by motion. Unanimous consent is of utmost importance, and its use is regulated by the majority leader in consultation with the minority leader.

Unanimous Consent Agreements

The Senate frequently dispenses with its cumbersome formal rules and instead follows privately negotiated agreements submitted to the Senate for its unanimous approval. The objective is to expedite work in an institution known for extended debate (the filibuster). Such agreements limit debate on the bill, any amendments, and various motions. Occasionally, they specify the time for the vote on final passage.

If unanimous consent agreements cannot be worked out, bills can be filibustered. On the other hand, the lack of such agreements can encourage bargaining. For example, there was no unanimous consent agreement governing the 1978 civil service reform bill. When Orrin Hatch, R-Utah, "presented the floor managers with what Percy [Charles Percy, R-Ill.] called 'a rather bulky package of amendments' the day of the debate, Percy and Ribicoff [Abraham Ribicoff, D-Conn.] aides and Civil Service Commission Chairman Alan K. Campbell met with Hatch...to work out compromises acceptable to both sides." [30] Very quickly the Senate passed the bill.

Example of a Unanimous Consent Agreement

Following are excerpts from a unanimous consent agreement that the Senate followed in debating S 2222, a bill extending the time for lawsuits on behalf of Indian tribes. The "Order No." refers to the bill's chronological position on the General Orders Calender.

Ordered, That when the Senate proceeds to the consideration of S 2222 (Order No. 607) ... debate on any amendment (except an amendment to be offered by the Senator from Oklahoma (MR. BELLMON), on which there shall be one hour); shall be limited to 30 minutes, to be equally divided and controlled by the mover of such and the manager of the bill; and debate on any debatable motion, appeal, or point of order which is submitted or on which the Chair entertains debate shall be limited to 20 minutes to be equally divided and controlled by the mover of such and the manager of the bill: *Provided,* That in the event the manager of the bill is in favor of any such amendment or motion, the time in opposition thereto shall be controlled by the minority leader or his designee: *Provided further,* That no amendment that is not germane ... shall be received.

Ordered further, That on the question of final passage of the said bill, debate shall be limited to 1 hour, to be equally divided and controlled, respectively, by the Senator from Montana (MR. MELCHER) and the Senator from Maine (MR. COHEN); *Provided,* That the said Senators, or either of them, may from the time under their control ... allot additional time to any Senator during the consideration of any amendment, debatable motion, appeal, or point of order.

SOURCE: U.S., Congress, Senate, *Congressional Record,* daily ed., 97th Cong., 1st sess., February 19, 1981, p. S1555.

The Senate's unanimous consent agreements are the functional equivalents of special orders from the House Rules Committee. They waive the rules of their respective chambers, and each must be approved by the members, in one case by majority vote and in the other by unanimous consent. However, whereas senators and aides draft unanimous consent agreements privately, the Rules Committee hears requests for special orders in public session.

Ways to Extract Bills Blocked in Committee

The Senate has four ways to obtain floor action on a bill blocked in committee. These are: 1) adding the bill as a nongermane floor amendment to another bill, 2) bypassing the committee stage by placing the bill directly on the calendar, 3) suspending the rules, and 4) discharging the bill from committee. Only the first procedure is effective; the other three are difficult to employ and seldom succeed.[31]

Because the Senate has no general germaneness rule, senators can take an agriculture bill that is stuck in committee and add it as a nongermane floor amendment to a pending health bill. "Amendments may be made," Thomas Jefferson noted long ago, "so as to totally alter the nature of the proposition." Most unanimous consent agreements, however, prohibit nongermane amendments.

In the Senate, germaneness essentially means barring the introduction of "new subject matter" into pending bills. For example, in 1978 a senator tried to amend an endangered species bill to authorize use of a pesticide against grasshoppers. The majority floor manager successfully objected that the amendment was not germane under the bill's unanimous consent agreement.

The "new subject matter" criterion is vague. In some respects, the Senate's germaneness principle is akin to what former Supreme Court Justice Potter Stewart said about hard-core pornography: "I know it when I see it."

SENATE FLOOR PROCEDURES

Senate procedures emphasize freedom of expression and individual rights. Its rules "magnify the views strongly held by a single Member of the Senate," observed former Senate Majority Leader Mike Mansfield, D-Mont. (1961-1977). Any senator who knows the rules can easily stymie floor action. In the House, on the other hand, a determined majority eventually can overcome minority opposition.

The Senate, like the House, regularly convenes at noon, although often it meets earlier. It typically opens with prayer; approval of the *Journal*; statements by the party leaders; routine business, such as the introduction of bills and receipt of messages; brief speeches by members; and then unfinished business or new business made in order by a unanimous consent agreement. For most bills, Senate procedure consists of these steps:

- The majority leader secures the unanimous consent of the Senate to an arrangement that specifies when a bill will be brought to the floor and the conditions for debating it.
- The bill is brought to the floor as scheduled.
- The presiding officer recognizes the majority and minority floor managers for brief opening statements.
- Amendments are then in order, with debate regulated by the terms of the unanimous consent agreement.
- There is a roll-call vote on final passage.

As in the House, amendments serve different purposes. A floor manager, for example, might accept "as many amendments as he can without undermining the purposes of the bill, in order to build the broadest possible consensus behind it." [32] Another calculation of floor managers is the timing of amendments. During 1978 Senate debate on the endangered species bill, John Culver, D-Iowa, persuaded William Scott, R-Va., to hold off an amendment until the next morning.

...Culver figures that most of his colleagues will assume that at this point, especially after a long day of taking up amendments—and major ones—yesterday, only routine, "housekeeping" amendments are being considered, and that they will pay less attention to the issue, be less eager to join the fray, than they might be later on. [33]

A bill is brought to a final vote whenever senators stop talking. This can be a long process, particularly in the absence of a unanimous consent agreement. Debate on the 1976 tax reform bill, which reached the floor without a time-limitation agreement, took 25 days, with 129 roll-call votes on 209 amendments or motions.

On some bills unanimous consent agreements are foreclosed because of deliberate obstructive tactics, particularly the filibuster. In these instances, bills cannot be voted upon until the talkathon is ended.

The right of extended debate is unique to the Senate. Any senator or group of senators can talk continuously in the hope of delaying, modifying, or defeating legislation. In 1957 Strom Thurmond, R-S.C., then a Democrat, set the record for the Senate's longest solo filibuster—24 hours and 18 minutes—trying to kill a civil rights bill.

Defenders say filibusters protect minority rights, permit thorough consideration of bills, and dramatize issues. Critics contend that they permit small minorities to extort unwanted concessions.

During most of its history, the Senate had no way except unanimous consent to terminate debate. In 1917 the Senate adopted Rule

XXII, its first cloture (debate-ending) rule.[34] After several revisions, Rule XXII now permits three-fifths of the Senate (60 of 100 members) to shut off debate on substantive issues. Once cloture is invoked, the Senate has 100 hours of debate time remaining before finally voting on the pending matter. Many considerations affect cloture proceedings, some of which Democratic leader Byrd, then Senate majority leader, discusses in the box on the following page.

RESOLVING HOUSE-SENATE DIFFERENCES

The House and Senate must pass bills in identical form before they can be sent to the president. If neither chamber will accept the other's changes, a House-Senate conference committee must reconcile the differences.

Virtually every controversial bill is sent to conference, although there are exceptions. In 1980, for example, proponents of an Alaskan lands bill deliberately avoided a conference to prevent an end-of-session Senate filibuster that might have killed the legislation.

Conference committees meet to resolve the matters in dispute; they are not to reconsider provisions already agreed to. Neither are they to insert new matter. But because congressional rules are not self-enforcing, members must object on the floor to keep new matter from appearing in conference reports.

Selection of Conferees

Conferees usually are named from the committee or committees that reported the legislation. Congressional rules state that the Speaker and Senate presiding officer select conferees; actually, the decision is made by the respective chairmen and ranking minority members.

Each chamber may name as many conferees as it wants. In recent years, conference delegations have grown larger. The 1981 omnibus reconciliation conference set the record, with more than 250 conferees working in 58 subconferences.

In conference, each chamber has one vote determined by a majority of its conferees, who are expected to support generally the legislation as it passed their house. But as conference committees drag on, a senator said, the "individual attitudes of the various members begin to show." [35]

The ratio of Democrats to Republicans on a conference committee generally reflects their proportion in the House or Senate. Seniority frequently determines who the conferees will be, but in recent years it has become common for junior members to be conferees.

Openness

Secret conference meetings were the norm for most of Congress's history. In 1975, however, both houses adopted rules requiring open

---

Byrd on Legislative Strategy

...The important thing is to have the right Senators at the right place at the right time.... Strange as it may seem, he [Harry F. Byrd, Jr., of Virginia, an independent who sits with the Democrats] is not going to vote with the Democrats, who are trying to invoke cloture. He is going to vote with our Republican friends....

Now, why did I schedule that vote at 5 o'clock to accommodate a Democratic Senator who is not going to vote with me? ... Some Senators will not vote for cloture the first time around. Some will only vote for cloture the second time around or the third time around. So I know I am going to lose that vote on Monday.

But there are several Senators who will not vote for cloture the first time. This particular one; I want him to be here and vote, even though he is going to vote against me, because then I would hope that on Tuesday he would vote with me.

That is just a little interesting insight into how we have to weigh all things, how we have to schedule and program, calculate how we will get this vote and how we will get that one. That is the way it goes.

SOURCE: Remarks of Senate Majority Leader Robert C. Byrd, D-W.Va., in the *Congressional Record*, April 18, 1980, p. S3922.

---

meetings unless the conferees from each chamber voted in public to close the sessions. Two years later, the House went a step further by requiring open conference meetings unless the full House agreed to secret sessions. Some legislators hold that open conferences impair bargaining. Commented Senator Mark Hatfield, R-Ore.:

> When conferences were in executive [closed] session members didn't have to pound the table and make speeches they hope will be reported back home. They could sit there and say, "You know where I sit and I know where you sit so we've got to compromise." We do the same thing now but it takes much longer because we have to give all of our speeches first.[36]

This is another instance of individual-institutional cleavage. Under the watchful eye of lobbyists, conferees fight harder for provisions they might have dropped quietly in the interest of bicameral agreement.

Senators and representatives anticipate that certain bills will go to conference and plan their strategy accordingly. For example, it was observed that Senator Russell Long, D-La., then chairman of the Finance Committee, "usually comes to conference with a bill loaded up with amendments added on the Senate floor.... The result is that Long has plenty of things he is willing to jettison to save the goodies."[37]

The Conference Report

A conference ends when its report (the compromise bill) is signed by a majority of the conferees from each chamber. The House and

Senate then vote on this report without further amendment. At this stage, the incentives are to approve it. As Representative Richard Bolling, D-Mo., said about the compromise on the 1978 national energy act: "I think it is terribly important to remember that this is not a House bill coming from a committee to the floor. This is a conference report which, after months, has come through the mill, through the grinding mill of two very, very different institutions." [38]

If either chamber rejects the conference report, an infrequent occurrence, then a new conference could be called or another bill introduced. Once passed, the compromise bill is sent to the president for his approval or disapproval.

CONCLUSION

Persistence, strategy, timing, compromise, knowledge of rules and procedures, and plain luck are key elements in the lawmaking process. To make public policy requires building majority coalitions at successive stages where pressure groups and other parties can advance their claims. Political, procedural, personality, and policy considerations shape the final outcome. Passing laws, as one representative said, is like the "weaving of a web, bringing a lot of strands together in a pattern of support which won't have the kind of weak spots which could cause the whole fabric to fall apart." [39]

The president is also a vital "weaver" of our national laws. In our interdependent governmental system, the chief executive's power to recommend, promote, or veto laws looms large in legislative decision-making. In short, the participation of both branches is required to make national policy.

NOTES

1. U.S., Congress, *Congressional Record,* 95th Cong., 1st sess., October 3, 1977, pp. 31924-31943. See also "Natural Gas Filibuster Ties Up Senate," *Congressional Quarterly Weekly Report,* October 1, 1977, pp. 2059-2066.
2. *Constitution, Jefferson's Manual, and Rules of the House of Representatives,* House Doc. 95-403, 95th Cong., 2d sess., 1979, p. 111. The rules of the Senate are contained in *Senate Manual,* Senate Doc. 96-1, 96th Cong., 1st sess., 1979.
3. Donald R. Matthews, *U.S. Senators and Their World* (Chapel Hill: University of North Carolina Press, 1960), chap. 5; and Herbert B. Asher, "The Learning of Legislative Norms," *American Political Science Review* (June 1973): 499-513.
4. *U.S. News & World Report,* February 18, 1980, p. 60.
5. U.S., Congress, *Congressional Record,* daily ed., 97th Cong., 1st sess., May 28, 1981, p. E2582.
6. Woodrow Wilson, *Congressional Government* (Boston: Houghton Mifflin Co., 1885), p. 320.

7. Theodore Sorensen, *Kennedy* (New York: Harper & Row, 1965), p. 184.
8. Jack L. Walker, "Setting the Agenda in the U.S. Senate," in *Policymaking Role of Leadership in the Senate* (Papers prepared for the Senate, Commission on the Operation of the Senate, 94th Cong., 2d sess., 1976).
9. U.S., Congress, *Congressional Record,* daily ed., 95th Cong., 1st sess., May 17, 1977, p. E3076.
10. *Washington Post,* June 21, 1978, p. D7.
11. *Roll Call,* October 26, 1978, p. 4.
12. *New York Times,* August 17, 1977, p. 31.
13. George Gallup, "U.S. Public Opinion Shifts to Support of Panama Treaties," *The Gallup Poll,* February 2, 1978, p. 1.
14. Bertram M. Gross, *The Legislative Struggle* (New York: McGraw-Hill Book Co., 1953), p. 209.
15. T. R. Reid, *Congressional Odyssey: The Saga of A Senate Bill* (San Francisco: W.H. Freeman & Co., 1980), p. 17.
16. Figures refer to all public bills and resolutions and may be found for each Congress in the Final Daily Digest of the *Congressional Record* for the appropriate session.
17. Elizabeth Drew, "A Tendency To 'Legislate'," *New Yorker,* June 26, 1978, p. 80.
18. U.S., Congress, *Congressional Record,* daily ed., 96th Cong., 1st sess., April 4, 1979, p. E1514. See also Ann Cooper, "Legislative Parkinson's Law: House Use of Suspensions Grows Drastically," *Congressional Quarterly Weekly Report,* September 30, 1978, pp. 2693-2695.
19. Stanley Bach, "Special Rules in the House of Representatives: Themes and Contemporary Variations," *Congressional Studies,* vol. 8, no. 2, pp. 37-58.
20. Alfred Steinberg, *Sam Rayburn* (New York: Hawthorn Books, 1975), p. 313. See also James A. Robinson, *The House Rules Committee* (Indianapolis: Bobbs-Merrill Co., 1963).
21. Neil MacNeil, *The Forge of Democracy* (New York: David McKay, 1963), p. 411. See also Milton C. Cummings, Jr., and Robert L. Peabody, "The Decision to Enlarge the Committee on Rules: An Analysis of the 1961 Vote," in *New Perspectives on the House of Representatives,* ed. Robert L. Peabody and Nelson W. Polsby (Chicago: Rand McNally & Co., 1963), pp. 167-194; and William R. MacKaye, *A New Coalition Takes Control: The House Rules Committee Fight of 1961,* Eagleton Institute Case Study No. 29 (New York: McGraw-Hill Book Co., 1963).
22. Spark M. Matsunaga and Ping Chen, *Rulemaker of the House* (Urbana,Ill.: University of Illinois Press, 1976); and Bruce I. Oppenheimer, "The Rules Committee: New Arm of Leadership in a Decentralized House," in *Congress Reconsidered,* 1st ed., edited by Lawrence C. Dodd and Bruce I. Oppenheimer (New York: Praeger Publishers, 1977).
23. Bruce I. Oppenheimer, "Policy Implications of Rules Committee Reforms," in *Legislative Reform,* ed. Leroy Rieselbach (Lexington, Mass.: D. C. Heath & Co., 1978), p. 103.
24. *Washington Post,* June 22, 1981, p. A14; *Washington Post,* June 26, 1981, p. A1; and *New York Times,* June 26, 1981, p. A1.
25. *Washington Post,* July 3, 1980, p. A6. See also Nadine Cohodas, "Discharge Petition Derailed?" *Congressional Quarterly Weekly Report,* July 12, 1980, pp. 1966-1967.
26. *New York Times,* September 29, 1980, p. B4.
27. Andy Plattner, "Pacific Northwest Power Bill Cleared After House Breaks One-Man 'Filibuster'," *Congressional Quarterly Weekly Report,* November

22, 1980, p. 3410. See also Larry Light, "Congress Clears Legislation Allowing Some Exemptions To Endangered Species Act," *Congressional Quarterly Weekly Report,* October 21, 1978, p. 3045; and *Washington Post,* August 15, 1979, p. A10.
28. *Mt. Vernon* [Ohio] *News,* September 20, 1980, p. 2.
29. *Washington Post,* December 18, 1977, p. B1.
30. Ann Cooper, "Senate Approves Carter Civil Service Reforms," *Congressional Quarterly Weekly Report,* August 26, 1978, p. 2239.
31. Walter J. Oleszek, *Congressional Procedures and the Policy Process* (Washington, D.C.: Congressional Quarterly Press, 1978), pp. 174-178 . See also Lewis A. Froman, Jr., *The Congressional Process* (Boston: Little, Brown & Co., 1967).
32. Elizabeth Drew, *Senator* (New York: Simon & Schuster, 1979), p. 158.
33. Ibid.
34. Franklin L. Burdette, *Filibustering in the Senate* (Princeton: Princeton University Press, 1940), pp. 114-128. See also Raymond E. Wolfinger, "Filibusters: Majority Rule, Presidential Leadership, and Senate Norms," in *Readings on Congress* ed. Raymond E. Wolfinger (Englewood Cliffs, N.J.: Prentice-Hall, 1971); and Ann Cooper, "Senate Limits Post-Cloture Filibusters," *Congressional Quarterly Weekly Report,* February 24, 1979, pp. 319-320.
35. Randall B. Ripley, *Power in the Senate* (New York: St. Martin's Press, 1969), p. 128.
36. *Los Angeles Times,* December 22, 1979, p. 6.
37. Daniel J. Balz, "When the Man from Louisiana's There, It's a Long, Long Road to Tax Reform," *National Journal,* May 22, 1976, p. 694.
38. U.S., Congress, House, *Activity Report of the House Ad Hoc Committee on Energy,* House Report 95-1820, 95th Cong., 2d sess., 1978, p. 78.
39. Barber B. Conable, "Weaving Webs: Lobbying By Charities," *Tax Notes,* November 10, 1975, pp. 27-28.

Vice President Bush and House Speaker O'Neill share a
laugh with President Reagan as he addresses Congress.

10

Congress and the President

The Republican president and the Democratic-led House were
locked in a tense struggle over the size and shape of the federal
budget. President Reagan wanted deep cuts in domestic social
programs supported by most Democrats, including Speaker
Thomas P. O'Neill, Jr., D-Mass. Dissatisfied with the Democratic-
controlled committees' efforts to conform to his budgetary blue-
prints, the president decided to propose an eleventh-hour substitute plan of his own.

"I want a chance to send some substitute language up there on
the budget," Reagan told the Speaker over the phone. "The House
has worked hard and done a good job, but it hasn't gone far
enough, and I. . . ."

"Did you ever hear of the separation of powers?" O'Neill
interrupted. "The Congress of the United States will be responsible for spending. You're not supposed to be writing legislation."

"I know the Constitution," Reagan broke in testily.[1]

It was a classic face-off between the two branches of government. Congress jealously guards its power of the purse, and its
committees strive to shape the programs and agencies under their
care. If they are fortunate, presidents have the ability to force
issues and call forth public support. In this instance, Reagan had
his way, leaving the Democrats stunned and battered.

291

As this tale illustrates, tensions between the two branches are inevitable. The branches are organized differently; they have divergent responsibilities; they are jealous of their prerogatives; and they often view each other with suspicion. Executive officials see Congress as disorganized and inefficient. Legislators perceive the executive branch as insensitive and arbitrary. At times, these differences lead to conflicts that the media dramatize as "battles of the Potomac."

Yet, day in and day out, Congress and the president work together. Even when their relationship is guarded or hostile, bills get passed and signed into law. Presidential appointments are approved by the Senate. Budgets are enacted and the government is kept afloat. This necessary cooperation goes on even when the White House and the Capitol are controlled by different parties. Conversely, as we saw during Jimmy Carter's administration, partisan control of both branches is no guarantee of harmony.

Conflict between Congress and the president inheres in our "separation of powers" and "checks and balances" system. The Founders expected their governmental arrangement also to promote accommodation between the branches. The Framers sought to "prove that a rigid adherence to [the separation of powers] in all cases would be subversive of the efficiency of the government and result in the destruction of the public liberties." [2] Other interpreters of the Constitution have emphasized these themes: "While the Constitution diffuses power the better to secure liberty," wrote Supreme Court Justice Robert Jackson in 1952, "it also contemplates that practice will integrate the dispersed powers into a workable government." [3] The two branches worked together in the New Deal's early days (1933-1936), during World War II (1941-1945), and the brief Great Society years following John Kennedy's assassination (1964-1965). At other times they fought constantly, for example, during Woodrow Wilson's second term (1919-1921), after 1937 for Franklin Roosevelt, after 1966 for Lyndon Johnson, and for most of Richard Nixon's tenure. [4]

In this chapter we will review sources of cooperation and conflict between Congress and the president, as well as the president's legislative role.

THE PRESIDENT AS LEGISLATOR

The president is called the "chief legislator" because of his close involvement in congressional decisionmaking. The Constitution directs the president to "give to the Congress information of the state of the union, and recommend to their consideration such measures as he shall judge necessary and expedient." Soon after delivering the annual State of the Union address, the president sends to Congress draft "administration bills" for introduction on his behalf. By adding to the list of messages required from the president—annual budget and economic reports, for example—Congress has further involved the chief executive in planning legislation. Crises, partisan considerations, and public expectations all make the president an important participant in congressional decisionmaking. And the president's constitutional veto power assures that White House views will be listened to, if not always heeded, on Capitol Hill.

Setting the Agenda

Presidents, to varying degrees, have influenced Congress's agenda from the beginning. The First Congress of "its own volition immediately turned to the executive branch for guidance and discovered in [Treasury Secretary Alexander] Hamilton a personality to whom such leadership was congenial." [5] Two decades later (from 1811 to 1825) the "initiative in public affairs remained with [Speaker Henry] Clay and his associates in the House of Representatives" and not with the president.[6]

The two branches alternate as the predominant force in national policymaking. Strong presidents sometimes provoke efforts by Congress to reassert its own authority and attempt to restrict the executive's. Periods of presidential ascendancy often are followed by eras of congressional dominance.

Proposal and Disposal. Presidential recommendations to Congress—special messages, the State of the Union address, and other communications—serve various purposes. They identify national priorities, provoke public debate, and encourage congressional consideration of the administration's program. Modern Congresses expect the president to translate executive proposals into draft bills. "If the president wants to tell the people that he stands for a certain thing, he ought to come out with his proposal. He ought to come to the House and Senate with a message," commented a senator. "And he ought to provide a bill if that is exactly what he wants." [7]

Congress can influence what, when, how, or even whether executive recommendations are sent to Capitol Hill. This may explain the wide gap that often separates what a president wants from what he can get. "The president proposes, Congress disposes" is an oversimplified adage.

Central Clearance. In developing his legislative program, the president is deluged with advice. Party platforms, congressional suggestions, campaign promises, pressure group demands, and agency proposals are some of the overlapping sources of instruction. Coordinating and sifting through these recommendations (central clearance) is a responsibility primarily of the Office of Management and Budget. Central clearance enables the president "to monitor department requests to ensure that they are not in conflict with his own." [8]

Outside Events. National and international developments influence agenda-setting. The Great Depression of the 1930s demonstrates how events may promote the president's agenda-setting role. When Franklin Roosevelt took office in 1933, Congress wanted him to tell it what to do. And he did. During his first 100 days, Roosevelt sent Congress 15 messages and signed 15 bills into law.

The Constitution gives the president the authority to convene one or both houses of Congress "on extraordinary occasions." A few days after taking office, FDR called a special session of Congress to consider his emergency banking legislation. "The House had no copies of the bill; the Speaker recited the text from the one available draft, which bore last minute corrections scribbled in pencil." After 38 minutes of debate, "with a unanimous shout, the House passed the bill, sight unseen." [9] Passing President Reagan's revised budget package in 1981 took a little longer but featured the same kind of swift support of the While House.

Contrast this with the careful scrutiny given President Carter's 1977 energy proposals—and indeed most other major presidential initiatives. Early in his term, Carter went on television and called America's need for a new energy policy the "moral equivalent of war" (dubbed MEOW by critics). Carter wanted to focus congressional, media, and public attention on his program for reducing U. S. reliance on imported oil, encouraging energy conservation, and promoting energy production. Yet the public was slow to recognize the crisis, and there was little consensus about how to cope with it. In the end Congress enacted a 1978 energy package that included the phased deregulation of natural gas and tax incentives to produce and conserve energy.

Legislative Delegations. Congress frequently delegates legislative responsibility to the president, departmental officials, or regulatory agencies. In 1946, for example, Congress asked the president to recommend ways to keep the nation's economy healthy.[10] The decision to transfer such authority to the president typically occurs because Congress recognizes its own shortcomings—its decentralized committee structure that inhibits swift and comprehensive policy formulation, and its members' vulnerability to reelection pressures. Congress also appreciates the strengths of the executive—its capacity for fact finding and coordination, for example.

The Veto Power

Article I, Section 7, of the Constitution requires presidential approval or disapproval of bills passed by Congress. In the case of disapproval, the measure "shall be repassed by two thirds of the Senate and House of Representatives." Because vetoes are so difficult to override, the veto power makes the president a "third branch of the legislature," wrote Woodrow Wilson.[11] A president usually can attract one-third plus one of his own partisan supporters in Congress to sustain his vetoes, and so presidential vetoes generally are not overridden, as Table 10-1 shows.

The veto is more than a negative power, however. Presidents also use it to advance their policy objectives. Veto threats, for example, often encourage committees and legislators to accommodate executive preferences and objections. For its part, Congress can discourage vetoes by adding items strongly favored by the president to "must" legislation.

Once he receives a bill from Congress, the president has 10 days (excluding Sundays) in which to exercise four options:

1. He can sign the bill. Most public and private bills presented to the president are signed into law.

2. He can return the bill with his veto message to the originating house of Congress.

3. He can take no action, and the bill will become law without his signature. This option, seldom employed, is reserved for bills the president dislikes but not enough to veto.

4. He can "pocket veto" the bill. Under the Constitution, if a congressional adjournment prevents the bill's return, it cannot become law without the president's signature. There has been sharp conflict between Congress and the president over the meaning of "prevents." After several court suits during the 1970s, an informal agreement was reached in 1976 that pocket vetoes, which Congress has no opportunity to override, will be employed not during interim or intersession breaks but only after Congress has adjourned *sine die* (literally, without a day; that is, has adjourned finally).

The decision to veto is a collective administrative judgment. Presidents seek advice from agency officials, the Office of Management and Budget, and White House aides.[12] Five reasons commonly are given for vetoing bills: 1) they are unconstitutional, 2) they encroach on the president's independence, 3) they are unwise public policies, 4) they cannot be administered, and 5) they cost too much. Political considerations may permeate any or all of these reasons. A month before he won reelection in 1972, President Nixon told the nation by radio that "I will veto even bills whose purposes I agree with, if I conclude that the price tags of those bills are so high that they will lead to tax increases."

Just as there may be strong pressure on the White House to veto or sign a bill, there can be intense political heat on Congress after it receives a veto message. A week after President Nixon's 1970 televised Labor-HEW veto, House members received more than 55,000 telegrams, most urging support for the veto. Senator Edmund S. Muskie, D-Maine, observed that using television to veto the bill enabled the president to

Table 10-1   Number of Presidential Vetoes, 1789-1981

Years	President	Regular Vetoes	Pocket Vetoes	Total Vetoes	Vetoes Over-ridden
1789-1797	George Washington	2	—	2	—
1797-1801	John Adams	—	—	0	—
1801-1809	Thomas Jefferson	—	—	0	—
1809-1817	James Madison	5	2	7	—
1817-1825	James Monroe	1	—	1	—
1825-1829	John Q. Adams	—	—	0	—
1829-1837	Andrew Jackson	5	7	12	—
1837-1841	Martin Van Buren	—	1	1	—
1841	W. H. Harrison[1]	—	—	0	—
1841-1845	John Tyler	6	4	10	1
1845-1849	James K. Polk	2	1	3	—
1849-1850	Zachary Taylor	—	—	0	—
1850-1853	Millard Fillmore	—	—	0	—
1853-1857	Franklin Pierce	9	—	9	5
1857-1861	James Buchanan	4	3	7	—
1861-1865	Abraham Lincoln	2	5	7	—
1865-1869	Andrew Johnson	21	8	29	15
1869-1877	Ulysses S. Grant	45	48	93	4
1877-1881	Rutherford B. Hayes	12	1	13	1
1881	James A. Garfield[2]	—	—	0	—
1881-1885	Chester A. Arthur	4	8	12	1
1885-1889	Grover Cleveland	304	110	414	2
1889-1893	Benjamin Harrison	19	25	44	1
1893-1897	Grover Cleveland	42	128	170	5
1897-1901	William McKinley	6	36	42	—
1901-1909	Theodore Roosevelt	42	40	82	1
1909-1913	William H. Taft	30	9	39	1
1913-1921	Woodrow Wilson	33	11	44	6
1921-1923	Warren G. Harding	5	1	6	—
1923-1929	Calvin Coolidge	20	30	50	4
1929-1933	Herbert Hoover	21	16	37	3
1933-1945	Franklin D. Roosevelt	372	263	635	9
1945-1953	Harry S. Truman	180	70	250	12
1953-1961	Dwight D. Eisenhower	73	108	181	2
1961-1963	John F. Kennedy	12	9	21	—
1963-1969	Lyndon B. Johnson	16	14	30	—
1969-1974	Richard M. Nixon	26	17	43	7
1974-1977	Gerald R. Ford	48	18	66	12
1977-1981	Jimmy Carter	13	18	31	2
	Total	1,380	1,011	2,391	94

[1] W. H. Harrison served from March 4 to April 4, 1841.
[2] James A. Garfield served from March 4 to September 19, 1881.

SOURCE: *Presidential Vetoes, 1789-1976,* compiled by the Senate Library (Washington, D.C.: U.S. Government Printing Office, 1978), p. ix; *Presidential Elections Since 1789,* 2d ed. (Washington, D.C.: Congressional Quarterly, 1979), p. vi; and *1980 CQ Almanac* (Washington, D.C.: Congressional Quarterly, 1981), p. 7.

"build momentum on an issue or on a confrontation with the Congress ... that's very difficult to offset." Congress upheld the veto.[13]

Congress need not act at all upon a vetoed bill. The chamber that receives it may refer it to committee or table it, if party leaders feel they lack the votes to override. And if one house musters the votes to override, the other body may do nothing. No amendments can be made to a vetoed bill—it is all or nothing at this stage—and votes on vetoed bills are required by the Constitution to be recorded.

SOURCES OF LEGISLATIVE-EXECUTIVE COOPERATION

Unlike national assemblies where executive authority is lodged in the leader of parliament, called the prime minister or premier, Congress is truly separate from the executive branch. Yet the executive and legislative branches are mutually dependent in policymaking, and they cooperate in many other ways. Tying the branches together are parties, public pressures, and the need for bargaining to achieve results.

Party Links

Presidents and congressional leaders have met informally to discuss issues ever since the First Congress, when George Washington frequently sought the advice of Representative James Madison. But regular meetings between the chief executive and House and Senate leaders did not become common until Theodore Roosevelt's administration. Today, congressional party leaders are two-way conduits, communicating legislative views to the president and, conversely, informing members of executive preferences and intentions. *(See box, p. 298.)*

There is also presidential-congressional interdependence in initiating legislation, scheduling measures for floor action, and mobilizing votes. In 1981, for example, President Reagan relied heavily on Senate Majority Leader Howard H. Baker, Jr., R-Tenn., to marshal support for the administration's economic program. With Republicans controlling the Senate for the first time in 26 years, the majority leader quickly established himself as a critical ally. "Before we move on anything up there, we pick up the phone and get Howard Baker's judgment on what will or won't fly," said White House Chief of Staff James Baker (no relation to the senator).[14]

Bargaining Relationships

The interdependence of the two branches provides each with the incentive to bargain. Legislators and presidents have in common at least three interests: choosing good public policy, winning elections, and attaining influence within the legislature. In achieving these goals,

Byrd Describes Leadership Meetings With President Carter

The President of the United States often consults with the leaders of the two parties of both Houses. There is normally, under the Carter administration, a leadership breakfast that is held about once every 2 weeks. Generally, it occurs on Tuesdays. At that breakfast, the President and some of the people in his administration will sit down with the Speaker and the leaders of the other body and the President pro tempore and the leaders in this body. President Carter will sound out the leaders within his own party in the two Houses and get their information with respect to the possibilities and the problems that will confront specific pieces of legislation within the respective bodies.

Those meetings will often indicate to the leaders of his own party, the President's wishes with respect to particular pieces of legislation, his desires as to priorities to be given legislation. The leaders may or may not, as they proceed to schedule the actions within their respective bodies, follow his desires.

I assign, as a usual thing, great importance to the desires, the feelings, and the opinions of committee chairmen in this body, and the Members of the body who have amendments to measures, in my scheduling of measures to be taken up. That is not to say that I disregard the wishes of the President. They are certainly taken into consideration. But they are not the absolute top priority in every instance, by any means.

I try to keep in mind that the Senate and the House are two separate but equal bodies and that the legislative branch and the executive are separate but equal bodies.

Of course, when the President is a member of the party that is in control of the Senate and House, the relationship between the President and the majority leader of his own party in the Senate is going to be much closer than if the two individuals are of different parties.

With respect to the leadership meetings at the White House, the President from time to time also meets with the minority leadership of both Houses, separate and apart from the Democratic leaders.

There are occasions when the President will meet with the joint leadership of both Houses, including both parties.

SOURCE: Remarks of Senate Majority Leader Robert C. Byrd, D-W.Va., *Congressional Record*, May 2, 1980, pp. S4494-S4495.

members may be helped or hindered by executive officials. Agency personnel, for example, can seek legislators' advice in formulating policies and help them get favorable publicity back home. Executive officials, on the other hand, rely on legislators for help in pushing administrative proposals through the legislative process.

An illustration of effective presidential bargaining with Congress occurred on May 7, 1981, when the Democratic-controlled House adopted President Reagan's controversial budget package, intended to cut federal spending for social programs and raise military spending. The plan easily passed the House because of Reagan's popularity and adroitness in dealing with representatives. The "greatest selling job I've ever seen," said Democratic Speaker O'Neill. On the key House vote, all 191 GOP members and 63 Democrats backed the president's budget approach.

The president's victory was made possible by a multipronged strategy. He bolstered the support of wavering Republicans. He convinced several governors to meet with representatives from their states who were opposing the program. He met or phoned conservative Democrats whose support was needed. Top executive officials were sent into targeted Democratic districts to drum up public support. Finally, a few days before the House vote, and in his first public appearance since March 30 when he was shot in an assassination attempt, President Reagan made a nationally televised address before a joint session of Congress and appealed for support of his economic program.

South Carolina Democrat Butler Derrick, who saw Reagan at the White House, experienced the "two Congresses" dilemma we have been discussing in this book. He described the "inside-outside" pressures he was under prior to the House vote.

> We've had all sorts of conservative proposals to come before the Congress that were not here a year ago or six or eight months ago. They're here because Reagan was a catalyst. Most people I talk to, and

President Reagan, center, meets at the Capitol with congressional leaders, including, from left, Senate Majority Whip Ted Stevens, R-Alaska; House Speaker Thomas P. O'Neill, Jr., D-Mass.; Senate Majority Leader Howard H. Baker, Jr., R-Tenn.; and Senate Minority Leader Robert C. Byrd, D-W.Va.

I think they're right, back in the district, say, "You know, I don't know if he's right or he's wrong, but I'm not pleased with what we've done up to now, so I say let's give the guy a chance to see if it'll work."

I've had a lot of pressure on me. I'm considered, I guess as a member of the Rules Committee, part of the Democratic leadership and I have had a good bit of pressure put on me from members of the leadership and what not. And I've just explained it to them. Quite frankly, to vote other than to vote for [the president], which I plan to do, would be like throwing gasoline in the face of my constituents. [15]

In short, President Reagan shrewdly encouraged representatives to back his national budget while pleasing their constituents. He even suggested how legislators might reconcile their budget-cutting and program-spending instincts. Vote for my austerity budget, he told House members, but fight in committee or on the House floor for favored programs.

Informal Ties

Some presidents woo Congress more adeptly than others. Lyndon Johnson assiduously courted members. He invited legislators to the White House for private meetings, danced with their wives at parties, telephoned greetings on their birthdays, and invited them to his Texas ranch. Johnson was known to "twist arms" to win support for his programs. But his understanding of what moved members and energized Congress was awesome.

In contrast, President Carter, elected as a Washington "outsider," never developed close ties with Congress. Although by one measurement Congress backed Carter 75 percent of the time on votes where he took a position during 1977, the margin was low for a first-year president whose party also controlled the Congress. *(See Figure 10-1.)* Part of Carter's problem was his inability to establish close relations with the members. A House Democrat recalled:

When I came here President Kennedy would have six or seven of us down to the White House every evening for drinks and conversation. Johnson did the same thing, and they created highly personal, highly involved relationships. With Carter, he has 140 people in for breakfast and a lecture.[16]

President Reagan, on the other hand, is so far at ease with members. He enjoys talking about issues and swapping stories with Democrats and Republicans alike. Indeed, during two months in early 1981, the president "met face to face with 400 Congressmen and ostentatiously courted the most powerful Democrat among them, Speaker of the House Thomas P. (Tip) O'Neill, Jr., who was invited for dinner and to the President's surprise birthday party for intimates." [17] Reagan aides said that informal sessions with legislators were part of a strategy of holding "potential enemies close, so close that they can't move their arms." [18]

SOURCES OF LEGISLATIVE-EXECUTIVE CONFLICT

Congress and the presidency are independent yet interlocked institutions. Each branch is in a position to thwart the other; yet they must bargain and cooperate with each other to achieve common objectives. Ninety-four volumes of the *United States Statutes at Large* underscore the cooperative impulses of the two branches. Each volume contains the joint product of Congresses and presidents over the years, from the 108 public laws enacted by the First Congress (1789-1791) to the 613 enacted by the 96th Congress (1979-1981).

What is not shown in these compilations are the many hours of work, and the conflict and compromises, that are built into each law. Legislative-executive conflicts are a recurrent theme of American politics. They were evident in 1789, they are present today, and they can be expected in the future. Many factors contribute to this central reality of national decisionmaking, including constitutional ambiguities, differences in the constituencies that presidents and Congresses serve, and variations in the timetables of the two branches.

Constitutional Impact

The Constitution, replete with ambiguities, does not specify the precise roles of Congress and the president in policymaking nor the manner in which they are to share power. Article I invests Congress with "all legislative Powers," but it also authorizes the president to veto

Figure 10-1 Presidential Success on Votes, 1953-1980

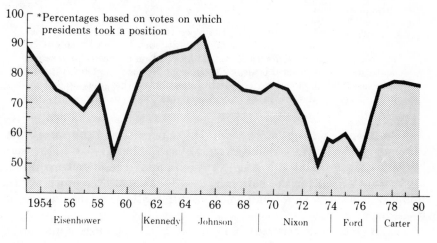

SOURCE: *President Carter 1980* (Washington, D.C.: Congressional Quarterly, 1981), p. 100.

legislation. In a number of specific areas, the Constitution also splits authority between the president and Congress. The Senate, for example, is the president's partner in treatymaking under the "advice and consent" clause. Before treaties can take effect, they require the concurrence of two-thirds of the Senate. The Constitution, however, is silent on how or when the Senate is to render its advice to the president.[19]

In 1919 and 1920 a classic confrontation occurred when the Senate vehemently opposed the Treaty of Versailles negotiated by President Wilson. The treaty contained an agreement involving the United States in the proposed League of Nations. Earlier, many senators had warned the president against including the league provision in the treaty; during floor deliberations, the Senate added several "reservations" to the treaty that the president strongly opposed.

Unable to break the Senate deadlock, Wilson launched a nation-wide speaking tour to mobilize popular support for the treaty. Not to be outdone, senators opposed to the pact organized their own "truth squad," followed the president, and rebutted his arguments. In the end, the treaty was rejected. The Constitution, in short, intermingles presidential and congressional authority and also assigns each branch special duties.

Different Constituencies

Presidents and their vice presidents are the only public officials elected nationally. To win, they must create vastly broader electoral coalitions than legislators, who represent either states or districts. Only presidents, then, can claim to speak for the nation at large; legislators are limited to speaking for smaller groups of voters. It is important to note, however, that

> There is no structural or institutional or theoretical reason why the representation of a "single" broader constituency by the President is necessarily better or worse than the representation of many "separate" constituencies by several hundred legislators. Some distortion is inevitable in either arrangement, and the question of the good or evil of either form of distortion simply leads one back to varying value judgments. [20]

Presidents and legislators tend to view policies and problems from different perspectives. Members often subscribe to the view that "What's good for Seattle is good for the nation." Presidents are apt to say: "What's good for the nation is good for Seattle." In other words, public officials may view common issues differently when they represent diverging interests.

A vivid example occurred in February 1977 when President Carter proposed to terminate 19 congressionally approved dams and other water projects as environmentally and economically unsound. The president's unexpected action incensed many legislators. "To a member of Congress—with rare exceptions," wrote Elizabeth Drew, a "good project is what puts money in your district." [21] The different outlooks of Congress and the president do not mean that one branch is wiser than the other in making policy judgments. Nor are voters of one mind in choosing between general and local values. Voting for presidents, the electorate chooses candidates espousing broad national and international goals. Voting for representatives and senators, citizens often choose candidates who can "bring home the bacon." [22]

For example, a president might wish to reduce international trade barriers. A representative from a district where the automobile industry is threatened by imported products from Japan is likely to oppose the president's policy. The importer and retailer of shoes from Italy, however, is likely to support the president. The challenge to national policymaking is achieving consensus within an electorate that simultaneously holds membership in two or more competing constituencies.

Different Time Perspectives

Congress and the president operate on different timetables. Presidents have four years, and possibly eight (no president from 1961 to 1981 has served two complete terms), to win adoption of their programs. They are usually in a hurry to achieve all they can before they have to leave office. In practice, they may have even less time—in view of the typical falloff of presidential support. Thus Reagan and his advisers assumed they had less than a year to sell the president's basic program.

Congress, on the other hand, is slow-moving. Seldom does Congress pass presidential initiatives quickly. Moreover, many legislators are careerists. Once elected, House members are likely to be reelected, and senators serve six-year terms. Most members, then, will hold office a good deal longer than presidents. Skeptical legislators reluctant to follow the president realize that, if they resist long enough, another person will occupy the White House. In short,

> The President is intent on the problem of the moment, which is to pass high-priority items in his program. He asks his congressional allies to spend power in behalf of this goal. The congressman, who has to worry about the possibility of a future transfer to a desirable committee or a private bill that may mean political life or death in the future, is naturally inclined to hoard power or to invest it so as to increase his future stock of resources. [23]

LOBBYING THE CONGRESS

"Merely placing a program before Congress is not enough," declared President Johnson. "Without constant attention from the administration, most legislation moves through the congressional process at the speed of a glacier." [24] Johnson regularly admonished his aides and departmental officers to work closely with Congress. "[Get off] your ass and see how fast you can respond to a congressional request," he told his staff. "Challenge yourself to see how quickly you can get back to him or her with an answer, any kind of answer, but goddamn it, an answer." [25]

White House liaison activities, patronage services, and public appeals for support are three important ways presidents enhance their bargaining power with Congress. They help presidents exercise their constitutional and persuasive powers, and they may also serve to avoid the delay and deadlock built into executive-legislative relationships.

White House Liaison

Presidents have always maintained informal contacts with Congress. Washington dispatched Treasury Secretary Hamilton to consult with members; Jefferson socialized with his congressional allies. But not until the Truman administration in 1949 did any president create an office to maintain ties with Congress. Truman's liaison unit consisted of two persons inexperienced in legislative politics.

In 1961 President Kennedy transformed the congressional relations unit. He realized that without aggressive liaison his New Frontier program faced tough sledding in a Congress controlled by conservatives. He appointed Lawrence F. O'Brien to the highest staff level in the White House and named him to head the Office of Congressional Relations. As a result, O'Brien said, "I could speak for the president with the Congress and deal directly with the Leadership of the House and Senate on behalf of the president." [26]

O'Brien worked diligently to establish cordial relations with the members. He designated certain staff to be responsible for the House or Senate and for regional and partisan blocs. Liaison staff became familiar with the members from each geographical area, understanding their interests and calculating how their votes might be won for the president's program. O'Brien also coordinated departmental and agency liaison activities with Congress.

> We surveyed Congressional Relations in the Departments and Agencies and established a procedure whereby each Cabinet Member and Agency Head submitted to me by Monday noon of each week, a written report detailing his Department's activity on the Hill during the previous week and a projection of activity for the current week. We summarized these reports during Monday afternoon and sent the summary to the President for his night reading on Monday evenings along with a suggested agenda for his use when he met with the Democratic Leadership each Tuesday. In addition, we called the Congressional Liaison Heads of the Departments and Agencies, numbering about 40, to the White House periodically for in-depth discussions of our program and specific assignments. [27]

Presidents after Kennedy added different lobbying dimensions. Johnson urged an activist approach. Nixon elevated his first liaison head (Bryce Harlow) to cabinet status. Ford enlarged the congressional relations staff from about 6 in 1972 to approximately 16. And President Carter for a while organized his staff differently from previous administrations.

Carter first organized his liaison staff of more than 20 persons (headed by Georgian Frank Moore) along issue lines—health, energy, and other specialties—rather than by geographical area. That arrangement was dropped in less than six months. As one White House liaison officer explained:

> I don't think that the issue-based organization of the liaison office was a very good idea. Too many members simply fall through the cracks. You might be assigned an issue, and that issue might never come up during the entire two years of a congressional session. Also, with the issue-based system, you don't get around to talking to many members until it's too late. You won't talk to the lowest-ranking member of the Energy Subcommittee until you need his vote, and that's not when we should be talking with him. Our job is to serve the members' needs, to hold their hands, to stroke their egos. We have to do all kinds of little things with them that have nothing to do with issues. It's sort of like we're in the Green Stamps business. But we have to give out a lot of stamps before the members will trade them in. [28]

Later Carter reorganized the liaison unit into House-Senate specialists, allowing the staff to work with the members they knew from previous contacts. Another Carter innovation was likely to have lasting impact. His liaison unit employed computers to analyze congressional votes and thus target members who were perhaps "gettable" for certain issues. [29]

Carter's congressional relations office got off to a rocky start because of its inexperience. Speaker O'Neill was denied extra tickets to the Carter inaugural and met with top Carter aide Hamilton Jordan (whom he dubbed "Hannibal Jerkin") only three times in four years. By comparison, during the Reagan administration's first 100 days, the Speaker met many times with the president and his top aides. The Reagan legislative liaison unit, headed by Max L. Friedersdorf, quickly won plaudits from Democrats and Republicans alike on Capitol Hill for its skill and sophistication in dealing with Congress. [30]

Patronage Services

To win congressional support for their programs, presidents commonly grant or withhold their patronage resources. Broadly conceived, patronage involves not only federal and judicial positions, but also federal construction projects, location of government installations, offers of campaign support, access to strategic information, plane rides on Air Force One, White House meetings for important constituents of members, and countless other favors both large and small. Their actual or potential award enables presidents to amass political IOUs they can "cash in" later for needed support in Congress. A story illustrates the dynamics of trading.

> John Kennedy was trying to make a case to Senator Robert Kerr for an investment credit tax bill that was bottled up in the Senate Finance Committee, of which Kerr was an influential member. Kerr responded by asking why the administration opposed his Arkansas River project and by demanding a trade. Kennedy smiled and replied, "You know, Bob, I never really understood that Arkansas River bill before today." Kerr got his project as well as several other benefits. In return, he provided Kennedy with important support and managed the president's high-priority Trade Expansion Act in the Senate.[31]

Senator Everett Dirksen, R-Ill., an influential minority leader from 1959 to 1969, insisted that patronage was a "tremendous weapon" of the president. "It develops a certain fidelity on the part of the recipient," he said.[32] Yet there are limitations, including the shrinkage of patronage jobs, in attractiveness if not in numbers. Presidents try to avoid the sharp irritation of members whose requests are turned down, sometimes assigning to other officials the job of saying "no."

Public Appeals for Support

To generate grass-roots or indirect support for their programs, presidents may take their case to the people. The assumption is that citizens and pressure groups energized by a president's "fireside chat" or nationally televised address will lobby their representatives and senators to back the president. "With public sentiment, nothing can fail; without it nothing can succeed," said Abraham Lincoln.[33]

Presidents employ various means to win support and reduce opposition for their actions. The White House can sponsor regional conferences to drum up public support for the administration's program. Or groups from members' states and districts can be invited to the White House by the president's public liaison aide (Elizabeth Dole for Reagan) to receive briefings from high-level officials. Or the president can undertake a nationwide speaking tour, woo press and media correspondents, conduct "town meetings," or dispatch high aides and executive officers to address groups around the country.

"Going public" on an issue is not without its risks. The president can raise expectations that cannot be met, make inept presentations, lose control over issues, infuriate legislators whose support he needs, or offer poorly conceived proposals. "We used to be frightened to death that he [President Carter] would go over the top of Congress and appeal directly to the people," said Democratic Representative Timothy Wirth of Colorado. "But there's not enough cohesion in his program to do that. There's no reason to feel threatened." [34]

Also, many legislators are more popular than the president in their districts or states. The president "goes public" to seek support, for "if he had the votes he would pass the measure first and go to the public only for the bill-signing ceremonies." [35]

THE BALANCE OF POWER

"The relationship between the Congress and the presidency," wrote Arthur M. Schlesinger, Jr., "has been one of the abiding mysteries of the American system of government." [36] Part of the mystery is inherent in the Constitution, which enumerates many powers for Congress as well as those "necessary and proper" to carry them out, while leaving the president's powers largely ambiguous. Who has ultimate authority to determine public policy depends upon a wide variety of circumstances.

Where does the balance of power lie? There is no easy answer, but some perspective on the legislative-executive tug-of-war can be gained by examining the history of the relationship and the roles of the branches in domestic and foreign policymaking.

Swings of the Pendulum

Shifts of power between Congress and the president have been a regular feature of American politics. Scholars even designate certain periods as times of "congressional government" or "presidential government." [37]

Several points need to be made about the ups and downs of Congress and the presidency. First, the power relationship is in constant flux. The stature of either branch can be influenced by issues, circumstances, or personalities. And even during periods when one branch is called the "junior partner," the actual relationships in specific policy areas may be exactly the reverse.

The mid-1960s and early 1970s, for example, are cited as a time of imperial presidents and weak Congresses. [38] But Congress's role during this period was not minuscule. It enacted much of President Johnson's "Great Society" program and initiated scores of laws (including consumer, environmental, health, and civil rights legislation). Executive actions did not go entirely unchallenged. Nationally televised hearings conducted in 1966 by the Senate Foreign Relations Committee helped mobilize congressional and public opposition against President Johnson's Vietnam war policies.

Second, legislative-executive relationships are not zero-sum games. If one branch gains power, it does not necessarily mean that the other loses it. If one branch is up, the other may not be down. The expansion of the federal government since World War II has augmented the authority of both branches. Their growth rates differed, but each expanded its ability to address complex issues, initiate legislation, and frustrate proposals of the other.

Third, events contribute importantly to policymaking power. Conventional wisdom states that wars, nuclear weapons, and public demands fostered the imperial presidency. Such factors certainly enlarge the possibilities for executive predominance, but we should note that in the wars of 1812 and 1898, military action was encouraged in part by strong Congresses. Nor did economic panics and depressions under Presidents Monroe, Buchanan, or Grant lead to losses of congressional power.

Fourth, shifts of power occur within each branch. In Congress, aggressive leaders may be followed by less assertive leaders. In the executive branch, the forces for agency centralization regularly battle the forces for agency decentralization.[39] These internal power fluctuations clearly affect policymaking. As recently as the Eisenhower presidency, powerful committee and party leaders could regularly deliver blocs of votes to pass legislation. More recent presidents are never quite sure which of the 540 members can assemble winning coalitions.

Finally, pendulum swings affect issue areas and how they are addressed by the two branches. In foreign relations cycles of isolationism and internationalism, noninterventionism and interventionism, have succeeded each other at fairly regular intervals. Debates on health policy may shift from emphasizing government-run programs to approaches stressing private-sector competition. In short, our political system gives plenty of room to Congress and the president to initiate policies jointly or separately and to coexist as strong and active branches of government.

Domestic Policymaking

It is somewhat artificial to divide public policymaking into domestic and international components because many domestic and foreign issues are interrelated. One scholar coined a new word, "intermestic"— from *inter*national and do*mestic*—to emphasize that certain international problems "strike instantly into the economic and political interests of domestic constituencies." [40] Notwithstanding their interdependence, it may be helpful to distinguish between the two.

Congress is a durable partner in domestic policymaking. Many studies have concluded "not that the President is less important than generally supposed but that Congress is more important" as a policy formulator.[41] As a Brookings Institution study determined after examining seven urban issues:

> The case studies, then, cast considerable doubt on the stereotype of a passive legislature simply responding to presidential initiatives. When opposing parties control the presidency and the Congress, the political environment for policy making invites and positively encourages the exercise of congressional initiative. Moreover, even when the political environment would tend to dampen congressional initiative—for example, when a young, aggressive President occupies the White House and his party is in full command of both House and Senate—even then Congress may prove to be the dominant force in advancing new program ideas in some policy fields, in shaping certain bills and guiding them through to enactment.[42]

Policymaking, as we shall see in Chapter 14, involves many steps: conceiving an idea, gathering information, publicizing the proposal, mobilizing support, gaining its passage, and implementing the law. Congress is involved at every stage, but its role is often stronger at one point than another. For example, conceiving, ventilating, and sustaining ideas are special strengths of Congress that flow from its representative character. At the mobilization and implementation stage, however, Congress frequently requires help from the executive branch and pressure groups.

Congress's influence also varies from one issue area to another. For example, "Congress has viewed [the water resource] area as peculiarly their domain, far more than any other program I can think of," remarked a veteran official of the Office of Management and Budget.[43] Thus, many members rose up against President Carter's 1977 cancellation of 19 ongoing water projects.

Reelection incentives frequently account for Congress's activist role in certain domestic areas and highlight the two Congresses problem. As aides to Senator Thomas Eagleton, D-Mo., discovered during his 1980 reelection campaign:

> [M]uch of his current support stems from his image as a politician who "comes through for Missouri." [Campaign aides] note that an early "benchmark" poll taken for the Eagleton campaign last spring by pollster William Hamilton showed that Missouri voters overwhelmingly view the role of their Senator as "someone who helps with my problems" and "a person who brings federal dollars into my state." Other possible attributes—such as "statesman" or "effective legislator"—trailed far behind. [44]

In short, the legislative branch can initiate on its own, prod the executive into action, or transform an executive proposal into its own product.

Finally, public expectations that Congress ought to assert its authority, especially in domestic policy, encourage it to do so. *(See Table 10-2.)* This condition—combined with activist-oriented legisla-

Table 10-2　The Role of Congress and the President in Policymaking

Who should have the major responsibility?	Energy Policy	Economic Policy	Foreign Policy	General Responsibility
Congress	40%	40%	27%	36%
Equal	19	20	18	22
President	35	34	49	37
Don't know	6	6	6	5
	100	100	100	100

QUESTION ASKED: Now I would like to ask you some questions about the President and Congress. Some people think that the President ought to have the major responsibility for making policy, while other people think that Congress ought to have the major responsibility. In general, which do you think should have the major responsibility for setting policy?

SOURCE: Gallup Poll; Thomas E. Cronin, "A Resurgent Congress and the Imperial Presidency," *Political Science Quarterly* (Summer 1980): 211.

tors who want to make policy and institutional norms and procedures that promote such activity—further buttresses Congress's ability to conceive domestic policies and to pass, modify, or kill proposals.

Foreign Policymaking

Many citizens and foreign nationals believe that international and military policymaking is exclusively the president's domain. That is not the case. The constitutional separation of powers is "an invitation to struggle for the privilege of directing American foreign policy." [45]

Congress has a large number of explicit constitutional duties, such as the power to declare war, regulate foreign commerce, and raise and support armies. The president's only specific international powers are to be commander-in-chief, to negotiate treaties and appoint ambassadors (shared with the Senate), and to receive ambassadors.

Throughout American history, presidents have claimed responsibilities not spelled out in the Constitution. Whether they are called implied, inherent, or emergency powers, presidents have used them to control foreign policy. This development occurred in part because of the innate advantages of the office. As John Jay wrote in *The Federalist* (No. 64), the unity of the office, its superior information sources, and its capacity for secrecy and dispatch gave the president daily charge of foreign intercourse. Moreover, Congress was at that time not in session the whole year; by contrast, the president was always available to make decisions.

Congress seldom has been a "rubber stamp," as Woodrow Wilson discovered when the Senate rejected the Treaty of Versailles. From World War II through the 1960s, however, Congress assented to presidential control of foreign policy. "There were some disputes between the two branches over international issues during that period," said House Foreign Affairs Chairman Clement Zablocki, D-Wis. "But it is safe to say that the presidents who served then—Roosevelt, Truman, Eisenhower, Kennedy, and Johnson—seldom, if ever, found themselves blocked on a major foreign policy matter by a 'nay-saying' Congress." [46]

Legislative-executive relations turned a corner during the late 1960s and early 1970s. With the Vietnam war and Watergate acting as catalysts, Congress became heavily involved in international relations. It passed, for example, numerous statutes that both constrained the president and expanded Congress's policymaking role. Several examples include:

—A 1972 law that requires executive agreements to be reported to Congress. To avoid Senate involvement, presidents commonly entered into secret "executive agreements" with foreign countries. Such agreements require no congressional action and can be just as binding as treaties.

—The 1973 War Powers Resolution, which limits the president's authority to engage U.S. troops abroad for prolonged periods without legislative consent.

—The 1974 Trade Act containing the Jackson-Vanik Amendment (after Senator Henry Jackson, D-Wash., and Representative Charles Vanik, D-Ohio) that prohibited U.S. trade concessions for the Soviet Union as long as it restricted Jewish emigration.

—Several laws that place restrictions on U.S. arms sales abroad.

—Legislation that requires intelligence agencies to keep certain congressional committees informed of their activities.

What makes this thrust different from earlier ones is that Congress took important steps to strengthen its capacity for initiating and monitoring international issues. It hired more and better foreign policy staff; it augmented its information sources; and it lost its inferiority complex. Many legislators hold the view that Congress can do as well as the president in making foreign policy.

The House, long the Senate's junior partner in this field, added to its foreign policy role during this period. Traditionally, the Senate has led in foreign affairs because of its constitutional role in ratifying treaties and confirming diplomatic personnel. But the House's recognition of the "intermestic" factor, the activism of many members and staff aides, and increased lobbying by special interest groups (American Jews and the Greek lobby, for example) partially account for expanded House participation.[47] In addition, today's foreign policy requires money—aid, loans, and arms sales are examples—where the House historically has predominated.

Congress also strengthened its financial capability over international (and domestic) issues. The new budget process, initiated in 1974, better enables Congress to examine and alter administration proposals, to control and oversee military and foreign programs, and to take a comprehensive view of international commitments. Congress's revamped budget process is "one of the most important government reforms in decades," said Stuart Eizenstat, then President Carter's chief domestic aide. "But it increases the power of Congress vis-à-vis the Executive. They've set up a competing power system which makes it more difficult for the President to have his way." [48]

Congress's greater assertiveness in international relations causes some political commentators, who worried earlier about the imperial presidency, to be concerned that Congress now intrudes too deeply into presidential prerogatives. The critics say Congress has a legitimate role in *making* policy but not in *conducting* it. *(See box, p. 313.)*

For long-range planning, executive officials want flexibility, discretion, and commitments from Congress. They prefer few controls and consultations with only a small number of legislators. Congress, on the other hand, responds to other imperatives.

Congress is a messy, disorganized branch. However, one of its fundamental strengths is to give voice and visibility to diverse viewpoints that may have been overlooked or ignored by the executive branch. The dispersion of power can slow down decisionmaking, but it can also promote public understanding of the nation's policies. "No foreign policy will stick unless the American people are behind it," observed seasoned diplomat Averell Harriman, "and unless Congress understands it, the American people aren't." [49]

There are virtues, in short, for what people view as Congress's vices in foreign policy. Two congressional experts summarize the foreign policy role of Congress: "it can help formulate policies; it can act to check the growing powers of the presidency; it can support the president, when necessary and desirable, in his foreign policy initiatives; it can monitor the attitudes of the American people; it can convey the view of the people to the President; and it can help inform and educate the people on foreign policy." [50]

CONCLUSION

Several themes endure in legislative-executive relations: accommodation, conflict, and flux. Of these, the central reality is mutual accommodation. Neither branch is monolithic. Presidents find supporters in Congress even when they are opposed by a majority of either

---

President Ford on Congress's
Foreign Policy Weaknesses

First, they have so many other concerns: legislation in committee and on the floor, constituents to serve, and a thousand other things. It is impractical to ask them to be as well versed in fast-breaking developments as the President, the National Security Council, the Joint Chiefs of Staff, and others who deal with foreign policy and national security situations every hour of every day.

Second, it is also impossible to wait for a consensus to form among those congressional leaders as to the proper course of action, especially when they are scattered literally around the world and when time is the one thing we cannot spare. Again, we should ask what the outcome would be if the leaders consulted do not agree among themselves or disagree collectively with the President on an action he considers essential.

Third, there is the risk of disclosure of sensitive information through insecure means of communication, particularly by telephone. Members of Congress with a great many things on their minds might also confuse what they hear on the radio news in this day of instant communication with what they are told on a highly classified basis by the White House.

Fourth, the potential legal consequences of taking executive action before mandated congressional consultation can be completed may cause a costly delay. The consequences to the President, if he does not wait for Congress, could be as severe as impeachment. But the consequences to the Nation, if he does wait, could be much worse.

Fifth, there is a question of how consultations with a handful of congressional leaders can bind the entire Congress to support a course of action — especially when younger Members of Congress are becoming increasingly independent. A survey reported by Congressional Quarterly last November indicated that an overwhelming majority of the Congress believed the legislative branch had an inadequate role in the international crises I have mentioned.

Sixth, the Congress has little to gain and much to lose politically by involving itself deeply in crisis management. If the crisis is successfully resolved, it is the President who will get credit for the success. If his efforts are not successful, if the objectives are not met or if casualties are too high, the Congress will have seriously compromised its right to criticize the decisions and actions of the President.

Finally, there is absolutely no way American foreign policy can be conducted or military operations commanded by 535 Members of Congress on Capitol Hill, even if they all happen to be on Capitol Hill when they are needed.

* SOURCE: *Congressional Record*, April 25, 1977, pp. S6360-S6361.

---

house. Both branches seek support for their policy preferences from each other and outside allies in an atmosphere usually free of acrimony.

However, it is also true that confrontation is a recurring theme in dealings between Capitol Hill and the White House. The Framers consciously distributed and mixed power among the branches. They left it unclear how Congress or the president were to assert control over the bureaucracy and over policymaking. No wonder they tend to be adversaries even when they are controlled by the same party. "[W]e are not going to roll over and play dead just because Jimmy Carter is President," declared the Democratic chairman of the House Foreign Affairs Committee shortly before Carter took office in 1977.[51]

Finally, legislative-executive relations are constantly in flux. Either branch may be active on an issue at one time, and passive on the same or different issues at another time. So many circumstances affect how, when, what, or why changes are brought about in their relationship that it is impossible to predict the outlook.

It is clear, however, that during the past decade Congress equipped itself with a formidable array of resources. As a result, it can play a more active role and even initiate policies of its own. This development need not be a formula for stalemate. "Our proper objective," counseled former Senator J. William Fulbright, D-Ark., "is neither a dominant presidency nor an aggressive Congress but, within the strict limits of what the Constitution mandates, a shifting of the emphasis according to the needs of the time and the requirements of public policy." [52]

Another important aspect of legislative-executive relations is how Congress deals with the bureaucracy. In recent decades, there has been an enormous growth of federal agencies, regulations, and payments to individuals and subnational governments. In 1976 Jimmy Carter campaigned successfully on the theme of reorganizing the national government to eliminate waste and promote efficiency. Ronald Reagan went even further in his victorious 1980 campaign, promising to lop off whole departments. After taking office Reagan ran into congressional and bureaucratic resistance when he tried to make good on some of his more drastic promises to cut government spending. The role of the bureaucracy, Congress's oversight function, and the budget process are the topics we address in the next chapter.

NOTES

1. Hedrick Smith, "Taking Charge of Congress," *The New York Times Magazine*, August 9, 1981, p. 16.
2. Joseph Story, *Commentaries on the Constitution of the United States*, 5th ed., vol. 1 (Boston: Little, Brown & Co., 1905), p. 396.
3. *Youngstown Sheet & Tube Co. v. Sawyer*, 343 U.S. 579, 635 (1952).
4. See Wilfred E. Binkley, *President and Congress* (New York: Alfred A. Knopf, 1947); William S. Livingston et al., eds., *The Presidency and the Congress: A Shifting Balance of Power?* (Austin, Texas: Lyndon B. Johnson School of Public Affairs, 1979); and Richard E. Neustadt, *Presidential Power: The Politics of Leadership From FDR to Carter* (New York: John Wiley & Sons, 1980).

5. Leonard D. White, *The Federalists* (New York: Macmillan, 1948), p. 55. See also Paul C. Light, "The President's Agenda: Notes on the Timing of Domestic Choice," *Presidential Studies Quarterly* (Winter 1981): 67-82.
6. Leonard D. White, *The Jeffersonians* (New York: Macmillan, 1951), p. 35.
7. Bertram M. Gross, *The Legislative Struggle* (New York: McGraw-Hill Book Co., 1953), p. 189.
8. Richard M. Pious, *The American Presidency* (New York: Basic Books, 1979), p. 159. See also Larry Berman, *The Office of Management and Budget and the Presidency, 1921-1979* (Princeton, N.J.: Princeton University Press, 1979).
9. William Leuchtenburg, *Franklin D. Roosevelt and the New Deal, 1932-1940* (New York: Harper & Row, 1963), pp. 43-44.
10. Stephen K. Bailey, *Congress Makes a Law* (New York: Columbia University Press, 1950). On legislative delegations, see Sotirios A. Barber, *The Constitution and the Delegation of Congressional Power* (Chicago: University of Chicago Press, 1975); and Louis Fisher, "Delegating Power to the President," *Journal of Public Law* 19 (1970): 251-282.
11. Woodrow Wilson, *Congressional Government* (Boston: Houghton Mifflin Co., 1885), p. 52. See Louis Fisher, *The Constitution Between Friends* (New York: St. Martin's Press, 1978), chap. 4; and Robert L. Peabody et al., *To Enact A Law: Congress and Campaign Financing* (New York: Praeger Publishers, 1972), chap. 7.
12. Stephen J. Wayne, *The Legislative Presidency* (New York: Harper & Row, 1978).
13. *Congressional Quarterly Weekly Report*, February 6, 1970, p. 348.
14. *Wall Street Journal*, April 8, 1981, p. 1.
15. *Washington Post*, May 10, 1981, p. A3.
16. *New York Times*, May 27, 1979, p. E4.
17. Steven R. Weisman, "A Test of the Man and the Presidency," *The New York Times Magazine*, May 3, 1981, p. 56.
18. *Washington Post*, March 17, 1981, p. A5.
19. See Richard E. Webb, "Treaty-Making and the President's Obligation to Seek the Advice and Consent of the Senate With Special Reference to the Vietnam Peace Negotiations," *Ohio State Law Journal* (Summer 1970): 490-519; Joseph P. Harris, *The Advice and Consent of the Senate* (Berkeley: University of California Press, 1953); and G. Calvin Mackenzie, *The Politics of Presidential Appointments* (New York: The Free Press, 1981).
20. James Macgregor Burns, *Presidential Government* (Boston: Houghton Mifflin Co., 1966), p. 284.
21. Elizabeth Drew, "Engagement With the Special-Interest State," *The New Yorker*, February 27, 1978, p. 64.
22. Willmoore Kendall, "The Two Majorities," *Midwest Journal of Political Science* (November 1960): 317-345.
23. Nelson Polsby, *Congress and the Presidency*, 2d ed. (Englewood Cliffs, N.J.: Prentice-Hall, 1971), p. 103.
24. Lyndon B. Johnson, *The Vantage Point* (New York: Holt, Rinehart & Winston, 1971), p. 448.
25. Jack Valenti, "Some Advice on the Care and Feeding of Congressional Egos," *Los Angeles Times*, April 23, 1978, p. 3.
26. U.S., Congress, House, *Congressional Record*, daily ed., 89th Cong., 2d sess., October 10, 1966, p. H24928.
27. Ibid. See also John F. Manley, "Presidential Power and White House Lobbying," *Political Science Quarterly* (Summer 1978): 255-275.

28. Eric Davis, "Legislative Liaison in the Carter Administration," *Political Science Quarterly* (Summer 1979): 289.
29. *Congressional Quarterly Weekly Report,* February 11, 1978, p. 366.
30. *Congressional Quarterly Weekly Report,* May 2, 1981, pp. 747-751; and Dick Kirschten, "The Pensylvania Avenue Connection—Making Peace on Capitol Hill," *National Journal,* March 7, 1981, pp. 384-387.
31. George C. Edwards III, *Presidential Influence in Congress* (San Francisco: W. H. Freeman & Co., 1980), p. 129.
32. Neil MacNeil, *Dirksen: Portrait of a Public Man* (New York: The World Publishing Co., 1970), p. 343. See also Stanley Kelley, Jr., "Patronage and Presidential Legislative Leadership," in *The Presidency,* ed. Aaron Wildavsky (Boston: Little, Brown & Co., 1969), pp. 268-277.
33. Roy P. Basler, ed., *The Collected Works of Abraham Lincoln,* vol. 3 (New Brunswick, N.J.: Rutgers University Press, 1953), p. 27.
34. *New York Times,* May 27, 1979, p. 4E.
35. Pious, *The American Presidency,* p. 194.
36. Arthur M. Schlesinger, Jr. and Alfred de Grazia, *Congress and the Presidency: Their Role in Modern Times* (Washington, D.C.: American Enterprise Institute for Public Policy Research, 1967), p. 1.
37. Wilson, *Congressional Government*; and James McGregor Burns, *Presidential Government.*
38. See Joseph S. Clark, *Congress: The Sapless Branch* (New York: Harper & Row, 1964); and Arthur M. Schlesinger, Jr., *The Imperial Presidency* (Boston: Houghton Mifflin Co., 1973).
39. Ronald C. Moe, *The Federal Executive Establishment: Evolution and Trends,* Senate Committee on Governmental Affairs, 96th Cong., 2d sess., 1980.
40. Bayless Manning, "The Congress, the Executive and Intermestic Affairs: Three Proposals," *Foreign Affairs* (January 1977): 306-324.
41. Lawrence H. Chamberlain, *The President, Congress and Legislation* (New York: Columbia University Press, 1946), pp. 453-454. See also James L. Sundquist, *Politics and Policy* (Washington, D.C.: The Brookings Institution, 1969); Ronald Moe and Steven Teel, "Congress as Policymaker," *Political Science Quarterly* (September 1970): 443-470; David E. Price, *Who Makes the Laws?* (Cambridge, Mass.: Schenkman Publishing Co., 1972); and John R. Johannes, "The President Proposes and the Congress Disposes But Not Always: Legislative Initiative on Capitol Hill," *The Review of Politics* (July 1974): 356-370.
42. Frederick N. Cleaveland et al., *Congress and Urban Problems* (Washington, D.C.: The Brookings Institution, 1969), p. 356.
43. Dick Kirschten, "Congress Makes Waves Over Carter's Water Policy," *National Journal,* July 1, 1978, p. 1054. See also John A. Ferejohn, *Pork Barrel Politics* (Stanford, Calif.: Stanford University Press, 1974); and James T. Murphy, "Political Parties and the Porkbarrel: Party Conflict and Cooperation in House Public Works Committee Decision Making," *American Political Science Review* (March 1974): 169-185.
44. *Wall Street Journal,* March 14, 1980, p. 21.
45. Edward S. Corwin, *The President, Office and Powers* (New York: New York University Press, 1940), p. 208.
46. U.S., Congress, *Congressional Record,* daily ed., 95th Cong., 1st sess., January 4, 1977, p. E49.

47. Holbert Carroll, *The House of Representatives and Foreign Affairs,* rev. ed. (Boston: Little, Brown & Co., 1966); and Fred M. Kaiser, "Oversight of Foreign Policy: The U.S. House International Relations Committee," *Legislative Studies Quarterly* (August 1977): 255-280.
48. *New York Times,* May 21, 1978, p. E4.
49. U.S., Congress, House, *Congressional Record,* daily ed., 95th Cong., 2d sess., August 28, 1978, p. H7765.
50. Lee H. Hamilton and Michael H. Van Dusen, "Making the Separation of Powers Work," *Foreign Affairs* (Fall 1978): 32. See also Alton Frye, "Congress: The Virtues of Its Vices," *Foreign Policy* (Summer 1971): 108-125.
51. U.S., Congress, *Congressional Record,* 95th Cong., 1st sess., January 4, 1977, p. 246. See also I. M. Destler, "Dateline Washington: Congress as Boss?" *Foreign Policy* (Spring 1981): 167-180.
52. J. William Fulbright, "The Legislator As Educator," *Foreign Affairs* (Spring 1979): 726.

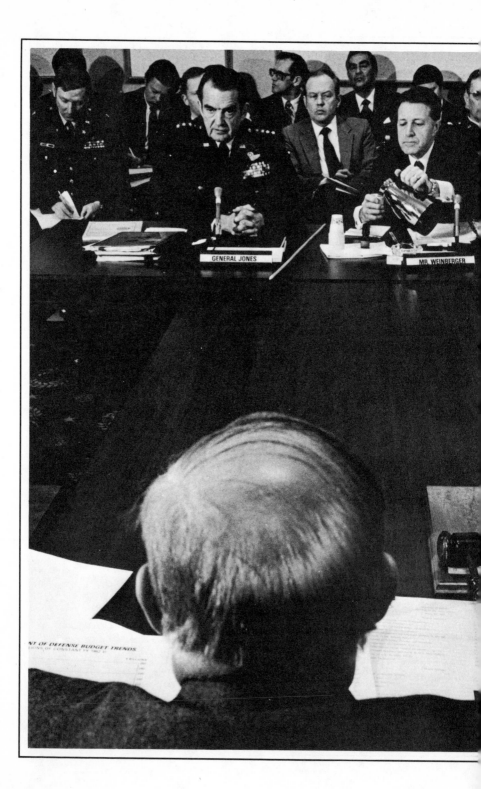

11

Congress, the Bureaucracy, and the Budget Process

A local business owner was baffled by a federal application form that said: "List all your employees broken down by sex." Not knowing what to reply, the businessman scratched his head then wrote, "We don't have any employees broken down by sex, but we do have a couple of alcoholics, and it is just killing them." [1] In an earlier and simpler time, there would have been no such form. Today, however, bewildering rules and regulations govern most federal programs. Overlaid are broad government-enforced requirements—equal employment opportunities, environmental standards, and citizen participation, among others.

Many private concerns have turned into public issues. Teenage pregnancy and the Chrysler Corporation's future are two examples. Neighborhood problems such as crime and waste disposal have become national questions. In short, the national government's agenda has expanded so that there is virtually no area that it does not address.

In 1921 the federal budget was $5 billion. Sixty years later it was nearly $700 billion. Contributing to this phenomenal growth were:

• The 1930s Depression that provoked citizens to look to the national government for economic assistance.

• The two world wars and the Korean and Vietnam wars that required national mobilization of people and material.

• The heavy involvement of the United States in international affairs ever since World War II.

• The nationalization of issues—air and water pollution, for example—that do not respect state or local boundaries.

• The decline of ideological barriers against federal involvement in such areas as education, health, civil rights, welfare, employment, and consumer protection—matters traditionally left to state and local governments or to the private sector.

Presidential recommendations and the demands of special interest groups also caused the government to grow. Both Carter in 1976 and Reagan in 1980 campaigned against big government, pledging to "streamline the bureaucracy." Yet in 1979 Congress helped Carter keep a campaign promise to a teacher's union by creating a new Department of Education. The Department of Energy was also established during the Carter administration. And Reagan, while slashing domestic social programs, promised an expanded military establishment.

Public judgments about the bureaucracy usually depend on "whose ox is being gored." Beneficiaries resist curtailing or eliminating favorite agencies or programs. Liberals applaud government intervention to achieve economic welfare, social equality, consumer rights, and so forth; conservatives bridle at these programs but welcome government subsidies to producers and intervention to promote law, order, and national defense. True libertarians—who oppose government intervention on principle—are few and far between, it seems.

CONGRESS AND THE BUREAUCRACY

Both the president *and* Congress are responsible for the "fourth branch of government," the bureaucracy. The Constitution requires the president to implement the laws and by tradition he must give managerial direction to the executive branch.[2] However, Congress "has at least as much to do with executive administration as does an incumbent of the White House."[3] Congress is constitutionally authorized to organize the executive branch, confirm presidential appointments, and control the purse strings.

Executive Organization and Reorganization

The Constitution's Framers could not have foreseen that their sparse references to "executive departments" would nurture the huge structure of modern bureaucracy. Where George Washington supervised three departments (State, War, and Treasury), President Reagan heads 13 departments, from the oldest (State and Treasury, 1789) to the newest (Education, 1979). *(See Figure 11-1.)* Besides the departments, Congress also has a hand in creating independent agencies, government corporations and intergovernmental commissions. Some of the characteristics of each type are given in the box below.

The complex federal structure periodically undergoes four basic forms of reorganization. First, executive agencies are abolished or

---

Executive Units

The federal government comprises many administrative units of varying autonomy and authority. These units fall into the following categories:

Cabinet Departments. The heads, or secretaries, of the 13 federal departments (such as State, Defense, or Energy) form the "cabinet." The departments contain an array of bureaus and other subunits, some of which act independently from departmental leaders, depending on their constituency and congressional support.

Independent Agencies. Some agencies are outside the formal departmental structure. They are created to promote administrative flexibility, to underscore concern for a major policy area, or to respond to the concerns of outside groups, as in the case of the Veterans Administration. Other examples include the Environmental Protection Agency and the Central Intelligence Agency.

Government Corporations. Initially created to carry out commercial-type functions (the Panama Canal Company, for example), some newer government corporations perform activities outside regular channels of governmental accountability. Examples include the Legal Services Corporation and the Corporation for Public Broadcasting.

Intergovernmental Commissions. To address federal and regional issues, Congress has set up several permanent commissions composed of federal, state, and local officials. The Advisory Commission on Intergovernmental Relations, for example, was established in 1959 to monitor and recommend improvements in the federal system.

Independent Regulatory Commissions. These agencies have broad authority from Congress to issue rules and regulations that govern economic activity (such as rail and telephone rates), public health and welfare (such as consumer product safety), and the expenditure of federal funds by state and local governments (grants-in-aid, for example). These groups, often viewed as "arms of Congress," are run by several commissioners with overlapping terms, and are called "independent" because the president cannot fire any commissioner as he can a cabinet secretary. Examples include the Federal Trade Commission and the Consumer Product Safety Commission.

Figure 11-1 Organization of the Federal Executive Branch

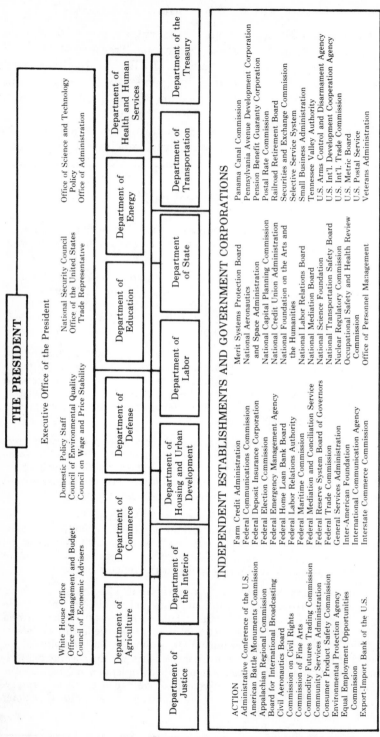

SOURCE: U.S., Department of Commerce, Bureau of the Census, *Statistical Abstract of the United States: 1980*, 101 ed. (Washington, D.C.: U.S. Government Printing Office, 1980), p. 254. The chart has been updated to 1981.

created by law, as in the case of the Education Department in 1979. Second, the president may order administrative changes, as President Reagan did when he all but abolished the Council on Wage-Price Stability. Third, Congress can authorize departments and agencies to reorganize themselves. Finally, Congress may authorize the president to propose reorganization plans subject to legislative veto.[4]

President Carter used his reorganization authority extensively. Old-line agencies such as the Civil Service Commission, U.S. Information Agency, and Defense Civil Preparedness Agency were replaced by the Office of Personnel Management, the International Communication Agency, and the Federal Emergency Management Agency.

On taking office, President Reagan moved quickly to undo some of Carter's work. While he did not immediately seek to abolish the Energy and Education departments, as he had suggested during his campaign, he cut their budgets and left some top offices unfilled.

Reorganizations can have political as well as administrative results. Congress is unlikely to approve such plans if they disrupt committee relations with favored agencies and programs. "If by this [executive] reorganization you affect in a major way the powers of the various committees in the Congress, you may as well forget it," a House committee chairman, Chet Holifield, D-Calif., told President Nixon.[5]

The Personnel System

Congress wields wide authority—constitutionally, legally, and informally—over the federal personnel system. In 1883 it curbed abuses of the "spoils system" (handing out federal jobs to supporters of the party that had won the presidency). The assassination of President Garfield by a disgruntled job seeker triggered passage of the first civil service law that substituted merit for patronage. Almost 100 years later, at President Carter's request, Congress revised the federal employment system, making it somewhat easier to fire incompetent workers and setting up the Senior Executive Service, a pool of top federal officials.

Constitutionally, high-level federal appointments are subject to the Senate's"advice and consent." Literally tens of thousands of government positions require confirmation, although the vast majority are military appointments that receive scant Senate attention. During the 96th Congress (1979-1981) a record 154,141 nominations were offered.[6]

The confirmation process makes career administrators accountable to political officials, gives the Senate a direct hand in approving or rejecting top national officers, influences presidential selection, and allows the Senate to extract policy and program commitments from prospective nominees. In the 1973 "Saturday Night Massacre," for example, Attorney General Elliot Richardson resigned rather than obey

President Nixon's order to fire the Watergate special prosecutor, Archibald Cox. Richardson had pledged during his confirmation hearings to respect the prosecutor's independence.

Political, policy, and patronage considerations permeate the confirmation process. "We are following President Reagan's policies and that is why the people we are appointing are so different from Jimmy Carter's appointees," said the White House personnel director.[7] But this did not stop the GOP-controlled Senate Foreign Relations Committee from rejecting the president's nominee to a human rights position at the State Department.[8] The Senate may also refuse to consider a nominee if members invoke "senatorial courtesy." This tradition, dating from President Washington's administration, generally means that the Senate will delay or not act upon nominations if a senator of the president's party opposes those appointments.[9]

By law, Congress has wide control over federal employees. It can establish special requirements for holding office; terms of principal officers; employee performance standards; wages, benefits, and cost-of-living adjustments; protections from reprisals for "whistleblowers" (employees who expose waste and corruption); or personnel ceilings.

The "two Congresses" clash when pay raises are proposed for members and other federal employees. Few issues place senators and representatives in a more precarious position. Public criticism of pay hikes is real, as is the threat that potential opponents will seize upon the issue in the next election.

Congressional committees also explore agency recruitment practices. In 1976, for example, the House Post Office and Civil Service Committee published a staff study alleging that personnel procedures in certain agencies were manipulated to "provide preferential treatment for favored candidates for career appointments."[10] The study contributed to passage of the 1978 civil service reform act.

There is considerable circulation of members, legislative staffers, and lobbyists between Congress and the executive branch. When Representative George Bush, R-Texas, (Reagan's vice president) lost a Senate race to Lloyd Bentsen, D-Texas, President Nixon appointed him ambassador to the United Nations. President Carter named many Hill employees to top federal positions, including Michael Pertschuk, long-time general counsel of the Senate Commerce Committee, as chairman of the Federal Trade Commission.

Independent Executive Units

Congress is largely responsible for the growth of executive units independent of direct presidential control. Take the 1980 Synthetic Fuels Corporation. Three years before, Congress created the Department of Energy to give the nation's energy policy focus and direction.

The new department soon was embroiled in controversy over its management and effectiveness. As a result, rather than assign synthetic fuels production to the Energy Department, Congress established an independent corporation to handle the "crash" program. Such units usually are exempt from requirements imposed on the other federal departments, such as civil service rules, salary limitations, presidential orders, or Office of Management and Budget (OMB) clearance of their legislative and most regulatory proposals.[11]

Executive disunity works to the advantage of congressional committees and members. It helps them acquire information, influence executive decisions, and gain access to key policymakers. On the other hand, it inhibits the administrative branch from providing Congress with integrated approaches to national problems.

Private Organizations

Despite the nationalization of scores of issues (and contrary to many people's ideas), the federal civilian work force has remained constant at about 2.8 million employees for 25 years. How can the government do more but keep the size of its work force relatively stable? The answer is that many subnational governments and private organizations perform federal functions indirectly.

Only about 15 percent of federal spending "is directed to activities that the federal government performs itself." [12] Weapons systems are built by private companies under contract to the government. The job of Defense Department personnel, like that of many other federal workers, "consists of planning, coordinating, preparing and issuing regulations and contracts for, negotiating, paying for, overseeing, inspecting, auditing, and evaluating the work of others." [13] The "others" include state and local governments, universities, businesses, and hospitals.

The political urge to avoid public criticism of bloated bureaucracies largely accounts for the cosmetic budget games that conceal the true number of indirect federal employees. The advantages to the federal establishment of this so-called "third-party" government are offset by serious problems of accountability, because the persons exercising federal authority are not directly responsible to Congress.[14]

The Electoral Connection

Some observers suggest that Congress enlarged the executive establishment by passing vague laws that bureaucrats had to flesh out with rules and regulations. Many regulatory laws, for example, call for a "reasonable rate," without defining "reasonable." Frustrated by government rules, people then turn to their congressmen for help. Lawmakers thus "take credit coming and going" by claiming credit both for getting programs enacted and for ironing out bureaucratic snarls they create.[15]

The electoral explanation of bureaucratic growth is disputable, however. There is little support for the argument that "congressmen's incessant quest for local benefits has somehow contributed to growth in government spending." [16] Federal expenditures have grown only slightly as a percentage of gross national product (18.1 percent in 1955 to 21.7 percent in 1980). Further, there has been a decline in emphasis on federal programs that benefit localities. Instead, the newer programs, such as medicare, medicaid, and revenue sharing, "deliver benefits as a matter of right, not privilege, and congressmen have fewer opportunities to claim responsibility for them." [17]

Public Works Projects. For many federal programs, Congress leaves it to administrators to decide how funds are to be spread among legislative districts. This is a resource that bureaucrats can employ to maintain and expand their influence in Congress.

> It is a mutually rewarding system. Congressmen can claim credit for whatever benefits flow into their districts, but at the same time they have insulated themselves from their constituents' anger when certain benefits cannot be secured. If Congress itself allocated benefits, constituents might well blame their congressmen for failing to acquire benefits, but as long as bureaucrats have the final say, congressmen are partially protected from their wrath....[18]

Many things affect how federal projects are distributed. Crucial states might be awarded projects just before a presidential election; an agency might process quickly the requests of the president's congressional backers, while others' proposals are mired in red tape; or key members of the committees with jurisdiction over certain agencies might receive the lion's share of federal benefits. Some scholars conclude that committee members receive more district benefits from the agencies they supervise than do noncommittee members.[19] Other studies challenge this judgment.[20]

Of course, not all federal projects are worth attracting. Members compute the political risks of backing a missile base, nuclear power plant, or other project strongly resisted by their constituents. Thus, Nevada and Utah senators led the counterattack against the Air Force's elaborate MX missile basing plan, opposed by many local influentials including the Mormon Church.

Casework. Legislators frequently act as intermediaries between constituents and federal agencies. Constituent problems are handled by personal staff aides called caseworkers. Beyond the electoral payoff of effective casework, members appreciate its value in oversight. "The very knowledge by executive officials that some Congressman is sure to look into a matter affecting his constituents acts as a healthy check against bureaucratic indifference or arrogance," wrote a former senator.[21]

CONGRESS AND THE BUDGET PROCESS

Congress's power of the purse is constitutionally rooted and crucial to its lawmaking and oversight tasks. True to its pluralistic nature, Congress came slowly to centralized control of federal spending. Today's budget process, which received a dramatic test in the early days of the Reagan administration, dates from the mid-1970s and was designed to bring coherence to the way standing committees handle the president's budget.

The Pre-1974 Budget Process

Every committee wants a hand in budget making. Hence, Congress has a two-step financial procedure: *authorizations* and *appropriations*. Congress first passes authorization laws that establish federal agencies and programs and recommend funding them at certain levels. Congress then enacts appropriation laws that allow agencies to spend money. An authorization, then, is akin to an "IOU" that needs to be validated by an appropriation.

There are different kinds of authorizations and appropriations: annual, multi-year, and permanent. By the end of World War II, most federal agencies and programs were permanently authorized; they were reviewed annually by the appropriating committees but not the authorizing panels. In recent years, there has been a trend toward short-term authorizations, giving the authorizing committees more chances to control agency operations. During the 1970s, for example, the State and Justice departments were subjected to annual review.

The authorization-appropriation sequence is an invention of Congress. It is required by House and Senate rules, not by the Constitution. Historically, the dual procedure stemmed from inordinate delays caused by adding "riders"—extraneous policy amendments—to appropriation bills. "By 1835," wrote a legislator, "delays caused by injecting legislation [policy] into these [appropriation] bills had become serious and John Quincy Adams suggested that they be stripped of everything save appropriations." [22] Two years later, the House required authorizations to precede appropriations. The Senate followed suit.

Here is what happens after an authorizing committee—Agriculture, Banking, Commerce, and the like—approves a new program. Our hypothetical example is based on an actual bill (reported from the House Agriculture Committee in 1977, recommending $20 million for an Agriculture Department small farm research and development program). Under the authorization-appropriation procedure, the bill must pass both houses and become law before the Agriculture Department has the "authorization" to establish the program.

Then the House Appropriations Committee (in effect, one of its 13 virtually autonomous subcommitees) must propose how much money ("budget authority") the small farm program should actually receive. The Appropriations Committee can provide all $20 million (but not more), propose cuts, or refuse to fund the program at all. Let's assume that the House goes along with Appropriations in approving $15 million. Then the Senate Appropriations Committee, acting like a "court of appeals," hears agency officials asking the Senate to approve the full $20 million. If the Senate does so, a House-Senate compromise is worked out, under the procedure described in Chapter 9.

In practice, it is hard to keep the two stages distinct. There are authorizations that carry appropriations (called "backdoors") and appropriation bills containing legislation. In the House, "limitations" riders make policy under the guise of restricting agency use of funds. Always phrased negatively ("None of the funds. . . ."), limitations bolster congressional control of bureaucracy. They are employed frequently. In 1980, 67 limitations riders were offered and three-fourths of them were adopted.[23]

Among the authorizing committees, the tax committees—House Ways and Means and Senate Finance—have especially strong roles in the budget process.[24] Both panels have access to the staff experts of the Joint Taxation Committee.[25] Because the House initiates revenue measures, it typically controls whether Congress will act on measures to raise, lower, or redistribute taxes. There are occasions, however, when the Senate takes the lead. The Senate can technically comply with the Constitution by taking a minor House-passed revenue bill and adding to it a major Senate tax measure. In 1981 the Republican-controlled Senate acted first on President Reagan's sweeping tax plan by employing this tactic.[26] To be sure, the House jealously guards its tax authority and may return to the Senate bills that violate the origination clause.[27]

Problems With the Process

During the early 1970s the existing budget process on Capitol Hill failed to cope with new trends: the weakening of Congress's guardianship of the public purse, President Nixon's challenges to spending programs, and the sagging national economy. Pulling and hauling between authorizing, taxing, and funding panels made it difficult for Congress to control federal expenditures.

To sidestep the appropriations axe, authorizing committees evolved "backdoor" spending techniques—funding provisions outside the appropriations process. There are three types of backdoors.

> One form of backdoor spending is "contract authority," which allows agencies to enter into contracts before they receive appropriations. Congressional funding to liquidate the contract obligations

when they come due is perfunctory because the good faith and credit of the federal government is at stake. A second form of backdoor spending is "borrowing authority," which allows agencies to obligate and spend funds that they borrow directly, through authority to spend agency debt receipts, or indirectly, through authority to spend Treasury debt receipts. A third form of backdoor spending is authorized by the system of "mandatory entitlements" which requires payments to any person or government that meets standards established by law.[28]

Entitlements, the fastest-growing of the "backdoors," establish judicially enforceable rights without reference to dollar amounts. That is, spending for entitlement programs (medicare, black lung, and social security, for example) is determined by the number of citizens who qualify for benefit levels established by law. Entitlement programs cost the taxpayers about $340 billion in 1980. "The share of the federal budget taken up by entitlements has grown by two-thirds in the past 13 years—from 36.1 percent in 1967 to 59.1 percent...."[29]

The backdoor devices weakened Congress's capacity to control federal spending. Interest on the federal debt was another uncontrollable expenditure. By 1973 only 44 percent of the federal budget was handled by the appropriating committees. Practically every committee could mandate federal spending, but no single panel calculated the overall effect of the scattered spending decisions.

Congress's motivation in giving up annual appropriations review is to "pursue other budget values: efficiency, stability, and financial security."[30] The net effect, however, is that Congress controls spending for a shrinking portion of the federal budget (see Figure 11-2). In short, even if Congress adjourned on its very first day in session, the government is legally entitled to spend huge sums (in 1980, 76 percent of an annual federal budget of nearly $700 billion).

The loosening of Congress's purse strings opened it to charges of being spendthrift and financially irresponsible. President Nixon blamed Congress for annual deficits, consumer price hikes, high joblessness, and inflation. He also impounded (refused to spend) monies appropriated by Congress, and challenged the legislative branch to do something about it.[31] Although the administration lost every court challenge to the impoundments, Nixon won the political high ground. He made Congress's haphazard budget process a major issue of the 1972 presidential campaign. In October Nixon told a nationwide radio audience:

> But, let's face it, Congress suffers from institutional faults when it comes to Federal spending. In our economy, the President is required by law to operate within the discipline of his budget, just as most American families must operate within the discipline of their budget.
>
> In the Congress, however, it is vastly different. Congress does not consider the total financial picture when it votes on a particular spending bill, it does not even contain a mechanism to do so if it wished.[32]

Figure 11-2 Controllability of Budget Outlays, 1972-1982

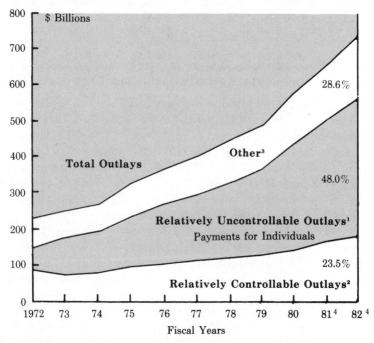

¹ "Relatively uncontrollable" outlays are those the federal government is committed by law to undertake. These outlays can be controlled only if Congress changes the basic law that authorizes the expenditures. Most uncontrollable expenditures arise from entitlement programs for individuals, such as Social Security, Medicare, and welfare.

² "Relatively controllable" outlays are those subject to annual increases or decreases through the appropriations process.

³ "Other" includes uncontrollable outlays required by prior-year contracts and other obligations.

⁴Estimated.

SOURCE: *Fiscal 1982 Budget of the United States Government,* pp. 41 and 596-597.

These diverse pressures prompted Congress to restructure its budget procedures in 1974.

The 1974 Budget Act

When Congress enacted the Budget and Impoundment Control Act of 1974, it stretched jurisdiction over financial matters and accommodated its own fragmentation. Instead of abolishing or consolidating committees, the act added new institutions and procedures. Institutionally, Congress created the House Budget Committee, the Senate Budget Committee, and the Congressional Budget Office (CBO). These entities are charged with providing members and other committees information and independent assessments of the president's annual budget.

Procedurally, the 1974 Act established a rigorous timetable for Congress and its committees to act on authorization, appropriation, and tax measures (see Table 11-1).

The revamped budget procedure requires Congress to adopt annually at least two concurrent budget resolutions. These housekeeping

Table 11-1 Congressional Budget Timetable

Deadline	*Action to be Completed*
15th day after Congress convenes	President submits his budget, along with *current services estimates.*[1]
March 15	Committees submit views and estimates to Budget committees.
April 1	Congressional Budget Office (CBO) submits report to Budget committees.[2]
April 15	Budget committees report first concurrent resolution on the budget to their Houses.
May 15	Committees report bills authorizing new budget authority.
May 15	Congress adopts first concurrent resolution on the budget.
7th day after Labor Day	Congress completes action on bills providing budget authority and spending authority.
September 15	Congress completes action on second required concurrent resolution on the budget.
September 25	Congress completes action on reconciliation process implementing second concurrent resolution.
October 1	Fiscal year begins.

[1] *Current service estimates* are estimates of the dollar levels that would be required next year to support the same level of services in each program as this year's budget. The Budget Act originally required submission of the current services estimates by November 10 of the previous year. Since the president was still in the midst of developing his budget proposals for the next year, Congress later agreed to permit simultaneous submission of the current services and executive budgets in January.

[2] The Budget committees and CBO have found April 1 too late in the budget process to be useful; hence, CBO submits its report(s) in February, although April 1 remains the date required by law.

SOURCE: Allen Schick, *Budget Handbook, Congressional Quarterly's Seminar: The Congressional Budget Process* (Washington, D.C.: Congressional Quarterly, 1981), p. 4.

NOTE: Congress has not always adhered to these deadlines. In recent years, Congress has fallen increasingly behind schedule.

devices for Congress, which overlay the existing authorization-appropriation procedure, are organized into two basic parts: fiscal aggregates and functional categories. The first consists of dollar figures for total federal spending, revenue, debt, and surplus; the second part identifies dollar figures for 19 areas ("functional categories"), such as national defense, agriculture, and health.

Under the 1974 Act, Congress adopts a spring (May 15) budget resolution. This measure recommends targets for overall federal spending during the fiscal year. The targets are financial guidelines for the committees. With adoption of the spring budget resolution, Congress acts on its money bills. Then the Budget committees report a second resolution by September 15 that is shaped by Congress's previous spending decisions and the needs of the economy. This resolution sets binding budgetary totals for Congress. And if the spring and summer spending decisions of Congress exceed these binding totals, then budgetary discipline can be imposed through a "reconciliation" process. Congress can direct appropriate committees to report bills that raise revenue or reduce spending.

Operation of the New Process

Congress's revised budget process is not self-enforcing, and Congress frequently ignores some of its features. Members complain about the tight budget deadlines, delays in enacting authorization and appropriation bills, jurisdictional intrusions of the budget panels, and, prior to 1981, Congress's hesitancy to make tough spending decisions. "It's just too easy," said Robert Giaimo, D-Conn., then chairman of the House Budget Committee, "to borrow the money or print the money that you need to make the special interest groups happy." [33]

On the other hand, Congress's revamped procedures have increased member sophistication and knowledge of budgetary matters. They have permitted Congress to relate tax and spending policy, balance the pressures for more spending against its guardianship of the treasury, review the budget's effect on the economy and the economy's impact on the budget, and assess short-term financial decisions against their long-term implications. The new process also has defined presidential use of impoundments and enhanced Congress's capacity to evaluate the president's budget. [34] Neither evaluation nor deliberation, however, marked Congress's 1981 review of President Reagan's budget.

Reagan and Reconciliation

When Reagan took office, he moved quickly to implement a favorite campaign theme: getting government off everyone's back. In February 1981 he recommended that Congress cut more than $130 billion over three years from numerous social programs outlined by OMB Director David Stockman (a former GOP House member and congressional aide) in a three-pound black book entitled, *America's New Beginning: A Program for Economic Recovery.*

Reagan, Stockman, and their congressional allies conceived the strategy of using the reconciliation procedure to achieve their spending goals. Under the budget act, reconciliation was to occur at the end of the budget process to bring spending into line with the binding targets of the second budget resolution. Instead, the administration had Congress employ reconciliation at the beginning of the budget process as it had done the year before, forcing Congress in one bill to make dramatic cuts in spending for social programs. "Without reconciliation," said Senate Budget Chairman Pete Domenici, R-N.M., "it would be absolutely impossible to cut the budget by this dimension." [35]

The two-stage reconciliation process works this way: During stage one, Congress adopts a concurrent budget resolution giving each designated committee a dollar figure for savings and a deadline for reporting legislation to achieve the savings. During stage two, the budget panels compile the legislative recommendations of the instructed committees into an omnibus reconciliation bill. The 1980 and 1981 reconciliation instructions to legislative committees differed in several important respects as Table 11-2 indicates.

Reagan's economic plan dominated the reconciliation process, and his victories were particularly noteworthy in the Democratic-led House. During stage one, Reagan and Stockman objected that the Democrats' cuts were not deep enough. Representatives Phil Gramm, D-Texas, and Delbert Latta, R-Ohio, developed a Reagan-endorsed substitute that the House adopted. The instruction resolution (Gramm-Latta I) passed Congress and House and Senate panels were given three weeks to report

Table 11-2   A Comparison of Reconciliation Instructions, 1980-1981

	1980	*1981*
Number of instructed committees	9 House 11 Senate	15 House 14 Senate
One-year savings	$8.3 billion est.	$37 billion est.
Multi-year savings	—	Nearly $140 billion over three years
Savings in	Appropriations and entitlements	Appropriations, entitlements *and* authorizations (lowering the financial levels in the basic laws that establish programs)

their reconciliation bills. Working under pressure, almost every congressional committee complied, but Reagan and Stockman charged that several of the cuts made by Democratic-controlled House committees were unrealistic or even phony.

Working with Stockman, Representatives Gramm and Latta hastily drafted a substitute reconciliation package (Gramm-Latta II) the day before the vote (the GOP package was filled with penciled-in additions, crossed-out items, misnumbered pages, and even the name and phone number of a budget staff aide). This effort infuriated Democrats. "A popular President is attempting to tyrannize a whole Congress," declared Representative Richard Bolling, D-Mo.[36] Added Majority Leader Jim Wright, D-Texas:

> There has never been an administration that has demanded to dictate so completely to the Congress, certainly not Lyndon Johnson in his heyday or Franklin Roosevelt in his. I don't know what it will take to satisfy them, I guess for the Congress to resign and give them our voting proxy cards.[37]

Once again the House went along with President Reagan after the White House successfully wooed key southern Democrats.

After the dust had settled, many Democrats and Republicans wondered how Congress could reconcile itself to reconciliation. "Nobody is particularly happy about this procedure," said Representative Barber Conable, R-N.Y.[38] The hectic pace and confusion led some members to question the procedure's future. On the other hand, as economic analyst Robert Samuelson pointed out:

> Congress wouldn't be Congress if it always knew what it was doing. Many of the things that were recently undone in obscurity, misunderstanding and deceit were probably enacted in similar circumstances. As for the timing and scope of the reconciliation package, they reflected the changed political climate. Nothing in the 1974 Congressional Budget Act said these things couldn't happen.[39]

CONGRESSIONAL CONTROL OF THE BUREAUCRACY

Congress delegates large discretionary responsibility to federal administrators. These delegations occur, as Chapter 10 noted, for a variety of reasons, such as the executive branch's capacity to handle technical policy areas (licensing interstate communications, for example). "Congressional power, like chastity," explained a scholar, "is never lost, rarely taken by force, and almost always given away." [40] Hence the need for Congress to watch over its programs, lest they be redefined erroneously through administration. No wonder David Truman stated that "administration of a statute is, properly speaking, an extension of the legislative process." [41] Given the size and reach of the executive establishment, Congress's oversight role is more important today than when Woodrow Wilson wrote that "Quite as important as lawmaking is vigilant oversight of administration." [42]

Congress thus has formalized its oversight duties. The Legislative Reorganization Act of 1946 directs all House and Senate committees to exercise "continuous watchfulness" over the programs and agencies under their jurisdiction. Several subsequent statutes and House and Senate rules extend Congress's authority and resources for oversight. *(See box, p. 336.)*

Hearings and Investigations

Many of Congress's most dramatic moments have involved legislative inquiries into administrative misconduct, such as the Teapot Dome Scandal of 1923 and the 1973-1974 Senate Watergate hearings. But Congress's investigative authority is neither granted by the Constitution nor without limits. As Chief Justice Earl Warren wrote in *Watkins v. United States* (1957):

> There is no general authority to expose private affairs of individuals without justification in terms of the functions of Congress.... Nor is the Congress a law enforcement or trial agency. These are functions of the executive and judicial departments of government. No inquiry is an end in itself; it must be related to, and in furtherance of, a legitimate task of the Congress.[43]

Administrators are sensitive to even the threat of hearings and inquiries. "When an oversight committee is upset at something that the [FTC] is doing and wants to drag me up and embarrass me substantially in public," said Michael Pertschuk, then Federal Trade Commission chairman, "the first reaction is to call in the [FTC] staff and say, cure that problem, cure that problem if you can." [44] Hearings and investigations have large potential for influencing agency policies and priorities. They can spawn new laws or their functional equivalent: "unwritten" laws that change bureaucratic operations.

Congressional Vetoes

Hundreds of laws allow Congress to veto executive branch actions. First employed in a 1932 law authorizing President Hoover to reorganize executive agencies, congressional vetoes delay carrying out an executive decision for a certain period, usually 30 to 60 days. During this time, one or both houses of Congress (in some cases, committees of both or either) can vote to approve or disapprove the executive action.

Congressional vetoes have become increasingly popular devices, largely because of Congress's distrust of the executive branch and public clamor against excessive federal regulation. By 1980 there were 200 laws

---

Measures Affecting Oversight

Legislative Reorganization Act, 1970

- Increased staff assistance for all House and Senate committees.

- Recommended that House and Senate committees ascertain whether programs within their jurisdiction could be funded annually.

- Required most House and Senate committees to issue oversight reports every two years.

Budget and Impoundment Control Act, 1974

- Strengthened the General Accounting Office's role in acquiring fiscal, budgetary, and program-related information from federal agencies.

- Authorized the General Accounting Office to establish an Office of Program Analysis to develop and recommend to Congress methods for the review and evaluation of programs.

- Permitted committees to evaluate programs "by contract, or require a Government agency to do so and furnish a report thereon to Congress."

House Rule Changes, 1975

- Authorized committees to create oversight subcommittees.

- Permitted committees to triple the size of their staffs.

- Granted several committees "special oversight" authority: the right to conduct comprehensive reviews of subject areas even if they fall within other committees' jurisdiction.

Senate Rule Changes, 1977

- Granted several committees "comprehensive policy oversight" responsibilities (comparable to special oversight in the House).
- Required committees to include in reports accompanying measures the regulatory impact of each bill or joint resolution.

---

containing more than 250 legislative veto provisions, one-third of them enacted since 1975.[45] One law, the Energy Security Act of 1980, embodies more than 20 veto provisions.

Congress often directs agencies to formulate regulations and the Administrative Procedures Act of 1946 tells them how to do it. The routine includes: agency preparation of draft regulations; publication of draft regulations in the *Federal Register,* a daily publication of regulatory decisions; public hearings and public comment periods on the draft regulations; and publication of the final regulations in the *Federal Register* 30 days before their effective date.

Critics argue that the congressional veto 1) imposes needless burdens on committee staff who must review complex executive regulations within a specified time period and without benefit of the agency's fact-finding process, 2) affords special interests another chance to thwart unwanted rules, and 3) violates the constitutional separation of powers.[46] In 1978 President Carter said legislative vetoes are "intrusive devices that infringe on the Executive's constitutional duty to faithfully execute the laws." [47] The constitutionality of legislative vetoes has not been directly addressed by the Supreme Court.

Some legislative veto advocates want to subject all executive rule-making to congressional review. They argue that the device 1) strengthens Congress's control of delegated authority, 2) checks the growth of burdensome federal rules, and 3) enables Congress to assert its prerogatives against unelected regulators.[48]

Mandatory Reports

Congress requires the president, agencies, and departments to assess programs and report their findings.[49] Although sometimes only marginally useful, reports can be important oversight tools. A counsel of the Senate Appropriations Committee's Subcommittee on Foreign Operations effectively uses reports to monitor activities of the Agency for International Development:

> He [William Jordan] is the overseer of a remarkable reporting system he has imposed on the agency. During the past decade, more than 50 provisions have been plugged into AID's enabling legislation requiring the agency to report everything from detailed spending justifications to line-item breakouts of administrative and consulting expenses. Reports go directly to the subcommittee—that is, to Jordan. The system even requires AID to send Jordan 15 days' advance notice before transferring money *within* accounts. "It gives Jordan, essentially, veto power over any AID decision," says Tim Lovaine, lobbyist for New Directions, a pro-foreign-aid group.[50]

Nonstatutory Controls

Congressional committees also use informal means to review and influence administrative decisions. These range from telephone calls, letters, personal contacts, and informal understandings to statements in committee and conference reports, hearings, and floor debates. Committee reports frequently contains phrases such as:

"The committee clearly intends that the matter be reconsidered. . . ."

"The committee clearly intends for the Secretary to promote. . . ."

"The committee clearly expects. . . ."

There is no measure of their usage, but nonstatutory controls may be the most common form of congressional oversight. Administrators are well advised to consider carefully such informal instructions. Courts and agencies also rely on background information found in committee and conference reports to interpret Congress's intent. In 1980 the U.S. Court of Appeals for the District of Columbia raised questions about this practice. It avoided use of legislative history and stated: "We must assume that if Congress had intended to limit the [Civil Aeronautics] Board's ... authority ... it would have said so in unmistakable language" *(National Small Shipments Traffic Conference, Inc. v. Civil Aeronautics Board)*. The decision might encourage Congress to write more specific laws.

Impeachment

A rarely used oversight device is impeachment. Under the Constitution, Congress can remove federal officials for "treason, bribery, or other high crimes and misdemeanors." The House has the authority to impeach an official; it then tries the case before the Senate. A two-thirds vote in the Senate is required for conviction. Only a dozen officials have been impeached, two executive officers and ten federal judges. The House impeached President Andrew Johnson in 1868, but the Senate acquitted him by a single vote. President Richard Nixon resigned in 1974 after the House Judiciary Committee voted articles of impeachment.

Some Barriers to Effective Oversight

Each oversight technique has limitations. Hearings, for example, tend to be episodic with minimal follow-up; the appropriations process is hemmed in by programmatic needs for financial stability; and statutes are often blunt instruments of control.

Congress's capacity and willingness since the 1970s to do more oversight stems from several factors.[51] They include public dissatisfaction with big government; the rapid growth of congressional staff; revelations of executive abuses by agencies such as the FBI, CIA, and IRS; the influx of new legislators skeptical of government's ability to perform effectively; and recognition that in a time of fiscal and resource scarcity Congress must make every dollar count.

Despite the surge of interest, many legislators and scholars charge that Congress oversees ineffectively.[52] "Members like to create and legislate," Speaker O'Neill said, "but we have shied from both the word and deed of oversight."[53] In short, barriers inhibit committees and members from conducting regular and close review of agency activities.

Lack of Incentives. Some doubt there are enough institutional or political incentives to reward those who conduct oversight. There is a "high cost and low benefit . . . ratio in the oversight effort," said John B. Anderson, R-Ill., then a House member. The "high cost in terms of the time that must be expended, you might even call it drudgery, and the low benefit in any real public recognition." [54] Members see political support as a payoff for introducing and passing laws; few legislators attract attention for oversight.

Cozy Relationships. "Sweetheart" alliances often develop between the committees that authorize programs and the agencies that administer them. Many committees are biased toward the programs or agencies they oversee; they frequently want to protect and nurture their progeny and make program administration "look good." Absent allegations of fraud or mismanagement, committees may lack the incentive to undertake critical scrutiny of their programs.

Unclear Program Objectives. A standard rationale for oversight is ensuring that laws are carried out according to congressional intent. In practice, however, many laws are vague and imprecise, which thwarts assessment.

Committee Limits. Other obstacles include inadequate coordination among the committees sharing jurisdiction over the same programs and agencies, unsystematic committee review of departmental activities, and frequent turnover among committee staff aides, which limits their understanding of programs passed by Congress.

Proposed Improvements

To remedy these defects, some legislators and critics advocate various oversight reforms. "Sunset" legislation, for example, would direct committees to review all programs and agencies under their jurisdiction within a prescribed time period. Unless the programs and agencies were formally reauthorized, the "sun would set on them." [55]

Another proposal, dubbed "sunrise," would require committees to identify the goals of bills and specify planned annual achievements. Unlike sunset, sunrise focuses on the start of the authorizing process, not the end of it. A further suggestion would create groups independent of the authorizing or appropriating committees to investigate agency performance. [56] Attempts to improve legislative oversight seek to buttress but not replace traditional review processes.

CONCLUSION

Many factors account for Congress's increased monitoring of administrative matters, but one stands out: Given an enormous executive establishment that both initiates and implements public policy, oversight affords Congress its best chance of controlling the enterprise.

Some say that Congress enters "more and more into the details of administration." [57] The age-old issue of executive independence vs. congressional scrutiny cannot be settled conclusively because of continual shifts in the balance between legislative and executive prerogatives. The recent resurgence of oversight has had little discernible impact on the size and scale of the executive branch. After all, committees are not disinterested overseers but frequently guardians of the agencies and programs under their jurisdiction. Together with their satellite interest groups, committees and agencies form "subgovernments" or "issue networks" that dominate many policymaking areas. Our next chapter focuses on these complex relationships.

NOTES

1. U.S., Congress, Senate *Congressional Record,* daily ed., 96th Cong., 1st sess., June 5, 1979, p. S6893.
2. Richard P. Nathan, *The Plot That Failed: Nixon and the Administrative Presidency* (New York: John Wiley & Sons, 1975).
3. Richard E. Neustadt, "Politicians and Bureaucrats," in *The Congress and America's Future,* 2d ed., edited by David B. Truman (Englewood Cliffs, N.J.: Prentice-Hall 1973), p. 119. See also Louis Fisher, *The Politics of Shared Power: Congress and the Executive* (Washington, D.C.: Congressional Quarterly Press, 1981).
4. See Herbert Emmerich, *Essays on Federal Reorganization* (University, Ala.: University of Alabama Press, 1950); Peter Szanton, ed., *Federal Reorganization: What Have We Learned?* (Chatham, N.J.: Chatham House Publishers, 1981); and Harold Seidman, *Politics, Position, and Power,* 3d ed. (New York: Oxford University Press, 1980).
5. Harold Seidman, "Congressional Committees and Executive Organization," in *Committee Organization in the House,* House Doc. No. 94-187, 94th Cong., 1st sess., p. 823.
6. Compiled from Daily Digests of the *Congressional Record.* See Judith H. Parris, "Consideration of Presidential Nominees by Senate Committees," Report No. 80-34, Congressional Research Service, January 21, 1980.
7. *New York Times,* July 3, 1981, p. A8.
8. Richard Whittle, "Lefever Withdraws After Committee Vote," *Congressional Quarterly Weekly Report,* June 6, 1981, p. 985.
9. See Joseph P. Harris, *The Advice and Consent of the Senate* (Berkeley: University of California Press, 1953); Ronald C. Moe, "Senate Confirmation of Executive Appointments," in *Congress Against the President,* ed. Harvey C. Mansfield, Sr. (New York: Academy of Political Science, 1975), pp. 141-152; and G. Calvin Mackenzie, *The Politics of Presidential Appointments* (New York: The Free Press, 1981).
10. U.S., Congress, House, Committee on Post Office and Civil Service, *Final Report on Violations and Abuses of Merit Principles in Federal Employment,* Committee Print No. 94-28, 94th Cong., 2d sess., December 30, 1976, p. 245.
11. Ronald C. Moe, "Government Corporations and the Erosion of Accountability: The Case of the Proposed Energy Security Corporation," *Public Administration Review* (November/December 1979): 566-571; Lloyd D.

Musolf, "The Blurred Boundaries of Public Administration," *Public Administration Review* (March/April 1980): 124-130; and *The Federal Executive Establishment: Evolution and Trends*, Senate Committee on Governmental Affairs, 96th Cong., 2d sess., 1980 committee print.

12. Frederick C. Mosher, *The GAO: The Quest for Accountability in American Government* (Boulder, Colo.: Westview Press, 1979), p. 297.

13. Ibid.

14. U.S., Congress, *Congressional Record*, daily ed., 96th Cong., 2d sess., July 1, 1980, p. E3320.

15. Morris P. Fiorina, *Congress: Keystone of the Washington Establishment* (New Haven: Yale University Press, 1977), p. 48.

16. R. Douglas Arnold, "The Local Roots of Domestic Policy," in *The New Congress*, ed. Thomas E. Mann and Norman J. Ornstein (Washington, D.C.: American Enterprise Institute for Public Policy Research, 1981), p. 284.

17. Ibid.

18. R. Douglas Arnold, *Congress and the Bureaucracy: A Theory of Influence* (New Haven: Yale University Press, 1979), p. 209.

19. Arthur Maass, *Muddy Waters* (Cambridge, Mass.: Harvard University Press, 1951); John Ferejohn, *Pork Barrel Politics* (Stanford: Stanford University Press, 1974); Leonard G. Ritt, "Committee Position, Seniority, and the Distribution of Government Expenditures," *Public Policy* (Fall 1976): 463-489; Gerald S. Strom, "Congressional Policy Making: A Test of a Theory," *Journal of Politics* (August 1975): 711-735; and Barry S. Rundquist and David E. Griffith, "The Parochial Constraint on Foreign Policy-Making," *Policy Studies Journal* (Winter 1974): 142-146.

20. Barry S. Rundquist and David E. Griffith, "An Interrupted Time-Series Test of the Distribution Theory of Policy-Making," *Western Political Quarterly* (December 1976): 620-626; Arnold, *Congress and the Bureaucracy*, pp. 217-224; and Bruce A. Ray, "Military Committee Membership in the House of Representatives and the Allocation of Defense Department Outlays," *Western Political Quarterly* (June 1981): 222-234.

21. Joseph S. Clark, *Congress: The Sapless Branch* (New York: Harper & Row, 1964), pp. 63-64. See also Robert Klonoff, "The Congressman As Mediator Between Citizens and Government Agencies: Problems and Prospects," *Harvard Journal on Legislation* (Summer 1979): 701-734; and John R. Johannes, "The Distribution of Casework in the U.S. Congress: An Uneven Burden," *Legislative Studies Quarterly* (November 1980): 517-544.

22. Robert Luce, *Legislative Problems* (Boston: Houghton Mifflin Co., 1935), p. 426. See also Louis Fisher, "The Authorization-Appropriation Process in Congress: Formal Rules and Informal Practices," *Catholic University Law Review* (Fall 1979): 51-105; Richard F. Fenno, Jr., *The Power of the Purse* (Boston: Little, Brown & Co., 1966); Stephen Horn, *Unused Power: The Work of the Senate Committee on Appropriations* (Washington, D.C.: The Brookings Institution, 1970); and John S. Saloma, *The Responsible Use of Power: A Critical Analysis of the Congressional Budget Process* (Washington, D.C.: American Enterprise Institute for Public Policy Research, 1964).

23. *Congressional Quarterly Weekly Report*, November 1, 1980, p. 3252. Based on figures through September 26, 1980.

24. John F. Manley, *The Politics of Finance: The House Committee on Ways and Means* (Boston: Little, Brown & Co., 1970); Richard Spohn, *The Revenue Committees: A Study of the House Ways and Means and Senate Finance Committees and the House and Senate Appropriations Committees* (New York: Grossman Publishers, 1975); "Federal Tax Policy and the

Tax Legislative Process," *National Tax Journal* (September 1979); and Catherine E. Rudder, "The Policy Impact of Reform of the Committee on Ways and Means," in *Legislative Reform,* ed. Leroy N. Rieselbach (Lexington, Mass.: Lexington Books, 1978), pp. 73-89.

25. John F. Manley, "Congressional Staff and Public Policy-Making: The Joint Committee on Internal Revenue Taxation," *Journal of Politics* (November 1968): 1046-1067. In 1976 the panel was renamed the Joint Taxation Committee.
26. *Washington Post,* July 3, 1981, p. A7; *Washington Star,* July 9, 1981, p. A1.
27. T. R. Reid, *Congressional Odyssey: The Saga of a Senate Bill* (San Francisco: W. H. Freeman & Co., 1980), pp. 69-72; and·*New York Times,* July 13, 1981, p. D1.
28. Louis Fisher, "Congressional Budget Reform: The First Two Years," *Harvard Journal on Legislation* (April 1977): 415.
29. Eric Hemel, "The Expansive Myth of 'Uncontrollable' Spending," *Journal of Contemporary Studies* (Winter 1981): 16.
30. *Congressional Control of Expenditures,* Study Prepared for the House Budget Committee, 95th Cong., 1st sess., January 1977, p. 7. This report was written by Allen Schick of the Congressional Research Service.
31. Louis Fisher, *Presidential Spending Power* (Princeton: Princeton University Press, 1975), chaps. 7 and 8.
32. *Public Papers of the Presidents of the United States, Richard Nixon, Containing the Public Messages, Speeches, and Statements of the President, 1972* (Washington, D.C.: U.S. Government Printing Office, 1974), pp. 965-966.
33. *National Journal,* October 10, 1980, p. 1761.
34. A thorough account of the budget process's development can be found in Allen Schick, *Congress and Money* (Washington, D.C.: The Urban Institute, 1980). See also Joel Havemann, *Congress and the Budget* (Bloomington: Indiana University Press, 1978); Aaron Wildavsky, *The Politics of the Budgetary Process,* 3d ed. (Boston: Little, Brown & Co., 1979); James P. Pfiffner, *The President, the Budget, and Congress: Impoundment and the 1974 Budget Act* (Boulder, Colo.: Westview Press, 1979); Lance T. LeLoup, *The Fiscal Congress* (Westport, Conn.: Greenwood Press, 1980); John W. Ellwood and James A. Thurber, "The Politics of the Congressional Budget Process Re-examined," in *Congress Reconsidered,* 2d ed., edited by Lawrence C. Dodd and Bruce I. Oppenheimer (Washington, D.C.: Congressional Quarterly Press, 1981); Allen Schick, "The Three-Ring Budget Process: The Appropriations, Tax, and Budget Committees in Congress," in *The New Congress*; and Joseph P. Harris, *Congressional Control of Administration* (Washington, D.C.: The Brookings Institution, 1964).
35. *Wall Street Journal,* June 9, 1981, p. 35.
36. *New York Times,* June 17, 1981, p. A25. See also Richard Bolling and John E. Barriere, "Budget-Making Gone Awry," *Washington Post,* June 28, 1981, p. D7; *Washington Post,* June 14, 1981, p. A9; Stuart E. Eizenstat, "The Hill's Budget Stampede," *Washington Post,* June 21, 1981, p. C1; Donald T. Rotunda, "Reconciliation: Not Better the Second Time Around," *Washington Post,* June 28, 1981, p. D5; and Senator Richard G. Lugar, R-Ind., "Reconcile Now," in *Congressional Record,* daily ed., 97th Cong., 1st sess., July 9, 1981, pp. S7315-S7316.
37. Ibid.
38. Dale Tate, "Reconciliation Conferees Face Slim Choices," *Congressional Quarterly Weekly Report,* July 4, 1981, p. 1168.

39. Robert J. Samuelson, "Budget Mythology," *National Journal*, July 4, 1981, p. 1216.
40. David B. Frohnmayer, "The Separation of Powers: An Essay on the Vitality of a Constitutional Idea," *Oregon Law Review* (Spring 1973): 330.
41. David B. Truman, *The Governmental Process*, rev. ed. (New York: Alfred A. Knopf, 1971), p. 439.
42. Woodrow Wilson, *Congressional Government* (Boston: Houghton Mifflin Co., 1885), p. 297.
43. *Watkins v. United States*, 354 U.S. 178 (1957). See also James Hamilton, *The Power to Probe* (New York: Vantage Books, 1976).
44. U.S., Congress, House, *Workshop on Congressional Oversight and Investigations*, H. Doc. 96-217, 96th Cong. 1st sess., 1979, p. 58.
45. Clark F. Norton, "Congressional Veto Provisions and Amendments: 96th Congress," Issue Brief 79044, Congressional Research Service, March 2, 1981; and "Statistical Summary of Congressional Approval and Disapproval Legislation, 1932-1980," Congressional Research Service, July 15, 1981.
46. Harold H. Bruff and Ernest Gellhorn, "Congressional Control of Administrative Regulations: A Study of Legislative Vetoes," *Harvard Law Review* (May 1977): 1369-1449; and John B. Henry, "The Legislative Veto: In Search of Constitutional Limits," *Harvard Journal on Legislation* (Summer 1979): 735-762.
47. U.S., Congress, Senate, *Congressional Record*, daily ed., 95th Cong. 2d sess., June 22, 1978, p. S9443.
48. Richard E. Cohen, "Junior Members Seek Approval for Wider Use of the Legislative Veto," *National Journal*, August 6, 1977, pp. 1228-1232.
49. John R. Johannes, "Study and Recommend: Statutory Reporting Requirements as a Technique of Legislative Initiative—A Research Note," *Western Political Quarterly* (December 1976): 589-596.
50. Gregg Easterbrook, "The Most Powerful Nobody in Washington," *The Washington Monthly*, September 1980, p. 58.
51. Michael W. Kirst, *Government Without Passing Laws* (Chapel Hill: University of North Carolina Press, 1969).
52. Seymour Scher, "Conditions for Legislative Control," *Journal of Politics* (August 1963): 526-551; and John D. Lees, "Legislatures and Oversight: A Review Article on a Neglected Area of Research," *Legislative Studies Quarterly* (May 1977), pp. 193-208.
53. *Workshop on Congressional Oversight and Investigations*, p. 3.
54. Ibid., p. 78. See also Morris S. Ogul, *Congress Oversees the Bureaucracy* (Pittsburgh: University of Pittsburgh Press, 1976); Morris S. Ogul, "Congressional Oversight: Structures and Incentives," in *Congress Reconsidered*, 2d ed.; and Morris P. Fiorina, "Congressional Control of the Bureaucracy: A Mismatch of Incentives and Capabilities," in *Congress Reconsidered*, 2d ed.
55. Bruce Adams, "Sunset: A Proposal for Accountable Government," *Administrative Law Review* (Summer 1976): 511-542; and Robert D. Behn, "The False Dawn of the Sunset Laws," *The Public Interest* (Fall 1977): 103-118.
56. Lawrence C. Dodd and Richard Schott, *Congress and the Administrative State* (New York: John Wiley & Sons, 1979).
57. Wilson, *Congressional Government*, p. 45.

Senior citizens protest cuts in social security programs.

12

Congress and Interest Groups

At a hearing on communications issues, a House member surveyed the spectators and asked any employees of the American Telephone & Telegraph Company to please stand. "Amid the quiet shuffling of polished shoes, a large portion of the audience rose," wrote a journalist.[1] Such a scene, with varying actors, could be repeated all over Capitol Hill.

Lobbyists regularly fill committee hearings and markups, jam into conference committee rooms, and pack House and Senate galleries. These representatives do more than observe congressional events for their clients. They wield their many resources— money, personnel, information, and organization—to bend the course of legislation. "Lobbyist Williams Is Part of the Power Process," trumpeted a December 31, 1980, *Washington Star* story about J. D. Williams, a politically savvy lawyer considered to be one of the capital's most effective lobbyists.

Practically every major corporation, trade association, and professional group has Washington lobbyists. They even have their own association: the American Society of Association Executives (ASAE).[2] Like many other groups, ASAE is based in Washington—the home of more national associations (28 percent) than New York (23 percent) or any other city.

More than 500 corporations employ Washington lobbyists, compared with 100 a dozen years ago. Lobbyists annually spend about $1 billion to influence Washington opinion, "plus another $1 billion to orchestrate public opinion across the nation." [3]

The American penchant for joining groups was observed long ago by the French chronicler Alexis de Tocqueville. Americans of all "conditions, minds, and ages, daily acquire a general taste for association and grow accustomed to the use of it," he wrote in 1825.[4] Today, more than 65 percent of the population belongs to at least one organization. Table 12-1 lists some of the more popular types of groups that people join.

Not all groups seek to influence congressional policymaking, but each has the right to do so. The First Amendment protects the people's right to "petition the Government for a redress of grievances." Throughout American history, groups speaking for different subsets of

Table 12-1   Membership in Various Groups, 1980

Organization	Percent of Population Who Belong
Church-Affiliated Groups	30.0
Sports Groups	17.0
Labor Unions	13.0
Professional or Academic Societies	12.8
Fraternal Groups	10.4
School Service Groups	9.9
Service Clubs	8.9
Hobby or Garden Clubs	8.4
Literary, Art, Discussion, or Study groups	8.4
Youth Groups	8.0
Veterans Groups	7.4
School Fraternities or Sororities	4.2
Farm Organizations	4.0
Political Clubs	3.1
Nationality Organizations	2.5
Any Other Groups	10.0

SOURCE: National Opinion Research Center, General Social Surveys, *1972-1980: Cumulative Codebook*, July 1980.

"the people" have swayed public policies and politics. Such groups have included the Abolitionists of the nineteenth century and their fight to end slavery, the Anti-Saloon League's 1900s crusade for prohibition, the anti-Vietnam war and environmental movements of the 1960s and 1970s.[5]

In a free society, politically active groups are inevitable—"Liberty is to faction [groups] what air is to fire," wrote James Madison in *The Federalist* Number 10. Until recent years, a few well-organized, well-financed groups dominated national policymaking: farm, labor, business, and medical interests. The current era has seen an explosion of narrower-based groups that focus their energies on a single issue, such as abortion or gun control.

> It is the advent, then, of this newer type of pressure group concerned with largely social, moral, and environmental topics along with the growing proliferation of programmatic groups (paralleling the enactment of more and more excessively specific [federal programs]), and the final arrival of all the generalist public interest groups (including the towns and townships), that has created the impression (and the reality) of contemporary Washington awash with specialized interests.[6]

Since the New Deal, the government has launched thousands of programs, taxes, subsidies, regulations, and entitlements. These in turn foster specific groups that ardently advocate or combat the actions that affect them. These groups can provide expertise that hard-pressed committees and members need. As one legislative aide observed:

> I think there's a new breed of lobbyist around. There's less of the slap-on-the-back, "I've been dealing with you for 15 years, let's go duck hunting" kind of approach. Now it's "Here's a 20-page paper full of technical slides, charts showing the budget impact, a table on how it meets the threat situation and some language in case you'd like to introduce an amendment."[7]

In the view of many, then, lobbyists "foster rich and useful dialogue between the people and their government."[8] In the fragmented Congress lobbyists sometimes act as brokers and coordinators among competing or insulated House and Senate committees.

On the other hand, lobbyists are often seen as sinister manipulators of policies. A December 1980 ABC News-Louis Harris poll indicated that 84 percent of adults believe that "special interests get more from government than the people do." A 1980 *U.S. News & World Report* survey of senators and representatives found that almost half (42.1 percent) agreed that "lobbies have too much influence over decisions by Congress." Clearly, group activity in policymaking is both critical and controversial.

GROUPS AND THE CONGRESSIONAL PROCESS

Congress is an open, decentralized institution with numerous entry points. The mere fact that bills must pass both the House and Senate affords lobbyists two cracks at determining their fate. Groups also affect, directly or indirectly, key features of the congressional environment such as committee activities, selection of party leaders, legislative agendas, and floor decisionmaking.

Groups and the Committee System

Structure. As we have seen, many congressional committees reflect the concerns of specific groups such as farmers, teachers, or veterans. As long as the outside group wields political clout, Congress is unlikely to eliminate the committee it supports. For example, in 1977 the Senate considered abolishing its six-year-old Veterans' Affairs Committee and merging its functions with those of other standing committees, but veterans' groups adamantly objected and the committee remains. Congress's problem, observed Senator Robert Packwood, R-Ore., is that "if everybody has an ear, a direct ear in the form of a committee, we are not going to have any kind of coherent [committee] structure." [9]

Membership. As noted in Chapter 7, legislators sometimes enlist the support of outside groups in their campaigns for choice committee assignments. Texas Democrat Phil Gramm, for example, mounted a successful effort in 1979 to win a seat on the House Energy and Commerce Committee, a panel important to Texas's oil and gas interests. Gramm's strategy involved contacting outside groups and individuals. "I knew insurance men in Boston, bankers in Chicago and others in Los Angeles," Gramm said. "I asked them to contact their local representatives who could help me." [10]

Lobbyists also encourage friendly legislators to bid for committees and subcommittees that handle issues important to the group's interests.

> [O]il and gas lobbyists were aghast when their favorite freshman, Senator David Boren of Oklahoma, lost his bids for both the Finance and Energy committees. Senator Russell B. Long of Louisiana, the finance chairman and a Boren supporter, was so furious that he called in his political "due bills" and pushed through a decision to expand the committee and give Mr. Boren the extra seat. [11]

White House lobbyists sometimes get into the act and consult House and Senate leaders about crucial assignments. "We had 18 or 19 votes on Ways and Means last time [in 1977] and then there were five vacancies [two years later]," said William Cable, chief House lobbyist for President Carter. "We want(ed) these vacancies to be filled with pro-Jimmy Carter people." [12] The Carter forces were only partly successful. Three of the five new Democrats on Ways and Means were considered supporters of the Democratic leadership. The other two were more conservative, as were the two new Republicans.

'Subgovernments'

Committees often form alliances with the bureaucrats and lobbyists who regularly testify before them and with whom members and staff aides periodically meet. Personnel flow among committees, agencies, and groups. Scholars and journalists have called the three-way policy-making partnerships *subgovernments* or subsystems. Other names for the alliances include "cozy little triangles," "triple alliances," "policy whirlpools," or "iron triangles." [13] These triple alliances can directly affect program development.

> Committee members want campaign contributions, help in their election campaigns, and honoraria for speeches. They rely on expertise of lobbyists in writing laws. Interest groups expect members of committees to provide them with formal and informal access to the bureaus and funds for programs that benefit them. They expect committee members to help them win the nomination of group members by the president to the department level.[14]

The influence of subgovernments varies with different policy areas depending on the nature of the issue, its visibility, conflict among alliance members, and the existence of competing subgovernments. Veterans' programs, for example, are well protected "by a traditional alliance of lobby groups, the veterans' committees, and the (Veterans Administration)—an alliance so invincible that 'lobbying' hardly describes it." [15] Even this autonomous subgovernment, however, is affected by other forces—the decline in the number of legislators who are veterans, budgetary pressures, and internal divisions—that can limit its ability to dominate policymaking.

Some scholars hold that subgovernments are less powerful than they once were. Subgovernments, argues Hugh Heclo, connote arrangements that are small, stable, and autonomous. Newer arrangements that he calls "issue networks"—knowledgeable individuals and groups that flow in and out of several policy areas—have somewhat replaced the old triangles. Issue networks include

> a large number of participants with quite variable degrees of mutual commitment or of dependence on others in their environment; in fact it is almost impossible to say where a network leaves off and its environment begins. . . . Participants move in and out of the networks constantly. Rather than groups united in dominance over a program, no one, as far as one can tell, is in control of the policies and issues.[16]

Like the rise of subcommittee government in Congress, *issue networks* reflect large growth in the number of individuals and interests that need to be consulted and accommodated in policymaking. "Everything that happens on this hill is a seamless web," observed veteran Representative Richard Bolling, D-Mo.[17]

The courts have also begun to play a role. Martin Shapiro suggests that a new iron triangle has appeared—the courts, executive agencies, and interest groups. "Congress initiates the triangle by creating a statutory right, but then withdraws," he said.[18] The statutory right might be an adequate education for handicapped children. If the Department of Education promulgates regulations to achieve this objective that are unsatisfactory to the affected parties, they can bring suit in court. With active judicial "administration" of statutes, interest groups and individuals are emboldened to make demands on agencies to secure their rights. The new alliance, according to Shapiro, resists outside control and weakens presidential authority.[19]

Groups and Leadership Selection

Group involvement in campaigns for party offices is common in competitive situations. In 1971, when Carl Albert, D-Okla., was elected Speaker, five Democrats campaigned hard for the majority leader post Albert had vacated. The eventual winner, Hale Boggs, D-La., had mobilized group support for his candidacy.

> The majority whip [Boggs] also activated the many political ties and interest group contacts he had built up during 20 years on the Ways and Means Committee and his service as party leader. The AFL-CIO, the UAW, and other large unions considered Boggs a known quantity, generally sympathetic to their interests. During the last two weeks of the campaign, they "covered their bets"—"If (Jim) O'Hara (Mich.) isn't going to make it, then Boggs is our second choice." The Seafarers' Union, through its principal Washington lobbyist, Phillip Carlip, contacted several members on Boggs' behalf, concentrating upon those who served on the Committee on Merchant Marine and Fisheries. Several oil company representatives talked to members of the Texas delegation. The mayor of an East Coast city was prevailed upon to telephone his Democratic delegation. Tobacco and textile interests in the Carolinas actively supported the majority whip.[20]

Framing the Legislative Agenda

Groups help to set Congress's policy and oversight agenda by pushing the House and Senate to address their concerns. Many legislative preoccupations of the past two decades—civil rights, environmental and consumer protection, and occupational safety among them—stemmed at least in part from vigorous outside lobbying.

Interest groups help "bring matters to the attention of sympathetic congressmen who would not otherwise have taken any action." [21] In 1981, for instance, industries as diverse as banking and shrimping pushed their concerns onto Congress's agenda. The U.S. League of Savings Associations dramatized the plight of savings and loan banks (S&Ls) and campaigned vigorously for federal aid. From 1979 to 1981, billions of dollars shifted from S&Ls into higher yielding investments. Faced with huge losses, the S&Ls persuaded Congress's tax committees to include special interest provisions in President Reagan's tax plan.[22] Imports were hurting the shrimp industry. As a result, a new group was formed—the Shrimp Harvesters Coalition of the Gulf and South Atlantic States—to promote passage of the American Shrimp Industry Development Act, which was the focus of committee hearings chaired by a friendly Louisiana representative.[23]

Floor Action

Lobbyists are active during all phases of the legislative process. When major measures reach the House and Senate floor, groups focus on influencing votes. They plan strategy with their friends in Congress, prepare arguments for and against expected floor amendments, work to get their supporters on the floor for key votes, and draft floor statements and amendments. A 1979 newspaper report described one such scene:

> There is a flurry in the Senate gallery, where a group of wealthy western farmers and their lawyers is watching the debate. The Senate is trying to decide if these landowners will be exempted from legislation putting sharp limits on the amount of federal irrigation water they can receive.
>
> Their champion is Sen. Alan Cranston (D-Calif.), arguing mightily against Gaylord Nelson (D-Wis.), who views the exemption and the water subsidy with some outrage.
>
> In the gallery, Sen. Rudy Boschwitz (R-Minn.) is talking with the farmer-lobbyists. In the hallway, one of their lawyers is drafting language that Cranston will use to make his case. A Cranston aide runs relays between the gallery and the Senate floor.[24]

For their part, members sponsor bills and amendments that win them group support—the "two Congresses" again. Senator Jesse Helms, R-N.C., is a case in point. Regularly, Helms offers controversial social amendments (abortion, school prayer, etc.) and forces votes on them. "His amendments," wrote Elizabeth Drew, "gave him a kind of publicity that was useful, firmed up his relationships with a cluster of 'New Right' groups, helped him raise money, and provided material with which he and his allies could try to defeat opponents." [25]

INFORMAL GROUPS AND SPECIAL INTERESTS

Legislators complain about single-issue lobbying groups, yet they follow the same trend in forming their own groups. Since the 1970s, members have established so many informal caucuses that Speaker Thomas P. O'Neill, Jr., D-Mass., was led to complain that the "House has over-caucused itself." [26] A week after the 97th Congress convened on January 5, 1981, Representative Fred Richmond, D-N.Y., announced formation of a new "Arts Caucus," intended to be a "powerful voice in passing legislation on the arts."[27]

Congress always has had informal groups, caucuses, coalitions, clubs, alliances, blocs, and cliques.[28] Some state delegations meet regularly—perhaps a weekly breakfast or luncheon—to discuss state and national issues and internal congressional politics, mobilize support to capture their share of federal funds and projects, champion colleagues for coveted committee assignments, or back candidates for party leadership positions. When delegations are unified, members can count on the support of their state's colleagues, sometimes even on a bipartisan basis. "When a member has his chips on the line for something that affects his district, the others pretty much fall into line and help him," said House Majority Leader Jim Wright, speaking as a member of the usually cohesive, mostly Democratic Texas delegation.[29]

What makes today's groups different from earlier ones is their number (more than 70 by 1981); diversity (there are partisan, bipartisan, and bicameral groups, for example); institutionalized character (many have paid staff, office space, dues-paying members, bylaws, and elected officers); and capacity to monitor federal activities that affect their interests.

Growth of Groups

Many factors underlie the spread of unofficial congressional groups, technically called "legislative service organizations." Most are House groups but some also have Senate members (see Table 12-2).

Interest Group Sponsorship. Outside interests impel informal legislative groups in at least three ways. First, the lobbying successes of many outside groups encouraged legislators to imitate them. Second, most informal legislative groups have ties with outside interests. Not surprisingly, the Steel Caucus maintains links with the steel industry, and the Textile Caucus with textile manufacturers. Some outside groups. provide staff and financial support to the informal legislative associations.

Finally, some interest groups are instrumental in the formation of legislative counterparts. The idea for the Mushroom Caucus (to protect mushroom producers from foreign imports) originated at a May 1977 luncheon sponsored for House members by the American Mushroom Institute.[30] The Ancient Order of Hibernians, an Irish-Catholic organization of about 1.5 million members, wrote a representative of Italian descent, Mario Biaggi, D-N.Y., and asked him to create and chair an Irish Caucus. He was asked to do this, said Biaggi, because the Hibernians "recognized that I had been concerned for the 10 years I have been in the Congress with the troubles in Northern Ireland." [31] Differences within the American-Irish community led to formation of another legislative group, "Friends of Ireland," that favors a more conciliatory approach toward Irish problems.[32]

Legislators and outside groups want recognition and clout in Congress. The Black, Women's, and Hispanic caucuses manifest these objectives for their national constituencies. The Congressional Hispanic Caucus, created in 1976, said that "The fact that we have joined together is a sign of the growing power of our community, and we are looking forward to strengthening the Federal commitment to Hispanic citizens." [33]

Regional and Economic Rivalry. The decline of certain regions and industries galvanizes their legislators to form ad hoc groups such as the Northeast-Midwest Economic Advancement Coalition and the Steel Caucus. Members from Frost Belt states, for example, want to retain their share of energy supplies and federal aid to cities. The South's recent economic improvement, said Representative Donald Mitchell, R-N.Y., "has been financed on a basis of northern tax dollars." [34] Each move to protect a region's interests is likely to prompt a countermove. The Sun Belt Caucus, a southern representative explained, was established in 1979 "in large part to counter lobbying and information-disseminating activities of the Northeast-Midwest Coalition." [35]

Structural Weaknesses. Committee flaws also foster informal legislative groups. Congress has few devices to integrate related legislation considered by its many committees. Ad hoc groups can act in a coordinative role. "One joins these caucuses," observed Representative Thomas Daschle, D-S.D., "because the committees don't go far enough in bringing together people with the same interests or experience on the issue. I believe [the] gasohol caucus has done that. When I came here, over 100 members had different gasohol bills, but they had no communication or coordination among themselves. The caucus gives us a way to find a consensus." [36]

A goal for some ad hoc groups is to help legislators anticipate issues and provide analytical support. The House's Environmental and Energy Study Conference, for example, acts as a clearinghouse for information in these fields. There is even a Clearinghouse on the Future to promote forecasting of trends.

Table 12-2   Informal Congressional Groups, 1981

HOUSE

Democratic

Conservative Democratic Forum
Democratic Research Organization
Democratic Study Group

New Members' Caucuses for
95th, 96th, and 97th Congresses
United Democrats of Congress

Republican

'Gypsy Moths'
Republican Study Committee

Republican Clubs for 95th, 96th,
and 97th Congresses
Wednesday Group

Bipartisan

Ad hoc Congressional Committee
for Irish Affairs
Alcohol Fuels Caucus
Auto Task Force
Congressional Ad hoc Monitoring
Group on South Africa
Congressional Arts Caucus
Congressional Black Caucus
Congressional Coal Caucus
Congressional Port Caucus
Congressional Shipbuilding
Coalition
Congresswomen's Caucus
Domestic Energy Supply Coalition
Export Task Force
Fair Employment Practices Com-
mittee

Federal Government
Service Task Force
Great Lakes Conference
Hispanic Caucus
Industrial Innovation Task Force
Metropolitan Area Caucus
Missing in Action Task Force
Mushroom Caucus
New England Congressional Caucus
Northeast-Midwest Economic
Advancement Coalition
Rural Caucus
Steel Caucus
Suburban Caucus
Sun Belt Caucus
Textile Caucus

SENATE

Democratic

Midwest Conference of
Democratic Senators

Moderate/Conservative
Democrats

Republican

Republican Steering Committee

Wednesday Club

Bipartisan

Coal Caucus
Concerned Senators for
the Arts
Copper Caucus
Export Caucus

Freshman Senators
Northeast-Midwest Coalition
Rail Caucus
Steel Caucus
Western State Coalition

BICAMERAL, BIPARTISAN

Children's Lobby
Coalition for Peace
Through Strength
Congressional Clearinghouse on
the Future
Environmental and Energy Study
Conference
Friends of Ireland
High Altitude Coalition

Jewelry Manufacturing Coalition
Members of Congress for Peace
Through Law
North American Trade Caucus
[Pentagon] Reform Caucus
Pro-Life Caucus
Solar Coalition
Tourism Caucus
Vietnam Era Veterans in Congress

SOURCE: Adapted from David P. Mulhollan, Susan Webb Hammond, and Arthur G.
Stevens, Jr., "Informal Groups and Agenda Setting" (Paper delivered at the annual
meeting of the Midwest Political Science Association, Cincinnati, Ohio, April 16-18, 1981).

Electoral Incentives. Members form informal groups to gain political strength back home and leverage on Capitol Hill. The House Coal Caucus, for example, was an initiative of Representative Nick Rahall, D-W.Va. "By providing a congressional forum for the major industry in his district," wrote two scholars, the "Coal Group offered Mr. Rahall significant political benefits." [37]

Membership in an informal group can be an asset on the campaign trail. Representative Daschle stresses his support of gasohol to voters because the grain alcohol to be mixed with gasoline can be made from the corn, rye, wheat, and potatoes grown by South Dakota's farmers.

> "You and I are in the driver's seat," [Daschle] told a Farmer's Union picnic July 1. He talked about efforts to create a gasohol caucus in the House and how the caucus now has 85 members. The audience gave him a standing ovation.
>
> Later that day, stopping in Clark, S.D., he conferred with a local farmer who is seeking federal help for a million-dollar plant that would make gasohol from potatoes. [38]

Some legislative groups, such as the House Democratic Study Group, also provide campaign and fund-raising assistance for their members. [39]

Legislative Impact of Ad Hoc Caucuses

The impact of informal groups on policymaking is not clear. Some legislators criticize them. Representative John Erlenborn, R-Ill., opposes the spread of caucuses because they "lead to nothing but increased expenses, increased staff, decreased available working space, and a further growth of purely provincial points of view." [40] Others believe informal groups undermine party unity and lead to the "Balkanization" of Congress.

Although their overall achievements are hard to assess, caucuses have influenced the passage (or defeat) of specific bills. "We made the phone calls to alert [the House Textile Caucus] members that the [1978] trade bill was coming up at the 11th hour," commented caucus member Margaret Heckler, R-Mass. "We also were able to keep together a nucleus of people who could make speeches and carry the vote." [41]

Informal groups serve as contact points for liaison officers in the executive branch. Informal groups provide executive and White House officials with a focal point for information exchange, strategy coordination, and coalition-building. "[A]t least a caucus is an organized group you can make a presentation to," declared Frank Moore, congressional liaison chief in the Carter White House. [42]

Finally, ad hoc caucuses permit members to discuss common issues and join with other groups to pass or defeat legislation. Paradoxically, informal groups foster both decentralizing and integrative tendencies in Congress.

PRESSURE GROUP METHODS

Groups have influenced congressional decisions from the beginning. During the nation's early technological and industrial expansion railroad interests lobbied for federal funds to build the transcontinental railroad. Some of the lobbyists' tactics—offering bribes, for example—helped foster the traditional public suspicion of the "pressure boys." In 1874 Senator Simon Cameron, R-Pa., commented that "An honest politician is one who, when he is bought, stays bought." [43]

Lobbying methods during the twentieth century became more varied, urbane, and publicly acceptable. Significantly, the move from limited to big government reinforced the mutual dependence of legislators and lobbyists.

> Groups turn to Congress as an institution where they can be heard, establish their positions, and achieve their policy goals. Members of Congress in turn rely on groups to provide valuable constituency, technical, or political information, to give reelection support, and to assist strategically in passing or blocking legislation that the members support or oppose. Groups need Congress, and Congress needs groups. [44]

Groups' modern-day methods vary according to the nature and visibility of the issue and the groups' financial and other resources. Common practices include using direct and social lobbying, group alliances, and grass-roots support.

Direct Lobbying

In the traditional method, lobbyists present their client's case directly to members·and congressional staff. If a group hires a prominent lawyer or lobbyist, such as Clark Clifford or Charls E. Walker, the direct approach will involve personal discussions with senators or representatives. "I called Russell [Senator Russell Long, D-La.] at his apartment this morning," said Charls Walker, "but he had a senator with him. His wife told me that. I usually talk to him in the mornings at his apartment two, three times a week." [45] Former members of Congress are particularly effective at direct lobbying and so are much in demand among lobbying organizations.

Alternatively, lobbyists may direct their attention to staff aides. Because senators are less available, lobbyists devote ample attention to their staffs. In the House, there are more chances for lobbyists to contact members directly.

The direct approach involves lobbyists in diverse tasks: monitoring committees and testifying at hearings; interpreting Hill decisions to clients and client interests to legislators; performing services for members, such as speech-writing; reinforcing attitudes of members committed to their group's interests; attempting to persuade fence sitters; and providing campaign assistance to members.

The direct approach has limitations, however. From the client's perspective, rapid turnover in Congress weakens a lobbyist's personal rapport. From the legislator's perspective, it is sometimes unclear whether a lobbyist actually "speaks" for an organization. Lobbyists, observed former Senator John Culver, D-Iowa,

> recognize that they are subject to challenge from within the ranks on the charge that they were not sufficiently true to the organization's professed goals, that they "sold out." In the process, they can end up preventing a resolution of a conflict, and thus fail to represent their groups' true interests.[46]

A particularly effective direct technique is member-to-member lobbying. No outsider has the same access to members as another colleague. In 1980, for instance, Representative Butler Derrick, D-S.C., stayed "on or just off the Senate floor for more than nine hours. . .grabbing key senators, persuading them" that a nuclear waste policy bill should be enacted.[47] He was successful. Only members, former members, and a few others can go onto the House and Senate floor.

Social Lobbying

The Washington social circuit is vastly overrated, but some lobbyists gain access to members at dinner parties or receptions. "When you want to make an end run, meet someone at a party," explained an experienced power dealer.[48] Some lobbyists have been famous (or infamous) social hosts. Until his downfall in the 1977-1978 "Koreagate" scandal about influence-buying on Capitol Hill, South Korean lobbyist Tongsun Park was a noted Washington host. "His flamboyant social style earned him enormous good will and access in the Washington political community," noted a commentator. "That could often be cashed in for reciprocal good will and generosity toward the country he represented." [49]

A variation of social lobbying is offering legislators gifts or campaign contributions. Congressional rules prohibit senators and representatives from taking anything worth more than $100 from a lobbyist or organization with a direct interest in legislation pending before Congress.

This standard can be murky in application, however. "We've seen a subtle shift," said a congressional aide. "For instance, an organization will give only a couple of hundred dollars for a speech—less than in the past—but then the congressman will be shown a truly good time with an all-expense-paid holiday." [50]

Lobby Coalitions

There is an oft-repeated statement that applies to lobbyists: "We have no permanent friends or permanent enemies—only permanent interests." This philosophy helps to explain why lobbying rivals, public interest and business groups, for example, sometimes forge temporary coalitions to promote or defend shared goals. These combinations, because of their great financial, personnel, and grass-roots clout, are formidable political forces.

In 1981 Wilbur Cohen, former Johnson administration cabinet officer, helped reactivate a coalition of more than 100 national organizations to oppose President Reagan's proposed cuts in Social Security benefits.

> Called SOS for "Save Our Security," the group was formed two years ago to fight the Carter administration when it proposed a series of Social Security cutbacks. With Cohen and others tramping the halls of Congress, it helped stave off all the Carter proposals except reduction of disability insurance benefits.[51]

Some of the organizations associated with SOS included the United Auto Workers, the National Conference of Catholic Charities, American Association of Retired Persons, and Paralyzed Veterans of America.

Administration officials and legislators often work closely with lobby coalitions. The landmark Elementary and Secondary Education Act of 1965, for instance, was largely crafted by the U.S. commissioner of education, Francis Keppel, key Catholic and Protestant legislators, and representatives of two major groups, the National Education Association and the United States Catholic Conference.[52]

Grass-roots Lobbying

Instead of contacting members directly, many organizations seek to mobilize citizens to pressure their senators and representatives. Here is what one lobbyist said when he called a woodsman about a proposal to make hunting a nondeductible business expense: "Hello, Johnny Bob? This is J. D. in Washington. Got a pencil handy? Now, this is who your congressman is. This is how you write him. You write this son-of-a-bitch and tell him this is going to ruin you. How are you going to guide people if. . . ."[53]

Legislators understand that lobby groups orchestrate "spontaneous" outpourings of letters and postcards. Pressure mail is easily recognized, because each piece is nearly identical to all the others. Members may discount the content of such mail, but its volume is sure to attract their attention as they think about the next election.

Grass-roots lobbying is not new, but it has become more prevalent, effective, and sophisticated. Many groups use computers to identify supporters, target specific constituencies, or address mass mailings. Mass-mail moguls like Richard Viguerie can generate sudden political pressure.

> [Viguerie] has compiled a detailed list of some 4 million conservative activists. Operating out of a handsome office building in McLean, Va., Viguerie and his 300 employees man two IBM computers that can break out lists of likely contributors with details of how they stand on particular issues and what they have given to which candidates or legislative drives in the past. He considers his magnetic tapes so valuable that they are guarded 24 hours a day—and duplicates are kept in a secret mountain hideaway. His company grossed an estimated $3 million [in 1977] from the use of his tapes to stimulate mass mailings.[54]

Groups have the capability today to pinpoint (the "rifle" as opposed to "shotgun" approach) people (doctors, union members, previous contributors) in a state or district who might write letters supporting or opposing legislation. The U.S. Chamber of Commerce boasts a network of KRPs (key resource people) all across the country.

> A KRP is an individual member of the National Chamber—through his company or local chamber—who has direct "access" to a representative or senator. The KRP's access may be derived from personal friendship, large campaign contributions, or family relations. The Chamber field staff carefully nurtures each KRP, reserving them only for important issues.[55]

Finally, grass-roots lobbying is related to the decline of party organization and loyalty. Today, lobbies, pollsters, and media consultants are critical to the election of many legislators. As a result, parties are less able to protect members from pressure campaigns linked "directly to the electoral fortunes of individual Members." [56] As Representative Mike Synar, D-Okla., explained: "Through their computers these groups get to more of my voters, more often and with more information than any elected official can do. I'm competing to represent my district against the lobbyists and the special interests." [57]

GROUPS AND THE ELECTORAL CONNECTION

Groups are integral to the election process. Group support and electoral leverage come in a variety of forms, but at least three are worth noting: raising funds, making financial contributions through political action committees (PACs), and rating the voting record of legislators.

Fund-raising Assistance

Many legislators thoroughly dislike raising money, finding it demeaning and offensive. Thus they turn to lobbyists or professional fund-raisers to sponsor parties, luncheons, dinners, or other social events where admission is charged. Lobbyists buy tickets or supply lists of people who should be invited.

Legislators and lobbyists alike sometimes question the propriety of fund-raising practices. Members are concerned about implied obligations when they accept help or money from groups. "Whether it's lending an ear or more than lending an ear, I don't know," said Representative Donald Pease, D-Ohio.[58] For their part, lobbyists may resent it when the subcommittee chairman who handles their group's concerns asks them to buy tickets to his fund-raiser.

Despite such complaints, fund-raisers are likely to remain popular. The situation could change if Congress provided for public financing of congressional elections. This proposal, however, faces stiff opposition from incumbents who feel that public funding would underwrite their challengers.

Money and PACs

Political action committees, as Chapter 3 notes, are not new. Business, labor, medical, and other groups have had them for decades. What is new about PACs is their rapid growth (1,204 corporate PACs in 1980, more than 13 times the number in 1974), and the sharp public concern about whether PACs can "buy" congressional seats through enormous financial contributions.

Growth. "As the government moves closer and closer to partnership with an industry, the result of that liaison is a PAC, mothered by industry but unmistakably sired by government," commented a Business-Industry Political Action Committee (BIPAC) spokesman.[59] Table 12-3 shows the rapid growth of business and other PACs.

In the 1972-1978 period, PAC donations rose from $8.5 million to $35 million.[60] PAC money forms an ever-larger portion of House candidates' election budgets—about a quarter of their campaign funds,

Table 12-3   Growth of Political Action Committees, 1974-1980

Year	Labor PACs	Corporate PACs	Miscellaneous PACs	Total PACs
1974	201	89	318	608
1976	224	433	489	1,146
1978	217	784	652	1,653
1980	297	1,204	1,050	2,551

SOURCE: Federal Election Commission, Press Office, January 1981.

on the average. Its proportional role in Senate spending has not risen so rapidly.[61]

PAC donations to all congressional candidates in 1980 were estimated by Common Cause at $55 million to $60 million. The biggest givers were the National Association of Realtors and the United Auto Workers ($1.5 million apiece), American Medical Association ($1.3 million), National Auto Dealers Association ($1 million), and Machinists and Aerospace Workers ($0.8 million).

Following the 1980 elections, when right-wing PACs such as the National Conservative Political Action Committee (NCPAC) helped defeat several Democratic senators, liberals stepped up fund raising by their own PACs, including a new Progressive Political Action Committee (PROPAC).[62] Some GOP leaders have sought to distance themselves from NCPAC and other groups that wage largely negative campaigns. GOP National Chairman Richard Richards remarked that such groups "create mischief" because candidates could be hurt by inept efforts over which they had no control.[63]

Bills to limit PAC spending have been put forward, but few who benefit from PAC efforts are about to bite the hands that feed them. Thus, curbs on independent spending are quite unlikely, and in any event might violate the Constitution.

Partly because of PACs, the mix of funding sources has shifted over the past decade. According to figures compiled by Michael Malbin, no more than 6 or 7 percent of the average House or Senate candidate's funds come from the parties.[64] In 1980 party spending revived mainly because of aggressive GOP efforts. Republicans outspent their Democratic counterparts by about five to one in the 1979-1980 election cycle. This includes efforts of the Republican House and Senate campaign committees, as well as the National Committee itself.

Rating Legislators

Many groups keep pressure on legislators by issuing "report cards" on their voting records. Groups select key issues and then publicize the members' scores (from 0 to 100) based on their "right" or "wrong" votes on those issues. The liberal Americans for Democratic Action (ADA) and the conservative Americans for Constitutional Action (ACA) issue among the best-known of such ratings. Environmental groups used to target a "dirty dozen," members with low scores on particular votes. PACs sometimes rate members to help determine which ones they want to support or try to defeat.

> [The Business-Industry Political Action Committee] "targets" incumbents by compiling their votes on selected issues. For example, a senator who voted for the new Department of Education, against exempting small businesses from Occupational Safety and Health

Members Disagree on PACs' Role

'Lawful Evil'

I think the present system, whereby special interest groups contribute enormous sums to congressional candidates, has probably produced more bad legislation and ruined more good legislation than any other single factor in our political life. Indeed, I believe that in our political life PACs are the greatest evil that is still lawful.

What does the public think when, time after time after time, a certain candidate in every election gets enormous contributions from one or another trade, business, labor union, or whatever special interest it might be, and the vote follows the legislation as day follows night.

—Representative Millicent Fenwick, R-N.J.

'Serve Constituency'

I do not share the opinion that congressional seats are up for sale to the highest bidder or that contributions from political action committees (PACs) have an "evil" influence on those who serve in office. Contrary to what many would like us to believe, PACs are not monolithic, evil conspirators that engage in pressure politics and clandestine electoral activities. In fact, PACs are individual in nature, each with a different objective and each with a different strategy to achieve that objective. PACs are basically representative institutions that rely on a specific constituency for support. Like political parties, they solicit contributions from that constituency and use the funds raised to express the views of that constituency in the political arena.

—Representative Philip Crane, R-Ill.

SOURCE: *Business and Society Review* (Summer 1980): 13-14.

Administration inspections and for mandatory industrial energy efficiency standards would have voted "wrong" on three of BIPAC's 11 Senate votes.[65]

Many legislators are critical of the "ratings game." The selected issues, they say, are often biased, oversimplified, self-serving, and inadequate to judge a member's record. Some legislators charged with crimes, for example, have received high morality scores from religious groups. *(See box, p. 363.)*

REGULATION OF LOBBYING

For more than 100 years Congress intermittently considered ways to regulate lobbying, a right protected by the Constitution. Not until 1946, however, did Congress enact its first—and only—comprehensive lobbying law: the Federal Regulation of Lobbying Act, Title III of the Legislative Reorganization Act of that year.

Business Lobby Ratings Stir Furor

Groups that rate Congress typically hope to reap fringe benefits of publicity and power, but none has carried that wish as far as the National Federation of Independent Business (NFIB). The small business lobby has a rating scheme that combines polling, computers, campaign gifts and pewter statuettes in an elaborate effort to build legislative influence. "I like to say we have a complete system," boasts John J. Motley, deputy director of the federation.

Some rival business lobbyists and members of Congress have said less flattering things about the NFIB formula. "An extremely unfair and slanted voting index," was the judgment of Senator Russell B. Long, D-La., who fared poorly with NFIB. But those who score well revel in the rewards.

NFIB begins with a periodic polling of its 620,000 members on upcoming issues to determine the federation's position. Each member of Congress is sent a breakdown of the poll results.

As a measure approaches a floor vote, NFIB first sends all members of Congress a personalized letter stating the group position and then a green-edged, oversized postcard indicating that the issue will be a "key small business vote" and probably will appear in the annual rating. At the end of a session, NFIB counts up the votes and publishes the results with all the fanfare it can muster. A member who scores 70 percent or better is declared a "Guardian of Small Business" and receives a pewter minuteman trophy to display in his office. The award is accompanied, if the member wishes, with a publicity blitz aimed at hometown press. . . .

The final component in NFIB's "system" is a political action committee, which last year [1980] gave $217,222 to candidates. A 70 percent rating automatically entitles an incumbent to an endorsement and, if he is in a close race, a contribution. Conversely, a score lower than 40 percent sends a donation to the challenger. . . .

Last September [1980], Long, then chairman of the Senate Finance Committee, took the Senate floor to denounce the rating as "a flagrant misrepresentation of the work we have done in this Congress to help small business . . . biased, superficial and deceiving." Long's rating was 42, but he made no mention of that. His complaint was that NFIB had given Gaylord Nelson, D-Wis. (1963-1981), chairman of the Small Business Committee, the lowest rating in the Senate—22.

To question Nelson's devotion to small business, Long declared, was as preposterous as "to challenge the credentials of Jesus Christ as a moral leader to us Christians."

But NFIB was unrepentant. The group shot off a reply to its Wisconsin members defending the rating and pointing to its pre-vote polling as justification for its stands. The letter raked Nelson's record over the coals, concluding the senator had "not been an effective or true advocate of small business."

SOURCE: Excerpted from Bill Keller, "Small Business Lobby Plays Trick or Treat," *Congressional Quarterly Weekly Report*, March 21, 1981, p. 509.

The 1946 Lobbying Law

The main objective of the 1946 Act was public disclosure of lobbying activities. It required persons trying to influence Congress to register with the Clerk of the House or Secretary of the Senate and to report quarterly on the amount of money received and spent for lobbying. The law's authors, although loathe to propose direct control of lobbying, believed that "professionally inspired efforts to put pressure upon Congress cannot be conducive to well considered legislation." Hence the law stressed registration and reporting:

> The availability of information regarding organized groups and full knowledge of their expenditures for influencing legislation, their membership and the source of contributions to them of large amounts of money, would prove helpful to Congress in evaluating their representations without impairing the rights of any individual or group freely to express its opinion to the Congress.[66]

The lobby law soon proved ineffective, however. In 1954 the Supreme Court upheld its constitutionality, but the decision *(United States v. Harriss)* significantly weakened the law. First, the Court said that only lobbyists paid to represent someone else must register, exempting lobbyists who spend their own money. Second, the Court held that registration applies only to persons whose "principal purpose" is to influence legislation. As a result, many trade associations, labor unions, professional organizations, consumer groups, and Washington lawyers avoid registering, because lobbying is not their principal purpose.[67] There are even lobbyists who say they are not covered by the law because their job is to inform—not influence—legislators.

Finally, the Court held that the Act applies only to lobbyists who contact members directly. This interpretation excludes lobbying activities that generate grass-roots pressure on Congress. Critics say also that the Act is weakly enforced; the Clerk of the House and Secretary of the Senate simply compile the lobbyists' quarterly reports and publish them in the *Congressional Record,* but lack authority to investigate or enforce compliance.

Efforts to Revise the 1946 Law

As a result of campaign fund scandals, Congress has tried several times to plug the lobby law's gaping loopholes. These attempts foundered largely because it is difficult to regulate lobbying without trespassing on citizens' rights to contact their elected representatives.

Other practical and political obstacles hamper revision of the law. There is disagreement about what constitutes lobbying. Nor is there consensus on a threshold to trigger the revamped registration and reporting requirements, such as number of hours or days spent lobbying, or the amount of money expended during a quarter. Groups agree that a threshold covering almost every lobbying activity would cause certain organizations to "opt out of the political process for any of a number of reasons: the cost of compliance; the stigma of being labeled a lobbyist; the fear of government meddling in the organization's affairs; the assessment by the organization that the benefit of contacting Washington might be outweighed by the burdens of complying with the registration and reporting requirements." [68]

CONCLUSION

From the nation's beginning, lobbyists and lobbying have been an integral part of lawmaking. Lobbying "has been so deeply woven into the American political fabric that one could, with considerable justice, assert that the history of lobbying comes close to being the history of American legislation." [69] Yet the influence of lobbyists on lawmaking still arouses controversy.

In his farewell address President Carter called special interests and single-issue groups "'a disturbing factor in American political life." In reply, others contend that "more lobbying from a wider spectrum of society is not only constitutionally mandated, but leads to better, more open, and more responsive government." [70]

In recent years, there has been an explosion in the number and types of groups organized to pursue their ends on Capitol Hill. Compared with a decade ago, there are more public affairs lobbies (such as Common Cause) and single-issue groups (pro- and anti-gun control, and the like), political action committees, and agents representing foreign governments. Some of these employ new grass-roots lobbying techniques. Today, many issues are won in Washington because of sophisticated lobbying campaigns back in home states or districts.

Few people question that groups and lobbyists have a legitimate public role. "I don't believe you can build a consensus without outside support," commented Representative James Jones, D-Okla. "You should use the resources of lobbyists to enact your legislative program." [71] But other aspects of lobbying warrant concern. Groups do push Congress to pass laws that benefit the few and not the many. And lawmakers who defy single-issue groups find at election time that these organizations pull out all the stops to defeat them.

Built-in checks limit group pressure, however. First, there often are competing groups on any issue, and legislators can play one off against the other. As former Democratic Representative (now New York City mayor) Edward Koch said:

> I learn a lot from lobbyists because after they have given me all the arguments on their side I invariably ask this question: "What are the

three major arguments your opponents use and how do you respond to them?" This sometimes causes consternation. Then I will say, "If you don't tell me, they will." This usually provides me with additional information which would not otherwise come to my attention.[72]

Second, knowledgeable staff aides can challenge the lobbyists' arguments. Still another informal check on lobbyists is lawmakers' own expertise. Finally, there are self-imposed constraints. Lobbyists who misrepresent issues or mislead members soon find their access permanently closed off.

In addition to groups, many other forces shape a member's vote—constituency, conscience, or party membership among them. The next chapter examines these and other significant elements of decision-making in Congress.

NOTES

1. *Los Angeles Times,* September 29, 1980, p. 42.
2. Michael Macdonald Mooney, "Nation of Lobbyists," *Harper's,* November 1980, pp. 24-32.
3. "The Swarming Lobbyists," *Time,* August 7, 1978, p. 15.
4. Alexis de Tocqueville, *Democracy in America,* ed. Phillips Bradley (New York: Alfred A. Knopf, 1951), p. 119.
5. See Peter H. Odegard, *Pressure Politics: The Story of the Anti-Saloon League* (New York: Columbia University Press, 1928); V. O. Key, Jr., *Politics, Parties and Pressure Groups* (New York: Thomas Y. Crowell Co., 1953); David B. Truman, *The Governmental Process* (New York: Alfred A. Knopf, 1951); Lester W. Milbrath, *The Washington Lobbyists* (Chicago: Rand McNally & Co., 1963); James Deakin, *The Lobbyists* (Washington, D.C.: Public Affairs Press, 1966); Abraham Holtzman, *Interest Groups and Lobbying* (New York: Macmillan, 1966); J. David Greenstone, *Labor in American Politics* (New York: Alfred A. Knopf, 1969); Lewis Anthony Dexter, *How Organizations Are Represented in Washington* (Indianapolis: Bobbs-Merrill Co., 1969); Bruce I. Oppenheimer, *Oil and the Congressional Process* (Lexington, Mass.: Lexington Books, 1974); Carol S. Greenwald, *Group Power* (New York: Praeger Publishers, 1977); Jeffrey M. Berry, *Lobbying for the People* (Princeton, N.J.: Princeton University Press, 1977); and Harold D. Guither, *The Food Lobbyists, Behind the Scenes of Food and Agri-Politics* (Lexington, Mass.: Lexington Books, 1980).
6. David B. Walker, "Constitutional Revision, Incremental Retrenchment, or Real Reform: An Analysis of Efforts to Curb Federal Growth," *The Bureaucrat* (Spring 1980): 41.
7. Bill Keller, "In a Bull Market for Arms, Weapons Industry Lobbyists Push Products, Not Policy," *Congressional Quarterly Weekly Report,* October 25, 1980, p. 3203.
8. U.S., Congress, *Congressional Record,* daily ed., 96th Cong., 2d sess., November 12, 1980, p. E4886.
9. *Committee System Reorganization Amendments of 1977,* Hearings before the Senate Committee on Rules and Administration, 95th Cong., 1st sess., p. 21.

10. Richard E. Cohen, "The Mysterious Ways Congress Makes Committee Assignments," *National Journal*, February 3, 1979, p. 187.
11. *New York Times*, January 24, 1979, p. A15.
12. *Congressional Quarterly Weekly Report*, February 3, 1979, p. 196.
13. There is an extensive literature on subgovernments, a term coined by Douglass Cater, *Power in Washington* (New York: Random House, 1964). For other studies see: J. Leiper Freeman, *The Political Process: Executive Bureau-Legislative Committee Relations*, Revised edition (New York: Random House, 1965); Roger H. Davidson, "Breaking Up Those 'Cozy Triangles': An Impossible Dream?" in Susan Welch and John Peters, eds., *Legislative Reform and Public Policy* (New York: Praeger Publishers, 1977); Richard Rose, "Government Against Sub-Governments: A European Perspective on Washington," in Richard Rose and Ezra N. Suleiman, eds., *Presidents and Prime Ministers* (Washington, D.C.: American Enterprise Institute for Public Policy Research, 1980); James R. Temples, "The Politics of Nuclear Power: A Subgovernment in Transition," *Political Science Quarterly* (Summer 1980): 239-260; Randall B. Ripley and Grace A. Franklin, *Congress, the Bureaucracy and Public Policy*, 2d ed. (Homewood, Ill.: Dorsey Press, 1980); Gordon M. Adams, "Disarming the Military Subgovernment," *Harvard Journal on Legislation* (April 1977): 459-504; and Timothy B. Clark, "The President Takes on the 'Iron Triangles' and So Far Holds His Own," *National Journal*, March 28, 1981, pp. 516-518.
14. Richard Pious, *The American Presidency* (New York: Basic Books, 1979), p. 222.
15. Bill Keller, "Chinks in the 'Iron Triangle'? How a Unique Lobby Force Protects Over $21 Billion In Vast Veterans' Programs," *Congressional Quarterly Weekly Report*, June 14, 1980, p. 1627.
16. Hugh Heclo, "Issue Networks and the Executive Establishment," in Anthony King, ed., *The New American Political System* (Washington, D.C.: American Enterprise Institute for Public Policy Research, 1978), p. 102. For another interesting critique, see Graham K. Wilson, "Are Department Secretaries Really a President's Natural Enemies?" *British Journal of Political Science* (July 1977): 273-299.
17. Cited in Godfrey Hodgson, *All Things To All Men, The False Promise of the American Presidency* (New York: Simon & Schuster, 1980), p. 160.
18. Martin Shapiro, "The Courts v. the President," *Journal of Contemporary Studies* (Winter 1981): 5. In 1981, several members introduced measures to limit the authority of federal courts to hear cases in several controversial areas, such as school busing and abortion. For an overview, see Nadine Cohodas, "Members Move to Rein in Supreme Court," *Congressional Quarterly Weekly Report*, May 30, 1981, pp. 947-951.
19. Ibid.
21. John W. Kingdon, *Congressmen's Voting Decisions*, 2d ed. (New York: Harper & Row, 1981), p. 172.
22. Robert G. Kaiser, "Behind the Saving of America's Savings and Loans," *Washington Post*, July 5, 1981, p. A1.
23. Ward Sinclair, "American Shrimp Industry Lobbies on Hill For Five-Year Quota and Tariff on Imports," *Washington Post*, July 21, 1981, p. A3.
24. *Washington Post*, September 23, 1979, p. A1.
25. Elizabeth Drew, "A Reporter At Large, Jesse Helms," *The New Yorker*, July 20, 1981, p. 80. See also Albert R. Hunt, "Man on the Right," *Wall*

Street Journal, July 16, 1981, p. 1 and Dom Bonafede, "Though He's Riding a Conservative Tide, Jesse Helms Remains the Lonely Maverick," *National Journal,* July 18, 1981, pp. 1284-1288.

26. *U.S. News & World Report,* February 4, 1980, p. 59.
27. *Washington Post,* January 13, 1981, p. B1.
28. See, for example, James Sterling Young, *The Washington Community, 1800-1828* (New York: Columbia University Press, 1966); Sven Groennings, "The Clubs in Congress: The House Wednesday Group," in Sven Groennings and Jonathan P. Hawley, eds., *To Be A Congressman* (Washington, D.C.: Acropolis Books, 1973); and Ross K. Baker, *Friend and Foe in the U.S. Senate* (New York: The Free Press, 1980).
29. *Congressional Quarterly Weekly Report,* April 7, 1973, p. 771. For information on state delegations, see, for example, John H. Kessel, "The Washington Congressional Delegation," *Midwest Journal of Political Science* (February 1964): 1-21; Barbara Deckard, "State Party Delegations in the U.S. House of Representatives: A Comparative Study of Group Cohesion," *Journal of Politics* (February 1972): 199-222; Alan Fiellin, "The Group Life of a State Delegation in the House of Representatives," *Western Political Quarterly* (June 1970): 305-320; Aage R. Clausen, "State Party Influence on Congressional Party Decisions," *Midwest Journal of Political Science* (February 1972): 77-101; and Richard Born, "Cue-Taking within State Party Delegations in the U.S. House of Representatives," *Journal of Politics* (February 1976): 71-94.
30. *Washington Star,* May 22, 1978, p. A1.
31. U.S., Congress, House, *Congressional Record,* daily ed., 95th Cong., 2d sess., February 23, 1978, p. H1471, and Sarah E. Warren, "The New Look of the Congressional Caucuses," *National Journal,* April 29, 1978, p. 678.
32. U.S., Congress, Senate, *Congressional Record,* daily ed., 97th Cong., 1st sess., March 17, 1981, p. S2266.
33. *New York Times,* December 8, 1976, p. 32. See Marguerite Ross Barnett, "The Congressional Black Caucus," in Harvey C. Mansfield, Sr. ed., *Congress Against the President* (New York: Proceedings of the Academy of Political Science, 1975); Robert C. Smith, "The Black Congressional Delegation," *Western Political Quarterly,* June 1981, pp. 203-221; and Deborah Churchman, "Congresswomen's caucus wields clout beyond its size," *Christian Science Monitor,* June 11, 1981, p. 17.
34. Neal R. Peirce and Jerry Hagstrom, "Regional Groups Talk About Cooperation, But They Continue to Feud," *National Journal,* May 27, 1978, p. 844.
35. U.S., Congress, House, *Congressional Record,* daily ed., 96th Cong., 1st sess., April 3, 1979, p. H1904. See Dan Balz, "Sun Belt States Form House 'Counterforce'," *Washington Post,* April 18, 1981, p. A3.
36. *Washington Post,* October 7, 1979, p. C2.
37. Daniel P. Mulhollan and Arthur G. Stevens, "Special Interests and the Growth of Information Groups in Congress," (Paper presented at the Midwest Political Science Convention, April 24-26, 1980, p. 15.) Also see Burdett A. Loomis, "Congressional Caucuses and the Politics of Representation," in Lawrence C. Dodd and Bruce I. Oppenheimer, eds., *Congress Reconsidered,* 2d ed. (Washington, D.C.: Congressional Quarterly Press, 1981); Arthur G. Stevens, Jr., Daniel P. Mulhollan, and Paul S. Rundquist, "U.S. Congressional Structure and Representation: The Role of Informal Groups," *Legislative Studies Quarterly* (August 1981): 415-437; and Pat

Lewis, "Caucuses: Playing Political Football on Capitol Hill," *Washington Star*, August 6, 1981, p. D1.

38. *Washington Star*, July 9, 1979, p. A9.
39. For information on the Democratic Study Group, see Kenneth Kofmehl, "The Institutionalization of a Voting Bloc," *Western Political Quarterly* (June 1964): 256-272; Mark F. Ferber, "The Formation of the Democratic Study Group," in Nelson W. Polsby, ed., *Congressional Behavior* (New York: Random House, 1971) and Arthur G. Stevens, Jr., Arthur H. Miller, and Thomas E. Mann, "Mobilization of Liberal Strength in the House, 1955-1970: The Democratic Study Group," *American Political Science Review* (June 1974): 667-681.
40. John Erlenborn, "Rep. Erlenborn on the Caucus Delecti," *Roll Call*, April 27, 1978, p. 4.
41. *U.S. News & World Report*, February 4, 1980, p. 59.
42. Ibid.
43. Elise D. Garcia, "Money in Politics," *Common Cause*, February 1981, p. 11.
44. Norman J. Ornstein and Shirley Elder, *Interest Groups, Lobbying and Policymaking* (Washington, D.C.: Congressional Quarterly, 1978), p. 224.
45. Elizabeth Drew, "Reporter At Large," *The New Yorker*, January 9, 1978, p. 56.
46. Elizabeth Drew, *Senator* (New York: Simon & Schuster, 1979), p. 147.
47. Andy Plattner, "Congress Passes Low-Level Nuclear Waste Bill, Leaves Broader Solution for Future," *Congressional Quarterly Weekly Report*, December 20, 1980, p. 3623.
48. *New York Times*, January 20, 1981, p. B3.
49. Norman J. Ornstein, "Lobbying for Fun and Policy," *Foreign Policy* (Fall 1977): 160.
50. *U.S. News & World Report*, December 1, 1980, p. 47.
51. *Washington Post*, January 21, 1981, p. B3.
52. Eugene Eidenberg and Roy D. Morey, *An Act of Congress, The Legislative Process and the Making of Education Policy* (New York: W. W. Norton & Co., 1969).
53. *Washington Star*, December 31, 1980, p. C2.
54. *Time*, August 7, 1978, p. 21.
55. Mark Green and Andrew Buchsbaum, "How the Chamber's Computers Con the Congress," *The Washington Monthly*, May 1980, p. 49.
56. James Q. Wilson, "American Politics, Then and Now," *Commentary*, February 1979, p. 44.
57. *New York Times*, January 24, 1980, p. A16.
58. Bill Keller and Irwin B. Arieff, "Money and Munchies: As Campaign Costs Skyrocket, Lobbyists Take Growing Role in Washington Fund-Raisers," *Congressional Quarterly Weekly Report*, May 17, 1980, p. 1346.
59. Bernadette A. Budde, "Business Political Action Committees," in Michael Malbin, ed., *Parties, Interest Groups, and Campaign Finance Laws* (Washington, D.C.: American Enterprise Institute for Public Policy Research, 1980), p. 11. See Edwin M. Epstein, "The Emergence of Political Action Committees," in Herbert E. Alexander, ed., *Political Finance* (Beverly Hills, Calif.: Sage Publications, 1979), pp. 159-198.
60. Michael J. Malbin, "Of Mountains and Molehills: PACs, Campaigns, and Public Policy," in Malbin, ed., *Parties, Interest Groups, and Campaign Finance Laws*, pp. 154-155.
61. Common Cause, press release, March 12, 1981. See *New York Times*, March 29, 1981, p. 31.

62. See, for example, Jack W. Germond and Jules Witcover, "Democrats Aim At '82 Recovery With PACs," *Washington Star,* February 16, 1981, p. A3; "Center for Democratic Policy Formed," in *Congressional Record,* daily ed., 97th Cong., 1st sess., February 27, 1981, pp. S1677-S1679; Richard E. Cohen, "Democrats Take a Leaf from GOP Book With Early Campaign Financing Start," *National Journal,* May 23, 1981, pp. 920-925; and Maxwell Glenn, "Liberal Political Action Committees Borrow a Page from the Conservations," *National Journal,* July 4, 1981, pp. 1197-1200.
63. *Washington Post,* June 14, 1981, p. A3.
64. Malbin, "Of Mountains and Molehills: PACs, Campaigns, and Public Policy," pp. 154-155.
65. *Wall Street Journal,* September 17, 1980, p. 33. See Bill Keller, "Congressional Rating Game Is Hard To Win," *Congressional Quarterly Weekly Report,* March 21, 1981, pp. 507-512.
66. U.S., Congress, House, *Organization of the Congress,* House Report 1675, 79th Cong., 2d sess., 1946, p. 26.
67. See Daniel P. Mulhollan, "An Overview of Lobbying By Organizations," in U.S., Congress, Senate, *Senators: Offices, Ethics, and Pressures,* Commission on the Operation of the Senate, 94th Cong., 2d sess., 1977, pp. 157-192.
68. Hope Eastman, *Lobbying: A Constitutionally Protected Right* (Washington, D.C.: American Enterprise Institute for Public Policy Research, 1977), p. 19.
69. Edgar Lane, *Lobbying and the Law* (Berkeley: University of California Press, 1964), p. 18.
70. Ornstein and Elder, *Interest Groups, Lobbying and Policymaking,* p. 229.
71. Richard E. Cohen, "The Business Lobbying Discovers That in Unity There Is Strength," *National Journal,* June 28, 1980, p. 1052.
72. *Washington Star,* December 16, 1975, p. A1.

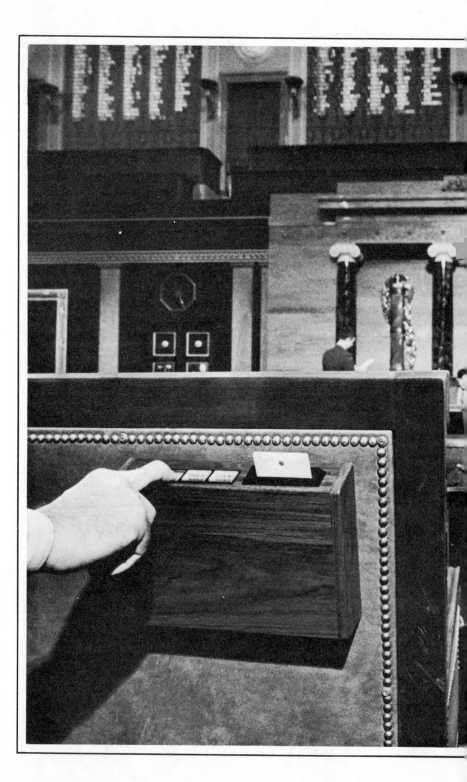

Representatives vote at stations located throughout the
House chamber, with a running tally displayed on electronic
screens above the Speaker's chair.

13

Decisionmaking in Congress

The day before the climactic vote, Senator Wendell H. Ford,
D-Ky., secluded himself in his Senate office. One of a handful of
senators still undecided on the historic Panama Canal treaties, he
and his colleagues would determine whether President Carter
could muster the necessary 67 votes—two-thirds of the Senate—
for ratification. Ford had good reason to seek quiet reflection. The
previous day his suite in the Dirksen Office Building was "under
almost continual siege by pro- and anti-treaty forces" seeking his
vote.[1]

The assault had begun at 7:15 a.m. when Vice President
Walter Mondale, trailed by White House heavies Robert Strauss
and Hamilton Jordan, arrived to plead for the treaty—not only for
its merits but also for the president's credibility with the rest of
the world. President Carter himself conveyed the same message by
phone; he gave Ford an open invitation to talk things over at the
White House. After Mondale's early morning visit, longstanding
treaty supporter Abraham Ribicoff, D-Conn., phoned. Newly announced supporter Russell B. Long, D-La., whose state, like
Ford's, disliked the idea of ceding the canal to the Panamanians,
also urged him to vote for ratification.

Meanwhile, the treaty's foes were busy. Throughout the day
Ford's switchboard buzzed with calls from all parts of the country;
staff aides passed in and out of the office carrying armloads of
letters and telegrams, most of them opposing the treaties.

373

Earlier Ford had requested 15 minutes of floor time to announce his vote, but in the afternoon he notified Senate leaders that he would not use his time. "I had fully intended to make a statement today," the senator explained. "After the visits I've had, though, I decided to take a step back and look at it again." He called the vote "one of the toughest decisions in all my political life." When the vote occurred the next day—March 16, 1978—Ford voted "nay." Doubts about U.S. defense of the canal and the cost of the transfer, not to mention the opposition of a majority of Kentuckians, overrode the White House appeals. Some observers believed Ford would have given the treaties his vote if needed. As it happened, President Carter had gathered enough support elsewhere: the treaties were ratified by a vote of 68 to 32—one vote more than was needed.

THE POWER TO CHOOSE

The Panama Canal vote reflects the extraordinary power and freedom of individual House or Senate members. Although few votes command such public attention, every decision has the capacity to shape government. In both chambers, every legislator has the right, even the obligation, to vote. (Delegates and resident commissioners in the House may vote in committee but not on the floor.) Legislators vote for themselves; no colleague or staff aide may do it for them. "In the end," observed Senator Ford on the eve of the Panama Canal vote, "you can get all the advice in the world; but those who give you advice don't vote." [2] To exchange that vote for money or any other thing of value would be to accept a bribe, a federal crime.

Recorded votes on the House or Senate floor, while a legislator's most visible decisions, are imperfect clues to a legislator's views; sometimes they are downright misleading. For an accurate measure of members' stewardship, one must study their entire range of decisions. These include such choices as: participating in floor debate, taking part in committee deliberations, gaining expertise on issues, attending to party or caucus affairs, allocating time between legislative and constituent duties, hiring and supervising staff, and gathering and utilizing information supplied by scores of agencies or interested parties. Countless such decisions—a few reached with the agony of Senator Ford's Panama Canal vote, others made hastily or inadvertently—define what it means to be a member of Congress.

In making such choices, members of Congress are relatively free and unfettered. There are no pat formulas for being a senator or a representative. Legislators are chosen from individual, discrete constituencies. Although virtually all wear party labels, they wear them loosely at best. Speaker Thomas P. O'Neill, Jr., once described House

Democrats as "an organization of convenience." [3] Loyalty to the president, even when of the legislator's own political party, is not always expected or even rewarded. Although many lawmakers prefer to support the president, especially on foreign policy questions, they are free to dissent when drawn by conscience or constituency pressures.

Capitol Hill norms strongly underscore members' independence.[4] Party leaders may plead, cajole, or warn; but using "roughhouse" tactics against members is frowned upon and if tried probably would backfire. Presidents also woo members, but their powers are limited. A Carter cabinet member's suggestion that members who failed to support the president's reelection drive risked their districts' federal funds was roundly criticized in the press and on Capitol Hill. Nor are there legal grounds for attacking legislators for performing their duties, at least legislative deliberations and votes. Anxious to prevent reprisals against legislators in the conduct of office, the Constitution's authors specified in Article I, Section 6, that "for any speech or debate in either House, they shall not be questioned in any other place."

TYPES OF DECISIONS

Allocating Scarce Resources

Legislators must allocate their time and energy among countless demands competing for their attention. For one thing, lawmakers must decide how much time to spend in the nation's capital. Members within 500 or 600 miles often remain at their home base, commuting to Washington during the Tuesday-Thursday period and returning home every weekend. House Ways and Means Chairman Daniel Rostenkowski, D-Ill., reportedly spent only nine weekends in Washington during his first 22 years in office, preferring to return to Chicago to be with his family and attend to political duties.[5] For such members, Washington life beyond Capitol Hill is as alien as a foreign country. Others, with varying degrees of enthusiasm, plunge into the capital's social and political life. Such individuals rarely "go back to Pocatello," as the saying goes. Between these two extremes are many degrees of "at homeness" in Washington, roughly measured by the amount of time spent in the home state or district.

A more subtle question is how to spend one's time and energies while in the nation's capital. A major decision is whether to focus attention on legislative issues or on constituency relationships. Some members work hard to digest the mountains of reports and analyses that cross their desks; in the parlance of Capitol Hill, they "do their homework." By comparison, others seem to know or care little about legislative matters. They prefer to stress different aspects of the job like correspondence, outreach, and visits with constituents or lobby groups. Such members rarely contribute to committee or floor deliberations; their votes are usually influenced by cues from colleagues, staff members, the White House, or interested groups.

Although either of these strategies can be successfully pursued, and relatively few voters can tell the difference, most legislators claim to prefer legislative tasks, as we saw in Chapter 4. When faced with competing constituency demands, many legislators are impatient and dissatisfied. Whatever the distractions, they strive to emphasize legislative work. David Kovenock's legislative communications audit indicated that, while staff aides may spend much of their time running errands for constituents, lawmakers themselves typically do not. Nearly two-thirds of all the messages read or heard by Kovenock's six representatives concerned legislation and congressional procedure—the heart of traditional lawmaking. Only one in six messages had to do with case work, patronage, or routine office matters.[6]

Specializing

Within the legislative realm, members may dig deeply in a particular area or become involved in a wide range of policies. Senators are more apt to be generalists, while representatives are inclined to cultivate a few specialties.

In both houses, the key policymaking roles are played by those whom David Price calls *policy entrepreneurs:* those recognized for "stimulating more than . . . responding" to outside political forces in a given field.[7] Often nearly invisible to the mass of citizens, these legislators are known to specialized publics for their contributions to specific public policies—for example, Senators Edmund Muskie, D-Maine, in environmental and "sunset" proposals, Sam Nunn, D-Ga., in military personnel, Pete Domenici, R-N.M., in waterway user fees; or Representatives Paul Rogers, D-Fla., in health care, Phillip Burton, D-Calif., in trusts and territories, and Claude Pepper, D-Fla., in rights for the elderly.

What determines members' legislative specialties? First, committee assignments may determine a member's interest. Thomas J. McIntyre, D-N.H., former mayor of the small city of Laconia, became the Senate's leading expert on military research and development after he was assigned to the Armed Services Committee. Senator Dick Clark, D-Iowa, a former Hill staff member, became an expert on African affairs. Neither specialty proved attractive to home-state voters (both men were defeated for reelection in 1978); but both were acknowledged to have served their country well in their respective areas.

Second, a policy may be linked to member's constituency interests. Representative Fred Richmond, D-N.Y., assigned to the House Agriculture Committee, gravitated to consumer issues and food stamp programs because of his Brooklyn constituency. Alaska senators have focused on the issue of government-controlled Alaskan lands, crucial to the state's development.

Third, specializations may reflect personal interests nurtured by background or experience. Sidney Yates, D-Ill., whose parents took him to concerts as a child and who now collects modern art, easily cultivated the role of shepherding government funding for the arts through the House. Former Representative Mike McCormack, D-Wash., a nuclear physicist, concentrated on nuclear power issues.

Whatever a member's specialty, the ability to influence the decisionmaking process is what really counts. "Power, power," declared former Senator Muskie.

> People have all sorts of conspiratorial theories on what constitutes power in the Senate. It has little to do with the size of the state you come from. Or the source of your money. Or committee chairmanships, although that certainly gives you a kind of power. But real power up there comes from doing your work and knowing what you're talking about. Power is the ability to change someone's mind.... The most important thing in the Senate is credibility. *Credibility! That* is power." [8]

Sponsoring Bills

Bureaucrats, lobbyists, or staff aides may do the drafting, but only members of Congress may introduce bills and resolutions in their respective chambers. Given the large number of bills and resolutions, patterns of legislative sponsorship vary widely. Studying the post-World War II Senate, Donald Matthews found that most senators confined their bills mainly to committees on which they sat. Senators who deviated from this norm tended to come from larger and more urban states that were more electorally competitive. They tended also to be more liberal and to have had briefer pre-Senate political careers. Matthews contended that senators who specialized in bill sponsorship were more effective in pushing their legislation through the Senate. This specialization norm has faded as more senators represent populous, diverse states, and are expected to command a broad range of issues. [9]

Do legislators actually favor the bills and resolutions they introduce? Normally they do, but as Sportin' Life, the *Porgy and Bess* character, said, "It ain't necessarily so." Members may introduce a measure to stake out jurisdiction for a committee or to form the basis for hearings and deliberations that will air a public problem. In such instances members are interested in the topic but not wedded to the specific remedy embodied in the draft legislation. Or members may introduce measures they do not personally favor to oblige an executive agency or to placate a given interest.

According to Senate and House rules, bills and resolutions may have an unlimited number of cosponsors. Cosponsorship, no less than sponsorship, is politically motivated. Normally cosponsors are sought out and welcomed. A bill's author will circulate a "Dear Colleague" letter detailing the virtues of the bill and soliciting cosponsors. Names of cosponsors are listed on the bill; new cosponsors are sometimes announced in the *Congressional Record,* as we saw in Chapter 9, to demonstrate broad support and encourage committee action.

Occasionally, however, cosponsors are shunned. Introducing his waterway users' fee bill, Senator Domenici decided against seeking cosponsors for several reasons.[10] First, as ranking Republican on the subcommittee, he felt he could arrange hearings without cosponsors' support. Second, single sponsorship would be easier. ("If you've got cosponsors you have to clear every little change with them.") Third, if the bill became law, he would get full, undiluted credit. And finally, if by chance he found no cosponsors, his effort might suffer a devastating initial setback. Thus, for a time, Domenici fought alone for his bill. In the end, it was signed into law by President Carter at a Democratic rally crowded with politicians who initially had opposed it; Domenici's role was barely mentioned. Such are the ironies of politics.

Casting Votes

Lawmakers' most visible decisions are the votes they cast. Voting is a central ritual in any legislative body. Members place great stock in their voting records, under the assumption (sometimes valid) that constituents will judge these votes at reelection time. Outside groups are assiduous followers of votes on specific measures. Scholars, too, exhibit a longstanding love affair with legislative voting, no doubt because votes provide concrete, quantitative indicators that lend themselves to statistical analysis.

Most senators and representatives strive to be present for as many floor votes as they can. The average member participates in 9 out of every 10 recorded votes on the floor.[11] A few members boast perfect voting records. The all-time champion is Representative William Natcher, D-Ky., whose unbroken string of some 8,000 floor votes began when he came to the House in 1954 and was still in progress in 1981. By contrast, some members may vote less than half the time, perhaps because they are ill or are running for another office. Most legislators, however, are diligent in casting floor votes, if only to forestall charges of absenteeism by potential opponents.

In Congress, there are at least four methods of voting: roll-call, teller, division, and voice. On roll calls each member's vote is recorded separately. In the Senate and in committees, the clerk calls the names of members, who may vote "Yea," "Nay," or "Present." The roll may be repeated to allow time for members to make their way to the chamber. Since 1973 the House has employed an electronic voting system, with members' votes displayed on panels above the press gallery behind the Speaker's desk. Members insert a personalized, plastic card into one of more than 40 voting stations throughout the chamber and press one of three buttons: Yea, Nay, or Present. The system is also used to ascertain quorums.

In a teller vote the chair appoints one or more members from each side of the question to act as "tellers" or vote counters. Members file up the center aisle toward the rear of the chamber—the yeas first, followed by the nays—between the tellers who count them and report the results to the chair. In the House, recorded votes were precluded prior to 1971 in Committee of the Whole deliberations, where many crucial amendments are decided. Teller votes were the most accurate records of decisions reached there. Unrecorded votes were defended as promoting compromise and permitting members to vote the national interest beyond the glare of publicity. Secrecy was not absolute, but journalists and others in the galleries found it difficult to identify all the members who passed through the tellers. In the late 1960s "gallery spotters" from groups opposed to the Vietnam war made concerted efforts to recognize and record members as they voted. Sometimes the spotters made mistakes, provoking protests from members who were erroneously recorded in news reports. Finally, a combination of member dissatisfaction, bipartisan reform efforts, and public pressure succeeded in attaching a recorded teller vote provision to the 1970 Legislative Reorganization Act. Today, such a vote may be demanded by 25 representatives, one-fourth of a quorum in the Committee of the Whole.

With the advent of electronic voting in 1973, the recorded teller vote lost its special character. Electronic voting has cut House balloting time in half—to 15 minutes—and has encouraged doubling of the pre-1970s floor votes. It also places members "on record" on a greater number of issues. Finally, it probably helps dilute the power of committee leaders: with so many recorded votes in the Committee of the Whole, more members are drawn to the floor to cast their votes—not just a handful of members from the committee reporting the measure being considered.

Offering Amendments

A chief strategy for shaping legislation during floor deliberations is to offer amendments. Sometimes amendments are intended to provide a test of strength. During Senate debate on President Reagan's tax bill, for example, the floor manager, Robert Dole, R-Kan., moved to table his own amendment offsetting the windfall profits tax on oil companies. He thought his motion would be heavily defeated, but a narrow margin indicated that opponents of oil-tax loopholes were strong and could even sustain a filibuster.[12] Other amendments are intended to counteract the biases of the committees that drafted and reported the legislation.

In some cases, amendments are designed to force members to declare themselves on symbolic issues that hold public attention. Amendments on abortion funding or budget-balancing are prime examples. When the House debated creation of the Department of Education in 1979, the bill was laden with amendments having little to do with the new agency's charter or structure—on such matters as abortion, busing, school prayers, and racial quotas. Although the amendments were widely publicized and passed by wide margins, they were unceremoniously dropped by conferees before the measure could gain final approval.

In the Senate, which cherishes the individual senators' prerogatives, amendments have always been a central part of floor debate, even though some amendments are designed to delay action. After the Senate's cloture rule was tightened in 1975, some senators found they could evade it by introducing delaying amendments after cloture had been invoked. Some of these loopholes have been closed, but floor participation in the Senate remains high. Rules are generous, and very little is heard of earlier folkways that frowned upon participation by junior members or those not on the committee dealing with the particular bill.

If members can't vote in person, they can still be recorded on an issue. Of course, they may announce their views in floor statements or press releases. Also, both chambers permit members to be recorded in the *Congressional Record,* even though they do not count in tabulating the votes. This is *pairing,* a voluntary arrangement between two legislators on opposite sides of an issue, one or both of whom are absent when the vote is taken. Pairs take several forms. A "general pair" means that two members are listed without any indication of how either might have voted. A "specific pair" indicates how the two absent legislators would have voted, one for and the other against. A "live pair" matches two members, one present and one absent. The member who is there casts a vote and then withdraws it to vote "present," announcing that he or she has a live pair with a colleague and identifying how each would have voted on the issue. A live pair subtracts one vote, yea or nay, from the final tally and occasionally influences the outcome of closely contested issues.

During committee deliberations, absent members often vote by *proxy,* entrusting their votes to an ally who is present at the session. Proxy rules vary by committee. A few prohibit proxies altogether. Some require written proxies, others do not; some require separate proxies for each vote, while others allow general proxies in which the member in attendance casts the votes on any matter that comes up. Given scheduling difficulties and erratic attendance patterns, legislators leading the fight for or against a particular measure take care to gather proxies beforehand and use them according to the applicable rules.

What Do Votes Mean?

Like other elements in the legislative process, voting is open to various interpretations. A given vote by a certain legislator may or may not be what it seems to be. Therefore, students of politics must be very cautious in analyzing legislative votes.

Votes are frequently taken on procedural matters that evoke responses independent of the issue at hand. Certain senators, for example, refuse to vote in favor of cloture, regardless of the substantive issue. They cherish individual senators' right to speak at length on matters of intense concern—to filibuster, if necessary, to put their case before the final court of public opinion. Once thought the exclusive property of southern segregationists intent on blocking civil rights legislation, the filibuster is now employed by senators of every ideological stripe to block legislation they vehemently oppose. Hence, not every senator who favors a measure is willing to vote for cloture.

House and Senate floor votes offer imperfect channels for registering members' views. Members may favor a measure but feel constrained to vote against it in the form it is presented on the floor. Conversely, members unhappy with portions of a measure may support it because "on balance" it is a step forward. Or they may support a proposal they disagree with in order to prevent enactment of something worse. Or they may support an amendment they oppose with the expectation that the other body or conference committee will kill it. Or they may go along with party leaders on measures they disagree with as long as their actions don't adversely affect their constituency. And so on.

In some cases, recorded votes are totally misleading. A favorable vote may really be negative or vice versa. A 1979 Senate vote to attach a school prayer amendment sponsored by Jesse Helms, R-N.C., to a measure dealing with Supreme Court jurisdiction was really a vote to kill the amendment because it was expected that the House would scuttle the court bill. A vote later that year against automobile air bags was only a token vote because it was tied to an authorizing bill that would expire before the National Highway Traffic Safety Administration's air-bag regulations were to take effect. In such cases the meaning of a legislator's vote is, to say the least, very much in doubt.

Not infrequently, voting obscures a legislator's true position. Given the multiplicity of votes—procedural as well as substantive—on many measures, it is entirely possible for a lawmaker to come out on both sides of the issue or at least appear to do so. For instance, members may vote to authorize a program but against funding it. Or they may vote against final passage of a bill but for a substitute version. This strategy ensures the bill's supporters that the lawmaker favors the concept, while pleasing voters who oppose the bill. Such voting patterns may reflect a deliberate attempt to obscure one's position or careful thought about complex questions. As in so many aspects of human behavior, lawmakers' motivations can be fully judged only in light of specific cases.

Votes are occasionally cast in confusion. Lawmakers often face the situation of Representative Joe Fisher, D-Va., who was attacked by an opponent for a vote he hardly recalled casting. It had been a steamy August day, and Fisher had spent most of it in the Ways and Means Committee rooms, ironing out report language on a land conservation tax bill he had written. When the bells called him to the floor about 1:30 p.m., he found legislators wrangling over an amendment concerning bilingual education, one of some 30 riders to an educational appropriations bill. Making his way to the majority managers' desk, he examined the 75-word amendment and asked the floor manager, a trusted senior colleague, what it meant. "Vote against it, Joe," the colleague said. "It hasn't been through the committee." [13] This voting cue—and the fact that the amendment's rigid language came from a right-wing Republican with whom he rarely agreed—led Fisher to vote against the amendment and leave without learning the outcome. The amendment passed and was hailed as a litmus test on the bilingual education issue. Thus Fisher was accused of "voting for bilingual education," even though he had earlier gone on record as opposing the controversial federal regulations.

Fisher's vote on the bilingual education rider, in fact, tells us next to nothing about his views on that thorny question. His opponent charged that it proved his support of bilingual education. Yet the events suggest at least four other possibilities: 1) he thought the appropriations subcommittee should review the amendment before the floor vote; 2) he thought the amendment was inappropriate for a funding bill and should be part of an authorizing bill; 3) he thought the amendment was badly drafted, limiting the options for school districts that wanted to use bilingual programs; or 4) he was simply misinformed and had cast his vote by mistake. Any one or several of these explanations may be valid. Whatever the explanation, Fisher went down to defeat in 1980.

Where congressional votes are concerned, things are not always what they seem. Votes for or against abortion do not always test members' beliefs about the matter; the real issue behind some abortion votes is federal health plans or welfare policy. Similarly, a member may oppose "forced busing" of school pupils but balk at supporting a constitutional amendment forbidding the practice. Legislators may have reasons for voting that are hard to explain to outsiders. In such cases members face a dilemma: either swallow their reservations and vote for appearance's sake or vote their convictions and take the consequences. Regarding the 1973 clean elections bill, former Senator George Aiken, R-Vt., explained, "A common excuse for voting for [it] was that it was easier to vote for it than to explain why one did not vote for it." [14]

This point is important for students because scholars often treat votes as if they were unambiguous indicators of legislators' views. It is important for citizens because lobbyists and reporters frequently assess incumbents on the basis of floor votes. Some groups construct voting indices for labelling "friendly" or "unfriendly" legislators. Citizens are well advised to examine such indices closely. Have the votes been chosen fairly? Have they been interpreted accurately? Have they been weighted to distinguish between key votes and those of lesser importance? How have absences been counted?

Interest groups often employ questionable methods in portraying lawmakers' voting records. Favoring creation of a federal Department of Education, the National Education Association pegged its 1980 campaign support almost exclusively on that issue.[15] The NEA's "single-vote" standard was applied to aid members even if they had voted against the group on other matters. Representative Patricia Schroeder, D-Colo., who received no NEA funds, complained, "On every other issue, I've been on NEA's side, but they went nuts on this one." The Environmental Action Coalition's "dirty dozen" list of anti-environment incumbents, it was charged, targeted members who were vulnerable at the polls—a tactic that would enhance the group's prestige if the members were in fact defeated. After he lost a bitter reelection contest in 1980, Senator Robert Morgan, D-N.C. submitted a "white paper" detailing how his voting record had been used in the campaign. "I found myself faced with a constant barrage of distortions and misstatements regarding my voting record," he said. "Procedural votes were taken to be substantive votes on an issue, even though in the final analysis I cast my vote directly opposite the intent of the procedural vote." [16] Needless to say, it takes longer to answer such charges than it does to make them.

The lesson of these examples is skepticism. Votes, particularly on single issues, should be examined and interpreted cautiously. With these caveats in mind, we turn to several factors that shape congressional voting: party affiliation, constituents' views, ideological leanings, and presidential leadership.

DETERMINANTS OF VOTING

Party and Voting

One way for members to reach voting decisions is to consult the views of their political party colleagues. Party affiliation remains the strongest single correlate of members' voting decisions.

Unlike parliamentary systems, the United States Congress rarely witnesses straight party-line votes and never has votes resulting in the fall of the government in power (unless one counts impeachment of the president). In a typical year from one-third to one-half of all floor votes could be called "party unity votes," defined by Congressional Quarterly as votes in which a majority of voting Republicans oppose a majority of voting Democrats. In a typical year the minority party wins about a third of all party-unity votes—indicating the looseness of party ranks. Figure 13-1 depicts the composite (House and Senate) party votes from 1954 to 1980. The sawtooth pattern of recent years suggests that party votes are most frequent early in the two-year Congresses, falling off as the next election approaches and members pick their own way through controversial end-of-session votes. Party votes show a long-term decline. Around 1900 about two-thirds of all roll calls were party-unity votes. In several sessions a majority of the votes saw 90 percent of one party ranged against 90 percent of the other; today such sharp partisan divisions appear in no more than one in ten roll-call votes.

Individual members' "party unity scores" can be calculated—the percentage of party-unity votes in which they vote in agreement with the majority of their party colleagues. According to these scores, the average legislator votes with party about two times out of three. Democratic and Republican party-unity scores from 1960 to 1980 are displayed in Figure 6-3 on page 194. Partisan voting blocs are prominent also in many committees: from their painstaking study of voting in eight House committees during the mid-1970s, Glenn and Suzanne Parker concluded that partisanship was a key explanatory variable in all of the panels except for Foreign Affairs, which has a bipartisan tradition.[17]

Partisan voting patterns have been extensively studied by scholars, although their conclusions are by no means in total agreement. As Figure 6-3 suggested, party voting levels in both houses were relatively high in the 1950s, fell in the 1960s, and rose again perceptibly in the 1970s. Republicans tend to be more cohesive than Democrats, a cohesiveness that has gathered strength in recent years. Democrats have often been badly divided—first by the historic northern-southern split, in the late 1960s by the Vietnam war, and today by a host of social and economic issues. High points of Democratic cohesion occurred in 1965, at the zenith of President Johnson's "Great Society," and when opposition to President Nixon galvanized in the early 1970s.

Partisan strength in voting is rooted in several factors. Some students argue that party loyalty is mainly a shorthand term for constituency differences.[18] That is, partisans vote together because they reflect the same kinds of political and demographic areas. According to this reasoning, legislators stray from party ranks when they feel their constituents will not benefit from the party's policies.

Figure 13-1 Party Votes in Congress, 1954-1980

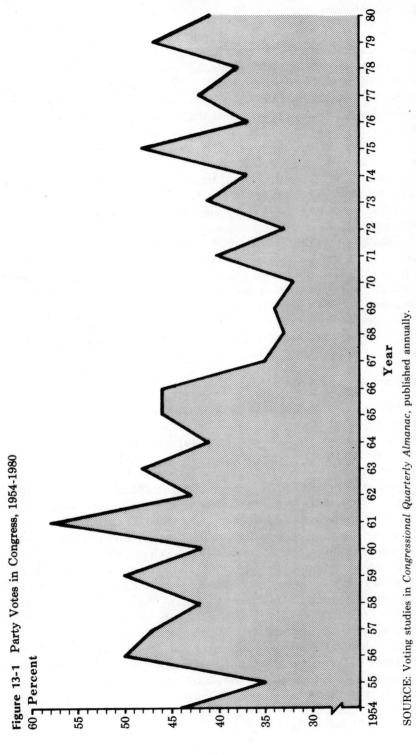

SOURCE: Voting studies in *Congressional Quarterly Almanac*, published annually.

NOTE: Votes are defined as "party unity votes" or those in which a majority of the party is found in opposition to a majority of the other party.

Party cohesion may also flow from shared policy goals shaped as candidates emerge early in their careers. Those who entered politics through the civil rights, environmental, or antiwar movements tend to cluster within the Democratic party, reflecting shared values in their voting. By contrast, individuals who became active to lower taxes or combat big government often gather under the GOP banner, underscoring the party's historic approach to such issues.

Such factors as constituency or recruitment are reinforced by partisan activities on Capitol Hill. New members rely upon party mechanisms for committee assignments and usually organize into partisan "class clubs." When seeking out cues for voting, moreover, legislators tend to choose party colleagues as guides for their own behavior.[19]

Finally, as we saw in Chapter 6, partisan voting is encouraged by party leaders who contact members to solicit views and urge them to support the party. The more visible an issue, the harder party leaders must compete against other pressures for members' votes.[20] They are more likely to gain votes if the issue is defined in procedural terms than if the issue is presented substantively. Whatever the legislator's personal leanings, the institutional push toward partisan voting cannot be ignored.

Constituency and Voting

While the impact of constituency upon individual decisionmaking has been studied extensively, the conclusions from these studies are not altogether clear. As we have seen, constituency traits often take partisan form. Certain types of areas are more likely to elect Democrats while other areas tend to elect Republicans. Issue cleavages flow from these basic differences between "Democratic districts" and "Republican districts."[21] Representatives who deviate from their party's norms more likely than not represent constituencies atypical for that party. According to one study, representatives' roll-call voting differs because their constituencies diverge demographically and electorally.[22]

Constituencies can control lawmakers' choices in two ways. First, people can elect representatives whose views so mirror their own that floor votes automatically represent the will of the constituents. In other words, representatives vote their constituency because they are simply transplanted locals. Representatives' actions are constrained also by the threat of defeat. Occasionally members voice policies or views at odds with those of their district's voters; often (but not always) incumbents subsequently shift their stands to retain their seats. Largely because of voter outcries, Representative Al Ullman, D-Ore., publicly renounced his earlier support of the value-added tax (VAT) in his intense but unsuccessful 1980 reelection drive.

Apart from such vivid examples of constituency pressure, the precise impact of constituencies on congressional voting is hard to measure. Most constituents, after all, are unaware of most issues coming up for votes in the House or Senate chamber. Or constituency opinions may conflict so sharply that a clear mandate is lacking. Finally, legislators adopt varying strategies to interpret constituency interests and then explain their positions back home.

Ideology and Voting

According to conventional wisdom, ideologies are out of place on Capitol Hill. Reporter-turned-novelist Ward Just voiced this view in one of his short stories:

> It was not a place for lost causes. There were too many conflicting interests, too much confusion, too many turns to the labyrinth. . . . This was one reason why it was so difficult to build an ideological record in the House. A man with ideology was wise to leave it before reaching a position of influence, because by then he'd mastered the art of compromise, which had nothing to do with dogma or public acts of conscience. It had to do with simple effectiveness. . . .[23]

Thus members are counseled to steer a middle course. The spirit of compromise, it is argued, supplies oil for the gears of the legislative process. Because grass-roots voters tend to cluster in the middle of the ideological spectrum, moderation appears to be prudent politics.

Some research studies, however, reveal striking ideological divisions in Congress. On the basis of roll-call votes and interviews, Jerrold Schneider concluded that congressional voting is ideological, that voting coalitions form because members carry with them well-developed ideological positions. Another study found that ideology affected voting more than state benefits or party commitments.[24]

One notable ideological grouping is the so-called "conservative coalition" of Republicans and southern Democrats. The coalition emerged in the late 1930s as a reaction against the New Deal and enjoyed its greatest successes between 1939 and 1954.[25] Figure 13-2 shows the percentage of record votes in each chamber in which the coalition has appeared and the proportion of votes won by the coalition. A conservative coalition vote is defined as one in which a majority of voting Republicans and a majority of voting southern Democrats oppose a majority of voting northern Democrats. The coalition appears in roughly one out of every five House votes and one out of every four Senate votes. Historically the coalition has appeared more frequently in the Senate than in the House. Its success rate in both chambers is relatively high, with the conspicuous exception of the 89th Congress (1965-1967), when the anti-Goldwater landslide brought a horde of Democratic liberals to boost President Lyndon Johnson's "Great Society" programs.

Figure 13-2 Conservative Coalition Votes and Victories, 1957-1980 (In Percentages)

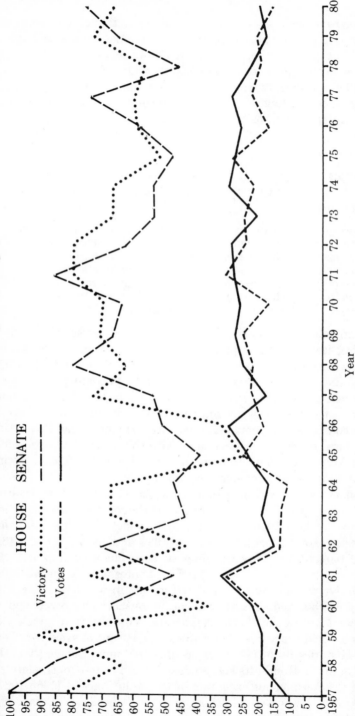

SOURCE: *Congressional Quarterly Almanac*, various years, and *Congressional Quarterly Weekly Report*, January 10, 1981, p. 85.

NOTE: "Votes" is the percentage of all roll call votes on which a majority of voting southern Democrats and a majority of voting Republicans—the conservative coalition—opposed the stand taken by a majority of voting northern Democrats. "Victories" is the percentage of conservative coalition votes won by the coalition.

In the 1980s the coalition reappeared as President Reagan captured votes of conservative Democrats on budget and tax issues, while pulling mainstream Democrats toward conservative positions on other issues.[26]

Ideological cleavages are also uncovered in voting indices prepared by the liberal Americans for Democratic Action (ADA), the conservative Americans for Constitutional Action (ACA), and various labor and business organizations. These indices reveal striking differences in the records of individual members and political parties. Such measures reflect not so much pure ideologies as current definitions of liberalism or conservatism. As such, they are useful clues to opinion leaders' perceptions of Congress.

The Presidency and Voting

In many areas of policymaking, Congress responds to presidential leadership. Although Congress often pursues an independent course and few members feel a deep loyalty to the occupant of the White House, incumbent presidents do influence decisions reached by individual senators and representatives.[27] Not only does the president shape the legislative agenda, but he can mount pressure for members to lend their support. Figure 10-1 on page 301 depicts the mean "presidential support scores"—the percentages of times members voted with the president on issues on which the president announced a position— of Eisenhower, Kennedy, Johnson, Nixon, Ford, and Carter. This index embraces issues of varying gravity, including many routine and noncontroversial matters. Still, the index roughly gauges the president's standing on Capitol Hill and suggests several patterns.

First, modern presidents achieve at least half of their legislative objectives. This success probably flows not so much from popularity or skill as from the routine nature of many of their initiatives. Yet some presidents, like Eisenhower and Johnson during their early years and Kennedy during his abbreviated term, enjoy special success in steering their proposals through Congress.

Second, partisan swings affect presidential success rates. When their party controls Congress, presidents win at least three of every four votes on which they have taken positions; with divided government, presidents average well below that level. Shifts in partisan strength in Congress sometimes have dramatic effects. President Eisenhower's success rate fell 24 percent following the Democrats' victories in the 1958 congressional elections. Building on the 1964 Democratic landslide, President Johnson achieved a modern high of 93 percent success. (Johnson's success rate was boosted by his habit of sending up messages supporting measures he already knew would pass.)

Third, presidents tend to lose congressional support as their administrations age. The only exception to this generalization was

Kennedy, who seemed to be building momentum before his tragic death.

Fourth, congressional support for the president's issue positions sagged in the 1970s. According to one count, Presidents Nixon and Ford—facing large Democratic majorities in Congress—succeeded in persuading Congress to enact only a third of their important legislative proposals.[28] In most other countries, such a poor legislative record would force the chief executive into a general election; here, tension between the two branches is a frequent state of affairs. Loyalty sometimes pulls the president's own partisans away from their traditional ideological positions. In foreign policy, for example, the president's partisans, Democrat or Republican, gravitate toward "internationalist" positions issuing from the White House.[29]

Although presidents have taken clear-cut stands on an increasing *number* of issues over time, these represent a declining *percentage* of congressional votes.[30] In 1979 President Carter took a position on about one out of every five House and Senate votes; at a comparable stage in his administration, President Eisenhower was taking positions on about three out of five congressional votes. In other words, although presidential position-taking has expanded, it has been outrun by the congressional workload. Both presidential influence and congressional independence are running strong.

CUE GIVING AND CUE TAKING

Party, constituency, ideology, and presidential support—external influences on members' voting decisions—are not the only forces that shape voting. Given the huge number of votes and limited information, lawmakers rely heavily on cues from others in deciding how to vote. Several intriguing studies have illuminated patterns of influence internal to the two chambers.

In a model of congressional voting devised by Cleo Cherryholmes and Michael Shapiro, decisionmaking is divided into two phases: *predisposition* and *conversation*.[31] In the initial phase, party, region, committee, and other variables *predispose* each legislator for or against each measure. If the predisposition is indecisive, the lawmaker seeks cues from colleagues—the *conversation* stage. Cherryholmes and Shapiro assign weights to various predispositions as well as to the probability that members would accept cues from colleagues. When applied to 1963-1964 votes on federal activism and foreign aid, this simulation predicted 84 percent of the results in both areas.

A model constructed by Donald Matthews and James Stimson covers selected votes in the 1958-1969 period.[32] They estimated the significance of nine different types of cues that members might seek out:

state party delegations, party leaders, party majority, president, House majority, committee chairman, ranking minority members, the conservative coalition, and the liberal Democratic Study Group. State party delegations proved to have the highest correlations with voting in both parties. Party and committee leaders were also effective cue givers, as were party and House majorities. Democratic presidents were potent positive cue-givers for the Democrats, and Republican presidents were moderately powerful in influencing their Hill partisans. In short, partisan cues were most potent when the White House and Congress were controlled by the same party. Taken as a whole, the Matthews-Stimson model was able to predict 88 percent of the votes actually cast.

Statistical analysis of roll-call votes in the 1950s and 1960s form the basis of Aage Clausen's model.[33] He examined voting on government management, social welfare, international involvement, civil liberties, and agricultural aid. Scoring legislators on each policy dimension, Clausen discovered great stability in members' positions over time and in the impact of various cue sources. Political party was an effective predictor for some issues (especially government management). Constituency controlled others (civil liberties, in particular). In still other cases, a combination of factors were at work: party and constituency dominated social welfare and agricultural aid votes, while international involvement decisions were affected by a combination of constituency and presidential influence. Clausen's work demonstrated that stable forces such as party, constituency, and presidential support induce members to assume long-term positions on legislative policy.

These three models are based upon, or tested with, aggregate voting statistics. To compile these figures individual members' votes are compared with such factors as the party majority or the president's position; high correlations are described as influence. Thus the models are based on inferences gleaned from the conjunction of members' votes and other factors. A few researchers have tackled the arduous job of trying to tap the actual processes by which voting cues are given or received.

David Kovenock's "communications audit" of six members of a House subcommittee supports the notion of cue-giving and cue-taking within Congress. "Most of the messages congressmen received, and most of those which influence them," he found, "originate at least in the first instance from sources within the Congress."[34] Nearly two-thirds of all incoming communications originated on Capitol Hill—from fellow representatives, staff aides, or senators. Of those communications dealing with subcommittee business and regarded as influential, virtually 99 of every 100 messages came from members and staff, governmental agencies, or organized interest groups. The kinds of communications lawmakers received depended on their positions. For example, the more vulnerable their electoral position, the less they focused on lawmaking messages and the more they communicated with the folks back home.

John Kingdon's model of representatives' decisions is based on interviews with members immediately after their votes on specific issues.[35] Legislators have little difficulty making up their minds when they have strong personal convictions or when party leaders and interest groups agree and point them in the same direction. If all the actors in their field of vision concur, members operate in a "consensus mode" of decisionmaking. Fellow members emerge as the most influential cue-givers, with constituencies ranking second. Party leaders and interest groups by contrast are relatively unimportant. When members deviate from the consensus stance indicated by their cue givers, it is usually to follow their own conscience. Adding up these short-term forces, Kingdon's model successfully predicts about 90 percent of the decisions.

The models of legislative voting we have discussed are helpful, but ultimately they approximate rather than duplicate the real world of decisions. For one thing, subtle shifts in organizing or staffing the chambers affect cue-giving and cue-taking. The advent of closed circuit TV transmission of House floor proceedings, for example, has changed members' schedules and perhaps information trading as well. (Senators can follow audio transmissions of floor debates in their offices.) Four out of five representatives in a 1979 survey reported that they often followed proceedings on TV from their offices. About a quarter of the members said they spent more time in their offices and less time on the floor as a result. A majority claimed they and their staffs were better informed about legislative issues because of the TV coverage.[36] By allowing members to follow the drift of the debate on their own TV monitors, the system could dilute the influence of cue-givers—particularly leaders, committees, fellow members, informal caucuses, and staffs. As Representative Michael Barnes, D-Md., commented:

> It used to be that all a representative knew about the vote he was running to cast was, "If it's Tuesday, this must be Fisheries Management. . . ." But it's not quite so superficial anymore. It's on TV. If the member is in his office. . .he can leave the television turned on. . .and follow what's going on. . . . I think the case can be made that Congress has finally found a way to keep up with itself.[37]

Whether or not TV has changed things as radically as Barnes claims, there is little question that the flow of information is affected by just such innovations.

Legislative voting models, no matter how elegant, cannot capture the full range of factors shaping decisions. "The two biggest political lies," Senator Thomas Eagleton, D-Mo., declared, are "one, to say a senator never takes into account the political ramifications of a vote and secondly, almost an equal lie, is to say the only thing a senator considers is politics." [38] To unravel the chain of causality involved in congressional decisionmaking would require a comprehensive model embracing demographic, sociological, psychological, and political motivations. Simplified models, without a doubt, pinpoint important ingredients of legislators' decisions. As with all complex human behavior, however, such decisions elude wholly satisfactory description.

LEGISLATIVE BARGAINING

Legislators make choices on a staggering variety of matters, in a relatively short space of time, often with inadequate information. Two elements of this predicament are especially important. First, legislators harbor separate and sometimes conflicting goals and information. Second, whatever their goals or information levels, every legislator wields one vote with which to affect the outcome.[39]

Such a state of affairs—disparate goals and widely scattered influence—is hazardous. Conflict may flare out of control if the contending policy objectives are not adequately met. On the other hand, stalemate is a constant threat, as when irresistible forces clash with immovable objects. In such a predicament, members have to resort to politicking: that is, they must trade off goals and resources to get results. No wonder, then, that Congress is "an influence system in which bargain and exchange predominate." [40]

Bargaining is a generic term referring to several related types of behavior. In each case, an exchange takes place: goals or resources pass from a bargainer's hands in return for other goals or resources that he or she values. A simple typology of bargaining is shown in Table 13-1.

Bargains may be implicit or explicit. Implicit bargaining occurs when legislators draft a bill or deliver a speech designed to elicit certain reactions from others, even though no negotiation may have taken place. For example, legislators may introduce a bill or sponsor hearings not because they think the bill will pass, but because they hope the action

Table 13-1 Typology of Bargaining

Implicit	*Explicit*
Anticipated reaction	Compromise
Exchanges of cues	Logrolling (simple, time, side-payments)

SOURCE: Adapted from Robert L. Peabody, "Organization Theory and Legislative Behavior: Bargaining, Hierarchy and Change in the U.S. House of Representatives" (Paper presented at the annual meeting of the American Political Science Association, New York, New York, September 4-7, 1963).

will lead someone else—an executive branch official, perhaps, or a committee chairman with broader jurisdiction on the question—to take action on the problem. This is the so-called "law of anticipated reactions." Another example of implicit bargaining occurs when legislators seek out or accept the judgments of colleagues with expertise on a given matter, expecting to have the situation reversed in the future. As we have seen already, exchanges of voting cues are commonplace in both chambers.

Explicit bargains also take several forms. In *compromises*, legislators agree to split their differences. Thus conferees may settle on a $75 million bill when the House and Senate versions specified $50 million and $100 million, respectively. Compromise is most visible in measures embodying quantitative elements—for example, funding levels or eligibility criteria—that can easily be adjusted upward or downward. Compromise also occurs between factions. For example, members who favor a major new program and members who oppose any program at all may agree to a two-year pilot program to test the idea.

Logrolling is a bargaining strategy in which the parties trade off support so that each may gain its goal. In its most visible form, trading is embodied in a something-for-everyone enactment—known as "pork barrel"—on such subjects as public works, omnibus taxation, or tariffs and trade. President Reagan's 1981 budget and tax packages, although stunning victories, were replete with logrolls aimed at ensuring winning coalitions in both houses. Specifically, this meant luring votes from conservative Democrats (the so-called "Boll Weevils") while keeping the GOP ranks firm (especially northeastern moderates, dubbed "Gypsy Moths"). Thus the president's strategists agreed to withdraw their opposition to sugar price supports to please Louisiana members. And peanut acreage allotments and price supports were okayed for the Georgia delegation. For GOP moderates, the administration partially retreated in trying to eliminate social security minimum benefits and accepted softer language on student loan cutbacks. One lawmaker, Representative Bill Goodling, R-Pa., held off supporting the administration until he won pledges not to close a military installation in his district and to support a $37 million cleanup of the Three Mile Island nuclear plant.[41] Goodling was described as neither a Boll Weevil nor a Gypsy Moth—just a "caterpillar," holding out for the best deal for his constituents.

On a narrower scale, members may explicitly trade support for competing goals. Thus, when the Senate was rushing to consider loan guarantees for the Chrysler Corporation late in 1979, Senator Warren Magnuson, D-Wash., then Appropriations Committee chairman, used the occasion to interpose the problem of the Milwaukee Railroad's bankruptcy, an acute concern of legislators from northern-tier states. "I could foul this thing up pretty well" by offering a Milwaukee Road amendment, he declared, appealing bluntly for reciprocal support:

> We bailed out the railroads for all you people from New England. We bailed you out in the northeast corridor and we have appropriated millions of dollars to keep the northeast corridor alive. We have put out millions of dollars on ConRail and we have put out several million dollars on Amtrak. We are talking about a small amount of money to keep the Milwaukee Railroad viable.
>
> I am not going to present the amendment tonight, but I am hopeful that the Members of the Senate will help us convince the Department of Transportation, which has been against this bill all the time, and the [Office of Management of Budget] to help us out in keeping the Milwaukee Railroad a living, viable service for the whole Pacific Northwest.[42]

Similarly, when urban legislators support farm crop subsidies, the quid pro quo may be rural support for food stamp programs to help feed needy individuals. This urban-rural logroll in fact helped make food stamps the nation's second largest income maintenance program in the 1970s.

Logrolling sometimes transforms narrowly targeted programs into broad-scale ones. The late Senator Paul H. Douglas, D-Ill., sponsored a depressed-areas bill that underwent such a transformation. Originally drafted to provide aid to older industrialized regions, the bill met sharp resistance from rural and southern legislators who called it "special legislation for a few spots in Illinois, Pennsylvania, and a few other places." [43] To gain their support, Douglas reluctantly agreed to expand his bill to provide an equal amount for rural areas. He ruefully called the new provisions, "Pass the biscuits, Pappy." The senator's fears that broadened language would water down the bill to the point of ineffectiveness were not unfounded: once the measure was enacted two-thirds of all U.S. counties eventually qualified for aid.

In a *time logroll,* members agree to support one measure in exchange for later support for another measure. Sometimes the logroll embodies a specified exchange; at other times it is open ended, until the donor decides to try to "call in the chips." Both methods were needed in 1977 to approve a controversial pay raise for senators and representatives (and thousands of top civil servants whose salaries are linked to the congressional rate). Maneuvering to forestall disapproval of the pay raise, Senate Majority Leader Robert C. Byrd, D-W.Va., and House Speaker O'Neill called in scores of political debts accumulated from prior political battles. Moreover, they promised early action on congressional ethics resolutions to neutralize public backlash and give members a reason to defend the pay raise.

In a logroll with *side-payments,* support is exchanged for nonissue benefits—for example, a better committee assignment, an invitation to a prestigious conference, or a campaign appearance by party notables back home. Sometimes the benefits may seem petty or personal; yet in many if not most cases, such benefits are valued because they help the member achieve other valued goals.

Are there limits to negotiation? According to bargaining theory, a measure's sponsors will yield only what they absolutely must to gain a majority of supporters. Under this so-called "size principle," a *minimum winning coalition* will occur in legislative bargaining situations under ideal conditions—that is, when the bargainers act rationally and with perfect information.[44] In 1868 Representative Ransom Gillet, D-N.Y., recalled that enacting a tariff bill required protecting the local interests of just enough representatives to ensure the bill's passage. "Interest and not principle," he said,

> determines what shall be done. If votes from Louisiana and Texas are needed, sugar will come in for favor. If support is needed from Illinois, Wisconsin, Minnesota, and Michigan, lead, copper and pine lumber are provided for. If the votes of Pennsylvania are wanted, coal and iron receive full attention.... The principle of protection under a tariff never expands beyond the objects necessary to carry a bill.[45]

From the viewpoint of legislative strategists, this model assumes conditions rarely met in actual situations. For one thing, uncertainty about outcomes leads strategists to line up more than a simple majority of supporters. At many points in the legislative process, extraordinary majorities are required—for example, in constitutional amendments, veto overrides, or in ending Senate filibusters. Not surprisingly, therefore, minimum winning coalitions are not typical of Congress, even in the majoritarian House of Representatives.[46] Yet coalition size lies at the heart of legislative strategy. Bargainers repeatedly face the dilemma of how broadly or how narrowly to frame their issues or how many concessions to yield in an effort to secure passage.

Legislative bargaining offers a tempting target for criticism by the press and the public. Whatever the propriety of specific deals, however, bargaining is essential if multiple, contested goals are to be realized in the legislative arena. Constructing winning coalitions for bills or resolutions is an ongoing challenge. If bills are to be passed or policies ratified, then bargaining must occur. Bargaining is reflected not only in the substance of legislation but also in many attributes of the legislative process—delay, obfuscation, compromise, and such norms as specialization and reciprocity. It is no exaggeration to say that bargaining lies at the heart of the legislative way of life.

Legislative bargaining shapes the character of bills, resolutions, and other forms of congressional policymaking. It is yet another point of contact and conflict between the two Congresses—the Congress of individual members and the Congress of collective policy products. In the final section of our book, we return to the two Congresses concept to consider legislative policymaking and organizational change on Capitol Hill.

NOTES

1. John M. Goshko, "Swing Vote Sits Out High-Pressure Day," *Washington Post,* March 16, 1977, p. A19.
2. Ibid.
3. U.S., Congress, House, *Congressional Record,* daily ed., 96th Cong., 2d sess., 1980, p. H9699.
4. Randall B. Ripley, *Congress: Process and Policy,* 2d ed. (New York: W. W. Norton & Co., 1978), p. 120.
5. Curt Suplee, "The Ways and Means Broker: Dan Rostenkowski and the Tax Test," *Washington Post,* July 23, 1981, p. C1.
6. David M. Kovenock, "Influence in the U.S. House of Representatives: A Statistical Analysis of Communications," *American Politics Quarterly* (October 1973): 407-464.
7. David Price, *Who Makes The Laws?* (Cambridge, Mass.: Schenkman Publishing Co., 1972), p. 297.
8. Bernard Asbell, *The Senate Nobody Knows* (Garden City, N.Y.: Doubleday & Co., 1978), p. 210.
9. Donald R. Matthews, *U.S. Senators and Their World* (Chapel Hill: University of North Carolina Press, 1960), pp. 96, 115.
10. T. R. Reid, *Congressional Odyssey: The Saga of a Senate Bill* (San Francisco: W. H. Freeman & Co., 1980), p. 15.
11. Wayne Walker, "Attendance During Votes Increased During 1980," *Congressional Quarterly Weekly Report,* January 12, 1980, pp. 98-99.
12. Edward Cowan, "House Panel Completes Tax Action," *New York Times,* July 23, 1981, p. D7.
13. Ed Bruske, "The Making of an Issue," *Washington Post,* October 21, 1980, p. C3.
14. George D. Aiken, *Senate Diary* (Brattleboro, Vt.: The Stephen Greene Press, 1975), p. 208.
15. Albert R. Hunt, "Teachers Tie Election Cash to Single Issue," *Wall Street Journal,* October 17, 1980, p. 33.
16. U.S., Congress, Senate, *Congressional Record,* daily ed., 96th Cong., 2d sess., December 10, 1980, p. S16135.
17. Glenn R. Parker and Suzanne L. Parker, "Factions in Committees: The U.S. House of Representatives," *American Political Science Review* (March 1979): 85-102.
18. Lewis A. Froman, Jr., *Congressmen and Their Constituencies* (Chicago: Rand McNally & Co., 1963).
19. Helmut Norpoth, "Explaining Party Cohesion in Congress: The Case of Shared Policy Attitudes," *American Political Science Review* (December 1976): 1171.
20. Lewis A. Froman, Jr., and Randall B. Ripley, "Conditions for Party Leadership: The Case of the House Democrats," *American Political Science Review* (March 1965): 52-63.
21. Froman, *Congressmen and Their Constituencies.*
22. Thomas A. Flinn and Harold L. Wolman, "Constituency and Roll Call Voting," *Midwest Journal of Political Science* (May 1966): 193-199.

23. Ward S. Just, *The Congressman Who Loved Flaubert and Other Washington Stories* (Boston: Little, Brown & Co., 1973), pp. 13-14.
24. Jerrold E. Schneider, *Ideological Coalitions in Congress* (Westport, Conn.: Greenwood Press, 1979); and Robert A. Bernstein and William W. Anthony, "The ABM Issue in the Senate, 1968-1970: The Importance of Ideology," *American Political Science Review* (September 1974): 1203.
25. John F. Manley, "The Conservative Coalition in Congress," *American Behavioral Scientist* (December 1973): 223-247.
26. Robert J. Donovan, "For America, A New Coalition?" *Los Angeles Times*, July 6, 1981, pt 2, p. 4.
27. Ronald C. Moe and Steven C. Teel, "Congress as Policy Maker: A Necessary Reappraisal," *Political Science Quarterly* (September 1970): 443-470.
28. Samuel C. Patterson, "The Semi-Sovereign Congress," in *The New American Political System,* ed. Anthony King (Washington, D.C.: American Enterprise Institute for Public Policy Research, 1978), p. 171.
29. Leroy N. Rieselbach, "The Congressional Vote on Foreign Aid, 1939-1958," *American Political Science Review* (June 1964): 372-388.
30. John F. Bibby, Thomas E. Mann, and Norman J. Ornstein, *Vital Statistics on Congress* (Washington, D.C.: American Enterprise Institute, 1980), p. 96.
31. Cleo H. Cherryholmes and Michael J. Shapiro, *Representatives and Roll Calls* (Indianapolis: Bobbs-Merrill Co., 1969).
32. Donald R. Matthews and James A. Stimson, *Yeas and Nays* (New York: John Wiley & Sons, 1975).
33. Aage R. Clausen, *How Congressmen Decide* (New York: St. Martin's Press, 1973).
34. Kovenock, "Influence in the U.S. House of Representatives," p. 456. See also pp. 455, 457.
35. John W. Kingdon, *Congressmen's Voting Decisions,* 2d ed. (New York: Harper & Row, 1981).
36. U.S., Congress, House, Committee on House Administration, *Report on the Activities of the Committee on House Administration During the 96th Congress,* H. Rept. 96-1558, 96th Cong., 2d sess., January 2, 1981, pp. 7-12.
37. Michael Barnes, "What the House Didn't Know About TV," *Washington Post,* April 17, 1979, p. A21.
38. Albert R. Hunt, "Politicians Don't Play Politics All the Time," *Wall Street Journal,* May 14, 1981, p. 26.
39. Roger H. Davidson, *The Role of the Congressman* (Indianapolis: Bobbs-Merrill Co., 1969), pp. 22-23.
40. Robert L. Peabody, "Organization Theory and Legislative Behavior: Bargaining, Hierarchy and Change in the U.S. House of Representatives" (Paper delivered at the annual meeting of the American Political Science Association, New York, N.Y., September 4-7, 1963).
41. Elizabeth Wehr, "White House's Lobbying Apparatus Produces Impressive Tax Vote Victory," *Congressional Quarterly Weekly Report,* August 1, 1981, pp. 1372-1373; Steven V. Roberts, "Reagan Displays Deal-Making Skill," *New York Times,* July 30, 1981, p. D21; and Barton Gellman, "Reagan's Deal on the Budget: A Sweetener for the Sugar Industry," *National Journal,* August 8, 1981, pp. 1417-1421.
42. U.S., Congress, Senate, *Congressional Record,* daily ed., 96th Cong., 1st sess., 1979, pp. S19414-S19415.
43. Sar A. Levitan, *Federal Aid to Depressed Areas* (Baltimore: The Johns Hopkins University Press, 1964).

44. See William H. Riker, *The Theory of Political Coalitions* (New Haven: Yale University Press, 1962), p. 32. Theorists define legislative bargaining situations formally as n-person, zero-sum games where side payments are permitted. That is, a sizable number of participants are involved; when some participants win, others must lose; and participants can trade items outside the substantive issues under consideration.
45. *Guide to Congress,* 2d ed. (Washington, D.C.: Congressional Quarterly, 1976), p. 613.
46. Russell Harden, "Hollow Victory: The Minimum Winning Coalition," *American Political Science Review* (December 1976): 1202-1214.

IV

Policymaking and Change in the Two Congresses

"To get along, go along," Speaker Sam Rayburn's famous adage, characterized much of Congress's policymaking during the twentieth century. A few powerful committee chairmen and party leaders exercised predominant influence in the House and Senate. This situation changed dramatically during the 1970s. Today, scores of legislators—junior and senior—have the opportunity to exercise initiative and creativity in lawmaking and oversight.

Changes of the past decade dispersed power to many more members and further opened Congress to public observation. The benefits and costs of these developments once again reflect the inherent tension between the "two Congresses." On the one hand, greater decentralization and openness enhance Congress's representative role. Members can easily hear diverse and competing constituent views. On the other hand, with so much democracy it frequently takes Congress longer to formulate public policies. Policy stalemate and immobility can result.

The coexistence of electoral and policymaking imperatives helps to explain much of Congress's behavior. Electoral incentives may promote congressional deference to the White House on some issues. For other problems Congress decisively exercises its prerogatives. In our final two chapters, we explore the characteristics of congressional policymaking and the adjustments Congress has made to changes in its internal and external environments.

14

Congressional Policymaking

When the bleary-eyed 96th Congress finally packed its bags
and went home in the predawn hours of December 16, 1980, few
members regretted its end. By most measures the Congress had
fallen short of success. Wrangling over issues both trivial
and momentous, it had been unable to approve appropriations
bills for the federal government, contenting itself finally with a
continuing resolution to ensure funding at the previous year's
level. When the Congress adjourned, other pressing business
remained unresolved. The month before, the Democrats, who had
controlled both the White House and Capitol Hill, had been
rejected at the polls. The men and women of the 96th Congress,
like their predecessors, would have to await history's verdict on
their efforts.

Thus far we have described the structure of Congress and its
procedures for making policy. However, as political scientists
are coming to realize more and more, the bottom line is the policies themselves. The topics we have already described in Parts I,
II, and III—the motivations and careers of legislators, and the
organization and procedure of legislating—both reflect political
realities and shape resulting policies. If one fully understands
these forces, the policies themselves will seem quite predictable.

405

WHAT IS POLICYMAKING?

Because policies are ultimately what government is about, it is not surprising that definitions of policy and policymaking are diverse and influenced by the beholder's eye. David Easton's celebrated definition of public policy as society's "authoritative allocations" of values or resources is one approach to the question.[1] Put another way, policies can be regarded as reflecting "who gets what, when, and how" in a society.[2] A more serviceable definition of policy is offered by Randall Ripley and Grace Franklin: policy is what the government says and does about perceived problems.[3] Thus policies are government actions or statements aimed at dealing with problems that have been identified as important to citizens.

How do we recognize policies when we see them? The answer is not as simple as it may seem. Many policies, of course, are explicitly labeled and recognized as being authoritative statements of what the government is doing, or intends to do, about a given matter. The 2,961 measures passed by the 96th Congress fall into this category. They may be far-reaching, like launching a national synthetic fuels program; they may be trivial, like proclaiming a "national doughnut week." Nonetheless, they are obvious statements of policy. They are written down, often in painfully precise legal language. Many have documented life histories in committee hearings, reports, or floor deliberations that indicate what legislators had in mind as they hammered out the policy's final provisions.

The other two branches have analogous bodies of formal policies: executive orders and regulations, and opinions of its Supreme Court and inferior courts. For example, "affirmative action" policies rest upon a 1965 Executive Order issued by President Lyndon Johnson. Judicial policies are numerous and well-documented.

Not all policies, however, are formal enough to be considered "the law of the land." Some are articulated by officials but for one reason or another are never set down in laws or rules. The "Monroe Doctrine," which declared U.S. resistance to European intervention in the Western Hemisphere, was developed by Secretary of State John Quincy Adams in the second decade of the nineteenth century and repeated for a century and a half by successive chief executives. Other policies, especially of a symbolic or exhorting nature, gain currency in the eyes of elites or the public without formal or legal elaboration.

Some policies stress substance—programs designed to build the nation's defense, for example. Others stress procedure, such as requiring multiyear contracting for military weapons, imposing personnel ceilings on federal agencies, or mandating improvements in program management. The Reagan administration, in one instance, recommended legislation that would make it easier for program managers to collect delinquent debts ($25 billion is past due) owed by citizens to the federal government.

Other policies are amalgams of rules or practices meeting specific demands but not perceived as comprising a whole. It was not until the 1970s that people began to talk of "energy policy"; but in truth the nation had such policy for at least two generations—a something-for-everything mixture of producers' tax advantages, artificially low consumer costs, and subsidies for mobility, suburban sprawl, and gasoline-powered transportation (e.g., highways). This hodgepodge of programs, which encouraged inefficient use of energy and guaranteed dependence upon foreign oil, haunts the nation's energy policy even today.

Finally, there are policies that are made by negation. Doing nothing about a problem often has results that are as profound as passing a law about it. The nation had no overall immigration law prior to 1924 and no medical care program before 1965, but its policies on those matters—in favor of unregulated private activity—were unmistakable.

The process of arriving at these policies is *policymaking*. This process may be simple or complex. It may be highly publicized or nearly invisible. It may be highly concentrated or diffuse. It may happen quickly, as when President Harry S Truman decided in 1950 to engage U.S. troops in the Korean conflict. It may require years or even decades to formulate, as in the case of medicare or civil rights.[4] Whatever the time frame, policymaking normally passes through several distinct stages or phases.

Stages of Policymaking

Agenda Setting. In this initial stage, public problems are identified and established as proper subjects for political discussion. In a large, diverse country such as the United States, the size and shape of the "national agenda" are constantly debated. This agenda is shaped by politicians, of course, but even more by events and by experts and concerned citizens from every walk of life—scientists, technicians, clergy, social activists, lawyers, and spokespersons for various interests. In the 1960s for example, pro-choice activists pushed the subject of abortion onto the agenda and lobbied for liberalized state and federal laws; a few years later, anti-abortionists succeeded in returning the subject to the agenda and reversing some of the pro-choice policies.

Political agendas are broader and more detailed than in earlier times. For better or worse, political leaders are expected to present "solutions" to "problems" expressed by constituents or organized groups. As might be expected, government action is often costly or ineffective in affecting large-scale physical or social forces—for example, technological innovations, global changes, population movements, or business cycles. When government actions fail to deliver the promised or hoped-for results, cynicism typically results. Still, politicians hesitate to tell voters that proposed solutions may not succeed in resolving public problems.

Policy Formulation. In the second stage of policymaking, problems on the political agenda are discussed and potential solutions explored. At this stage, members of Congress and their staffs play crucial roles by conducting hearings and writing committee reports. They are aided by policy experts in executive agencies, interest groups, and the private sector.

Congress's role as a policy formulator is enhanced when there is public and member consensus about the urgency of problems and how they ought to be resolved. Without consensus, there are limits to what Congress or the president can do to resolve major problems. "People can't agree on the facts, let alone the answer" to the energy crisis, once declared Representative Morris K. Udall, D-Ariz.[5] The intractability of many modern issues further complicates the consensus-building process. Representative Thomas Foley, D-Wash., finds issues today far more complicated than when he came to Congress in 1965:

> ...15 years ago, the civil rights issue facing the legislators was whether the right to vote should be federally guaranteed for blacks and Hispanics. Now members are called on to deal with more ambiguous policies like affirmative action and racial quotas.[6]

Another term for this stage is "policy incubation," which entails "keeping a proposal alive while it picks up support, or waits for a better climate, or while a consensus begins to form that the problem to which it is addressed exists."[7] Sometimes this process takes only a few months; more often it requires years. During the Eisenhower administration (1953-1961), for example, congressional Democrats explored and refined policy options that, while not immediately accepted, were ripe for adoption by the time the party captured the White House.[8]

Although policy incubation occurs in both chambers, it is especially promoted in the Senate because of that body's flexible rules, more varied constituent pressures, and greater news media coverage. The policy-generating role is particularly characteristic of senators with presidential ambitions, who need to capture both press and public attention.[9]

Policy Legitimation. Once policies are ripe for adoption, they must gain popular acceptance. This is the function of legitimation, the process through which policies are invested with an air of rightness or propriety. Inasmuch as citizens are expected to comply with laws or regulations—pay taxes, observe rules, or make sacrifices of one sort or another—the policies themselves must appear to have been properly considered and enacted. A nation whose policies lack legitimacy is in deep trouble.

Such symbolic acts as voting on the House or Senate floor or bill-signing by the president signal to everyone that policies have been duly adopted according to traditional forms. Hearings and debates, more-over, serve not only to fine-tune policies but also to cultivate support among affected interests. Answering critics of Congress's slowness in adopting energy legislation, Senator Ted Stevens, R-Alaska, asked:

> Would you want an energy bill to flow through the Senate and not have anyone consider the impacts on housing or on the automotive industry or on the energy industries that provide our light and power? Should we ignore the problems of the miner or the producer or the distributor? Our legislative process must reflect all of those problems if the public is to have confidence in the government.[10]

Legitimizing, in other words, often demands a measured pace and attention to procedural details.

Program Implementation. In the final stage, policies shaped by the legislature and the highest executive levels are put into into effect, usually by a federal agency.[11] Policies are not self-executing: they must be promulgated and enforced. A law or executive order rarely tells exactly how a particular policy will be implemented. Congress and the president usually delegate most decisions to the responsible agencies under broad but stated guidelines.

Implementation determines the ultimate impact of policies. Offi-cials at the sub-cabinet level can thwart a policy by foot-dragging or sheer inefficiency. By the same token, zealous administrators can push a policy far beyond its creators' intent. The ponderous rules for workplace safety were not part of the Occupational Safety and Health Act passed by Congress in 1970, but were regulations promul-gated later by the Occupational Safety and Health Administration (OSHA).

Although legislators do not directly implement policies, they often play crucial roles. Numerous statutes require executives to report to or consult with congressional committees; many include formal procedures for congressional approval and disapproval. Committee oversight is also employed to support—and not just criticize—agency activities. A study of medicare found that the Senate Finance Committee promoted certain administrative policies "through committee investigations, hearings, and reports which had been previously advocated by administrators within the Bureau of Health Insurance...but which were vetoed at higher levels of the bureaucracy."[12] Oversight of the executive branch is, as noted in Chapter 11, a cherished congressional prerogative, some-times honored more in the breach than in reality. Congress can and often does pass judgment on how policies are implemented by adjusting funding, introducing amendments, or recasting the basic legislation governing the policy.

A Shared Responsibility

Some policies follow faithfully the agenda-setting, formulation, legitimation, and implementation stages; others gestate quite rapidly, with the stages occurring simultaneously. Similarly, institutional involvement differs widely. Legislative activity is likely to be greatest in formulating and legitimating policies; moreover, formulation is typically identified with subcommittees and committees, whereas legitimation tends to occur in full chamber deliberation, voting, and bill signing. Congress is less apt to play a leading part at other policymaking stages: agenda setting is usually accomplished by presidents and by private individuals and groups, whereas implementation is historically the province of executive agencies. Yet here, too, distinctions are relative rather than absolute. Legislators, usually acting individually, strive to shape the national agenda; Congress participates in implementing policies through oversight and other techniques.

This flexibility is part of the constitutional design. The Founders clearly envisioned a government, *not* of separate structures performing separate functions, but of separate structures *sharing* functions. As James Madison expressed it, the Constitution created a government of blended powers.[13]

Bicameralism

Another influence on legislative policymaking is the existence of two separate chambers, each with its special character and dynamics. As noted in Chapter 2, the writers of the Constitution expected bicameralism to produce wiser laws, with the Senate's stability and expertise countering the House's popular sentiments. Whether or not these intentions have been borne out, bicameralism unquestionably makes lawmaking more complicated and time-consuming. With two separate sets of legislative hurdles to surmount, many potential laws are simply not enacted. At the end of the 96th Congress (1979-1981), 330 bills were left stranded after passing one house but not the other.

Several differences between the two chambers powerfully influence their policymaking biases: the terms of office, the size and character of the constituencies, and the size of the legislative body itself. Six-year terms, it is argued, allow senators to play the "statesman" for at least part of each term, before they are forced by oncoming elections to concentrate on fence-mending. This distinction may be more apparent than real, but empirical studies of senators' voting habits lend some support to it. The different constituencies unquestionably pull in divergent directions, as already noted. The more homogeneous House districts often promote clear and unambiguous position-taking on a narrower range of questions, whereas senators must weigh the claims of many competing interests on a broad range of matters. The size of the chambers, moreover, dictates procedural characteristics. House rules are designed to allow majorities to have their way, whereas Senate rules give individual senators lots of elbowroom in influencing action.

A striking instance of divergent House and Senate decisions occurred in the fall of 1980, when President Carter decided to ship nuclear fuel for a power plant in Tarapur, India. Under the statute, the sale would go forward unless both houses of Congress voted against it. Although the House voted 298 to 98 to reject the proposed shipment, the Senate approved it 48 to 46. Public opinion on this issue was not particularly strong. Why then were the House and Senate votes so different?

The leading reason for the divergence had to do with the House's greater reliance on its committees and subcommittees—partly because of its larger size, partly because its committee members cultivate deeper expertise than do their Senate counterparts. The House resolution of disapproval was sponsored by 25 of the 33 Foreign Affairs Committee members. Chairman Clem Zablocki, D-Wis., strongly opposed the sale, as did Jonathan Bingham, D-N.Y., the highly regarded representative who led the floor fight against the sale and whose International Trade Subcommittee voted unanimously against it. In contrast, the Senate Foreign Relations Committee was badly divided, voting 8 to 7 to disapprove the shipment, and its members lacked the clout of their House counterparts. Senators, too, were more inclined to support the president in a close foreign policy decision, no doubt partly because of their special constitutional role in foreign policy. Finally, White House lobbying focused on the Senate, where Secretary of State Edmund Muskie helped persuade a number of his former Senate colleagues to support the president.

Are the biases of the two bodies consistent? Probably not. In the post-World War II era, the Senate appeared more "liberal" than the House because of the presence of urban configurations in most of the states and the lingering effects of malapportionment favoring rural areas in drawing House districts.[14] Today, however, that generalization would be hard to sustain. In the 97th Congress (1981-1983), for example, Republicans controlled the Senate while Democrats retained a majority, however precarious, in the House. Viewing the mixed long-term results, Benjamin Page concludes that bicameralism is less important in promoting or discouraging particular kinds of policies than in "the furtherance of deliberation, the production of evidence, and the revealing of error."[15]

Federalism

In addition to the horizontal dispersion of power among the branches of government and legislative chambers, power is distributed vertically by levels—local, state, and national. The Constitution delegates to Congress an impressive array of explicit and implied powers. All powers not explicitly delegated, the Tenth Amendment adds, are reserved to the states or to the people. These reserved powers, although not enumerated, fall into four categories: 1) police powers—for protecting and promoting public health, safety, welfare, and morals; 2) taxing and spending powers; 3) proprietary power—to own and operate economic enterprises; and 4) the power to take private property for public use, with just compensation (eminent domain).[16]

Although the national government's policy role has grown, state and local governments have expanded far more. Only one out of every five governmental employees in this country works for the federal government. Federal grants to states and localities have risen both in absolute figures and in proportion to total federal outlays. Today, nearly 20 percent of federal outlays are in the form of grants to states and localities, representing more than one-quarter of the latter's expenditures. In short, while national and local policies are necessarily intertwined, public policies are more likely to be local in focus than national. Indeed, most policies that closely affect our daily lives are local in nature: police and fire protection, roads and utilities, zoning, schools, and delivery of unemployment and welfare benefits.

The level of government making a policy is important for several reasons. First, interest groups wield different degrees of influence at various governmental levels. Racial, ethnic, and labor groups, for example, traditionally prefer national legislation over local control; business and industry groups tend to prefer local action, which they feel more confident of bending to their purposes. This is the reality underlying debates over targeted "categorical programs" with standards closely specified by the federal government, and "block grant" programs, where local officials are granted leeway in spending federal monies. In 1980 there were about 500 categorical programs. One goal of the Reagan administration is to consolidate these programs into block grants controlled by the states. This effort has been only partly successful because Washington lobbyists, not to mention congressional policymakers, tend to prefer tight control over federal funds.

Second, policymakers are sensitive to local traditions, some of which may be far ahead of the "nationwide consensus" and others of which may lag behind. Members of Congress represent localities and often share local policymakers' views.

Finally, national policies can be advanced or hindered by state and local governments, which may adopt policies that contradict or hamper national policy. Debate over extending the Voting Rights Act of 1965, for example, raised the question of how far the federal government should go to ensure compliance with the law of the land—in this case, the Fifteenth Amendment's voting guarantees. States' rights advocates view the act as an insulting interference with local powers—for example, requiring 13 southern states and parts of 19 others to obtain Justice Department approval before changing voting procedures. Civil rights groups counter that blacks still face voting barriers and need the act's protection. At least one conservative, Representative Henry J. Hyde, R-Ill., switched his position after 1981 Judiciary Committee hearings detailing "horror stories" of obstacles confronting blacks who try to vote in the South. Despite his dislike of federal control, he concluded that "we have a long way to go before people will be fully enfranchised." [17]

Many policy debates therefore revolve around the governmental level at which they should be resolved. Such discussions are not confined to the efficiency of a given level but reflect differences over the content of policies as well.

The 'Subgovernment' Phenomenon

Subgovernment networks of bureaucratic agencies, congressional committees (or subcommitees), and interest groups often dominate policy within a given field so that outsiders (including the president and general public) have minimal leverage. If the principal actors are in agreement, they have a good chance of controlling policy outcomes that affect them. If these actors are able to conduct their business outside the glare of publicity, their chances of domination are even better.

Congressional committees and subcommittees are active partners in these triangular relationships. As we have already seen, committee memberships are frequently biased toward the interest handled by the committee. "It has generally been regarded," noted then Representative Charles Wiggins, R-Calif., "that the members of the committees should almost be partisans for the legislation that goes through the committee and for the interest groups that are affected by it." [18] Frequently this means avoiding oversight of programs and downplaying rifts or problems. If the Agriculture Committee were to make a thoroughgoing review of the Department of Agriculture, former Chairman W. R. Poage, D-Texas, once remarked,

> About all we would accomplish, as I see it, is to create hard feeling, a loss of confidence on the part of our farmers that the Department of Agriculture could render them a service, because we can be so critical of the Department...that there won't be any farmer in the nation that will have any confidence.[19]

No wonder, then, that authorizing committees agonized over the 1981 budget cuts, or that Reagan and his advisers decided to use the budget process as a lever to bring the committees into line.

Sometimes events break open these "cozy triangles" of power. A 1962 scandal over the controversial drug thalidomide, for example, pressured legislators to enact stricter drug-testing standards; Ralph Nader's activism in the mid-1960s persuaded Congress to adopt auto safety standards. The public's attention span is brief, however. After such upheavals, subgovernments often revert to their prior behavior, perhaps with a new balance of power imposed by the short-lived crisis. Not all public policy can be explained in terms of such segmented arenas, but a surprisingly large portion of policymaking conforms roughly to this picture.

DOMESTIC POLICIES

A key to understanding public policies is to understand the nature of the policies themselves. Scholars have classified policies in many different ways.[20] The typology we will use identifies three types of domestic policies—distributive, regulatory, and redistributive—and three types of foreign and military policies—structural, strategic, and crisis.

Distributive Policies

Distributive policies or programs are governmental actions that convey tangible benefits to private individuals, groups, or firms. Invariably there are subsidies to favored individuals or groups. The typical policymaking arrangement is the subgovernment, comprised of the congressional subcommittee (or committee), the executive agency, and the clientele group that expects to receive the benefit. The dominant decision mode is logrolling, in which benefits are separated and given directly to recipients. Typically the chief actors display unity and are low in visibility.

Distributive politics are highly attractive to Congress, which as a nonhierarchical institution must build coalitions in order to function. A textbook example was the $1-billion-plus National Parks and Recreation Act fashioned by Representative Phillip Burton, D-Calif., in 1978. Dubbed the "park barrel" bill, it created so many parks, historical sites, seashores, wilderness areas, wild and scenic rivers, and national trails that it sailed through the Interior Committee and passed the House by a 341 to 61 vote. "Notice how quiet we are. We all got something in there," said Representative Trent Lott, R-Miss., after the Rules Committee cleared the bill in five minutes flat. Another member explained: "If it had a blade of grass and a squirrel, it got in the bill." [21] Distributive politics of this kind throw into sharp relief the two Congresses notion: national policy as a mosaic of local interests.

Distributive politics assume various forms. In some instances, the subgovernments are tightly knit and can dominate policies. Agricultural price supports, for example, are upheld by firm alliances between commodity interests (producers of cotton, wheat, tobacco, and dairy products, among others), friendly members of Congress on the agriculture committees, and sympathetic officials in the U.S. Department of Agriculture.[22] Similarly, rivers and harbors projects have been dominated by local beneficiaries, relevant congressional committees (and appropriations subcommittees), and the Army Corps of Engineers—a powerful agency that has seized the initiative from rival federal entities.[23] The late Senator Paul Douglas, D-Ill., once characterized public works bills as

> built up out of a whole system of mutual accommodations, in which the favors are widely distributed, with the implicit promise that no one will kick over the apple cart; that if senators do not object to the bill as a whole, they will "get theirs." It is a process, if I may use an inelegant expression, of mutual backscratching and mutual logrolling.[24]

One virtually unbeatable subgovernment is veterans' affairs. The Veterans Administration is a large agency with a wide range of services—including life insurance, mortgage insurance loans, pensions, educational aid, disability compensation, and the nation's largest hospital and medical care system.[25] VA programs are stoutly supported by House and Senate veterans' committees, not to mention such groups as the American Legion, Veterans of Foreign Wars, and Disabled American Veterans. VA programs may duplicate similar programs for the general public and sometimes are delivered regardless of the recipient's need or the relation of the need to military service.

Even when assailed by competing forces, some subgovernments, such as the tobacco industry, maintain unity and are able to fight off or delay opposition. A. Lee Fritschler describes the tobacco subgovernment in the quiet days before health-related attacks upon cigarettes:

> The tobacco subsystem included the paid representatives of the tobacco growers, marketing organizations, and cigarette manufacturers; congressmen representing tobacco constituencies; the leading members of four subcommittees in Congress—two appropriations subcommittees and two substantive legislative committees in each house—that handle tobacco legislation and related appropriations; and certain officials within the Department of Agriculture who were involved with the various tobacco programs of that department. This was a small group of people well known to each other and knowledgeable about all aspects of the tobacco industry and its relationship with the government.
>
> As long as no one objected too loudly, the important and complex tobacco programs, like price supports and export promotion, were conducted without interference from those not included in this subsystem.[26]

By the 1960s, evidence of smoking's harmful effects led to demands from health organizations for curbing cigarette use. Gradually, advertising limits and health warnings were adopted, but they were slow to take effect and their impact upon the industry was slight. Nor did anyone dare remove agricultural subsidies for tobacco growers—an anomalous policy that benefits a number of congressional districts in southern and border states. Even in the face of 1980s assaults on federal spending programs, tobacco subsidies—like most other crop price supports—seemed to live a charmed life.[27]

In other instances, subgovernments are forced to adapt and accept compromises in their goals to survive external challenges. Take, for example, the plight of savings and loan associations that historically have financed the bulk of this country's residential housing. Recent inflation and soaring interest rates imperil the industry, which must pay out more in interest than their old mortgages are bringing in. In the short run the industry lobbied Congress to create an "all-savers' certificate"—a tax break for savers designed to lure back money that had flowed into other investments.[28] For the longer range, the industry and its allies—the congressional banking committees and the Federal Home Loan Bank Board—explored measures that would rescue the industry but alter fundamentally its ways of doing business. Whether the industry and its allies can successfully adapt to changed circumstances, only time will tell.

Some subgovernments compete for benefits. Such is the case in the research and development field, where researchers vie for federal funds, their fortunes roughly reflecting the perceived urgency of their findings. The physical sciences prospered in the post-World War II "cold war" period with its life-and-death emphasis upon nuclear superiority over the Soviet Union. When relations with the Russians thawed in the late 1960s and 1970s, federal support for such research dwindled. The same fate befell the biomedical and health research subgovernment composed of universities, medical schools, private research institutes, and the huge federal National Institutes of Health (NIH). During the 1950s and 1960s, key congressional committee leaders championed such research and made certain it had ample financial support.[29] After 1969, however, fiscal conservatism swung the pendulum against health research, forcing researchers to compete for funds. Cancer researchers, by far the biggest recipients of federal support, split off from other researchers, forcing those dealing with other diseases to lobby for more parity in research support. The two subgovernments—the cancer subgovernment and the one championing broader health funding—rivalled one another.

Distributive politics are attractive to elected politicians because they allow them to supply benefits from the public treasury to their constituents. Distribution is especially well suited to the congressional decisionmaking apparatus with its scattered centers of power and its reliance on logrolling for coalition-building. Nondistributive policies—regulatory or redistributive—are often transformed into distributions to make them more palatable and gain broad support for adoption. Thus regulation, typically instituted to control an industry or activity for the protection of consumers, may turn out to have built-in benefits for the industry itself. Redistributive issues, such as energy allocations, may be made more attractive by setting up new pork barrel mechanisms like the Synthetic Fuels Corporation, whose mission is to disperse funds to a burgeoning synfuels industry in the hopes of overcoming the nation's energy shortfalls.

Yet the government's distributive activities are far from static, and subgovernmental structures change over time. The size and influence of groups wax and wane. New governmental leaders, or the passing of old ones, can shift the subgovernment's access to government agencies. Periodic crises—scandals, labor disputes, natural disasters, or other important events—can fix public attention upon a subgovernment and precipitate changes, either temporary or long-range. Yet subgovernments persist in one form or other in most areas of domestic policy and even some foreign policy fields. And distribution as a policy mode is probably the most common governmental response to problems.

Regulatory Policies

Regulatory policies are designed to protect the public against harm or abuse that might result from unbridled activity. Thus the Food and Drug Administration monitors standards for foodstuffs and tests drugs for purity, safety, and effectiveness. The Federal Trade Commission guards against illegal business practices such as deceptive advertising. The National Labor Relations Board combats unfair labor practices by business firms.

Regulatory policies typically arise from public anger or agitation. A reformist, proregulation coalition forms around the proposition that "there oughta be a law" protecting the public against certain abuses. Federal regulation dates from the nineteenth century. The Interstate Commerce Act and the Sherman Antitrust Act were enacted to protect against transport and monopoly abuses. As the present century dawned, scandalous practices in slaughterhouses and food processing plants, colorfully reported by reform-minded muckraking reporters, led to meatpacking, food, and drug regulations. The 1929 stock market collapse and the Great Depression paved the way for New Deal legislation regulating the banking and securities industries and labor-management relations. Consumer rights and environmental protection came of age in the 1960s and 1970s. Dramatic attacks on unsafe automobiles by consumer crusader Ralph Nader led to new laws mandating tougher safety standards. Concern about smog produced by auto exhausts led to the Clean Air Act of 1970. Later, worry over dwindling fuel supplies produced a timetable for fuel economy standards.

In these cases, and many other similar ones, Congress responded to reformist pressure and passed a law to protect the public. Some theorists refer to such policies as *protective regulation* because their purpose is to protect the public and prevent anticipated abuses. In most cases, the industries stoutly opposed the regulatory thrusts, arguing that the public would be better off with self-regulation or mild guidelines than with tough, detailed standards and cumbersome reporting and enforcement procedures. Faced with stiff competition from efficient foreign cars, for example, the auto industry blamed its plight on the plethora of government regulations—safety, low pollution, and fuel economy.

Congress often enacts vague regulatory laws that state the problem to be resolved and set forth overall objectives. Details are delegated either to a regular cabinet department or a special "independent" regulatory agency. The agency then drafts detailed standards, reporting requirements, and enforcement mechanisms. Such standards and procedures are subject to public comment before they are promulgated in final form. "Over the past several years," noted Senator Lloyd Bentsen, D-Texas, "there has been an increasing tendency for agencies to write 50 pages of regulations to interpret one page of law." [30] Indeed, federal regulations have grown in the last 40 years at an astronomical rate. One indication of this is the growing size of the *Federal Register*, shown in Table 14-1.

Table 14-1 Pages in the *Federal Register,* Selected Years, 1936-1980

Year	Pages
1936	2,599
1946	14,736
1956	10,528
1966	16,850
1976	57,072
1980	87,012

SOURCE: Office of the Federal Register. The office does not keep separate statistics on the actual number of regulations issued each year by federal agencies.

For the first few years, the agency may be driven by zealous individuals (many drawn from the ranks of the proregulation movement) determined to enforce the law to the hilt. As time passes, public attention subsides and the proreform coalition dissipates. Then the regulating agency may evolve comfortable working relationships with the regulated industry, both to ease daily conflicts and to cultivate support for the regulations. Information and personnel flow back and forth between the private and public sectors. In time the industry may even learn to appreciate regulation, using it to discourage potential competitors or reassure the public about standards. Many commentators believe that regulatory agencies are vulnerable to "capture" by the industries with which they deal.[31]

Such trends are not inevitable, however. New events may rekindle an agency's regulatory zeal. Responding to the consumer movement of the 1970s, the Federal Trade Commission stepped up its activities in a variety of industries—textiles, funeral homes, cereals, and others. By the end of the decade, however, the pendulum had swung the other way. Industry complaints about "overregulation" fired congressional efforts to clip the agency's wings. When Congress adopted the Federal Trade Commission Improvement Act in 1980, therefore, it included a legislative veto provision allowing itself a chance to stop trade rules before they became operative.

Competitive regulation is regulatory policy that grants firms or organizations a favored place in the market and helps protect that place by limiting the entry of newcomers to the field. Only occasionally are protective and competitive regulatory policies clearly differentiated. One case is the airline industry, regulated by the Federal Aviation Administration (FAA) and the Civil Aeronautics Board (CAB). The FAA is primarily engaged in protective regulation—certifying aircraft and crews, operating a flight control system, and generally monitoring safety in the airlanes. The CAB, on the other hand, is primarily a regulator of competition—allocating routes and setting fares for various commercial airlines. When the "deregulation" wave hit the industry in the late 1970s, it was the CAB rather than the FAA whose mission came under attack and was curtailed.

Few regulatory activities are so neatly delineated. Most regulations serve the dual purpose of protecting the public while at the same time guarding the competitive position of firms within the regulated industry. The policy thus serves distributive as well as regulatory functions, and for this reason some analysts consider regulation a subtype of distributive politics. The line between distribution and regulation is in fact hard to draw. Many policies contain regulatory elements at least in their inception. Confusion on the airwaves demands licensing for the public's convenience as well as broadcasters'. Assigning airline routes protects competitors but also guards against chaos in air transportation. Many regulations thus serve the industry's convenience, which underscores the pervasiveness of distributive policies and the tendency of policies to slip into the distributive mode even though originated for other purposes.

Conflicts about deregulation began in the late 1970s over the competitive aspects of regulatory policies. The trucking, airline, and broadcasting industries were deregulated because economists and consumer groups concluded that federal regulations wasted resources and ultimately hurt consumers. Initially the industries and their allies, including the regulators and the relevant congressional committees, resisted deregulation. The predictable world of governmental protection seemed more comfortable than the unpredictable world of competition. In these cases the mounting costs of compliance, not to mention the consumers' benefits from competition, overcame the fears of the more conservative sectors of the industry, and Congress authorized pullbacks from earlier regulatory practices.

When leaders from a regulated industry condemn regulation, they usually mean protective regulation. In some industries, regulators and regulated firms engage in continual trench warfare. A reformist coalition led by labor unions and health groups gained passage in 1970 of the Occupational Safety and Health Act, intended to improve workplace safety. The resulting Occupational Safety and Health Administration, however, became bogged down in volumes of rules specifying everything from acceptable levels of harmful chemicals to the proper construction of ladders and the availability of toilets. By the early 1980s industries had succeeded in blunting many of the agency's bolder ventures. Foes of regulatory "red tape" are found not only among firms but also universities, local governments, and ordinary citizens.

Congressional involvement varies with the stage of regulatory policy. When new regulatory policies or major shifts in existing policies are pondered, the full Congress is engaged along with the White House and cabinet-level officials. Ever since the beginning, Congress has viewed regulation as closely allied with the legislative process; the independent regulatory commissions are even set up as multimember bodies like Congress itself. Once a regulatory law is in place, however, involvement tends to be at the level of the individual lawmaker or subcommittee. Frequently legislators lobby for adjustments or exceptions to accommodate certain individuals or firms. Legislators from the proregulation coalition may prod the agency to enforce the regulations more vigorously. If conflicts are unresolved at the subcommittee-bureau level, they may be appealed to higher levels—to the full committee or to the House or Senate chamber. When public attention is again turned on the regulatory policy, the full membership of Congress is engaged. The distributive aspects of regulation tend to be settled in the committee and subcommittee rooms, the protective regulatory aspects in the House or Senate chamber. As a general proposition, therefore, regulatory policies attract broader circles of Capitol Hill policymakers than do distributive policies.

Redistributive Policies

Redistribution is the most difficult of all political feats insofar as it shifts resources visibly from one group to another. Because it is controversial, redistributive policy engages a broad spectrum of politial actors—not only in the House and Senate chambers, but in the executive branch, interest groups, and even the public at large. Redistributive issues tend to be ideological. They often separate liberal and conservative factions because they concern relationships between social and economic classes. As Theodore R. Marmor described the 30-year fight over medical care for the aged:

> Debate [was] ... cast in terms of class conflict.... The leading adversaries ... brought into the opposing camps a large number of groups whose interests were not directly affected by the Medicare outcome.... [I]deological charges and countercharges dominated public discussion, and each side seemed to regard compromise as unacceptable.[32]

Of all public issues, redistribution is the most visible because it involves the most conspicuous allocations of values and resources. Most of the divisive socioeconomic issues of the last generation—civil rights, affirmative action, school busing, the war on poverty, aid to education, job training, tax reform—were redistributive problems. Invariably such issues involve the widest possible circle of political actors—legislators debating on the floor, presidents acting in their most public moments, interest groups articulating their most visceral concerns. Redistributive issues expose the very core of a society's class structure; too many of them appearing at once can rip a society apart with class strife.

Civil rights legislation is redistributive, shifting benefits from advantaged to disadvantaged groups. Many of the most dramatic moments of contemporary congressional policymaking have centered on civil rights—from the passage of major civil rights laws in the 1960s, through subsequent clashes over busing, affirmative action, and bilingual education.

The tax code is another redistributive policy. Tax provisions transfer wealth from one class of citizens to another. "Right now the code oozes with discriminatory provisions," wrote economic analyst Robert J. Samuelson.

> It treats homeowners more favorably than renters. It treats those over 65 more favorably than it treats everybody else. It treats those

who receive a high proportion of their compensation in fringe benefits—many of which aren't taxed—more favorably than those who don't.[33]

Such tax benefits may be defensible public policy; certainly all of them have vocal defenders. The point is that the tax code is easily broken down into a series of provisions benefiting specific groups—the so-called "Christmas tree" aspect of virtually every major tax revision. Thus the Reagan tax bill of 1981 embraced many benefits for the president's constituency—primarily the business community and individuals earning $50,000 or more a year. There were also specific sweeteners for savings and loan companies, commodity traders, and oil companies—among others. Like regulation, then, redistribution easily slips into distributive policy.

Chairman Dan Rostenkowski, D-Ill., at head of table, discusses 1981 tax cut legislation with members of the House Ways and Means Committee. Others from left: J. J. Pickle, D-Texas; Cecil Heftel, D-Hawaii; Sam Gibbons, D-Fla.; Ken Holland, D-S.C.; Thomas J. Downey, D-N.Y.; and Don J. Pease, D-Ohio.

FOREIGN POLICIES

Foreign policy is the sum total of decisions and actions governing a nation's relations with other nations. The major foreign policy ingredients are *national goals* to be achieved and *resources* for achieving them. Statecraft is the art of formulating realistic goals and marshaling appropriate resources.

Ascertaining a nation's goals is no simple matter. Historically, great congressional debates have broken out over divergent and even incompatible foreign policy goals: for example, over ties to old-world powers such as England and France during our nation's first decades, over high versus low tariffs, over American expansionism and industrialization abroad, over involvement in foreign wars. Any given issue is likely to pose a number of competing goals. Foreign policy goals are often articulated in congressional hearings or during debate on the House or Senate floor; however, linkages among goals are less frequently spelled out.

Bearing in mind the dilemmas of identifying national goals and balancing them with national resources, it is helpful to think of several types of foreign and defense policies. *Structural policies* involve deployment of resources or personnel; *strategic policies* advance the nation's interests militarily or otherwise; and *crisis policies* protect the nation's vital interests against specific threats.[35]

Structural Policies

Foreign and military programs require vast resources—millions of employees and billions of dollars annually. Deploying these resources is termed structural policymaking. Examples of these policies include specific weapons systems and procurement decisions, location of military installations, approval of specific weapons sales to foreign powers, sales of surplus goods to foreign countries, and decisions on specific trade restrictions to protect domestic industries. Structural policymaking for foreign and defense issues is virtually the same as distributive policymaking in the domestic realm.

Structural decisions engage a wide variety of political groups. Defense contracts and installations, for example, are sought by business firms, labor unions, local communities, and their representatives on Capitol Hill. The Defense Department's muscle is nurtured by the huge volume of structural, or distributive, decisions it controls. In contrast, the State Department makes relatively few such decisions, which constricts its ties with domestic interest-group clienteles.

As might be expected, structural decisions, like distributive ones, are typically reached in congressional subcommittees. Legislators from areas containing major military installations or defense contractors lobby with executive agencies for continued support, and subcommittee decisions are reached with local needs in mind.[36] Rarely do these issues leak out onto the floor, for interested members can usually reach accommodation on allocating defense resources. "People used to worry about the power of the military-industrial complex," said a retired admiral. But now, he says, the "congressional-industrial complex" often has a greater influence on boosting spending for military arms.[37]

Strategic Policies

Given the underlying need to protect the nation's interests, decision-makers face the job of designing strategies toward other nations. Examples of strategic policies include the basic mix of military forces and weapons systems; arms sales to foreign powers; trade inducements or restrictions; allocation of economic, military, and technical aid to less developed nations; the extent of treaty obligations to other nations; and our basic stance toward such international bodies as the United Nations and world banking agencies. Strategic policies embrace most of what are commonly thought of as major foreign policy questions.

Strategic policies engage not only top-level executive decision-makers, but also congressional committees and middle-level executive officers. The State Department is a key agency for strategic decision-making, as is the Office of the Secretary of Defense and the National Security Council. Strategic issues are generally accorded less public and media attention than crisis situations; however, they can engage citizens' ideological, ethnic, racial, or economic interests.[38]

Debate over the Panama Canal treaties in 1977 and 1978 is a classic instance of congressional participation in strategic policies. Built during an expansive period of U.S. history, the canal is a source of national pride. Throughout debate on the canal treaties, the bulk of U.S. public opinion opposed "giveaway" of the strategically important canal. To the Panamanians, however, the U.S.-run canal, and the 10-mile-wide U.S.-controlled zone cutting their nation in two, affronted their dignity and sovereignty. After years of unrest, the two countries agreed in 1964 to discuss replacing the old 1903 treaty, under which the U.S. owned and operated the canal and had perpetual sovereignty over the canal zone. After 13 years of negotiation, new treaties were signed by President Carter and the late Panamanian General Omar Torrijos. Under the new treaties the U.S. agreed to operate the canal jointly until 1999, when it would pass to Panamanian control; in return, U.S. usage of the canal would be guaranteed, along with the canal's neutrality.

Congressional involvement occurred at all levels, embracing individual legislators, committees, and the full chambers. Several executive agencies were engaged, and at crucial negotiating and ratifying stages the president, secretary of state, and key advisers were brought into the fray.[39] Within the government, opinion was divided on the direction of the negotiations. The State Department, worried about U.S.-Panamanian relations and world opinion, counseled a flexible U.S. position—a view reflected by the Senate Foreign Relations and House Foreign Affairs Committees. The army, which operated the canal and governed the canal zone, argued strongly for keeping the status quo; the Joint Chiefs of Staff, responsible for defending the area, worried about military base rights, access, and U.S. military personnel. On the Hill, the Armed Services committees tended to go along with this approach. The Panama Canal Company, facing abolition by the treaties, naturally opposed any change. Its view was echoed by the Merchant Marine and Fisheries Committee, which held jurisdiction over the canal in the House and which argued that the canal was U.S. property and therefore could not be disposed of by treaty, but only by legislation approved by both houses.

Once the treaties were signed, Congress conducted a meticulous review and forced some crucial changes in the provisions. The Senate Foreign Relations Committee's published record of hearings and deliberations comprised four volumes totaling 2,423 pages. Senate floor debate continued for two and a half months, to the virtual exclusion of other business—the longest such debate since the Treaty of Versailles was considered in 1919. In the process, senators offered some 192 changes to the treaties. Prior to the debate, almost half the Senate visited Panama and talked to General Torrijos and other Panamanian officials.[40] A group headed by then-Minority Leader Howard H. Baker, Jr., R-Tenn., advised General Torrijos that the treaty as signed could not be ratified, and that U.S. rights for protecting the canal would have to be spelled out. These alterations, which removed ambiguities in the treaties, were accepted. Later, a freshman senator, Dennis DeConcini, D-Ariz., successfully pushed an amendment allowing the U.S. to use military force in Panama or take other steps to keep the canal open after the year 2000. This amendment was accepted by President Carter and adopted by the Senate, even though it caused a furor among the Panamanians and had to be clarified by yet another round of talks. Other senators were wooed by administration concessions on matters quite unrelated to the treaties—one more instance of logrolling as a technique for gaining support.

When Senate debate concluded in April 1978, the two treaty documents—as revised—were finally ratified by identical votes of 68 to 32. To implement the treaties, however, legislation had to be passed by both houses. Here the House members, who had stood on the sidelines during the ratification debate, drove a series of hard bargains which in reality added further conditions to the treaties.

The Panama Canal treaties illustrate Congress's assertiveness in strategic affairs, even to the extent of having individual legislators take part in diplomatic negotiations. This was exemplified by the Senate ratification debate and the activities of individual senators under pressure in voting on the treaties. It extended, too, to the activities of several committees in the negotiation and postratification stages. Finally, the case illustrates the House's determination to deliberate on major foreign policy issues, despite the Senate's historic role in ratifying treaties. Because of the congressional input, the treaties were ratified in a form that preserved their original purpose while ensuring that U.S. security needs were met.

Crisis Policies

Self-preservation may not be the sole goal of foreign or military policy; but when it is directly threatened, other goals are shunted aside. One definition of an international crisis is a sudden challenge to the nation's safety and security. Examples range from the Japanese attack on Pearl Harbor in 1941 to the Iranian seizure of American citizens in 1979.

Crisis policies engage decisionmakers at the very highest levels: the president, the secretaries of state and defense, the National Security Council, and the Joint Chiefs of Staff. Occasionally, a few congressional leaders are brought into the picture; sometimes, as in the failed 1980 attempt to rescue the American hostages in Iran, no consultation is undertaken. Even more rarely, congressional advice is sought and heeded: congressional leaders' opposition dissuaded President Eisenhower from intervening in Indochina in 1954.[41] However, when executive decisionmakers fear congressional opposition, they often simply neglect to inform Capitol Hill.

As long as the crisis lasts, policymakers keep a tight rein on information flowing upward from line officers. Public and media attention is riveted upon crisis events. Patriotism runs high; citizens hasten to "rally 'round the flag" and support whatever course the decisionmakers choose.[42] When the crisis and its sense of urgency subsides, competing information is more readily available and the executive's monopoly of information and initiative is blunted. As the urgency passes, too, congressional critics may be emboldened to voice reservations about the president's course of action.

Most foreign and defense policymaking is aimed at deterring crises—that is, preventing direct challenges to the nation's survival or sense of honor. Yet, with public attention and support at their highest levels, crises give officials unique leadership opportunities. Thus leaders sometimes promote a crisis atmosphere in the hope of grabbing people's attention and mobilizing support. President Carter hoped to raise public awareness of the energy crisis by calling it "the moral equivalent of war." In the early months of the 1980 presidential campaign, Carter reaped benefits from the Iranian hostage crisis. However, sustaining a crisis psychology over a long period of time is virtually impossible short of an all-out war effort. President Johnson's failure to maintain a sense of crisis during the Vietnam war betokened a loss of support for the war itself. Although President Carter initially benefited from the rallying effect of the hostage crisis, the fact that the situation dragged on in the face of the administration's inability to resolve it ultimately harmed Carter's reelection prospects.

CONGRESS AND POLICYMAKING

As a policymaking machine, Congress displays several important traits. It is decentralized, having few mechanisms for integrating or coordinating its policy decisions. It is representative, especially where geographic interests are concerned. It is reactive, mirroring prevailing public or elite perceptions of problems. It looks to the present or the immediate past because its perspective is limited by electoral timetables. It responds to popular symbols. Members' careers rest as much or more upon public impressions as upon substantive achievements. And it typically involves contending sides who seek advantages over their opponents. No wonder journalists, scholars, and political commentators depict legislation as being "killed," "murdered," "stabbed," "gored," or "assassinated." These metaphors underscore that lawmaking is not child's play. It can be a rough, bruising process that determines the fate of personal goals and national policies.

To be sure, policies mirror Congress's institutional attributes. Policies are typically considered piecemeal, reflecting the patchwork of committee and subcommittee jurisdictions. Sometimes policies are duplicative or even contradictory; committees may sponsor price supports and agricultural research promoting tobacco production on the one hand and research on lung cancer on the other. Congress's segmented decisionmaking is typified by authorizing and appropriating processes in which committees consider individual programs, often with little consultation among them.

Congressional policies respond to constituents' needs, particularly those that can be mapped geographically. Sometimes these needs are pinpointed with startling directness. For example, a 1979 aviation noise control bill required construction of a control tower "at latitude 40 degrees, 43 minutes, 45 seconds north and at longitude 73 degrees, 24 minutes, 50 seconds west"—the exact location of a Farmingdale, N.Y., airport in the district of Democratic Representative Jerome A. Ambro, who requested the provision.[43] More commonly, programs are directed toward states, municipalities, counties, or geographic regions like metropolitan areas. Funds are often transferred directly to local governmental agencies, which in turn deliver the aid or services to citizens. Or local agencies may act, individually or in consortiums, as "prime sponsors" for a bundle of closely related services—in community development or worker training, for example—that can be tailored according to the decisions of local-level councils. Eligibility requirements are often written quite specifically to cover given groupings or geographic areas.

And regional agencies, such as the Economic Development Administration or the Appalachian Regional Commission, are quite popular on Capitol Hill—not only because they dispense federal funds, but because they boast a ready-made lobby of local senators and representatives.[44]

Congress is essentially a reactive institution. Members continually take soundings of constituent opinions; skillful legislators react as their constituents would do even without overt consultation. At any given moment, elected officials are seldom either far ahead or far behind the collective views of the citizenry. Hence it would be misguided to expect the national legislature to express "radical" solutions to problems. Not only are members unlikely to entertain such notions, but they know that these views would not attract widespread public support.

Congress is oriented to the present or, more accurately, to the immediate past and the foreseeable future. Because its members live or die by the ballot box, its timetable is dictated by elections. With their two-year terms, representatives face a continuous battle for support and reelection. With their longer terms, senators can stretch out their reelection efforts, but lapses in fence-mending efforts can still be costly. The pressures for publicity and results are immediate and relentless. If the voters' constant challenge is, "What have you done for us lately?" then the politicians' response must be, "This is what I am doing right now." Thus congressional policies often confer immediate benefits and shift costs into the future. This is true of federal budgets and deficits, taxes, social security, and pension plans.

Finally, congressional policymaking deals with appearances as much or more than substantive results. Symbolic actions are important to all politicians. This is not the same thing as saying that politicians are merely cynical manipulators of symbols. Words and concepts—like "equal opportunity," "affirmative action," "cost of living," or "parity"—are contested earnestly in committee rooms and on the House or Senate floor. Thus federal goals are frequently stated in vague, optimistic language, and not spelled out in terms of specific measures of success or failure. Often measures are passed to give the impression that action is being taken when the impact or efficacy of the measure is wholly unknown. From the lawmaker's vantage point, outside groups continually demand: "Don't just stand there, do something." Doing "something" is often the only politically feasible alternative, even when no one really knows what to do or when inaction might be just as effective. This need for action is responsible for the vast number of Capitol Hill speeches and reports, and also for the numerous specific laws and programs—often overlapping or duplicative, sometimes authorizing an agency or program for which the content of the service is unknown.

These attributes restrict Congress's ability to exert systematic policy leadership. Critics repeatedly stress that decentralization makes

Congress more suited for following strong executive initiatives than for shaping its own framework of policy. A striking example was the post-Watergate 94th Congress, which convened amidst high hopes that outsized Democratic majorities and a weakened presidency would lead to a new era of legislative initiative. Barely six months later, Capitol Hill leaders conceded failure. In a remarkable letter to all House committee chairmen, Speaker Carl Albert, D-Okla., confessed that the 94th Congress could not enact "programs and policies that will return us to full employment, economic prosperity and durable social peace and progress." He implored committee chairmen to come up with "something practical—politically, economically, socially and psychologically feasible," for consideration by the next Congress.[45] Senate Majority Leader Mike Mansfield, D-Mont., was even more pessimistic, declining to suggest changes because "the sense of independence each senator has is very important." Improvements, he said, would be a matter of decades.[46]

Recently Congress has moved haltingly toward taking a more systematic, longer-range view of the nation's problems and policies. The Employment Act of 1946 committed the nation to promoting "maximum employment, production, and purchasing power."[47] This would have been simply another vague objective had the act not created three institutions to monitor economic conditions: the Joint Economic Committee (as it is now called), the President's Council of Economic Advisers, and the president's annual economic report. Since then, other laws have been passed that require monitoring and assessment of emerging capabilities, opportunities, and issues. These include the National Environmental Policy Act of 1969; the Resources Planning Act of 1974 and the Resources Conservation Act of 1977; the National Science and Technology Policy, Organization and Priorities Act of 1976; and the Humphrey-Hawkins Full Employment and Balanced Growth Act of 1978—not to mention new analytical and forecasting responsibilities given to committees and congressional support agencies such as the Office of Technology Assessment, Congressional Budget Office, Congressional Research Service, and General Accounting Office.

Whether these developments will alter the character of congressional policymaking is open to question. Congress has been and remains an intensely political institution whose roots and concerns are as varied as the constituencies represented by its members. Its approach to policymaking is therefore segmental, many-sided, and short-range. It has, in short, all the strengths and weaknesses of a representative assembly.

In sum, Congress contributes to national policymaking by providing multiple points of access for diverse viewpoints; reconciling conflicting demands through compromise and bargaining; incubating future public policies; molding national consensus on issues; clarifying and publicizing problems; and reviewing policy implementation. Perhaps Congress's most important policymaking feature is its independence. Unlike many foreign parliaments, Congress can challenge executive actions. It has the power to say no, check unwarranted assertions of presidential authority, compel policy revisions, or even develop its own legislative initiatives.

NOTES

1. David Easton, *The Political System* (New York: Alfred A. Knopf, 1953).
2. Harold D. Lasswell, *Politics: Who Gets What, When, How* (New York: Meridian Books, 1958).
3. Randall B. Ripley and Grace A. Franklin, *Congress, the Bureaucracy, and Public Policy*, rev. ed. (Homewood, Ill.: Dorsey Press, 1980), p. 1.
4. Theodore R. Marmor, *The Politics of Medicare* (Chicago: Aldine Publishing Co., 1973).
5. *Wall Street Journal*, April 6, 1978, p. 2.
6. *Congressional Quarterly Weekly Report*, January 24, 1981, p. 173.
7. Nelson W. Polsby, "Strengthening Congress in National Policy Making," *The Yale Review* (Summer 1970): 481-497.
8. James L. Sundquist, *Politics and Policy: The Eisenhower, Kennedy, and Johnson Years* (Washington, D.C.: The Brookings Institution, 1968).
9. Robert L. Peabody, Norman J. Ornstein, and David W. Rohde, "The Senate as a Presidential Incubator," *Political Science Quarterly* (Summer 1976): 237-258.
10. American Enterprise Institute, *The State of the Congress: Can It Meet Tomorrow's Challenges?* (Washington, D.C.: American Enterprise Institute for Public Policy Research, 1981), p. 8.
11. George C. Edwards III, *Implementing Public Policy* (Washington, D.C.: Congressional Quarterly Press, 1980).
12. John P. Bradley, "Shaping Administrative Policy With the Aid of Congressional Oversight: The Senate Finance Committee and Medicare," *Western Political Quarterly* (December 1980): 493.
13. James Madison, Alexander Hamilton, and John Jay, *The Federalist Papers*, (New York: New American Library, 1961), no. 48.
14. Lewis A. Froman, Jr., *Congressmen and Their Constituencies* (Chicago: Rand McNally & Co., 1963).
15. Benjamin I. Page, "Cooling the Legislative Tea," in *American Politics and Public Policy*, ed. Walter Dean Burnham and Martha Wagner Weinberg (Cambridge, Mass.: MIT Press, 1978), pp. 171-187.
16. James Anderson, David Brady, and Charles C. Bullock III, *Public Policy and Politics in America* (North Scituate, Mass.: Duxbury Press, 1978).
17. Steven V. Roberts, "One Congressman Finds Pragmatism," *New York Times*, July 19, 1981, p. 15.
18. U.S., Congress, House, Select Committee on Committees, *Committee Organization in the House*, H. Doc. 94-187, 94th Cong., 1st sess., 1974, p. 38.
19. Ibid., p. 66.
20. Theodore Lowi, "American Business, Public Policy, Case Studies, and Political Theory," *World Politics* (July 1964): 677-715; Theodore Lowi, "Four Systems of Policy, Politics, and Choice," *Public Administration Review* (July/August 1972): 298-310; Samuel P. Huntington, *The Common*

Defense (New York: Columbia University Press, 1961); and Ripley and Franklin, *Congress, the Bureaucracy, and Public Policy.*

21. Mary Russell, " 'Park-Barrel Bill' Clears House Panel," *Washington Post,* June 22, 1978, p. A3.

22. Charles O. Jones, "Representation in Congress: The Case of the House Agriculture Committee," *American Political Science Review* (June 1961): 358-367; and Theodore Lowi, "Four Systems of Policy."

23. Arthur A. Maass, "Congress and Water Resources," *American Political Science Review* (September 1950): 576-593.

24. Elizabeth Drew, "Dam Outrage: The Story of the Army Engineers," *Atlantic,* April 1970, pp. 51-63.

25. See Sar A. Levitan, *Old Wars Remain Unfinished* (Baltimore: Johns Hopkins University Press, 1973).

26. A. Lee Fritschler, *Smoking and Politics,* 2d ed. (Englewood Cliffs, N.J.: Prentice Hall, 1975), pp. 4-5.

27. Ward Sinclair, "Hill Seen Plowing Under Crucial Farm Issues," *Washington Post,* May 30, 1981, p. A7.

28. Robert G. Kaiser, "Behind the Saving of America's Savings and Loans," *Washington Post,* July 5, 1981, p. A1.

29. Stephen P. Strickland, *Politics, Science, and Dread Disease* (Cambridge, Mass.: Harvard University Press, 1972).

30. U.S., Congress, Senate, *Congressional Record,* daily ed., 95th Cong., 1st sess., March 9, 1977, p. S3793.

31. Marver H. Bernstein, *Regulating Business by Independent Commission* (Princeton: Princeton University Press, 1955).

32. Marmor, *The Politics of Medicare,* pp. 108-109.

33. Robert J. Samuelson, "Dubious Conservatism," *National Journal,* August 8, 1981, p. 1428.

34. Thomas B. Edsall, "Reagan Wins May Be Far-Reaching," *Washington Post,* August 13, 1981, p. A2.

35. Ripley and Franklin, *Congress, the Bureaucracy, and Public Policy,* pp. 184-186; and Huntington, *The Common Defense,* pp. 5-7.

36. Huntington, *The Common Defense,* p. 135.

37. Kenneth H. Bacon, "The Congressional-Industrial Complex," *Wall Street Journal,* February 14, 1978, p. 22.

38. Charles McC. Mathias, Jr., "Ethnic Groups and Foreign Policy," *Foreign Affairs* (Summer 1981): 975-998.

39. Cecil V. Crabb, Jr., and Pat M. Holt, *Invitation to Struggle: Congress, the President and Foreign Policy* (Washington, D.C.: Congressional Quarterly Press, 1980), pp. 65-87.

40. Ibid., p. 79.

41. Chalmers M. Roberts, "The Day We Didn't Go To War," *The Reporter,* September 14, 1954, pp. 30-35.

42. John E. Mueller, *War, Presidents, and Public Opinion* (New York: John Wiley & Sons., 1973), pp. 208-213.

43. *Congressional Quarterly Weekly Report,* May 12, 1979, p. 916.

44. Bill Peterson, "Agencies Have Powerful Friends," *Washington Post,* February 9, 1981, p. A1.

45. David E. Rosenbaum, "Albert Concedes Congress's Failure to Achieve Goals," *New York Times,* June 22, 1975, p. 1.

46. David S. Broder, "Congress's Talk of Leadership: Well, What Happened to It?" *Los Angeles Times,* June 9, 1975, pt. II, p. 7.

47. Stephen K. Bailey, *Congress Makes A Law* (New York: Columbia University Press, 1950).

15

Change in the Two Congresses

Congress has a persistent image problem. The other branches of government have nothing quite like the comic image of Senator Snort, the florid and incompetent windbag. Pundits and humorists—from Mr. Dooley to Johnny Carson, from Thomas Nast to Pat Oliphant—find Congress an inexhaustible source of raw material. Seemingly, the public shares this disdain toward Congress. Since the mid-1960s, public approval Congress's performance has been notoriously low. Fewer than one-third of the respondents in a recent survey approved of the way Congress was handling its job.[1]

Serious commentators' view of Congress is often scarcely more flattering than the public's. Thomas E. Cronin persuasively argues that we have long been beguiled by the awesome image of an all-powerful "textbook president," a combination of Superman and secular saint.[2] If so, we are equally influenced by a stereotype of the "textbook Congress": an irresponsible and slightly sleazy body of people approximating Woodrow Wilson's caustic description of the House as "a disintegrated mass of jarring elements."[3] Legislators in their home states or districts often contribute to this shabby image by portraying themselves as gallant warriors against the dragons back on Capitol Hill: as Richard F. Fenno, Jr., puts it, they "run *for* Congress by running *against* Congress."[4]

Notwithstanding its reputation for inertia, Congress is now dramatically transformed. Changes wrought in the late 1960s and 1970s have reached into virtually every nook and cranny of Capitol Hill—its members, careers, structures, procedures, folkways, and staffs. If those legendary leaders of the 1950s, Sam Rayburn and Lyndon Johnson, were to return to visit the chambers they served with such distinction, they would doubtless be astounded at the transformations that have occurred—even though both men had a hand in bringing them about.

In assaying the current state and future development of Congress, it is important to understand the meaning of these changes. This is no simple task. Some changes were the result of pressures built up over many years; others occurred suddenly and almost offhandedly. Nor are the changes part of a whole cloth, but rather fragments of a puzzling patchwork. It is important to remember also that institutions do not change randomly, but rather in response to pressures either emanating from the external environment or generating from within.[5]

For our discussion of change, we refer once again to our notion of the "two Congresses"—Congress-as-Institution and Congress-as-Career-Entrepreneurs. Although analytically distinct, these two Congresses are inextricably bound together. What affects one sooner or later affects the workings of the other. What forces have affected the functioning of these two Congresses? What changes have occurred in them? What are the current problems of each, and what innovations are likely to be invoked in coming years to alleviate these problems?

CONGRESS AS INSTITUTION

Our age has been called antiparliamentary, and this is surely because of the staggering, shifting challenges emanating from the larger political and social environment. These include pressing national problems, rising public expectations, fast-moving events, competing institutions, and an exploding workload. In country after country, parliamentary forms have been overrun by military dictatorships or bureaucratic regimes after failing to cope with rapidly changing events or escalating political demands. Almost alone among the world's legislatures, the U.S. Congress strives to maintain its autonomy by crafting its own legislation and monitoring the governmental apparatus. Yet many people question whether, realistically, Congress can retain meaningful control, given the complex, interdependent character of current problems.[6]

Like most of the world's legislative bodies, Congress faces a prolonged crisis of adapting to its perplexing environment. Most analysts agree on this point although they differ over the exact causes and nature of the crisis. The crisis is typified by executive ascendancy, as Congress increasingly relies on the president and the bureaucratic apparatus for its legislative agenda and as it delegates ever larger chunks of discretionary authority to bureaucrats. Whatever the immediate sources of the crisis, it is acutely felt on Capitol Hill, and it stretches legislative structures and procedures to their limits if not beyond.

Origins of the Crisis

Many factors in Congress's external environment contribute to a sense of crisis. Government, and Congress in turn, is asked to resolve more problems in quicker fashion than ever before. Constituents are "not content to wait for the normal evolutionary process of debate, dialogue, compromise, resolution, and consensus," observed Representative Thomas S. Foley, D-Wash.[7] As we saw in Chapter 2, the congressional workloads—hours in session, committee meetings, and floor votes, for example—have increased dramatically in recent years.[8] A further complication is that many issues (controlling inflation, for example) are shaped by circumstances beyond Congress's control, such as natural disasters or price hikes by the Organization of Petroleum Exporting Countries (OPEC).

Relative to these policy demands, resources for resolving them in politically attractive ways have probably dwindled. It is vexing enough to shape policies for an affluent society; in an era of limits the task is excruciating, especially when there are so many well-organized and competing interest groups. Rather than distributing benefits, politicians find themselves having to assign costs or cutbacks. This represents a shift from distributive to redistributive policies—a disconcerting prospect for policymakers because it means higher levels of conflict and disaffection.[9]

The advance of the executive branch establishment causes acute stresses on Capitol Hill. Lawmakers expect sure-handed White House leadership and grumble when it is not forthcoming; yet they chafe under vigorous leadership, sensing a threat to legislative powers. The Nixon administration was a high-water mark in the constitutional struggle between White House and Capitol Hill, with presidential challenges in impoundment, executive privilege, war powers, dismantling of federal programs, and even abuse of the pocket veto. Although the pendulum swung toward Capitol Hill in the post-Watergate years, President Reagan's ability to put his economic proposals on a fast legislative track shows vividly that presidential leadership, backed by skill and grassroots support, can turn the institution around in short order.

Today's problems do not come in familiar packages or respond to traditional solutions. Many of them transcend conventional categories and jurisdictions, not to mention two-year legislative timetables. President Carter's 1977 energy package, embracing more than 100 separate legislative initiatives, was referred to five different House committees plus one ad hoc body. Nearly every House and Senate committee handles some phase of energy policy. What is true of energy is equally true of other broad-gauged topics, such as health, welfare, and international economics.

Longstanding warfare over federal spending levels rages among authorizing, appropriating, budget, and tax-writing committees. Although heightened by external stresses—for example, criticism from the Reagan White House in the early 1980s—this conflict also stems from a clash of committee norms.[10]

Another impetus for change—external in the sense that it emanates from electoral decisions—is the shifting partisan and factional structure manifested in the House and Senate. During the 1960s the tide favored the liberal wing of the Democratic party; 20 years later, conservatives of both parties were in the ascendancy. Party lines themselves have become somewhat blurred, and voting patterns are not as predictable as they once were. Interest groups are flooding into the vacuum left by the parties' decline—not just the few traditionally powerful lobbies, but a bewildering profusion of groups clustering around numerous issues and causes.

Institutional Responses

Attempting to cope with these shifts in its external environment, Congress has adopted several noteworthy innovations: adjustments in the legislative workload, committee and subcommittee proliferation, growth of staff bureaucracies, and "democratization" of the two houses.

Workload Adjustments. In the face of a workload expanding both in quantity and breadth of subject matter, Congress often responds by restricting the depth of its involvement—mainly by concentrating on fewer but more complex issues, delegating more decisions to executive-branch agents, and shifting its own role to that of monitor, vetoer, and overseer. The proliferation of reporting requirements, legislative approval and veto provisions, and oversight activities testifies to this strategic shift. Sometimes, as in the 1973 War Powers Resolution, the innovation takes the form of lending formal recognition to de facto shifts in the constitutional blend of powers. As seen in President Reagan's use of the budget process, shrewd chief executives can turn these innovations to their own purposes.

Heightened dependence upon the executive has not occurred without resistance from conscientious legislators and from those opposed to the drift of legislation. Congress counters by striving to regain control it senses has been lost. In the wake of the Watergate and Vietnam crises, a phase of vigorous reaction took place in which legislators proclaimed their loyalty to the concept of oversight, some even putting the concept into practice. Predictably, cries of congressional "meddling" were heard from the other end of Pennsylvania Avenue. For their part, legislators risk becoming entangled in their own efforts to maintain control: reporting requirements and veto provisions, not to mention more elaborate schemes such as mandated "sunset" for federal programs, could demand at least as much time and attention as drafting the original legislation.

Committee and Subcommittee Proliferation. Perhaps the most significant organizational development on Capitol Hill is the proliferation of work groups. In the 97th Congress (1981-1983), there were approximately 150 House work groups, with the average member serving on six of them. Since 1977 the Senate has succeeded in paring its 175 subcommittees to a little more than 100. This was achieved by coupling consolidation with limits on the number of subcommittee assignments and chairmanships each senator could hold, thus distributing committee posts more equitably.[11] The average number of assignments per senator was cut from approximately 18 (4 committees, 14 subcommittees) to approximately 10 (3 committees and 7 subcommittees).

Even so, the number of work groups in Congress is impressive. Senators and representatives are spread very thinly. Virtually any day the houses are in session, most legislators face conflicts in their meeting schedules. Members are tempted to committee-hop, quorums are hard to maintain, and deliberation suffers. Committee specialization and apprenticeship norms have been diluted, casting doubt on the committees' continued ability to give in-depth consideration to detailed measures that come before them.

Jurisdictional competition among committees is common, resulting in member complaints about the need for tighter scheduling and coordination. Attractive issues often cause an unseemly scramble for advantage—sometimes breaking into open conflict, more frequently simply raising decisionmaking costs by necessitating complicated informal agreements or awkward partitioning of issues. One clue is the number of measures referred to two or more committees—a procedure that gets more people into the act but can also frustrate action.[12]

'Democratization' of Congress. Democracy is in full flower on Capitol Hill. Formal posts of power remain, as do inequalities of influence. But the Senate boasts nothing like its bipartisan conservative "inner club" of the 1950s, which so vexed the little band of liberals. In that chamber the transformation was gradual, symbolized by the "Johnson rule" for spreading desirable committee assignments and the benign majority leadership of Mike Mansfield (1961-1977).[13]

In the House, revolts against senior leadership were spasmodic and occasionally fierce, punctuated by a series of intracommittee revolts against recalcitrant chairmen; dispersion of power into the subcommittees (1971 and 1973); and, finally, overthrow of three unpopular committee chairmen (1975).[14]

The seniority reforms have by no means eliminated seniority. As H. Douglas Price remarked, "Seniority, like monarchy, may be preserved by being deprived of most of its power." [15] That is only part of the story. Seniority has been preserved also by extending its benefits to far more members. In the 97th Congress, all Republican senators and a majority of Democratic representatives were committee or subcommittee chairmen. Thus, there are more seniority leaders in the House and Senate than ever before. If Woodrow Wilson were around to rewrite his classic treatise, *Congressional Government,* he no doubt would have to observe that "Congressional government is subcommittee government." [16]

These changes have made the House and Senate more open, democratic bodies. What the past generation of reform did not solve, however, is how to orchestrate the work of the disparate work groups into some semblance of a coherent whole. Indeed, the advent of subcommittee government compounds the dilemmas of congressional (and presidential) leadership. The next wave of innovation no doubt will focus on unifying what the last wave of changes dispersed.[17]

Growth of Staff Bureaucracies. The most lasting legacy of the Legislative Reorganization Act of 1946 was its commitment to equip Congress with more adequate staff to cope with its rising workload and compete with executive-branch expertise. No visitor to Capitol Hill can fail to be impressed by the number of people who work there. Nearly 17,000 staff aides now work for members and committees; some 23,500 work for the four support agencies: the Congressional Research Service, the Congressional Budget Office, the Office of Technology Assessment, and the General Accounting Office.[18]

The Capitol Hill bureaucracy has grown in ways that betray the character of Congress as a decentralized institution. Congress has begotten not one bureaucracy but many, clustered about centers of power and in a sense defining those centers. Efforts to impose a common framework on the staff apparatus have thus far been stoutly resisted. A 1975-1976 Senate panel (the Commission on the Operation of the Senate or the Culver Commission after its sponsor, Senator John Culver, D-Iowa) and a 1976-1977 House group (the Commission on Administrative Review or the Obey Commission after its chairman, Representative David Obey, D-Wis.) failed in their efforts to streamline the administrative structure of the two chambers.

The Future Agenda

Post-World War II shifts in congressional organization and procedures—shifts that came to a head in the 1970s—reinforced the historic decentralization of the House and Senate. Congressional history is a struggle of the general versus the particular, in which the particular seems the most powerful force. This particularism—so characteristic of Congress from its beginnings and with rare exceptions ever since—is underscored by recent developments.

Two related problems of coordination may very well form the pivots for innovative thrusts in the near future: strengthening the central leadership and recasting the committee system.

Struggle for Leadership. Most critics agree that stronger central leadership is required to orchestrate the activities of the scattered committees and subcommittees, schedule consideration of measures, and provide more efficient central services. Vigorous central leadership might also help Congress solve its image problem by giving the media and the public a handle for identifying what is to most people a confusing, faceless institution.

Today's congressional leaders are stronger, on paper at any rate, than any of their recent predecessors, even the legendary Sam Rayburn and Lyndon Johnson. Speakers exercise significant new powers under the House rules. They can schedule and cluster floor votes; they may make joint, split, or sequential referrals of bills to two or more committees with jurisdictional claims. In addition, the Speakers are empowered to create ad hoc legislative committees to handle bills claimed by two or more committees. These powers are often called into play: in 1977 and 1978 approximately 1,241 measures were multiply referred to committees.[19] Although these devices give Speakers certain leverage on committee scheduling, they have turned out to be a mixed blessing because they underscore the fragmentation and overlap that besets the committee system.

When they are Democrats, Speakers have added powers conferred by the Democratic Caucus. They chair the Democratic Steering and Policy Committee and appoint nearly half its members. They nominate all Democratic members of the House Rules Committee, subject to caucus ratification. For the first time since the days of Speaker Joseph Cannon at the turn of the century, in fact, the Rules Committee serves as a leadership arm in regulating access to the House floor.[20]

On the Senate side, although leadership trends have been less clear-cut, there are signs of real vigor. During his tenure as majority leader (1977-1981), Robert C. Byrd, D-W.Va., a tireless guardian of Senate rules, parlayed his procedural mastery and meticulous attention to detail into unprecedented controls over floor procedure. Recent Senate rules give the majority leader added leverage over bill referrals and committee coordination; and GOP leader Howard H. Baker, Jr., R-Tenn., working with a new team of committee leaders, labored similarly to achieve policy coordination. Precedents and rules limiting post-cloture filibusters give the majority leader and the presiding officer potent weapons to combat dilatory tactics.

Nevertheless, central leadership is suspect, and decentralizing forces still predominate. In the next few years, innovative efforts will probably center on leadership prerogatives.

Leaders, for their part, seem not to know which way to turn. Often they appear reluctant to accept new prerogatives, preferring to rely on informal powers like those that formed the basis of the vigorous leadership of Rayburn and Johnson. Yet House and Senate leaders sense that, although publicly held responsible for congressional performance, they lack adequate power to coordinate or schedule the legislative program. That is why virtually all leaders since Rayburn have supported reforms that promised to increase their leverage in the legislative process.

Committee Realignment. Reorganization efforts have thus far failed to recast House or Senate committees to dovetail with contemporary categories of public problems. The wide-ranging 1974 House committee realignment proposal by the Bolling Committee (House Select Committee on Committees, chaired by Richard Bolling, D-Mo.) fell victim to intense lobbying by committee leaders who opposed curbs on their jurisdictions. The Bolling plan was ambushed by a reverse-lobbying process in which committee members and staffs, seeking to preserve their positions, mobilized support from groups that had previously benefited from committee decisions.[21] A 1977 bid by the Obey Commission to revive committee reorganization was turned down summarily, as was a 1980 effort to create a new energy committee.

The Senate was somewhat more successful when a 1977 realignment package proposed by the Stevenson Committee (the Temporary Select Committee to Study the Committee System, chaired by Adlai E. Stevenson III, D-Ill.) was accepted with modifications. Like the 1946 realignment, the Stevenson package left jurisdictional lines almost untouched, concentrating instead on consolidating several obsolete committees. The scheme was accepted because, by limiting assignments and leadership posts, it succeeded in spreading the workload more equitably among the Senate's more junior members.[22]

Committee modernization is politically the roughest reorganization challenge. It severely upsets the institution's internal balance because it threatens not only individual legislators' committee careers but also their mutually supportive relationships with powerful outside groups.

Nevertheless, many members are profoundly dissatisfied with the existing committee system. In a 1979 survey of 184 House members conducted by the Patterson Committee (another select committee on committees, chaired by Jerry Patterson, D-Cal.) nearly three-quarters of the representatives advocated comprehensive changes in the committee system. At the same time, a similar proportion of the respondents admitted that their colleagues would accept no more than minor alterations.[23] In short, legislators are fully aware of the committee system's disarray, but they cannot bring themselves to pay the price for remedying the problem. The need to coordinate fiscal decisionmaking— scattered among the revenue committees (Senate Finance; House Ways and Means), House and Senate appropriations committees, and House and Senate budget committees—has not abated. The edifice proposed by the 1946 Legislative Reorganization Act—a legislative budget— crumbled even before it was fully erected. Later, prodded by President Nixon's budgetary thrusts, Congress enacted the Budget and Impoundment Control Act of 1974. It has forced legislators to adopt an overall fiscal point of view in making budgetary decisions; and its institutional legacies—the budget committees and the Congressional Budget Office—churn out sophisticated economic data.[24]

Dramatic evidence of the committee system's vulnerability occurred in the first months of the Reagan administration. Rather than choosing the lengthy, laborious path of pushing proposals through the authorizing committees, Reagan and his advisers shrewdly focused on the budget process as a short-cut way of shifting spending priorities. Time was short, they reasoned, and committees would be unwilling to curtail programs they had developed and nurtured. Committees were thus given spending ceilings and told to conform; and when the painful process yielded results somewhat short of the administration's goals, a new budget resolution was prepared and pushed through. Both the process and the product unsettled many lawmakers on both sides of the aisle—especially senior members with an investment in committee specialization. The budget mechanism may or may not be used this way again. But the experience bared the weaknesses of the committee structure, and few could blame the president and his advisers for seeking another way out.

For an institution reputed to be slow and tradition-bound, Congress has launched a surprisingly large number of major reorganization efforts in the past generation. There have been two joint committee investigations (1945 and 1965), three committee realignment efforts (the Bolling, Stevenson, and Patterson committees), two administrative review bodies (the Culver and Obey commissions), and major budgetary reform— eloquent testimony to the persistence of Congress's crisis of adaptation. The agenda of innovation is lengthy, and pressures for institutional innovation are likely to persist.

CONGRESS AS CAREER ENTREPRENEURS

Individual members harbor a variety of goals.[25] All of them, or virtually all, want to get reelected. But men and women—even politicians—do not live by reelection alone. They seek opportunities to contribute, to shape public policy, to see their ideas become reality, to influence others, and to work in dignity and sanity. In a body of 540 politicians, this jostling of individual goals and careers inevitably generates friction.

How fares the second Congress, this Congress-as-Career-Entrepreneurs? Here, the careful analyst faces a combination of puzzling and seemingly inconsistent developments. No less than the institution itself, the individual careers that converge on Capitol Hill are subject to novel stresses and strains. Yet they do not add up to a consistent picture, and there is reason to wonder if congressional careerism has not reached a turning point.

Trends in Congressional Careers

Party Decline. Of all the factors affecting today's politicians, the most conspicuous is the ebbing of political party organizations and loyalties. In only a few areas do party organizations still serve as sponsors and anchors for political careers. Nor do voters depend as heavily as they once did on party labels to guide their choices. Hence, politicians are thrust into the role of individual entrepreneurs, relying on their own resources for building and nurturing supportive constituencies. This yields something resembling a series of cottage industries— a situation very much at odds with the nationalized linkages that mark other sectors of our social and economic life.

Constituency Demands. Rising constituency demands have inundated individual legislators and their staffs. The average state now numbers about 4 million people, the average House district more than half a million. Educational levels have risen; communications and transportation are easier. Public opinion surveys show unmistakably that voters expect legislators to "bring home the bacon" in terms of federal largesse and services, and to communicate frequently with the folks back home.[26] Surveys suggest that constituents' demands will not diminish in the future.

Public Cynicism. Citizens' traditional ambivalence toward politicians turned into overt cynicism in the 1970s. Politicians of all persuasions felt a backlash following Watergate, the Vietnam war, various Capitol Hill scandals, and the seeming ineffectiveness of government programs. A few congressional careers have been halted by personal scandals, perhaps because a "new morality" spotlights practices that previously might have escaped censure. Campaign financing and ethical standards have been singled out by reformist groups such as Common Cause and Ralph Nader's Congress Watch. Members themselves display ambivalence toward such standards: they make the politician's life more difficult, but at the same time they are needed to bolster citizen confidence in elected officials.

The 'Incumbency Party'

Elected officials have countered these career demands by building personal machinery for communicating with constituents and cultivating reelection support. True, U.S. legislators have always been expected to run errands for constituents. In an era of limited government, however, there were few errands to run. In the past generation, the constituency service role has been quantitatively and qualitatively transformed. Responding to perceived demands, senators and representatives have set up veritable assembly lines for communicating with voters, responding to constituents' requests, and even generating those requests through newsletters, targeted mailings, and hot lines. Staff and office allowances have grown, district offices have sprouted over the landscape, and recesses are called "district work periods." This apparatus extends legislators' ability to communicate with constituents, and it provides badly needed help for citizens for whom coping with the federal bureaucracy can be a bewildering and frightening experience.

Constituency service is a profitable enterprise for legislators and their staffs. A 1977 survey found that 15 percent of all citizens (or members of their families) had requested help from a member of Congress. By more than a 2-to-1 margin, the citizens were satisfied with the service they had received.[27] No fewer than two-thirds of the respondents claimed to have received some communication from their representatives; half could correctly identify his or her name. As we explained in Chapter 5, citizens assess their own representatives far more favorably than they do Congress as a whole.

Congressional Careerism in Transition

Congressional careerism—mainly a twentieth-century phenomenon —recently has shown a perceptible downturn, as we saw in Chapter 2. Since 1969 a tide of new members has come to Capitol Hill, following two decades of uncommonly low turnover levels. When the 97th Congress convened in 1981, solid majorities in both chambers had served five years or less; three quarters had arrived on Capitol Hill since Richard Nixon's resignation in 1974.

In the House at least, the turnover did not result solely or even primarily from electoral competition. In the five congressional elections concluding with 1980, 213 representatives retired while only 150 were defeated in primaries or general elections. In 1980, 36 members retired voluntarily and 37 were defeated. Of those members seeking reelection, 91 percent were successful. Put in terms of total turnover, 16 percent of the body's membership changed as a result of retirements or defeats.[28]

In the Senate, reelection is more hazardous. In 1980 just more than half of the incumbent senators who ran for reelection were successful. This was a somewhat lower reelection rate than in other modern elections, but senatorial contests tend to be more competitive than House contests. Five senators retired and 13 were defeated in primaries or general elections in 1980. Total turnover was therefore nearly one-fifth of the Senate's total membership.

Legislators, it used to be said, "never go back to Pocatello." Recently, that has not been true. In unusually high numbers (for modern times), members in fact have chosen to retire from Congress or seek other jobs. Interestingly, a number of these retirements occurred in midcareer, when the legislator could look forward to years of service on Capitol Hill.

High levels of turnover may be transitional or they may signify alteration of congressional careerism. Certainly we have witnessed what journalist David S. Broder has termed the "changing of the guard": the passing of the post-World War II generation of leaders and the rise of a new generation of leaders steeped in the political movements of the 1960s and 1970s—anti-Vietnam war, environmentalism, consumerism, and anti-big-government, to name a few.[29] On the other hand, the turnover may herald a new period when congressional careerism is not so highly valued and members are more willing to leave Congress after a short time.

Some evidence suggests that careerism is threatened by weariness and alienation. In a survey of House members in the mid-1960s, a generally high level of satisfaction with the institution's performance was discovered—an attitude characterized as "a vote of aye—with reservations."[30] A survey conducted a decade later yielded not even such tempered optimism. That study, which focused on foreign policy, uncovered widespread discontent among members of both houses. Dissatisfaction was expressed by four-fifths of the legislators and extended to all groups and factions on Capitol Hill. And in a 1977 survey of House members, only 13 percent of the representatives thought the House was "very effective" in performing its principal functions.[31]

Comments from retirees in the late 1970s reveal disenchantment and relief. Representative James W. Symington, D-Mo., described leaving Congress as "a release from a kind of bondage." Thomas Rees, D-Calif., exulted that he no longer had "to listen to some hysterical person who calls me about an issue that I care nothing about."[32] Otis G. Pike, D-N.Y., retired reportedly because he was "tired of wasting time on drivel."

Perhaps lateral mobility—a phenomenon notably absent in the 1960s—has regained its appeal. It is not coincidental that three of

President Carter's original cabinet-level appointees and two of President Reagan's came from House or Senate posts. Congressional retirement benefits enacted in 1972 have made retirement more attractive than before.

Role Conflicts. Another source of trouble could be increasing conflict between legislative and constituency roles, given the steep escalation of expectations in both areas. Findings from a 1976-1977 member survey in the House convey the distinct impression that members experience severe strains between these two roles. On the whole, members *want* to spend more time on legislation than they actually do. Typically, they rate legislative tasks as more important than constituency service. But legislators cannot escape constituency demands, even if they wanted to do so. When asked to compare the ideal and actual role of a member of Congress, fully half of the representatives interviewed in 1977 stated that "constituent demands detract from other functions"—the most frequently mentioned obstacle.[33]

Nor are public demands likely to abate. We are fast approaching the day when 90 percent of all adults will have received a secondary education and perhaps 50 percent a postsecondary education. Thus, political activity is likely to remain at a high level or even rise—not the old-style activity of the political party cadres, but dispersive involvement in myriads of special-purpose groups and causes. These activists will expect their elected representatives to be responsive. In a recent national survey, citizens expressed the most dissatisfaction with legislators' efforts at public education and communication. Nine out of every 10 respondents said that Congress should do more to inform the public about its activities.[34]

Less obvious is the impact of constituent activities on the institutional life of Congress. It is at least arguable that ever more demanding electoral and ombudsman functions have helped erode the legislative and institutional folkways identified by observers in the 1950s and early 1960s—especially the folkways of specialization, apprenticeship, and institutional loyalty. At the very least, it has placed added demands on members' time and energies. Although most ombudsman activities are actually carried out by staff aides rather than by members themselves, there are inescapable costs to members' own schedules. Larger staffs, while helping lawmakers extend their reach of involvement, require supervision and have a way of generating needs of their own. And with high (and apparently still rising) constituent expectations, there inescapably are many symbolic functions that cannot be delegated to staffs—situations that require members' personal intervention and face-to-face presence.

The Question of Ethics. Post-Watergate morality also weighs heavily on public servants. Details of their lives are exposed, their motives are suspect, and they are often subject to snickering comparisons with such scandals as the Abscam affair. Disclosure and ethics rules have become more stringent. Stung by press and public criticism and wishing to justify a congressional pay raise, both the House and the Senate passed new ethics codes in early 1977. The codes limited the amount that any member may earn from a job outside of Congress to 15 percent of his or her salary. The time-honored practice of members' earning income by making public speeches was curtailed; unofficial office accounts were barred; and public disclosure of the amount and sources of members' incomes was mandated. *(See box, p. 154.)*

The ethics codes exacted a price in legislators' morale. The regulations are controversial (at least on Capitol Hill); reactions in both houses have been bitter, accounting partly for the Senate's delay of outside earnings limits in 1979 and the House's defeat of the Obey Commission's final recommendations in 1977. Whether or not legislators' reactions are justified is debatable; but there is little doubt that senators' and representatives' self-esteem has been damaged. Several members have cited the codes in explaining their decisions to retire from public life.

The past generation of career problems centered around Congress's low turnover rates and unrepresentative membership. This situation has been alleviated. Turnover rose in the 1970s more from voluntary than from involuntary retirements. Today's membership is more diversified: blacks, women, minorities, young people, and nonlawyers are better represented than in prior years.

The next generation's problem could well be how to enhance the attractiveness of the congressional career. With other pursuits becoming more tempting, with leadership within Congress more easily and rapidly attained, with congressional life showing new tensions, tomorrow's critics could conceivably be talking about a problem no one would have taken seriously 20 years ago: how to make certain that the jobs of senators or representatives remain desirable enough so that top-flight individuals are attracted to them and so that their loyalty is commanded once they are there. At the same time, it would be healthy if a greater degree of electoral competition could be fostered.

CONCLUSION

Are the two Congresses ultimately compatible? Or are they diverging, each detrimental to the other? The burden placed on both Congresses is vastly heavier than it was a generation ago. Congress-as-Institution is expected to resolve all sorts of problems—not only in processing legislation, but also in monitoring programs and serving as an all-purpose watchdog. By all outward signs of activity—such as numbers of committees and committee assignments, hearings, votes, and hours in session—legislators are struggling valiantly to keep abreast of these demands.

At the same moment, Congress-as-Career-Entrepreneurs is busier than ever. Partly because of the sheer scope of modern government, partly because of constituents' keener awareness, citizens are insisting that senators and representatives communicate more often, benefit their states or districts materially, and play the role of ombudsmen. It is a function legislators have accepted and profited from, but not without misgivings and not without detriment to their legislative tasks.

The intensified demands upon the two Congresses could well lie beyond the reach of normal men and women. Reflecting on the multiplicity of presidential duties, Woodrow Wilson once remarked that we might be forced to pick out leaders from among "wise and prudent athletes"—a small class of people. The same might now be said of senators and representatives. And if the job specifications exceed reasonable dimensions, can we expect our most talented citizens to volunteer for, and remain at, these jobs?

In the longer view, the question is whether an institution embracing so many disparate motives and careers can continue to function as a coherent whole. Can policies patched together out of so many discrete interests really guide the nation on its perilous course? Ever since 1787, people have wondered about these questions. History is only mildly reassuring; and the future poses new and delicate challenges for which the margin of error may be narrower than in the past. And yet, representative democracy itself is a gamble; the proposition that representation can yield wise policymaking remains a daring one. As always, it is an article of faith whose ultimate proof lies in the future.

NOTES

1. Associated Press/NBC News Poll 66 (April 1981).
2. Thomas E. Cronin, *The State of the Presidency,* 2d ed. (Boston: Little, Brown & Co., 1980).
3. Woodrow Wilson, *Congressional Government,* rev. ed. (New York: Meridian Books, 1956), p. 210.
4. Richard F. Fenno, Jr., *Home Style: House Members in Their Districts* (Boston: Little, Brown & Co., 1978), p. 168.
5. Roger H. Davidson and Walter J. Oleszek, *Congress against Itself* (Bloomington, Ind.: Indiana University Press, 1977).
6. See, for example, Kevin Phillips, "An American Parliament," *Harper's,* November 1980, pp. 14-21; and Lloyd N. Cutler, "To Form A Government," *Foreign Affairs* (Fall 1980): 126-143.

7. U.S., Congress, *Congressional Record,* daily ed., 94th Cong., 2d sess., February 25, 1976, p. E832.
8. U.S., Congress, House, Commission on Administrative Review, *Final Report,* 2 vols., H. Doc. 95-272, 95th Cong., 1st sess., December 31, 1977, 2: 634; and U.S, Congress, Senate, Commission on the Operation of the Senate, *Policy Analysis on Major Issues,* committee print, pp. 5-6.
9. Lester Thurow, *The Zero-Sum Society* (New York: Basic Books, 1980).
10. Allen Schick, *Congress and Money* (Washington, D.C.: The Urban Institute, 1980).
11. Judith H. Parris, "The Senate Reorganizes Its Committees, 1977," *Political Science Quarterly* (Summer 1979): 319-337.
12. U.S., Congress, House, Select Committee on Committees, *Final Report,* H. Rept. 96-866, April 1, 1980, p. 442.
13. Michael Foley, *The New Senate: Liberal Influence on a Conservative Institution, 1959-1972* (New Haven: Yale University Press, 1980).
14. David W. Rohde, "Committee Reform in the House of Representatives and the Subcommittee Bill of Rights," *Annals of the American Academy of Political and Social Sciences* (January 1974): 39-47; and Norman J. Ornstein, "Causes and Consequences of Congressional Change: Subcommittee Reforms in the House of Representatives, 1970-1973," in *Congress in Change,* ed. Norman J. Ornstein (New York: Praeger Publishers, 1975), pp. 88-114.
15. H. Douglas Price, "Congress and the Evolution of Legislative Professionalism," in *Congress in Change,* p. 19.
16. Wilson, *Congressional Government.*
17. Roger H. Davidson, "Subcommittee Government: New Channels for Policy Making," in *The New Congress,* ed. Thomas E. Mann and Norman J. Ornstein (Washington, D.C.: American Enterprise Institute for Public Policy Research, 1981), pp. 99-133.
18. Harrison W. Fox, Jr., and Susan Webb Hammond, *Congressional Staffs* (New York: The Free Press, 1977), pp. 168, 171.
19. House, Select Committee on Committees, *Final Report,* p. 442.
20. Spark M. Matsunaga and Ping Chen, *Rulemakers of the House* (Urbana, Ill.: University of Illinois Press, 1976).
21. Davidson and Oleszek, *Congress against Itself.*
22. Parris, "The Senate Reorganizes."
23. House, Select Committee on Committees, *Final Report,* p. 284.
24. Schick, *Congress and Money.*
25. Richard F. Fenno, Jr., "If, as Ralph Nader Says, Congress is 'the Broken Branch,' How Come We Love our Congressmen So Much?" in *Congress in Change,* pp. 277-287.
26. Glenn R. Parker and Roger H. Davidson, "How Come We Love Our Congressmen So Much More than Our Congress?" *Legislative Studies Quarterly* (February 1979): 53-61.
27. House, Commission on Administration Review, *Final Report,* 2: 830-831.
28. Joseph Cooper and William West, "Voluntary Retirement, Incumbency, and the Modern House," *Political Science Quarterly* (Summer 1981): 279-300.
29. David S. Broder, *Changing of the Guard* (New York: Simon & Schuster, 1980).
30. Roger H. Davidson, David M. Kovenock, and Michael K. O'Leary, *Congress in Crisis* (Belmont, Calif.: Wadsworth Publishing Co., 1966).

31. Commission on the Organization of the Government for the Conduct of Foreign Policy, *Report* (Washington, D.C.: Government Printing Office, 1975); and House, Commission on Administrative Review, *Final Report,* 2: 867.
32. Ann Cooper, "Ex-Members of Congress: Some Go Home, Many Don't," *Congressional Quarterly Weekly Report,* September 17, 1977, pp. 1970-1971.
33. House, Commission on Administrative Review, *Final Report,* 2: 875.
34. Ibid., 2: 884.

450   *Appendix Table*

Party Control of the Presidency, Senate, House, 1901-1983

Congress	Years	President	Senate D	Senate R	Senate Other*	House D	House R	House Other*
57th	1901-1903	McKinley T. Roosevelt	31	55	4	151	197	9
58th	1903-1905	T. Roosevelt	33	57	—	178	208	—
59th	1905-1907	T. Roosevelt	33	57	—	136	250	—
60th	1907-1909	T. Roosevelt	31	61	—	164	222	—
61st	1909-1911	Taft	32	61	—	172	219	—
62nd	1911-1913	Taft	41	51	—	228	161	1
63rd	1913-1915	Wilson	51	44	1	291	127	17
64th	1915-1917	Wilson	56	40	—	230	196	9
65th	1917-1919	Wilson	53	42	—	216	210	6
66th	1919-1921	Wilson	47	49	—	190	240	3
67th	1921-1923	Harding	37	59	—	131	301	1
68th	1923-1925	Coolidge	43	51	2	205	225	5
69th	1925-1927	Coolidge	39	56	1	183	247	4
70th	1927-1929	Coolidge	46	49	1	195	237	3
71st	1929-1931	Hoover	39	56	1	167	267	1
72nd	1931-1933	Hoover	47	48	1	220	214	1
73rd	1933-1935	F. Roosevelt	60	35	1	310	117	5
74th	1935-1937	F. Roosevelt	69	25	2	319	103	10
75th	1937-1939	F. Roosevelt	76	16	4	331	89	13
76th	1939-1941	F. Roosevelt	69	23	4	261	164	4
77th	1941-1943	F. Roosevelt	66	28	2	268	162	5

*Excludes vacancies at beginning of each session.

**The 437 members of the House in the 86th and 87th Congresses is attributable to the at-large representative given to both Alaska (January 3, 1959) and Hawaii (August 21, 1959) prior to redistricting in 1962.

Congress	Years	President	Senate			House		
			D	R	Other*	D	R	Other*
78th	1943-1945	F. Roosevelt	58	37	1	218	208	4
79th	1945-1947	Truman	56	38	1	242	190	2
80th	1947-1949	Truman	45	51	—	188	245	1
81st	1949-1951	Truman	54	42	—	263	171	1
82nd	1951-1953	Truman	49	47	—	234	199	1
83rd	1953-1955	Eisenhower	47	48	1	211	221	1
84th	1955-1957	Eisenhower	48	47	1	232	203	—
85th	1957-1959	Eisenhower	49	47	—	233	200	—
86th**	1959-1961	Eisenhower	65	35	—	284	153	—
87th**	1961-1963	Kennedy	65	35	—	263	174	—
88th	1963-1965	Kennedy Johnson	67	33	—	258	177	—
89th	1965-1967	Johnson	68	32	—	295	140	—
90th	1967-1969	Johnson	64	36	—	247	187	—
91st	1969-1971	Nixon	57	43	—	243	192	—
92nd	1971-1973	Nixon	54	44	2	254	180	—
93rd	1973-1975	Nixon Ford	56	42	2	239	192	1
94th	1975-1977	Ford	60	37	2	291	144	—
95th	1977-1979	Carter	61	38	1	292	143	—
96th	1979-1981	Carter	58	41	1	276	157	—
97th	1981-1983	Reagan	46	53	1	243	192	—

☐ Republican Control   ☐ Democratic Control

SOURCE: U.S., Department of Commerce, Bureau of the Census, *Statistical Abstract of the United States* (Washington, D.C.: U.S. Government Printing Office, 1980), p. 509 and *Members of Congress Since 1789*, 2d ed. (Washington, D.C.: Congressional Quarterly, 1981), pp. 176-177. Reprinted from Barbara Hinckley, *Congressional Elections* (Washington, D.C.: Congressional Quarterly Press, 1981), pp. 144-145.

Suggested Readings

This list of suggested readings is not intended to be exhaustive. Journal articles, papers delivered at meetings, doctoral dissertations, and individual essays in books are not included. We have listed those books we feel are most useful and accessible to students.

Chapter 1 Introduction: The Two Congresses

Dodd, Lawrence C., and Oppenheimer, Bruce I., eds. *Congress Reconsidered.* 2d ed. Washington, D.C.: Congressional Quarterly Press, 1981.

Kozak, David, and McCartney, John, eds. *Congress and Public Policy: A Sourcebook of Documents and Readings.* Homewood, Ill.: Dorsey Press, 1982.

Mann, Thomas E., and Ornstein, Norman J., eds. *The New Congress.* Washington, D.C.: American Enterprise Institute for Public Policy Research, 1981.

Miller, Clem. *Member of the House: Letters of a Congressman.* Edited by John W. Baker. New York: Charles Scribner's Sons, 1962.

Chapter 2 Evolution of the Modern Congress

Cunningham, Noble, Jr., ed. *Circular Letters of Congressmen, 1789-1839.* 3 vols. Chapel Hill: University of North Carolina Press, 1978.

Galloway, George B. *History of the House of Representatives.* rev. ed. by Sidney Wise. New York: Thomas Y. Crowell Co., 1976.

Haynes, George H. *The Senate of the United States: Its History and Practice.* 2 vols. Boston: Houghton Mifflin Co., 1938.

Josephy, Alvin M., Jr. *On the Hill: A History of the American Congress.* New York: Simon & Schuster, 1980.

MacNeil, Neil. *Forge of Democracy: The House of Representatives.* New York: David McKay, 1963.

Rothman, David J. *Politics and Power: The United States Senate, 1869-1901.* Cambridge: Harvard University Press, 1966.

Young, James S. *The Washington Community, 1800-1828.* New York: Columbia University Press, 1966.

Chapter 3   Making It: The Electoral Game

Alexander, Herbert E. *Financing Politics: Money, Elections and Political Reform.* 2d ed. Washington, D.C.: Congressional Quarterly Press, 1980.

Clem, Alan L. *The Making of Congressmen: Seven Campaigns of 1974.* North Scituate, Mass.: Duxbury Press, 1976.

Hinckley, Barbara. *Congressional Elections.* Washington, D.C.: Congressional Quarterly Press, 1981.

Jacobson, Gary C. *Money in Congressional Elections.* New Haven: Yale University Press, 1980.

Jones, Charles O. *Every Second Year: Congressional Behavior and the Two-Year Term.* Washington, D.C.: The Brookings Institution, 1967.

Kingdon, John W. *Candidates for Office: Beliefs and Strategies.* New York: Random House, 1966.

Mann, Thomas E. *Unsafe at Any Margin: Interpreting Congressional Elections.* Washington, D.C.: American Enterprise Institute for Public Policy Research, 1978.

Chapter 4   Being There: Hill Styles and Home Styles

Davidson, Roger H. *The Role of the Congressman.* Indianapolis: Bobbs-Merrill Co., 1969.

Drew, Elizabeth. *Senator.* New York: Simon & Schuster, 1979.

Fenno, Richard F., Jr. *Home Style: House Members in Their Districts.* Boston: Little, Brown & Co., 1978.

Fiorina, Morris P. *Congress: Keystone of the Washington Establishment.* New Haven: Yale University Press, 1977.

Mayhew, David R. *Congress: The Electoral Connection.* New Haven: Yale University Press, 1974.

Chapter 5   Looking Good: The Two Congresses and the Public

Bagdikian, Ben H. *The Information Machines: Their Impact on Men and the Media.* New York: Harper & Row, 1971.

Blanchard, Robert O., ed. *Congress and the News Media.* New York: Hastings House, 1974.

Cater, Douglass. *The Fourth Branch of Government.* New York: Vintage Books, 1965.

Graber, Doris A. *Mass Media and American Politics.* Washington, D.C.: Congressional Quarterly Press, 1980.

Hess, Stephen. *The Washington Reporters.* Washington, D.C.: The Brookings Institution, 1981.

Chapter 6   Leaders and Parties in Congress

Hasbrouck, Paul D. *Party Government in the House of Representatives.* New York: Macmillan Publishing Co., 1927.

Jones, Charles O. *The Minority Party in Congress.* Boston: Little, Brown & Co., 1970.

Peabody, Robert L. *Leadership in Congress.* Boston: Little, Brown & Co., 1976.

Ripley, Randall B. *Party Leaders in the House of Representatives.* Washington, D.C.: The Brookings Institution, 1967.

_____. *Majority Party Leadership in Congress.* Boston: Little, Brown & Co., 1969.

Truman, David B. *The Congressional Party.* New York: John Wiley & Sons, 1959.

Chapter 7   Committees: Workshops of Congress

Fenno, Richard F., Jr. *Congressmen in Committees.* Boston: Little, Brown & Co., 1973.

Goodwin, George. *The Little Legislatures.* Amherst: University of Massachusetts Press, 1970.

Morrow, William L. *Congressional Committees.* New York: Charles Scribner's Sons, 1969.

Price, David E. *Who Makes the Laws?* Cambridge, Mass.: Schenkman Publishing Co., 1972.

Shepsle, Kenneth A. *The Giant Jigsaw Puzzle: Democratic Committee Assignments in the Modern House.* Chicago: University of Chicago Press, 1978.

Wilson, Woodrow. *Congressional Government.* reprint of 1885 ed. Baltimore: The Johns Hopkins University Press, 1981.

Chapter 8   Congressional Staff

Fox, Harrison W., Jr., and Hammond, Susan Webb. *Congressional Staffs.* New York: The Free Press, 1977.

Kofmehl, Kenneth. *Professional Staffs of Congress.* 3d ed. West Lafayette, Ind.: The Purdue University Press, 1977.

Malbin, Michael J. *Unelected Representatives: Congressional Staff and the Future of Representative Government.* New York: Basic Books, 1979.

Mosher, Frederick C. *The GAO: The Quest for Accountability in American Government.* Boulder, Colo.: Westview Press, 1979.

Chapter 9   Congressional Rules and Procedures

Bailey, Stephen K. *Congress Makes a Law: The Story Behind the Employment Act of 1946.* New York: Columbia University Press, 1950.

Froman, Lewis A., Jr. *The Congressional Process: Strategies, Rules, and Procedures.* Boston: Little, Brown & Co., 1967.

Matsunaga, Spark M., and Chen, Ping. *Rulemakers of the House.* Chicago: University of Illinois Press, 1976.

Oleszek, Walter J. *Congressional Procedures and the Policy Process.* Washington, D.C.: Congressional Quarterly Press, 1978.

Redman, Eric. *The Dance of Legislation.* New York: Simon & Schuster, 1973.

Siff, Ted, and Weil, Alan. *Ruling Congress: How House and Senate Rules Govern the Legislative Process.* New York: Grossman Publishers, 1975.

Vogler, David J. *The Third House: Conference Committees in the U.S. Congress.* Evanston, Ill.: Northwestern University Press, 1971.

Chapter 10   Congress and the President

Binkley, Wilfred. *President and Congress.* New York: Alfred A. Knopf, 1947.

Chamberlain, Lawrence. *The President, Congress and Legislation.* New York: Columbia University Press, 1946.

Edwards, George C., III. *Presidential Influence in Congress.* San Francisco: W. H. Freeman & Co., 1980.

Fisher, Louis. *The President and Congress: Power and Policy.* New York: The Free Press, 1972.

_____. *The Constitution Between Friends: Congress, the President, and the Law.* New York: St. Martin's Press, 1978.

_____. *The Politics of Shared Power: Congress and the Executive.* Washington, D.C.: Congressional Quarterly Press, 1981.

Sundquist, James L. *Decline and Resurgence of Congress.* Washington, D.C.: The Brookings Institution, 1981.

Wayne, Stephen J. *The Legislative Presidency.* New York: Harper & Row, 1978.

Chapter 11   Congress, the Bureaucracy, and the Budget Process

Arnold, R. Douglas. *Congress and the Bureaucracy: A Theory of Influence.* New Haven: Yale University Press, 1979.

Dodd, Lawrence C., and Schott, Richard. *Congress and the Administrative State.* New York: John Wiley & Sons, 1979.

LeLoup, Lance T. *The Fiscal Congress.* Westport, Conn.: Greenwood Press, 1980.

Mackenzie, G. Calvin. *The Politics of Presidential Appointments.* New York: The Free Press, 1981.

Ogul, Morris S. *Congress Oversees the Bureaucracy.* Pittsburgh: University of Pittsburgh Press, 1976.

Schick, Allen. *Congress and Money.* Washington, D.C.: The Urban Institute, 1980.

Seidman, Harold. *Politics, Position, and Power.* 3d ed. New York: Oxford University Press, 1980.

Wildavsky, Aaron. *The Politics of the Budgetary Process.* 3d ed. Boston: Little, Brown & Co., 1979.

Chapter 12   Congress and Interest Groups

Alexander, Herbert E., ed. *Political Finance.* Beverly Hills, Calif.: Sage Publications, 1979.

Bauer, Raymond A., de Sola Pool, Ithiel, and Dexter, Lewis Anthony. *American Business and Public Policy: The Politics of Foreign Trade.* New York: Atherton Press, 1963.

Freeman, J. Leiper. *The Political Process: Executive Bureau-Legislative Committee Relations.* rev. ed. New York: Random House, 1965.

Gross, Bertram M. *The Legislative Struggle: A Study in Social Combat.* New York: McGraw-Hill Book Co., 1953.

Malbin, Michael J., ed. *Parties, Interest Groups, and Campaign Finance Laws.* Washington, D.C.: American Enterprise Institute for Public Policy Research, 1980.

Oppenheimer, Bruce I. *Oil and the Congressional Process.* Lexington, Mass.: Lexington Books, 1974.

Ornstein, Norman J., and Elder, Shirley. *Interest Groups, Lobbying and Policymaking.* Washington, D.C.: Congressional Quarterly Press, 1978.

Truman, David B. *The Governmental Process, Political Interests and Public Opinion.* 2d ed. New York: Alfred A. Knopf, 1971.

Chapter 13   Decisionmaking in Congress

Brady, David W. *Congressional Voting in a Partisan Era.* Lawrence, Kansas: The University Press of Kansas, 1973.

Clausen, Aage R. *How Congressmen Decide: A Policy Focus.* New York: St. Martin's Press, 1973.

Kingdon, John W. *Congressmen's Voting Decisions.* 2d ed. New York: Harper & Row, 1980.

Matthews, Donald R., and Stimson, James A. *Yeas and Nays: Normal Decisionmaking in the U.S. House of Representatives.* New York: John Wiley & Sons, 1975.

Schneider, Jerrold E. *Ideological Coalitions in Congress.* Westport, Conn.: Greenwood Press, 1979.

Chapter 14   Congressional Policymaking

Asbell, Bernard. *The Senate Nobody Knows.* Garden City, N.Y.: Doubleday & Co., 1978.

Crabb, Cecil V., Jr., and Holt, Pat M. *Invitation to Struggle: Congress, the President and Foreign Policy.* Washington, D.C.: Congressional Quarterly Press, 1980.

Levine, Erwin L., and Wexler, Elizabeth M. *PL 94-142: An Act of Congress.* New York: Macmillan Publishing Co., 1981.

Orfield, Gary. *Congressional Power: Congress and Social Change.* New York: Harcourt Brace Jovanovich, 1974.

Reid, T. R. *Congressional Odyssey: The Saga of a Senate Bill.* San Francisco: W. H. Freeman & Co., 1980.

Ripley, Randall B., and Franklin, Grace A. *Congress, the Bureaucracy, and Public Policy.* rev. ed. Homewood, Ill.: The Dorsey Press, 1980.

Sundquist, James L. *Politics and Policy: The Eisenhower, Kennedy, and Johnson Years.* Washington, D.C.: The Brookings Institution, 1968.

Chapter 15   Change in the Two Congresses

Davidson, Roger H., Kovenock, David M., and O'Leary, Michael K. *Congress in Crisis: Politics and Congressional Reform* Belmont, Calif.: Wadsworth Publishing Co., 1966.

Davidson, Roger H., and Oleszek, Walter J. *Congress against Itself.* Bloomington: Indiana University Press, 1977.

Ornstein, Norman J., ed. *Congress in Change.* New York: Praeger Publishers, 1975.

Rieselbach, Leroy N. *Congressional Reform in the Seventies.* Morristown, N.J.: General Learning Press, 1977.

———. ed. *Legislative Reform.* Lexington, Mass.: Lexington Books, 1978.

Index

468 Index

Randall, Samuel J. (D-Pa.) - 34
Rankin, Jeannette (R-Mont.) - 103
Ranney, Austin - 93, 200
Rarick, John (D-La.) - 189
Ray, Bruce A. - 341
Ray, Elizabeth - 259-260
Rayburn, Sam (D-Texas) - 10, 15, 28, 31, 48, 137, 170, 196, 276, 434, 439, 440
Reagan, Ronald - 39, 153, 163, 185, 187, 193, 197, 203, 208, 210, 236, 258-259, 269-270, 276-277, 291, 294, 297, 299, 300-301, 303, 305, 314, 320, 321, 323, 324, 328, 332-334, 379, 389, 394, 406-407, 412, 413, 422, 435, 436, 441
Reed, Thomas B. (R-Maine) - 34, 184, 191
Rees, Thomas (D-Calif.) - 444
Redman, Eric - 232
Reid, T. R. - 262, 288, 342, 397
Representation - 9, 10, 39-40, 108-109, 113-115
Republican Campaign Committee, House - 191, 361
Republican Campaign Committee, Senate - 190, 361
Republican Committee on Committees, House - 191, 212
Republican Committee on Committees, Senate - 190, 212, 214
Republican Conference, House - 172, 189-191
Republican Conference, Senate - 139, 180, 183, 189-190
Republican National Committee - 72, 91, 361
Republican Personnel Committee, House - 191
Republican Policy Committee, House - 172, 191
Republican Policy Committee, Senate - 180, 183, 189-190
Republican Research Committee, House - 172, 191
Resources Conservation Act of 1977 - 429
Resources Planning Act of 1974 - 429
Reynolds v. Sims (1964) - 61
Rhodes, John J. (R-Ariz.) - 171, 236
Ribicoff, Abraham (D-Conn.) - 282, 373
Richards, Richard - 361
Richardson, Elliot - 323-324
Richmond, Fred (D-N.Y.) - 212, 352, 376-377
Riddick, Floyd M. - 198
Rieselbach, Leroy N. - 288, 342, 398
Riker, William H. - 129, 399
Ripley, Randall B. - 49, 130, 176, 198-200, 289, 367, 397, 406, 430, 431
Ritt, Leonard G. - 341
Ready, Elston - 201
Roberts, Chalmers M. - 431

Roberts, Steven V. - 398, 430
Robinson, Donald Allen - 200
Robinson, James A. - 288
Robinson, Michael J. - 87, 93, 95, 143, 146, 148-150, 155, 157-159
Rodino, Peter W., Jr. (D-N.J.) - 211, 219, 230
Rogers, Lindsay - 48
Rogers, Paul (D-Fla.) - 376
Rohde, David W. - 129, 200, 230, 231, 430, 448
Roosevelt, Franklin Delano - 39, 163, 292, 294, 311, 334
Roosevelt, Theodore - 38, 169, 297
Roper, Burns W. - 158
Rose, Richard - 367
Rosenbaum, David E. - 431
Rosenthal, Alan - 230
Rosten, Leo C. - 157
Rostenkowski, Dan (D-Ill.) - 172, 375
Rotunda, Donald T. - 342
Roukema, Margaret S. (R-N.J.) - 109
Rousselot, John H. (R-Calif.) - 163
Royce, Richard - 262
Rudder, Catherine E. - 342
Rules, House Committee on - 169, 170, 172, 208, 213, 216, 228, 272, 274-277, 278, 279, 283, 300, 414, 439
Rules and Administration, Senate Committee on - 218, 249
Rundquist, Barry S. - 49, 341
Rundquist, Paul S. - 368
Russell, Mary - 431
Russell, Richard B. (D-Ga.) - 177-178
Rutkus, Dennis Stephen - 156

Salisbury, Robert H. - 263
Saloma, John S., III - 341
Samuelson, Robert J. - 334, 343, 421-422, 431
Sarbanes, Paul S. (D-Md.) - 78
Savings and loan industry - 351, 416
Schattschneider, E. E. - 232
Scher, Seymour - 343
Schick, Allen - 48, 262, 331, 342, 448
Schlesinger, Arthur M., Jr. - 307, 316
Schmitt, Harrison "Jack" (R-N.M.) - 100
Schneider, Jerrold E. - 387, 398
Schott, Richard - 343
Schroeder, Patricia (D-Colo.) - 214, 383
Schuck, Peter H. - 262
Science and Technology, House Committee on - 218
Scott, William (R-Va.) - 284
Seidman, Harold - 340
Senate Committee System, Temporary Select Committee to Study the (Stevenson Committee) - 224, 239, 440, 441
Senior Executive Service - 323